A History of
The Expansion of Christianity

Volume II
THE THOUSAND YEARS
OF UNCERTAINTY

A History of
THE EXPANSION OF CHRISTIANITY

(*Volume II*)

THE
THOUSAND YEARS
OF UNCERTAINTY

A.D. 500 - A.D. 1500

by

KENNETH SCOTT LATOURETTE

*D. Willis James Professor of Missions
and Oriental History in Yale University*

HARPER & BROTHERS PUBLISHERS

New York and London

In memory of

HARLAN PAGE BEACH

1854-1933

Contents

vii

CONTENTS

Chapter VII

Chapter VIII

Chapter IX

Chapter X

Preface

THE purpose and scope of the survey of which this is the second volume have been fully stated in the introduction to the first volume. Here, therefore, they need not be repeated. At the very outset, however, the author craves the privilege of expressing his deep appreciation of the generous assistance which has facilitated his task. Among the libraries which have placed their resources at his disposal he is particularly indebted to the British Museum and to the various collections of Yale University. The unfailing courtesy of the staffs, and particularly of Professor R. P. Morris, is a very pleasant memory. As in the preceding volume, so in this, Mrs. Charles T. Lincoln has made an invaluable contribution through her skill in copying into typescript a frequently nearly illegible manuscript and through suggestions as to style. Professors J. T. Addison, R. H. Bainton, A. B. Benson, M. Spinka, G. Vernadsky, H. Watt, and K. B. Westman have read various sections of the typescript. Without their kindly criticisms the volume would have been guilty of far more errors than it now displays. Moreover, any work of the scope of this one would be impossible but for the labours of hundreds of scholars through the centuries—from the authors of chronicles and letters in the Middle Ages, through the care of librarians and copyists who transmitted their writings, to those who have prepared careful editions of these sources and to the many modern scholars who have treated sundry phases of our story. The names of many are recorded in the footnotes and bibliographies, but those of others must remain forever unknown. To all of these the author desires to express his profound gratitude.

A History of
The Expansion of Christianity

Volume II
THE THOUSAND YEARS
OF UNCERTAINTY

Chapter I

FROM THE CLOSE OF THE FIFTH TO THE BEGINNING OF THE SIXTEENTH CENTURY. INTRODUCTORY. THE WORLD IN WHICH CHRISTIANITY EXPANDED, WHY CHRISTIANITY SPREAD, THE CHRISTIANITY WHICH SPREAD, THE MEANS BY WHICH IT WAS PROPAGATED

AS WE move out of the fifth into the sixth century we begin to find ourselves in a different world. The Roman Empire was dwindling and becoming Greek and Byzantine. The great state which throughout the lifetime of Christianity had dominated the Mediterranean world was breaking up. The culture into which the faith had been born was being profoundly altered. In many of its aspects the change was due largely to Christianity. Yet in some of its features it had its inception before the advent of Jesus. Beginning as a minor cult, Christianity had eliminated all of its rivals except its parent, Judaism, and had made itself a major and integral part of the Græco-Roman world—only to find that world crumble about it. In no other large cultural area had it yet become more than an intermittently persecuted minority group. In Persia the Sassanids were closely allied with Zoroastrianism and still looked askance at Christianity as the faith of the Syriac-speaking subject populations. Even though it had become Nestorian in creed and national in its organization, they could not forget that it was akin to the religion of the hereditary enemy, Rome. China probably had not yet been touched by the missionary vanguard, and in India, so far as we know, Christian groups were found only on the coastal and north-west fringes.

What fate was Christianity to have? Was it to be identified with the waning power which still called itself the Roman Empire and with such local, fading cultures as those of the Copts and the Syriac-speaking peoples, and was it, in alliance with them, to wage a slowly losing battle against the forces of the new day? That this was a very real danger is clear. Some forms of Christianity so coalesced with these besieged remnants of a passing age that they have survived only as the faith of encysted and slowly dwindling minorities. We see them in the Armenian, the Jacobite, the Coptic, and the Nestorian communities of today, the last bulwarks of ancient nationalities. Or was Christianity to

1

display sufficient vitality to reach out into fresh areas and hitherto untouched peoples, and aid in constructing new and vigorous cultures?

The issue was not quickly decided. In the thousand years between A.D. 500 and A.D. 1500 Christianity was forced to surrender about as much territory and as many adherents as it gained. It won the peoples of Northern Europe, but it lost practically all of the northern coast of Africa, much of the Nile Valley, part of South-eastern Europe, most of Asia Minor, Syria, and Palestine, whatever it had held in Arabia, and nearly all of such ground as it had once occupied in Persia and Central Asia. Our statistics of population and our historical records are too uncertain to permit of exact comparisons. It may be that in 1500 the number of Christians was actually smaller than it had been a millennium before. In the interim the boundaries of the territory partially or completely possessed had suffered extensive changes. They had expanded in some directions and had contracted in others. The centuries had seen both ebb and flow. In the thirteenth century the area in which Christians were found was more extensive than it had been in the year 1000 or than it was to be at the beginning of the sixteenth century. Probably in A.D. 1500 it was more restricted than it had been in A.D. 500.

During much of the time, moreover, the lands in the hands of the Christians were not the undisputed centre of the highest civilization of the Mediterranean world. Christianity divided that honour with Islam.

Nor was Christianity the only faith which was spreading in these years. Islam, younger by six centuries, was gaining ground much more rapidly and was even winning from the Church its native home and some of the peoples among whom it had been earliest and most firmly established. As late as A.D. 1500, nearly nine hundred years after the birth of Islam, Western Christendom was at times still in fear of the Moslem hosts. In Central and Southern Asia and in Japan Buddhism was making extensive strides. While, like Christianity, it was losing ground in the land of its birth, elsewhere it was largely recouping its losses.

Through much of the period it was not at all clear that Christianity had a future or that its days were not numbered. It had become largely identified with subject populations and with recent converts among the semi-civilized peoples of Northern Europe. The main current of civilization seemed to be passing it by.

Yet in the thousand years Christianity became the avowed faith of North-west Europe. In South-west Europe it won back practically all of the territory which it had temporarily lost to Islam. Partly under the influence of Christianity and because of the stimulus given by it, the peoples of Western Europe developed a new set of cultures which were much more profoundly shaped by the faith than had been the Mediterranean world of the fifth century. Then, at about the close of the fifteenth century, they embarked upon a succession of geographical discoveries and conquests which were to carry them and their cultures and with them Christianity over much of the surface of the globe. So, likewise, in Eastern Europe, in the interval between the years 500 and 1500, Christianity had become the professed faith of the Russians. Not far from 1500 the Russians also began a process of expansion which in the ensuing four centuries was to lead them into Central Asia and across Northern Asia to the Pacific and into North America. They, too, took their religion with them. If, then, in 1500 the hypothetical visitor from Mars might not have been able to determine whether in the ten centuries since the year 500 Christianity had won more than it had lost, had he returned again in 1600, or 1700, or 1800, or 1900, he would have discovered that the gains made in what once seemed the indeterminate millennium had become the basis of an unprecedented expansion.

The thousand years between A.D. 500 and A.D. 1500 were marked by vast movements of peoples. The human animal is notoriously restless and mobile. Migrations have punctuated all its known history. Now and again particular groups have acquired possession of especially desirable areas and have been able for some centuries to hold them against all comers. Sooner or later, however, their defences have crumbled and they have been forced to share with new invaders their fertile valleys and salubrious plains. The era in which Christianity appeared had been marked by comparative security in some of the great cultural areas. From the birth of Jesus until near the close of the second century the Roman arms insured for the Mediterranean world a large measure of internal peace. In China the Han Emperors were maintaining an extensive, prosperous, and fairly stable realm. In India the Andhra and Kushan rulers were according something of peace and prosperity to wide areas. The Arsacids gave an uneasy coherence to much of the territory between the Roman and the Kushan domains. It was in this period of relative stability of great empires that Christianity first made its way. As we have seen, it succeeded in winning the richest and most populous of them, that of Rome. However, about the year 200 several of the realms began to disintegrate and migrant invaders pushed in over their weakened defences. Insecurity mounted. Beginning in the fifth and sixth centuries, the movements of peoples were notably increased in the Euro-Asiatic land mass. For a thousand years and more the centres of civilization were disturbed again and again by incursions of semi-civilized and barbarous peoples.

To every student of history these movements are so familiar that to repeat their main outlines must appear a gratuitous banality. Yet so moulded was the course of Christianity by them that they must be at least summarized. It was they which largely determined the waxing and waning of the boundaries of the faith. We must note, then, although briefly, those which affected the fate of that religion.

In the fifth century, it will be remembered, came the irruptions of the Germanic peoples into the Roman Empire. It was in 410 that Rome was taken and sacked by Alaric and his Goths. It was in the fifth century that the Visigoths established themselves in Spain, that the Vandals moved into North Africa, that the Burgundians, the Alamanni, and the Franks carved out estates for themselves in Gaul, and that the Angles and Saxons effected permanent settlements in Britain. The last decade of the fifth century witnessed the founding by Theodoric of the Ostrogothic Kingdom in Italy. The middle of the fifth century saw the invasion of the west by Attila and his Huns. Attila, indeed, led only one wave of those Hunnic peoples who during these centuries were pressing not only into Europe, but into India and China. From north of the Caspian came the Alani, a Sarmatian folk, who were later associated with the Vandals in the African adventure. In the fifth and sixth centuries many of the Celts migrated from Britain to Armorica, in Gaul, the present Brittany. In the sixth century the Lombards, of Teutonic stock, conquered Northern Italy and established a kingdom which endured into the eighth century. It was in that same century that a people known as the Avars, probably mainly Uighurs, who for generations were prominent on the frontiers of China, established their dominion over much of Central Europe, made frequent incursions into the Balkans, and menaced the borders of some of the Teutonic states of Western Europe. For part of the sixth century the Avars were the most formidable power in Central Europe, and even in the first half of the seventh century remained strong enough to attack Constantinople. In the seventh century a branch of the Bulgars, another folk originally from the steppes of Asia, wrested from the Eastern Roman Empire territory south of the Danube and founded a regime which under one dynasty or another was to endure for centuries. Like the Avars, they were gradually absorbed by the subject Slavic majority, but they long maintained a redoubtable Balkan state. The Slavs, too, were moving. Divided into many groups, they were very widely spread. Of their early migrations we know little. Early in the sixth century, however, they were in possession of much of what is now the north-eastern part of Germany. In the seventh century they were overrunning the Balkans and were penetrating into Greece. To the Emperors in Constantiʌople they constituted a major menace. Usually they were peasants, subject to Germans, Huns, Avars, Bulgars, and other aggressive folk. Never or almost never did they form themselves into large political groups of their own accord. Yet, atomized though they were into many small bands and tribes and inter-mixed with other stocks, they became widely diffused and often gave their language and much of their blood to their conquerors.

All the peoples mentioned in the last paragraph either eventually accepted Christianity or, like the Huns, disappeared as a distinct entity from the Euro-pean scene. In the seventh century, however, a wave of invaders broke into the Mediterranean world of whom this was not true. The Arabs brought with them their new faith, Islam, and made it dominant in much of the Orient, in North Africa, and in most of Spain. They ruled Sicily and threatened Italy. In Mesopotamia and Persia they overthrew the Sassanian dynasty and from there penetrated far into Central Asia.

The Arab advance into Europe had been stemmed only about a half-century when from the opposite direction came a fresh incursion of non-Christians which threatened the Christianity and the remnants of Græco-Roman civiliza-tion which had been impressed upon the Germanic invaders of Western Europe. It is from near the end of the eighth century that we have the first reliable reports of the Viking raids. In the ninth century the Scandinavians became a widespread plague. Ireland, Great Britain, the Carolingian domains, the Iberian Peninsula, the shores of Morocco and of Southern Gaul, and the rivers of Russia knew these pillaging men of the North. In places, as in Great Britain and Normandy, they established their rule over fairly wide areas. In the eleventh century some of their descendants, now become Chris-tian, mastered England, Sicily, and part of Southern Italy.

In the eleventh century, too, began those eastward movements of various Western European peoples which we know by the name of the Crusades. Reinforced by the commerce of the Italian cities, for some centuries they left colonies on the islands and shores of the Eastern Mediterranean. Merchants and missionaries went far beyond the fringes of military occupation and in the thirteenth and fourteenth centuries even reached China.

In the East these crusading and trading Western Europeans came in con-tact with peoples who in successive tides had issued out of Central Asia. They fought the Seljuk Turks, who, coming from Central Asia in the eleventh and twelfth centuries, were a formidable power in the Near East. In the thirteenth century the great Mongol eruption broke forth, led by Jenghiz Khan and his descendants. Crusading and Mongol outposts almost touched each other. But the Mongol exploits in Persia and Mesopotamia were only a part of the amazing achievement. China was conquered. Much of Russia was overrun. For a time even Western Europe seemed threatened. Many of the earlier Mongol conquerors were not unfriendly to Christianity. Later, however, most of those in Persia and what is now Russian Central Asia became Moslems. The latest of the line to make a great military record, Timur, of the end of the fourteenth and the first few years of the fifteenth century, wiped out much of what remained of Christianity in the lands scourged by him.

Then in the fifteenth and sixteenth centuries the Ottoman Turks became prominent. They established a huge empire in the eastern end of the Mediterranean world and for a time threatened Central and even Western Europe.

At the end of the fifteenth century began that most remarkable of all migrations of mankind, the expansion of Northern and Western European peoples, which in the ensuing four and a half centuries was to carry Western culture and Christianity into all portions of the globe. These Europeans, equipped with a culture which was in part the product of Christianity, and some of them professing as a motive a missionary purpose, made themselves masters of the larger part of the land surface of the earth. For extent the conquests were without precedent. It was largely because of this association that in the past four and a half centuries Christianity has been extended more widely than has ever been any other faith professed by man.

At first thought, the millennium of migrations might seem to be highly unfavourable to the spread of Christianity. The greater proportion of the conquerors were at the outset barbarous or only semi-civilized. They tended to destroy orderly life and with it the structure of society with which Christianity was closely associated. The kind of life they stood for, with its ruthless use of rough force, was quite contrary to the spirit and teachings of the founder of Christianity. For them and their followers real conversion to the faith would entail a revolution in motives and manners so complete as to be almost inconceivable. In the New Testament a type of life was set forth which was a categorical negation of nearly all that these rude migrants esteemed most highly. Christianity as it was at its inception seemed quite out of place in this new and crude world. What chance did it have of being understood? Or, if understood, what hope could there be of its adoption, even by a minority? It is not strange that many of the conquerors were scornful of even that modified Christianity which they knew. Some were antagonistic to it.

A closer examination, however, discloses a number of factors which made for the expansion of the faith. The first of these arose out of the very fact that most of the migrants were semi-barbarous folk who were moving into lands with a much more complex culture. The invaders stood in awe of the civilization which they conquered while they robbed and affected disdain for the peoples who possessed it. Even if at the outset they came only for plunder and had little respect for what they were looting, before many generations their leaders desired to acquire many of the manners and customs of their subjects. By the year 500, as we have seen, Christianity had become an integral part of the culture of the Mediterranean world. It was, then, not surprising that the Northern peoples who adopted that culture should with it take over the Christian faith.

The conversion was facilitated by the fact that most of these peoples had religions which offered little effective resistance to Christianity. Usually the more nearly primitive types of religion, such as animism and polytheism, offer feeble opposition to newer forms. The only exceptions seem to be in regions where they are part and parcel of a resistant social structure. In India, for instance, crass types of polytheism and many primitive religious beliefs are intimate parts of a culture which is organized by castes and which has long presented a sturdy and on the whole effective wall to such faiths as Christianity and Islam. Usually animism and the more elementary forms of polytheism have been unable to stand before Islam, Christianity, and Buddhism. The more advanced religions, like the more advanced cultures, tend to supplant the more nearly primitive ones. Most of the invaders of this period had a polytheism of a somewhat crude type. As they gave up their hereditary culture for that of the Mediterranean basin, they also rather easily abandoned their old gods and took over the religion which was integrated with the type of civilization that they were adopting. One series of exceptions there was, and this most notable. Numbers of the migrants took on Islam. Here was a faith which has won millions of converts from Christianity, but which, except in the Iberian Peninsula, Sicily, and Southern Italy, has lost very few adherents to Christianity.

Another reason for the acceptance of Christianity was in the types of that faith which the migrants of the sixth and succeeding centuries came to know. What was now called Christianity had, as we have seen, been greatly changed from that of the New Testament. It had been modified by its environment, and that environment was the decaying Roman world, which in turn was being transformed by the infiltration, through the armies, of Northern barbarians. Already the Christianity of the multitude and even of many of the leaders was being adjusted to the mental outlook and the desires of a population with a declining civilization. Its belief in the miraculous, its reliance upon the magic power of the sign of the Cross and the rites of the Church to expel demons, to cure disease in man and beast, and to fend off physical disaster, had an appeal to the untutored mind. Its imposing ceremonial inspired awe, and its claim to determine the eternal destiny of the human soul awakened both fear and hope. It must be noted, however, that, along with accretions from the environment, much of the original content of Christianity persisted. While for many Christianity must have seemed to do what had been expected of the older religions, only more powerfully, and while it opened up vistas of heaven and hell, it also presented a way of life which condemned that in the midst of which it was set. It created a tension between the ideal and the actual, a conflict which still exists in those cultures which it helped to produce. From this, as we shall see, were to come some of the most striking effects both of Christianity on individual lives and on institutions, and of the environment on Christianity.

One last reason for the spread of Christianity in this millennium of migrations, and by no means the least important, was the nature of the faith itself. The inner vitality continued which from the beginning was so marked a characteristic of the movement that originated in Jesus. Through the thousand years between the fifth and the sixteenth century a practically continuous flow of missionaries poured out into non-Christian territory. Not always did it issue from the same spot. Now one and now another region became the source. At some periods it was much fuller than at others. Without it, however, the other factors would probably have proved insufficient to guarantee the expansion of Christianity. But for the missionary, the non-Christian folk who invaded the South, or who, remaining in their own lands, came under the spell of the culture of the Mediterranean world, might, in adopting that culture, have failed to take over the religion associated with it. Indeed, they might have been much slower in appropriating its non-religious phases. Had the missionary not been present, they might even have failed entirely to enter the circle of what became Western civilization. This is not to attempt to pass judgment on the worth of this Occidental civilization or to say whether it was fortunate or unfortunate that it developed and that the peoples of Northern Europe adopted it. What is meant is that the spread of Christianity in this period was not due simply to the proximity of barbarous or semi-barbarous peoples to a more complex culture which inspired awe and aroused a desire to win admission to its charmed circle. Nor was it merely because of the contrast between a more advanced and a more nearly primitive religion. Without these factors, to be sure, the missionary would have found his task much more difficult and at times impossible. What we are here saying is that these factors are not alone sufficient to account for the expansion of Christianity.

The missionary and the religious impulse which sent him forth were indispensable.

The professional missionary seems to have been much more prominent in these ten centuries than in the first five hundred years of the expansion of the faith. This impression may be due to our imperfect knowledge of the precise ways in which Christianity spread in much of the earlier period. However, when allowance is made for this element in our judgment, the conviction still remains that between A.D. 500 and A.D. 1500 men who gave the major part of their time to propagating their faith had a much larger share in the expansion of Christianity than in the days when the Græco-Roman world was being won.

It was, then, due to a variety of factors that Christianity, instead of retreating and slowly dying out with the decay of the political order with which it had become so intimately associated, continued to spread, and that it won new footholds which were to prove of primary importance in much of the future expansion of the faith.

It must be noted that the conditions which surrounded the spread of Christianity in the years between A.D. 500 and A.D. 1500 presented a sharp contrast to those of its first five centuries. In the earlier period Christianity had entered a highly civilized world whose inherited official faith was for millions of individuals disintegrating under the influences of a changing age. Deracinated men and women living in a day when old institutions and beliefs were being challenged, and thrown into a newly emerging cosmopolitan world, were seeking replies to questions which the official polytheism could not answer. Various philosophies and cults were competing for their attention. Among these came Christianity. Youthful, at the outset a small and persecuted sect, it ultimately won its way until it joined forces with the state and in some regions outlived it. Now in this new day the cosmopolitan world which Christianity helped to create was crumbling. Christianity was associated with a culture which was passing and, like the polytheism which it had supplanted, was in danger of being outmoded. At the outset of the thousand years it enjoyed the prestige of being affiliated with the high civilization of the Mediterranean world. In that was both an advantage and a peril—an advantage of prestige and a peril of identification with a disappearing order. Christianity entered that fresh era, not as an obscure and numerically feeble Jewish sect, but as the professed faith of the largest civilized group of mankind. It was partly as a representative of ancient civilization and partly as its vehicle that it confronted the migrants, and it was largely in these capacities that it won its way.

It is important not only to ask why Christianity spread in this new era, but to observe the types of Christianity which expanded. As we have seen, the religion which owed its initial impulse to Jesus took on many different forms in its first five centuries. The founder had formulated no creeds, had entrusted his message not to books, but to the memory of disciples, and, so far as our written records tell us, had given little or no attention to devising an organization which could perpetuate his vision. The experiences which came to his disciples after the crucifixion—the resurrection appearance and especially what they called the Holy Spirit—by their very nature led to variety and to extensive proliferation. The movements which sprang from Jesus were, as we have noted, very numerous. Probably from no other initiator of a religion have so many schools and groups arisen as those which trace their origin to him. By the year 500, it will be recalled, the vast majority of those who professed to owe their faith to Jesus were found in a few main communions. Of these the largest was what called itself Catholic. The Arians, it may be remarked, also laid claim to this title, but it is usually accorded to the others. This Catholic Church, while still theoretically preserving intercommunion and doctrinal unity within its widely flung borders, was in effect becoming divided—chiefly between a body in the West which looked to the Bishop of Rome as its head and which usually employed Latin as its language, and one in the East which was predominantly Greek in speech and in which the Patriarch of Constantinople exercised a certain primacy.

It was the Catholic Church from which most of the expansion of the faith came. Arianism disappeared, leaving the field to its rival. Such minority groups as the Donatists, the Marcionites, the Montanists, and the Gnostics had either died out before the year 500 or remained, dwindling movements, largely out of touch with the immigrants and conquerors from the North. Manichæism seems never to have had any attraction for the uncivilized peoples of Europe. Of the two great branches of the Catholic Church, that which looked to Rome as its centre won far more converts and became the source of many more vigorous movements than did that which looked to Constantinople for direction.

In Africa and most of Asia, however, most of the extension of the faith did not emanate from the Catholics. From the Monophysite church in Egypt Christianity spread southward up the Nile into the Sudan and brought Ethiopia within its sphere of influence. A branch of Syrian Monophysites usually known as Jacobites displayed a missionary zeal which carried them southward and eastward. The majority of the Christians in the Persian domains were

Nestorians and as such conveyed their faith into India, Central Asia, and China.

Of these missionary branches of Christianity, the most successful in winning a permanent following was the western portion of the Catholic Church, with the eastern a somewhat distant second. For a time the geographic frontiers of Nestorianism were more far-flung than either, but before A.D. 1500 they had disastrously and, at the end, rather rapidly contracted. The Monophysites of Syria and Egypt were the least successful and by A.D. 1500 their borders, too, had narrowed.

Why did these particular types of Christianity gain converts rather than the others? Why among these missionary churches the differing degrees of success? Some of the reasons must be fairly obvious. The Catholic form of the faith was, as is clear from its very name, that of the large majority of the population of the Græco-Roman world. It enjoyed the endorsement and support of the state. As the prevailing religion of the centres of civilization with which the peoples of Northern Europe were chiefly in touch, it quite naturally was the type of Christianity adopted by them. Arianism seems to have owed its progress among the Teutonic peoples to the fact that it was the official cult of the emperors when the Goths first came extensively in touch with Christianity. Since it never possessed any strong foothold among the Roman population in the West, and since it lost official support and its following in the East, it could scarcely hope for a long life or a growing constituency. The Germanic folk who professed it were usually minorities who eventually conformed to the customs of their civilized subjects, the descendants of the old Roman provincials. Their adoption of Catholicism, like that of the language of the majority, was almost a foregone conclusion. The other minority offshoots of Christianity, such as Gnosticism and Montanism, had either died out before the year 500 or were not in intimate touch with the main bodies of non-Christians. Manichæism, if we admit that faith to the Christian circle, was the one exception, but it had the misfortune never to capture the allegiance of any important people. Among the Uighurs, in Central Asia, it obtained a numerous following, and through them made a strong impression on the Chinese, but the Uighurs were not long a major power and even they were divided in their religious allegiance.

As between the Roman Catholicism of the West and the Greek Catholicism of the East, the advantage clearly lay with the former. In the East, where the political structure of the Roman Empire outlasted that in the West, the Church had less freedom. Always it was largely under the control of the state. In it the Roman tradition of religion as a function of government tended to persist. The Byzantine Church by no means completely lost the features distinctive of Christianity, but the missionary initiative was decidedly less marked than in the Western wing of the Church. Then, too, through all but the first century and a half of the millennium, this Catholic Church of the East was facing an aggressive Islam. Against the latter on some of its borders it was engaged in a slowly losing struggle.

On the other hand, Roman Catholicism, because of the collapse of the imperial structure in the West, fell heir to much of the prestige and the spirit of Rome. Through a large proportion of the thousand years it carried some of the functions formerly assumed by the state. Its efforts to maintain its independence of the local kingdoms and of the Empire which appropriated the Roman name were often extraordinarily successful. At times it even made good a claim to superiority over the civil authorities. Many portions of the Church showed no missionary enthusiasm. Usually, however, on the frontiers where it bordered on non-Christian peoples some of its members displayed a zeal to extend the faith. Then, too, Islam was by no means the grave menace that it proved to be to the sister Church of the East. In contrast with the latter, where its frontier touched non-Christians, the Church of the West had chiefly to do not with Moslems, but with folk of primitive religions which might resist but could not permanently oppose Christianity.

Armenian Christianity, like its adherents, was always on the defence against powerful neighbours. It gave coherence and strength to Armenian national consciousness and helped to prevent absorption into other peoples, but it evinced little or no tendency to reach out among non-Armenians for converts. Nestorianism possessed the advantage of having its centre in Mesopotamia and of being strong in the major political and commercial cities of that region, Seleucia-Ctesiphon and Baghdad. The former was the capital of the powerful Sassanian Empire and the latter of the Abbasid caliphs. Each in its day was a metropolis to which trade routes converged from both East and West. Nestorians, traversing these routes, went to Central Asia, India, and China. Among them were earnest missionaries who sought to make converts from non-Christians. Yet the Nestorians usually were in touch chiefly with peoples of advanced religions—Persian Zoroastrians, Arab Moslems, Indian Hindus and Buddhists, and Chinese Confucianists, Taoists, and Buddhists. From these they won relatively few. Among Central Asiatic tribes of more primitive cults they attracted numerous followers, only to lose out a few centuries later to Buddhism, which had long been entrenched in that region, and to the politically more powerful Islam. Never, except for some of these tribes, was Nestorianism the predominant faith of an independent people.

In Mesopotamia, its stronghold, the rulers were first Zoroastrian and later Moslem. As compared with both Western and Eastern Catholicism, it was at a decided disadvantage.

The Jacobite Monophysites of Syria, like the Nestorians, were in cities—such as Edessa and Antioch—at strategic points on important trade routes. Along these their missionaries travelled far and wide. However, even less than Nestorians were they in touch with primitive polytheists or animists. Soon after their Church was organized their land was conquered by the Moslem Arabs. Most of their success appears to have been in winning fellow Christians to their views.

On their southern borders, the Monophysite Copts were in contact with semi-civilized peoples whose polytheism offered no very effective resistance to the missionary faith of the more highly civilized North. It was not strange that Monophysitism won an extensive following over a wide area in the Sudan and Ethiopia. Yet the Copts, like their fellow Monophysites in Syria, were politically always a tributary people, first to the Catholic Greeks and then to the Moslem Arabs.

During most of the thousand years between A.D. 500 and A.D. 1500, all the churches of the East confronted a younger Islam professed by aggressive peoples who were politically the overlords of most of the area. It was among the folk in Northern and especially in North-western Europe that Christianity found its greatest opportunity for expansion. Of the various branches of the Church, the advantage lay with those who had freest access to them.

To one surveying the world scene in the sixth century, and especially in the seventh century, after the first amazing conquests of Islam, the future of Christianity might not seem particularly promising. By the beginning of the eighth century, Christianity had distinctly lost ground among civilized peoples. The contemporary observer might be pardoned if to him the outlook appeared dark for a faith which had been identified with a now waning and dismembered culture and whose most promising outlet for expansion was among the barbarians of the forest and plains of Northern Europe. At the close of the fifth century Christianity had become master of the Mediterranean world, still, in spite of its decay, the major cultural centre of mankind. Within the next three centuries it had lost about half of this area, and in the portion which still professed the faith the level of civilization had distinctly fallen. The most brilliant cultures were to be found not in the basin of the Mediterranean, but in Mesopotamia and China. The gains which Christianity had made among the barbarians in Gaul, the Rhine Valley, and the British Isles seemed poor compensation for the losses. In subsequent chapters we shall wish to ask how far the later brilliant attainments of these apparently un-promising peoples were due to the faith which achieved its greatest strongholds among them. Even in the fifteenth century, however, China was probably richer, more prosperous, and more highly civilized than Europe. Not until after the sixteenth century was the cultural area which professed the Christian name relatively as prominent among the other civilized regions of the world as in the fourth and fifth centuries.

We have appeared to content ourselves with the obvious answers to the query as to why it was that certain types of Christianity rather than others expanded in this critical millennium. While true, so far as they go, they may be only partial and superficial replies. Back of them lies the problem of why these, rather than one of the other forms of Christianity, prevailed in their respective areas. That carries us back into the period before the sixth century. There, it will be recalled, the query was at least partially dealt with. Behind all the reasons which the historian is wont to give, however, may lie still others. In the last analysis the spread of a faith depends not only upon externally congenial circumstances, but upon inward vitality, something in the nature of the religion or the sect which commands such enthusiastic devo-tion that it impels its adherents to propagate it. No matter how favourable the environment, where this inward dynamic is wanting no expansion takes place. The inquiry, then, must be pushed back still further. Why, we must ask, is this vitality? Obviously it is because certain deep springs in human nature are tapped. Again one must inquire the origin of those qualities of the religion or the sect which, more than its rivals, have enabled it to reach these hidden springs of conduct. The answer to that question may carry us far beyond the domain to which the historian is supposed to be restricted. At most he can only recognize the possible existence of realms into which the canons of his craft forbid him to venture. It may well be that the ultimate reply is to be given by the metaphysician and the theologian. Whatever that may be, certain facts are clear. It was from the types which we have indicated that in its next stage the expansion of Christianity proceeded.

It is important that in these thousand years no radically new schools devel-oped which attracted an extensive following. To be sure, such variants as the Bogomils of the Balkans and the Cathari of Southern Europe appeared, but they remained minority groups. Possibly, moreover, they had their origin in part from impulses derived from Manichæism or Gnosticism. Such sects as that of Peter Waldo, the Lollards, and the Hussites also succeeded in attracting only relatively few adherents. From time to time from within the existing bodies, notably the Catholic West, new movements issued. Usually, however, like the Cistercians, the Franciscans, and the Dominicans, they remained inside the parent Church.

In the year 1500 Christianity was in the main represented by the same great churches that it had been in the year 500. The relative numerical strength had somewhat altered. The Catholic Church of the West had forged ahead of its sister communion of the East. The Nestorians, after a wide extension, had suffered disastrous losses which had reduced their strength below that of the sixth century. After a somewhat similar expansion, both the Jacobite Monophysites and the Coptic Monophysites were yielding ground. Some internal changes there had been. Especially had the Catholic Church of the West displayed the sort of life which led to new monastic orders, to fresh formulations of theology, to modifications in ritual, and to new forms of religious art and architecture. However, except for the development of monastic communities, in the outstanding features of creed and of organization the communions who embraced the vast majority of those who called themselves Christians had changed little in the course of the thousand years. In most of its main outlines the Christianity of the end of the fifteenth century was substantially that of the Christianity of the end of the fifth century. Not until the Protestant Reformation, in the sixteenth century, were major new forms of the faith to appear.

Yet, while it is true that in creeds and the chief features of its formal organization Christianity was little altered, within this framework it underwent changes. The miraculous, with veneration of relics as having magic potency and of certain signs and words as powerful theurgic agents, loomed much larger than in some of the previous centuries. Popular movements, such as the Franciscans, the Waldenses, and the Lollards developed. Schools of mysticism arose. Creeds were bulwarked by voluminous theological systems. Liturgies were elaborated. If in creeds, sacraments, and episcopate Christianity in the fifteenth century was substantially that of the fifth century, in many other respects it was far different at the end of the millennium from what it had been at the beginning.

Before we proceed to a more detailed description of these thousand years, it remains to summarize in anticipatory fashion the process by which Christianity won its new territories. It is remarkable what similarities the course of conversion displayed from region to region and from people to people. Variations there were, as we shall see, but in general an almost monotonous uniformity prevailed. First of all, a few individual converts were won, by either merchants, captives, or monks. These constituted small, scattered minorities, usually persecuted. Upon the country as a whole they seemed to have little or no effect. In general, this corresponded to what had taken place in the Mediterranean basin the first three centuries. Next, after a longer or shorter time, was seen a mass movement into the Church. Within a few years, perhaps less than a generation, an entire people or kingdom would come. This was akin to the process of conversion in the Roman Empire in the two centuries after Constantine. In that case, however, the numbers and territory involved were much larger and the time consumed longer. Usually, in contrast, it was only with groups of a few thousand that we here have to do. As in the Roman Empire, this mass movement was led by the rulers—the king or the chief. Often, too, as in Rome, some of the aristocracy held out for a time. Occasionally their opposition seems to have been as much from resentment against the growing power of the king and against the king's attempt to use the new faith to bulwark his authority as from preference for the old customs. Repeatedly, on the other hand, the aristocracy joined the king in heading the new movement. Under these circumstances, a people entered the new faith as a body, led by those whom they were accustomed to follow. Conversion became not so much a matter of individual conviction as of group action. Precedent for this had already been established in Armenia and in the Roman Empire of the fourth and fifth centuries. It represented, however, a marked departure from the original nature of Christianity and from the usual processes of expansion in the first three centuries. It was conformity to what seems to have been, until the time of Christ, a prevailing conception of religion. Religion was generally thought of as a tribal or national affair. It was, naturally, of use to the individual, but the individual did not have the right to reject it. To depart from the cult of one's group was to be guilty of disloyalty. It was with this concept of religion that most of the converts of these thousand years adopted the Christian faith.

Not infrequently mass conversion was hastened by the use of force. For instance, more than one Scandinavian Christian king resorted to arms to defend himself against the pagan opposition or to overwhelm the recalcitrants. Often baptism was imposed as a sign of submission to a foreign conqueror. A Christian monarch in seeking to extend his domains sought to assimilate his new subjects to his religion and required baptism and, perhaps, the support of Christian clergy. More than once the ecclesiastical authorities or some outstanding Christian clergyman denounced the use of the sword and insisted that it was quite contrary to the spirit of the Gospel. Usually, however, these protests availed little. The age was rough and the Christian leaven could not quickly transform it. Instead, the two often existed side by side and in incongruous and illogical contrast. The same individual might at one moment

exhibit warm religious emotion with care for the poor and deep appreciation
of Christian moral and spiritual ideals, and at the next give himself over to
cruelties and gross coarseness and immorality which were the complete
negation of Christian ethics.

While conversions were often *en masse* and engineered by the recognized
rulers, the preliminary preparation, the winning of the first individual converts, and the actual task of instruction of the throngs of new Christians were
the work of missionaries. The large majority of the missionaries were monks.
But for monks, indeed, it is hard to see how in most regions the expansion of
Christianity could have been carried on. But for them it would have proceeded
much more slowly and would have remained more superficial. In some places
the secular clergy had a share, but as a rule monks were the pioneers and the
seculars became important only as an orderly church life was developed with
its territorial parishes. The missionary function was originally not a primary
aim of monasticism. Monks had, supposedly, separated themselves from society
to achieve the salvation of their own souls and not for the purpose of helping
others. Many, perhaps the majority of monks, held to this purpose and had
little or no interest in the peoples outside their cells. However, some monks
almost inevitably became missionaries. The monastic movement attracted those
who were not content with the superficial religion which went by the name
of Christianity, but were resolved to give themselves entirely to the faith.
What more natural than that some of them should be caught by that desire to
propagate the faith which from the beginning has been so integral a part of
the genius of Christianity? Many, moreover, in search of solitude, pressed out
beyond the borders of the society in which they had been reared, and built
cells in neighbourhoods where the only other inhabitants were non-Christians.
Numbers acquired reputations for sanctity which attracted visitors and these
contacts led to conversions. Some went out deliberately as missionaries. Then,
too, the monastic congregation often proved an admirable missionary agency.
Its fellowship strengthened the purpose of its members. In the West the prevailing Benedictine rule and the various reforming movements which arose
out of it, like the Cistercians, stressed the importance of labour. In many a
nominally converted region monks established themselves in fresh communities which cleared the forests, drained the swamps, introduced some of the
arts of civilization, and gave religious instruction to the people about them.
Yet the process of conversion and of raising the level of Christian living of
the many neophytes of the mass movements might have proceeded more
rapidly had missions been the primary monastic purpose. The monastery tended
to remain somewhat aloof from the world and to pursue a self-contained routine.

The character of the Christianity of the peoples brought into the Church in these thousand years was largely determined by the processes by which the faith was adopted. The fact that conversions were so largely the result of group action under the direction of the civil authorities made for a very superficial and formal Christianity. At the outset few had even an inkling of the original nature of that which they were accepting. When they learned more about it, it was chiefly from monks. The current Christianity, therefore, strongly smacked of monastic ideals. The perfect Christian, thus the belief ran, was the ideal monk. Not for centuries, and then not everywhere, did a lay Christianity develop which held to another view of the faith. Slowly the masses acquired more knowledge of the faith. Increasingly in Europe Christianity was woven into the fabric of life and culture. Yet never did it entirely escape from the consequences of the method of its introduction. Only the minorities, whether of lay folk, or of monks, or of clergy, entered whole-heartedly into the inward spirit of Christianity as it was preached and lived in the ancient world by the greatest of the early disciples.

The financial support of missionaries was seldom derived from contributors in some homeland. No organizations maintained by the gifts of millions of lay donors formed the base of the missionary enterprise. These were not to appear in any prominent fashion until the eighteenth and nineteenth centuries. Usually the missionary asked for support from the local prince. Often this was given in the form of lands for the use of the monastic community or for the endowment of a church.

Moreover, usually the infant Church quickly passed through the stage of dependence on foreign personnel. To a few regions, as in some of the Baltic lands, for several generations foreign missionaries continued to come. Yet in other instances, such as the Italian mission to Great Britain and the English mission to Germany, within two generations the work of the alien was practically completed and the Church was manned by sons of the soil. The transient function of the foreigner was in striking contrast with the prolongation of his prominence in many of the communities established by Christian missions after 1500.

Still another feature of the process by which Christianity was extended in these years was the part played by the ecclesiastical heads of the various communions. In the Catholic West the Papacy performed an important function. At times, when the Papal throne was occupied by such vigorous administrators as Gregory the Great and Innocent III, it actually initiated missions. This, however, was exceptional. Always, however, the Papacy provided a centre of reference and of unity. Disputes which crippled the work of missions could be referred to it for settlement. Its endorsement accorded a certain amount of prestige to missionary bishops and clergy. Then, in a day when feudalism and rising monarchies threatened to dismember and secularize the Church, making it ancillary to the civil authorities, the Papacy fought to maintain the independence of the spiritual authority and the supremacy of the Christian conscience as embodied in the Church.

The importance of this Papal contribution is difficult to exaggerate. The age was one in which Christianity owed its spread largely to the patronage of rulers. The Church, endowed munificently by the gifts of those who thus sought security in the world to come, proved tempting to aspirants for wealth and power. Kings tended to place in its leading offices favourites who had little or no interest in the essential message of Christianity and who in their lives contradicted its tenets. The multitudes who had moved into the Church *en masse* possessed only the most superficial knowledge of their new faith. Under such circumstances Christianity was in danger of becoming quickly denatured and of disappearing. Against this peril the Papacy constituted an important, if not an always effective, safeguard. Through it some of those reformers could act who wished to see the Church true to its original purpose. In it was a power strong enough and sufficiently free from the state to seek to enforce the Church's autonomy. Repeatedly the Papacy fell into the hands of men who were either too weak or of too un-Christian character to hold it to this purpose. Sometimes in its struggle with the secular arm it was compelled to yield. Often it compromised. Always, however, it was there as a symbol of a community which in its aspirations overpassed national lines and of ideals which were above the control of the state. Occasionally, moreover, the Papal throne was occupied by a strong man who embodied something of what the dreamers hoped of it.

For the eastern part of the Catholic Church the Emperor and the Patriarch of Constantinople provided a point of reference, important but less influential than the Papacy. Occasionally the Emperor directed missions. The Patriarch enjoyed a certain primacy in the bodies which derived their Christianity from this Church of the East. Yet in lands which inherited the Byzantine tradition the spiritual were more subject to the temporal authorities than was the rule in the West. No central officer could stand effectively for the autonomy and unity of the Christian community. Frequently the civil rulers sought to render the Church in their domains autocephalous, quite independent of any control from Constantinople. Each wished to have authority over the head of the Church in his domains in the same fashion that the Patriarch was dominated by the Emperor. As a result, in those regions which derived their

Christianity from the eastern branch of the Catholic fellowship the Church was much less independent and united than in the West.

Among the Nestorians the Catholicos, who resided first in Seleucia-Ctesiphon and later in Baghdad, exercised some control over the wide-flung dioceses of the Church, including those in recently entered territories. Somewhat similarly the Coptic Patriarch in Alexandria enjoyed a primacy among all the branches of the Monophysites who stemmed from Egypt. Neither, however, wielded authority comparable to that of the Pope of Rome.

Again and again the student who surveys these centuries is impressed by the leisurely pace at which Christianity made its way among new peoples. With all the aid given by secular rulers, and in spite of the zeal of the hundreds of ardent missionaries, even the superficial conversion of the Northern European peoples required most of the thousand years between the fifth and the sixteenth century. Clovis was baptized, as we have seen, towards the end of the fifth century. Yet it was two and a half centuries more before the majority of the Germans of the Rhine Valley became even nominally Christian. Not until the end of the twelfth century could the conversion of the Scandinavian peoples be called substantially completed. In the thirteenth century paganism was still unsubdued in some of the Baltic lands. Moreover, the populations involved were not numerically nearly as large as in the Europe of today or, probably, even in the Roman Empire of the first five centuries. As against the gains of the initial five hundred years, the expansion of Christianity was slowing down. Not only were many regions being lost to the faith, but in those which were being added the rate of growth was much less rapid than at the outset. Only after 1500 was it once more accelerated.

However, while in Europe the expansion of the faith, measured by centuries, was slow, it was fairly steady. The sixth century saw the completion of the conversion of the Franks. The sixth and seventh centuries witnessed the conversion of the Angles and Saxons and of most of those Celtic folk in Britain who had heretofore been pagan. In the eighth century the conversion of the Rhine Valley was brought to a conclusion. The eighth and ninth centuries cover the baptism of the Saxons. The ninth century was marked by the rapid spread of the faith among the Slavs of Central Europe and the Balkans, a process which was continued in the tenth century. In the eleventh century most of the Danes, Norwegians, and Magyars entered the fold of the Church, and the mass conversion of the Russians began. The twelfth century marked the final victory of Christianity in Poland and Sweden and among the Wends (the Slavs of Eastern Germany). In the thirteenth century such Baltic peoples as the Estonians, the Letts, and the Prussians were forcibly brought to the baptismal font. In the thirteenth and fourteenth centuries the faith became firmly planted in Northern Russia and in Lithuania.

It was chiefly where Christianity's territories bordered on Islam that the violent fluctuations occurred. Most of the Iberian Peninsula was overrun in the seventh century, only to be slowly regained, and much of South-eastern Europe was lost in the fifteenth century. Outside of Europe, due again chiefly to Islam, the flow and ebb were even more extreme, with gains in the Nile Valley in the sixth century, great losses in North Africa and Western Asia in the seventh century, wide extension of the borders of Nestorianism in Central Asia, India, and the Far East between the seventh and the fourteenth century, a Roman Catholic missionary enterprise from the eleventh to the fourteenth century which carried this branch of the Church clear across Asia, and then in the fourteenth and fifteenth centuries sudden disastrous contraction.

As we proceed to the detailed account of the expansion of Christianity in these years it is not possible to preserve a precisely chronological order. Although it spread slowly, Christianity was often making headway on many fronts. At times, moreover, while it was gaining ground in one region it was suffering vast losses in another. In general we will tell our story by an outline which is partly according to topography and arranged partly in a time sequence. First we will describe the conversion of those peoples who came into the faith through Roman Catholicism, next of those who derived their faith from Greek Christianity, and then recount the territorial progress of the Nestorians and of the Syrian and Coptic Jacobites. Then chronologically we will double back on our tracks and tell of the spread of Islam and of the reverses which it brought to Christianity. Next we will narrate the efforts of Christians to regain the ground lost to Islam and to carry their faith beyond the eastern bounds of Islam into the lands of the Far East. Finally we will note the fresh outburst of Moslem peoples which in the fourteenth and fifteenth centuries wiped Christianity from the map in much of Asia and threatened it in South-eastern Europe. Following this account of the varying fortunes in the expansion of the faith we will address ourselves to the questions of the effect of Christianity upon its environment and of the effect of the environment upon Christianity.

Chapter II

THE SPREAD OF ROMAN CATHOLIC CHRISTIANITY AMONG THE PEOPLES OF WESTERN EUROPE: ITALY; SPAIN TO THE MOSLEM INVASION; GAUL; THE IRISH; SCOTLAND, WALES, AND ENGLAND; FRISIA; THE RHINE VALLEY; THE SAXONS; THE SCANDINAVIANS

IN THE geographic division of our story between the years 500 and 1500 we have chosen to treat first of all those regions and peoples in Europe among whom the Latin form of Catholic Christianity spread. We must remind ourselves again that this arrangement is not chronological. Simultaneously other forms of Christianity were being propagated in other portions of the world. Even in recounting the expansion of Latin Christianity we cannot, without undue confusion, follow a strictly chronological order. Often events with which we have to do were occurring contemporaneously in many different lands.

In this chapter, however, we can keep roughly to a time sequence. First we will speak of the progress of Latin Catholicism in Italy and Spain to the time when, in the seventh century, the Arab Moslem incursions brought sharp reverses. Then we will turn to Gaul, to the completion of the conversion of the Franks and the elimination of Arianism. Next we must describe the Irish missions which had so much to do with the spread of Christianity in the Frankish domains, in the British Isles, and in Germany. Following that we must recount the conversion of the peoples of Great Britain, notably the Angles and Saxons. From these our story naturally continues among the Frisians and in the Rhine Valley and adjacent lands, where the leading agents in the completion of the work of conversion were from the English, who themselves were not yet all even nominally Christian when missionaries from their number began to go to the Continent. From Frisia and the Rhine Valley we must logically proceed to the Saxons, and thence to the Scandinavians. That will complete the story of the conversion of the Celtic and Teutonic peoples. It forms, therefore, a convenient grouping for a chapter.

In the succeeding chapter we will proceed to those Slavs who became Roman Catholics, to the Magyars who planted themselves in the midst of the Slavs, and to the peoples on the south-eastern shores of the Baltic who were late in accepting the Christian faith.

Without more preliminaries, then, we turn to Italy and the adjacent islands of Sicily, Sardinia, and Corsica. By the end of the fifth century, paganism in the guise of formal cults had been largely eliminated. Yet it had not been completely eradicated. Moreover, the dominance of Catholicism was challenged by the Arianism of the Teutonic invaders. Toward the end of the fifth century, the Ostrogoths, Arians, established a kingdom in Italy which lasted until the middle of the sixth century. Then came the Lombards, mostly Arian, who founded a kingdom which survived until 774. Indeed, fragments of the Lombard power in the form of local nobles persisted for centuries after the downfall of the kingdom. The Lombards had their chief stronghold in the North of Italy, but they held important centres in the South, particularly in and around Beneventum, not far from Naples. Throughout the thousand years between 500 and 1500 and for centuries thereafter, the political situation was extraordinarily complicated. Over the Alps came invader after invader. The Emperors in Constantinople long ruled part of the peninsula. The Papacy became an important political power.

Fortunately, we need not enter upon all the main features of even the main outlines of the confused political fortunes of Italy. We can content ourselves with noting some of the steps by which the surviving pagan cults gave way to Christianity and by which the Arians were absorbed by Catholicism. Yet here our knowledge is tantalizingly fragmentary. Only now and then do we catch glimpses of what, if all its details could be known, would make a long and interesting story.

Decades before the year 500 the hold of paganism on Italy had been broken. The capture of the Eternal City by Alaric and his Goths early in the fifth century had, as we have seen, dealt the final blow to the aristocratic circles which still proudly adhered to the gods of ancient Rome.

Yet here and there the old cults lingered. Down into the seventh century we read of missionary efforts to eliminate the last traces of the now outmoded worship. Thus, as we have seen, when in 529 Benedict first reached Monte Cassino, soon to be famous because of his monastery, he discovered peasants still honouring Apollo. He turned the temple into a shrine to Martin, constructed an oratory to St. John where the altar had been, and cut down the wood.[1] An Irish monk of the sixth century, Finnian, as Bishop of Lucca

---

[1] *Gregorii Magni Dialogi*, Book II, Chap. 8 (edition Umberto Moricca, pp. 95, 96).

laboured for the conversion of the Lombards, and with marked success.[2] Barbatus, in his later days Bishop of Beneventum, spent years among the Lombards in and near that city who, though baptized, were paying worship to the image of a snake and to a tree. Not until after the city was delivered from a siege by an enemy army, a happy event which Barbatus had assured the defenders would follow if they abandoned their idolatry, did they consent to the destruction of these objects of their cult.[3] In the pontificate of Gregory the Great (590-604) pagans were still to be found in Sicily,[4] Sardinia,[5] and Corsica.[6] Here as in some other regions the vigorous statesman-prelate-saint was at pains to encourage the work of conversion. He actually sent two missionaries to Sardinia, although he usually confined himself to stirring up the local authorities to greater activity. Some of the Lombard hosts who invaded Italy in the sixth century seem to have been pagan,[7] but of their conversion we know little or nothing. In the first half of the eighth century we read of legislation against "country folk who worshipped a tree or a fountain, calling it their sacramentum."[8]

Arianism proved a much more formidable opponent of Catholicism than did the weak remnants of the moribund pagan cults. It enjoyed the prestige of being the faith of the politically powerful Ostrogoths, and, when these had been eliminated, of their successors, the Lombards. Both peoples had been won to that form of the faith before entering Italy.[9] The exact history of their conversion, especially that of the Lombards, is shrouded in obscurity, but of the fact there is no doubt. As a rule, both Ostrogoths and Lombards seem to have been fairly tolerant of Catholicism. The greatest of the Ostrogoths, Theodoric, who headed the Italian kingdom from 493 to 526, was notably so. Until almost the end of his reign he refused to bring any influence to bear on Catholics to adopt his creed and is reported to have inflicted the death penalty upon a Catholic priest who sought the royal favour by coming over to Arianism.[10] About two years before his death, perhaps partly because of

[2] Stokes, *Six Months in the Apennines,* pp. 36-39.

[3] *Acta Sanctorum,* Feb. 19, Vol. VI, pp. 142-147; Hodgkin, *Italy and Her Invaders,* Vol. VI, pp. 293-299.

[4] Gregory the Great, *Epist.,* III, 62 (in Migne, *Pat. Lat.,* Vol. LXXVII, col. 659).

[5] Gregory the Great, *Epist.,* IV, 24, 25, 26 (in Migne, *Pat. Lat.,* Vol. LXXVII, col. 693-695).

[6] Gregory the Great, *Epist.,* VIII, 1 (in Migne, *Pat. Lat.,* Vol. LXXVII, col. 903-905).

[7] Villari, *The Barbarian Invasions of Italy,* Vol. II, p. 279; Hodgkin, *Italy and Her Invaders,* Vol. V, p. 157.

[8] Hodgkin, *Italy and Her Invaders,* Vol. VI, p. 407, gives the Latin text.

[9] On the conversion of the Ostrogoths to Arianism, see Hodgkin, *Theodoric the Goth,* pp. 175-180. On the conversion of the Lombards to Arianism, see Hodgkin, *Italy and Her Invaders,* Vol. V, pp. 157, 158.

[10] Hodgkin, *Theodoric the Goth,* pp. 128, 181, 182.

mental unbalance, Theodoric, angered at the persecution of Arians by the Emperor Justin, instituted tyrannical measures. Then, perturbed by the fear of an alliance between Pope and Emperor, he imprisoned the Pope and ordered all Catholic churches in Italy to be handed over to the Arians. On the very day on which the latter decree was to be carried out, he died, but not before the Pope had succumbed in prison.[11] With Theodoric's passing—which, to his Catholic contemporaries, seemed a judgment of God—all thought of carrying out the transfer of the churches to the Arians was dropped.[12]

About the middle of the century, the Gothic rule was destroyed by Narses, the commander of the forces of the Emperor. However, the Byzantine triumph was short-lived. In 568 began the dominion of the Lombards. These new barbarians were never to control all Italy, but they mastered large sections of it. Of much ruder culture than the Ostrogoths, their regime was more disastrous to civilization. As we have suggested, at their advent into Italy some of them were pagans but the majority were Arians. The sufferings which the Catholics endured at their hands were probably due more to the exigencies of conquest and to differences of race and culture than to diversities of religion. The Lombards kept their own laws and cults.[13] While they might seek to enjoy the spoil of their swords in a somewhat ruthless manner and were not averse to sacking churches, apparently they undertook no extensive measures for the conversion of the Catholics to Arianism or for the restoration of paganism.

Although religiously the rule of Ostrogoths and Lombards was usually fairly tolerant, it could not but bring some distress to the Catholic Church. Arian churches were built. Theodoric, we know, constructed a number in Ravenna, his capital.[14] An eighth-century Lombard Catholic historian declared that in the first half of the seventh century each city had both a Catholic and an Arian bishop.[15] The accuracy of this statement has been challenged,[16] but it is clear that the Arians, supported by the prestige of the ruling group, must have been powerful. Theodoric attempted, with some slight temporary degree of success, to bring the Teutonic Arians together in a kind of league.[17] This, had it been given reality and lasting form, might long have divided the Christian forces in the West.

[11] Hodgkin, *Theodoric the Goth*, p. 285.

[12] Hodgkin, *Theodoric the Goth*, pp. 286, 294.

[13] At least one Lombard king forbade Catholic baptism of Lombard children, obviously in an attempt to keep his people a distinct group and to prevent their assimilation.— Schubert, *Geschichte der christlichen Kirche im Frühmittelalter*, pp. 249-251.

[14] Hodgkin, *Theodoric the Goth*, pp. 246-253.

[15] Paul, *Hist. Langob.*, Book IV, Chap. 42.

[16] Foulke's translation of *History of the Langobards by Paul the Deacon*, p. 194, n. 3.

[17] Hodgkin, *Theodoric the Goth*, pp. 175 ff.

Yet the ultimate triumph of Catholicism in Italy was probably never seriously in doubt. After all, the Arians, whether Goths or Lombards, were in the decided minority. The great mass of the population was Catholic. The invaders were inferior in culture to the conquered and must almost inevitably be assimilated by them. As the amalgamation proceeded, Arianism would disappear. Moreover, in its organization Arianism was at a disadvantage. It tended to split into churches dependent on monarchs. In contrast with it was Catholicism, with its hierarchy strongly entrenched in the life of Italy, its bishops often the chief representatives of Roman culture. Then, too, the Arians had nothing equivalent to the Papacy. While that had not yet developed all the powers which it later possessed, it was a centre around which Catholics, and especially those of the city of Rome, could rally, and under a Pontiff like Gregory I it gave aggressive leadership to their forces.

Of the process by which the Arians became Catholics we have only occasional glimpses. Towards the end of the sixth and the beginning of the seventh century a combination of circumstances seems to have led to a good many conversions to Catholicism. On the Papal throne sat Gregory the Great, who ably upheld the Catholic cause and encouraged those who supported it. Contemporaneously with him, Theudelinda, a Bavarian princess and a Catholic, was successively the queen of two of the Lombard kings, Authari and Agilulf, and regent during the reign of her son, a minor.[18] A Lombard historian declares that Agilulf became a Catholic,[19] but that has been questioned.[20] It seems certain, however, that Agilulf's son by Theudelinda was baptized a Catholic.[21] Authari had already found it necessary to forbid Lombards to have their children baptized as Catholics—evidence that this was being done.[22] After Agilulf's death and under the regency of Theudelinda, churches, presumably Catholic, were restored and rich gifts made them.[23] It was, too, while Agilulf was King and Theudelinda Queen, and only a few years after the death of Gregory the Great, that there came to Italy the distinguished Irish monk, Columban. He was shown favour by the King and must have strengthened the Catholic cause. During a sojourn at Milan he felt his soul stirred by the presence of the Arians and composed a work against them.[24] He founded a monastery at Bobbio,[25] in the Ligurian Apennines between

---

[18] Paul, *Hist. Langob.*, Book III, Chaps. 30, 35; Book IV, Chap. 41.
[19] Paul, *op. cit.*, Book IV, Chap. 6.
[20] Hodgkin, *Italy and Her Invaders*, Vol. VI, pp. 143, 144.
[21] Hodgkin, *op. cit.*, Vol. VI, p. 144.
[22] Schubert, *op. cit.*, pp. 249-251.
[23] Paul, *op. cit.*, Book IV, Chap. 41.
[24] Jonas, *Life of St. Columban*, 59.
[25] Jonas, *op. cit.*, 60.

Milan and Genoa, which became an important centre of Catholic influence. The strong anti-Arian conviction of its founder, the favour shown it by the princes and the Lombard kings,[26] and the fact that in 628 it was placed directly under the Pope,[27] all strengthened its position. Theudelinda's son became insane and was deposed.[28] After her regime the Arian influence at court may have revived.[29] However, the work of conversion could not be long delayed. By the end of the seventh century Arianism seems to have disappeared among the Lombards in North Italy and in the Lombard strongholds in Central and South Italy of Spoleto and Beneventum.[30] By the middle of the eighth century the Lombard king in his laws gave strong expression to his conviction that the Pope was "head of the churches of God and of the priests in the whole world."[31]

In the Iberian Peninsula the problem was, in general, the same as in Italy. Probably not much open paganism survived into the sixth century. We do hear that the Synod of Toledo of 589 complained that idolatry was growing.[32] Presumably, however, the great majority of the Teutonic invaders were Christian or had become so by the beginning of the sixth century. As in Italy, they were Arians and so in religion as in race were distinct from the Catholic Roman provincials. At the outset the Suevi, who settled in the North-west, were pagan, then were converted to the Catholic form of Christianity, and later exchanged it for Arianism.[33] The dominant Teutonic people in Spain were not the Suevi, but the Visigoths, and these were Arian when they entered the peninsula. As in Italy, the Teutonic Arians were of inferior culture. Assimilation to the majority was only a matter of time and with it the adoption of Catholicism.

At first the Visigoths, like the Ostrogoths, seem usually to have been very tolerant of the faith of their Catholic subjects. They did not rule all the peninsula and it may be that they deemed it unwise, by drastic measures against them, to drive their Catholic subjects into alliance with the forces of the

[26] Paul, *op. cit.*, Book IV, Chap. 61. On Bobbio at the close of the nineteenth century, see Stokes, *Six Months in the Apennines*, pp. 152 ff.

[27] Schubert, *op. cit.*, pp. 249-251.

[28] Paul, *op. cit.*, Book IV, Chap. 41.

[29] Paul, *op. cit.*, Book IV, Chap. 42; Foulke, *History of the Langobards by Paul the Deacon*, p. 190, n. 2.

[30] Schubert, *Geschichte der christlichen Kirche im Frühmittelalter*, pp. 249-251.

[31] Hodgkin, *op. cit.*, Vol. VI, p. 394.

[32] Schultze, *Geschichte des Untergangs des griechisch-römischen Heidentums*, Vol. I, p. 403.

[33] *Cambridge Medieval History*, Vol. II, p. 165.

Eastern Emperor, who still controlled a large portion of it.[34] Occasionally, however, there were persecutions.[35] King Leovigild, who reigned in the second half of the sixth century and who greatly extended the Visigothic rule in Spain, had varying religious policies. At times he was conciliatory. At others, in the vicissitudes of politics, he was a persecutor. In 580 he convened at Toledo a synod of the Arian bishops and induced it to facilitate the conversion of Catholics by eliminating the requirement of rebaptism. Apparently this procedure met with some success, for we hear that many Catholics, among them a bishop, came over to the Arian fold.[36] However, the movement to Arianism was against the trend of the times and could be only temporary. Indeed, the process of assimilation to Catholicism had already begun. The year before the Arianizing synod convened, Hermenegild, a son of Leovigild and a Catholic mother, had married a Catholic wife, and, shortly after, himself adopted that form of the faith.[37] Not far from this time, too, Gothic names appear among the lists of Catholic bishops.[38] Hermenegild's course was stormy. Some of the Spanish-Romans proclaimed him king and in the ensuing war with his father he was defeated, imprisoned, and killed.[39]

Under Recared, a son and the successor of Leovigild, Catholicism triumphed. There is even a report that Leovigild embraced Catholicism shortly before his death.[40] Recared, like his father, desired unity of religion among his subjects, but decided that it must be on the basis of Catholicism. He himself came over to that branch of the Church. Under him, in 589, scarcely a decade after the synod which seemed to mark a fatal reverse for Catholicism, another ecclesiastical gathering was convened, also at Toledo, but this time of Catholic prelates. Here Recared formally declared his own conversion and was followed by eight Arian bishops, many Arian priests, and numbers of Gothic nobles.[41] Catholicism now became the official religion of the Visigothic kingdom.

Numbers of the Goths, however, remained recalcitrant. The Visigothic nobles were notoriously restive under royal authority. Their recurring resistance to their kings was a chronic weakness of the Visigothic state. Many of them, together with numbers of Arian bishops and many of their Gothic followers, refused thus to abandon the faith of their fathers at the behest of their mon-

[34] *Cambridge Medieval History*, Vol. II, p. 164.
[35] *Cambridge Medieval History*, Vol. II, p. 163.
[36] *Cambridge Medieval History*, Vol. II, p. 169; Leclercq, *L'Espagne Chrétienne*, p. 259.
[37] *Cambridge Medieval History*, Vol. II, p. 168; Leclercq, *op. cit.*, pp. 253-262.
[38] Schubert, *op. cit.*, pp. 174-185.
[39] *Cambridge Medieval History*, Vol. II, p. 168.
[40] *Cambridge Medieval History*, Vol. II, p. 171.
[41] Leclercq, *op. cit.*, pp. 275-285; *Cambridge Medieval History*, Vol. II, pp. 171, 172; Schubert, *op. cit.*, pp. 174-185.

arch. Conspiracies and rebellions broke out. While in his lifetime Recared succeeded in suppressing them, recusancy continued. Recared's son and successor
was also a Catholic, but an Arian rebellion cost him his throne and his life.
Within less than a decade the Catholics were again in power, but Arianism
continued to claim a following right up to the erasure of the Visigothic kingdom by the conquering Moslems.[42] To the religious division in Spain must be
attributed part of the weakness which prepared the way for the Moslem triumph.
However, it seems to have been only incidental and to have been as much a
symptom as a cause of the lack of cohesion of the Visigothic regime.

In Gaul we have already noted the conversion of Clovis, the King of the
Franks, towards the end of the fifth century. As we have suggested, Clovis did
not force his people to conform to his example. Some were very slow in following him to the baptismal font.

Neither for Clovis nor for the masses of the Franks did the nominal acceptance of the faith mark any great revolution in character. Indeed, not only
the fifth, but the sixth, the seventh, and much of the eighth century were a
time of turbulence in the history of Gaul. In moving into former Roman territory and adopting some of the manners and the outward guise of the Christian religion, the Franks seem to have deteriorated. They had abandoned much
of their old culture, and with it whatever restraint it may have imposed upon
them. Yet they had not been mastered by the new. They gave evidence of
the demoralization which may attend the transition from one cultural milieu
to another.

A vivid picture of sixth-century Gallic society is preserved in the history by
Gregory, Bishop of Tours. Gregory himself was of that period. From a prominent Gallo-Roman family, widely travelled in his native land, head of the
diocese in which reposed the body of Martin of Tours (one of the most fre-
quented and venerated objects of an age which made much of relics), Gregory
was in a position to know whereof he wrote. At the outset of his work he
declares that liberal culture was perishing in the cities of Gaul, that kings
were growing more cruel, and that while in general the Christian faith was
being cherished, among some it was growing cold.[43] His pages bear out the
truth of this generalization, and quite as much so in their unconscious witness
as in the deeds which he deliberately records. His own Latin is evidence of the
decay of polite letters. He declares that he is weary of narrating the details of

---

[42] *Cambridge Medieval History*, Vol. II, pp. 172, 173; Leclercq, *op. cit.*, p. 295.
[43] Gregory of Tours, *Hist. Franc.*, preface.

the civil wars which plague the nation.[44] He tells of callous murders by princes, of concubinage, rape, and adultery in high places,[45] of a bishop who was often so befuddled by drink that four men could hardly take him away from dinner,[46] and of other bishops who were unchaste, gluttonous, and bibulous.[47] His own religion was a curious compound of energetic loyalty to the Catholic creed, esteem of asceticism, denunciation of the Arians, credulous belief in the magic efficacy of relics, and eager readiness to note the miraculous.[48]

Disorder and the decay of society were the natural results of the invasions of the fifth century. The inroads of barbarians, the wars which devastated much of the land, the settlement on the soil of Germanic peoples who had barely begun to take on a smattering of Roman culture and at best were only superficially Christian, could not but bring on a decline in civilization.

The picture of sixth-century Gallic society given by Gregory of Tours is but the continuation of a similarly gloomy portrayal by Salvian. Salvian, whose life spanned much of the fifth century, told of mounting taxes, of the purchase and sale of justice, of free citizens parting with all their possessions to buy the protection of the mighty and then sinking into slavery, and of a superficial Christianity which filled the churches but which, except for the monks, wrought little or no change in the morals of its professors.[49]

Allowance must be made for bias both in Gregory and in Salvian. From other sources we hear, even in the sixth century, of smiling valleys with villas and meadows, of great lords decorating their country seats with new baths, porticoes, and fountains, of church building, of the continued use of Roman roads, and of expeditious travel by those who could pay for it.[50] After all, in many parts of Gaul much of Gallo-Roman culture continued.

In the upheavals of the times the bishops often became the main bulwark of the old order. Roman civil government had collapsed or had passed into the hands of the Germanic invaders. The Gallo-Roman populace, now predominantly Christian, looked to the Church for protection. Not all the bishops rose to the high demands of their office, but in the main, much more than the civil officials, they preserved a sense of public responsibility and unselfishly served their flocks. Drawn, as they were in the early days of the Frankish rule,

[44] Gregory of Tours, op. cit., Book V, first two lines.
[45] As in Gregory of Tours, op. cit., Book IV, Chap. 28; Book VIII, Chap. 36; Book IX, Chaps. 27, 34; Book X, Chap. 8.
[46] Gregory of Tours, op. cit., Book IV, Chap. 12.
[47] Gregory of Tours, op. cit., Book IV, Chap. 20.
[48] As in Gregory of Tours, op. cit., preface, Book V, Chaps. 6, 14, 21, 23; Book VI, Chap. 29; Book VII, Chap. 44; Book VIII, Chap. 33.
[49] Salvian, De Gubern. Dei, Book III, Chaps. 9, 10; Book IV, Chap. 4; Book V, Chaps. 4, 5, 7; Book VI, Chaps. 2, 3, 5.
[50] Dill, Roman Society in Gaul in the Merovingian Age, p. 236.

largely from the upper classes of the Gallo-Roman stock,[51] they came forward as protectors of widows and orphans, and as dispensers of charity to the poor.[52] Monasticism, too, was growing and provided an outlet for many who sought a better way of life.

When all has been said that the records justify to offset the shadows, the fact remains that the Gaul of the sixth century was a very different world from that of the fourth. The masses who adhered to the Church seem to have displayed a declining quality of Christian living. Even the nominal Christianity of the times had not yet won universal acceptance. Pagan cults were widespread and had many adherents. The Church itself was divided. The Burgundians who dominated the Rhone Valley and the Goths who ruled in much of the south of Gaul were Arians. The Gallo-Roman population and such of the Franks as had followed Clovis into the Church were Catholics. It was a quarrelsome and largely superficial Christianity which faced the perils of surviving paganism and declining civilization.

Against these dangers Christianity for a time made decided gains. The weakness first eliminated was the division between Catholics and Arians. In Gaul, even sooner than in Italy and Spain, Arianism early ceased to be formidable. The conversion of Clovis was decisive. We have already seen that Clovis gave his adherence not to the Arianism which most of his fellow German princes espoused, but to Catholicism. The Franks followed his lead. The hope of a league of Arian Teutonic peoples, always chimerical, was finally dissipated.

Before the baptism of Clovis, Catholicism had begun to win the Arian Burgundians. Presumably that process would have been completed even without the influence of the Franks. Clothilde, a Burgundian princess and the wife of Clovis, came to him a Catholic. For at least a time, Catholic bishops held high place at the Burgundian court and were spiritual directors of the queen and princesses.[53] Mixed marriages with the Gallo-Romans were frequent. The Latin tongue gained headway.[54] With assimilation in blood and language, conformation to the Catholic faith of the majority came almost as a matter of course. Early in the sixth century, Sigismund, a Catholic, was on the Burgundian throne and encouraged the Council of Epaône, held in 517, to take drastic measures against Arianism.[55] In 534 two sons and a grandson of Clovis, the then rulers of the Franks, conquered Burgundy and divided it

[51] Dill, *op. cit.*, p. 479.
[52] Hauck, *Kirchengeschichte Deutschlands*, Vol. I, pp. 77-81.
[53] Dill, *op. cit.*, p. 83; Schubert, *Geschichte der christlichen Kirche im Frühmittelalter*, pp. 88, 89.
[54] Schubert, *op. cit.*, pp. 88, 89.
[55] *The Cambridge Medieval History*, Vol. II, p. 117.

among themselves.[56] This insured the elimination of whatever of Arianism may have survived.

Not far from the same time Provence and most of such other portions of Southern Gaul as had been controlled by the Arian Ostrogoths were conquered by the Frankish rulers.[57] Even earlier, under Clovis, the Franks had eliminated the Visigothic rule in much of Southern Gaul.[58] These political conquests, naturally, were followed by the triumph of Catholicism.

In the fifth and sixth centuries fresh migrations occurred which transformed the Gallo-Roman Armorica into Brittany, but these seem only to have strengthened the hold of Christianity upon that region. In the first half of the fifth century an exodus began of the Celtic peoples of South-west Britain, largely from the present Cornwall, Devon, Somerset, and parts of Wales, to the promontory which temptingly jutted out from Gaul and was so conveniently reached by crossing the English Channel. Presumably the movement was due, at least in part, to the pressure of the Anglo-Saxon invasions of Britain. Most of the emigrants went to Armorica, but some went to the Iberian Peninsula.[59] The exodus continued into the sixth century and resulted in submerging or eliminating most of the earlier life and institutions of Armorica.[60] In the days before the migrations, the region had at least three bishoprics, although probably not all the population were Christian.[61] The British immigrants, rough plunderers though many of them were, brought their own form of Christianity. In doctrine it was identical with the rest of Catholicism, but in organization it differed from that which prevailed in Gaul. It had its own type of monasticism, and its bishops were usually abbots who exercised jurisdiction primarily over the monastery and were not territorial magnates as were the members of the Gallo-Roman episcopate. The founders of the Breton bishoprics were all monks of British origin and it is probable that most of their clergy were regulars rather than seculars. They came from Britain to minister to the spiritual needs of their fellow countrymen.[62] Until the ninth century the Breton Church was practically independent of the rest of the Church in Gaul.

Arianism early ceased to be formidable and the Breton migration seems to have strengthened rather than weakened Christianity in the portions of Gaul which it occupied. Pagan cults, however, were long in dying. Against them Catholic Christianity made only slow progress. In Brittany the old faiths lingered

---

[56] *Ibid.*
[57] *The Cambridge Medieval History,* Vol. II, p. 118.
[58] Gregory of Tours, *Hist. Franc.,* Book II, Chap. 37.
[59] Gougaud, *Christianity in Celtic Lands,* pp. 104-112.
[60] Taylor, *Life of St. Samson of Dol,* pp. xxv-xxix.
[61] Taylor, *op. cit.,* pp. xxix-xxxi.
[62] *Ibid.;* Gougaud, *op. cit.,* pp. 121-128.

late: we hear that in 658 the Council of Nantes ordered the destruction of druidical stones and sacred trees.[63] In the northern portions of Gaul paganism was especially persistent, probably partly because the Teutonic barbarians were more numerous there and the disappearance of the Gallo-Roman Christian order had been more nearly complete.[64] In the sixth century, a deacon, a contemporary of Martin of Tours, found in the region of Treves an image which was still worshipped and which he induced the country folk to help him destroy.[65] Towards the end of the sixth century, a man from Treves on a voyage to Italy found himself the only Christian on board the ship.[66] Again and again Church councils of the sixth century found it necessary to denounce paganism.[67] To be sure, some of the practices forbidden were not the outright worship of the old deities, but divination and auguries, and taking an oath on the head of an animal.[68] However, more than once we read of penalties prescribed for the reversion of baptized Christians to the cults of the gods.[69] It was not only among the lowly that paganism continued, but also among some of the mighty of the land.[70] Sixty years after the baptism of Clovis, King Childebert, who had his capital in Paris, denounced landowners who allowed images of the gods on their holdings.[71] A decade or so later, in 567, at a synod in Tours it was reported that paganism was still alive, and that trees, rocks, and springs continued to be reverenced.[72] Somewhere between 550 and 560 we hear of a Frankish queen discovering, while on a journey, a pagan temple not far from the road. She had it destroyed, in spite of the armed opposition of its Frankish constituency.[73] When Vaast, a contemporary of Clovis, became Bishop of Arras, in Northern Gaul, he found much of the city non-Christian.[74] From a synod in 626 and 627 we hear of the continuation of pagan feasts.[75]

Against these cults the authorities of the Church continued the work of

---

[63] Dupouy, *Histoire de Bretagne*, p. 34.

[64] Dill, *Roman Society in the Merovingian Age*, pp. 86-89.

[65] Gregory of Tours, *Hist. Franc.*, Book VIII, Chap. 15.

[66] Dill, *op. cit.*, pp. 86-89.

[67] *Ibid.*

[68] Hauck, *Kirchengeschichte Deutschlands*, Vol. I, p. 115. The Latin texts (Conc. Aurel. I, a. 511, can. 30; IV, can. 16) are given in footnote 3.

[69] Hauck, *op. cit.*, Vol. I, p. 115. The Latin texts (Conc. Aurel. II, a. 533, can. 20; IV, a. 541, can. 15) are given in footnote 2.

[70] Hauck, *op. cit.*, Vol. I, p. 115. The Latin text (Conc. Aurel. V, a. 549, can. 22) is given in footnote 5.

[71] *Praecept. Childeberti*, in *Mon. Germ. Hist., Capit. Reg. Franc.*, Vol. I, pp. 2, 3.

[72] Hauck, *op. cit.*, Vol. I, p. 117. The Latin text is given in footnote 3.

[73] *Vita S. Radegundis*, Book II, Chap. 2, in *Mon. Germ. Hist., Script. rer. Meroving.*, Vol. II, p. 380.

[74] *Vita Vedastis*, Chaps. 5, 6 in *Mon. Germ. Hist., Script. rer. Meroving.*, Vol. III, pp. 409, 410.

[75] Hauck, *op. cit.*, Vol. I, p. 119. The Latin text is given in footnote 2.

extirpation. Indeed, most of our knowledge of the persistence of paganism is from the ecclesiastical legislation which was enacted against it. In this the synods were again and again supported and encouraged by the Merovingian rulers. Active missionaries there were, too. Sometimes these were bishops who carried on the task of winning the pagans of their dioceses as part of their episcopal functions. At least one was a bishop without a specific diocese.[76] Amandus, born near Nantes not far from the end of the sixth century, became a monk, was consecrated as a missionary bishop, and through a long life laboured, largely as a missionary, in various regions. In the present Flanders, among the Frisians in the Low Countries, among the Slavs on the Danube, and among the Basques he sought to win converts. For a time he was Bishop of Maastricht, in a region where much of paganism survived, but he could not long be tied to any one place. He fearlessly rebuked his patron, one of the Merovingians, for the latter's polygamy and concubinage, and for his pains was expelled from the kingdom.[77] A monk and the founder of monasteries, he was one of the many members of the monastic movement who had a part in the propagation of Christianity in the domains of the Franks.

Not always were monasteries centres of missionary effort. Probably in Gaul the majority had little or no interest in it. However, from some of them went those who sought to win the pagans of the land.[78]

By the beginning of the seventh century Christianity seems to have become the faith of the vast majority in Gaul, not only of the Gallo-Roman population, but of the descendants of the invaders. The assimilation of the latter by the former and with it the process of conversion were approaching completion. It was chiefly on the northern and eastern borders of the Frankish domains and north and east of the Rhine Valley that formal non-Christian cults survived.

Although both the upper and the lower classes had become nominally Christian, the religion of both rulers and ruled must have presented a medley of observances which had a Christian heritage and of customs with a non-Christian provenance. To the ordinary believer, Christianity seems to have been largely a matter of outward observances with something of the aspect of magic, more powerful than that of the older faiths, to be sure, but not different in kind. It was also a way to escape the pains of hell and attain the blessings of heaven.

The Church suffered by its very success. In the closing days of Roman rule,

[76] Moreau, in Descamps, *Histoire Générale Comparée des Missions*, p. 153.

[77] *Vita Amandi*, in *Mon. Germ. Hist., Script. rer. Meroving.*, Vol. V, pp. 431-483; Édouard de Moreau, *Saint Amand* (Louvain, 1927), *passim*.

[78] Moreau, in Descamps, *op. cit.*, p. 153.

as we have seen, the bishops became the chief support of law and order and the leading representatives of the old Roman culture. In that manner they acquired great authority. As we have suggested, they were drawn largely from aristocratic families who represented the Gallo-Roman tradition.[79] Property was given the Church by many benefactors, and the bishops became its administrators. In these troublous times many sought the protection of the Church, entrusting their lands to it. The Church was exempt from taxation. As monasteries increased,[80] bishops brought them under their control. Then when the barbarian conquerors accepted baptism, they, too, endowed the Church with lands and established monasteries.[81] However far they might be from presenting ideal examples of Christian living, many of the successors of Clovis were lavish in their donations to the Church. Thus monasteries became rich and bishops increased in power.[82] Bishops, too, performed many functions formerly reserved to the civil authorities.[83] The offices of bishops and abbot attracted men who desired wealth and power.

During the sixth century, if one may judge by the names, bishops were still drawn predominantly from the Gallo-Roman rather than from the German stock.[84] During that century, too, synods continued to wrestle with the problem of cleansing the Church of abuses.[85]

As the sixth century passed, the Merovingian ruling line showed lamentable signs of decay. Before the close of the first half of the seventh century, the descendants of Clovis had become *rois fainéants*. As the authority of the crown declined, that of the local magnates rose. In the decentralization and the attendant disorder, the morale of the Church deteriorated. The buying and selling of the episcopal office became common. Frequently ecclesiastical positions were spoils to be awarded by the mighty to their supporters. On occasion, young men who had not yet attained the canonical age were placed in the episcopacy. Both bishops and priests rode with sword and lance and some felt no compunction over ignoring their ordination and returning to lay life. No longer did synods struggle against the secularizing tide. Indeed, eventually they ceased to be held.[86]

[79] Gregory of Tours, *Hist. Franc.,* Book V, Chap. 49, says that up to his time, with five exceptions, all the Bishops of Tours had been connected with his own family. See also Gregory of Tours, *Hist. Franc.,* Book V, Chap. 37; Book VI, Chap. 7; Book X, Chap. 31.

[80] In the sixth century alone, about two hundred monasteries are said to have arisen.— Moreau, in Descamps, *op. cit.,* p. 153.

[81] As an example, see Gregory of Tours, *op. cit.,* Book II, Chap. 18.

[82] Hauck, *Kirchengeschichte Deutschlands,* Vol. I, pp. 123-156, 226-243, 366.

[83] C. Pfister in *Cambridge Medieval History,* Vol. II, p. 144.

[84] Hauck, *op. cit.,* Vol. I, p. 144.

[85] Hauck, *op. cit.,* Vol. I, p. 375.

[86] Hauck, *op. cit.,* Vol. I, pp. 364-388; Schubert, *Geschichte der christlichen Kirche im Frühmittelalter,* pp. 260-263.

Under these circumstances, no very great ardour could be expected in the Frankish Church to communicate the Christian faith to the pagans who still bordered it on the north and the east, much less to take it across the Channel to the Anglo-Saxons of Britain. It was from other quarters and from branches of the Western Church numerically much weaker that most of the chief missionary movements of the seventh and eighth centuries arose. Indeed, when finally it came, the revival of religious life in the Frankish domains owed a large debt to men who had been nourished in churches which in age, wealth, and numbers were vastly inferior to that sister body which they helped to quicken.

In the seventh century the chief centre of missionary impulse in Western Europe was the distant island of Ireland. To this, in the eighth century, was added what was in part a child of the Christianity of Ireland, that of the English.

In an earlier chapter we have recounted what little is known of the entrance of the faith into Ireland. Here, as we have seen, for the first time in the West a strong Christian Church arose outside what had once been the political borders of the Roman Empire. Of the details of the founding of the Church, it will be recalled, we know very little. Even the part which Patrick played is debatable. For the generation or two after the probable time of Patrick we know practically nothing of the Christian communities with whose early days he is believed to have had so much to do.

When the mists begin to clear, the type of Christianity which is disclosed is different from anything we know on the Continent. Presumably Patrick had encouraged the development of the Church after the pattern with which he had become familiar in Gaul. When, however, we first begin to catch glimpses of Irish Christianity in the sixth century, it is of a Church which in many ways was quite unlike what had been known in Gaul. In creed it was the same.[87] It also knew monasticism. However, the territorial organization under diocesan bishops was absent and instead was a strongly monastic Christianity in which the bishop as such possessed no executive responsibilities, administratively was often subordinate to the abbot, and had the function simply

[87] Moreau, in Descamps, *Histoire Générale Comparée des Missions,* p. 155. How far Irish Christianity was submissive to the Pope and was consciously a part of the Catholicism of the West is debated. Toynbee, *A Study of History,* Vol. II, p. 333, holds that it took a very independent attitude toward Rome. McNaught, *The Celtic Church and the See of Peter,* argues that the Celtic Church was in communion with the Bishop of Rome, acknowledged him as head of the Church, and in all points of doctrine was in agreement with Rome. The debate is complicated by the ecclesiastical views of the writers, modern Roman Catholics tending to emphasize the Roman connexion and Anglicans to belittle it.

of ordaining priests. Sometimes the abbot was also a bishop.[88] In contrast with Gaul, where the bishop controlled the monastery, in Ireland the monastery controlled the bishop.[89] This differed somewhat even from the practice in the neighbouring Celtic Christianity in Wales and South-western Britain, where more generally the bishop seems also to have been an abbot.[90] Moreover, in such matters as the form of the tonsure and in the date for observing Easter, the Irish Church varied from customs sponsored by Rome.[91] These two peculiarities, apparently trivial, were later to assume major importance.

How the Church in Ireland came by these characteristics we do not know. One theory suggests that they were a development from colleges of Druids, resulting from the transfer of the allegiance of these spiritual leaders of the masses from the old to the new faith.[92] That, however, is by no means clearly established.[93] Another theory derives them from the monastic movement of Gaul and holds that Christianity spread chiefly to Ireland through a faith which stemmed from Martin of Tours and which reached Ireland by way of the spiritual sons of Ninian and through Brittany and Wales.[94] This, too, while ingenious, seems unproved. It is also said that after the death of Patrick Christianity in Ireland suffered a relapse and was reintroduced from Britain, and especially Wales, where it had taken on the distinctive forms which, with modifications, were found in Celtic Christianity wherever the latter spread.[95] This post-Patrician pagan reaction, however, is not universally conceded.[96] A factor which obviously entered was the separation of Ireland from the Christianity of the Continent by the barrier of paganism injected by the Anglo-Saxon conquests in Britain. Another which obviously proved important was the contrast between the social and political structure of Ireland and that which prevailed on the Continent. Gaul inherited the Roman civil administrative organization. In time this was erased by the consequences of the Germanic invasions, but not before the Church had been permanently moulded by it. In contrast, Ireland was divided into many petty states and socially and po-

[88] Gougaud, *Christianity in Celtic Lands*, pp. 220-223; Hauck, *op. cit.*, Vol. I, p. 243; Duke, *The Columban Church*, pp. 45-54; Meissner in Phillips, *A History of the Church of Ireland*, Vol. I, pp. 128-130.

[89] Hauck, *op. cit.*, Vol. I, p. 243.

[90] Taylor, *Life of St. Samson of Dol*, p. xv.

[91] McNaught, *op. cit.*, p. 83.

[92] Bertrand, *Nos Origines. La Religion des Gaulois. Les Druides et le Druidisme*, pp. 417-424.

[93] Gougaud, *op. cit.*, p. 62.

[94] Gougaud, *op. cit.*, p. 63.

[95] Bund, *The Celtic Church in Wales*, p. 24. Gougaud, *op. cit.*, pp. 70, 71, gives a bibliography of those maintaining this position.

[96] Gougaud, *op. cit.*, pp. 70-73, argues strongly against it.

litically was organized around the tribe.[97] Often the tribe entered the new faith as a body, led by its chief.[98] Whether or not it came through Ninian, obviously the monastic ideal was regarded as the perfect Christianity and proved very attractive. The tribe, therefore, tended to centre its religious life around a monastery, and monasteries became the fundamental units of the ecclesiastical organization.[99]

In the sixth century Irish monasteries were notable for scholarship and for a religious life of abounding vitality. We do not know by what steps the Irish monasteries were led to devote so much energy to learning nor just how it came about that Latin was studied so extensively.[100] It seems a fair conjecture that here was a normal outgrowth of the religious life. The monks and nuns naturally gave much time to the Christian Scriptures and to services in which the Psalter had a prominent part. Both the Bible and the service books presumably came to them in Latin, the ecclesiastical language of the Church on the adjacent Continent. To read these books Latin was necessary. The chief subject on the curriculum was the Bible. Some of the Latin Fathers were read and several of the celebrated non-Christian authors of Rome may have been perused. Much attention was paid to copying and embellishing religious books. Penmanship and illumination were brought to perfection.[101]

In general, the monasteries observed the three principles of poverty, chastity, and obedience, but each establishment tended to have its own rule, and one which differed in some details from those of its neighbours.[102] Extreme forms of ascetic discipline were practised.[103]

Around these monasteries, so full of vigour, a Christian Celtic culture developed.[104] From them for several centuries streams of influence issued to the Anglo-Saxons and the Continent with important results. From them Irish monks, missionaries, and scholars went forth, and to them came students from many lands who either were themselves in turn inspired to be missionaries to foreign peoples, or who carried home with them something of what they had learned.

Of particular importance were the Irish who went to other lands. In this age of migrations here was one strangely unlike its fellows. None of the

[97] Bund, op. cit., p. 58.
[98] Gougaud, Christianity in Celtic Lands, p. 65.
[99] Ibid.
[100] Gougaud, op. cit., pp. 240-256. Gougaud, op. cit., pp. 247, 248, maintains that the evidence that Greek was taught is very slight. Duke, The Columban Church, pp. 45-54, says that Latin, Greek, and Hebrew were studied.
[101] Gougaud, Gaelic Pioneers of Christianity, pp. 56-59.
[102] Gougaud, Christianity in Celtic Lands, p. 78.
[103] Gougaud, Christianity in Celtic Lands, pp. 89-98.
[104] Toynbee, A Study of History, Vol. II, p. 332.

other great movements of peoples of the fifth and sixth centuries appear to have been from predominantly religious motives. Even in the Arab explosion of the seventh century the religious factor seems to have been mixed with others. The closest contemporary parallel was that of the missionaries from India and Central Asia who were propagating Buddhism in China. In proportion to the population of the homeland, however, the Irish migration was probably much larger than this latter. What all of the impulses back of it were we may not know. It seems a fair guess that one of them was the desire to see new lands, the *wanderlust* to which groups of mankind have repeatedly been subject. The monastic life must often have become irksome and some may have sought refuge from it in travel. Of one of the most famous of the *peregrini* it was said by an early biographer that "after he had been many years in the cloister he longed to see strange lands, in obedience to the command which the Lord gave to Abraham: 'Get thee out of thy country, and from thy kindred, and from thy father's house, to a land which I will show thee.' "[105] It seems clear, however, that the religious motive was prominent. Probably it was dominant.

For many, perhaps most of these adventurers of the spirit, the missionary purpose was either minor or was entirely lacking. It was not from a burning desire to preach the Gospel that most of the wanderers travelled. Incidentally, some, finding themselves among non-Christians, preached to them, or, stirred by the lax living of those who bore the name of Christian, addressed themselves to the task of reform. The professed motive of most of the voluntary expatriates was ascetic. They left home "for the love of God," "for the name of the Lord," "for the love of the name of Christ," "for the healing of the soul," or "in order to win the heavenly fatherland"—or so the biographers declare.[106]

They went far. To the Orkneys, the Faroes, the rough coasts of Scotland they voyaged, and perhaps even to Iceland before the Vikings. The forests of Germany and the rugged hills of Gaul, the foothills of the Alps, the Rhine and the Danube, and the cities and the remote mountain valleys of Italy knew them.[107] Sometimes they gathered in communities. Often they established hermitages and sought salvation in solitude. A few of them were summoned as scholars and spiritual advisers to the courts of kings. Among

[105] Jonas, *The Life of St. Columban,* 9.
[106] Gougaud, *Christianity in Celtic Lands,* pp. 129, 130.
[107] Gougaud, *Christianity in Celtic Lands* is the best survey of these Celtic missionaries. An older, less critical, strongly pro-Irish, readable account is H. Zimmer, *The Irish Element in Mediaeval Culture* (New York, G. P. Putnam's Sons, 1891, pp. vii, 131, translated from the *Prussische Jahrbücher* of Jan., 1887).

their number were those who showed no hesitation in rebuking the mighty. For centuries they fared forth. Often they travelled afoot, choosing to follow the Apostolic example.[108]

Largely restless individualists, the Irish *peregrini* must have been a picturesque feature of the age, sometimes inspiring and often annoying to the churchmen of the Continent. Usually they proved more irritating than invigorating. They did not tamely conform to the ecclesiastical organization of the lands to which they went. Their wandering bishops probably had little understanding and less patience with the Roman-inherited territorial diocesan organization. Accustomed as they were to monasteries which subordinated the bishop to the abbot, when the Irish founded similar establishments on the Continent they sometimes proved reluctant to place them under the local bishops. Their unwillingness was probably reinforced by outraged disapproval and contempt for the worldliness of the secularized Merovingian prelates. They helped, accordingly, to nourish the precedent for the independence which so many monasteries came to have of episcopal visitation and control.[109] Wandering bishops weakened diocesan organization by going about as and when they pleased, consecrating and ordaining whom they would.[110] Some of the *peregrini* were accused by clerical opponents of irregularities in doctrine. We hear of one who was reported to have taught that when Christ descended into hell he delivered all who were confined there, both good and bad.[111] It may be, incidentally, that this was an attempt to remove what to so many pagans proved a stumbling-block to the acceptance of Christianity, the fate of their non-Christian ancestors. On the other hand, some of the Irish made notable contributions to the scholarship of the Continent. Here was one of the many examples in the history of the expansion of Christianity of the effort of adherents of one strain of the faith to bring those of another to their own way of life and thought.

Of the Irish we shall have more to say as we pass from land to land in our narrative of the propagation of Christianity. Here, however, we must pause to note the contributions of those who laboured in an area and period of which we have already spoken, Gaul under the Merovingians.

The most famous of these missionaries was Columban. He was born two

---

[108] Gougaud, *Gaelic Pioneers of Christianity,* pp. 72-74.

[109] Robinson, *The Conversion of Europe,* p. 200. Yet Helen Robbins Bitterman, "The Influence of Irish Monks on Merovingian Diocesan Organization," in *American Historical Review,* Jan. 1935, Vol. XL, pp. 232-245, holds that the Irish did not weaken the power of the diocesan authorities.

[110] Gougaud, *Gaelic Pioneers of Christianity,* pp. 24-30. But see, for a contrary view, Bitterman, *op. cit.*

[111] Gougaud, *Christianity in Celtic Lands,* p. 164.

or three generations after the death of Patrick, about the second quarter of the sixth century, in South-eastern Ireland, in the present county of Leinster.[112] The son of a Christian mother, he seems to have been reared from childhood in the atmosphere of religion. He was early studious, avid for the scholarship which could then be had in his native land. He appears also to have been a full-blooded and handsome youth, attractive to and attracted by the opposite sex. But he heard the call of the ascetic life. In the face of his mother's earnest entreaties and tears, he left home with the resolution never to see it again.[113] For a time he studied the Scriptures with one Sinell. Thence he joined himself to the famous monastic community of Bangor, in County Ulster.

After some years at Bangor, driven by an inward urge, Columban led a band of twelve across the sea. He landed in Brittany, the goal of so many of the British Celts, but passed on into the Merovingian domains. Stirred by the superficiality of the nominal Christianity of the populace, he preached a more earnest Christian life, presumably setting forth by word and example the exacting ascetic virtues which he had learned in Ireland.[114] Eventually, at the request, so it is said, of one of the rulers, he and his companions settled down in a ruined castle at Annegray in a lonely spot in the foothills of the Vosges.[115] He was sought out by so many who wished to undertake the ascetic life under his leadership that he was forced to find still another location for a monastery. This he determined upon in a place, still in the Vosges, which formerly had been a fort, Luxeuil. This became his chief centre. The community continued to grow, recruited at least in part from the scions of

---

[112] Jonas, *Vita Col.,* Chap. 9, gives his birthplace. On the date of his birth, see Martin, *Saint Columban,* pp. 11, 12, where the year is given as *c.* 540. Schubert, *Geschichte der christlichen Kirche im Frühmittelalter,* p. 211, says *c.* 530. The standard early life of Columban is by Jonas, a monk of Bobbio, the monastery which Columban founded in his later years, and was written about a generation after Columban's death. The Latin text is in *Mon. Germ. Hist., Script. rer. Meroving.,* Vol. IV, pp. 65-108. An English translation of Jonas (*Life of St. Columban*) by D. C. Munro, was published in Philadelphia in 1902. The *Vita* by Jonas is also in Migne, *Pat. Lat.,* Vol. LXXXVII, cols. 1009-1046. Most of Columban's writings are in Migne, *Pat. Lat.,* Vol. LXXX, cols. 201-296. His letters are in *Mon. Germ. Hist., Ep. Mer. et Kar. Aevi,* Vol. I, pp. 154-190. Modern biographies are E. Martin, *Saint Colomban* (Paris, Victor Lecoffre, 2d ed., 1905, pp. vi, 198), Johann Joseph Laux, *Der hl. Kolumban* (Freiburg i.B., Herdersche Verlagshandlung, 1919, pp. xvi, 290), and Mrs. Thomas Concannon, *The Life of St. Columban* (Dublin, The Catholic Truth Society of Ireland, 1915, pp. xxxii, 338). Of the many brief accounts the following may be mentioned: Hauck, *Kirchengeschichte Deutschlands,* Vol. I, pp. 244-266; Gougaud, *Gaelic Pioneers of Christianity,* pp. 8-16; Maclear, *A History of Christian Missions during the Middle Ages,* pp. 234-248; Montalembert, *The Monks of the West,* Book VII (Vol. II, pp. 385-549); Addison, *The Medieval Missionary,* pp. 5-8.

[113] Jonas, *Vita Col.,* Chap. 8.

[114] Jonas, *Vita Col.,* Chaps. 9-11.

[115] Jonas, *Vita Col.,* Chap. 12.

prominent families, and he founded one more offshoot, at Fontaines.[116] These monasteries lived under a rule which Columban framed and which was more severe than that of Benedict.[117] It exacted even more absolute obedience to the head of the monastery; it commanded as much silence as possible; it reduced food to a minimum and enjoined rising before the monk had slept sufficiently; and it had an enumeration of sins with a list of penalties more Draconian than the Benedictine.

So energetic a leader, with such strong convictions, set in an alien society, and especially in one so at variance with his principles as was the Merovingian realms, could not avoid conflicts. Columban was not the man to evade them. Impatient of contradiction, passionate, and uncompromising, he rather invited them. He did not hesitate to dissent vigorously even from Pope Gregory the Great.[118] He fell out with the bishops of Gaul over the date of Easter and in 602 or 603 was summoned before a synod. While his letter to the episcopate was conciliatory and in good temper, pleading for love and for reciprocal tolerance on the question at issue, it displayed no sign of yielding.[119] Apparently the bishops either assented or proved unable to oust him.

Far otherwise was his contest with royalty. Since 596 the nominal ruler of Burgundy, in whose territory Columban's monasteries lay, was one Theuderich or Theodoric, who apparently held the abbot in high respect. However, the real master of the realm was Brunhilda, Theuderich's grandmother, a dominating woman with a thirst for power. Columban aroused her ire by his unyielding and open disapproval of her grandson's habit of taking to himself concubines. Stormy scenes with the Queen Dowager and the King followed. Eventually Theuderich commanded the monk to return to his own land.[120] The ostensible charge was that Columban was violating the customs of the country and may indicate that differences in ecclesiastical practice may have been as prominent as the abbot's disapproval of the monarch's morals.[121] For a time Columban held out against deportation, but eventually yielded rather than imperil others, and was taken as far as Nantes. In some way—by a miracle, so the biographer declared—at the very port of debarkation he avoided being shipped out of the country and resumed his wanderings through the Continent. These eventually brought him to Italy.

---

[116] Jonas, *Vita Col.*, Chap. 17. On Luxeuil as it was near the close of the nineteenth century, see Stokes, *Three Months in the Forests of France,* pp. 20-70.

[117] The rule is given in Migne, *Pat. Lat.,* Vol. LXXX, cols. 210-224. See also Montalembert, *The Monks of the West,* Vol. II, p. 405.

[118] Columban, *Epist.* 1, in Migne, *Pat. Lat.,* Vol. LXXX, cols. 259-264.

[119] Columban, *Epist.* 2, in Migne, *Pat. Lat.,* Vol. LXXX, cols. 264-268.

[120] Jonas, *op. cit.,* Chaps. 31-33.

[121] Jonas, *op. cit.,* Chap. 33; Joynt, *The Life of St. Gall,* p. 5.

There, as we have seen, he was received with honour by the Lombards and, with faithful followers, established a monastic community at Bobbio, in the mountains between Milan and Genoa, where, after a few more years, he died, probably in 615.[122]

Columban was not allowed to live out his days in the monasteries in the Vosges to which he had given twenty years or so of his life.[123] Yet he and his labours had a profound effect upon the Merovingian domains and even beyond them. Under the inspiration of his example other monasteries were founded which followed his rule and which kept alive his ideals.[124] Moreover, he helped to summon the masses of nominal Christians outside the monasteries to a more exacting standard of living. He and his Irish fellows encouraged lay folk to come to them for confession, and as a moral discipline and a means of salvation imposed penance for concrete sins.[125] By the earnestness and the compelling force of his character Columban attracted to him clergy and laymen. Here was a foreigner who held no office in the Frankish Church, who did not seek its thoroughgoing reformation, and who ignored and even condemned some of its ecclesiastical customs. Yet bishops whose consciences were burdened with the guilt of simony, and clergy troubled by the sins of their youth, came to him for spiritual counsel. To members of a society notorious for cruelties, murders, gluttony, drunkenness, and flagrant sexual irregularities he presented the rebuke of an austere life which exemplified the virtues which the Merovingians and their subjects at once praised and profaned. To raw consciences and fearful souls he brought the medicine of confession and penance.[126] The penitentiary which he left with its enumeration of sins and of the penances to be imposed for each seems to have had a wide influence.[127] After his exile and death disciples continued his form of the monastic rule, the types of confession and penance which he introduced, and his emphasis on scholarship.[128]

Columban made his deepest impression upon the nominal Christians of the Merovingian realms. However, from him emanated impulses which led

[122] Jonas, op. cit., Chaps. 34-61. On the date of his death see Martin, Saint Columban, p. 173, n. 1.

[123] Jones, op. cit., Chap. 38.

[124] Hauck, Kirchengeschichte Deutschlands, Vol. I, pp. 270-274, gives a list of at least some of these. See also Jonas, op. cit., Chap. 22. The number of monasteries under the influence of Columban is estimated at more than fifty. Wilhelm Levison, Die Iren und die fränkische Kirche, p. 6 (in Historische Zeitschrift, Vol. CIX, 1912, pp. 1-22).

[125] Levison, op. cit., pp. 10-12.

[126] Hauck, op. cit., Vol. I, pp. 253-260.

[127] The text of the penitentiary is in Migne, Pat. Lat., Vol. LXXX, cols. 223-230.

[128] Gougaud, Gaelic Pioneers of Christianity, pp. 12-16; Meissner, in Phillips, A History of the Church of Ireland, Vol. I, p. 294.

to missions among some of the pagans who were still in the mountains of what are now the western part of France, Southern Germany, Switzerland, and Austria. Luxeuil was geographically so located that from it fairly easy access could be had to the valleys of the Rhone, the Rhine, the Seine, and the Danube.[129] From it went missionaries not only to Christians, but also to non-Christians. Thus Valery (Walaricus), gardener at Luxeuil under Columban, later won converts from among pagans in North-western Gaul.[130] Eustace, who succeeded Columban as Abbot of Luxeuil, laboured among non-Christians not far from the monastery, and later among the Boii.[131] Omer (Audomar), a monk at Luxeuil and subsequently Bishop of Thérouanne in North-west France,[132] is said to have striven for the conversion of pagans in the north-western portions of the Frankish domains. To one of the Irish companions of Columban, Gall, is attributed missionary effort among non-Christians near the head of Lake Zürich, in the present Switzerland. Here Columban, in his wanderings after his expulsion from Luxeuil, came upon idolaters whom he and his companions endeavoured to teach the Christian faith. Gall in his zeal set fire to the shrines and threw the offerings into the lake, an act which not unnaturally aroused enmity. Later, on Lake Constance, the company found images which were still being worshipped, and Gall, who is said to have had some knowledge of the vernacular, destroyed them and told their devotees of Christianity. Some, we are informed, were converted and others antagonized. Columban and his group remained there for three years. When Columban eventually passed on to pursue his course towards Italy, Gall, ill, remained behind[133] and established a monastery. Columban himself, so it is said, won some of the Suevi, and at one time contemplated going to the pagan Wends (Slavs).[134]

Columban and the men whom he inspired were not the only channels through which the stream of Irish Christianity entered the Frankish domains. Thus a generation or so after Columban's death Fursa came to Gaul after labours in his own country and in East Anglia.[135] The monastery at his burial place in Peronne, in North-western Gaul, became a centre for Irish

[129] Toynbee, *A Study of History*, Vol. II, p. 330.
[130] *Vita Walarici*, Chap. 22, in *Mon. Germ. Hist., Script. rer. Meroving.*, Vol. IV, pp. 168, 169.
[131] Jonas, *Vita Eustasii*, in *Mon. Germ. Hist., Script. rer. Meroving.*, Vol. IV, pp. 121, 122.
[132] *Vita Audomari*, in *Mon. Germ. Hist., Script. rer. Meroving.*, Vol. V, p. 756.
[133] Joynt, *The Life of St. Gall*, Chaps. 4-9.
[134] Jonas, *Vita Col.*, Chaps. 53, 56.
[135] *Vita Fursei*, edited by B. Krusch in *Mon. Germ. Hist., Script. rer. Meroving.*, Vol. IV, pp. 434-440. On Fursa see also Stokes, *Three Months in the Forests of France*, pp. 87 ff.

monks.[136] In the eighth century, on the advice of Boniface, who was reforming the Carolingian church, an Irishman was made Archbishop of Rheims, and in the seventh and ninth centuries we hear of two Irish Bishops of Angoulême.[137] Irish had a significant part in the revival of letters under the Carolingians, and the Irish colony at Laon became an important centre of scholarship. One of the most notable thinkers of the Carolingian age and, indeed, of the Middle Ages was Johannes Scotus Erigena, of Irish extraction.[138]

As we pass to Great Britain and Germany we shall hear still more of these Irish *peregrini*. For centuries they remained a picturesque and sometimes an important feature of the religious life of Western Europe. More than once they constituted for harassed bishops problems of regulation and discipline. On occasion they contributed notably to deepening the religious earnestness of the communities among whom they settled. Repeatedly we read of them as missionaries to non-Christians.[139]

To the monasteries and the religious life of Ireland the raids and conquests of the North brought great changes. Ireland was not far from Scandinavia and its internal divisions among many jealous tribes and chieftains helped to make it an easy victim to the Vikings. Norse settlements were effected in various places in the island. Scotland, the Shetland and Orkney Islands, and the Hebrides, where the Irish were represented, were also victims of the northern pirates. One of the early effects of the Norse raids was to quicken the migration of Irish monks to the Continent. There many of them sought refuge, carrying with them their precious manuscripts and their learning. Another and disastrous result was injury and even destruction to the monasteries in Ireland. These religious houses with their defenceless and peaceful inmates must have aroused the cupidity and the contempt of the warriors of the North. At the outset, too, the Vikings were pagans, and while in the course of centuries they became Christian and their descendants tended to amalgamate with the Irish, the first effect of their conquests was the decay of Christianity and the reintroduction of paganism.[140]

In the tenth and eleventh centuries a slow improvement began once more in the religious life of Ireland. Some of the Norse became Christian. Early

[136] Gougaud, *Christianity in Celtic Lands*, p. 147.
[137] Gougaud, *Gaelic Pioneers of Christianity*, pp. 22, 23.
[138] Gougaud, *Gaelic Pioneers of Christianity*, pp. 42-54, contains a list of some of these scholars and of their activities.
[139] For some of these Irish with brief comments on them see Gougaud, *Christianity in Celtic Lands*, pp. 146-180.
[140] Gougaud, *Christianity in Celtic Lands*, pp. 390-398; Gougaud, *Gaelic Pioneers of Christianity*, pp. 37, 38; Phillips (editor), *A History of the Church of Ireland*, Vol. II, pp. 3-8; Stokes, *Ireland and the Celtic Church*, pp. 251-266.

in the eleventh century their political power in the island was broken. Once again connexions with the Continent were re-established or increased. Students from abroad began to seek out the monastic schools of Ireland and Irish pilgrims became a more familiar sight in other lands.

The religious revival and the strengthening of the connexions with Continental and English Christianity were accompanied by a change in the structure of the Irish Church. The monastic bishop and an ecclesiastical administration centred in the monastery disappeared, and in their place came the territorial diocese with its bishop. The peculiarities which had distinguished Irish Christianity largely disappeared and at about the same time the flow of Irish religious emigrants to the Continent dwindled and at last ceased.[141]

Probably the causes for the end of the Irish migration and for the termination of the prominence of Ireland in the religious life of Western Europe must be sought even more outside than within Ireland. By the eleventh century the conversion of England and Scotland had been completed and that of the Continent had proceeded much further than in the sixth and seventh centuries. Moreover, the level of religious life on the Continent had risen. The Cluny movement was giving new life to the Church. The eleventh-century improvement in the Irish Church was due as much to impulses from Cluny as to the waning of the power of Viking paganism. From now on the flow of religious life was to be from England and the Continent to Ireland and not from Ireland to other lands.

From Ireland and its contribution to the Christianity of Western Europe we turn naturally to Great Britain. We do this not just because of the geographic propinquity of the two islands, but because the Irish had so large a share in the conversion of the peoples of the present England and Scotland and because English Christianity had much to do with the conversion of the peoples of the Low Countries, Germany, and Scandinavia. It was from England rather than from the larger and presumably more civilized and populous domains of the Franks that most of the missionaries came who created and organized the Church in the Rhine Valley and in some of the closely associated German territory. From England, too, were derived the monks and the ecclesiastics who had a major part in founding and giving form and

[141] Gougaud, *Christianity in Celtic Lands,* pp. 398-409; Phillips, *op. cit.,* Vol. II, p. 32; Lawlor, *St. Bernard of Clairvaux's Life of St. Malachy of Armagh,* pp. xii-xix; Stokes, *op. cit.,* pp. 305-349. In the date of Easter and in liturgy, conformation of Irish practice to that of Rome began in the seventh century.—N. J. D. White in Phillips, *op. cit.,* Vol. I, p. 114; Browne, *The Conversion of the Heptarchy,* p. 32.

depth to the Christianity of Denmark, Norway, and Sweden. It was also to the English that the Carolingians looked for the outstanding leaders in the reform of the Church and the revival of scholarship in their realms. The conversion of the English began in the sixth century, and almost before it was completed their missionaries were going to the Continent to spread the faith which had so recently come to them.

As we have seen in an earlier chapter,[142] Christianity was still spreading among the partially Romanized population of Britain when invasions of barbarians from the Continent and from the north of the island wiped out much of what had been accomplished in the four centuries of Roman rule. How nearly complete had been the nominal conversion of the British provincials we do not know. It is not an entirely baseless conjecture that here as elsewhere in the course of the fifth century practically all who called themselves Romans had accepted the Christian name.[143]

For a century or more following the collapse of Roman rule in the island, recorded history is almost a blank. Civilization did not immediately come to an end nor did Christianity completely die out. Yet the morale of rulers, clergy, and people declined. From the sixth century comes a gloomy picture by one Gildas, who seems to have known whereof he spoke, which is a scathing indictment of the clergy of the land.[144] It may well be overdrawn, for those who denounce the evils of their age seldom view them in balanced perspective. The very fact of the jeremiad indicates a conscience not yet seared into indifference to moral turpitude. However, more than a century of a slowly losing struggle against a barbarian invader, marked probably by dissensions among the defenders, must have lowered the quality of what at the outset had been for the majority only a superficial Christianity. Very possibly the British resistance was more stubborn than has sometimes been assumed.[145] Even in the east of England some Romano-British culture and Christian communities may have persisted until very late. Hundreds of years after the event a mediæval chronicle declared that the last British Bishop of London retired to Wales, and with him such of the clergy as had survived. It also said that the Bishop of York fled, presumably about

[142] Vol. I, Chap. 5.

[143] Patrick, a British Christian, in his *Letter* seemed to assume that Roman and Christian were identical, which appears to imply that all the Romano-British he knew were of that faith.

[144] See the text of Gildas in Haddan and Stubbs, *Councils and Ecclesiastical Documents Relating to Great Britain and Ireland,* Vol. I, pp. 44-115. See especially p. 74.

[145] Foord, *The Last Age of Roman Britain, passim,* contends that the Romano-British culture persisted long after the departure of the Roman legions and that not until about 582 was the final death blow given to whatever remained of Roman Britain.

the same time. The date ascribed to these events is 586.[146] If correct, this means that organized British Christianity continued in London and York until only slightly over a decade before the coming of those missionaries from Rome who had so much to do with the conversion of the invaders. Even should this late report prove unreliable, it is possible that much of the British population remained on,[147] enslaved, in the areas occupied by the Germanic conquerors, and many may have clung to their faith.

When every allowance is made for the slowness of the disappearance of the culture and the Christianity of the Roman era, the British Church must have suffered severely in the invasions and have vanished in large areas. Moreover, even before the end of Roman rule it is likely that most of what is now Scotland, lying as it did outside the control of the imperial system, remained untouched by the faith. Yet, while that is true, it seems probable that a Roman-Christian culture was widely diffused in the southern part of Scotland and persisted in scattered communities down into the sixth century.[148] At the beginning of the sixth century, Christianity had its strongholds in those parts of Great Britain where the ancient British people still maintained their independence—the West.

It was in the sixth and seventh centuries that the conversion of the non-Christian peoples of Great Britain was largely accomplished. On the surface it would have seemed normal to have had it achieved by missionaries from Gaul. It was probably from Gaul that Christianity had first come to Roman Britain. What more natural than that it should come to Anglo-Saxon Britain from the same quarters—where was the largest neighbouring body of Christians? In fact, however, it arrived chiefly from elsewhere. The conversion of England and the pagan Celts in the northern part of the island was the work of missionaries from two directions, the Celtic West and North and the Italian South. While, in the end, the Christianity of Great Britain was closely tied to Rome and in its customs and its diocesan organization conformed with that of the Continent, it owed a great debt to Celtic missionaries. Indeed, the actual conversion must be ascribed more to them than to the missionaries from Italy.

Much of the story of the labours of the Celtic missionaries has been lost. From the fragments which survive we can attempt to reconstruct the whole,

---

[146] *Flores Historiarum,* edited by Henry R. Luard, in *Rerum Britannicarum Medii Aevi Scriptores,* Vol. I, p. 280. On a possible persistence into the fifth and sixth centuries of a Romano-British town on the site of London see R. H. Hodgkin, *A History of the Anglo-Saxons* (Oxford, The Clarendon Press, 2 vols., 1935), Vol. I, pp. 137-147.

[147] Browne, *The Conversion of the Heptarchy,* p. 10; Hodgkin, *op. cit.,* Vol. I, p. 155.

[148] Simpson, *The Celtic Church in Scotland,* pp. 46, 47. Duke, *The Columban Church,* p. 141, believes that the earliest Christian monuments in Scotland do not go back to the Roman occupation, but to the activities of Ninian.

but many sections elude us, nor are we sure of the relative importance of some of the most prominent figures.

In an earlier chapter we have noted the name of Ninian.[149] We know very little of him, and an account two centuries or so after the probable time of his death records what is frankly labelled as oral tradition.[150] According to this report he was British by race, a bishop, and had been instructed in the faith while in Rome. His episcopal see was famous for a church which was known as *Candida Casa*, or the White House (or Whithorn, near the north shore of the Solway), was dedicated to Martin, and later became the burial-place of Ninian. Ninian is also reported to have won to the faith the Southern Picts. From this it appears clear that he was profoundly influenced by that early inspirer of monasticism in Gaul, Martin of Tours. Likewise it seems a fair inference that he did much to encourage the spread in Britain of a monastic type of Christianity.

How far the effects of Ninian's labours were felt has been a matter of debate. The Picts were the Celtic folk who predominated in Scotland in the days of the Roman occupation of Britain.[151] When, early in the fifth century, the legions were withdrawn, they ravaged northern portions of the Romanized section of the island.[152] How large a proportion of the Picts accepted the message preached by Ninian is not clear. It is sometimes said, from evidence drawn from a variety of sources, that Ninian's enterprise extended widely among the Picts and even to Ireland. It is also said that *Candida Casa* became an important missionary centre and that from it Ninian's disciples and successors continued the work of conversion which he began.[153] It may be, indeed, that Christianity had been found among the Picts even before the time of Ninian, coming in association with the Romano-British culture which for years had been filtering in among the non-Romanized Celts of the northern part of the island.[154]

As we have earlier suggested,[155] the movement initiated by Ninian may

[149] Vol. I, Chap. 5.

[150] Bede, *Eccles. Hist.*, Book III, Chap. 4. The accuracy of some of Bede's statements has been challenged. His knowledge of Scottish geography is said probably to have been vague.—Simpson, *op. cit.*, pp. 17, 58. His statement that *Candida Casa* as a church of stone was unique in Celtic practice is also declared to be inaccurate.—Scott, *The Pictish Nation: Its People and Its Church*, pp. 73, 74; Simpson, *op. cit.*, pp. 51, 61. See also on Ninian, Skene, *Celtic Scotland*, Vol. II, pp. 2-4.

[151] Simpson, *op. cit.*, p. 40; Scott, *op. cit.*, pp. 1-14.

[152] Simpson, *op. cit.*, p. 42.

[153] Simpson, *op. cit.*, pp. 63-72.

[154] Simpson, *op. cit.*, pp. 31-34, 47.

[155] Vol. I, Chap. 5.

have reached to Ireland. Several reports declare that a number of Irish leaders studied at *Candida Casa*.[156]

How far south Ninian's influence penetrated we do not know. For our accounts of the early leaders of the Celtic Church in the west of England and in Wales, we are dependent upon biographies the oldest of which were written four or five centuries after the death of their subjects.[157] These, then, give us little safe ground for an accurate appraisal of Ninian's contribution. It has been conjectured and even asserted as probable that some of the men who came out of his movement had much to do with the introduction of Christianity and the development of monasticism in the southern and western parts of Britain.[158] So imperfect is our evidence, however, that this must be put down as an interesting but quite unproved theory.

That Christianity existed among the Celts in the west of England and in Wales, and probably continuously from the time of the collapse of Roman power, is clear. Such names as those of David and Illtyd have come down to us from that period. The earliest accounts which we have of these worthies date from several centuries after their day. It seems probable, however, that such men actually lived, even though the details about them escape us. Most of them are said to have been monks and many of them bishops. They indicate a monastic Christianity.[159]

Another Celtic missionary whose influence is said to have extended through much of Scotland and into Wales was Kentigern, who was probably the same as Mungo. Kentigern is placed in the sixth century and so was between a century and a half and two centuries after Ninian. Our earliest extant biographies of him are from the twelfth century and must be used with the greatest caution. At best he is a shadowy figure. His headquarters are reported to have been at Glasgow, of which he is the reputed founder and where he is said to have been bishop, but his activities may have extended very widely— from north of Aberdeen in Scotland southward into Wales.[160] Kentigern's sojourn in Wales is reported to have been the result of a temporary exile from

[156] Haddan and Stubbs, *Councils and Ecclesiastical Documents Relating to Great Britain and Ireland,* Vol. I, pp. 120, 121.

[157] Haddan and Stubbs, *op. cit.,* Vol. I, pp. 156-161, gives a list of these biographies and in a footnote on p. 161 declares that none of them "can claim to approach to history."

[158] Bund, *The Celtic Church of Wales,* p. 153; Robinson, *The Conversion of Europe,* p. 154.

[159] Haddan and Stubbs, *op. cit.,* Vol. I, pp. 156-161; Taylor, *Life of St. Samson of Dol,* p. ix. Wade-Evans, *Life of St. David,* gives an eleventh-century biography which claims (p. xiv) to be based on "very old writings."

[160] Skene, *op. cit.,* Vol. II, pp. 180-184; Scott, *op. cit.,* pp. 246-255; Simpson, *op. cit.,* pp. 85-89; Duke, *op. cit.,* pp. 28-31; Anderson, *Early Sources of Scottish History,* Vol. I, pp. 130-138, gives a translation of the mediæval *Life of Kentigern.* Haddan and Stubbs, *op. cit.,* Vol. II, Part I, pp. 4, 5, has a note on the founding of Glasgow by Kentigern.

Glasgow due to a hostile king. Most of his activity seems to have been not far from this see. From the names of church sites it seems possible, however, that at least two of his Welsh disciples carried on extensive missions in the area north of the Mounth and of Aberdeen.[161]

Some time after the collapse of Roman rule, the Picts were harassed by fresh invaders. Many of these were Scots, Celts from Ireland. Others were Teutonic folk, part of that wave of conquest which submerged and eradicated the Romano-British culture in so much of the present England. From the south came in British, perhaps seeking a way of escape from the Anglo-Saxons, and established themselves in what is now the south-western part of Scotland. The Picts, hard pressed, may have lost much of whatever of Christianity had been theirs, whether from Ninian or from other sources. It is possible that Kentigern and the missionaries whom he inspired helped to stem the tide and even extended the borders of the Church. Probably, too, many of the Irish and British invaders were nominally Christian when they arrived.[162]

One of the most powerful of the movements which checked the rising flood of paganism is associated with the name of Columba, or Columcille. A contemporary of Kentigern, he stands out much more vividly than does the saint of Glasgow. This is largely because of the good fortune which handed down his memory to posterity through a biography by Adamnan, written about a century after the great missionary's death. Adamnan was abbot of the monastery on Iona which Columba founded and had the advantage of both written and oral sources. The biography is full of anecdotes, among them tales which were told him by eye-witnesses concerning the acts, the miracles, the visions, and the sayings of its hero.[163] Other and later biographies give us more information, but much of it legendary and unreliable.[164]

Columba, so we learn, was born in Ireland, in Donegal, probably on Dec. 7, 521.[165] Both his parents were of royal stock, and the son seems always to have had something of the prestige and the air of an aristocrat. From infancy he was reared in the Christian faith. For a time he was the pupil of a Bishop

---

[161] Simpson, *The Celtic Church in Scotland,* p. 88.

[162] Simpson, *op. cit.,* pp. 73-75.

[163] *Vita Sancti Columbae.* An English translation by William Reeves, together with a Latin text, is in *The Historians of Scotland,* Vol. VI (Edinburgh, 1874, pp. clxxxiv, 385).

[164] The text and translation of a sixteenth-century biography which incorporated all of the old Irish *Life* and part of Adamnan's is *Betha Colaim Chille. Life of Columcille Compiled by Manus O'Donnell in 1532,* edited by A. O'Kelleher and G. Schoepperle (University of Illinois, 1918). *The Old Irish Life of St. Columba* is translated by W. M. Hennessy in Skene, *Celtic Scotland,* Vol. II, pp. 467-507. An early brief notice of Columba's life and works is in Bede, *Eccles. Hist.,* Book III, Chaps. 4, 25.

[165] From Adamnan, *Vita Sancti Columbae,* preface, 521 seems the likely year. Other dates range from 518 to 523. On the year and the day of the month see Reeves, *op. cit.,* p. xxxiii; Anderson, *op. cit.,* Vol. I, p. 6, n. 3.

Finnio.[166] Of his boyhood and early manhood we have little detailed information from our earliest sources. His name Columba, "a dove," may not have been the one with which he was christened, but was possibly given him because of the character which he displayed as a child.[167] He was also known as Columcille, reported to be a compound of Columba and Cella.[168] The Cille or Cella meant church or cell, but no agreement exists as to how he came by the appellation.[169] Apparently Columba early dedicated himself to the monastic life. In due time he was ordained deacon and priest, but he was never made a bishop.[170] We know that he was early reported to have organized at least one monastery[171] and later accounts declare that he travelled much in his native island, founding many churches and monasteries.[172]

The course of Columba's life was not untroubled. Adamnan admits that he was once excommunicated by a synod, but beyond declaring that the action was unjust and for some very trifling reasons, gives no clue as to the cause.[173] We hear elsewhere that Columba stirred up his fellow clansmen to avenge in battle two insults he had suffered. Although his supporters won, remorse for the lives which they had taken and popular condemnation of the act, so it was declared, sent him from Ireland to Scotland.[174] Another account alleges that it was for his part in bringing about the war that he suffered excommunication.[175] The whole story of the battle is, however, dubious.[176]

Why Columba left Ireland we do not know. Adamnan simply says that it was "for the love of Christ."[177] We can only conjecture that it was because of something of that same wandering spirit reinforced by an ascetic impulse which sent so many of his countrymen to the Continent. Whatever the motive, it was in 562 or 563, when he was already in middle life, in his forty-second year, that he departed.[178] Nor was it a permanent leave-taking. More than once, apparently, he recrossed the sea to his native land.

[166] Adamnan, *op. cit.,* Book III, Chap. 5.

[167] Duke, *The Columban Church,* p. 58. His baptismal name may have been Crimthann, or "Fox."—Wapon in *The Aberdeen University Review,* Vol. XV, p. 138.

[168] Bede, *Eccles. Hist.,* Book V, Chap. 9.

[169] For various explanations see Reeves, *op. cit.,* p. xxxiii; Duke, *op. cit.,* p. 58; Simpson, *The Historical Saint Columba,* p. 2.

[170] Adamnan, *op. cit.,* Book II, Chap. 1; Duke, *op. cit.,* p. 59.

[171] Bede, *Eccles. Hist.,* Book III, Chap. 4.

[172] Simpson, *The Historical Saint Columba,* pp. 4, 5; Duke, *op. cit.,* p. 60.

[173] Adamnan, *Vita S. Columbae,* Book III, Chap. 4.

[174] O'Donnell, *Betha Colaim Chille* (edited by A. O'Kelleher and G. Schoepperle, University of Illinois, 1918), Chaps. 167-180.

[175] Skene, *Celtic Scotland,* Vol. II, p. 82.

[176] Skene, *op. cit.,* Vol. II, p. 83.

[177] Adamnan, *op. cit.,* second preface.

[178] *Ibid.*

With Columba in his first pilgrimage went twelve companions,[179] the same number with which, probably only a little later, Columban landed in Brittany. In Scotland he made his headquarters on Hy or Iona, an island about three miles long and from a mile to a mile and a half wide. Although the island was mostly low-lying, its highest hill rose to three hundred and thirty feet and commanded a magnificent view of the sea and of a neighbouring larger island.[180] On Iona Columba built a monastery. Much of his time must have been spent in the ordinary routine of the monk's life—in labour and prayer. He was said always to have been occupied—with study, prayer, writing, fasting, and watching.[181] Yet we must not allow the word "monastery" to bring to our minds the picture of a pretentious institution. The establishment on Iona must have been a simple one. It was more in the nature of a centre in which missionaries could be trained and from which they could conveniently be sent forth.

From Iona Columba made numerous journeys into Scotland. On his travels he was often a missionary to non-Christians. Presumably at least some of the Scots who had settled in the portion of Great Britain to which they gave their name were Christian. Perhaps, indeed, all the Scot immigrants were Christian and their kingdom from the beginning a Christian one. However, pagans were also in Scotland, whether only Picts or including Celtic folk of other strains we do not know. Columba is accredited with having won to the faith the Picts who dwelt north of the Grampians, the southern branch, so it is said, being already Christian through the labours of Ninian.[182] Adamnan tells of more than one occasion on which his hero addressed himself to the task of conversion. We hear of him baptizing the entire family of a peasant[183] and of hurrying to give the sacred rite to a dying pagan for whose character he entertained great respect.[184] We read of contests with the Druids.[185] Apparently these priests of the old faith were his bitter enemies. He is said to have met their magic with miracles which proved, by the tests they were accustomed to regard as valid, that the power on his side was greater than that which they could wield.[186] Perhaps a belief that Columba's miracles evidenced a God superior in power to the old ones had something to do with

---

[179] Adamnan, op. cit., Book III, Chap. 5. On the frequent use of twelve by early Irish Christians see Reeves, Life of Saint Columba, by Adamnan, pp. lxxi-lxxvi.
[180] Duke, op. cit., pp. 67, 68.
[181] Adamnan, op. cit., second preface.
[182] Bede, Eccles. Hist., Book III, Chap. 4.
[183] Adamnan, op. cit., Book II, Chap. 33.
[184] Adamnan, op. cit., Book III, Chap. 15.
[185] As in Adamnan, op. cit., Book II, Chaps. 10, 33, 34.
[186] As in Adamnan, op. cit., Book II, Chaps. 10, 35.

the readiness of his hearers to accept the new faith. Certainly Columba's disciples never tired of telling of his works of wonder. It was as much a religion of miracles as of ethics and even more than of formal creeds which made headway. Columba succeeded in winning the respect of Brude, the Pictish king,[187] and this may have stood him in good stead in gaining access to the Picts for himself and for other missionaries.

Of the characteristics of Columba we have much evidence. He must have possessed marked gifts of leadership. He seems to have been of impressive appearance and to have had a ready and eloquent command of language.[188] Clearly he shared in the beliefs of his day which peopled the world with demons and angels.[189] His disciples were convinced that he had the gift of forecasting events and of being aware of what was transpiring at a distance.[190] "He was not a gentle hero," said an old Gaelic eulogy:[191] he was capable of invoking condemnation upon his opponents and the unrighteous.[192] Yet he had a tender pity for the poor which expressed itself in active deeds of kindness.[193] He cherished a love for the brute creation, an affection which animals seem to have returned. We hear of him blessing a knife, with the request that it never be used to take animal or human life,[194] and of an old horse in the Iona community which showed signs of grief at the saint's failing strength.[195] We read of his tender solicitude for a storm-beaten crane.[196] He was a mystic with a simple trust in God. His disciples treasured as a sacred memory the words which he transcribed just before consciously putting aside his pen for the last time: "They that seek the Lord shall not want any good thing," and told the story of how, at the very end, he sought the foot of the altar and, dying, "looked round him from side to side, with a countenance full of wonderful joy and gladness, no doubt," so the biographer comments, "seeing the holy angels coming to meet him."[197]

How much share Columba had in the conversion of the peoples of modern Scotland is a matter of debate. Some insist that the larger part of the task was achieved by movements other than those which sprang from Iona. It

[187] Adamnan, op. cit., Book II, Chap. 36.
[188] Adamnan, op. cit., second preface.
[189] Adamnan, op. cit., Book III, Chaps. 9, 15.
[190] As in Adamnan, op. cit., Book I, Chap. 35, Book III, Chap. 15.
[191] Quoted in Taylor, The Mediæval Mind, in the sketch of Columba in Vol. I, pp. 134-137.
[192] Adamnan, op. cit., Book I, Chap. 31, Book II, Chaps. 25, 33.
[193] Adamnan, op. cit., Book II, Chap. 28.
[194] Adamnan, op. cit., Book II, Chap. 30.
[195] Adamnan, op. cit., Book III, Chap. 24.
[196] Adamnan, op. cit., Book I, Chap. 35.
[197] Adamnan, op. cit., Book III, Chap. 24. The date of his death seems to have been 596 or 597.—Reeves, Life of St. Columba by Adamnan, p. lxxix.

is declared that through the work of Ninian Christianity had already won many of the Picts and that Columba's contemporaries, Kentigern and his disciples, quite independently of Columba, were planting churches in Pictland as far north as Aberdeenshire, and that other Celtic monks were founding churches and monasteries even in the neighbourhood of Iona. The Pictish Church, so it is said, was chiefly the result of efforts from three centres, Ninian's foundation of *Candida Casa*, Kentigern's Glasgow, and Bangor in Ulster.[198] On Iona itself, so it is asserted, Christianity had been represented before the arrival of Columba.[199] Columba's missionary labours, it is declared, were confined almost entirely to the Scots who had settled in Scotland and to the Picts on their borders.[200] The Picts, so it is said, already possessed of a church, would scarcely receive the faith from one of the hated race of Scots who were invading their shores.[201]

All this, of course, is quite contrary to the traditional story and to the impression made by the reading of our oldest sources, the *Ecclesiastical History* of Bede, and Adamnan's *Life of Saint Columba*. More than one recent writer has taken up the cudgels for the older views. They deny that the evidence is sufficient to postulate any such extensive Pictish Church as the theory presupposes. They contend that the records do not support so wide-spread a missionary effort from *Candida Casa* as is necessary to substantiate the hypothesis. They hold that the hostility of the Picts for the Scots was not great enough to preclude the lasting friendship which Adamnan declares the Pictish king came to feel for Columba. They also deny that the archæological evidence adduced to support the new radical views is convincing.[202]

A detailed examination of the controversy is out of place in a work of this length. Perhaps it may be said that an impressive amount of evidence has been amassed and persuasively presented to show a wide extension of a non-Columban Christianity in Scotland contemporaneously with, if not prior to, the time of the founder of Iona. Much of it, however, is derived from written sources compiled centuries after the event. While these may embody authentic tradition, their reliability is decidedly open to question and it seems almost

[198] Simpson, *The Historical Saint Columba*, pp. 17 ff.; Simpson, *The Celtic Church in Scotland*, pp. 73 ff.; G. A. Frank Knight, *Archeological Light on the Early Christianizing of Scotland* (London, James Clarke and Co., 2 vols., 1933), *passim*.

[199] Simpson, *The Historical Saint Columba*, p. 20.

[200] Simpson, *The Historical Saint Columba*, p. 28; *The Old Irish Life of Saint Columba*, in Skene, *Celtic Scotland*, Vol. II, p. 491.

[201] Scott, *The Pictish Nation: Its People and Its Church*, pp. 223-225.

[202] Duke, *The Columban Church*, pp. 150-158; W. J. Watson in *The Aberdeen University Review*, Vol. XV (March and July, 1928), pp. 134-140, 234-236. See also a reply by Simpson in *The Aberdeen University Review*, Vol. XV, pp. 233, 234.

impossible to separate the wheat from the chaff. Moreover, many of the archæological data appealed to are of uncertain date and significance.

It is clear that Columba and the movements emanating from him were not the only source of the Christianity in what later became Scotland. Others had laboured before him as missionaries. Still others, like Columba, belong to the sixth century but worked independently of him.[203] Some missionaries who came after him were quite out of the Ionan stream. So we hear of Maol Rubha of Bangor in Ulster who arrived in Scotland in 671, won to the faith much of the extreme northern part of the land, and died in 722.[204]

The chief division of opinion is over the extent and the importance of the activity of Columba in the conversion of the Picts. The present writer is as yet unconvinced by the arguments which would so pronouncedly demote him from the position which has long been his.

Yet the scene is very confused. Even could we know it completely it would doubtless seem complicated. It may be that Columba has been traditionally assigned too prominent a place. As we have seen, we have so much information about Columba largely because of the full biography by Adamnan and because of Bede. Both sources may be inclined to exaggerate his importance, the one because of the admiration of a successor for the founder of the Iona community, the other because so much of the Christianity which he knew came through the Ionan stream of influence.

Whatever may be the truth concerning the geographic extent of the labours of Columba in his own lifetime, it is clear that from Iona went a missionary movement which carried the influence of that centre beyond both the Scots and the Picts and had much to do with the conversion of some of the pagan Teutons who had so rudely wiped out the Romano-British culture on the eastern side of Britain. The Ionan mission to the English began about a generation after one from Rome. In actual influence on the conversion of the English, however, it proved more important than the latter.

The story as we know it is quickly told. In the struggles for power which punctuated the history of the petty states founded by the Germanic invaders, some of the defeated party in the northernmost of these kingdoms, Northumbria, sought refuge with the Scots and the Picts. Among these were two young princes of the blood royal. They were there instructed in the Christian faith and baptized. From the sequence it appears fairly certain that this happened in the Columban circle. When the tide turned and the princes returned home, one of them, Eanfrid, who first became king, apostatized,

---

[203] W. J. Watson in *The Aberdeen University Review,* Vol. XV, pp. 134-140; Duke, *op. cit.,* pp. 32-38, 111.

[204] Duke, *op. cit.,* pp. 109, 110.

but the other, Oswald, remained true. Eanfrid was slain by a prominent British king, Cædwalla. When, in about 633 or 634, Oswald succeeded his brother, he and his forces in turn defeated and slew the victorious Briton.[205] Shortly before the decisive battle, or at least so he later reported, Oswald in a dream saw Columba in glory and was assured by him of victory.[206] Before the battle, so we are told, Oswald had a cross erected, knelt before it, and asked aid for himself and his army.[207] It was natural that, when his faith was rewarded by the utter rout of his enemy, he should be confirmed in it. He thereupon sent north for a bishop to instruct his followers in the tenets of the religion whose power had been so signally attested.[208] As we shall see in a moment, Christianity had already been introduced into Northumbria from Rome, but the conversion was far from complete and it is probable that it had lapsed in a pagan reaction.

It was to Iona that Oswald made his appeal. The first bishop delegated to him proved ill adapted to his task and, returning home, reported his flock as intractable.[209] In his place was appointed one Aidan. Aidan proved of a more winsome temperament and met with signal success. To him Oswald granted headquarters in the island of Lindisfarne. The place must have been suggested by the precedent of Iona, an island relatively undisturbed by the instability on the adjoining shore, yet near enough to be a convenient centre for a mission. Unlike Iona, Lindisfarne could be reached on foot at low tide from the mainland.[210] Aidan is reported to have made his journeys on foot, as seems often to have been the practice of the Irish *peregrini* on the Continent, both winning pagans to Christianity and confirming believers in their faith. He is said to have been deeply concerned for the welfare of the poor and to have devoted much attention to ransoming slaves. Many of the latter he educated and ordained as priests.[211]

In 642 Oswald was killed in battle by Penda, the famous pagan ruler of Mercia, the Anglo-Saxon kingdom which dominated the central part of England.[212] Oswald, it may be noted, became famous for his sanctity, and after his demise his cult spread to Ireland and the Continent.[213] His untimely death did not halt the work of conversion. Aidan survived him by about nine

[205] Bede, *Eccles. Hist.,* Book III, Chap. 1.
[206] Adamnan, *Vita S. Columbae,* Book I, Chap. 1.
[207] Bede, *op. cit.,* Book III, Chap. 2.
[208] Bede, *op. cit.,* Book III, Chap. 3.
[209] Bede, *op. cit.,* Book III, Chap. 5.
[210] Bede, *op. cit.,* Book III, Chap. 3.
[211] Bede, *op. cit.,* Book III, Chap. 5.
[212] Bede, *op. cit.,* Book III, Chap. 9.
[213] Bede, *op. cit.,* Book III, Chaps. 9-12.

years.[214] On Aidan's death Iona appointed a successor, one Finan,[215] who held the post for ten years.[216]

The decade of Finan's administration saw the spread to still other regions of the Christianity which derived its immediate impulse from Iona. Penda's son Peada sought the hand of the daughter of the King of Northumbria. His suit was accepted on the condition that he become a Christian and induce his people to do likewise. He acceded, and he and his retinue were baptized by Bishop Finan. Peada asked for missionaries to return to Mercia with him. Four priests were sent, three of them English and one a Scot. Penda offered no opposition to their activities, apparently asking only that those who accepted the new faith do so sincerely and show its fruits. Many of his subjects, therefore, both high and low, were baptized. In time Finan consecrated the Scottish priest as bishop.[217] After the death, in battle, of Penda (655) Christianity seems to have spread rapidly in the central part of England.[218]

Under Finan the faith was renewed among the East Saxons, in Essex. The King of the East Saxons, on frequent visits to the King of Northumbria, was brought by the latter into the Church. The East Saxons had already become acquainted with Christianity through missionaries from Rome. They had, however, lapsed, and it was from Northumbria that they were permanently won to the faith. At his request the Northumbrian King provided the King of the East Saxons priests to teach his people. In time one of the latter was consecrated bishop, receiving ordination at Lindisfarne. Instruction and baptism in Essex apparently proceeded apace.[219]

It is interesting to note that some time before the arrival of these missionaries from Northumbria, the Irish Fursa, whom we have mentioned as labouring in North-western Gaul, paused for a time in the adjoining East Anglia (the present Norfolk and Suffolk) on his way to the Continent, and both made converts and strengthened in the faith the Christians whom he found there.[220]

In the stream which came from Iona belongs Cuthbert, who had much to do with extending the work of conversion in the North and in deepening the faith of those who in times of adversity were inclined to relapse into paganism.[221] Cuthbert's race we do not know, his alleged Irish birth being

[214] Bede, op. cit., Book III, Chap. 17.
[215] Ibid.
[216] Bede, op. cit., Book III, Chap. 26.
[217] Bede, op. cit., Book III, Chap. 21.
[218] Bede, op. cit., Book III, Chaps. 21, 24.
[219] Bede, op. cit., Book III, Chap. 22.
[220] Bede, op. cit., Book III, Chap. 19.
[221] Bede, op. cit., Book IV, Chap. 27.

quite unproved.[222] We do know, however, that at Melrose, where he first entered a monastery, he was within the spiritual circle of Lindisfarne and so of Iona, and that he was later chosen Bishop for Lindisfarne.[223]

It was in part from Lindisfarne, and therefore from Iona, that the impulse came which brought into the faith the last of the Anglo-Saxon groups to accept baptism. Bishop Wilfrid, who had been educated at Lindisfarne but had also been at Rome, during one of the exiles of his stormy career lived among the South Saxons. This folk, then mostly pagan, and separated from the now Christian peoples about them by marsh and forest,[224] he led to the baptismal font. He also helped them in time of famine by teaching them improved methods of fishing.[225] It was Wilfrid, too, who entered the Isle of Wight in the wake of its conquest by the King of Wessex (686) and apparently directed its conversion. The actual work of the mission was performed by Wilfrid's nephew with a priest as an assistant. The Isle of Wight, Bede declares, was the last of the "provinces" of Britain to receive the faith.[226]

Lindisfarne, then, like Iona, proved a notable training school for missionaries. Its influence, and so that of its parent, Iona, was widely extended. Through the support of the Northumbrian kings it was felt over the major part of the portions of the island which had been occupied by the Anglo-Saxons.[227]

It was not only through Iona that the Celtic churches contributed to the planting and nourishing of Christianity among the English. In the South we hear of a small monastery in the modern Sussex founded by one who is called a Scot, but whether from Ireland or Scotland is unknown. Apparently, however, it had little effect upon the peoples among whom it was set.[228] In the South, too, among the West Saxons, laboured for many years as their second bishop one Agilbert. He was a native of Gaul, but he had long been in Ireland, and it was from that island that he came to England. Apparently Agilbert never learned the language of the Saxons, or at best only imperfectly, for we read that the West Saxon king wearied of his "barbarous tongue" and divided his realm with a bishop who had command of the native speech.

---

[222] Skene, *Celtic Scotland*, Vol. II, pp. 203-205.

[223] Bede, *op. cit.*, Book IV, Chaps. 27, 28.

[224] Robinson, *The Conversion of Europe*, p. 142.

[225] Bede, *op. cit.*, Book IV, Chap. 13; Book V, Chap. 19; Eddius Stephanus, *The Life of Bishop Wilfrid*, Chap. 41 (Colgrave's edition, pp. 81-85). Howorth, *The Golden Days of the Early English Church*, Vol. I, p. 115, suggests that when Wilfrid arrived in Sussex the king and queen and probably some of the nobles were already Christian.

[226] Bede, *op. cit.*, Book IV, Chap. 16; Bright, *Chapters of Early English Church History*, pp. 393, 394.

[227] Macewen, *History of the Church in Scotland*, Vol. I, p. 83.

[228] Bede, *op. cit.*, Book IV, Chap. 13.

Agilbert, so it is said, disgruntled, retired to Gaul and became Bishop of Paris.[229]

It is interesting and significant that the only Celtic missionaries to the English of whom we have record were from parts of the British Isles which had little or no direct contact with the Teutonic invaders. Indeed, it is expressly stated that the Christian British who were in immediate touch with them made no effort to convert them[230] and that when the English finally became Christian through other agencies they declined to have any friendship with them.[231] This is not surprising. The Anglo-Saxons were the intruding conquerors who had dispossessed the British of their lands and the shifting frontier between the two races was the scene of frequent battles. It may be that quiet missionary work existed of which we do not know. If, as seems probable, in some regions British Christian communities held out in territory which was becoming predominatingly English, a few conversions among the Anglo-Saxons may have taken place through them. Possibly, too, some enslaved British captives clung to their faith and here and there won some of their masters. Of this, however, no evidence has come to light. So far as we know, none of the Anglo-Saxons accepted the Christian faith through their British neighbours. It was by Celts, but from Ireland and the modern Scotland, that the English were chiefly introduced to Christianity.

In the work of conversion missionaries from the Continent had a relatively smaller, but important, part. In the fifth century, when the Anglo-Saxon invasion began, the Church of Gaul was too hard pressed by pagan and Arian Germanic invaders to spare much energy and attention for other lands. In the sixth and seventh centuries, as we have seen, when the conversion of the English was in progress, the Frankish Church was too badly in need of reform and too nearly secularized to take much interest in peoples across the Channel. We do hear of a Frankish bishop in pagan Kent, but he came to give spiritual care to its Christian Frankish Queen and we have no evidence of mission work by him.[232] In the latter part of the sixth century, however, a mission from a more distant part of the Continent began which was to have a share in the conversion of the English and which was to have the still more important result of knitting a close bond between English and Continental Christianity and of bringing the former into conformity with the latter. It was

[229] Bede, op. cit., Book III, Chap. 7.

[230] Bede, op. cit., Book V, Chap. 22.

[231] Bede, op. cit., Book II, Chap. 20; Book V, Chap. 22.

[232] Bede, op. cit., Book I, Chap. 25. Browne, The Christian Church in These Islands before the Coming of Augustine, pp. 9-26, suggests that this bishop had been there some time before the coming of Augustine and had done missionary work.

the type of organization and of life developed by Christianity in Roman rather than in Celtic lands which was to prevail in England. This, in its turn, had momentous consequences for the Christianity of Germany and Scandinavia.

The story of the Italian mission to England has often been narrated, but its importance for Great Britain, Germany, and Scandinavia makes it necessary to tell it again. A striking fact is that the mission was originated by a Pope. So far as our records show, never before had a Bishop of Rome sent forth an expedition for the purpose of converting a pagan people. Moreover, measured by its results through the generations, the mission was extraordinarily successful. Without it presumably the English, the Rhine Valley and adjacent lands on the North and East, and Scandinavia would ultimately have been brought within the orbit of Roman Christianity and would have conformed to it both organizationally and creedally. This mission, however, was chiefly the actual enterprise through which, as a matter of history, these events followed.

The initiator and early director of the mission was one of the most remarkable of the men who have occupied the See of Peter. Gregory I is rightly accorded the title of Great. The English mission was only one of his many achievements. He was born in Rome about the year 540,[233] of a senatorial family distinguished for its aristocratic lineage, its wealth, and its piety. Among his progenitors was a Pope Felix.[234]

It was a decaying Rome in which Gregory was reared. The capital of the Empire had long since been moved elsewhere and the city had largely lost its political importance. Even before his birth the public buildings were falling into disrepair and, by breaks in the aqueducts, the traditional water supply of the palaces and the baths had been cut off. In Gregory's boyhood the city experienced a disastrous siege and despoiling by the Goths. Before Gregory was thirty it had suffered again and again at the hands of several armies. The population had shrunk sadly since the days of the city's glory. Many of the wealthy families had died out or had migrated to Ravenna or to Constantinople.[235] Yet Gregory's family retained at least part of its extensive possessions and gave the lad the training in grammar, rhetoric, and dialectic prescribed for the high-born youths of the day.[236] So decadent were

---

[233] Batiffol, *Saint Gregory the Great,* p. 12, thinks he was born a little before 540. Dudden, *Gregory the Great,* Vol. I, p. 3, believes the date to have been about 540. Howorth, *Saint Gregory the Great,* p. 6, says that "it has been generally supposed it was about the year 540." Also on Gregory the Great see Horace K. Mann, *The Lives of the Popes in the Middle Ages* (London, Kegan Paul, Trench, Trubner and Co., 18 vols., 1925-1932), Vol. I, pp. 1-250.

[234] Bede, *Eccles. Hist.,* Book II, Chap. 1.

[235] Dudden, *op. cit.,* Vol. I, pp. 32-51; Howorth, *op. cit.,* p. 10.

[236] Dudden, *op. cit.,* Vol. I, pp. 69-79.

the times, however, that Gregory's education, though probably the best that Rome could afford, included no Greek, he seems to have read but little in the Latin classics, and his own Latin style was clear but not polished.[237]

For a time, in about 573, Gregory served as Prætor or Prefect of the city,[238] the highest civil dignity in Rome.

While still in his early thirties Gregory renounced his wealth. Less than a generation before Gregory's birth, Benedict of Nursia had formulated his famous rule. In this monastic movement, then still in the first flush of its youth, the able and earnest Gregory was caught up.[239] From his inherited estates he founded and endowed six monasteries in Sicily and one on the Coelian Hill in Rome to which he gave his ancestral mansion. The balance of his fortune he is said to have distributed among the poor.[240] However, so able and prominent a man was not permitted to enjoy for long the quiet of a monastery. Against his inclination he was forced into active life. He was made the leading one of Seven Regionary Deacons in whose hands was the administration of the alms for the city. From 579 to 586 he served as the Papal ambassador at the imperial court at Constantinople.[241] Some time after his return he was elected abbot of the monastery which he had founded in Rome.[242] From this post, in 590, he was called, by popular acclaim and much against his will, to become Bishop.[243]

The little less than fourteen years that Gregory sat on the Papal throne are among the most notable in the entire history of the See of the Fisherman. Gregory seems never to have been in robust health and to have been chronically subject to indigestion, gout, and attacks of fever.[244] Yet he accomplished

[237] Batiffol, op. cit., pp. 52, 53; Howorth, op. cit., p. 7.
[238] John the Deacon, Vita Gregorii, Book I, Chap. 4 (Migne, Pat. Lat., Vol. LXXV, col. 64). On the date and on the functions of the office see Dudden, op. cit., Vol. I, pp. 101-103.
[239] Paul the Deacon, Vita Gregorii, Chaps. 3, 4 (Migne, Pat. Lat., Vol. LXXV, col. 43); John the Deacon, op. cit., Book I, Chaps. 5, 6, 7 (Migne, Pat. Lat., Vol. LXXV, col. 65); Dudden, op. cit., Vol. I, p. 107. Howorth, op. cit., pp. 11, 12, while agreeing that Gregory entered a monastery and lived the life of an ascetic, believes that he did not become a monk.
[240] Gregory of Tours, Hist. Franc., Book X, Chap. 1; John the Deacon, op. cit., Book I, Chaps. 5, 6 (Migne, Pat. Lat., Vol. LXXV, col. 65); Paul the Deacon, op. cit., Chap. 4 (Migne, Pat. Lat., Vol. LXXV, col. 43). Batiffol, op. cit., p. 23, suggests that the statement that he sold his property and distributed the proceeds to the poor may be a form of rhetoric.
[241] Paul the Deacon, op. cit., Chap. 7 (Migne, Pat. Lat., Vol. LXXV, col. 44); John the Deacon, op. cit., Book I, Chap. 26 (Migne, Pat. Lat., Vol. LXXV, col. 72); Dudden, op. cit., Vol. I, pp. 123-157.
[242] Dudden, op. cit., Vol. I, pp. 187-222.
[243] Batiffol, op. cit., pp. 58-62.
[244] Dudden, op. cit., Vol. I, p. 243.

what for a physically strong man would have been a prodigious amount of work. He displayed energy, imagination, initiative, devotion, and great administrative capacities. He showed foresight, prudence, tenacity of purpose, and ability to rise above difficulties. He supervised with skill the great landed estates of the Papacy and used their huge revenues largely for the care of the poor and of the indigent refugees who thronged the city.[245] Upon him, indeed, devolved the chief burden of what had once been the task of the Emperors, the provision of food for the populace. He preached frequently. He carried on an enormous correspondence. His writings, both before and after he entered upon his pontificate, have made him one of the so-called Doctors of the Latin Church. He actively used the authority which as Patriarch he possessed in portions of Italy and the adjacent islands.[246] Over the other churches of the West he exerted himself to maintain and strengthen the primacy which he believed to be at once the right and the sacred trust of the Papacy.[247] In this he used tact, but showed firmness. In him the Roman genius of empire building and administration lived again, but turned into ecclesiastical channels.

No more noteworthy instance is seen of the creative imagination of Gregory, devoted to religious ends and implemented by high courage and determination, than in the mission dispatched to England. When and how Gregory first concerned himself with the enterprise we do not know. We have a story recounted by Bede, but which that conscientious historian is careful to record merely as tradition.[248] Gregory, so it is said, chanced to see in the Roman market some boys of fair complexion exposed for sale. On inquiry, he learned that they were from Britain and from pagan peoples. Asking the name of their nation, he was told that they were called Angles. "Right," said he, "for they have angelic faces and it is meet that such should be co-heirs with the angels in heaven." Upon further inquiry, he was told that they came from Deiri, and he declared that they were saved from wrath. The alleged name of their king, Aelli, suggested to him that Allelujah, the praise of God, should be heard there. Gregory is said to have asked the Pope to be allowed to go himself as a missionary to those parts, but to have been prevented by the unwillingness of the populace to lose him from the city. The incident, if it occurred at all, probably belongs to the period of Gregory's abbacy. Less romantic but more credible is the suggestion that Gregory became interested in England through Anglian slaves from Britain, some of whom he had had

---

[245] Dudden, *op. cit.*, Vol. I, pp. 246 ff.
[246] Dudden, *op. cit.*, Vol. I, pp. 357 ff.
[247] Dudden, *op. cit.*, Vol. I, pp. 402 ff.
[248] Bede, *Eccles. Hist.*, Book II, Chap. 1, gives the most frequently quoted form of the story. See Howorth, *Augustine the Missionary*, pp. 11-13.

redeemed with the funds of the Church and put into monasteries.[249] In one letter he declares that it had come to his attention that the Angles desired the Christian Gospel, but that the priests (presumably British) who might normally have given it to them had been negligent.[250] The source of his information—or misinformation—we do not know.

Whatever may have been the origin of the idea, it is clear that, once he had conceived it, Gregory set about its execution with his customary energy and care. For agents to carry it out, he went, as was natural, to the Roman monastery which he had founded in his ancestral mansion and of which he had been abbot. To lead them he chose one Augustine, who had been head of the community.[251] The group set out from Rome in 596, an even century after the baptism of Clovis. It was, too, the year before the death of Columba, and thus almost at the close of the life of him from whose community on Iona went forth those influences which had so much to do with the conversion of the English whom Augustine had set out to reach. When Augustine was traversing Gaul, Columban was already at his task of bringing new life to the Church there. Thirty-nine years later, in 635, at almost the other extreme of the Euro-Asiatic Continent, A-lo-pên, the first Christian missionary whom we know to have gone to China, arrived at Ch'ang-an, the capital of the recently founded T'ang Dynasty. Moreover, it was not far from the time when in Arabia a faith was in process of birth which was to deal to this expanding Christianity the most serious reverses it had yet known.

The little band commissioned by Gregory was to undertake a new conquest of Britain by Rome. To the casual observer the time would have seemed inopportune. As a city Rome had ceased to be an effective political power. Repeatedly in the past generation it had fallen a victim to its enemies and its supposed defenders. Its population had shrunk and its ancient buildings were crumbling. The contrast between the comparatively small paternal mansion of Gregory, the monastery from which the mission set forth, and the mighty palaces of the Cæsars which it faced across a valley on the Palatine Hill and from which Britain had once been ruled, must have been striking.

---

[249] See the discussion and the instances cited in Howorth, *Augustine the Missionary*, pp. 5-10. See especially a letter of Gregory in *Gregorii I Papae Reg. Ep.*, VI, 10 in *Mon. Germ. Hist., Epis.*, Vol. I, pp. 388, 389, and in Mason, *The Mission of St. Augustine to England*, pp. 17, 18. Moreau, in Descamps, *Histoire Générale Comparée des Missions*, p. 158, believes this purchase of slaves may have been the basis on which grew Bede's story.

[250] Letter of Gregory to Theodoric and Theodebert. Text and translation in Mason, *The Mission of St. Augustine*, pp. 31, 32.

[251] Bede, *op. cit.*, Book I, Chap. 23. Gregory, Letter to Syagrius (in *Gregorii I Papae Reg. Ep.*, IX, 222, in *Mon. Germ. Hist., Epis.*, Vol. II, p. 213) speaks of Augustine as "formerly præpositus of my monastery, now our brother and co-bishop."

If the empire centring in these structures had faded and the dominion it had once exercised over Britain had vanished, what hope had these weak monks and this quiet monastery of re-establishing it? Moreover, the group sent to initiate the conquest were not very promising. They were a small company, without military support or the powerful backing of any monarch. They themselves were oppressed by the apparent futility of their undertaking. While in Gaul they became terrified by the dangers in the way and dispatched Augustine to Rome to ask of Gregory permission to abandon the mission. Gregory was of sterner stuff and sent Augustine back with a kind but firm letter ordering them on.[252]

Yet the expedition proved extraordinarily successful. It initiated an enterprise which was to bring more of Britain and its adjoining islands under the direct sway of Rome than had ever even seen the eagles of the legions. Unlike the earlier conquest, achieved by force of arms, and which lasted for only about four centuries, this was to endure, unbroken, for over nine hundred years and in parts of the islands has never disappeared. Moreover, the English who were won by it were to be important agents in extending the spiritual rule of Rome over portions of Germany which the Rome of the Emperors had never been able to subdue and in carrying it into Scandinavia, a region which the Cæsars had apparently never even dreamed of conquering.

Remarkable though the achievement was, it is not inexplicable. Nor was it due entirely to the superiority of the arm of the spirit over the sword of the flesh. But for the earlier Roman political dominion Christianity would probably not have spread among the Celts of the British Isles—certainly not as soon as it did. As we have seen, it was by this Celtic Christianity that the conversion of the English was chiefly accomplished. Moreover, British and Irish Christianity, although going on its way without much reference to Rome, had seemingly never broken formally with the See of Peter, but, when it thought about it at all, looked with reverence upon the only church in the West which could substantiate a claim to direct connexion with the Apostles. Then, too, while politically the city of Rome had become impotent, the name of Rome was one to conjure with. It still stood for the mightiest civilization which Europe had known. To the mind of Europe the Roman Empire had not disappeared. It continued, even though its political centre had been transferred. Only lately it had enjoyed a fresh blooming under Justinian. The Roman Church was inheriting the prestige of the Empire. This was the more easily acknowledged because now, in North-western Europe, the acceptance

[253] Bede, *Eccles. Hist.*, Book I, Chap. 23. See also letters of Gregory in *Gregorii I Papae Reg. Ep.*, VI, 50a, in *Mon. Germ. Hist., Ep.*, Vol. I, pp. 425, 426, and Howorth, *Augustine the Missionary*, pp. 29, 30.

of the suzerainty of Rome in its ecclesiastical form did not involve a compromising of political independence.

It would be a mistake, however, to ascribe the triumph of the Church of Rome in Britain, Germany, and Scandinavia entirely or even chiefly to the magic of the Roman name. But for the inward urge which historically has been part of the essence of Christianity and which traces its source to the founder of the faith, Gregory would not have sent Augustine, the Celtic missions would not have been, and English missionaries would not have gone to the Continent. So far as we have a record of Augustine's message, no plea was made on the basis of the superiority of Roman culture. The Christian faith was presented on its own merits and as a way of insuring an entrance to heaven. It was the terrors of hell, the bliss of heaven, and the authentication of the faith by miracles which made the greatest appeal.

Augustine and his band, their purpose restored by Gregory's courage and their way presumably smoothed by Papal letters to important people in the Frankish domains,[253] pursued their journey. When they finally reached Britain, however, it was not to Northumbria and the Angles of Gregory's original purpose that they went, but to the more accessible Kingdom of Kent. It was both natural and fortunate that they landed here. It was natural because Kent lay nearest to the Continent. It was fortunate because, of all the Teutonic kingdoms of Britain, it had already been most touched by influences from the mainland. Its ruler, Ethelbert, had for wife a Christian Frankish princess, Bertha.[254] As a condition of the marriage, Ethelbert had promised that she should be allowed to observe her religion, and a Bishop Luidhard had accompanied her.[255] She worshipped at Canterbury, the capital of Kent, in a church dedicated to St. Martin which is said to have been built in Roman times.[256]

Augustine and his party, armed with interpreters supplied by the Franks, landed on what was then the Isle of Thanet, on the north-eastern corner of Kent and not far from Canterbury. They sent word to Ethelbert telling of their arrival and announcing their message. The King ordered them to remain

[253] For one of these letters see Bede, *Eccles. Hist.*, Book I, Chap. 24. See also texts and translations in Mason, *The Mission of St. Augustine*, pp. 23-35. See Howorth, *Augustine the Missionary*, pp. 31-37. For texts see Haddan and Stubbs, *Councils and Ecclesiastical Documents Relating to Great Britain and Ireland*, Vol. III, pp. 5-11.

[254] Bede, *op. cit.*, Book I, Chap. 25. Bede says that Ethelbert's domains extended to the Humber. He was probably the leading Anglo-Saxon king of his time. His marriage to a Frankish princess shows that the Franks must have esteemed him a personage of note. Howorth, *Augustine the Missionary*, p. 39; Cutts, *Augustine of Canterbury*, p. 53. See also Hole, *Early Missions to and within the British Islands*, pp. 69-72.

[255] Bede, *op. cit.*, Book I, Chap. 25. Luidhard may have been dead when Augustine arrived.—Howorth, *Augustine the Missionary*, p. 42.

[256] Bede, *op. cit.*, Book I, Chap. 26. On St. Martin's Church, see Howorth, *Augustine the Missionary*, pp. 43-48.

on the island until he could decide their fate. After some days of waiting, Ethelbert himself came to the island and received the missionary band—in the open air, for fear of possible magic. Augustine and his companions approached, chanting litanies and offering prayers for the salvation of themselves and those to whom they had come. Then Augustine presented the Christian message. Ethelbert promised the group liberty to preach and to win converts, and assured them of provision for their physical needs.[257] Augustine and his colleagues were established in Canterbury and used for worship the Church of St. Martin.

At first converts seem to have come slowly. Presently, however, Ethelbert himself was baptized, and while he compelled none of his subjects to follow his example, it is not surprising that the accessions rapidly increased. The missionaries thereafter had still greater freedom and travelled widely, preaching and erecting and repairing churches.[258] A letter of Gregory, undated, speaks of ten thousand as having been baptized by Augustine on one Christmas.[259] The knowledge of Christianity possessed by these converts must have been very superficial, derived as it was through interpreters and in large groups. In the meantime Augustine had gone to Gaul for consecration as archbishop and had received the rite at the hands of the Archbishop of Arles.[260]

Gregory continued to take an active interest in the mission. Augustine sent to Rome two of his company, Lawrence and a lay brother, to report progress.[261] Gregory, in reply, dispatched him reinforcements, among them Mellitus, later successively Bishop of London and Archbishop of Canterbury, Justus, eventually Bishop of Rochester and finally Archbishop of Canterbury, Paulinus, and Rufianus.[262] He also sent vestments, sacred vessels, relics, and manuscripts.[263] He granted Augustine the use of the *pallium* and authorized him to appoint twelve diocesan bishops and to place a bishop in York who, as the Christians increased in that region, should also enjoy metropolitan privileges and ordain twelve bishops.[264] Thus was extended to England the

---

[257] Bede, *op. cit.*, Book I, Chap. 25. See also Bright, *Early English Church History*, pp. 51-55; Howorth, *Augustine the Missionary*, pp. 56-64; Browne, *Augustine and His Companions*, pp. 28-48.

[258] Bede, *op. cit.*, Book I, Chap. 26; Bright, *op. cit.*, pp. 56-58.

[259] Letter of Gregory to Eulogius, Bishop of Alexandria; text and translation in Mason, *The Mission of St. Augustine*, pp. 44, 45. Cutts, *Augustine of Canterbury*, pp. 57-60, suggests that Augustine was consecrated archbishop Nov. 16, 597, that the baptism of the ten thousand was at Christmas, 597, and that the conversion of Ethelbert followed.

[260] Bede, *Eccles. Hist.*, Book I, Chap. 27.

[261] *Ibid.*

[262] Bede, *op. cit.*, Book I, Chap. 29; Book II, Chaps. 2, 9.

[263] Bede, *op. cit.*, Book I, Chap. 29.

[264] *Ibid.*

system of the hierarchical diocesan episcopate which had developed within the framework of the Roman Empire, a sharp contrast with the Celtic monastic episcopate which almost contemporaneously was entering Anglo-Saxondom from the North. The two systems might well clash, especially since Gregory placed under Augustine all the bishops of Britain.[265] Gregory wrote both Ethelbert and his queen to confirm them in their faith and to encourage them to assist in its spread.[266] Gregory, too, was careful to reply at length to Augustine's specific questions concerning the administration of the Church[267] and to send through Mellitus some instructions on missionary methods.[268] In these he displayed a practical combination of tolerance and firmness. In ritual he advised no slavish adherence to that which prevailed in Rome, but a willingness to select whatever Augustine found anywhere which commended itself to him. While holding to the traditional rules of the Church concerning marriage, he would not exclude from the communion those who before their conversion had contracted unions within the forbidden degrees of relationship. He directed, moreover, that pagan temples be transformed into churches rather than destroyed and that festivals be organized, with feasting, as a substitute for the ceremonies and sacrifices of pre-Christian days. In this Gregory was but following the practice widely current in the days when the Roman Empire was being converted.

That the Italian missionaries followed the injunction to put pagan shrines to a Christian use is evidenced in excavations on the site of the monastery founded by Augustine in Canterbury. It is quite obvious, both from what can be seen today and from the written record, that the community took over a temple.[269]

Geographically the permanent successes of the Italian missionaries in effecting conversions were confined chiefly to Southern England. Augustine himself seems not to have extended his labours outside of Kent. For years Gregory's dream of an episcopal see in York remained unfulfilled. Nor did Augustine consecrate the twelve bishops authorized by the Pope. He sent Mellitus to

[265] Bede, *op. cit.,* Book I, Chap. 27.

[266] The letter to Ethelbert is in Bede, *op. cit.,* Book I, Chap. 32. Texts and English translation of both letters are in Mason, *op. cit.,* pp. 57-65. The texts are in Haddan and Stubbs, *Councils and Ecclesiastical Documents Relating to Great Britain and Ireland,* Vol. III, pp. 17, 18, 30, 31.

[267] Bede, *op. cit.,* Book I, Chap. 27.

[268] Bede, *op. cit.,* Book I, Chap. 30; Haddan and Stubbs, *op cit.,* Vol. III, pp. 18-28.

[269] The records declare that the temple was transformed into the Church of St. Pancras and that adjoining it was built a church and a monastery, the latter being St. Augustine's monastery in the grounds of the present St. Augustine's College. See Thomas of Elmham, *Historia Monasterii S. Augustini Cantuariensis* (ed. C. Hardwick), Titulus I, sections 7-10.

the East Saxons, whose territory lay north of the Thames and embraced London. They were then subject to Ethelbert and ruled by his nephew. It was natural that many of them should accept the new faith of their overlord.[270] This seems to have been the extent of the conversions effected by the Italian missionaries in the lifetimes of Gregory and Augustine.

The great Pope died March 12, 604.[271] Augustine's death occurred not far from the same time, probably in 604 or 605.[272] About a decade later, in 616, Ethelbert, the first Christian king among the Anglo-Saxons, followed them to the grave.[273]

After Ethelbert a pagan reaction set in. This was not strange. Less than twenty years had elapsed since Augustine had landed. For most of the thousands who had been swept into the Church conversion must have been nominal. Many doubtless resented the passing of the traditional customs. When once the strong hand of Ethelbert was removed, the opposition came to the fore. In Kent Ethelbert's successor, Eadbald, was a pagan who balked at the Christian marriage regulations.[274] Among the East Saxons the rule of pagan sons succeeded that of a Christian father, the populace apostatized, and Bishop Mellitus was driven out of London to Kent, whence, with Justus, he fled to Gaul.[275] Lawrence, who had succeeded Augustine in the See of Canterbury, was about to follow them, but is said to have been dissuaded by a dream and to have been encouraged by the conversion of Eadbald.[276]

When Eadbald finally became a Christian he gave vigorous support to his new faith. Unlike Ethelbert, who presumably, although himself a convert, offered no violence to the old cults, Eadbald ordered that the idols throughout his realm be destroyed. One of his daughters became a nun.[277]

Before many years what seemed a hopeful extension of the Italian mission was made. Edwin, the powerful King of Northumbria, asked the hand of the daughter of Ethelbert. Her brother, then King of Kent and himself by this time a Christian, objected to her marriage to a pagan and let her go only on Edwin's promise that he would not interfere with the religion of herself

---

[270] Bede, *op. cit.,* Book II, Chap. 3.

[271] Batiffol, *St. Gregory the Great,* p. 280.

[272] Bede, *op. cit.,* Book II, Chap. 3. Bede gives the month and the day (May 26th) but not the year of his death. Howorth, *Augustine the Missionary,* p. 177, thinks that it was probably 604. Bright, *Early English Church History,* p. 105, says that "probability would point to 605." Haddan and Stubbs, *op. cit.,* Vol. III, p. 4, declare that it could not have been before 604 nor after 610.

[273] Bede, *op. cit.,* Book II, Chap. 5.

[274] *Ibid.*

[275] *Ibid.*

[276] Bede, *op. cit.,* Book II, Chap. 6.

[277] Bede, *op. cit.,* Book III, Chap. 8.

and her entourage. With her went Paulinus, consecrated bishop (July 21, 625) for that purpose.[278] Edwin did not at first become a Christian, but he consented to the baptism of his infant daughter.[279] The successors of Gregory the Great continued to take an interest in the infant mission in England,[280] although not always were they so active as its founder had been. One of them, said to have been Boniface V, now wrote to Edwin urging him to accept the Christian faith[281] and to his queen encouraging her to pray and to labour for the conversion of her husband.[282] Edwin, after presenting the issue to a council of his leading men, received baptism, together with other outstanding persons of the kingdom and a large number of the populace. It was group action, apparently decided upon in a manner consonant with the customs of the land. The baptism was at York and of this city Paulinus became Bishop.[283] Pope Honorius I (625-638) wrote to Edwin to encourage him to persevere in the path he had entered.[284]

The powerful influence of Edwin aided the extension of the faith in East Anglia. Christianity had earlier penetrated there from Kent, but the nominally Christian king worshipped both Christ and the ancient gods. Now his son, through Edwin, became a Christian and his people followed him. For a time after the son's death paganism revived, but another son, who had become a Christian while in Gaul, on coming to power reinforced Christianity and brought in Felix, a Burgundian, from the mission in Kent. Teachers from Kent assisted in the work of instruction.[285]

Six years after his conversion, Edwin was killed in a joint attack upon him of the Britons and the pagan Penda of Mercia. Northumbria was thrown into great confusion. Paulinus returned to Kent with Edwin's widow.[286] Edwin's immediate successors lapsed into paganism.[287] When, a few years later, the nascent Christianity was revived and extended, it was not by missionaries from Italy, but, as we have seen, by emissaries from Iona.

To another branch of the invaders, the West Saxons, came a missionary directly commissioned by a Pope. Birinus, of whose origin we know noth-

---

[278] Bede, *op. cit.,* Book II, Chap. 9.
[279] *Ibid.*
[280] As in Bede, *op. cit.,* Book II, Chap. 8, when Boniface IV sent the *pallium* to Justus.
[281] Bede, *op. cit.,* Book II, Chap. 10.
[282] Bede, *op. cit.,* Book II, Chap. 11.
[283] Bede, *op. cit.,* Book II, Chaps. 12-14.
[284] Bede, *op. cit.,* Book II, Chap. 17.
[285] Bede, *op. cit.,* Book II, Chap. 16; Book III, Chaps. 18-20; Browne, *The Conversion of the Heptarchy,* p. 76.
[286] Bede, *op. cit.,* Book II, Chap. 20.
[287] Bede, *op. cit.,* Book III, Chap. 1.

ing,[288] is said to have gone to Britain at the suggestion of Pope Honorius I. Also at the suggestion of Honorius, he was consecrated Bishop by the Archbishop of Milan, then residing at Genoa.[289] He promised the Pope to go to a part of England where no other missionary had been. He found that the West Saxons, who held much of the South of England, were still pagan. To them, therefore, he gave himself, and succeeded in winning both king and people. He was assigned for his episcopal seat a town not far from the present Oxford.[290] Birinus was followed by a native of the Continent, Agilbert, of whom we have already spoken.

The conversion of the Anglo-Saxons, then, required approximately a century. So far as we know it, it began with the coming of the mission from Rome, led by Augustine, in 597. The last important section to be won seems to have been the Isle of Wight, entered by Wilfrid in the wake of the conquering King of Wessex, in 686. At the same time the baptism of the Celts of what is now Scotland was continuing.[291]

The conversion, so rapidly achieved, suffered occasional reverses. Among the East Saxons, who once before had been led into apostasy by their rulers, another relapse into paganism occurred shortly after the middle of the seventh century. The return to the old deities, as in the case of so many of the conversions to the new faith, was led by one of the kings. The cause seems to have been a pestilence, presumably because the new religion had failed to protect the nation against the epidemic and the ancient gods were turned to as a last resort—or perhaps because the disease was supposed to have come as a punishment for defection from them.[292] The incident opens to us a window into what the populace expected of a religion.

While the work of conversion was achieved fairly rapidly and defections were not unknown, many of the English took up Christianity with great enthusiasm. We hear of a number of women of royal blood entering monasteries. Some, indeed, sought the houses in the Frankish domains because of the paucity, at the outset, of such establishments in their own land.[293] We read,

[288] Browne, *op. cit.*, p. 48, suggests that the name is identical with the Irish Byrne. Rudborne, a fifteenth-century writer, says that he was from St. Andrew's monastery in Rome (cited in Hole, *Early Missions to and within the British Isles*, p. 165). See also Bright, *Early English Church History*, p. 168.

[289] Bede, *Eccles. Hist.*, Book III, Chap. 7; Bright, *op. cit.*, p. 168.

[290] Bede, *op. cit.*, Book III, Chap. 7; Howorth, *The Golden Days of the Early English Church*, Vol. I, p. 43, thinks that the importance and the extent of his success have been exaggerated. See also T. S. Holmes, "The Conversion of Wessex," in *The English Historical Review*, Vol. VII, pp. 437-443.

[291] Scott, *The Pictish Nation: Its People and Its Church*, pp. 301 ff.

[292] Bede, *op. cit.*, Book III, Chap. 30.

[293] Bede, *op. cit.*, Book III, Chap. 8.

too, of a distinguished King of the West Saxons, a famous warrior, who made a pilgrimage to Rome and was there baptized (on Easter Day, 689). His successor also undertook a similar pilgrimage, a custom which we are told was followed by many of both sexes, by clergy and laity, and by those of high and low degree.[294] Moreover, long before the seventh century was out, English missionaries were beginning to go to the pagans on the neighbouring shores of the Continent.

This conversion of Britain, as we have indicated, proceeded chiefly from two sources. One was Rome. From this centre of the Western Church, on the initiative of Gregory the Great, came small bands of missionaries. They began work among the Anglo-Saxons slightly earlier than did the Celts. Through them the permanent conversion of Kent was effected, the first but abortive conversion of Essex and London, and the initial spread of the faith into Northumbria and East Anglia. From Rome, too, came the missionary who was chiefly responsible for the winning of the West Saxons. Yet, after the death of the great Gregory, the Roman mission did not grow as rapidly as it had before. Reinforcements were few and the lesser men who followed on the Papal throne were too preoccupied with urgent tasks nearer at hand to give much energetic attention to distant England. Gregory's ambitious dream of a hierarchy extending over England was, for the time, left unfulfilled.[295] About a generation after the beginning of the Roman mission the other stream broke forth, the one mentioned first on the preceding pages. It issued from Iona and through it the conversion of Northumbria was completed, that of Essex renewed and made permanent, that of the central part of England effected, and the last of the pagan Anglo-Saxons, in Sussex and the Isle of Wight, drawn into the Christian Church. A little assistance came directly from Ireland and from the Frankish domains.

Of the two main sources, Rome and Iona, the latter, as we have seen, was probably responsible for the major portion of the baptisms. Indeed, had the Roman mission never come, the conversion of the English would probably have been accomplished by Celts from Scotland and Ireland and by a scattered few from the domains of the Franks. Moreover, it might have been completed almost as early as it was even without Roman aid.

What the Italian mission did was to extend the Roman form of ecclesiastical organization and Roman usages to England and to tie up the churches of Britain more closely with those of the Continent than would otherwise have been done—at least for several generations.

[294] Bede, *op. cit.,* Book V, Chap. 7.
[295] Browne, *The Conversion of the Heptarchy,* p. 185; Cutts, *Augustine of Canterbury,* pp. 202, 203.

Between the two types of Christianity some conflict arose. In creed no difference seems to have been present. Nor do the Celtic Christians appear to have denied the primacy of the Bishop of Rome.[296] The ostensible issues were mainly the date of Easter and the form of the tonsure. More important was the style of church government. Should that be through the monastery and bishops who were either abbots or had no defined territories, as was the practice in regions with the Ionan tradition,[297] or should it be through bishops of the type which had developed in the Roman Empire, with precise dioceses?

We must not attempt to narrate the complete story of the controversy, even in summary fashion, but must content ourselves with noting some of the main steps. Gregory the Great had placed under Augustine not only the bishops whose consecration he authorized in England, but all the prelates in Britain.[298] This design probably had in it the seeds of trouble, for we have little if any evidence that Papal authority had been exercised over these Celtic churches, long isolated as they had been from Continental Christianity by the barrier of pagan Anglo-Saxondom. Augustine, we are told, held conferences with leading British ecclesiastics and urged them to join with him in missions to the English and to conform their practices to those of Rome. The meetings were stormy. The sensitive Britons felt that Augustine displayed unapostolic arrogance in receiving them sitting and so refused to acknowledge his archiepiscopal jurisdiction. Augustine is reported to have threatened them with war—a prophecy which Bede held was fulfilled by the slaughter of many of the British monks by a Northumbrian King not long thereafter.[299]

These conferences of Augustine were with leaders of the Christianity of those Britons whom the Anglo-Saxons sought to displace. It is not strange that agreement proved impossible. Racial barriers and hereditary hatreds made fellowship between English and British Christians difficult. The two did not mingle much, if at all, in the same areas.

However, since the English had come into the faith partly through missionaries of the Ionan stream, and partly through those from Rome, these two types of Christianity were thrown together intimately in English domains. The issue between them came to a head in the Northumbrian state, where Iona was represented by Bishop Colman and the Roman tradition had its leading champion in a young Englishman of good birth, Wilfrid, whom we have already met and who had studied in Rome and had received the tonsure

---

[296] Duke, *The Columban Church*, pp. 132-138.
[297] Schubert, *Geschichte der christlichen Kirche im Frühmittelalter*, pp. 209, 210; Duke, *op. cit.*, pp. 119-123.
[298] Bede, *Eccles. Hist.*, Book I, Chap. 29.
[299] Bede, *op. cit.*, Book I, Chap. 34; Book II, Chap. 2.

in Gaul. The views of the two parties were presented at a synod at Whitby, in 664, in the presence of the Northumbrian King. After hearing both sides, the King gave his decision in favour of Rome.[300] Bishop Colman retired to Scotland, accompanied by some of those who wished to hold to the Ionan practice.[301]

Whitby is sometimes said to have marked the decisive step which guaranteed the triumph of Rome.[302] Others declare that the importance of Whitby can easily be exaggerated. The decision, so it is asserted, applied only to Northumbria, and even there Celtic monastic communities and some of the Ionan practices persisted.[303] It must be remembered, however, that Northumbria was the original centre of Ionan influence among the English. The victory there of Rome could not fail to have repercussions in other places, such as the contiguous Midland region of Mercia, where the Celtic influence predominated.

Important in the extension among the English of the Continental system and the authority of Rome were the labours of Theodore, Archbishop of Canterbury from 668, four years after the synod of Whitby, until his death, in 690.[304] An Englishman, Wighard, had been sent to Rome by the Kings of Kent and Northumbria to receive consecration for the post.[305] Wighard died in Rome before he could be consecrated and the Pope wrote the King of Northumbria that he was searching for a successor.[306] The Pope eventually picked Theodore, a native of Tarsus and well educated in Greek and Latin and in secular and ecclesiastical literature. Although sixty-six years of age, Theodore accepted the arduous post and was to fill it until the ripe age of eighty-eight. He was consecrated by the Pope and proceeded to England accompanied by Hadrian, an African by birth and formerly abbot near Naples.[307]

In 667, the year before Theodore's arrival, only three bishops were living in all the domains of the English. The Italian mission had broken down. Neither Rome nor Canterbury had much influence.[308] About 664 a pestilence

---

[300] Bede, *op. cit.*, Book III, Chap. 25; Eddius Stephanus, *The Life of Bishop Wilfrid*, Chap. 10 (ed. Colgrave, p. 21).

[301] Bede, *op. cit.*, Book III, Chap. 26.

[302] Toynbee, *A Study of History*, Vol. I, p. 29.

[303] Bede, *op. cit.*, Book III, Chap. 26; Meissner, *The Celtic Church in England after the Synod of Whitby*, pp. vii, viii; Duke, *op. cit.*, pp. 100-118; Howorth, *The Golden Days of the Early English Church*, Vol. I, pp. 200-204.

[304] For the date of consecration see Bede, *op. cit.*, Book IV, Chap. 1. For the date of Theodore's death see Bede, *op. cit.*, Book V, Chap. 8.

[305] Bede, *op. cit.*, Book III, Chap. 29.

[306] Bede, *op. cit.*, Book III, Chap. 29.

[307] Bede, *op. cit.*, Book IV, Chap. 1.

[308] Browne, *The Conversion of the Heptarchy*, pp. 115 ff.; E. W. Watson in Thompson, *Bede*, p. 57.

had carried off numbers of the clergy along with many of the populace.[309] Theodore became "the first Archbishop whom all the English Church consented to obey."[310] He travelled throughout the land, creating new dioceses,[311] consecrating bishops, and reconsecrating at least one of the bishops concerning whose orders some doubt existed. Theodore and Hadrian spread church music, presumably of the type associated with the name of Gregory, and trained men in the Bible, Greek, Latin, astronomy, and mathematics.[312] Under Theodore, moreover, only eight or nine years after Whitby, a synod was held which attempted to regulate the English Church. Some of its enactments seem directly aimed at Celtic customs, such as that on the date for Easter, the prohibition of one bishop intruding into the diocese of another, and the attempt to restrict the freedom of monks, clergy, and bishops to wander about at will.[313] A few years later, also under Theodore, another synod was held which reaffirmed the Catholicism of the English, especially as a safeguard against the Eutychian heresy, which was agitating the Church in the East.[314] It seems probable that Theodore attempted to establish what we now call a parish system.[315] It is clear that he endeavoured vigorously to inculcate what he believed to be Christian standards of morals.[316] In the extreme old age of Theodore, the Celts made one last great effort to regain control of Britain, and this reacted on the Church and reduced the prestige of Canterbury. Wilfrid, however, restored the authority of Rome in the North.[317]

The work of Theodore, then, appears to have been highly important not only in extending Roman practices, but also in unifying the English Church, training clergy, and raising the level of education and of Christian living. As we have suggested, when Theodore arrived the young Church was at a low ebb. The pestilence which had decimated the island had deprived it of many of the clergy who had been trained by the early missionaries.[318] The divisions and frequent wars between the states kept it divided. Dioceses were too large to be managed efficiently. The elderly Theodore became the real organizer

[309] Bede, op. cit., Book III, Chaps. 13, 23, 27. On this pestilence, which may have been the bubonic plague, see Creighton, A History of Epidemics in Britain, pp. 4-8.

[310] Bede, op. cit., Book IV, Chap. 2.

[311] Haddan and Stubbs, Councils and Ecclesiastical Documents Relating to Great Britain and Ireland, Vol. III, pp. 127, 165.

[312] Bede, op. cit., Book IV, Chap. 2.

[313] Bede, op. cit., Book IV, Chap. 5.

[314] Bede, op. cit., Book IV, Chap. 17. On the work of Theodore see also Cutts, Augustine of Canterbury, p. 203; Meissner, op. cit., pp. 35-46.

[315] Haddan, Remains, p. 323.

[316] Haddan and Stubbs, Councils and Ecclesiastical Documents Relating to Great Britain and Ireland, Vol. III, pp. 176 ff., gives Theodore's Penitential.

[317] Meissner, op. cit., pp. 68-70.

[318] Bede, op. cit., Book III, Chaps. 13, 23, 27.

of the Church. He gave it a structure which was inclusive of all the English and which rose above the political divisions. He, with the assistance of Hadrian, laid the basis for some of the schools, which, with the Irish monasteries, helped to raise the level of education not only of the English clergy, but also, through them, of much of Western Europe. He multiplied the number of dioceses and so facilitated episcopal supervision and, by that and other measures, greatly improved the Church's morale.[319] Yet, even before his time, English were flocking to the monasteries of Ireland[320] and it is probable that without him the number of educated clergy and monks would rapidly have increased— though under a different type of ecclesiastical organization.

Added to these actions in England was the effect of the many pilgrimages by English folk to Rome. That city, although lamentably decayed since its days of imperial splendour, still made a profound impression upon visitors from the rude North. To them it was associated with the Apostles and the origin of their faith. That enthusiastic reverence must have hastened the spread of Roman practices in England.

How rapidly the effective control of Rome was extended over the churches in Great Britain outside Anglo-Saxondom we do not know. We have already seen that not until the eleventh century or later was the ecclesiastical structure of Ireland brought into full conformity with that of the Continent. Into parts of what is now Scotland the Roman date of Easter and the Roman tonsure spread early in the eighth century. Concerning the British Kingdom of Strathclyde, in the West, we have little information, except that before 731 Ninian's old seat at Whithorn became an episcopal see in the Northumbrian sphere and so supposedly came under the Roman influence which predominated in that area.[321] Among the Picts, we hear that about 710 a King Nechtan (or Naiton) became a convert to Roman customs and ordered in his realms adherence to the Easter and the tonsure of Rome.[322] Not long thereafter, in 716, an Englishman brought Iona, that centre of so many non-Roman influences, into accord with the Roman Easter.[323] In this he had more success than did an Abbot of Iona, Adamnan, who in 686, while visiting in Northumbria, became a convert to the Roman Easter and tonsure and on his return to his monastery endeavoured in vain to win the monks to his way of thinking—

[319] Howorth, *The Golden Days of the Early English Church*, Vol. II, pp. 172-179.
[320] Bede, *op. cit.*, Book III, Chap. 27.
[321] Bede, *Eccles. Hist.*, Book V, Chap. 23; Duke, *The Columban Church*, p. 107.
[322] Bede, *op. cit.*, Book V, Chap. 21. See also the work of a Romanized Celt, Boniface, in Simpson, *The Celtic Church in Scotland*, pp. 110, 111; Skene, *Celtic Scotland*, Vol. II, pp. 226 ff.
[323] Bede, *op. cit.*, Book III, Chap. 4; Book V, Chap. 21; Macewen, *A History of the Church in Scotland*, Vol. I, pp. 99, 100.

although he had had better fortune in Ireland.[324] From Iona the innovations may have spread through some other parts of Scotland.[325] In the ninth century the Norse invasions brought confusion. Through much of the country a modified type of the Celtic monasticism, in the form of religious communities whose members were known as Culdees, exercised a large proportion of the spiritual care of the people. Not until the twelfth and thirteenth centuries was the diocesan system of Roman lineage which prevailed in the West fully extended to Scotland.[326]

Probably the conversion of many of the English was not thoroughgoing. Bede, who wrote something more than a century after it was begun by Augustine, tells of large districts neglected, of bishops undertaking the supervision of far more extensive areas than they could attend to, of numbers of places which had not seen a bishop for years, and of the neglect of instruction in morals and of the rite of confirmation.[327] We hear, too, from Bede, that many monks and clergy did not know Latin[328] and so could not have direct access to the literature of the Church. He complained of the laziness and licentiousness of numbers of the monks.[329] Yet he himself is an example of high-minded living and scholarship and speaks of having often given to uneducated priests translations of the Apostles' Creed and the Lord's Prayer.[330]

The paucity of missionaries from older portions of the Church must have made for a superficial Christianity. The Irish and Scots and those trained by them were fairly numerous, but, so far as we know, the clergy sent by the Popes were few. Very early, even the episcopate became English. Within about a century after the arrival of Augustine, the coming of missionaries from Italy seems to have ceased.

Yet this infant English Christianity proved very vigorous. Probably the fact that the clergy were natives and not foreigners helped the English to regard the Church as their own. Certainly many of them were enthusiastic in their adherence to the faith.

Moreover, the missionaries from Rome, few though they were, had effectively connected the young Church with the See of Peter. The streams of

---

[324] Bede, *op. cit.*, Book IV, Chap. 15.

[325] Simpson, *op. cit.*, pp. 114-116.

[326] Macewen, *op cit.*, Vol. I, pp. 121-131, 194-226. Skene, *op. cit.*, Vol. II, pp. 226 ff., presents a partially different view of the character of the Culdees.

[327] Browne, *The Venerable Bede*, pp. 280, 281.

[328] Browne, *op. cit.*, pp. 191-195.

[329] *Ibid.* See also E. W. Watson, in Thompson, *Bede*, p. 57.

[330] Browne, *op. cit.*, pp. 191-195. The Penitential of Theodore, in Haddan and Stubbs, *op. cit.*, Vol. III, pp. 173 ff., witnesses both to a great deal of violation of Christian morality, even by the clergy, and to a vigorous effort on the part of the Church to improve it.

English pilgrims, lured by the shrines of Peter and Paul, helped to keep the connexion intact.

The conversion of England, it is well to note, was effected without any political pressure from abroad. Christianity did not come as the faith of a conqueror or as an agent of imperialism. Nor was much compulsion employed even by native rulers. To be sure, kings and the upper classes led the way, and the masses usually followed. Very infrequently, however, do we hear of the use of force, even in the destruction of pagan shrines. Much the same was true of Irish and Scottish Christianity. It was not imposed from the outside. Here may be one reason for the zeal which the English and the Irish early displayed in propagating their faith in other lands. It was something which they had freely adopted and which they had made their own that they were seeking to extend.

This, as we shall see, is in striking contrast with the method by which Christianity spread on the northern and eastern borders of the Frankish domains. Here the faith entered with the support of the Frankish rulers and was suspected of being a cloak for political imperialism. In much of Scandinavia, too, while it made its great gains without coercion from without, it was forced on the people by their kings.

From Great Britain and Ireland we turn, quite naturally, to the Continent, for here we shall find, as we have suggested, that among the Teutonic population north of the former possessions of the Roman Empire the faith penetrated chiefly through Celtic and English Christians from the British Isles.

In the sixth and seventh centuries the Church had won back practically all the ground that it had lost in Gaul and Britain through the barbarian invasions. In the British Isles, moreover, it had expanded past the bounds of the Roman Empire and had stretched its lines far beyond their fifth-century limits. In the eighth century it was to be carried into the Low Countries and Germany into ground which it had never effectively penetrated and which the Roman Empire had never succeeded in assimilating. In the ninth century its extension throughout the Teutonic peoples of Germany was completed by the forcible conversion of the Saxons, and in the tenth, eleventh, and twelfth centuries the Scandinavians were brought within its fold. In all of this, except the incorporation of the Saxons, the missionaries, as we have hinted, came chiefly from the British Isles. Both Celtic and English Christianity were represented, but it was the latter which prevailed—although often inspired to missionary endeavour by a period of residence in an Irish monastery. The English brought with them many of the Roman types of organization and practice, so that it was these, rather than the Celtic forms, which eventually won the day.

The fact that in all these areas except the lands of the Saxons, and to a less extent Scandinavia, the missionaries came chiefly from the British Isles and particularly from the English, bears witness to the great change which Christianity had wrought in the Anglo-Saxons. This transformation is particularly marked when it is contrasted with the backwardness of the Saxons who had remained on the Continent.[331] To be sure, some missionaries came from the Frankish domains, but the share of the Franks, except in the case of the Continental Saxons and of the Danes, was confined chiefly to the support accorded by the state to the English missionaries. The reason, as we have seen, must be sought partly in the Frankish Church. In the eighth century it was as yet too secularized and too low in spiritual vitality to display much missionary zeal. Columban and the other Irish missionaries had not aroused in it enough vitality to offset the forces of decay. Not until the eighth century was substantial reform accomplished, and then largely through the agency of English and Irish Christians. When the revival came, the Christian frontier had already been carried beyond the Rhine by English and Irish missionaries. As to Scandinavia, the resentment there was so great at the linking of Frankish imperialistic and missionary activities that the latter were seldom acceptable. When the Scandinavian kings at last decided to adopt the faith, it was from England, from which they had nothing to fear politically and with which they had close relations through their own conquests, that they sought bishops and clergy.

In a certain sense, these Anglo-Saxon missionaries constituted a migration which effected an English conquest of large portions of the Continent. That conquest, however, was not political or economic, but religious and cultural. It was usually achieved with the consent of those affected by it. Moreover, it was not a culture or a religion peculiarly English which was transmitted. The English missionaries were loyal to Rome. It was Roman and not Anglo-Saxon Christianity which they propagated.

First of the regions on the Continent touched by the English missionaries were the Low Countries, in the present Belgium and Holland.

Portions of what is now Belgium had been included in the Roman Gaul and had been penetrated by Christianity before the fifth century.[332] The barbarian invasions erased most of the Christian communities.[333] Much of the territory was occupied by the Franks in their pagan days. With them, in the present

[331] Carol, *L'Angleterre Chrétienne avant les Normands,* p. ii.
[332] Pirenne, *Histoire de Belgique,* Vol. I, p. 7.
[333] Pirenne, *op. cit.,* Vol. I, p. 15.

Flanders, were some Suevi and Saxons.[334] North of the Franks and holding a large part of what is now Holland and the German shores of the North Sea were the Frisians. North and east of the Frisians, in portions of what is now the north-western section of Germany, were the Saxons. All of these groups were of Teutonic stock and some were closely related in speech to the Anglo-Saxons.

The first missionaries to the Teutonic peoples in the present Belgium and southernmost portions of Holland were not Anglo-Saxons. We hear of some Irish monks.[335] The most famous of the early missionaries was one whom we have already mentioned, Amandus, from Aquitaine, in Southern Gaul, and presumably of Gallo-Roman stock. From his youth he had been a monk. For a long time he had lived in a cell on the city wall of Bourges. Then he had visited Rome and while there had apparently felt a call to preach. Returning north, not far from the year 625, he was commissioned by the Merovingian King Clotaire II, and, at the King's behest, was consecrated Bishop, but without a fixed diocese. He was also accorded the support of Clotaire's successor, Dagobert I, under whom the Merovingian power reached its zenith. Dagobert assisted him in the construction of churches and in a variety of other ways. Amandus made Ghent the centre of his mission field. He proved tactless. He wished Dagobert to make baptism compulsory. The King complied and popular tumults followed. Amandus left, perhaps because he was discouraged, and possibly because of the inward urge which drove him from place to place. For a time he attempted missions among the Slavs on the Danube. Soon he was back in Ghent, but he fell out with Dagobert and was banished (629). Before long he was once more in the realm, and was hard at work as a missionary among the Franks and as a founder of monasteries in the vicinity of Arras. In 647 he was made Bishop of Maastricht. Here, true to his past history, he aroused opposition in his attempt to institute reforms and left to preach to the Frisians near the mouth of the Schelde. In turn, restless soul that he was, he abandoned this task to preach to the Basques. As a missionary in the Low Countries his career had ended.[336]

For a time under Dagobert I the Bishop of Cologne was encouraged to undertake the conversion of the Frisians and a church was established as far

[334] Hauck, *Kirchengeschichte Deutschlands*, Vol. I, p. 300; Moreau, *Saint Amand*, p. 119.

[335] Gougaud, *Christianity in Celtic Lands*, pp. 159, 175; Ditchfield, *The Church in the Netherlands*, p. 27.

[336] On Amandus, see his earliest biography, anonymous, in *Mon. Germ. Hist., Script. rer. Meroving.*, Vol. V, pp. 431 ff.; E. de Moreau, *Saint Amand, Apotre de la Belgique et du Nord de la France;* Hauck *op. cit.*, Vol. I, pp. 301-304; Ditchfield, *op. cit.*, pp. 26, 27, 34-37.

north as Utrecht.[337] To some of the territory in which Amandus had laboured, in what is now the western part of Belgium, came, in about 641, a different type of man, Eligius, or Eloi. Trained as a goldsmith, he early showed integrity and charity. He used his wealth to free slaves, to relieve the needs of the poor, and to erect churches and monasteries. In 641 he was made Bishop of Noyon, a diocese which included part of what is now North-western France and Western Belgium. Here he found many non-Christians. By incessant travelling, preaching, and the founding of churches and monasteries, he strove to win them to the Christian faith and to nourish them in it.[338] Handsome, imposing, with a gift for attracting men and for practical administration, he pushed forward the work of the Church.

The first English missionary contact with the Frisians came in the latter part of the century through the much-travelled Bishop Wilfrid, whom we have already met in Sussex, in the Isle of Wight, and at Whitby. In 678, a quarter of a century or so after Eligius had been made Bishop of Noyon, Wilfrid, on one of his trips to Rome, landed in Friesland and was received in friendly fashion by Aldgisl (or Aldgils). With the latter's consent, he preached to the people and is said to have baptized many of the leading men and thousands of the masses. It is also reported that his cause was helped by an unusually large catch of fish and particularly fruitful harvests. These were attributed to his presence.[339]

We have no record of lasting results from these baptisms. Wilfrid, however, continued to be interested in Frisia. Willibrord, who became the outstanding missionary to the region, spent his boyhood at Ripon,[340] in a monastery which was the creation of Wilfrid; it was to Wilfrid that the group of English missionaries sent one of their number, Suidbert, for consecration as Bishop;[341] and on a later trip to Rome Wilfrid once more visited the land.[342] Indeed, it is not too much to say that out of his initial visit issued a series of events which had a large share in the conversion of the country. Since Wilfrid was an ardent partisan of Rome, it is not surprising that the Frisian mission early established intimate ties with the Papacy.

[337] Hauck, op. cit., Vol. I, p. 306.
[338] On Eligius, see Hauck, op. cit., Vol. I, pp. 306, 307; Migne, Pat. Lat., Vol. LXXXVII, Cols. 482-658; Maclear, A History of Christian Missions in the Middle Ages, pp. 159-166.
[339] Bede, Eccles. Hist., Book V, Chap. 19; Eddius Stephanus, The Life of Bishop Wilfrid, Chap. 26 (Colgrave's edition, pp. 52, 53).
[340] Alcuin, Vita Willibrordi, Chap. 2. The text of Alcuin's Vita Willibrordi is in Mon. Germ. Hist., Script. rer. Meroving, Vol. VII, pp. 81-141. A translation is Grieve, Willibrord. On Willibrord, see also Jung-Diefenbach, Die Friesenbekehrung bis zum Martertode des hl. Bonifatius, pp. 24-106.
[341] Bede, op. cit., Book V, Chap. 11.
[342] Bede, op. cit., Book III, Chap. 13.

The English mission which had so much to do with the conversion of the Frisians, while closely connected with Wilfrid, seems not to have arisen directly out of his first visit. It came about, rather, through Egbert. Egbert was from the English upper classes and was one of those who, in the early days of the Ionan mission to his nation, went to Ireland to study. In his youth there he had a severe illness and vowed that if he recovered he would live permanently outside his native land. It was a conception of what was involved in complete devotion which was probably derived from his Irish environment. He later became a Bishop and spent his long life of self-exile— for he lived to be ninety years of age—among the Picts and Scots.[343] He had wished to fulfil his vow of expatriation by becoming a missionary to the pagan tribes on the Continent, but when he was about to sail he was prevented by what he believed to be providential hindrances. One of his companions, Wictbert, persisted and preached for two years in Frisia, but without apparent results. The reason for the failure seems to have been the hostility of the Frisian King Radbod.[344] Presumably Radbod feared Christianity as an entering wedge for the imperialistic designs of the great Frankish state on his southern border.[345] That his fears were not baseless was seen in the sequel.

Egbert, undiscouraged by Wictbert's unhappy experience, sent other missionaries. Among these was one who became known as the Apostle to the Netherlands. Willibrord was from a devout English family. His father, indeed, became a monk and established an oratory out of which soon arose the monastery of which the great Alcuin was later to be head.[346] As we have seen, Willibrord was reared in a monastery, in Wilfrid's foundation at Ripon. At the age of twenty he went to Ireland, lured especially by tales of Egbert and Wictbert. It was, therefore, not strange that in his thirty-third year he entered on that mission to the Frisians with which the heroes of his youth had been connected.[347] Willibrord embarked with eleven companions,[348] the band thus totalling the twelve which was a favourite number for the missionary groups from Ireland. This was in the year 690,[349] less than a hundred years after Augustine had begun the conversion of the English.

[343] Bede, op. cit., Book III, Chap. 27.
[344] Bede, op. cit., Book V, Chap. 9; Flaskamp, Die Anfänge friesischen und sächischen Christentums, pp. 8, 9.
[345] Hauck, op. cit., Vol. I, p. 404.
[346] Alcuin, op. cit., Chaps. 1, 2; Hauck, Kirchengeschichte Deutschlands, Vol. I, pp. 404, 405.
[347] Alcuin, op. cit., Chaps. 1-5.
[348] Alcuin, op. cit., Chap. 5; Bede, op. cit., Book V, Chap. 10.
[349] On the date, see Hauck, op. cit., Vol. I, p. 406, n. 2. Hauck takes as his authority a note, possibly by Willibrord himself, in the Echternach Calendar. See Wilson, The Calendar of St. Willibrord, pp. xi, 13, 43, for text, translation, and note.

Willibrord and his companions landed near the mouth of the Rhine and went first to Utrecht. They apparently met with a chilly reception and Willibrord soon betook himself to Pepin of Heristal. Pepin was the second of his line to bear that name and as Mayor of the Palace to the decrepit Merovingians was rapidly augmenting the power of the Carolingians, as his family later came to be called. From now on for nearly a century and a half the spread of Christianity on the borders of the Frankish domains was intimately bound up with the policies and successes of this house. Pepin was extending his authority over the southern portions of the Frisian lands and welcomed the English missionary as a useful ally. Willibrord, in his turn, apparently found the support of Pepin essential to any extension of the Church's borders. It must be noted, however, that we do not know that Pepin or any of his successors compelled the Frisians to be baptized. Apparently no such drastic measures were employed as those resorted to among the Saxons by Charles the Great.

As soon as Willibrord had obtained the desired support of Pepin, he went to Rome to ask the authorization of the Pope. Why he felt this to be desirable we do not know, but it may have been because it seemed a natural step to one reared, as Willibrord had been, in circles under the influence of Wilfrid.

Returning with the Papal blessing and with relics, Willibrord and his companions set about the task which had brought them to the Continent. Presumably they met with success, for a few years later, at the direction of Pepin, Willibrord went to Rome with that prince's express request to the Pope for archiepiscopal consecration for the English missionary. This the Pope granted, in either 695 or 696.[350] It would be interesting to know whether the Pope remembered that only a century before a great predecessor had sent Augustine and his little band to the English, and thrilled with the realization that from these people, so recently pagan, missionaries were now going to other lands.[351]

On his return Willibrord received headquarters from Pepin in the Frankish fortress at what is now Utrecht.[352] Apparently in the six years or so which had elapsed since Willibrord first landed, that centre had passed from the control of Radbod to that of Pepin, and with it more territory in which the missionaries were free to work.[353]

One of the English group met with less success. Suidbert, at the request of

[350] Bede, *op. cit.*, Book V, Chap. 11, says 696. Hauck, *op. cit.*, Vol. I, p. 408, n. 3, and Grieve, *Willibrord*, pp. 47, 48 say 695 on the basis of the Echternach Calendar. See Wilson, *op. cit.*, pp. xi, 13, 43, for text, translation, and note.

[351] The chief sources for the last two paragraphs are Bede, *op. cit.*, Book V, Chap. 11, and Alcuin, *Vita Willibrordi*, Chaps. 5-7.

[352] Bede, *op. cit.*, Book V, Chap. 11.

[353] On the years between these two visits to Rome, see Grieve, *Willibrord*, pp. 39-46.

his colleagues, had been sent to England for episcopal consecration and had received it at the hands of Wilfrid. Returning to the Frisian mission, for some unexplained reason he soon left it and went to the Boructuari, who apparently lived east of Frisia. Here he won many converts, but was forced out by the pagan Saxons and took refuge on an island in the Rhine assigned him by Pepin.[354]

For about forty-four years, until the extreme old age of eighty-one, Willibrord continued his labours.[355] He did not live to see all the Frisians Christians. For decades the north-eastern portion of the people remained pagan.[356] By the time of his death, however, Willibrord had seen Christianity firmly rooted in the southern part of the country. To him more than to any other one man was due the establishment of the Church among the Frisians.[357]

Willibrord's achievements were not without their vicissitudes. In the mind of the Frisians, Christianity must have been fairly closely associated with Frankish rule. To the end of his days, apparently Radbod remained a pagan, although there is a story which declares that at one point in his career he actually started to enter the baptismal font and drew back when in response to his inquiry he was told by a missionary that his non-Christian ancestors were in hell.[358] Another account depicts him as making a death-bed repentance, sending for Willibrord to baptize him, and dying before the Bishop could arrive.[359] When Pepin of Heristal died, division and weakness in the Frankish state gave the Frisian nationalists a breathing space. Radbod had some success in winning back at least part of his lost territory. As he did so he destroyed Christian shrines, drove out their attendants, and restored paganism.[360] When, however, the youthful Charles Martel, a son of Pepin, gained control, he pushed

[354] Bede, op. cit., Book V, Chap. 11. On some of the difficulties created for the historian by this brief notice in Bede, see Hauck, op. cit., Vol. I, p. 407; Grieve, op. cit., pp. 34-39. Flaskamp, Suidbercht, Apostel der Brukterer, Gründer von Kaiserwerth, passim, has a monograph on him drawn partly from the brief account in Bede. Flaskamp thinks that Suidbert, consecrated in England, must have seemed an interloper to Pepin.

[355] On Willibrord's dates, see Grieve, op. cit., pp. 131, 132. Alcuin, op. cit., Chap. 5, says that Willibrord came to the Continent in his thirty-third year. Since this was in 690, he must have been born in 657 or 658. He seems, according to another life written by Alcuin in metrical style, to have died in his eighty-second year, or in November, 739 (Grieve, op. cit., p. 132).

[356] Boniface, Ep. 90; Migne, Pat. Lat., Vol. LXXXIX, Cols. 787, 788; Grieve, op. cit., p. 90.

[357] Grieve, op. cit., p. 90. Bede, op. cit., Book V, Chap. 11, speaks of Willibrord as building many churches and monasteries, winning numbers to the faith, and constituting other bishops. Hauck, op. cit., Vol. I, p. 416.

[358] Grieve, Willibrord, p. 45.

[359] Grieve, op. cit., p. 78.

[360] Willibald, Vita Bonif., Chap. 4; Grieve, op. cit., pp. 76, 77; Hauck, Kirchengeschichte Deutschlands, Vol. I, pp. 412-414.

back Radbod.[361] Charles showed great favour to Willibrord, had him baptize his infant son Pepin (the Short),[362] and restored him to his cathedral city, Utrecht.[363] Radbod's successor, Aldgisl II, was a Christian, and his accession must have opened wide doors to the English mission.[364] Later, in 726, Aldgisl II appears to have reverted to paganism and to have sought to drive out the Franks. Charles, however, soon brought him to time.[365]

Radbod seems usually to have treated Willibrord with respect.[366] Yet it would be surprising if at times the Archbishop had not wondered whether he ought not to seek other fields. We hear that once, when the situation seemed unusually forbidding, he turned his attention to the Danes. He actually journeyed to their land, only to find them fully as difficult as the Frisians. He did, however, bring back with him thirty boys, and instructed them in the faith. Even while on this trip he encountered Radbod on the Island of Heligoland and aroused the latter's ire by killing some of the sacred cattle and celebrating baptisms in a sacred spring.[367]

Of the details of Willibrord's long missionary life we have very few. We know little of his method.[368] Nor do we know many of his associates[369] or much that is trustworthy of contemporary Franks who laboured among the Frisians.[370]

However, we do know of one of the younger men who for a time worked under him and who eventually outstripped him in fame and in the extent of territory covered. This was Winfrith, more familiar under his later name of Boniface, and the most distinguished of the English missionaries to the Continent. With him our narrative moves out of the Low Countries, except at the beginning and the end of his career, and carries us into the middle reaches of the Rhine, north and east of the Rhine, and ultimately touches all the Frankish domains.

In Winfrith we have one of the most remarkable missionaries in the entire history of the expansion of Christianity. From the standpoint of character

---

[361] Alcuin, *Vita Willibrordi,* Chap. 13.

[362] Alcuin, *op. cit.,* Chap. 23.

[363] Alcuin, *op. cit.,* Chap. 13.

[364] Grieve, *op. cit.,* p. 78.

[365] Grieve, *op. cit.,* p. 85.

[366] Alcuin, *op. cit.,* Chap. 9.

[367] Alcuin, *op. cit.,* Chaps. 9-11.

[368] See a brief summary of what is known, in Jung-Diefenbach, *Die Friesenbekehrung bis zum Martertode des hl. Bonifatius,* pp. 95-106.

[369] Some other Anglo-Saxon missionaries are mentioned in Robinson, *The Conversion of Europe,* p. 338, and Maclear, *A History of Christian Missions during the Middle Ages,* p. 174.

[370] Such as Wulfram, Archbishop of Sens. The two earliest biographies of Wulfram are late and are usually considered untrustworthy.—Grieve, *op. cit.,* pp. 44-46.

and achievement he deserves to be ranked among the greatest of those who have given their lives to the spread and the strengthening of the faith.[371]

The exact date and place of Winfrith's birth are unknown. He was of a good Anglo-Saxon family and was born in the Kingdom of Wessex, possibly about 672 or 675, and perhaps at Crediton, not far from Exeter, in Devon.[372] This, it will be noted, was only a generation or so after Birinus had led the first great movement to the faith among the West Saxons. In early childhood Winfrith expressed a desire to enter that monastic life which then was capturing the imagination of many of the youth of his nation. His father opposed his desire, but later, as the result of severe illness, yielded. Winfrith was first, as a boy, in a monastery at Exeter and later at another, Nhutscelle, which probably was between Winchester and Southampton. He acquired a reputation for learning, for Christian character, for skill as a teacher, and for sound judgment in matters of administration. Presumably it was in these student days that he achieved that intimate knowledge of the Scriptures which throughout his life was to be seen in his letters. At the age of thirty he was ordained. He had before him an assured future in the Church.

Winfrith preferred, however, to become a missionary. Sailing from London, with a few companions, he went to the land of the Frisians, where so many

---

[371] The bibliography on Winfrith (Boniface) is very extensive. An excellent selected one is in Robinson, *The Life of Saint Boniface by Willibald*, pp. 11 ff. The earliest biography is Willibald, *Vita Sancti Bonifatii*, written a few years after the death of Boniface at the request of the latter's successor. What is probably the best edition of Willibald's *Vita* is by Levison in *Mon. Germ. Hist., Scriptores*, Vol. II, pp. 331-353. The text of Willibald's *Vita* is also in Migne, *Pat. Lat.*, Vol. LXXXIX, Cols. 603-634. An English translation is George W. Robinson, *The Life of St. Boniface by Willibald* (Harvard University Press, 1916, pp. 114). Boniface's Letters are in Migne, *Pat. Lat.*, Vol. LXXXIX, Cols. 687-803, and in the *Mon. Germ. Hist., Ep. Mer. et Kar. Aevi*, pp. 231-431. Some other works attributed to Boniface—a few sermons (whose authenticity has been rejected) and some poems—are in Migne, *Pat. Lat.*, Vol. LXXXIX, Cols. 813-892. An eleventh century biography by Othlon worked over Willibald's *Vita* and incorporated some other material, partly from manuscript sources. It is in *Mon. Germ. Hist., Scriptores*, Vol. II, pp. 357-359. Some of Boniface's letters are translated in E. Kylie, *The English Correspondence of St. Boniface* (London, Chatto and Windus, 1911, pp. xiv, 212). Recent biographies are G. F. Browne, *Boniface of Crediton and His Companions* (London, Society for Promoting Christian Knowledge, 1910, pp. x, 372) and Otto Fischer, *Bonifatius* (Leipzig, T. O. Weigel, 1881, pp. 295). F. Flaskamp, *Das hessische Missionswerk des hl. Bonifatius* (Duderstadt, Aloys Mecke, 2d ed., 1926, pp. xxiv, 143), and F. Flaskamp, *Die Missionsmethode des hl. Bonifatius* (Hildesheim, Franz Borgmeyer, 2d ed., 1929, pp. xviii, 62) are especially valuable for their extensive footnote references to sources and literature. Hauck, *Kirchengeschichte Deutschlands*, Vols. I and II, contains excellent chapters with valuable footnotes. A popular account for Roman Catholics, and with an excellent bibliography, is Godfrey Kurth, *Saint Boniface*, translated from the French by Victor Day and with insertions from the latest historical findings by F. S. Betten (Milwaukie, The Bruce Publishing Co., 1935, pp. xiii, 178). See also Addison, *The Medieval Missionary*, pp. 9-16, 89-98.

[372] On the date of birth, see Hauck, *op. cit.*, Vol. I, p. 419, n. 3; Fischer, *op. cit.*, p. 10. Browne, *op. cit.*, p. 1, gives the date as 679 or 680.

of his countrymen had preceded him. He arrived in 716, at the inopportune time after Pepin of Heristal and before Charles Martel had come to his full strength, when Radbod, taking advantage of the disorder in the Frankish realm, was regaining lost territory and destroying churches. With characteristic directness and courage, Winfrith went to Utrecht and attempted to obtain from Radbod an opportunity to preach. Summer and autumn passed and all doors seemed to be closed. He returned, accordingly, to England, and was there from the autumn of 716 to the spring of 718. He was urged to accept the headship of his monastery, but he still felt the urge to a missionary career and declined.[373]

In 718 Winfrith again turned his face to the Continent. He did not go directly to his old field. He went, rather, to Rome, there to seek Papal approval for his missionary dreams. Like Willibrord, he was true to the strong tie which was binding the English Church to the See of Peter. Although Winfrith was armed with a letter of introduction from his good friend, Bishop Daniel of Winchester, the Pope, Gregory II, did not immediately give his consent. In due time, however, Winfrith won the Papal confidence. Gregory saw in him a promising and mature agent—for Winfrith was then probably in his forties—not only for the winning of new regions to the faith, but, perhaps, for bringing order into the somewhat chaotic Christianity which was beginning to appear on the far side of the Rhine.

In the spring of 719 Winfrith, now with the added name of Boniface which had been given him by the Pope,[374] returned North armed with a Papal commission and provided with some of the relics which were then so highly esteemed. He went first of all to the parts of Germany which lay east of the Rhine and north of the Danube, and especially to Thuringia. There he attempted to improve the morale of the existing Christian communities.[375]

Before many months Boniface heard of the death of Radbod. Recognizing that the greatest obstacle to missions among the Frisians had been removed, he hastened to his old field and for the next three years, 719-722, worked under Willibrord, destroying pagan temples and building churches and oratories. Willibrord wished him for his successor. Boniface declined, pleading his Papal commission to Germany and the fact that he had not yet attained the canonical age of fifty, and insisting that he could not become a bishop without the con-

[373] Willibald, *Vita Sancti Bonifatii*, Chaps. 1-5. A letter of recommendation by Daniel in 718 is in Haddan and Stubbs, *Councils and Ecclesiastical Documents Relating to Great Britain and Ireland*, Vol. III, p. 302.

[374] Hauck, *op. cit.*, Vol. I, p. 427.

[375] Willibald, *Vita Sancti Bonifatii*, Chap. 5. The letter of Pope Gregory II to Boniface, May 15, 719 (calling him by the name of Boniface) is in Haddan and Stubbs, *op. cit.*, Vol. III, p. 303.

sent of the Pope. He asked, instead, to be sent back to Germany, and the older man at last gave his consent.[376]

To Germany, then, Boniface went, and entered upon what was to be the main work of his life.

As we have hinted, Boniface was not the first to introduce Christianity north and east of the Rhine. It long antedated him. Before we can proceed with the account of his achievements we must turn for a moment to the story of what had transpired there before him.[377]

What the religion of the Germans was before their conversion to Christianity we know only in fragmentary and very imperfect fashion.[378] There was a belief in spirits and in gods. The latter were in part the personifications of earth, water, fire, storm, the sun, the moon, and other forces and objects which affected the physical well-being of man. Certain springs and trees were held sacred, and temples for the gods were maintained. Ceremonies were celebrated at important times in the calendar, such as the winter solstice and the beginning of summer and autumn. Human sacrifices were not unknown.[379]

Centuries preceding the coming of Christian missionaries, the religion of those Teutons who were near the Roman borders underwent modifications through contact with the paganism of the powerful civilization to the south and was partially assimilated to the beliefs and practices of the Roman Empire.[380] The adoption of Christianity, therefore, was in some respects a continuation of a process already under way of the transformation of German culture by intercourse with the Mediterranean world. From this earlier Romanization the acceptance of Christianity displayed some notable differences. Unlike the former, it was due in part to the activities of zealous missionaries: it was followed by a much more nearly complete disappearance of the preceding cults.

In the previous volume we have seen that before the invasions of the fifth century Christianity had been widely adopted in what were later Bavaria, Baden, Württemberg, and parts of Switzerland and Austria. These regions had

[376] Willibald, *op. cit.,* Chap. 5.

[377] For a brief but excellent bibliography of the story, see Schmidlin-Braun, *Catholic Mission History,* pp. 157, 158. See also, for bibliography, the footnotes in Hauck, *Kirchengeschichte Deutschlands,* Vol. I, pp. 307-363.

[378] Timerding, *Die christliche Frühzeit Deutschlands,* Vol. I, pp. 8-15.

[379] Timerding, *op. cit.,* Vol. I, pp. 8-15; Schubert, *Geschichte der christlichen Kirche im Frühmittelalter,* pp. 4-16; H. Vordemfelde, *Die germanishe Religion in den deutschen Volksrechten. Erster Halbband. Der Religiöse Glaube* (Giessen, Alfred Töpelmann, 1923, pp. 165), *passim;* G. Steinhausen, *Germanische Kultur in der Urzeit* (Leipsig, B. G. Teubner, 4th ed., 1927, pp. 199), pp. 95-121.

[380] Timerding, *op. cit.,* Vol. I, pp. 8-15; Schubert, *op. cit.,* pp. 4-16.

been partially Romanized. In the fourth century, after Constantine, when mass movements brought into the Church most of the peoples within the Empire, many of the Roman provincials along the upper reaches of the Rhine and Danube were affected. We have also recorded the fact that the barbarian invasions resulted in the disappearance of most of the Roman culture and with it the larger part of the Christianity of these districts.

Generations before Boniface, Christianity had once more begun to expand into what are now Switzerland, Southern Germany, and the western portions of Austria. By his time, indeed, their peoples had largely become nominally Christian. Even as far north as Thuringia Christianity had penetrated. Only in the Slavic lands to the east, among the northern portions of Frisia, and among the Saxons and their neighbours in what are now the north-western sections of Germany did the old paganism remain practically unbroken.

The pre-Bonifacian spread of Christianity in these regions was effected through a number of channels. In some places the Romanized provincial populations survived and preserved their language and their faith.[381] From these centres the Church presumably here and there began to make gains among the new settlers. Some, too, of the invaders were probably Christian when they first arrived. Usually, however, their religion, if Christian at all, was of the Arian type.[382] We hear of what was called Bonosianism, but that may have been a variety of Arianism.[383] When, at the close of the sixth and the beginning of the seventh century, the Franks moved into the Church, they began carrying their new faith with them to their expanding frontiers. In the latter part of the sixth and in the seventh century the Alamanni, who occupied what are now roughly portions of Baden, Württemberg, and Northern Switzerland, came under the control of the Franks. This eventually made for the extension of Christianity among them, partly through Frankish rulers, partly through Frankish settlers, and partly through the encouragement given to bishoprics which had persisted from Roman days.[384] In the seventh century the Bavarians, too, passed under the Frankish influence and with that came accessions to Christianity.[385] Even the Thuringians were included within the Frankish political sphere: Frankish settlers, presumably Christian, made their

---

[381] Hauck, *op. cit.,* Vol. I, pp. 340-342; Schubert, *op. cit.,* pp. 289, 290; Neuss, *Die Anfänge des Christentums im Rheinlände, passim.*

[382] Schubert, *op. cit.,* p. 289; Hauck, *op. cit.,* Vol. I, p. 309.

[383] Schubert, *op. cit.,* p. 289; Hauck, *op. cit.,* Vol. I, pp. 343, n. 4, 344. The true Bonosianism took its name from a Bishop Bonosus, of the fourth century, who was adjudged a heretic, but propagated his type of the faith.—*Cath. Encyc.,* Vol. II, p. 677; Hefele, *History of the Councils of the Church,* Vol. II, p. 394.

[384] Hauck, *op. cit.,* Vol. I, pp. 309 ff.

[385] Hauck, *op. cit.,* Vol. I, pp. 344 ff.

way up the Main, and probably served as nuclei for the new faith.[386] In time the ruling families in all these areas tended to conform to Frankish ways, and with them to take on Christianity. Several of them were of Frankish stock or intermarried with it, and so were Christians.[387]

Then, too, missionaries entered. Among them were some Franks. Many of them were Irish or owed their zeal to contacts with the Irish. So Fridolin, who may have been Irish, is reported to have lived in the sixth century, to have laboured among the Alamanni in the Black Forest and the vicinity of Basel, and to have founded a monastery on an island in the Rhine.[388] We have already noted the manner in which Columban's foundation at Luxeuil became the source of a number of missions to pagan Germans. We have also seen that the wanderings of Columban after his expulsion from Luxeuil resulted in conversions in the present Switzerland and in the work of Gall among non-Christians near Lake Constance. We read of a contemporary of Boniface, Pirmin, a foreigner, perhaps an Anglo-Saxon, less probably Irish, who died about 753 and who, under the protection of Charles Martel, seems to have ranged over a wide territory among the Alamanni, from Lake Constance into Alsace. He was one of the wandering bishops without fixed diocese who were so prominent on the German frontiers of Christianity in the seventh and eighth centuries and seems to have given his efforts chiefly to a nominally Christian population. He was the reputed founder or reformer of a number of monasteries. It may be that Charles Martel used him to reinforce and extend the authority of the Carolingians.[389]

By the inception of the eighth century Bavaria was outwardly Christian.[390] Duke Theodo, of the end of the seventh and the beginning of the eighth century, interested himself in ecclesiastical matters and gave liberally to churches and monasteries. He encouraged one Rupert (Hrodbert), who is said to have been related to the Merovingians and to have been Bishop of Worms. In Bavaria Rupert served as a kind of itinerant bishop, but eventually made his chief centre at Salzburg, built there a church and monasteries, and extended his labours into the surrounding country.[391] We hear vaguely of a

[386] Hauck, *op. cit.*, Vol. I, p. 359.

[387] Schubert, *op. cit.*, p. 289; Hauck, *op. cit.*, Vol. I, pp. 344, 348, 359, 360.

[388] *Vita Fridolini*, in *Mon. Ger. Hist., Script. rer. Meroving.*, Vol. III, pp. 354 ff.; Hauck, *op. cit.*, Vol. I, p. 318; Gougaud, *Christianity in Celtic Lands*, p. 159.

[389] Hauck, *op. cit.*, pp. 323-333, the footnotes in these pages giving references to the sources. Gougaud, *op. cit.*, p. 161, says that the increasing tendency is to regard Pirmin as not having been a Scot. See also Schubert, *op. cit.*, pp. 292, 293.

[390] Hauck, *op. cit.*, Vol. I, p. 345.

[391] Hauck, *op. cit.*, Vol. I, pp. 348-352. For the sources on Rupert, see Hauck, *op. cit.*, Vol. I, p. 347, n. 3. See also Moreau in Descamps, *Histoire Générale Comparée des Missions*, p. 189. See *Vita Hrodberti episcopi Salisburgensis*, ed. Levison in *Mon. Germ. Hist., Script. rer. Meroving.*, Vol. IV, pp. 140-162.

number of other missionaries in Bavaria, some of them wandering monastic
bishops of the type developed by the Irish.[392] Duke Theodo went to Rome in
716 and with Pope Gregory II planned a more regular organization of the
Bavarian Church with a territorial hierarchy after the Roman plan. With his
death, however, the project seems to have lapsed.[393]

By the time of Boniface, then, Christianity had made considerable progress
in what had once been Roman territory on the upper courses of the Rhine and
the Danube in what is now Southern Germany and Switzerland. Much of the
land was professedly Christian and Catholic. Arianism had disappeared. Yet
the state of this Christianity left much to be desired. In some places overt
paganism remained. Many of the nominal Christians maintained religious
and magical observances which had come down from pre-Christian days. The
clergy were poorly trained and often did not adhere to the rule of celibacy.
The Church was imperfectly organized. The itinerant bishops of the Irish
tradition did not make for a stable and disciplined ecclesiastical life.[394] The
great contribution of Boniface lay partly in extending the faith into pagan
territory and partly in improving the morale of the existing Christianity and
giving it a hierarchical organization of the Roman type.

We resume, then, the story of Boniface. Declining the urgent request of
Willibrord that he remain with him, Boniface went farther into the interior,
to Hesse.[395] Apparently here, too, were some nominal Christians before him,
but practising a religion in which mingled elements of both the new and the
old.[396] Here outright pagan cults were still strong. Hesse was partly isolated
by natural barriers[397] and so less subject to influences from the South than
were the Thuringians. Boniface went first of all to the non-Christians and is
said to have won and baptized large numbers, even up to the Saxon borders.[398]

Mindful of his Papal commission, Boniface sent to the See of Peter a messenger to report his success and to seek instructions. In due time a reply came
which summoned him to Rome. He went and at the request of the Pope
wrote out a statement of his faith. This was found satisfactory and, the last
day in November, 722, he was consecrated Bishop.[399] Gregory II, although a

---

[392] Hauck, *op. cit.,* Vol. I, pp. 352-354; Gougaud, *op. cit.,* p. 163.

[393] Hauck, *op. cit.,* Vol. I, pp. 354-357.

[394] Hauck, *op. cit.,* Vol. I, pp. 330-333, 358, 362.

[395] Willibald, *Vita Sancti Bonifatii,* Chap. 6.

[396] Hauck, *op. cit.,* Vol. I, pp. 430, 431.

[397] Flaskamp, *Das hessische Missionswerk des hl. Bonifatius,* pp. 12-14.

[398] Willibald, *op. cit.,* Chap. 6.

[399] Willibald, *op. cit.,* Chap. 6. Willibald gives the day of the month, Nov. 30, but not
the year. As to the year, opinion is divided between 722 and 723.—Hauck, *op. cit.,* Vol. I,
p. 433, n. 1. Hauck holds to 722, as does Robinson, *The Life of Saint Boniface by Willibald,* p. 60, n. 2.

Roman by birth and with no missionary experience, seems to have understood and appreciated Boniface and to have given him his confidence.[400] Boniface was sent back to his field with letters of commendation to Charles Martel,
to all Christians, to the clergy and laity, to the Christians of Thuringia, and
to the Saxons, and with instructions to observe the laws and customs of the
Church.[401] On his return journey Boniface presented himself and his letters to
Charles and received the latter's approval of his Hessian mission.[402]

To Hesse, then, Boniface once more made his way. Here he resumed the
work of conversion. It was probably before many months, in 723, that he
achieved one of the most spectacular successes of his career. Following the
advice of some of the most stalwart of his converts, he went to Geismar and,
in the presence of a large number of pagans, began cutting down a huge
ancient oak held sacred to Thor. Before he had quite completed the task a
powerful gust of wind finished the demolition. The tree crashed to the ground
and broke into four sections. The pagan bystanders, who had been cursing
the desecrator, were convinced of the power of the new faith. Out of the
timber Boniface constructed an oratory to St. Peter.[403] The Geismar episode
may well have proved decisive evidence in terms which the populace could
understand of the superior might of the God of the Christians. Presumably,
too, it helped to wean from pre-Christian magical practices many of the
nominal converts who observed the rites of both the new and the old faith.[404]

So rapidly did the conversion of the Hessians progress that within a little
over a year after his return from Rome with episcopal consecration Boniface
felt free to pass on to other lands.[405] Armed with a fresh letter from Pope
Gregory II,[406] he went to Thuringia. Here his chief problem was not the
conversion of pagans, but the improvement of the quality of an existing
Christianity. He met opposition from the disciples of Celtic missionaries from
the British Isles who held to some of the same peculiarities which had proved
a bone of contention in England. He found, too, a Church suffering from
political disorder and Christians who adhered to pagan rites. Some priests
administered baptism with an improper formula, some said mass for pagans

---

[400] Flaskamp, *Das hessische Missionswerk des hl. Bonifatius*, pp. 36, 37.

[401] Willibald, *op. cit.*, Chap. 6; *Ep.* 17-21, in *Mon. Germ. Hist., Ep. Mer. et Kar. Aevi*,
Vol. I, pp. 266-269.

[402] Willibald, *op. cit.*, Chap. 6. See Charles' letter of commendation to all his officers,
Ep. 22 in *Mon. Germ. Hist., Ep. Mer. et Kar. Aevi*, Vol. I, p. 270.

[403] Willibald, *op. cit.*, Chap. 6; Hauck, *op. cit.*, Vol. I, p. 438; Flaskamp, *Auf hessische
Bonifatiuspfaden*, p. 13.

[404] Willibald, *op. cit.*, Chap. 6.

[405] Willibald, *op. cit.*, Chap. 6; Hauck, *op. cit.*, Vol. I, p. 440; *Ep.* 24 in *Mon. Germ.
Hist., Ep. Mer. et Kar. Aevi*, Vol. I, pp. 273, 274.

[406] *Ep.* 25, in *Mon. Germ. Hist., Ep. Mer. et Kar. Aevi*, Vol. I, pp. 274, 275.

or for Christians living in open sin, and among the clergy were those who were distributing Bible texts as amulets to be worn as a protection against disease. Worship of the old gods continued. Christians ate meat offered to idols after making over it the sign of the cross. The Church's marriage regulations were not always observed. Some young women had taken the vow of chastity, but instead of entering a nunnery were living in perilous fashion out in society.[407] These and other evils Boniface fought with marked success. Within a decade of his arrival in Hesse, the Church in that region and in Thuringia had been firmly established and regularized.[408]

In all of these herculean labours Boniface had support from Charles Martel, although not nearly so much as the latter gave to Willibrord.[409] He enjoyed the cordial backing of Rome. He referred many of his problems to Gregory II and received from him careful answers and loyal approval. Gregory II died Feb. 11, 731, and was succeeded by Gregory III. Of Syrian antecedents and apparently not so good a judge of men as his predecessor, Gregory III was inclined to hold Boniface with a tighter rein than had Gregory II.[410] Yet he, too, gave him his confidence and sent him an Archbishop's pall.[411]

Boniface had a marked capacity for enlisting the enthusiastic assistance of many helpers. Through correspondence he kept in close touch with friends in England. Among his letters are ones to bishops and abbesses. From Bishop Daniel of Winchester came detailed advice on missionary methods.[412] Archbishops of Canterbury and York were kept informed on his work and at least one sent him assistance.[413] From abbesses came books which they had copied and vestments which they had prepared.[414] Boniface craved the prayers of his English friends.[415] From England, too, came many missionaries, both men and women, to serve under him. Some of these were relatives of Boniface's.[416] One of the most famous of the men was Lul, who as a boy had Boniface for his teacher at Nhutscelle, then made a pilgrimage to Rome, and

[407] *Ep.* 26-28, 33, 43, 44, in *Mon. Germ. Hist., Ep. Mer. et Kar. Aevi,* Vol. I, pp. 275-280, 283, 291, 292; Hauck, *op. cit.,* Vol. I, pp. 441-445.

[408] Willibald, *op. cit.,* Chap. 6; Hauck, *op. cit.,* Vol. I, pp. 445-447.

[409] Hauck, *op. cit.,* Vol. I, p. 449.

[410] Flaskamp, *Das hessische Missionswerk des hl. Bonifatius,* p. 87. On Gregory III, see Gregorovius, *Geschichte der Stadt Rom im Mittelalter,* Vol. II, pp. 269-285.

[411] Willibald, *op. cit.,* Chap. 6.

[412] *Ep.* 23, in *Mon. Germ. Hist., Ep. Mer. et Kar. Aevi,* Vol. I, pp. 271-273; English translation in Kylie, *The English Correspondence of Saint Boniface,* pp. 51-55.

[413] Translations in Kylie, *op. cit.,* pp. 71-73, 135-137, 176-191.

[414] Translations in Kylie, *op. cit.,* pp. 90, 92.

[415] Translations in Kylie, *op. cit.,* pp. 130, 131.

[416] Willibald, *op. cit.,* Chap. 6; Kylie, *op. cit.,* pp. 12-14; Flaskamp, *Die Missionsmethode des hl. Bonifatius,* pp. 3 ff. On some of these companions, see Hauck, *op. cit.,* Vol. I, pp. 452-459, and Browne, *Boniface of Crediton and His Companions, passim.*

later, while still young, followed Boniface to Germany and eventually succeeded him as Archbishop of Mainz.[417] Still another was Willibald, possibly of the royal line of Kent and a relative of Boniface's, who had been on a pilgrimage to Rome and to Jerusalem and spent ten years in the mother house of the Benedictines, on Monte Cassino. Then Boniface asked him of the Pope for the German mission and he became Bishop of Eichstätt, in Bavaria.[418] Willibald's brother, Wunnibald, also much travelled, served in the German mission,[419] as did a sister, Walpurga.[420]

On the Continent itself Boniface recruited helpers. One of the most famous of these was Gregory, of a noble Frankish family, who joined him at the age of fourteen or fifteen and became his lifelong disciple and companion.[421] We shall hear more of him when we come to the completion of the conversion of the Frisians.

To this ability to attract and hold colleagues, and particularly to this stream of personnel and material from England, much of the success of Boniface was due.

In his methods of work, with one exception Boniface seems not to have developed much that was peculiar or new.[422] His strength lay, rather, in employing more effectively than did others the means familiar to the English missionaries on the Continent. He appears to have addressed himself first to the upper classes. Having won them, the masses followed the example of their accepted leaders. He and his colleagues travelled by the usual trade routes— rivers and existing roads and forest trails. They lived off the land, eating fish from the rivers, fruits from the forest, and native meats. Often they worked with their hands. This was the more natural because the Anglo-Saxon missionaries were coming to fellow Germans whose language and manner of life were akin to their own. Wherever a missionary was placed for any length of time, a log building was erected, or a cell or a cloister. Monasteries were established. They became important means of deepening the religious life of newly and superficially converted regions and of introducing fresh elements

---

[417] *Ep.* 49, 98, 110-139, in *Mon. Germ. Hist., Ep. Mer. et Kar. Aevi*, Vol. I, pp. 297, 298, 384-386, 396-424; *Lamperti Vita Lulli archiepiscopi Mogontiacensis*, in *Lamperti Monachi Hersfeldensis*, pp. 305-340, in *Scriptores rerum Germanicarum* (Hanover, 1894).

[418] *Vita S. Willibaldi* in *Philippi Ecclesiae Eystettensis XXXIX Episcopi de eiusdem Ecclesiae Divis Tutelaribus S. Richardo, S. Willibaldo, S. Wunibaldo, S. Walpurgæ* (Ingolstadt, 1617).

[419] *Ibid.*

[420] *Acta Sanctorum*, Vol. VI, Feb. 25, pp. 529 ff., contains a life by Wolfhard. Brief accounts of Willibald, Wunnibald, and Walpurga are in Browne, *op. cit.*, pp. 112-118.

[421] See Liudger, *Vita S. Gregorii*, in *Acta Sanctorum*, Aug., Vol. V, pp. 254-264, and in Migne, *Pat. Lat.*, Vol. XCIX, Cols. 749-770.

[422] Flaskamp, *Die Missionsmethode des hl. Bonifatius*, pp. 17-28.

of culture. The wholesale baptisms made for little immediate profound change in the manner of life. This might conceivably have been accomplished merely by a better diocesan and parish organization. Boniface, however, reproducing what he had known in England, depended not only on bishops, synods, and parish clergy, but upon monasteries to follow up the mass acceptance of baptism by instruction in the tenets and the way of life demanded by the new faith. Such foundations as Fulda and Fritzlar[423] became permanent centres from which radiated religious instruction, handicrafts, and improved methods of agriculture.

The one markedly new feature in Boniface's method was the place given to women. On the frontiers, unsettled as they were, men alone were used, but in regions where the populace was Christian and order fairly well established women were brought in. Many of these were English. One, Walpurga, we have already noted. Another was a relative of Boniface, Leoba, Leobgutha, or Leobgytha, an only daughter who had been trained in a monastery on the Isle of Thanet near where Augustine had landed more than a century before. Boniface especially asked for her as one of his helpers. She became head of a religious house for women at Bischofsheim, not far from Würzburg.[424] For the first time in a number of centuries we find women taking an active part in missions. Moreover, not again until the nineteenth century—unless it may be in the Moravian enterprise of the eighteenth century—do we find them so prominent as representatives of the faith among newly Christian peoples.

By about the age of sixty, Boniface had seen practically all of Hesse become nominally Christian and had brought order into the Church there and in Thuringia. As Archbishop he had reached as high a post in the Church as he could hope to attain. Many men would have considered their life work finished and would have rested on their laurels.

Not so Boniface. Restive, he looked around for other exploits. First he went to Bavaria, where he travelled widely, preached assiduously, and attempted to improve the existing Christianity.[425] Thence he passed on to Italy, for his

[423] Fulda and Fritzlar were founded after the work of nominal conversion had been begun, perhaps after it had been practically completed. They were means of deepening the faith of Christians and centres of civilization rather than agencies for conversion. The date of Fritzlar's founding is not certain.—Hauck, *Kirchengeschichte Deutschlands*, Vol. I, p. 459, n. 4. On Fritzlar see also Willibald, *Vita Sancti Bonifatii*, Chap. 6; Flaskamp, *Das hessische Missionswerk des hl. Bonifatius*, p. 82. Fulda, Boniface's favorite monastic foundation, was begun later than Fritzlar. Here Boniface was buried.—Browne, *Boniface of Crediton and His Companions*, pp. 142 ff.

[424] See letter of Boniface to Leoba, *Ep.* 96 in *Mon. Germ. Hist., Ep. Mer. et Kar. Aevi*, Vol. I, p. 382; Rudolph of Fulda, *Vita Leoba*, German translation by Tangl in *Die Geschichtschreiber der deutschen Vorzeit*, Vol. XIII (third ed., 1920), pp. 85-102. See also Hauck, *op. cit.*, Vol. I, pp. 456-459; Browne, *op. cit.*, pp. 166-172.

[425] Willibald, *op. cit.*, Chap. 6.

third and last visit to Rome. Perhaps he hoped to gain Papal support for a mission to the Saxons. Probably from about this time date letters of his to the bishops, clergy, and monks of all England, asking their prayers for the conversion of these folk, urging the blood relationship of the Continental Saxons to the Christian English as a basis of interest, and speaking of the favour with which two Popes had looked upon the mission.[426] Whatever may have been Boniface's hopes, they were not fulfilled. The conversion of the Saxons was to be deferred for more than a generation and was to be accomplished by such a use of force as Boniface never employed.

Boniface spent nearly a year in Rome, visiting the various shrines and praying.[427] Yet his months there were by no means entirely given to his personal religious devotions. He found in the Eternal City many German and English pilgrims. They were greatly impressed by him and he seems to have sought from among them labourers for Germany.[428] Of course he conferred with the Pope.

When, finally, he left Rome, laden with gifts and relics of the saints, it was to Bavaria that Boniface went, there to complete that purification, reinvigoration, and reorganization of the Church which he had already begun.[429] Into this story we must not attempt to go. We can merely take the time to say that, supported by the Pope and at the invitation of Odilo, the Duke of Bavaria, Boniface carried out the reorganization of the Bavarian Church. In doing so, he found it necessary to expel irregular bishops, presumably Celts from the British Isles. In their place he divided the realm into four dioceses and placed at their head bishops, three of whom he himself consecrated.[430] Thus a child of the Roman influence in England repeated what had been accomplished in his native land about the time of his own birth, and brought the Christianity of Bavaria into conformity with the canon law and the administrative system which had been developed in the Roman Empire.

From Bavaria Boniface passed on to the reform of the Frankish Church. Charles Martel died in 741, dividing his power and his domains between his sons Carloman and Pepin (the Short). To Carloman went the eastern portions of the realm and to Pepin the western. Both men had been educated by

---

[426] Hauck, *op. cit.*, Vol. I, p. 463, n. 3. For the letter see *Ep. 46, Mon. Germ. Hist., Ep. Mer. et Kar. Aevi*, Vol. I, p. 294.

[427] Willibald, *op. cit.*, Chap. 7.

[428] Willibald, *op. cit.*, Chap. 7, speaks of the attraction which he had for the Franks, Bavarians, and English in Rome. *Vita Wynnebaldi*, 4 (text given in Hauck, *op. cit.*, Vol. I, p. 467, n. 1) speaks of his asking many to go with him. One of those who responded was Wynnebald, who was a brother of Willibald, and a relative of Boniface.

[429] Willibald, *op. cit.*, Chap. 7. See Hauck, *op. cit.*, Vol. I, pp. 469-478, for a longer account, with footnote references to the authorities.

[430] Willibald, *op. cit.*, Chap. 7.

the monks of St.-Denis. Carloman especially was religious and in 747 retired to a monastery. With this disposition, it is not surprising that early in the six years of his reign he sought to improve the quality of the Church within his domains. Nor is it strange that Boniface was called to the task, for his activities had been chiefly within the portion of the realm which fell to Carloman and had made him the outstanding spiritual force of the region. Beginning in 742 and 743, various synods were held. The influence of Boniface was dominant and decrees were passed which sought to bring order into the Church and to raise the moral and religious level of the Christian community. The actions authorized were at least partially carried out, apparently largely because of the energy of Boniface, and the clergy whom he had recruited through the years, but not without opposition from some of the Frankish bishops.[431]

Pepin put through ecclesiastical reforms in his portion of the kingdom, but used Boniface less than did Carloman.[432] Yet Pepin was friendly to Boniface. One report has it that when, in 750, Pepin ceased to be Mayor of the Palace and was crowned King, Boniface officiated at the ceremony and anointed him.[433]

For many of the years of his episcopate and archiepiscopate, Boniface was without a specific See. In 744, however, it was proposed that he become Archbishop of Cologne. Later, because of interesting developments whose intricacies we must not take time to trace, Mainz was fixed upon.[434]

Boniface was now old in years. In his sixties, as we have seen, he had added to the achievements of youth and middle age an important share in the reform of the Church, notably in Bavaria and in the eastern and northern sections of the Frankish realm. Through all of his decades of self-exile, moreover, he continued to keep in touch with his native land. Even in his old age he headed a letter of several bishops to an English king, rebuking the latter for his immoralities.[435]

Yet all this did not exhaust the energy of the great Englishman. Once more he turned to the people among whom he had begun his missionary career. In the task to which he had dedicated the vigorous years of his late youth he determined to end his days. He was well aware that he would not return.[436]

[431] Willibald, op. cit., Chaps. 7, 8. Hauck, op. cit., Vol. I, pp. 478-535, gives references to other sources and to pertinent literature.

[432] Hauck, op. cit., Vol. I, pp. 504 ff.

[433] Annales Regni Francorum, in Scriptores Rerum Germanicarum (Hanover, 1895). The accuracy of this statement has been challenged. See Hauck, op. cit., Vol. I, p. 537, n. 3.

[434] For the story, with reference to the sources, see Hauck, Kirchengeschichte Deutschlands, Vol. I, pp. 522 ff.; Browne, Boniface of Crediton and His Companions, pp. 257-262.

[435] Ep. 73, in Mon. Germ. Hist., Ep. Mer. et Kar. Aevi, Vol. I, pp. 339-345. An English translation is in Kylie, The English Correspondence of St. Boniface, pp. 160-172.

[436] Willibald, Vita Sancti Bonifatii, Chap. 8.

With characteristic thoughtfulness he sent a request to Pepin that after the Archbishop's death the King would give subsistence and protection to the clergy, monks, and students, most of them foreigners, who looked to Boniface as their leader and the majority of whom he had probably been the means of bringing to Germany.[437] Pepin seems to have granted the petition and received the old man's thanks.[438]

The thirty years or so since Boniface had left the Low Countries had not seen the completion of the conversion of the Frisians.[439] Many were Christian, but large numbers were still pagan. With Boniface went a company of priests and monks. For some months, perhaps as much as two years,[440] Boniface travelled among the non-Christians. He seems to have met with marked success, for we read that he baptized many thousands, destroyed temples, and built churches. More than once he must have rejoiced in the contrast between the discouragement which he encountered in his first sojourn on the Continent and the rapid advance of the faith in his declining years.

It was probably in June, 754,[441] that the end came, apparently unexpectedly, but presumably as he had wished. Boniface had set a day for the confirmation of neophytes and had summoned them from far and wide to meet him at his camp on the banks of a river. In the early morning of the appointed day, probably before many of the expected company had arrived, a body of pagans fell upon the camp, probably lured at least partly by the prospect of easy plunder. Some of the company sprang to the defence, but Boniface sought to restrain them and encouraged those who stood by him to meet their martyrdom with stout hearts. Soon it was all over. The attackers, drunk with the wine which they found in the spoil, fell to fighting one another over the division of the booty and were disappointed to discover in the chests of the victims only books and relics. A few days later, the Christians assembled a punitive expedition and, heedless of Boniface's dying injunction to return good for

[437] *Ep.* 93 (753 or 754) in *Mon. Germ. Hist., Ep. Mer. et Kar. Aevi,* Vol. I, pp. 380, 381. It is not certain, however, that this request was sent with the Frisian expedition in mind. It may have been made because of a consciousness of old age, infirm health, and the necessity of making some provision for the workers before the death of their leader.

[438] At least we have a letter of thanks from Boniface, although not certainly in response to this particular request. *Ep.* 107 (753 or 754) in *Mon. Germ. Hist., Ep. Mer. et Kar. Aevi,* Vol. I, p. 394.

[439] On events between the death of Willibrord and the resumption in person by Boniface of the Frisian mission, see Jung-Diefenbach, *Die Friesenbekehrung bis zum Martertode des hl. Bonifatius,* pp. 107-115.

[440] Browne, *Boniface of Crediton and His Companions,* p. 273.

[441] Hauck, *op. cit.,* Vol. I, p. 549, gives the date as June 5, 754. Fischer, *Bonifatius,* p. 216, says June 5, 755. See Hauck, *op. cit.,* Vol. I, p. 549, n. 6, for a discussion of the year.

evil, worked such havoc among the assassins that of such of the latter as survived, many, perforce, accepted the Christian name.[442]

The martyrdom of Boniface rounded out a great career. Few, if any, Christian missionaries have more accurately presented by their conduct the ideals of the faith they have sought to propagate. Humble in spite of the temptations which come with high ecclesiastical position, above the breath of scandal, affectionate and possessed of a wide range of friends with whom he took the time and trouble to maintain his contacts, a man of prayer, self-reliant, courageous, burning with indignation against anything which caused simple Christians to stumble,[443] self-sacrificing, with a deep and loving concern for all for whom he was responsible and with a passion for righteousness, Boniface was one of the outstanding exemplars of the Christian life. He was fearless in denouncing evil in high places and was capable of taking King and Pope to task.[444] His was not the mind of a philosopher, although he had a creditable command of the scholarship in which he had been trained and was steeped in the Scriptures. He was, rather, a man of action and an exceptionally able organizer and administrator. He possessed, too, the capacity of attracting and holding the loyalty of men and women, including some of large ability. Yet, gifted though many of the circle of his followers were, none of them quite equalled him. He was not one of those who can inspire men to greater deeds than they themselves have performed.

As we have seen, Boniface made a deep stamp upon the Christianity of the Rhine Valley and Central and South Germany. Some districts owed to him their conversion. In others his achievement was the organization and the improvement of the morale of an already existing Christianity. He had a major share in the development of monasteries and of the ordered cloistered life. To him, more than to any other one man, was due the extension of the power of Rome and the Roman type of discipline and ecclesiastical polity over much of what is now Central and South Germany. Most of the regions in which he laboured are still predominantly Roman Catholic. It is fitting that the chapel which enshrines his tomb should still be the accepted meeting-place of the Roman Catholic bishops of Germany. It is interesting but quite futile to inquire whether the fact that the territories to which most of his energies

---

[442] Willibald, op. cit., Chap. 8, gives a vivid account of these last months, and especially of the martyrdom.

[443] In Ep. 50, in Mon. Germ. Hist., Ep. Mer. et Kar. Aevi, Vol. I, p. 301, Boniface asked the Pope to prohibit riotous scenes in Rome at the beginning of January, on the ground that these were seen by pilgrims from the North and formed an obstacle to uprooting paganism in Germany.

[444] As in Ep. 50 and 73, in Mon. Germ. Hist., Ep. Mer. et Kar. Aevi, Vol. I, pp. 301, 339-345.

were devoted were never swept fully into the Protestant movement is in any way attributable to the foundations which Boniface laid.

At the time of the death of Boniface the conversion of what is now Germany and the Netherlands was far from complete. The frontiers of Christianity had been pushed forward, but beyond them were the Saxons, some of the Frisians, and the great bodies of Slavs. To the north, too, was Scandinavia, still practically untouched.

After the death of Boniface, the boundaries of Christianity in Germany and the Low Countries continued to be enlarged. Much of the actual work of conversion was still performed by priests from England. While the proportion of Continental missionaries increased, neither Columban nor Boniface had been able to inject enough vigour into the Frankish Church to arouse a missionary enthusiasm in any but a scattering few. Yet from these few came many of those who carried to completion the dream of Boniface for the Frisians and the Saxons. However, it would be a mistake to picture the English Church, even of the age of Willibrord and Boniface, as enthusiastically committed to spreading the faith. Here, too, it was only a minority in whom the missionary passion burned high. In Boniface's letters, although these were usually concerned primarily with conditions on the Continent, glimpses of English Christianity are to be had which disclose serious moral lapses.[445]

While much of the work of the mission was performed by Englishmen, the active support which in the past was given by the Frankish state increased. This was due to Charlemagne. Charlemagne came to the throne in 768, less than fifteen years after the passing of Boniface. In 771, on the death of his brother, Carloman, he became sole monarch. Charlemagne died in 814 and during the nearly half a century of his reign the Frankish power reached its apogee. More than any of his predecessors, Charlemagne sought to raise the level of the Frankish Church. More than many of them, moreover, he employed Christian missions as a means of extending Frankish boundaries. Nor did he hesitate to use force.

To assist in his project for improving the scholarship of his realms Charlemagne attracted savants from the British Isles. Of these the most famous and influential was Alcuin. Trained in York, in spiritual descent from the Venerable Bede, he brought to the Continent the best of English Christian scholarship and character.[446]

Under Charlemagne the conversion of the Frisians was completed. The

---

[445] As in *Ep.* 73 and 78, in *Mon. Germ. Hist., Ep. Mer. et Kar. Aevi*, Vol. I, pp. 339-345, 349-356.
[446] On Alcuin, see C. J. B. Gaskoin, *Alcuin: His Life and His Work* (London, C. J. Clay and Sons, 1904, pp. xxii, 275) and the bibliography on pp. xiii-xxii of that book.

martyrdom of Boniface and his companions had not brought missions to an end. They were continued with Utrecht as the central station. Here, where Willibrord had once been Archbishop, Gregory, a Frank, but the favourite disciple of Boniface, carried on the Anglo-Saxon tradition. The monastery which he headed became a training-school. To it came both Germans and Anglo-Saxons for preparation and inspiration, and from it they went forth to fulfil the hopes of Willibrord and Boniface. Gregory maintained the English connexion and sent a companion to York for consecration and two of his pupils to England for ordination.[447] Among the Anglo-Saxons attracted by Gregory probably the most distinguished was Willehad. He achieved prominence among both the Frisians and the Saxons. Among the Frisians he laboured in the region in which Boniface had perished.[448]

Gregory was succeeded by his nephew Alberic. Alberic brought new vigour into the mission. Under him, moreover, the English connexion practically ceased. Probably with the support of Charlemagne, Alberic sent his monks through Frisia with the command to destroy idols and pagan shrines.[449] In 784 some of the Frisians joined the Saxons in an attempt to throw off the Carolingian yoke. Many apostatized, churches were burned, and priests were driven out. Charlemagne suppressed the outbreak. Liudger, the son of a Frisian who had suffered under Radbod, a pupil of Gregory, and, even before the outbreak, a missionary to his own people, returned from exile, renewed the destruction of pagan fanes, and built churches.[450] While the priests had been absent, a blind singer, Bernlef, had gone about baptizing children.[451] With Charlemagne's backing, Liudger even went to the Island of Heligoland and there administered the rite to neophytes in the sacred spring whose use in a similar fashion had once earned Willibrord his expulsion.[452]

By the close of the eighth century the Frisians had become at least nominally Christian.[453] About two centuries had been required to win to the faith the comparatively small area of the Low Countries. The opposition had been as much on political as on religious grounds, and it was as much by political

---

[447] On Gregory, see the oldest biography, by his pupil, Liudger, *Vita S. Gregorii*, in Migne, *Pat. Lat.*, Vol. XCIX, Cols. 749-770. See a brief summary of Gregory's work in Hauck, *Kirchengeschichte Deutschlands*, Vol. II, pp. 356-361.

[448] *Vita Willehadi*, Chap. 2 (translation in *Die Geschichtschreiber der deutschen Vorzeit achtes Jahrhundert*, Vol. III, pp. 93 ff.) ; Hauck, *op. cit.*, Vol. II, p. 362.

[449] Altfrid, *Vita S. Ludgeri*, Book I, Chap. 15 (in Migne, *Pat. Lat.*, Vol. XCIX).

[450] The standard old biography of Liudger is Altfrid, *Vita S. Ludgeri*, in Migne, *Pat. Lat.*, Vol. XCIX, Cols. 769-796. See also Hauck, *op. cit.*, Vol. II, pp. 361-368.

[451] Altfrid, *Vita S. Ludgeri*, Book II, Chaps. 1, 2.

[452] Altfrid, *op. cit.*, Book I, Chap. 19.

[453] Hauck, *op. cit.*, Vol. II, p. 369.

as by religious agencies that the victory had finally been achieved. Frankish imperialism combined with the zeal of·devoted missionaries had won.

Except for the Scandinavians, the last of the Germanic peoples to be drawn into the Christian fold were the Continental Saxons. This was not strange. Their lands lay north of the Frisians and the Hessians. Geography made them the latest of the Germans to be brought within the Frankish boundaries. Like the Frisians, they identified their religious with their political independence and resisted conversion as an instrument of Carolingian imperialism.

Both before and during the lifetime of Boniface, many Anglo-Saxons had sought the conversion of their Continental kinsmen, but without much lasting effect. We hear of two English priests, the Ewalds or Hewalds, who had long lived in Ireland and had perhaps there imbibed the missionary spirit. They went as missionaries to the Saxons on the Continent but were martyred very shortly after their arrival.[454] Others of the English seem to have come.[455] Boniface himself, as we have seen, for years dreamed of undertaking the mission. In 722 he received from the Pope a letter to the Saxons and full power to preach the Christian message among them.[456] He pleaded with Christians in England to unite for their conversion.[457] We read, too, of Lebuin, an Englishman who had laboured for the Frisians, making a brave but apparently fruitless effort (c. 775) to gain neophytes from among the Saxons.[458] Eventually a small Christian minority appears to have arisen.[459] The winning of the nation, however, was delayed until the time of Charlemagne and then was accomplished, like that of the Frisians, by a combination of armed force and of instruction by missionaries.

Charlemagne's conquests were largely to the north and east and in Italy. Whether, had the Moslems not been so firmly entrenched in Spain and North Africa, he would have directed his efforts more to these latter areas must remain a subject for interesting but inconclusive conjecture. In his program the conquest by his armies was to be followed by the Christianizing of his new subjects. How much his zeal for missions arose from religious conviction and

---

[454] Bede, *Eccles. Hist.*, Book V, Chap. 10. The year is not given.

[455] Alcuin, *Poema de Pontificibus et Sanctis Eccl. Eboracensis*, v. 1071, 1072, in Migne, *Pat. Lat.*, Vol. CI, Col. 834.

[456] *Ep.* 21, in *Mon. Germ. Hist., Ep. Mer. et Kar. Aevi*, Vol. I, pp. 269, 270.

[457] *Ep.* 46, in *Mon. Germ. Hist., Ep. Mer. et Kar. Aevi*, Vol. I, pp. 294, 295.

[458] Hucbald, *Vita Lebwini* (a tenth-century biography), Chaps. 11 ff., in Migne, *Pat. Lat.*, Vol. CXXXII, Cols. 887 ff.

[459] Hauck, *op. cit.*, Vol. II, p. 380.

how much from political policy Charlemagne himself would probably have found it difficult to say. Obviously it was compounded of both.

The subjugation of Saxony and its incorporation into the Carolingian version of Western Christendom was the work of a generation. The narrative is a repetition, with variations, of campaigns resulting in outward submission and followed by the peaceful efforts of missionaries, of revolts, of fresh campaigns, of more or less sullen acquiescence, of fresh revolts, and of eventual victory. With each cycle of the story more Saxons seem to have given their loyal adherence to the new faith. Gradually Christianity took firm root, presumably through the labour and example of missionaries. The process succeeded earliest in the portions of the Saxon lands nearest to the Christian sections of Germany. Recalcitrants long remained, especially in the North, and some of the most obdurate were transplanted to the Rhine Valley and scattered among a safely Christian population of non-Saxon stocks.

The details need not engage us. We must take time only for the main outlines. Charlemagne's first campaign was in 772. In it the Franks destroyed a number of pagan shrines. In 774 the Saxons took advantage of Charlemagne's absence from the North to seek their revenge and carried fire and sword into Hesse. Charlemagne sent reinforcements to the frontier and in 775 followed in his own person. The Saxons submitted and gave him their oath of allegiance. In 776 some of the Saxons rose again, apparently taking advantage of the King's absence in Italy. Others, however, remained true and the malcontents were suppressed. Beginning with 776 Charlemagne seems to have regarded the land as legally Christian and part of the Frankish domains.[460]

In the spring of 777 Charlemagne held an assembly at Paderborn, in Westphalia. To insure the completion of the work of conversion and the instruction of the neophytes, he divided the Saxon territories among some of the Frankish bishoprics, assigning to each sections for which they were responsible.[461] We know that in at least one of these areas, that in which the monastery of Fulda had a share, throngs of Saxons applied for baptism.[462] We know, too, that some of those who accepted the faith did so with sincerity. One of the Saxon nobles, for instance, ended his days in Fulda[463] and another won honour as a martyr.[464]

Some prominent Saxons, however, still were unwilling to acquiesce in the

---

[460] Hauck, *op. cit.*, Vol. II, pp. 380-385. The footnotes give references to the sources.
[461] Hauck, *op. cit.*, Vol. II, pp. 385-389.
[462] Eigil, *Vita Sturmi* (in *Mon. Germ. Hist., Script.*, Vol. II, pp. 365-377), Chap. 23.
[463] *Necrolog. Fuld. Scriptores,* cited in Hauck, *op. cit.*, Vol. II, p. 390, n. 7.
[464] *Vita Willehadi,* Chap. 6.

new order. One of them, Widukind, took refuge in Denmark. When, in 778, Charlemagne was engrossed in a Spanish campaign, Widukind returned. Under him the recalcitrants rose and churches were burned.[465] It was two years before Charlemagne had sufficiently restored his rule to permit the resumption of missions.[466]

Charlemagne now made a fresh ecclesiastical division of Saxon territory.[467] He called the Anglo-Saxon Willehad from the Frisian mission and assigned him the region between the North Sea, the Weser, and the Elbe. Here Willehad began building churches and installing priests. Even some of the Wends (Slavs) became Christian.[468]

In 782 Widukind again led an uprising and was joined by Wends as well as Saxons. Willehad escaped, but numbers of his disciples and colleagues were killed. Many of the newly baptized were compelled to renounce their faith.[469]

By no means all the Saxons followed Widukind. Charlemagne, grim and thoroughly roused, ruthlessly suppressed the revolt. Many of the rebels were killed. In 785, Widukind, recognizing the futility of further resistance, submitted and received baptism.[470] In his first capitulary for the Saxons, Charlemagne commanded that churches receive more honours than had been accorded pagan temples and gave to them extensive rights of asylum. He ordered the death penalty for the murder of a bishop, a priest, or a deacon, for pillaging or setting fire to a church, for refusing to receive baptism, for plotting against Christians, and for participating in pagan sacrifices.[471]

On the report that the Saxons had entered the Catholic fold, the Pope directed that a festival of thanksgiving be observed throughout Christendom.[472] In 787 Willehad was consecrated as the first Bishop of the Saxons. He fixed upon Bremen as his seat and there built a cathedral.[473] Other bishoprics were organized, parishes were delimited, churches were constructed,

---

[465] *Annales Laurissenses*, an. 778, in *Annales regni Francorum*, in *Scriptores rer. Germ.* (1895), pp. 50-52; *Annales Einhardi*, in *Annales regni Francorum*, in *Scriptores rer. Germ.* (an. 778), pp. 51-53.

[466] Hauck, *op. cit.*, Vol. II, p. 392.

[467] *Annales Laureshamenses, chr. Mois.* for the year 780, cited in Hauck, *op. cit.*, Vol. II, p. 392, n. 3.

[468] *Vita Willehadi*, Chap. 5.

[469] *Annales Laurissenses* and *Annales Einhardi* (an. 782), in *Annales regni Francorum*, in *Scriptores rer. Germ.*, pp. 58-65; *Vita Willehadi*, Chap. 6.

[470] Hauck, *op. cit.*, Vol. II, pp. 393-395. Hauck gives the citations to sources.

[471] Carlo de Clerq, *La Législation Religieuse Franque de Clovis a Charlemagne . . . 507-814* (Louvain, Bureaux des Recueil Bibliotheque l'Université, 1936, pp. xvi, 398), p. 167.

[472] *Codex Carolinus*, Part I, Sec. III, LXXXV, in Migne, *Pat. Lat.*, Vol. XCVIII, Cols. 387-390.

[473] *Vita Willehadi*, Chaps. 8, 9; Böttgar, *Die Einführung des Christentums in Sachsen durch den Frankenkönig Karl von 775 bis 786*.

and hundreds of Frankish and Anglo-Saxon priests strove to make real the nominal Christianity which had been forced on the land and to eradicate the pagan practices to which a large proportion of the population secretly clung.[474]

Still not all the Saxons were content. Although Widukind remained true to his oath of fealty, in 792 a revolt occurred in the North, in regions which had been least assimilated to the Frankish rule. The cause of complaint seems to have been in part the exaction of tithes for the support of the church.[475]

Charlemagne responded with his accustomed vigour. In 795, 797, 798, and 804 thousands of Saxons were deported into the Rhineland and settled among the Christian population.[476] Additional bishoprics were created in the Saxon regions. Over that of Münster was placed the seasoned Frisian missionary Liudger.[477] By the time of Charlemagne's death the work of conversion had been practically completed and organized opposition, if it existed at all, had ceased to be formidable.

In the civil strife which disturbed the Carolingian realms a quarter of a century after the death of Charlemagne, the anti-Christian forces in Saxony once more raised their heads. Their discontent seems now to have been quite as much economic as religious. They may have been made up in part of former freeholders who had been dispossessed by nobles who held their lands according to Frankish principles and who favoured Christianity and Frankish rule.[478] In spite of this uprising, the majority of the Saxons remained true to their Christian profession.

As we have suggested, the conversion of the Saxons was achieved by a combination of armed force and the zeal of missionaries. So far as we know, never before had the adherence of any people to the Christian faith been brought about by quite so drastic a use of the mailed fist and with so much blood-letting among reluctant pagans. The completion of conversion of the entire Roman Empire in the fourth and fifth centuries, accomplished though it had been under the urge of imperial legislation, had probably not entailed the killing of as many non-Christians as did the winning of this comparatively small area in North-western Germany. It was the first but not the last instance in which acceptance of baptism and of the Christian name was induced by a liberal application of the sword. We shall find the procedure repeated again and again in the thousand years between the eighth and the nineteenth century. We shall see it usually as part of the process of the conquest of one

---

[474] Hauck, *op. cit.*, Vol. II, pp. 400-411.
[475] Hauck, *op. cit.*, Vol. II, pp. 411, 412.
[476] Hauck, *op. cit.*, Vol. II, p. 412, especially the citation of sources in n. 3.
[477] Hauck, *op. cit.*, Vol. II, p. 416.
[478] Keary, *The Vikings of Western Christendom*, p. 241.

people by another—invaders and conquerors employing the Church and its agents as one of their tools. Sometimes we shall discover it as one of the means by which a monarch extended his power over his domains, particularly against protesting nobles.

How far the leaders of the Carolingian Church were aware that they were witnessing an innovation we do not know. The methods employed in the conversion of the Saxons were so natural and logical an outgrowth of the policies of Charlemagne's predecessors that few seem to have been shocked. After all, as a part of their political policy, the Pepins and Charles Martel had given protection to missionaries, even though it had not been at the cost of so many deaths of unbelievers. We do, however, hear of at least one voice raised in protest. Alcuin, the most brilliant of the literary lights with whom Charlemagne surrounded himself, spoke out plainly and fearlessly. He hoped that the adults would not be baptized until they had been carefully instructed. He argued against the exaction of tithes from the newly converted.[479]

However much the methods of Charlemagne may have been an innovation and a contradiction of the original spirit of Christianity, in the case of the Saxons they resulted in a permanent conversion. So loyal were the Saxons to the faith and the culture which they had been forced to accept that they became their champions against the pagan Scandinavians, Magyars, and Slavs. But for the Saxons, Western Christianity would have suffered much more severely in the invasions of the tenth century than it did. Moreover, in the tenth and eleventh centuries Saxon monarchs reformed the German Church and helped to lift the Papacy from the low estate to which it had then fallen.

It would be interesting and pertinent to inquire whether the conversion of the Frisians, Central Germany, and the Saxons would have been achieved without the support of the Carolingians. Like all of the might-have-beens of history, no assured answer can be given. However, it must be noted that the conversion of the English was in part accomplished without exterior political pressure. In Frisia the fear of Frankish imperialism may have retarded the acceptance of the faith. It seems not improbable that, even without Carolingian support, the spread of Christianity into Germany and the Low Countries would have been long delayed.

We now come to the last of the great groups of the Teutonic peoples to accept Christianity—the Scandinavians. The earliest and one of the most persistent efforts to bring about the conversion of these peoples was made in connexion with Carolingian imperialism, but eventually, as we have hinted,

[479] Alcuin, *Ep.* 33, in Migne, *Pat. Lat.,* Vol. C, Cols. 188, 189.

it was accomplished largely by the efforts of native monarchs and through clergy from England. It is so closely related to the story which we have just been telling that it must be included in an already overlong chapter.

For almost exactly three centuries, from the conversion of Clovis in 496 to nearly the close of the eighth century, Western Christendom had not been successfully invaded by pagan peoples from the North. Non-Christian peoples had broken across its borders—notably the Moslems in Africa and Spain and the Avars in Central Europe. In the North-west, however, far from being seriously menaced, Western Christianity had been extending its frontiers. Now came a fresh irruption which threatened to wipe out all its gains. On the coasts of the British Isles, and along the Continental side of the North Sea and the English Channel from the northern borders of the Saxons to Brittany, marauders from the pagan North worked havoc. They penetrated even to the Mediterranean. At first they came as raiders, slaying and plundering. Eventually they made permanent settlements, notably, so far as Christian lands were concerned, in Normandy, Great Britain, and Ireland. For two and a half centuries, from shortly before 800 to about 1050, the movement continued. It carried the Northmen not only to regions occupied by Christian peoples, but to the heretofore unsettled or sparsely populated Orkneys, Shetlands, Faroes, Iceland, and Greenland, to the eastern shores of the Baltic and its tributary bays and rivers, and along the rivers of what is now Russia to the Black Sea and Constantinople. Nor did it end in 1050. After that date, descendants of Viking settlers, now Christian, conquered England, established themselves as a ruling power in Sicily and Southern Italy, and joined in the Crusades.

In the troubled ninth and tenth centuries the Scandinavians were not the only menace to Christendom. The pagan Slavs were pressing in from the East. From the East, too, toward the close of the ninth century came the Magyars. Internally, moreover, Western Christendom seemed crumbling politically and dwindling in morale. The Carolingians, the strongest ruling house in the West, were losing their vigour and their realm was breaking up. The Papacy suffered from unworthy incumbents. The Church was in imminent danger of secularization and the loss of all religious vitality. A cultured traveller from a foreign land might have believed that, paralyzed by internal weaknesses and submerged in fresh inundations of barbarism, Occidental Christianity was perishing.

Even at the beginning of their raids the Scandinavians were by no means completely uncivilized. They had developed a culture of their own and had

had contacts with that of the Mediterranean.[480] The wave of Slavs which inundated much of what is now Germany had partly cut them off from the South,[481] but they seem to have had some commerce with the Frankish domains.[482] However, they were pagans, and were not disposed to respect the sacred places of the Christians. Often, indeed, they appear to have singled out monasteries as easy and rich spoil. Some of their earliest recorded depredations were on the buildings and communities of Lindisfarne and Iona.[483] It is possible that this predilection for ecclesiastical establishments arose from a special antipathy to Christianity. This in turn may have been born partly of prejudice arising from the manner in which Charlemagne had forced the faith on their neighbours, the Saxons.

More than any of the invasions and internal weaknesses of the ninth and tenth centuries, the Viking expeditions, therefore, wrought desolation in Western Christendom. Apparently in few if any areas, and those not very large, was the Christianity of the native inhabitants erased as effectively as had been that of the British by the Anglo-Saxon conquest. However, in Ireland, Scotland, and England, and in parts of the Carolingian domains, the morale of the Church, already weakened, was badly shaken.

In Ireland, as we have seen, the Norse raids, followed by some permanent settlements, disrupted much of that monastic life which had had so marked an effect upon Great Britain and the Continent.[484]

Scotland was nearer to Scandinavia than either Ireland or England and suffered severely. The invaders laid waste monasteries and churches. Again and again the Northmen ravaged Iona, that source of the Christianity of so much of Scotland and England.[485] Whether Christianity actually disappeared in any of the areas held by the native populations is doubtful. However, its quality must have markedly deteriorated. Learning declined. The defenders returned in kind the cruelties of the invaders and in spite of the Christian name often lapsed into barbarism or near barbarism. In some sections, notably on the northern tip of Scotland, in Galloway, and in the islands to the north and west, pagan Scandinavians settled and became dominant. Not until the

---

[480] Svanström and Palmstierna, *A Short History of Sweden*, pp. 3-8; Hallendorff and Schück, *History of Sweden*, pp. 9-13; Gjerset, *History of the Norwegian People*, pp. 8-41.
[481] Toynbee, *A Study of History*, Vol. II, p. 341.
[482] Hallendorff and Schück, *op. cit.*, pp. 1-9.
[483] Raids on Iona are recorded in 795, 802, 806.—Anderson, *Early Sources of Scottish History*, Vol. I, pp. 256, 258. In 793 Northmen raided Lindisfarne.—Alcuin, *Ep.* 9, in Migne, *Pat. Lat.*, Vol. C, Cols. 150-152; *Anglo-Saxon Chronicle* (Thorpe's edition), Vol. I, p. 101, Vol. II, p. 48.
[484] Gougaud, *Christianity in Celtic Lands*, pp. 390-396.
[485] For a list of depredations on monasteries in Scotland, see Scott, *The Pictish Nation: Its People and Its Church*, pp. 454-461.

tenth century did the darkness begin to lift. When our records once more give us clear pictures of the scene, they disclose an altered Scotland and a somewhat different Scottish Church.[486]

Raid after raid was made and permanent Scandinavian colonies were planted in Wales, to the detriment of the Christianity of that land.[487]

In England a decay of religion and morals seems to have set in even before the invasions.[488] The repeated incursions of the Northmen brought a near approach to ruin. The exuberant religious life which had sent so many missionaries to the Continent flickered and almost went out. Throughout most of the North and East of England, in Northumbria, the Midlands, and East Anglia, the vitality and organization of the Church were shattered. Churches and monasteries were destroyed, clergy and monks were slain, and bishoprics long lay vacant, some of them never to be revived. In some places, notably in Cumberland, Northumbria, Mercia, and East Anglia, Scandinavians, avowedly non-Christian, effected permanent settlements. Only in the South, among the West Saxons, especially after the invaders were fought off by Alfred the Great (871-901), did the Church remain strong.[489]

The Frankish domains also suffered acutely. In the course of the ninth century, as the Carolingian line decayed, civil war and incompetent rulers plagued the land. The realm fell an easy prey to the determined and ruthless invaders. The shores of the newly converted Saxons were ravaged. The lands of the Frisians were severely dealt with. In 856 Utrecht was taken and pillaged and many of its churches demolished.[490] Through much of the Low Countries monasteries were plundered.[491] The Vikings made their way along the coasts and rivers of what is now France. Up the Seine they came to besiege Paris, up the Loire to Orléans, along the Garonne to Toulouse, and by the Rhone as far as Valence. As usual, churches and monasteries were singled out for attack.[492] In Italy a number of cities, including Pisa, fell to their arms.[493]

In none of their many incursions do the Vikings seem to have sought to

[486] On the effect of the Norse raids upon Christianity in Scotland, see Scott, *op. cit.*, pp. 447 ff.; Macewen, *A History of the Church in Scotland*, pp. 113 ff.; Skene, *Celtic Scotland*, Vol. II, pp. 332 ff.
[487] Kendrick, *A History of the Vikings*, pp. 323-327.
[488] Patterson, *A History of the Church of England*, pp. 40-42.
[489] Patterson, *op. cit.*, pp. 43-50; Hunt, *A History of the English Church from Its Foundation to the Norman Conquest*, pp. 247-267.
[490] Ditchfield, *The Church in the Netherlands*, p. 90.
[491] *Ibid.*
[492] *Cambridge Medieval History*, Vol. III, p. 320; Kitchin, *History of France*, Vol. I, pp. 174, 175; Kendrick, *op. cit.*, pp. 197 ff.
[493] *Cambridge Medieval History*, Vol. III, p. 320.

convert their victims to their gods. They were pillagers, not religious fanatics. Much of the time, moreover, they raided with no serious effort at permanent settlement. They weakened the Church and wrought great damage to the quality of its life. Yet seldom, if ever, do they appear deliberately to have sought to stamp it out and to replace Christianity by another faith.

By the end of the ninth century Western Christianity had begun to recover from the blows dealt it and to make headway among the invaders.

In some regions the Vikings established colonies. Where they did so, before the tenth century was out they had begun to conform to the culture of their new home and to accept the faith of the land. Their hereditary cults proved too weak to resist the religion of the South. In 979 we hear of a Danish chief from Dublin going to Iona on a pilgrimage and dying there, a report said to be the earliest evidence of a leading Dane of Ireland being a Christian.[494] In the latter half of the tenth and in the eleventh century most of the Viking colonists in Ireland seem to have accepted the Christian faith. They entered the Church after a period of religious indifference in which they had ceased to believe in the old gods but did not yet adhere to the new.[495] Nearly a century before that time, in 878, Alfred, in defeating the Danish army, required Guthrum, its head, and twenty-nine others of its leaders to be baptized.[496] Guthrum ruled in East Anglia, apparently as a Christian king.[497] In the North of England, too, many of the invaders, when they became permanent settlers, accepted Christianity. In less than a hundred years after the conquest they had given three archbishops to the English Church.[498]

On the Continent the invaders adopted the faith of the lands occupied. In 882 one of the Viking leaders made his peace with the Carolingian Emperor Charles the Fat, received baptism, and was assigned territory on the lower Rhine.[499] Here, however, no lasting Scandinavian state followed. Otherwise was the fate of the lower part of the basin of the Seine. There and in adjacent regions the Vikings created the Duchy of Normandy. The first Duke, known variously as Rollo, Hrolf, and Hrolfr, in 911 concluded a treaty with King

[494] Haddan and Stubbs, *Councils and Ecclesiastical Documents Relating to Great Britain and Ireland,* Vol. II, Pt. 1, p. 150, citing *Ann. IV Mag.,* an. 979.

[495] Gjerset, *History of the Norwegian People,* Vol. I, p. 158. In Dublin the transition to Christianity took place about 1039. The first Bishop of Waterford was consecrated in 1096 and the first Bishop of Limerick in 1104 or 1106. All three were Danish settlements. —Lawlor, *St. Bernard of Clairvaux, Life of St. Malachy of Armagh,* pp. xvi-xix. This, it will be noticed, was later than similar movements in Denmark.

[496] Gjerset, *op. cit.,* Vol. I, p. 58; Schubert, *Geschichte der christlichen Kirche im Frühmittelalter,* pp. 468-479.

[497] Hunt, *op. cit.,* p. 266.

[498] Hunt, *op. cit.,* p. 267.

[499] Keary, *The Vikings of Western Christendom,* p. 409; *Cambridge Medieval History,* Vol. III, p. 321.

Charles the Simple whereby his holdings were legitimatized and whereby, in return, he and some of his followers accepted baptism.[500] In the course of the first generation after Rollo's baptism some attempts were made to revive paganism. Under Rollo's successor, William Longsword, a rebellion of pagan *jarls* broke out, apparently a protest against innovations, both in religion and in the growing monarchical power of the Duke. In 943 a fresh Scandinavian invasion of Normandy took place. Some of the earlier settlers were induced to apostatize and an effort was made by pagans to gain control of the infant Duke Richard I.[501] However, in spite of the spasmodic attempts to restore the ancient faith, those who gave Normandy its name soon became loyally Christian and developed a vital church life. Here, as in England and the Low Countries, the original motive which led to the acceptance of baptism may have been political, but ultimately the faith so assumed, even if imperfectly understood and in practice far removed from its original content, was esteemed a normal part of civilization.

Centuries before the conversion of the Scandinavians was accomplished Christianity had been filtering into the North. It may be that some of the Danes were baptized on trading trips to Frisia.[502] Presumably some of those converted in Ireland, England, and the Continent returned to the fatherland. While we do not know that extensive Christian communities arose in Scandinavia until the tenth century,[503] before that time the culture of the North had been modified by Christian influences.[504] The poem Völuspá of the Elder Edda is said to show both Christian and pagan background.[505] Before Christianity was formally adopted, its effect can be traced in burial customs, and in the custom of sprinkling a child with water when it was given its name.[506] The idea of divine administration of justice, especially of a retribution beyond the grave, gained more and more credence.[507] To pre-Christian mythology, too, Christianity made contributions.[508] For instance, Balder, the son of Odin and the noblest of the gods, almost certainly reflects the virtues of Christ, and Heimdal, the keeper of the gates of Heaven, may embody some ideas of Christian origin.[509] Some of the Scandinavians made room for Christ in their

[500] Maurer, *Die Bekehrung des norwegischen Stammes zum Christenthume,* Vol. I, p. 59; *Cambridge Medieval History,* Vol. III, p. 322.
[501] *Catholic Encyclopedia,* Vol. XI, p. 104; Kendrick, *A History of the Vikings,* p. 225.
[502] Keary, *op. cit.,* p. 188.
[503] Maurer, *op. cit.,* Vol. I, pp. 13, 14.
[504] Gjerset, *op. cit.,* Vol. I, p. 94.
[505] Olrik, *Viking Civilization,* pp. 131-139.
[506] Snorre Sturlason, *Heimskringla,* Book III, Chaps. 38, 42; Book IV, Chap. 11.
[507] Olrik, *op. cit.,* pp. 129, 130.
[508] Gjerset, *op. cit.,* Vol. I, p. 94.
[509] Williams, *Social Scandinavia in the Viking Age,* p. 376.

pantheon. We hear of one who, while on his farm in Iceland, worshipped Christ, but when at sea or in danger sacrificed to Thor.[510]

Probably, moreover, for many Scandinavians, especially those who engaged in overseas raids or who settled abroad, contact with other cultures had brought a loss of faith in their hereditary cults but no belief in the Christians' God or in any might save their own and, perhaps, magic.

Indeed, through much of Scandinavia and the Scandinavian settlements formal conversion to Christianity was preceded by a period in which the personal religion of many was a compound of the old beliefs and the new.[511] Nowhere else in the conversion of Northern European peoples do we have so many hints of a twilight zone between the pagan and the Christian period. Probably for many individuals and in some sections the transition was so gradual that when conversion was finally registered by baptism no sharp break in customs and beliefs occurred.

Efforts were made through formal missions to win the Northmen in their native plains and mountains. These, however, long remained almost barren of results. Not until the tenth, eleventh, and twelfth centuries did Scandinavia become avowedly Christian. The delay may have been due to the fact that the ethics of Christianity ran so counter to much of Scandinavian practice. The new faith was not adopted simply as a matter of course, as a constituent of the culture of the South. When it was accepted, it was with a Scandinavian colouring. One of the chief attractions was the belief in Christ as a mighty god who had risen triumphant over death. The converts went into battle in full trust in him and his power to give them the victory.[512]

When the mass movement into the Church began, it occurred not far from the same time in all three of the major Scandinavian lands—Denmark, Norway, and Sweden.

Except in Norway little force was employed to encourage conversion. The leading men accepted the new religion and by their example drew others after them. Often the *thing*, or assembly, debated the wisdom of the step. When finally taken it was in a manner in which custom decreed that the community should act.[513]

We have already noted the effort of Willibrord to win converts in Denmark. The mission was of short duration and we hear of no permanent results. We do not even know the fate of the youths who were brought from Denmark, although Willibrord expected to train them as missionaries.[514]

[510] Willson, *History of the Church and State in Norway*, p. 19.
[511] Williams, *op. cit.*, p. 393.
[512] Olrik, *op. cit.*, pp. 143, 188.
[513] Olrik, *op. cit.*, p. 140.
[514] Alcuin, *Vita Willibrordi*, Chaps. 9-11.

After Willibrord, the next serious attempt to carry the Christian message into Scandinavia of which we read was that associated with the name of Anskar.[515] Liudger, with whom we have become familiar in Frisia, wished to undertake a mission to the North and asked Charlemagne's permission.[516] Charlemagne, however, was unwilling, perhaps because he felt the conversion of the Saxons to be too insecure to risk another venture on that border of his realm.[517] It remained for Anskar and a later monarch to make the endeavour.

Anskar (or Ansgar) was born in the north-western part of France in 801.[518] He is said to have been of Saxon stock, a descendant of immigrants to Flanders.[519] From his early boyhood he was sent to school and was deeply religious. The death of Charlemagne, whom he had seen in his might, made a profound impression upon the sensitive child and led him more fully to a devout life.[520] Throughout his career he was given to visions and dreams which helped to determine his actions.[521] He possessed, too, a combination of humility, of self-forgetfulness, and of undaunted courage and energetic initiative. In due course he received the tonsure at the monastery of Corbey,[522] a foundation not far from his home, which owed its origin to a group of monks from Luxeuil[523] and which was one of the most important religious houses in the Carolingian domains.[524] He thus was in the spiritual succession of Columban and of Irish monasticism. In his young manhood he was sent to the land of the recently converted Saxons to help found a new monastery. This, called New Corbey, or Corvey (in Saxon speech), was on the Weser, in Westphalia, was a daughter house of the one in which he had been reared, and became very prominent in

---

[515] The early standard life of Anskar is by Rimbert, his colleague and successor, *Vita Anskarii*, of which the text, edited by G. Waitz, is in *Scriptores rerum Germanicarum* (Hanover, 1884). An English translation is by C. H. Robinson, *Anskar, The Apostle of the North, 801-865* (Westminster, Society for the Propagation of the Gospel in Foreign Parts, 1921, pp. 139). See also Holger Rafn, *Ansgar* (Copenhagen, Det Danske Missions-selskab, 1926, pp. 195); Philippus Oppenheim, *Der heilige Ansgar und die Anfänge des Christentums in den nordischen Ländern* (Munich, Max Hueber, 1931, pp. viii, 207); E. de Moreau, *Saint Anschaire* (Louvain, Editions du Museum Lessianum, 1930, pp. xiii, 152); Hauck, *Kirchengeschichte Deutschlands*, Vol. II, pp. 694-706. See also G. Goyau, *La Politique Missionaire de l'Empereur Louis le Pieux* (*Revue d'Histoire des Missions*, Sept. 1929, pp. 321-334).

[516] Altfrid, *Vita S. Ludgeri*, Book II, Chaps. 3, 6, in Migne, *Pat. Lat.*, Vol. XCIX, Cols. 781-783.

[517] Hauck, *op. cit.*, Vol. II, p. 689.

[518] Hauck, *op. cit.*, Vol. II, p. 694, n. 1.

[519] Moreau, *Saint Anschaire*, p. 7.

[520] Rimbert, *Vita Anskarii*, Chap. 2.

[521] As in Rimbert, *op. cit.*, Chaps. 2-6, 9, 25, 37.

[522] Rimbert, *op. cit.*, Chap. 3.

[523] Robinson, *Anskar*, p. 9. The first abbot of Corbey came from Luxeuil.—*Vita Balthildis*, Chaps. 7, 8, in *Mon. Germ. Hist., Scrip. rer. Merov.*, Vol. II, pp. 490-492.

[524] Moreau, *Saint Anschaire*, p. 13. In Anskar's boyhood Corbey was presided over by a cousin of Charlemagne.

the Saxon Church. Here he was the first master of the monastic school and held the office of preacher.[525]

From Corvey Anskar was called to the great work of his life. The way to this momentous step was prepared by an interesting chain of circumstances. During the reign of Charlemagne a struggle broke out over the succession to the throne of Denmark. One of the contestants, Harald, had the sympathy,[526] but not the active support of the Emperor. Charlemagne was not prepared to extend his boundaries into Scandinavia. Harald was unsuccessful. Soon after Charlemagne's death he took refuge at the Frankish court and sought the aid of the new ruler, Louis the Pious. Louis went beyond his father's policy and promised Harald assistance in the reconquest of the kingdom. Harald proved luckless and perforce contented himself for a time with only a part of the Danish realm.[527] As a result, Carolingian prestige in the North suffered.[528] Louis, however, used Harald's partial success as a step towards beginning a mission in Denmark. By laying it before the assembly of the realm, he made the undertaking a matter of state policy. For its head he chose one of his favourites, Ebo, Archbishop of Rheims. Ebo was dispatched to Rome to obtain Papal authorization and returned with an appointment as Legate to the North. Thus equipped, Archbishop Ebo proceeded to Denmark, probably in the spring of 823. The immediate results were disappointing. Louis did not back his missionary with an army. The Danish nobles held aloof and even Harald remained a pagan.[529] However, Harald decided to accept baptism, perhaps in the hope of support by a Frankish army. For it he came to Mainz, and here, in 826, amid great pomp, he and his entourage received the rite.[530] Louis wished to send some one back to Denmark with Harald, to confirm the neophytes in their new faith and to win additional converts. No one seemed ready to assume the dangerous mission until the Abbot of Corvey stepped forward and suggested Anskar. Anskar was summoned to the palace, assented to the proposal, and was thus introduced to a task to which he was to devote the remainder of his days. Missionary interest in the Frankish Church must have been low, for many sought to dissuade him from the step and even reproached him for it. Only one colleague seemed enough impressed to offer to go with him.[531]

With the cordial endorsement of Louis the Pious, then, Anskar went north

[525] Rimbert, *op. cit.*, Chap. 6; Oppenheim, *op. cit.*, pp. 33 ff.; Moreau, *op. cit.*, p. 19.
[526] *Ann. Einh.* for the year 813.
[527] *Ann. Einh.* for the years 814, 815.
[528] *Ann. Einh.* for years 816, 819; Hauck, *op. cit.*, Vol. II, p. 690.
[529] Hauck, *op. cit.*, Vol. II, pp. 690-692.
[530] Rimbert, *op. cit.*, Chap. 7; Hauck, *op. cit.*, pp. 692, 693.
[531] Rimbert, *op. cit.*, Chap. 7.

with Harald, accompanied by a brother from Corvey. Harald could not return to Denmark, but Louis assigned him territory "beyond the Elbe," just where is debated, and there Anskar and his colleague laboured. They seem to have made something of an impression, but with what permanent results we do not know.[532] After two years, Anskar's colleague returned to Corvey, fatally ill.[533]

About this time the Swedish envoys came to the court of Louis, bringing word that their King desired Christian missionaries. Anskar was summoned, and, with an assistant, was sent to respond to the request. A substitute was dispatched to Harald.[534] On their way north Anskar and his companion fell in with pirates and were robbed of their possessions. They did not allow this misfortune to deter them, but persevered until they reached Sweden. The King received them in friendly fashion and granted them liberty to preach and to make converts. Some Christians were discovered among the captives, presumably the victims of Viking raids. A number of pagans asked for baptism, among them the leading man of Birka, an island in Lake Malar, where was a port, not far from the present Stockholm. After a few months the missionaries returned to the imperial court.[535]

Louis the Pious now conceived an ambitious plan for missions north of the Elbe. He had Anskar consecrated Archbishop of the new see of Hamburg, with power to appoint bishops and priests. Louis gave Anskar a monastery in Flanders, perhaps as a source of financial support.[536] He also sent him to Rome for Papal confirmation. Pope Gregory IV granted his approval, with the pallium, and with a commission as Legate to the Swedes, Danes, Slavs, and other races of the North. This latter authority Anskar was to share with Archbishop Ebo, on whom had already been conferred the same powers.[537]

Here, then, was a project for the conversion of the entire North, an area larger than the lands of the Saxons and even than the British Isles. The dreamers apparently thought that the region was to be won by spiritual weapons only, and not, as had been the Saxons, by the sword. To be sure, the plan was not unlike that by which Utrecht had been made a central station with Willibrord as Archbishop. Scandinavia, however, was much more extensive than Frisia and not so likely to be brought under Frankish political control. For a century or more the project seemed fantastic. The frontiers of

[532] Rimbert, op. cit., Chaps. 7, 8.
[533] Rimbert, op. cit., Chap. 8.
[534] Rimbert, op. cit., Chaps. 9, 10.
[535] Rimbert, op. cit., Chaps. 11, 12.
[536] Rimbert, op. cit., Chap. 12.
[537] Rimbert, op. cit., Chap. 13.

Christianity were rolled back, not pushed forward. For more than a hundred years the archiepiscopal see was an anomaly, without suffragan bishops. Hamburg itself was wasted by the invaders. Yet in the end the daring of Louis the Pious, Anskar, and the Pope was partly justified. Even though ecclesiastically all the North was not ruled from Hamburg, from the centre of Christianity established by these three proceeded missionaries who had a share, even though not always an important one, in the conversion of the region.

Nor were immediate efforts lacking to make the dream come true. Ebo, with the concurrence of Anskar, appointed a relative, Gauzbert or Gautbert, as Bishop of Sweden. Bishop Gauzbert was well received in his new post and began the construction of a church.[538] Anskar proceeded to his own diocese. Here he bought Danish and Slavic boys to train for the service of the faith. To him, moreover, came as assistants some of the monks of Corvey.[539] Reverses overtook the mission. Pirates captured and burned Hamburg with its church and monastery.[540] A popular uprising drove Bishop Gauzbert and his assistants out of Sweden,[541] and for nearly seven years the Christians in that land were left without pastoral care.[542] Yet Anskar did not despair. In time he was able to send a priest to minister to the Swedish flock.[543] In spite of some opposition, and after a considerable amount of ecclesiastical red tape had been unwound, the diocese of Bremen was placed under Anskar, partly to provide him with financial support, and was joined with Hamburg into an archiepiscopal see.[544] Perhaps because he came as an envoy of the Carolingian monarch, Louis the German, Anskar so far succeeded in winning the friendship of the Danish King Horic that the latter granted him permission to erect a church near a commercial centre. Many were there baptized. Others were signed with the cross—"primesigning" it was called—and officially became catechumens.[545] Anskar again visited Sweden. The priest whom he had sent there had left,[546] and Bishop Gauzbert declined to return to a land which had been so inhospitable. The way being thus cleared, Anskar himself went, armed with a recommendation from King Horic to the King of Sweden.[547] The latter monarch referred to the casting of lots before the gods and to an assembly, as he declared he was legally bound to do, the question of whether Anskar should

[538] Rimbert, *op. cit.,* Chap. 14.
[539] Rimbert, *op. cit.,* Chap. 15.
[540] Rimbert, *op. cit.,* Chap. 16.
[541] Rimbert, *op. cit.,* Chap. 17.
[542] Rimbert, *op. cit.,* Chap. 19.
[543] *Ibid.*
[544] Rimbert, *op. cit.,* Chap. 23.
[545] Rimbert, *op. cit.,* Chap. 24.
[546] Rimbert, *op. cit.,* Chap. 20.
[547] Rimbert, *op. cit.,* Chap. 25.

be allowed to preach. Both the lots and the assembly were favourable. Anskar, leaving a priest, a nephew of Bishop Gauzbert, to carry on, returned to his see.[548]

A curious tale is told by Anskar's colleague and biographer which, if true, sheds light on the manner in which pagan Scandinavians regarded the Christian faith and on the motives which may have led some to accept it. An army of non-Christian Swedes in besieging a town faced a discouraging outlook. They cast lots to inquire whether any of their gods would help them. The answer was unfavourable and the Swedes were much disheartened. However, some merchants who recalled Anskar's teaching suggested that lots be cast to see whether Christ, the God of the Christians, would assist them. The outcome was propitious, the beleaguered purchased peace, and the victors, returning home, honoured Christ by observing fasts and giving alms to the poor.[549] As so often in the spread of Christianity, pagans were attracted to the faith because it seemed to accomplish in better fashion than the old gods what they traditionally expected of religion.

Throughout most of his days, Anskar appears to have seen continued progress in his mission, although not without many handicaps and occasional reverses. He or Bishop Gauzbert sent several priests to Sweden.[550] The fact that at least two of these were of Danish descent is proof that Christianity was taking root among some of the Scandinavians. In Denmark, Horic's successor, another Horic, at first unfriendly because some claimed that the misfortunes which had overtaken the dead King arose from neglect of the old gods, eventually showed Anskar favour.[551] The coasts of his diocese were periodically ravaged by pirates,[552] presumably Vikings. Yet Anskar persisted and, when he realized that his end was at hand, on the day and night before his death (Feb. 3 or 4, 865) gave repeated charges for the continued conduct of the northern mission.[553]

How far the Christian communities established by Anskar persisted and contributed to the eventual conversion of Scandinavia we do not know. Anskar's was not the spectacular success of Boniface. The latter had lived in the time of the expansion of the Carolingian state and had been greatly aided by its renown. Anskar, on the other hand, laboured in the age of the disintegration and waning prestige of the Carolingian Empire. His was the generation of

---

[548] Rimbert, *op. cit.*, Chaps. 26-28.
[549] Rimbert, *op. cit.*, Chap. 30.
[550] Rimbert, *op. cit.*, Chap. 33.
[551] Rimbert, *op. cit.*, Chaps. 31, 32.
[552] Rimbert, *op. cit.*, Chap. 34.
[553] Rimbert, *op. cit.*, Chap. 41.

the first victorious raids of the Vikings. Those whom he was seeking to reach became the plunderers of the lands of the Christians. Forthright pagans that they were, they probably had scant respect for either the culture or the religion of those who were so helpless before their attacks. It is not surprising that the immediate numerical results of his efforts were so slight. Yet Anskar was not forgotten. In the lands which he sought to reach, his memory was eventually held in high esteem.

For more than a generation after his death, the story of the mission which Anskar had founded is one of discouragement and decline.[554] The tide of Scandinavian expansion was rising. The outposts of Christianity, far from being able to stem it, seemed in danger of being submerged or swept away.

Anskar was succeeded by his favourite disciple and biographer, Rimbert.[555] Rimbert tried to carry out the designs of Anskar and visited both the Danes and the Swedes.[556] In 873 Vikings plundered the coasts of Frisia and in 888 they wasted the banks of the Elbe with fearful cost in Saxon blood. To the Northmen were added dangers from the Wends and the Magyars.[557] The territories of Rimbert were the most exposed and suffered accordingly. Much of Rimbert's energy was spent in rescuing the Christian captives of the pagan raiders. To ransom them he even parted with the vessels of the altar.[558] Rimbert died in 888 and was succeeded by Adalgar, a monk of Corvey.[559] He was really only Bishop of Bremen. The archiepiscopal see of Hamburg-Bremen was without suffragans, and the suggestion was made that it be abolished. To have complied would have been to admit the defeat of the Church in the North. When the matter was referred to Rome, the Pope demurred, and the see was allowed to continue in the hope that happier days might dawn and the dream expressed in its establishment be fulfilled.[560] Early in the tenth century, King Gorm of Denmark, an inveterate enemy of Christianity, attempted to shut out of his realm all Christian priests. Not a few of them were martyred.[561] He destroyed the churches in Schleswig down to their foundations.[562] Gorm was

---

[554] Moreau in Descamps, *Histoire Générale Comparée des Missions*, pp. 226, 227.

[555] *Vita Rimberti* (text, edited by G. Waitz, in *Vita Anskarii Auctore Rimberto Accedit Vita Rimberti*, in *Scriptores rerum Germanicarum*, Hanover, 1884), Chaps. 11, 12.

[556] *Vita Rimberti*, Chaps. 18, 20.

[557] Adam of Bremen, *Gesta Hammaburgensis Ecclesiæ Pontificum*, Book I, Chap. 55; Schubert, *Geschichte der Christlichen Kirche im Frühmittelalter*, pp. 508, 509.

[558] *Vita Rimberti*, Chap. 17.

[559] *Vita Rimberti*, Chaps. 21, 24; Hauck, *Kirchengeschichte Deutschlands*, Vol. II, p. 709, n. 2.

[560] Hauck, *op. cit.*, Vol. II, pp. 709, 710.

[561] Adam of Bremen, *Gesta Hammaburgensis Ecclesiæ Pontificum*, Book I, Chap. 55; Hauck, *op. cit.*, Vol. III, p. 80.

[562] Saxo Grammaticus, *Gesta Danorum*, Book IX, 468.

not a man to be trifled with, for he apparently ruled well and long and made his realm the most powerful of the northern kingdoms.[563]

The turn of the tide was to wait until more than forty years after Rimbert's death. Even before Rimbert's passing, however, a new Christian state was gathering strength in the North. The Saxons, more and more independent of the decadent Carolingians who had all but abandoned them to the Vikings and the Slavs, were being organized under their own leaders and were becoming doughty champions of the Christian cause. Their Duke, Henry the Fowler, became King of the Germans in 919 and extended the Saxon frontier. In 934 he gained the upper hand over the Danes and compelled one of their rulers to accept Christianity.[564] Since 919 the vigorous Unni had occupied the see of Hamburg-Bremen.[565] Taking advantage of Henry the Fowler's victory, he sought to renew the work of Anskar. He went to the court of Gorm, and while he did not succeed in winning that hardy pagan to the Christian faith, he seems to have made something of an impression on Gorm's heir and successor, Harald Bluetooth. With Harald's favour he sought to reassemble the remnants of Christian communities on the Danish isles and placed priests in the long-neglected churches.[566] Unni went on to Sweden, only to find that the little Christian groups there had ceased to be. In Sweden, in Birka, the scene of Anskar's earlier successes, he fell ill and died (Sept. 17, 936).[567]

The Saxon power continued to grow under Henry the Fowler's son and successor, Otto I (the Great), who became king in 936, in 962 was crowned Roman Emperor, and is usually regarded as the founder of the Holy Roman Empire.

Moreover, in the Western Church a revival was beginning. In 910 was founded in what is now East-central France the monastery of Cluny, from which a wave of reform spread which brought new devotion and enthusiasm into Western Christianity. The Saxon monarchs aided the reform of the Church in their own lands and, in time, that of the Papacy. The Church was recovering from both its internal weaknesses and the storms without.

The new movements had their repercussions in the North. Harald Bluetooth succeeded his father as King of Denmark and seems greatly to have extended his realm and to have become overlord of Norway. He was friendly

[563] Gjerset, *History of the Norwegian People*, Vol. I, pp. 170-174.

[564] Widukind, *Res Gestae Saxonicae* (in *Scriptores rerum Germanicarum*, Hanover, 1904), Book I, Chap. 40; Adam of Bremen, *op. cit.*, Book I, Chap. 57.

[565] Adam of Bremen, *op. cit.*, Book I, Chaps. 54, 62 (56, 62); Hauck, *op. cit.*, Vol. III, pp. 80-82.

[566] Adam of Bremen, *op. cit.*, Book I, Chap. 59.

[567] Adam of Bremen, *op. cit.*, Book I, Chaps. 60-62; Hauck, *op. cit.*, Vol. III, p. 82.

to Christianity and eventually was himself baptized.[568] One account has it that Otto defeated him and that he and his wife were then baptized.[569] Harald may have sought to emulate the Saxon monarchs and to make of Denmark a powerful Christian state such as he saw rising on his southern border.[570] He seems to have endeavoured to bring his subjects into the Christian fold, and many of them appear to have acceded.[571] In a monument which he erected to his father he claimed to have "made the Danes Christian."[572] In 948 we first hear of bishops among the Danes.[573] The Archdiocese of Hamburg-Bremen, after a century of waiting, at last possessed suffragan sees. Yet many of the Danes still honoured both Christ and the old gods.[574]

Under Harald's son Sweyn (or Svend I) something of a pagan reaction took place. Sweyn is said to have been baptized in his youth,[575] but he rose in rebellion against his father and the latter perished in the struggle (c. 986). In that conflict, indeed, Danish apostates from Christianity are reported to have sided with Sweyn.[576] Sweyn's policy towards Christianity was not constant. As we have suggested, he appears to have been borne to the throne on the wave of a pagan reaction. For a time he severely persecuted Christians.[577] At one stage in his career, moreover, he married Sigrid, a domineering woman who was passionately devoted to the old gods.[578] Repeatedly he invaded England, eventually conquered a large part of it, and died there in 1014. During much of his English career he was regarded as an inveterate enemy of Christianity. Yet as the years passed, in Denmark his regime became more friendly to the Church.

During one period of his reign Sweyn was driven out of Denmark by

[568] Widukind, op. cit., Book III, Chap. 65; Snorre Sturlason, Heimskringla, Book VII, Chaps. 25-27; Arup, Danmarks Historie, p. 122; Maclear, A History of Christian Missions during the Middle Ages, p. 251. The date of Harald's baptism is variously given and is uncertain. See Hauck, op. cit., Vol. III, p. 101, n., and Cambridge Medieval History, Vol. III, p. 202, n. 2.

[569] Adam of Bremen, op. cit., Book II, Chap. 3. See another account in Snorre Sturlason, Heimskringla, Book VII, Chaps. 25-27. It is not certain whether the Otto spoken of there was Otto I or Otto II.

[570] Gjerset, op. cit., Vol. I, pp. 170-174.

[571] Adam of Bremen, op. cit., Book II, Chaps. 25, 26 (23, 24).

[572] Kendrick, A History of the Vikings, pp. 100, 101.

[573] Adam of Bremen, op. cit., Book II, Chap. 26 (24); Hauck, op. cit., Vol. III, pp. 99-102.

[574] Widukind, op. cit., Book III, Chap. 65.

[575] Snorre Sturlason, Heimskringla, Book VII, Chap. 28, says that Otto stood godfather to him.

[576] Adam of Bremen, op. cit., Book II, Chap. 27 (25).

[577] Adam of Bremen, op. cit., Book II, Chap. 29 (27).

[578] Snorre Sturlason, Heimskringla, Book VI, Chaps. 61, 91; Larson, Canute the Great, p. 163.

King Eric of Sweden.[579] Although Eric was a pagan and hostile to Christians,[580] apparently he felt it best to keep on amicable terms with the powerful Christian German monarchy which bordered on Denmark.[581] Moreover, he was an ally of Christian Boleslaw of Poland.[582] He therefore received in cordial fashion a Bishop Poppo sent officially by the Archbishop of Hamburg and the German ruler. Poppo became famous as a missionary in Denmark and is said to have won "many thousands" to the Christian faith.[583] A Bishop Odinkar, of Danish stock, laboured not only in Denmark, but in Sweden and elsewhere. We also hear of Odinkar's nephew and disciple, Odinkar Junior.[584] Missionaries, too, both priests and bishops, are said to have come from England.[585] Later, after his return from England, Sweyn himself became more friendly to Christianity. Apparently he encouraged the coming of English clergy to assist in the conversion of Scandinavia.[586]

It was under Sweyn's son Canute (Knud or Knut) that the Church was at last firmly established in Denmark. Canute had a Polish mother and seems to have been reared a Christian. Like so many others in that stormy age, he had to make his way by his sword and his wits. In 1013, when probably about nineteen years of age, he shared with his father in the conquest of Wessex. On Sweyn's death, in 1014, Canute was left without a kingdom, for to his brother Harald went the crown of Denmark. Canute, however, conquered much of England, and in 1016, on the death of the Saxon Edmund Ironside, was elected King of all England. In 1018, when still a young man, the death of his brother Harald gave him the throne of Denmark. In 1019 he sailed to claim it and until his death, in 1035, he was King of both England and Denmark. For a time he was also master of Norway.[587]

Canute was a Christian. We do not know when he was baptized, but it may have been in childhood.[588] In the first years of his reign he seems not to have been an especially ardent advocate of his faith, but that may have been because much of his army was pagan.[589] As a shrewd statesman he may

[579] Adam of Bremen, *op. cit.*, Book II, Chap. 30 (28).
[580] Adam of Bremen, *op. cit.*, Book II, Chap. 35 (33).
[581] Hauck, *Kirchengeschichte Deutschlands,* Vol. III, p. 635.
[582] Adam of Bremen, *op. cit.*, Book II, Chap. 35 (33), Schol. 24.
[583] Adam of Bremen, *op. cit.*, Book II, Chap. 35 (33).
[584] Adam of Bremen, *op. cit.*, Book II, Chap. 36 (34).
[585] Adam of Bremen, *op. cit.*, Book II, Chap. 37 (35).
[586] Adam of Bremen, *op. cit.*, Book III, Chap. 41 (39).
[587] Larson, *Canute the Great,* pp. 32, 58, 107, 138. The date of Canute's birth is very uncertain. It seems to have been about 995. On Canute's Polish mother see Samuel H. Cross, *Scandinavian-Polish Relations in the Late Tenth Century* (in *Studies in Honor of Hermann Collitz,* Baltimore, 1930, pp. 114-140).
[588] Larson, *op. cit.*, p. 164.
[589] Larson, *op. cit.*, pp. 162, 163.

have believed it impolitic at once to ally himself too openly with the Church. When, however, by 1020 he felt himself firmly seated in both England and Denmark, he energetically espoused the cause of Christianity. In England he gave rich gifts to churches and monasteries and came out with laws favouring Sunday observance and church attendance.[590] In Denmark he actively aided the Church. In 1022, presumably at his suggestion, the Archbishop of Canterbury consecrated three bishops for Danish sees.[591] Although the names appear to have been German rather than English, this step seemed to the Archbishop of Hamburg to infringe on his rights. One of the three was captured on his way north, taken before Archbishop Unwan of Hamburg, and made to do him homage.[592] Canute was induced to agree that in the future the jurisdiction of the Archbishop of Hamburg would be respected.[593] Canute himself made a pilgrimage to Rome, an expedition which must greatly have increased his zeal.[594] He is reported to have been so friendly to bishops that he seemed almost to be one of them.[595] He is said to have commanded his subjects to learn the Lord's Prayer and to go to communion three times a year.[596]

The death of Canute (1035) did not halt the progress of Christianity. The number of bishoprics increased.[597] Monasticism entered. It is said to date from the closing years of the eleventh century, with the coming of twelve monks from Evesham in England at the request of the Danish King to found a house at Odense,[598] but it may have begun earlier. The strength of the English influence in forming the Christianity of Denmark is seen in part, too, in the language of the Danish ritual, in the numbers of churches named after the Anglo-Saxon saints, and in monasteries founded by English monks.[599]

Early in the twelfth century Denmark was removed from the supervision of the Archbishop of Hamburg and was given its own Metropolitanate. For some years this had been in prospect. From 1043 or 1045 to his death in 1072 Hamburg had as its Archbishop an able and ambitious ecclesiastical prince, Adalbert. Adalbert cherished grandiose plans for his see and from time to time enjoyed large influence in the imperial court. However, in Denmark, Norway,

[590] Larson, *op. cit.*, pp. 177-179, 341-344, giving a translation of the text of the proclamation of 1020.
[591] Adam of Bremen, *op. cit.*, Book II, Chap. 55 (53).
[592] *Ibid.*
[593] *Ibid.*
[594] *Cnutonis Regis Gesta* (in *Scriptores rerum Germanicarum*, Hanover, 1865), Book II, Chap. 20; Larson, *op. cit.*, p. 224.
[595] *Cnutonis Regis Gesta*, Book II, Chap. 19.
[596] Hauck, *op. cit.*, Vol. III, p. 641, citing *Geist. Gesetze* 19, p. 267, 22, p. 267.
[597] Adam of Bremen, *Gesta Hammaburgensis Ecclesiæ Pontificum*, Book IV, Chaps. 2, 8.
[598] Larson, *Canute the Great*, p. 191.
[599] Leach, *Angevin Britain and Scandinavia*, pp. 76-80.

and Sweden opposition developed to this German domination. The King of Denmark pressed Rome for a Metropolitan of his own. Adalbert was willing to give his consent if at the same time Hamburg were raised to a Patriarchate of the North—thus preserving its outstanding position. To this Rome would not agree. The whole issue was complicated by the struggle between Pope and Emperor—then at an acute stage. Rome did not wish to strengthen a friend of the Emperor and was not unwilling to have a Metropolitanate in Scandinavia independent of Hamburg-Bremen. Not until after the death of all the original chief disputants (except the Emperor Henry IV) did Denmark attain its desire. In 1104 a Cardinal Legate was sent north to carry into effect a decision reached about 1100. He fixed upon Denmark's leading city, Lund, for the seat of the new archiepiscopal see and raised to it a Danish bishop.[600] It is significant that Hamburg was not compensated by the suggested Patriarchate. Although Denmark had long been considered a Christian country, here was formal recognition that the missionary era had ended and that an ecclesiastical organization comparable to that of other Christian lands was now possible. The last tie which bound Scandinavia to Hamburg-Bremen was severed. Ecclesiastical independence from the Germans had been obtained.

The conversion of Norway had a much more stormy course than that of Denmark. Chronologically the two partly coincided, and at points they were intertwined, but that of Norway began later than that of the southern kingdom. The delay was to be expected. In spite of its contacts through Vikings, Norway was slightly farther removed from Christian peoples than was Denmark. The latter bordered on the Christian Saxons and the Archdiocese of Hamburg found in it an adjacent mission field. Hamburg had not nearly so large a share in the conversion of Norway as it seems to have had in Denmark. Nor did much of Christianity come to Norway from either Denmark or Sweden.[601] Yet the conversion of Norway was completed at almost the same time with that of Denmark and about a century earlier than that of Sweden. The Church in Norway was the offspring of the English Church. In terminology and institutions the English lineage was clearly discernible. English missionaries laboured in Norway and some of the Norwegian monasteries were founded by Englishmen.[602]

Partly for geographic reasons, the British Isles were prominent as a goal of the raids from Norway. In the tenth century, however, the English Church had begun to recover from the demoralization wrought by them. The renewal

[600] Hauck, *op. cit.*, Vol. III, pp. 658-661; *Catholic Encyclopedia*, Vol. IX, p. 434.
[601] Willson, *History of the Church and State in Norway*, pp. 19-21, emphasizes the fact that the Church of Norway was a daughter of the Anglo-Saxon Church.
[602] Leach, *op. cit.*, pp. 85-100.

was begun by Alfred the Great in the last quarter of the ninth century. A reform of which Archbishop Dunstan of Canterbury was the most prominent figure led to a revival of monasticism and a stricter observance of the Benedictine rule and to an improvement in both morals and education.[603] The English Church was once more displaying enough vitality to be the source of missions. The movement which resulted seems not to have had anything like the vigour of the earlier one in which Willibrord and Boniface were the most prominent figures. It was more dependent upon the initiative of secular rulers. Yet it had important consequences in all of the Scandinavian lands, and especially in Norway.

It is interesting that the Christianity of England had a much larger part in the conversion of Norway—and of the rest of Scandinavia—than did that of either Ireland or Scotland. This may well have been because the Church in these two lands recovered much more slowly from the blows dealt by the Northmen than did that in England. Then, too, in Ireland the conversion of the Northmen took place rather later than in England. Indeed, it was after the conversion of Denmark and about contemporary with that of Norway.

Yet while the Christianity of Norway was largely the child of that of England, it had a different history. Much more violence attended the spread of the faith in Norway than in England, or, for that matter, than in Denmark or Sweden. This may have been because of the character of the kings who led in the process. It may have been, too, because at times acceptance of Christianity was identified with submission to the authority of the King and opposition came in part from local chieftains and landowners who fiercely prized their old liberties and identified these with the traditional religion.

The conversion of Norway began shortly before the middle of the tenth century, or more than two generations after the death of Anskar. The Norwegian Kingdom was the creation of Harald Haarfager ("Fairhair"), who died in 933. By dint of much fighting he made himself "the only ruler in all Norway."[604] On his death a struggle for the succession ensued. At first Eric "Bloodax" held the lead, but Haakon, "the Good," the child of Harald's old age, was brought into power under the ægis of the "wisest man in Norway," Sigurd the Jarl. He promised to restore to the landowners some of their rights which had been curtailed under the monarchy.[605] Haakon had been sent while a young child to England to the court of Aethelstan and had been a kind of

---

[603] For a brief summary of these changes in the English Church, see Patterson, *A History of the Church of England,* pp. 44-58.

[604] Snorre Sturlason, *Heimskringla,* Book III, is an account of Harald Fairhair. See especially Chap. 20.

[605] Snorre Sturlason, *op. cit.,* Book IV, Chap. 1.

foster son of the King. Here he had been baptized and had been reared a Christian. As a Christian he returned to Norway. About fifteen years of age, handsome, tall, athletic, and popular, he gave promise of being an ideal leader of his people.[606] In 935, thanks largely to Sigurd and through prowess in battle, Haakon had been accepted as King by most if not all of Norway.

Haakon attempted to win his people to his faith. At first he practised it without much ostentation, keeping Sunday and the Friday fast. Then he essayed fixing the Yuletide at the same time with the Christmas festival. He soon won to baptism some of his immediate entourage. Later, when he felt strong enough, he sent to England for clergy and proceeded to build churches and to place priests in them. It was perhaps about 950,[607] when he had been reigning fifteen years, that he took the further step of proposing to a *thing*, or local assembly, that the landowners adopt Christianity. They referred the question to a larger *thing*. Here Haakon presented his case and urged young and old, men and women, rich and poor, landowners and labourers, to become Christians. The bonders, or landowners, refused and complained bitterly at the threatened departure from the old ways. Apparently the issue was now joined. Although Haakon did not force through his measures, the leading men kept urging him to participate in the pagan sacrifices. They seem to have had vested interests in the old religion. The local chieftains were also priests and much of their power would be lost if the traditional faith disappeared.[608] Haakon at first declined to compromise, but after some months, under threats from some who had shown their enmity by destroying a church, at a great pagan sacrifice he ate a bit of the horse flesh and partook of the ceremonial drink. He did so, however, very reluctantly, and apparently because he faced rebellion and the loss of his throne if he did not comply.[609] Some time later, in 961, Haakon was mortally wounded in battle. On his death-bed he is said to have declared that if he were to live he would go to a Christian land and do penance for his sins.[610]

Haakon was succeeded by his nephews, the sons of Eric "Bloodax." Of these, Harald Graafell was the chief. Years before, the new rulers had, with their father, as part of a treaty of peace, been baptized in England.[611] How convinced Christians they were is not clear, but they are reported to have broken

---

[606] Snorre Sturlason, *op. cit.,* Book III, Chaps. 40, 41.

[607] Willson, *op. cit.,* p. 26.

[608] Gjerset, *History of the Norwegian People,* Vol. I, p. 166.

[609] Snorre Sturlason, *op. cit.,* Book IV, Chaps. 14, 15.

[610] Snorre Sturlason, *op. cit.,* Book IV, Chaps. 31, 32. He is said to have regretted very much his departure from the Christian faith.—*Fagrskinna,* p. 26, cited in Gjerset, *op. cit.,* Vol. I, p. 167.

[611] Snorre Sturlason, *op. cit.,* Book IV, Chap. 3, Book V, Chap. 2.

down pagan temples wherever they went. Misrule and bad seasons, however, may have led the populace to hate the faith thus violently championed.[612]

About 969 or 970, Harald Graafell was lured to Denmark and slain.[613] After his death, Harald Bluetooth, the King of Denmark, made himself the over-lord of Norway and ruled the land through Haakon the Jarl, a son of that Sigurd the Jarl who had been the chief adviser of Haakon the Good.[614] Haakon the Jarl may have represented a reaction of the pagan aristocracy against the centralizing and Christianizing efforts of Haakon the Good and the sons of Eric. Harald Bluetooth, as we have seen, submitted to baptism and propagated Christianity in his realms.[615] Having taken this step, he induced Haakon the Jarl and his followers to follow his example. Harald gave Haakon "priests and other learned men" and instructed him to bring them to Norway and use them for the conversion of his subjects. Haakon, as soon as he saw an opportunity of going to sea, put the missionaries ashore and went off on a raiding expedition.[616] Under Harald Bluetooth other attempts were made to spread Christianity in Norway which seem to have met with slightly more success.[617] However, little permanent result appears to have followed from his efforts or from the labours of missionaries under the Archbishop of Hamburg.[618]

The effective introduction of Christianity to Norway was the work of Olaf Tryggvason. As a great-grandson of Harald Haarfager he was in the line royal. He was born about 963 or 964. His was an adventurous and colourful life. From his infancy he had known danger. He was a posthumous child and his mother was in hiding when he was born. He was early captured by Vikings and sold as a slave, but was rescued by an uncle and grew to man-hood in a Scandinavian colony in Russia. It was in Russia that he began his military career, and he early fared forth as a Viking.[619] His raids carried him to England. Fairhaired, handsome, huge of stature, daring, and fearless, he was the embodiment of the Viking ideal. It may be that, reared away from Norway, he was never a zealous adherent of the old gods, but had very little

---

[612] Snorre Sturlason, *op. cit.,* Book V, Chap. 2.

[613] Snorre Sturlason, *op. cit.,* Book VII, Chaps. 14, 15.

[614] Snorre Sturlason, *op. cit.,* Book VI, Chap. 1; Book VII, Chap. 23.

[615] Snorre Sturlason, *op. cit.,* Book VII, Chap. 27.

[616] *Ibid.*

[617] Adam of Bremen, *Gesta Hammaburgensis Ecclesiæ Pontificum,* Book II, Chap. 25 (23), Scol. 147 (142); Willson, *History of the Church and State in Norway,* pp. 35, 36. Snorre Sturlason, *op. cit.,* Book VII, Chap. 53, says that Harald sent two jarls and a force of men to Norway to order the land to become Christian and that in Viken (not far from Denmark) many were baptized, only to apostatize under the Sweyn pagan reaction.

[618] Willson, *op. cit.,* p. 36.

[619] Snorre Sturlason, *op. cit.,* Book VII (*Olaf Tryggvasonssaga*), Chaps. 1-7.

faith in anything except his own strength and in magic.[620] While in the Scilly Islands he came in touch with a hermit who to Olaf's mind displayed an uncanny ability to forecast the future. By him he and his followers were baptized. Olaf remained there for a time and when he left he took priests with him.[621] It was as a Christian that he returned to England.[621]

For a time Olaf seems to have continued to harry England, although this is in doubt.[622] However, he appears to have made peace with Aethelred, to have been confirmed by the Bishop of Winchester, and to have agreed never again to wage war there.[623]

In the summer of 995 Olaf sailed for the land of his fathers. Presumably he had determined both to claim the crown and to bring his people into the Christian faith. On the way north he paused in the Orkneys and there compelled the Jarl to accept baptism and to acknowledge him as overlord.[624]

Norway was apparently weary of Haakon the Jarl and that sturdy pagan was soon eliminated.[625] At a general *thing* Olaf was elected King and as he went through the land it quickly submitted to him.[626]

Olaf now set about carrying out his purpose of making the country Christian. He began in Viken, where his father had ruled and the faith had been planted from Denmark. Here he naturally found loyalty among his kin and a ready acceptance of his suggestion of baptism. In a part of Viken he encountered opposition, but met it with force, exiling, maiming, or killing the recalcitrants.[627] He proceeded through his domains, carrying out his mission. Usually he seems to have presented to a local *thing* his argument for Christianity. In at least one instance the assembly assented without the application of force. In another he purchased compliance by giving his sister in marriage to one of the prominent youths. Some yielded when the King gave them the choice of battle or baptism. On one occasion Olaf threatened to sacrifice the most prominent of the opposition to the old gods, and the company, seeing the futility of resistance, accepted baptism. On another he obtained consent by a gift of a chieftainship and of rents. Sometimes he destroyed temples and once he met hesitancy by boldly striking down an image of Thor. More than once he slew members of the opposition.[628] The acceptance of Christianity was

[620] Undset, *Saga of Saints*, p. 49.

[621] Snorre Sturlason, *op. cit.*, Book VII, Chaps. 21, 22, 30-32.

[622] Snorre Sturlason, *op. cit.*, Book VII, Chap. 32, seems to indicate that he did not again raid England. However, on his harrying England in 994, see Gjerset, *op. cit.*, Vol. I, p. 177. Plummer (editor), *Two of the Saxon Chronicles*, Vol. I, pp. 126, 128.

[623] Plummer (editor), *Two of the Saxon Chronicles*, Vol. I, pp. 126, 128.

[624] Snorre Sturlason, *op. cit.*, Book VII, Chap. 47.

[625] Snorre Sturlason, *op. cit.*, Book VII, Chaps. 48-50.

[626] Snorre Sturlason, *op. cit.*, Book VII, Chap. 51.

[627] Snorre Sturlason, *op. cit.*, Book VII, Chap. 53.

[628] Snorre Sturlason, *op. cit.*, Book VII, Chaps. 54-80.

at least sometimes identified with the acknowledgement of Olaf's rule.[629] Within about four years, or in 999, the process of nominal conversion appears to have been completed.[630] Through Olaf, moreover, the faith was carried to Iceland and Greenland.[631]

The clerical agents whom Olaf used seem to have been bishops and priests from England.[632] One of these, Thangbrand, was so headstrong and violent that he aroused opposition in both Norway and Iceland and proved a real embarrassment to the King.[633]

Olaf's career came to its end in a characteristic manner. A powerful coalition against him was organized by Sweyn of Denmark, whose acquaintance we have already formed. In it joined the King of Sweden and two sons of Haakon the Jarl, with many of the disaffected Norwegians. Olaf was trapped into a naval battle (A.D. 1000) against a force vastly superior to his own, was overwhelmed, and at the end leaped overboard to his death.[634]

The victors divided among them parts of Olaf's possessions. Other portions of the realm were ruled by independent princes. The violence of the political union with its curtailment of the traditional rights of chieftains and landowners and its religious innovations was followed by reaction.[635]

Yet Olaf's work was not entirely undone. Two of the victorious jarls accepted Christianity and in the portions of Norway which they administered gave religious liberty to both the old and the new faith.[636]

The completion of the mission of Olaf Tryggvason was to wait for several years and was to be the achievement of another of the line of Harald Haarfager, this time a great-great-grandson of that founder of the Norwegian Kingdom. He, too, was an Olaf—Olaf Haraldsson, or St. Olaf. Like Olaf Tryggvason, he was a posthumous child. He is said to have been baptized, with Olaf Tryggvason for godfather,[637] but it is also alleged that his baptism occurred later, in Normandy.[638] He was stocky, strong, skilful in sports, keen of mind, good to look upon, fair of hair, ruddy of face, and with eyes before which, when they lighted up with anger, strong men quailed.[639] At the age of twelve,

---

[629] As in Snorre Sturlason, *op. cit.*, Book VII, Chap. 77.

[630] Willson, *History of the Church and State in Norway*, p. 52.

[631] Snorre Sturlason, *op. cit.*, Book VII, Chaps. 73, 81, 84, 86, 101.

[632] Adam of Bremen, *op. cit.*, Book II, Chap. 37.

[633] Snorre Sturlason, *op. cit.*, Book VII, Chaps. 73, 84.

[634] Snorre Sturlason, *op. cit.*, Book VII, Chaps. 108-122.

[635] Snorre Sturlason, *op. cit.*, Book VII, Chap. 123.

[636] *Ibid.*

[637] Snorre Sturlason, *op. cit.*, Book VII, Chap. 60.

[638] Willson, *op. cit.*, p. 61, citing the *Chronicle of William of Jumièges* and the *Passio et Miracula Beati Olaui*, Chap. 1; Gjerset, *History of the Norwegian People*, Vol. I, p. 247.

[639] Snorre Sturlason, *op. cit.*, Book VIII (*Saga of Olaf the Saint*), Chaps. 1, 3.

under tutelage, of course, he began a career of seafaring and plunder.[640] He raided the shores of Sweden. He fought in England, part of the time assisting King Aethelred. He also fought in France.[641]

Having thus served an apprenticeship abroad, in his early twenties he went to Norway (1015) to claim the throne. Here, in a decisive battle in 1016, he defeated his principal enemy and was acknowledged by *thing* after *thing*. In 1019 he obtained from Sweden the recognition of the independence of his realm.[642]

Olaf Haraldsson set himself to make his newly won kingdom Christian not only in name but in fact. He sought to strengthen the Christian faith and to suppress non-Christian soothsayers. He had with him many priests and bishops from England whom he had instruct his people and conduct missions in the islands and even in Sweden.[643] However, none of the four bishops from England of whom we hear specifically had an Anglo-Saxon name. Three of them seem to have been of Scandinavian descent.[644] Olaf appears also to have established friendly relations with the see of Hamburg, within whose sphere his realms traditionally lay.[645] With the advice of ecclesiastical counsellors he framed laws according to what he believed to be Christian principles, and directed them against paganism and anti-Christian customs.[646] In the South, in Viken, he found his task easier than in the North, for here was greater familiarity with things Christian.[647] He travelled through the land to see that the conversion was completed and that churches were built and priests set over them.[648] Like Olaf Tryggvason, he did not hesitate to threaten the recalcitrants with force[649] and in at least one instance burned the houses of the opposition.[650] Unlike the other Olaf, however, he seems to have done little of the actual preaching himself, but to have left most of that to the clergy who accompanied him. Nor does the use of force loom quite so prominently in the

[640] Snorre Sturlason, *op. cit.*, Book VIII, Chap. 4.

[641] Snorre Sturlason, *op. cit.*, Book VIII, Chaps. 6-20.

[642] Snorre Sturlason, *op. cit.*, Book VIII, Chaps. 32 ff.; Willson, *op. cit.*, pp. 63, 64; Gjerset, *op. cit.*, Vol. I, pp. 250-253.

[643] Adam of Bremen, *Gesta Hammaburgensis Ecclesiæ Pontificum*, Book II, Chap. 57 (55).

[644] Larson, *Canute the Great*, p. 192.

[645] Adam of Bremen, *op. cit.*, Vol. II, Chap. 57 (55). This turning to Hamburg may have been brought about by the fact that Canute controlled England and that Olaf feared that more English clergy might mean subjection to Canute.—Willson, *op. cit.*, p. 78; Hauck, *Kirchengeschichte Deutschlands*, Vol. III, p. 645.

[646] Snorre Sturlason, *op. cit.*, Book VIII, Chaps. 58, 64.

[647] Snorre Sturlason, *op. cit.*, Book VIII, Chap. 64.

[648] Snorre Sturlason, *op. cit.*, Book VIII, Chap. 114.

[649] Snorre Sturlason, *op. cit.*, Book VIII, Chaps. 113, 121.

[650] Snorre Sturlason, *op. cit.*, Book VIII, Chap. 121.

accounts of his methods of conversion.[651] Presumably something more of an understanding of the contents of Christian doctrine came through his methods than through those of the earlier missionary King. Yet he did not succeed in bringing about universal baptism. In his last campaign numbers of his recruits were pagan, and while some of these, at his request, submitted to the rite, others left him rather than do so.[652]

Olaf Haraldsson, however, fell on evil days. He endeavoured not only to bring over his people to Christianity, but also to strengthen the power of the throne at the expense of the local lords and landowners. Opposition was aroused. Yet it is significant evidence of the progress of the faith that at least some of Olaf's enemies were Christian and that a Danish bishop sought to urge them on against him.[653] He was attacked not on religious grounds, by a heathen party, but for political and personal reasons and by those who were aggrieved by his centralizing tendencies. Canute of Denmark wished to extend his rule over Norway and his agents helped to stimulate the discontent. Olaf was driven out of his kingdom. Then, returning, he faced his enemies with a force greatly inferior to theirs and in a decisive battle (1030) was slain.[654]

Norway now became subject to Denmark. Shortly, however, a reaction took place. A story relates that the following year (1031) Olaf's old friend and companion, Bishop Grimkel, had the King's body disinterred and found it uncorrupted. It was thereupon placed in a church and miracles were reported to have followed.[655] The cult spread rapidly and soon Olaf came to be regarded as a national saint and hero. To his shrine pilgrims flocked and churches were built in his honour.[656] On the tide of national feeling against Danish rule Olaf was swept into canonization and his young son, Magnus, was placed on the throne.

With Olaf Haraldsson the conversion of Norway may be said to have been completed. Probably at his death many unbaptized were still to be found. From his time on, however, the predominant faith professed in Norway was Christianity. Still, the training of a body of native clergy, the development of a lasting ecclesiastical organization, and the instruction of the neophytes and their children in the faith could scarcely be accomplished in the five years

[651] Undset, *Saga of Saints*, p. 51.
[652] Snorre Sturlason, *op. cit.*, Book VIII, Chap. 204.
[653] Snorre Sturlason, *op. cit.*, Book VIII, Chaps. 217, 218.
[654] Snorre Sturlason, *op. cit.*, Book VIII, Chaps. 146-236. On the date of his death, see Willson, *op. cit.*, p. 88.
[655] Snorre Sturlason, *op. cit.*, Book VIII, Chaps. 245, 246.
[656] Gjerset, *History of the Norwegian People*, Vol. I, pp. 265-269; Willson, *History of the Church and State in Norway*, pp. 92, 93.

of Olaf Tryggvason's reign nor even in the fifteen years that Olaf Haraldsson held the throne.

Christianity continued to spread. Sometimes its agents were the clergy. In the early days the native-born priests must have been relatively few and most of them poorly trained, with slight knowledge of the faith for which they stood. The word of respected laymen and the song of the *scald*, the traditional poet and bard, must have been major means of instruction.[657] It was in part through channels to which the populace were accustomed that the new ways were propagated. In the process, naturally, pre-Christian conceptions entered and amalgamated with the imported message to make a new compound which was unlike either the Christianity of England or Norse paganism, yet contained elements from both.[658]

Not until the latter half of the eleventh century, a generation after the death of Olaf Haraldsson, does Norway seem to have had a diocesan organization. The earlier prelates were missionary bishops, without fixed sees.[659] A parochial system was not immediately perfected. Monks came in who, like the seculars, were largely from England[660] and helped to present the monastic idea of Christianity. Presumably, too, they assisted in raising the educational level of the Church. Only beginning with the twelfth century, however, was the monastic life firmly established.[661]

When in time an ecclesiastical structure came into being, in its geographical outlines it partly conformed to the pre-Christian religious and social framework. A major division of the country had been the *fylke*, or canton, and in pagan days each *fylke* had its temple. The *fylke* was divided into *herreds*, or hundreds, each of which in turn possessed a temple. In addition were private shrines which local chieftains or landowners maintained.[662] We know all too little of details of the early Christian centuries, but it seems probable that often the churches were built on or near the sites of the pre-Christian shrines and that at times temples were transformed into churches.[663] Moreover, the first three territorial bishoprics corresponded to the centres where the chief *things* were held.[664] The phenomenon is one which recurs again and again

[657] Olrik, *Viking Civilization*, p. 146.

[658] For hints at the adjustments made in the imported Christianity, see Larson, "Problems of the Norwegian Church in the Eleventh Century," in *Church History*, Sept., 1935 (Vol. IV), pp. 159-172.

[659] Adam of Bremen, *op. cit.*, Book IV, Chap. 34 (33).

[660] Willson, *History of the Church and State in Norway*, pp. 130, 136.

[661] Willson, *op. cit.*, p. 126.

[662] Willson, *op. cit.*, p. 6.

[663] Willson, *op. cit.*, pp. 121, 122; Olsen, *Farms and Fanes of Ancient Norway*, pp. 233, 300.

[664] Willson, *op. cit.*, p. 120.

in our story. It was, indeed, natural that the Church should conform its structure to the existing political and religious framework of a land or community. Nor did such adjustment necessarily entail the transfer of pre-Christian religious ideas and customs.

Almost inevitably a conflict arose between the Norwegian monarchs and the Archbishops of Hamburg-Bremen. The King wished to appoint his own bishops and to control the Church. This, indeed, he usually did.[665] The Archbishop of Hamburg-Bremen, however, as we have repeatedly seen, claimed jurisdiction over the churches of the North. The conflict became particularly acute about the middle of the eleventh century, or in the generation after Olaf Haraldsson, when both the throne of Norway and the see of Hamburg were held by exceptionally autocratic and aggressive men. From 1046 to 1066 the King of Norway was Harald Haardraade ("the Ruthless"), and from 1043 or 1045 to 1072 the Archbishop of Hamburg-Bremen was the Adalbert who, as we have noted, was an ecclesiastical prince combining energy and ability with vaulting ambition. Harald was in the habit of having his bishops consecrated in Gaul and England. To this Adalbert objected. Harald angrily declared that he alone was archbishop and master in Norway. The Pope admonished him by letter to respect the authority of Adalbert as Papal Legate, but how much heed Harald paid is doubtful.[666] Eventually, in 1104, not long after the death of the two men, Norway was assigned to the newly created Archiepiscopal See of Lund.[667] Half a century later, in 1152, after an abortive move the preceding year, Norway was given an Archiepiscopate of its own and so placed on a basis of equality with other nations which were recognized as Christian.[668]

To the west of Scandinavia lay islands in which Norwegian influence was strong. The conversion of their populations was closely knit with that of Norway. An early account declares that Olaf Tryggvason Christianized not only Norway, but also the Orkneys, the Faroe Islands, the Shetlands, Iceland, and Greenland.[669] Before the coming of the Vikings, the Faroes and Shetlands may have had a sparse Christian population, but presumably it had little importance for later history.[670]

Before the Norse invasions the Orkneys probably had seen some Christians. They had a Pictish population, some of whom may have been of that faith.

[665] Willson, *op. cit.,* pp. 122, 123.
[666] Adam of Bremen, *op. cit.,* Book III, Chap. 17 (16), Schol. 68 (69), 69 (70).
[667] Willson, *op. cit.,* p. 104.
[668] Willson, *op. cit.,* pp. 136-138.
[669] *Fagrskinna* (edited by F. Jónsson), p. 113.
[670] Maurer, *Die Bekehrung des norwegischen Stammes zum Christentums.* Vol. I, pp. 42-48.

We hear of an Irish monk, a "soldier of Christ," as he was called, who in the time of Columba seems to have gone there.[671] However, in the tenth century the inhabitants were at least predominantly Scandinavian and pagan. We have seen that in 995 Olaf Tryggvason, on his way to Norway, halted in the islands and compelled the Jarl Sigurd Lodverson and his people to accept baptism.[672] In the time of Olaf Haraldsson Christianity seems to have existed in the Orkneys, the Shetlands, and the Faroes, but not in a condition which pleased the missionary monarch.[673]

Ecclesiastically the Orkneys became a bone of contention. About the middle of the eleventh century the ambitious and princely Archbishop Adalbert of Hamburg-Bremen consecrated and sent a Scandinavian bishop to them.[674] It is said that earlier they had had English and Scottish bishops.[675] We read also that in 1073 the Archbishop of York prepared, with the concurrence of his brother of Canterbury (Lanfranc), to consecrate as Bishop for the Orkneys a priest who had brought a letter from the Earl of the islands. This appointee was, however, not recognized either by his flock or the King of Norway and remained at York. Later York consecrated other bishops who were equally unacceptable to Norway and the people of the islands. Not even Papal letters could induce the kings of Norway to acknowledge the Bishop of the Orkneys as a suffragan of York. About 1102 a line of Norwegian bishops began which apparently continued until the fifteenth century—or as long as the Orkneys continued to belong to Scandinavia.[676]

Unwillingness to submit to the unification of Norway under Harald Haarfager led many to migrate to the Hebrides, the Faroes, the Shetlands, the Orkneys, and Iceland.[677] Harald is said to have pursued the recusants to the Orkneys, the Hebrides, and the Shetlands, and in the Shetlands to have killed all the Vikings whom he found.[678] As we have seen, Olaf Tryggvason is credited with having won to the faith the Faroes and the Shetlands. Sigmund Brestesson, the ruler and national hero of the Faroes, came to Norway at Olaf's invitation, was baptized, and at the King's request returned to the

[671] Adamnan, *Vita S. Columbae,* Book II, Chap. 42.
[672] Snorre Sturlason, *Heimskringla,* Book VII, Chap. 47. On Christianity in the Orkneys after Olaf Tryggvason, see a popular account in Undset, *Saga of Saints,* pp. 163 ff.
[673] Snorre Sturlason, *op. cit.,* Book VIII, Chap. 58.
[674] Adam of Bremen, *Gesta Hammaburgensis Ecclesiæ Pontificum,* Book III, Chap. 77; Book IV, Chap. 36.
[675] Adam of Bremen, *op. cit.,* Book IV, Chap. 36.
[676] Haddan and Stubbs, *Councils and Ecclesiastical Documents Relating to Great Britain and Ireland,* Vol. II, Pt. 1, pp. 153, 162, 167, 212; Macewen, *History of the Church of Scotland,* Vol. I, p. 167.
[677] Snorre Sturlason, *op. cit.,* Book III, Chap. 19.
[678] Snorre Sturlason, *op. cit.,* Book III, Chap. 22.

islands and brought the inhabitants to accept baptism, using force on some.[679] Olaf Haraldsson appears to have found Christianity still in existence on the two groups.[680]

Iceland seems not to have received a Scandinavian population until the second half of the ninth century. The first large immigration appears to have been by those who disliked the rule of Harald Haarfager. They desired to preserve the customs which Harald was restricting. Some settlers brought their temples with them. Others set up temples. The ownership of temples meant power, for worship in them was not a free right but purchasable and by a certain degree of submission to the proprietor.[681] Previously a few Irish monks and anchorites had made their way to the island, but had not, of course, brought with them a population which could reproduce itself.[682]

When Christianity first reached Scandinavian Iceland we do not know. It may well have been that the first Christians there were from the British Isles, perhaps slaves in the households of Viking masters.[683] An early record says that those expert in the lore of the past declared that some of the early settlers had been baptized, that among them were those who held to their faith until their death, but that they usually failed to transmit it to their descendants, and that the land remained pagan for about a century.[684]

The first serious effort of which we know for the conversion of Iceland was in about 981. Thorwald, who was off cruising the seas, fell in with a Bishop Frederick of Saxony and was baptized by him. At Thorwald's request, Bishop Frederick accompanied the neophyte to Iceland. There the two worked together for four or five years, both of them preaching. Some success attended their efforts. Tradition has it, however, that the Bishop parted company from Thorwald and returned to Saxony because his truculent convert was too ready to take life.[685]

---

[679] Gjerset, *History of the Norwegian People*, Vol. I, p. 190.

[680] Snorre Sturlason, *op. cit.*, Book III, Chap. 19.

[681] Ari Thorgilsson, *Islendingabók*, Chap. 1; Snorre Sturlason, *op. cit.*, Book III, Chap. 15. Hermannsson, *The Book of the Icelanders (Íslendingabók)* (Cornell University Library, 1930), pp. 2-5, gives the date of the earliest settlement as about 870. The officially accepted date is 874. See also on the settlement Gwyn Jones, *Four Icelandic Sagas. Translated with an Introduction and Notes* (Princeton University Press, 1935, pp. viii, 164), pp. 10, 13-16.

[682] Ari Thorgilsson, *op. cit.*, Chap. 1; Gougaud, *Christianity in Celtic Lands*, p. 132; Keary, *The Vikings of Western Christendom*, p. 186, citing Deculius, *De Mensura Orbis Terrarum*.

[683] Hermannsson, *op. cit.*, p. 8; Maurer, *op. cit.*, Vol. I, pp. 90-107.

[684] *Landnámabók*, c. 399, p. 231, translated in Anderson, *Early Sources of Scottish History*, Vol. I, pp. 342-344. It may have been that more Christianity early existed in Iceland than *Landnámabók* acknowledges.—Kendrick, *A History of the Vikings*, p. 347.

[685] *The Saga of King Olaf Tryggwason*, translated by J. Sephton (London, David Nutt, 1895, pp. xxviii, 500), Chaps. 131-138 (pp. 177-188); *Kristnisaga*, Chaps. 1-4. See a

A much more active attempt to bring Iceland into the faith began in the time of Olaf Tryggvason. That vigorous monarch interested himself in the island. Some of the Icelanders came to Norway and there were induced by him to accept baptism.[686] In 996 Olaf sent one Stevne Thorgilsson to Iceland as a missionary. The agent followed the King's methods, but without the same skill. He destroyed temples and altars, but the island assembly, the Althing, decreed that any one speaking disrespectively of the gods should be outlawed and under this legislation Stevne was forced to leave.[687]

Another missionary, even less tactful, was Thangbrand, an Anglo-Saxon priest who is said to have been something of a scholar. As we have seen, he was one of Olaf's assistants in Norway, but proved too violent even for that forceful King. Apparently to remove him from a land where he was proving a nuisance, Olaf sent him to Iceland to preach Christianity. Thangbrand was in the island two years and baptized many of the leading men. However, his violent temper brought him difficulty, for he slew three men, two of them for deriding him. Thangbrand returned to Olaf and lodged a complaint against the Icelanders. Olaf, angry, was about to retaliate by killing or maiming the islanders who happened to be in Norway. The vicarious victims expostulated, however, told of the priest's violent ways, were let off, and were baptized.[688] Moreover, two Icelanders came to the King and mollified him by promising their good offices to obtain a better hearing for the new faith in their home land. They returned with a priest.

When these new emissaries of Olaf and Christianity arrived and presented their religion to the Althing, for a time open war between the Christian and the pagan party seemed imminent. One of the leading men, after prolonged meditation, suggested that the two sides compromise and so avoid needless bloodshed. A law was enacted to the effect that all the population should be Christian and the unbaptized be baptized, but that existing regulations concerning infanticide and the eating of horse flesh should stand, and that secret sacrifices to the old gods should be met only with a minor penalty. This was

---

popular account in Sveinbjorn Johnson, *Pioneers of Freedom: An Account of the Icelanders and the Icelandic Free State, 874-1262* (Boston, The Stratford Co., 1930, pp. vii, 361), pp. 186-191.

[686] Snorre Sturlason, *Heimskringla,* Book VII, Chaps. 81, 82; Gjerset, *History of the Norwegian People,* Vol. I, p. 191. See also on the conversion of Iceland, Gjerset, *History of Iceland,* pp. 48 ff.

[687] Gjerset, *History of the Norwegian People,* Vol. I, p. 192.

[688] Snorre Sturlason, *op. cit.,* Book VII, Chaps. 73, 84; Ari Thorgilsson, *Íslendingabók,* Chap. 7; *Kristnisaga,* Chaps. 7-9. *Kristnisaga,* Chap. 5, declares that Thangbrand was a son of the Count of Bremen.

in the year 1000, that of Olaf's death.[689] Christians and such pagans as survived long lived together in comparative harmony.

A few winters later paganism was officially abolished.[690] Olaf Haraldsson interested himself in having the laws altered that protected the remnants of heathenism.[691] Olaf gave, too, a bell and timber for a church.[692] At least one bishop was sent there by him.[693] For years the infant Christianity of the island suffered from a shortage of clergy. Some chieftains who had built churches received ordination and so combined, as in pagan times, the functions of priest and civil leader. Other priests were chosen from among boys who had little training and remained in subjection to the chiefs.[694] For a time, too, Iceland depended on foreign Bishops.[695] However, within a few years Isleif, a native said by some to have been baptized as a child by Thangbrand, was consecrated Bishop and began a line of Icelandic prelates. His own son was later Bishop for many years and was greatly respected.[696] These native Bishops helped to improve the status of the Church. Isleif was consecrated by Adalbert, the famous Archbishop of Hamburg-Bremen,[697] who thus extended his archiepiscopal influence to that distant island. Bishops were regularly elected by the island assembly, the Althing, and sent to the Continent for ordination.[698]

The suggestion has been made that in spite of the nominal conversion, much of paganism long persisted. The evidence offered is in sagas, the best of them written in the thirteenth century, which so perfectly portray pre-Christian conditions and are so little affected by Latin influence that it is assumed that they could have been composed only in an environment in which the old customs persisted in but little altered form.[699]

The great explosion of energy which distributed the Scandinavians through much of Europe and westward to Iceland sent emigrants to Greenland. The first settlements of the Norsemen in Greenland were made towards the end of the tenth century, from Iceland. The leader was Eric the Red. He seems to have been a restless individualist of violent temper, for he and his father had

---

[689] Ari Thorgilsson, *op. cit.*, Chap. 7; Snorre Sturlason, *op. cit.*, Book VII, Chap. 95.
[690] Ari Thorgilsson, *op. cit.*, Chap. 7.
[691] Snorre Sturlason, *op. cit.*, Book VIII, Chaps. 60, 124.
[692] Snorre Sturlason, *op. cit.*, Book VIII, Chap. 124.
[693] Gjerset, *History of Iceland*, pp. 64, 65.
[694] Gjerset, *History of Iceland*, pp. 65, 66.
[695] Ari Thorgilsson, *op. cit.*, Chap. 8.
[696] Ari Thorgilsson, *op. cit.*, Chap. 9.
[697] Adam of Bremen, *Gesta Hammaburgensis Ecclesiæ Pontificum*, Book IV, Chap. 36 (35); *Kristnisaga*, Chaps. 12, 13; *Thattr of Isleifi Biskupi, passim*. Through Isleif Adalbert's jurisdiction is said to have been extended to Greenland.—Adam of Bremen, *op. cit.*, Book IV, Chap. 36 (35).
[698] Gjerset, *op. cit.*, p. 68.
[699] Gjerset, *History of the Norwegian People*, Vol. I, pp. 193, 194.

been compelled to leave Norway for manslaughter, and he himself had been outlawed from Iceland for a similar offence.[700] The Norse settlements were on the west coast of Greenland. Their population probably never much exceeded two thousand.[701] Eric was a pagan,[702] but it may be that Christianity first came through one of the early immigrants.[703] However, it was Leif, a son of Eric, who propagated Christianity among the new settlements. Leif had gone to Norway, had there come in contact with Olaf Tryggvason, had become a Christian, and had spent a winter with the King. In the spring Olaf sent him to Greenland, to bring the settlers to the faith. With him went a priest. Eric took Leif into his house, but was unfriendly to his son's strange God and declared the priest "a hurtful person." However, the new creed seems to have won speedy acceptance from many and a church was soon built.[704] Here, as in Iceland after the initial friction, Christians and pagans seem not to have allowed the division in faith to have added much disharmony.

As the years passed, other churches and a cathedral were erected. In 1123 the Greenlanders sent one of their number to Norway to obtain the establishment of a diocese of their own. In response to his request a Norwegian was consecrated and eventually reached Greenland.[705] He gave such prestige to the Episcopate that the Bishop henceforth became the chief personage of the island and was its civil as well as its ecclesiastical head.[706] The colony appears to have had its most prosperous years in the eleventh and twelfth centuries. In the fourteenth century it declined and in the sixteenth century it seems to have become extinct. Bishops continued to be appointed, but did not reach their see.[707] In 1492 a Papal letter declared that for about eighty years no bishop or priest had resided there and that Christianity had almost died out.[708] Cut off from Iceland and Europe and from clerical ministrations, probably pressed by an increasingly unfavourable climate, the survivors seem gradually to have died out, some of them killed by the Eskimos. Yet even in the fifteenth century, so archæology has shown, the feeble remnant retained their faith. Amalgamation

[700] Ari Thorgilsson, *op. cit.*, Chap. 6; Snorre Sturlason, *op. cit.*, Book VII, Chap. 86; *The Saga of Eric the Red*, translated in Reeves, *The Finding of Wineland the Good*, pp. 29, 30.

[701] Hovgaard, *The Voyages of the Norsemen to America*, p. 26; Gjerset, *History of the Norwegian People*, Vol. I, p. 198.

[702] Snorre Sturlason, *op. cit.*, Book VIII, Chap. 96.

[703] Snorre Sturlason, *op. cit.*, Book VII, Chap. 97. The date of the Christian settler from the Hebrides and its chronological relation to Leif's missionary labours is uncertain.

[704] Snorre Sturlason, *op. cit.*, Book VII, Chaps. 86, 96; *The Saga of Eric the Red*, translation in Reeves, *op. cit.*, pp. 36, 37.

[705] Hermannsson, *The Book of the Icelanders*, p. 83, citing *Einars Tháttr Sokkasonar*.

[706] Kendrik, *A History of the Vikings*, p. 365.

[707] Hovgaard, *The Voyages of the Norsemen to America*, p. 40.

[708] *Ibid.*; Gjerset, *History of the Norwegian People*, Vol. I, p. 202.

with the Eskimos may eventually have taken place, both in blood and in manner of life.[709] In the end, nothing but ruins remained to confirm the evidence of the fragmentary literary records of the former existence of a Christian population.[710]

It was from Greenland that the first known introduction of Christianity to the Americas was made. On the way to Greenland on his errand from Olaf, Leif is said to have been driven off his course and to have discovered a new land where vines, trees, and self-sown wheat were growing. In that generation, voyages, one of them by Leif himself, were made to what appears to have been the shores of North America. The region was called Vinland or Wineland. We need not enter into the debate over the validity of the details of the stories or over the precise parts of North America which were reached. Here we need simply note that no permanent settlements seem to have been effected. Nor does any attempt appear to have been made to convert the aborigines. The latters' first contacts with the white man were largely accompanied by violence. Yet it is of interest that among these explorers were Christians and that they seem to have been the converts of Leif and his priest. Their new faith made little difference in their conduct, but at least they bore the Christian name.[711]

We must return from these far-flung western frontiers of Scandinavian exploration and settlement to Scandinavia itself. Of the three major kingdoms, the last fully to enter the Christian fold was Sweden. This was partly because of geography. Sweden was more remote from Christian lands than either of its two neighbours. Across the Baltic it was faced by pagan peoples. Perhaps for this reason it was later in having Christian monarchs. When Christian kings came to the throne, they had a much larger area to deal with than did the Christian kings of Denmark and were less disposed to use force to obtain conversions than were the two Olafs of Norway. Here, too, we know much less of the part of the *thing* in the process of conversion than we do in Norway and Iceland.

As we have seen, the introduction of Christianity into Sweden goes back at least to the time of Anskar and to Christian captives whom he found there. As we have also seen, in the ninth century Anskar visited the land more than

[709] Hovgaard, *op. cit.*, pp. 41-50; Gjerset, *op. cit.*, Vol. I, pp. 202-204; Kendrick, *op. cit.*, pp. 365-367.

[710] For a brief account of these ruins, including those of churches and the cathedral, see Hovgaard, *op. cit.*, pp. 26-35.

[711] The texts which deal with the Norse expeditions to Vinland are translated in Hovgaard, *op. cit.*, and in Reeves, *op. cit.* Comments on the texts are to be found in these two books, and Hovgaard attempts to locate the regions to which the Norsemen went. He professes to identify them as far south as Cape Cod.

once and won converts. In Anskar's time, moreover, a Bishop Gauzbert was consecrated for Sweden, and priests resided in the land for longer or shorter intervals. Again as we have said, by 936 the Christian communities appear to have disappeared, for Archbishop Unni of Hamburg, who visited Sweden in that year and died there, could not find them.

When, finally, the conversion of Sweden took place, England seems to have had a larger part in the process than did the Germans and the See of Hamburg-Bremen—or, for that matter, than did even the Danes and Norwegians. Yet from all of these peoples and regions came contributions to the nascent Swedish Christianity. In some way, just how and whence are not known, but probably through commercial contacts, Christianity appears to have been introduced to the island of Gotland, which was a prominent trading centre.[712] Early in the tenth century, or before the death of Archbishop Unni, Swedes who had gone to England as merchants or soldiers and had there been baptized returned to their fatherland and brought their newly-found faith with them.[713] Archbishop Unni's successor, Adaldag, consecrated as Bishop to Sweden Odinkar, senior, of noble Danish stock.[714] Somewhat later we hear of a Bishop Folkward, consecrated by the Archbishop of Hamburg-Bremen, who, driven out of the Slavic lands in the present northern Germany, went to Sweden.[715] Whether permanent results followed the work of these two bishops we do not know. Bruno of Querfurt, who had been made a missionary archbishop by the Pope, who had laboured in Central Europe, and who in 1009 suffered martyrdom among the Prussians, sent a bishop to Sweden who is said to have baptized hundreds.[716] By the command of King Olaf Haraldsson some of the missionaries from England who assisted him in Norway went also to Sweden and there preached to the pagans.[717] Not far from the year 1030, or in the days of Olaf Haraldsson, one Wolfred from England preached in Sweden and died for the faith.[718]

A little earlier than these last events we hear of the baptism of a King of Sweden. King Eric, as we have seen, at one time drove King Sweyn out of his Danish realms. Eric was a pagan, but is said to have been baptized in Denmark, perhaps persuaded by Otto III of Germany, who had defeated him.

[712] Wordsworth, *The National Church of Sweden*, p. 58.
[713] Hallendorff and Schück, *History of Sweden*, pp. 25-29.
[714] Adam of Bremen, *Gesta Hammaburgensis Ecclesiæ Pontificum*, Book II, Chap. 26 (23).
[715] Adam of Bremen, *op. cit.*, Book II, Chap. 46 (44).
[716] Hauck, *Kirchengeschichte Deutschlands*, Vol. III, pp. 630, 646, citing a letter of Bruno to Henry II; Robinson, *The Conversion of Europe*, p. 426.
[717] Adam of Bremen, *op. cit.*, Book II, Chap. 57 (55).
[718] Adam of Bremen, *op. cit.*, Book II, Chap. 62 (60).

Missionaries took the opportunity to go to Sweden, but Eric is reported later to have reverted to his old gods.[719]

The first King of Sweden who can really be called a Christian or who did much to further the spread of the faith was Olof Skötkonung, a contemporary of Olaf Tryggvason. It was he who joined with Sweyn to defeat the Norwegian King. How Olof Skötkonung became a Christian we do not know. One theory declares that he was baptized in 1008, or eight years after his defeat of Olaf Tryggvason. Or the rite may have been administered by one Sigfrid, who is said to have been English.[720] However, Olof seems to have been a Christian some years earlier than this, when, before the year 1000, he made his compact with Sweyn.[721] Olof is reported to have been zealous in spreading his faith and to have desired to destroy the temple at Upsala, the chief fane of the old gods. The pagans quite naturally objected and what seems to have been a compromise was effected. Olof was allowed to practise his Christian faith and was permitted to rule in the best part of the realm and there to build the Church as he liked. He was not, however, to compel any one to accept his creed. Olof's religious activities, then, were largely confined to Västergötland, in the region next to the portion of Norway in which the Church was most firmly established. Here, in Skara, he inaugurated an episcopate and had its Bishop, Thurgot, consecrated by Archbishop Unwan of Hamburg-Bremen.[722] Thus, while Olof recognized the jurisdiction of Hamburg-Bremen, he retained control over the nomination of Swedish bishops. Even though Olof left the shrine at Upsala undisturbed, his adherence to Christianity must have dealt it a severe blow, for presumably he would no longer participate in its sacrifices. Not far from Upsala, moreover, he made of the town of Sigtuna the chief commercial centre of the land, and must have given to it something of a Christian aspect.[723]

Not only during the time of Olof, but after it English missionaries laboured in Sweden. We hear especially of Eskil and David, who were later esteemed as saints. Much of the ecclesiastical terminology and architecture showed English influence.[724] Several English saints, such as St. Alban, St. Botulf, and St. Dunstan, were venerated.[725]

[719] Adam of Bremen, *op. cit.*, Book II, Chap. 38 (36).

[720] Wordsworth, *op. cit.*, p. 71. Snorre Sturlason, *Heimskringla*, Book VII, Chap. 114, seems to imply that the Swedes were pagans at the time of Olaf Tryggvason's death.

[721] Adam of Bremen, *op. cit.*, Book II, Chap. 39 (37).

[722] Adam of Bremen, *op. cit.*, Book II, Chap. 58 (56). On the temple in Upsala, see Adam of Bremen, *op. cit.*, Book IV, Chaps. 26, 27; Keary, *The Vikings of Western Christendom*, p. 36.

[723] Hallendorff and Schück, *History of Sweden*, pp. 25-29.

[724] Svanström and Palmstierna, *A Short History of Sweden*, pp. 19-23.

[725] Hallendorff and Schück, *op. cit.*, pp. 25-29.

Olof was succeeded about 1021 by his son Anund Jakob, who enjoyed a relatively quiet reign of about thirty years (to 1051). Under Anund Jakob Christianity continued to spread. It is from this time that some of the Christian runic monuments probably date, evidence that the faith was gaining.[726] Yet he is said to have had to leave the kingdom for a time because he refused to offer sacrifices to the old gods.[727] Anund Jakob was followed by his half-brother Emund, who, a Christian, made a determined effort to free himself from the jurisdiction of Hamburg-Bremen. That see was then presided over by the dynamic Adalbert, who entertained such ambitious dreams of enhancing its authority throughout the North. One Osmund, an Englishman, a nephew of Sigfrid who had studied at Bremen, had obtained ordination from an arch-bishop in Poland and claimed to have been consecrated by the Pope as Arch-bishop for Sweden. Emund supported Osmund. An unseemly contest fol-lowed, but eventually a reconciliation appears to have been achieved, with the recognition of the rights of Adalbert and the consecration by him of several bishops for Sweden. Emund was followed in about 1057 by Stenkil, who was favourable to Hamburg-Bremen. It seems probable that Osmund went to Ely, in England. At least we hear of an Osmund who had been Bishop in Sweden coming to Ely and dying there.[728] Stenkil was warmly Christian. Yet in his day and even after it Upsala continued to boast its famous temple with its priests and sacrifices.[729] A Bishop Adalward the Younger, consecrated by the Archbishop of Hamburg-Bremen, fixed his seat at Sigtuna, which, it will be remembered, was near Upsala. He won many to the Christian faith. He wished, too, to destroy the Upsala temple, but the King hesitated to take the step lest it lead to a pagan reaction and to his own expulsion from the realm.[730] After Stenkil's death (1066) disorder broke out and a persecution of Christians followed.[731]

Stenkil's son Inge reigned for some years (died c. 1111?). He attempted to abolish sacrifices and to require baptism of at least some of his subjects. In consequence, he was forced to abdicate, and his brother-in-law, Sweyn, or Blotsweyn, ruled for a time and endeavoured to restore paganism. It was under Sweyn that the English missionary Eskil suffered martyrdom—

[726] Adam of Bremen, op. cit., Book II, Chaps. 59 (57), 73 (71). On the runic monuments a large literature has come into existence. A recent work edited by an outstanding author-ity is Otto v. Friesen, Runorna (Nordisk Kultur, VI) (Stockholm, Albert Bonniers Verlag, 1933, pp. 264).

[727] Adam of Bremen, op. cit., Schol. 84 (85), 140 (136).

[728] Adam of Bremen, op. cit., Book II, Chap. 15 (14); Book IV, Chap. 77; Liber Eliensis (London, 1848, pp. viii, 299), Book II, Chap. 99 (pp. 220, 221).

[729] Adam of Bremen, op. cit., Book IV, Chaps. 26, 27.

[730] Adam of Bremen, op. cit., Book IV, Chap. 30.

[731] Adam of Bremen, op. cit., Book III, Chap. 53 (52), Book IV, Chap. 9.

at Strängnäs, the *thing* place for Södermanland, on the site now occupied by the Bishop's residence. In general, Christianity was stronger in the South, nearer Christian lands, and paganism more persistent in the North. Inge later fought his way back to power. With his restoration Christianity finally triumphed. Paganism was not yet extinct. Not until the close of the twelfth century did the remoter districts of Sweden become Christian. Yet the doom of the old gods was sure. Inge became the real organizer of the Church in Sweden. Under him appeared bishoprics which persisted. Buildings from his time still exist.[732]

Beginning about two years after Inge's death a period of civil strife ensued. However, in about the year 1130 one Sverker mounted the throne. He was an ardent Christian and in the quarter of a century of his reign he and his wife called in the Cistercians. The Cistercian movement was then in the first flush of its youth and of that reforming zeal which attracted to it throughout Western Europe so many of the ardent souls who sought a perfect Christian life. The Cistercians seem to have been the earliest to establish monasticism in Sweden. It was therefore through their houses and not through the corrupt and easy-going older foundations that Sweden came to know monastic Christianity.[733] This meant on the part of Sverker the desire for a closer connexion with Rome and for stricter standards in the Church. It was also Sverker who began the construction of a cathedral at Upsala, where half a century before the most famous pagan temple of Scandinavia had been.[734] When, in 1164, after the death of Sverker, Sweden was given its first Metropolitan, the seat of the Archiepiscopate was fixed at Upsala, and the first holder of the see was a Cistercian.[735] Thus the chief centre of Swedish religious life remained where it had been, but the first head of the new hierarchy was from the strictest of the Christian groups.

Christianity in Sweden, then, in its formative years felt the effect of the new tides of life which were stirring in the Church of the West. Even before the coming of the Cistercians it had done so. In 1080 the great Pope Gregory VII (Hildebrand), who represented the reforming movements of his day, wrote to Inge, among other things asking that he send a bishop and priest to Rome to acquaint the Apostolic See with the Swedes and to receive Papal instruc-

---

[732] Wordsworth, *The National Church of Sweden*, p. 81; Hallendorff and Schück, *op. cit.*, p. 32; Svanström and Palmstierna, *op. cit.*, p. 25; Robinson, *The Conversion of Europe*, pp. 482, 483.

[733] Svanström and Palmstierna, *op. cit.*, p. 25.

[734] Wordsworth, *op. cit.*, p. 81, citing E. Benzelius Filius, *Monumenta Hist. Vet.*, p. 20 (Upsala, 1709).

[735] Svanström and Palmstierna, *op. cit.*, p. 26.

tions.[736] This is the first Papal letter of which we know addressed to a Swedish monarch.

Yet Christianity in Sweden reproduced in part the organizational texture of pre-Christian times. Under the new order, as under the old, as we have said, Upsala was the spiritual centre of the kingdom. In general, the dioceses corresponded to the provinces and the seat of the Bishop and the cathedral were at the *thing* place of the province. Bishops, indeed, were long elected by the *things* and confirmed by the King.[737]

The Swedes were the last to come into the Christian Church, not only of the Scandinavian but of the Teutonic peoples. The story of the winning of the Germanic folk is a long one. It begins in the fourth century and continues into the twelfth—a span of about eight centuries. Geographically it stretches from the Goths north of the Black Sea to the Norse settlers in Iceland and Greenland.

This chapter has, perforce, been very prolonged, for it has covered all but the first fifth of this time chart. In it, too, has been included the intimately related account of the completion of the conversion of the Celts—a process which was much further along in the year 500 than was that of the Teutons. We have watched the disappearance of the last remnants of the formal pagan cults in Italy and Spain and the incorporation of the Arian Teutons—mainly Goths and Lombards—into the Roman Catholic Church. We have surveyed a similar series of events in Gaul—the passing of the Arianism of the Goths and Burgundians and the triumph of Roman Catholicism. We have witnessed the continuation of the conversion of the pagan Franks and have seen the Frankish state, now officially Christian and Roman Catholic, become the dominant political power in Western Europe. We have traced the impact upon the Christianity of Western Europe of the remarkable monastic life of Ireland. We have watched Irish monks and anchorites bring increased earnestness into the Church of the Frankish domains and of Northern Italy. We have seen them, too, plant centres of an advancing Christianity among the Teutonic peoples in parts of the valleys of the Rhine and the Danube, in Central Germany, and especially in the modern Scotland and Northern England. We have repeated the story of the conversion of the Germanic settlers in England. We have

---

[736] Letter of Gregory VII, in Migne, *Pat. Lat.*, Vol. CXLVIII, Cols. 584, 585. A letter of Gregory VII, in 1081, addressed to "the Kings of the Visigoths" (Migne, *Pat. Lat.*, Vol. CXLVIII, Cols. 617, 618), seems also meant for the Swedes.—Wordsworth, *op. cit.*, p. 83.

[737] Hallendorff and Schück, *History of Sweden*, p. 41.

watched Christianity spread northward beyond the regions where once were the frontiers of the Roman Empire into the Low Countries and Central and Western Germany—especially in Frisia, Thuringia, Hesse, and the lands of the Saxons. Then we have seen it survive the blows dealt it by the violent and prolonged inroads of the Scandinavians, win the Scandinavian emigrants, eventually triumph in the very homes of the invaders, and successfully follow them into their distant colonies in Iceland and Greenland.

The order followed has not been entirely chronological. Yet in the main the geographical and the time sequence have tended to coincide.

Here is to be found part of the answer to one of the questions which we propounded at the outset of this study and to which we recur again and again: By what processes did Christianity spread?

In the first place it must be said that towards the North-west Christianity tended to advance from frontier to contiguous frontier.

In the second place, and as a corollary, the faith was propagated largely by the peoples most recently won to the faith, and not by those who had long been Christian. Only among the Anglo-Saxons did Italian missionaries play an important part in the conversion of the North. It was Arian Goths who spread the faith among their fellow Goths. Presumably it was through the Goths that the Vandals, Burgundians, and Lombards first entered the Christian fold. From the Irish, converts of the fifth and sixth centuries, came the majority of the missionaries of the sixth and seventh centuries. They were especially important in the winning of what are now Scotland, Northern England, and parts of Germany. The Anglo-Saxons, converts of the seventh century, were the source of the leading missionaries to the Low Countries, to much of the Rhine Valley, and to Hesse and Thuringia. From their number came some of the missionaries to the Saxons. Clergy from England, many of them Anglo-Saxons, and others, judging by their names, from recently converted Scandinavian immigrant stock, had a leading place in spreading the faith in Denmark, Norway, and Sweden. Centres in the lands of the Saxons, especially the monastery of Corvey and the Archiepiscopal See of Hamburg-Bremen, had an important share in the propagation of Christianity in Scandinavia. Some Danes were missionaries in Norway and Sweden, and recent converts from Norway had a prominent part in the establishment of the Church in Iceland and Greenland.

In the third place, this spread from frontier to frontier is not surprising. In an era when travel was arduous and often dangerous, and when commerce had dwindled far below its levels in Roman times, it was to be expected that the faith would be propagated by those most immediately in touch with pagan peoples. Moreover, Italy, which would have been a natural source of missions, was wasted again and again by invasions and wars. In the Frankish domains, as we have seen, the Church, because of its accumulated wealth, tended to fall under the control of those whose chief interests lay in its material possessions. A secularized ecclesiastical structure could scarcely be the source of new missionary movements. Fresh life, when it broke out, directed its energies chiefly to the reform of the Church and not to the extension of its borders.

In the fourth place, the share of the Papacy in the spread of the faith diminished roughly in proportion to the distance from Rome. It was marked in South-eastern England, in the Low Countries, in the Rhine Valley, and in Central and Southern Germany, important but less marked in Northern England, decidedly less prominent among the Saxons, and practically negligible in Ireland, Scotland, Scandinavia, Iceland, and Greenland. In Scandinavia Rome appears not to have concerned itself with the work of conversion until after that had been completed. Only to England did the Papacy take the initiative in inaugurating a foreign mission. Elsewhere it was content with placing its imprimatur upon labours already in progress or with seeking to bring newly emerging churches into conformity with its pattern of ecclesiastical life.

So, too, in the fifth place, in Scandinavia, monasteries had a much smaller share in the actual process of conversion than in England or among the Germans. When, later, the monastic system entered, presumably it aided in shaping the Christianity of the newly converted populations. It did not, however, have the part in the actual introduction of the faith that it possessed in the missions sprung from the Irish tradition. In missions which stemmed from Columba and Columban, or those led or inspired by Willibrord and Boniface, Englishmen more or less directly in the stream of Irish influence, monasteries were the chief centres of missionary enthusiasm and monks the main agents. Indeed, from the time of St. Martin of Tours, Roman Catholic Christianity had been propagated largely by monks. By the time of the conversion of the Scandinavians, however, Irish monasticism had suffered too severely from the inroads of the Vikings to be a source of missions. Then, too, the older English monasticism was decayed or secularized, and the revival associated with the name of Dunstan appears not to have led to the type of monastery which nourished the missionary passion.

In the sixth place, as we have again and again seen, conversion was largely by groups. Repeatedly it was engineered by the natural leader of a people, the monarch. Occasionally the king used force. Of this some of the Scandinavian monarchs were notable examples. Often the ruler consulted legally recognized assemblies of leading men. At least once, as in Iceland, where no king was recognized, an assembly took the question of conversion under advisement. Sometimes the king obviously acted from religious conviction. In some instances, as in the case of Harald Bluetooth of Denmark and Olaf Tryggvason and Olaf Haraldsson of Norway, the religious appears to have been mixed with the political motive. The monarch was attempting to increase his authority and encountered his chief resistance among local magnates who identified their privileges with the old faith. Occasionally monarchs, most notably those of the Carolingian line, furthered missions as agencies of political conquest.

Another of the recurring questions of our study is: Why did Christianity spread? For the Teutonic peoples of Western Europe our evidence is too fragmentary for satisfactory answers. Obviously several factors entered and no one or simple reply suffices. Thousands among the Saxons and Scandinavians accepted baptism because they were compelled to do so. For many Scandinavians the inherited faith disintegrated through contact with the culture to the South. They were, accordingly, more receptive to the Christian message than if they had held fanatically to paganism. Another reason must probably be sought in the prestige of the civilization which the Vikings, even while they raided it, held in awe. Some pagans came to the conviction that Christianity could do for them what they had asked of the old gods and do it more effectively. So Christ became a more potent help in war than Thor, or was esteemed as a hero who had conquered death. Many appear to have been attracted by the more satisfying answers which Christianity gave to the haunting questions of the meaning of human life and the fate of man beyond the grave. Closely allied with this may have been the desire to enter the Christian heaven and the fear of the pangs of hell. Such, at least, may be the inference from some of the stories in Bede. Undoubtedly the conviction and enthusiasm of the missionaries proved contagious. It may have been, too, that the lives of missionaries, with an austerity and a self-control alien to much of pagan life, first awakened disdain, then wonder, and eventually admiration.

Many of the records of the conversions and the missions of this period are contemporary documents, or only one generation removed from the events. As one reads them, he is impressed chiefly by the enthusiasm and the conviction with which the faith was propagated. Here seems to have been one of the basic reasons for the spread of Christianity to the Northern peoples. Its agents were not intent upon incorporating barbarian folk into a higher culture. Nor did most of them come with any arrogance born of the contempt of civilized for uncivilized peoples. An assurance of the truth of the religion which they professed, a zeal for the destruction of its rivals, and a desire to give its benefits to others seem to have constituted the driving power of the missions of the period. In this appears to have been the major cause of the spread of Christianity.

Almost as difficult is a question which perhaps ought to have been placed first: What was the Christianity which spread? To this a part of the answer is obvious. It was Roman Catholic Christianity with its creeds, its Scriptures, its sacraments and ceremonies, its monasticism, and its hierarchy. In formal outlines it was altered very little in the centuries covered by this chapter. Probably the chief changes were those involved in the partial adaptation of the Church to the developing feudal system and in the emergence of the new monastic movements associated with the names of Cluny and Citeaux. Missionary monks and clergy sought to bring their converts into conformity with this official Christianity. In laws enacted by Christian monarchs to enforce Christian practices and in the actions of synods we have some hint of what moral, ritual, and social standards were deemed essential. Almost always, however, these were formulated a generation or more after the work of conversion had been completed and do not give us clear assurance of the content of the message first preached to the pagans. Since none, or almost none, of the non-Christians were literate, no books or pamphlets were addressed to them. An apologetic literature such as that composed in the years when the Græco-Roman world was being won did not exist. We have no first-hand transcripts of addresses or sermons directed to the pagans or the neophytes. The penitentials composed by the Irish monks arose out of efforts to improve the standards of Christian living and acquaint us with both the ideals inculcated and the current departures from them. Yet they were designed for Christians, some of them of many generations' standing, and not for non-Christians. We need to remember, moreover, that in many regions missionary priests were usually few in proportion to the population, that baptisms were frequently wholesale, and that the masses of the converts must at the outset have had only the most rudimentary acquaintance with the faith they were adopting. In Norway and Iceland the King and other laymen seem to have made most of the first approaches to pagans, and presumably their knowledge of the faith was far from extensive. Probably, therefore, acceptance of the faith appeared to the convert chiefly to entail the abandonment of his old gods for the new, the substitution of one religious ritual for another, and a few alterations in his morals and family relations. This for the average neophyte was probably the Christianity which was adopted.

In joining the Christian community no such sharp break with the past and with surrounding society was entailed as in the first three Christian centuries.

Only in the course of several generations could the Church assimilate the thousands who had so quickly and with so little instruction been gathered into its fold. As we are to see more fully in a later chapter, in the process the Church itself, and with it popular Christianity, was altered. The formal creeds remained the same. The official machinery of the Church was stern against departure from them or anything which it deemed heresy. Gradually, too, the main outline of the type of ecclesiastical machinery developed in the Roman Empire, with its priesthood and its hierarchy, was adopted in the newly won lands. Quickly, however, an indigenous clergy arose who inevitably reflected much of the popular Christianity out of which they sprang.

As Christianity spread from frontier to frontier, it was unavoidably modified and reflected in part the cultural atmosphere to which it had last been acclimated. Into this influence of the environment we must not go until a subsequent chapter. Here, however, we must note that it helped to determine the type of Christianity which spread. That which won the Anglo-Saxons was not quite that which the English missionaries propagated in the Low Countries and among the Germans. Nor was that which was transmitted to Scandinavia exactly the kind of English Christianity which a Willibrord and a Boniface knew. In the two centuries and more between Boniface and the conversion of the North, England had passed through bitter experiences. The Church and the popular Christianity of the England of the tenth century were not those of the eighth. We must repeat, however, that in its creeds and in the main outlines of its organization the Christianity of the West had not been changed in the nearly seven centuries covered by this chapter.

The Western branch of that type of Christianity which had become dominant in the Roman Empire of the first five centuries had achieved a noteworthy series of triumphs. It had, to be sure, gradually drawn apart from the Catholic Christianity of the East, and it had lost to Islam practically all of North Africa and much of the Iberian Peninsula and of Sicily. On the other hand, it had eliminated Arianism, for a time a dangerous rival, and in North-western Europe its boundaries had been extended far beyond those of that Empire which it had survived. It had outlived the collapse of the political, economic, social, and intellectual structure with which it had been closely associated and had gained more territory than it had lost. It had won peoples who, centuries later, were to have a large share in carrying Christianity into lands of which the Church of the Roman Empire had never heard. Indeed, judged by later developments, for the future history and expansion of the faith, next to the Roman Empire, North-western Europe proved the most important territorial accession in all the centuries of the spread of Christianity. In it were to develop some of the most powerful movements which that religion has known. From it and its colonies was to take place the major part of the expansion of Christianity in the nineteenth and twentieth centuries. Since the fifth century the regions covered in this chapter, together with their colonies, have been the scene of most of the vigorous life of the Christian movement.

It was chiefly from Western Europe that Christianity spread into Central Europe and to the southern and eastern shores of the Baltic. To that phase of our story we must now turn.

Chapter III

THE SPREAD OF ROMAN CATHOLIC CHRISTIANITY AMONG THE PEOPLES OF CENTRAL EUROPE AND ALONG THE SOUTHERN AND EASTERN SHORES OF THE BALTIC—THE AVARS, THE SOUTHERN SLAVS, THE MORAVIANS, THE BOHEMIANS, THE MAGYARS, THE POLES, THE WENDS, THE FINNS, THE LAPPS, THE ESTS, THE LETTS, THE PRUSSIANS, AND THE LITHUANIANS—AND ATTEMPTS OF ROMAN CATHOLICS TO WIN THE JEWS

IT WAS not alone among the Celts and the Teutonic peoples of Western Europe that the Roman form of Catholic Christianity spread in the thousand years between the fifth and the sixteenth century. In Central Europe it regained territory lost during the barbarian invasions of the fifth century and there and on the southern and eastern shores of the Baltic it won peoples and areas which never before had been within the Christian sphere of influence.

The majority of these peoples were Slavs. As we have seen, in the early Christian centuries the Slavs had been spreading until in the sixth century they became sufficiently prominent on the Roman frontiers to attract the attention of the Mediterranean world. In the course of time they moved into the Balkans, into what are now Eastern Germany, Czecho-Slovakia, Poland, some of the regions along the Baltic, and over much of Russia. Eventually the western portions of the Slavs adopted the Roman type of Catholicism and the eastern groups the form of Catholicism which had Constantinople for its centre. In addition to the Slavs, the tier of peoples east of the Teutons who accepted Roman Catholic Christianity included fragments of the Avars and the Magyars, a few of the Lapps, and some of the Baltic peoples.

In the story of the expansion of Roman Catholic Christianity into Central Europe and along the southern and eastern shores of the Baltic, a chronological arrangement would prove very confusing. In Western Europe Christianity, as we have seen, spread from people to people in what was, although only roughly and with exceptions, an orderly time sequence. In Central Europe and the eastern shores of the Baltic it advanced from frontier to frontier, but not in such fashion that the various peoples can always be arranged according to the years of their conversion. Here along its borders Christianity was expanding at approximately the same time in a number of places. The order of treatment must be by regions and groups. Yet, so far as possible, the narrative will be made to conform with the calendar.

This non-chronological, fragmentary treatment must not be allowed entirely to obscure the comprehensive view which a strictly synchronized or annalistic account might give. Simultaneously great movements were taking place on a number of fronts, not only in Central Europe, but elsewhere. In the West the ninth century saw the completion of the conversion of the Saxons. In Central Europe it witnessed the entrance of the first large numbers of Slavic converts into Roman Catholic Christianity. Both accessions to Christianity were associated with the expansion of the Franks under the Carolingians. In the Balkans and the regions north of the Black Sea the ninth century was marked by the extension of Greek Orthodox Christianity among the Slavic invaders, the Bulgars, and the Turkish Khazars. It saw the loss, however, of some territory in Sicily to the Moslems. The tenth century was signalized in the West by the beginning of the conversion of the Northmen, not only in their colonies within Christendom, but in their homelands. It included the further extension of Roman Catholic Christianity among the Slavs of Central Europe and of Greek Christianity in the Balkans and among the Northmen and their Slavic subjects in Russia. In Asia, however, it watched the temporary extinction of Nestorian Christianity in China. The eleventh and twelfth centuries saw the completion of the conversion of the Scandinavians, more gains of Roman Catholic Christianity among the Slavs, the conversion of the Magyars, the elimination of Moslem political dominion in Sicily and Southern Italy, and the amazing efforts of Western Christians through the Crusades to establish themselves against the Moslems in Syria and Palestine. In Russia, Greek Orthodox Christianity was being consolidated and extended. In Central Asia the Nestorians were registering gains. The thirteenth and fourteenth centuries embraced the completion of the conversion of the Slavs and of the peoples on the Baltic—so far as these entered the Roman Catholic fold. They also saw a fresh threat to Christian civilization in the great Mongol invasions and, in Western (but not in Eastern) Russia, the beginning of recovery from the Mongols. In Asia they were marked by a rapid extension of Nestorianism in China. They embraced, too, the far-flung missions of the Dominicans and Franciscans in Eastern Europe and through much of Asia. The fifteenth century witnessed fresh losses on a huge scale to the Moslems. The Mongols, the Mongol converts to Islam, and Timurlane erased much of Nestorian Christianity. The Ottoman Turks, Moslems, made an end of the Christian empire in Constantinople and established Islam successfully in South-eastern Europe. Only in the Iberian Peninsula did Christianity win back territory from the Moslems, and only in Russia and a few islands in the Atlantic did it make some fresh gains against primitive paganism.

The processes by which conversion took place in Central Europe and along the Baltic were, in general, those which we have already seen in Western Europe. This was to be expected, for from the eighth until the twelfth century, as we have suggested, the territorial advance of Latin Christianity was proceeding simultaneously in the West and in the adjoining tier of lands on the East. Entrance into the Church was generally by groups and *en masse*. Usually kings and other secular rulers took an active part in the initiation and conduct of missions and in the decision of the group. The majority of actual missionaries were monks. From time to time the Papacy had an important share, infrequently as a directing agency, more often as a stabilizing centre of reference making for uniformity and for a conscious fellowship of the many diverse and warring racial and national groups in one great community—"Christendom."

However, at least two marked differences in the processes of conversion must be noted between the two areas. In the first place, the conversion of Western Europe was begun and finished earlier. In the West, even in the fifth century the barbarians who could not be classed as Roman provincials were being baptized, and the faith had spread outside the bounds of the Empire to Ireland. Scandinavia, including Iceland and Greenland, the latest of the Teutonic regions to enter the Church, had become nominally Christian before the end of the twelfth century. In Central Europe, on the other hand, not until the eighth and ninth centuries did Christianity begin to make notable headway among the barbarian invaders, and it was the ninth century before it made important gains outside the areas once occupied by the Roman Empire. Not until late in the fourteenth or even until the fifteenth century could the initial step of formal conversion be called complete.

The relative retardation of the conversion of Central Europe must be ascribed largely to geography. Central Europe was nearer to the great plains and mountains of Europe-Asia from which issued so many of the pagan invaders. Huns, Avars, Bulgars, Magyars, Mongols, Turks—all came out of that reservoir of peoples and successively wrought havoc in Europe, wiping out Christian communities and retarding missions. Because of the distance and because intervening peoples acted as a buffer, the invasions had largely spent their force before reaching Western Europe. So, too, the Moslem Arab incursion, coming by way of North Africa, by the time it reached Southern France was so far from its base that it could be checked. When once the last of the Teutonic invaders, the Scandinavians, had accepted baptism, no further irruption of pagans from the North was to be anticipated. To the West lay the pathless Atlantic. It is not surprising, therefore, that, thus relatively sheltered by the accident of geography, with its nearest source of civilization the converted Roman Empire, Western Europe became Christian and that it became so earlier than did Central Europe. Nor is it strange that in time it was counted the main stronghold of Christianity. As we shall see again and again, Eastern Christianity, more exposed to attack, often permanently lost ground and, when it made conversions among the barbarians who invaded it or who lodged on its outskirts, usually was less successful in impressing itself deeply upon them than was Roman Christianity in Western Europe.

A second difference between Western and Central Europe in the processes by which conversion was effected was the larger amount of force employed in the latter area. We have seen that in the West the most extensive use of force was by Charlemagne in subduing the Saxons. Notable but less thoroughgoing were the drastic methods of Olaf Tryggvason and Olaf Haraldsson in Norway. In Central Europe, on the other hand, we shall find that again and again baptism was imposed at the point of the sword. This was largely because conversion became entangled in the clash between races and peoples, especially between Teuton and Slav or Teuton and Finn. Teutonic peoples, avowedly Christian, were expanding, usually by conquest and often by settlement, and were attempting to impose their rule upon non-Teutonic peoples on their eastern frontiers or to supplant them altogether. Especially were the Germans active as colonizers, conquerors, and missionaries. The German Holy Roman Empire was the outstanding political power in Western Europe, and its rulers and its border nobles sought to extend their domains eastward and northward. The Germans, too, were merchants and settlers. Their frontiers moved eastward into the present Austria and beyond, and northward to the Baltic. Attempts to convert the non-German peoples whom they touched were part of the process of expansion. In a similar fashion, but to a very much less extent, Danes and Swedes were active on the eastern shores of the Baltic. Teutonic peoples, whether Germans, Danes, or Swedes, sought to use the Church as an agency of conquest and insisted upon baptism as a symbol of the acknowledgment of overlordship and as a step towards assimilation. Quite naturally, conversion and baptism were vigorously resisted. In Central Europe and along the Baltic, therefore, the acceptance of Christianity was much more often an incident in a political movement and in the clash of rival races and peoples than in the West. It will be interesting to inquire whether the difference in the process of spread was reflected in the resulting Christianity of the two areas.

The order in which we will narrate the spread of Christianity in Central Europe is, first the Avars, then the South Slavs, so far as they became Roman Catholic, then the Moravians and Bohemians, next the Magyars, then the Poles, followed by the Wends, the Finns, the Lapps, the Ests, the Letts, the Prus sians, and the Lithuanians. To round out the story of the efforts of Roman Catholic Christianity to win the non-Christian peoples of Western and Central Europe we will add a few pages on the attempts at the conversion of the Jews. We will reserve for a later chapter the missionary efforts in Central and Eastern Europe of the Franciscans and Dominicans, for these came towards the end of the period and form part of a more comprehensive story.

The Avars, the first of the pagan peoples of whom we are to speak, issued from Asia and for a time constituted a serious menace. Like the Huns, but unlike the Magyars, who also came from Asia, they did not succeed in per petuating themselves as a permanent enclave in Europe. In the sixth century the Avars first appeared prominently on the frontiers of the Roman Empire.[1] Eventually they established a large domain in Central Europe. Late in the sixth or early in the seventh century their power began to decline. Yet they ravaged the Balkan territories of the Eastern Empire up to the very walls of Constantinople. In the seventh and eighth centuries they became a terror to both Italy and the Germans. Charlemagne broke their power, but for centuries fragments remained. They appear to have been relatively few in numbers, and constituted a kind of ruling aristocracy which was ultimately absorbed by the subjects. Since most of the latter were Slavs, the majority of the Avars were eventually lost in the Slavic population.

Scattered in small communities and relatively few, only here and there do groups of the Avars appear to have been converted *en masse*. We hear little of specific missions among them. Probably they tended to assume the Christian faith about the same time as did the peoples among whom they were found. In 795, under pressure from the Franks, one of the Avar chiefs declared him self prepared to accept Christianity and submitted to Carolingian rule.[2] In 796 Charlemagne's son Pippin gave the final blow to Avar power and the sur vivors agreed to become Christians.[3] A commission of bishops, summoned by the victorious Pippin in the summer of 796 to give counsel on the work of

[1] For instance, Evagrius, *Eccles. Hist.*, Book VI, Chap. 10, tells of an invasion of the Avars (in A.D. 590) when Rome was engrossed with Persia.

[2] *Ann. Lauriss., Einh.,* for the year 795; Hauck, *Kirchengeschichte Deutschlands*, Vol. II, p. 472.

[3] Hauck, *op. cit.,* Vol. II, p. 472.

conversion, declared that the neophytes must be taught before baptism—that the Scriptural order was not baptism and then belief, but belief and then baptism. Further instruction was to follow baptism. The episcopal commission also insisted that the faith must be truly accepted and not forced upon any one.[4] How far these principles were carried out we do not know. Nor are we informed as to how large a proportion of the Avars were baptized. Presumably, however, those who thus came within the fold of the Church were only that section about the capital city or camp, and did not necessarily include many scattered elsewhere through Central Europe and the Balkans.

The destruction of the main centre of pagan Avar power must have opened up a large area in Central Europe to the extension of Frankish influence and of Christianity.

To the east of the Germanic folk, as we have seen, were other peoples of whose movements we begin to become clearly aware in the fifth, sixth, and seventh centuries. The most prolific were the Slavs. As was natural, the western portions of the Slavs derived their Christianity from Italy and from the Germans. Also quite naturally, the eastern sections were indebted for their Christianity to the Church of the Eastern Empire. Between East and West was a border on which the two types of Christianity met, repeatedly with rivalry and ill temper. The competition was often accentuated and embittered by political and racial factors. On the one side was German imperialism or Papal ambition, and on the other Byzantine imperialism.

The Slavs seldom created a strong state able to cope for any length of time with their Teutonic neighbours. They tended to divide into many groups and into kingdoms and principalities troubled by endless factions. Moreover, they were later than the Germanic peoples in coming within the sphere of the culture of the Mediterranean area. They accepted that culture, together with Christianity, from their more highly civilized neighbours, the Roman Catholic Germans on the West and the Eastern Orthodox Byzantines on the South-east.

Even before the Carolingian victory over the Avars, the conversion of the Slavs had begun. In the sixth and seventh centuries the Slavs had been pressing into former Roman territory and into the eastern sections of the Alps, largely erasing Christianity.[5] Sporadic efforts were made by individual missionaries to win them, but met only with scattering success.[6] In the seventh century the conversion of many of the Croats and Serbs was accomplished by Italian

---

[4] Alcuin, *Ep.* 68 (Jaffé edition, in *Bibliotheca Germanicarum*, pp. 311 ff.).

[5] Hauck, *op. cit.*, Vol. II, pp. 466-468.

[6] Spinka, *A History of Christianity in the Balkans*, pp. 15, 16.

missionaries. At the port of Spolato was a Latin see. In the eighth century, however, part of this territory passed under Byzantine control and the influence of the Greek Church increased.[7] In the latter part of the eighth century numbers of the Slavs sought Bavarian protection against the Avars. That led some of them to accept the overlordship of the Franks and, with it, baptism. Virgil, Bishop of Salzburg from 767 to 784 and so head of a German see on the edge of Slavic territory, had an important share in the direction of the missions. He commissioned for them a bishop and several clergy. Through these the faith spread south-eastward in the present Carinthia. In accordance with the usual sequence of the missions of the Middle Ages, conversion seems to have begun with the princes and to have spread from them to the masses.[8]

After Pippin had given the *coup de grâce* to Avar power, the conversion, not only of the Avars, but of the Slavs in Carinthia, Carniola, and what had once been Pannonia proceeded apace. Charlemagne accorded it support, and Christianity rapidly followed Frankish political power. The chief directing centres were Salzburg, Passau, and Aquilea (not far from the present Trieste). Salzburg was the most active.[9]

From sometime in this early period come a few literary fragments in the Slovene language containing hints of what must have been the faith taught to the neophytes. They speak of the incarnation, the suffering for men, the last judgment. They term Christ "the medicine of our bodies and the saviour of our souls." They condemn robbery, calumny, and pagan sacrifices. They stress as obligations of Christians the giving of oneself to God, the observance of Sunday, the bringing of offerings to the church, just dealing, truthfulness, reliability, feeding the hungry, giving drink to the thirsty, and clothing the naked. One of the motives for Christian living was hope of mercy from the Judge on the last day.[10]

In the ninth century German power continued to be an important factor in Central Europe. This made for the extension of Latin Christianity. Among the Dalmatian Croats we hear of a missionary by the name of Ursius and of a Christian prince called Višeslav, who reigned about the year 800. The latter's capital was Nona, the present Nin. Nin became the seat of a bishop and from the saint to whom the cathedral was dedicated it seems probable that the

[7] Schmidlin-Braun, *Catholic Mission History*, p. 202; Spinka, *op. cit.*, p. 19; M. D. Krmpotič in *Catholic Encyclopedia*, Vol. IV, p. 510.

[8] Hauck, *op. cit.*, Vol. II, pp. 428, 429, 468-470; Moreau in Descamps, *Histoire Générale Comparée des Missions*, p. 236.

[9] Hauck, *op. cit.*, Vol. II, p. 476; Spinka, *op. cit.*, pp. 15, 16; Schubert, *Geschichte der christlichen Kirche im Frühmittelalter*, pp. 338-341.

[10] *Kopitar Glagolita Clozianus* (Vienna, 1836), pp. xxxv-xli, gives the text. For a brief summary and comments, see Hauck, *op. cit.*, Vol. II, pp. 479, 480.

dominant missionary influence in the region was Frankish.[11] The see of Nin was placed directly under the Pope, presumably to prevent its passing into the control of the Archdiocese of Spolato, which at this time was attached to the Greek Church.[12] In Dalmatia in the first part of the ninth century Franks and Byzantines both made their influence felt, and, in consequence, Latin and Greek Christianity were both present. The Croat prince found it politic to remain on good terms with the two branches of the Church.[13] The Venetians were also a factor. We read that in about the year 830 an envoy of the Slavs of Narenta, who were known as doughty pirates, came to Venice, made peace, and was baptized by the Doge.[14] In the ninth century the Croats were divided between pro-Byzantine and pro-Western groups, but by the year 900 the Croats, like the Slovenes, had definitely and finally cast in their lot with the West and so with Latin Christianity.[15] As we shall see in the next chapter, their neighbours, the Serbs and Bosnians, and practically all the other Slavs of the Balkans became converts to Greek Christianity.

In the ninth and especially in the tenth century German colonists poured eastward. Carinthia became increasingly German in blood and language, and, in consequence, Latin Christianity in that region was strengthened.[16]

If German influence assisted in the spread of Latin Christianity among the Slavs in the general region of Carniola and Carinthia, and in Croatia and along the Dalmatian coast, it constituted an even more important factor in the conversion of the Slavs of Central Europe whose seats lay immediately to the north, in which are now Austria, Hungary, and Czecho-Slovakia. These were more remote from Constantinople and thus were not so readily penetrated by Greek Christianity. Yet here, too, the latter proved important.

From the time of Charlemagne the frontier of German settlement advanced eastward and south-eastward, and for centuries the movement continued. German occupation meant the extension of Latin Christianity, whether by nobles, clergy, or simple farmers.[17] King Louis the German, son of the Emperor Louis the Pious and grandson of Charlemagne, ruled in Bavaria from 825 to his death in 876, and during the course of his reign received most of the Carolingian domains east of the Rhine. He was active in seeking to extend his

[11] Dvorník, *Les Slaves Byzance et Rome au IXe Siècle*, p. 78.

[12] Spinka, *op. cit.*, p. 20.

[13] Dvorník, *op. cit.*, p. 79.

[14] *Johannis Chronicon Venetum, an. 823*, in *Mon. Germ. Hist., Scriptorum*, Vol. VII, p. 16; Dvorník, *op. cit.*, p. 80.

[15] Spinka, *op. cit.*, p. 22.

[16] Hauck, *op. cit.*, Vol. III, pp. 154, 155.

[17] Hauck, *op. cit.*, Vol. II, pp. 711, 712; J. W. Thompson, *East German Colonization in the Middle Ages*, in *Annual Report of the American Historical Association for 1915*, pp. 126-130.

control over the Slavs. To this end he furthered the spread of Christianity. The first prince of the Moravians of whom we know, Mojmir, appears not to have been a Christian, but to have permitted the Bishops of Regensburg (Ratisbon) and Passau to send missionaries into his territories.[18] Another Slavic prince of this region, Pribina (or Privina), whose capital was at Nitra (Neutra) in the present Slovakia, driven out of his territory, took refuge with the Germans, and at the command of Louis the German was instructed in the Christian faith and baptized. Through Louis he was assigned territory in the vicinity of Lake Balaton, in the present Hungary. Pribina seems to have remained true to Christianity and to the Germans. He built at least one church in his new possessions.[19] It is said that when he recovered Nitra, he there constructed a church which he had dedicated by the Archbishop of Salzburg.[20] After his death, in 860 or 861, his son and successor Kocel (or Chozel) preserved the connexion with Salzburg.[21] Pribina and Kocel are said to have built thirty churches, and under their protection various missionaries laboured in their domains.[22]

Bohemia and the Czechs were much nearer the centres of German power than were the domains of Pribina and Kocel. Since the time of Charlemagne the Czechs seem to have acknowledged Carolingian overlordship. However, as late as 840 Bohemia was regarded as a pagan land. In 845 fourteen of the Bohemian princes were baptized, together with their retinues, presumably under the influence of Louis the German.[23] This is the earliest instance supported by authentic documentary evidence of the baptism of any of the Czechs.[24] Whether a continuing Christian community arose from these formal conversions is not clear. In 846 we hear of the Bohemians giving difficulty to Louis on a military expedition to the east,[25] and we read of a Bohemian uprising in 848.[26] The conjecture appears reasonable that this resistance, being against Louis, was also anti-German and anti-Christian.[27] We hear of bishops leading

---

[18] Moreau in Descamps, *Histoire Générale Comparée des Missions,* pp. 241, 242.

[19] Moreau in *op. cit.,* p. 242; Hauck, *op. cit.,* Vol. II, p. 714.

[20] Hauck, *op. cit.,* Vol. II, p. 713. It is, however, denied that Pribina ever recovered Nitra.—V. Novotný, *České Dějiny* (1912), Vol. I, p. 315, n. 2.

[21] Hauck, *op. cit.,* Vol. II, p. 714; Moreau in *op. cit.,* p. 242.

[22] Dvorník, *Les Légendes de Constantin et de Méthode vues de Byzance,* p. 261.

[23] *Annales Fuldenses,* an. 845. See also Hauck, *op. cit.,* Vol. II, p. 716, who says the baptism was at Regensburg, but the authority which he gives, *Annales Fuldenses,* an. 845, says nothing of that city.

[24] Naegle in *Historisches Jahrbuch,* Vol. xxxii (1911), p. 246.

[25] *Annales Fuldenses,* an. 846.

[26] *Annales Fuldenses,* an. 848.

[27] So at least Hauck, *op. cit.,* Vol. II, pp. 716, 717, conjectures.

German armies against the Bohemians,[28] but whether forcible conversions followed is not clear.

Shortly after the middle of the ninth century, a Moravian prince, Rastislav, took a step which was to have momentous consequences, not only for his own people, but also for most of the Slavs of Central Europe, the Balkans, and Russia. As a result of a request which he made to the Byzantine Emperor, two men, Constantine (Cyril) and Methodius, came and set in motion forces which made lasting contributions to the Christianity of most of the Slavic world.

Rastislav was a nephew of that Mojmir whom we have met as prince of the Moravians. In 846 Louis the German marched an army into Moravia and made him "Duke." [29] From later events we know that Rastislav was a Christian. We do not, however, know whether he was one when Louis the German accorded him support, nor do we know the agency by which he became one. Apparently under his rule Christianity continued to spread among his subjects, and from various directions. In 852 the Moravians were regarded as a newly converted nation.[30] About a decade and a half later, so it is reported, Rastislav declared that his people were Christian, and Italians, Greeks, and Germans had laboured among them.[31] Whether this tradition is correct is debatable. It is certain that for a number of years Rastislav was engaged in war with the Germans[32] and it is possible that in addition to missionaries of German blood who entered in the days of his Carolingian connexion, he welcomed those from other races to offset German influence.

The act for which Rastislav is best remembered, as we have suggested, was the petition sent about the year 861, 862, or 863 to the Emperor Michael III, "The Drunkard," of Constantinople, for missionaries to instruct his people. Why Rastislav asked this is not clear, but the conjecture seems eminently reasonable that it was for the purpose of counteracting the dominating German power. That he contemplated a formal alliance with the Eastern Empire or that he expected military assistance from it is, however, highly doubtful. The Emperor Michael III was more noted for his dissipations than his piety. However, the desire of Rastislav was heeded and two brothers, Constantine and Methodius, were sent in response to it. The appointment may have been made on the advice of the Patriarch Photius, one of the ablest churchmen of the

[28] See Hauck, *op. cit.*, Vol. II, p. 717, n. 1, for sources.

[29] *Annales Fuldenses*, an. 846.

[30] Hauck, *op. cit.*, Vol. II, p. 718, n. 2, citing *Conv. Mogunt.* 11, Chap. 2, p. 189, Nr. 249, and giving the Latin text.

[31] *Vita Methodii*, Chap. 5.

[32] *Annales Fuldenses*, an. 855, 858, 863, 866, 869.

century. These brothers were to have a more profound effect upon the nascent Slavic Christianity than did any others of whom we know.[33] In their present form, our earliest accounts of Constantine and Methodius probably date from many years after the events they record. They are, therefore, not above suspicion, and the reliability of some of their details has been sharply contested. However, on portions of the main outlines of the story a fairly general agreement exists.

Constantine and Methodius are said to have been sons of a prominent citizen of Thessalonica who had held a position in the army and is declared to have been orthodox in faith and scrupulous in the observance of religion. Constantine is better known as Cyril, the name which he assumed toward the end of his life. He was the younger of the brothers. Tradition pictures him as devoting himself to wisdom and, after a careful education and attaining some fame as a teacher and philosopher, as having been sent to debate with the Moslems and on a religious mission to the non-Chrisitan Khazars in Russia. As a result of Constantine's labours the Khazars are said to have become Christians.[34] The accounts which are nearest to the events present Methodius as having served for some time as a civil official and then, weary of that life, as having become a monk. He is reported to have accompanied his brother on the Khazar mission.[35] If these traditions are true, and they are the oldest and generally supposed to be the most nearly authentic accounts which we have, both brothers were experienced missionaries before their assignment to Moravia. It may be that this was one reason for their appointment.

If we are to believe the tradition, before the brothers actually left Con-

[33] The main sources for our knowledge of Constantine (Cyril) and Methodius are two Slavic (the so-called Pannonian) documents, *Vita Constantini* (text and Latin translation by Ernst Dümmler and Franz Miklosich, *Die Legende vom heiligen Cyrillus*, in *Denkschriften kaiserlichen Akademie der Wissenschaften, philosophisch-historischen Classe*, Vol. XIX [Vienna, 1870], pp. 205-248) and *Vita Methodii* (Latin translation by Ernst Dümmler in *Archiv für Kunde österreichischer Geschichts-Quellen*, Vol. XIII [Vienna, 1854], pp. 156-163 (French translations of both lives are in Dvornik, *Les Légendes de Constantin et de Méthode vues de Byzance*, Prague, 1933), and *Translatio S. Clementis* (Latin text in *Acta Sanctorum*, March 9, Vol. VIII, pp. 20-22). Specialists have debated the reliability of these accounts and on many of the details a difference of opinion exists. The literature is prodigious. For bibliographies, see Dvorník, *Les Légendes de Constantin et de Méthode vues de Byzance*, pp. 395 ff., and *Cambridge Medieval History*, Vol. IV, pp. 822 ff. Standard accounts are in the work by Dvorník just cited, in Dvorník, *Les Slavs, Byzance et Rome au IXe siècle*, and by V. Jagić in *Cambridge Medieval History*, Vol. IV, pp. 215-229. See also E. Dümmler, *Die pannonische Legende von heiligen Methodius* in *Archiv für Kunde österreichischer Geschichts-Quellen*, Vol. XIII (Vienna, 1854), pp. 147-199, and Hildegard Schaeder, *Geschichte und Legende im Werk der Slavenmissionare Konstantin und Method*, in *Historische Zeitschrift*, Vol. CLII (1935), pp. 229-255.

[34] *Vita Constantini*, Chaps. 1-13; *Vita Methodii*, Chap. 4; *Translatio S. Clementi*, Chap. 6.

[35] *Vita Methodii*, Chaps. 1-4.

stantinople, Constantine, perhaps with the collaboration of others, devised an alphabet for the writing of Slavonic and began the translation of the Gospels.[36] Whether this was the first reduction of a Slavic tongue to writing we do not know. Nor is it certain which of the Slavonic scripts, Cyrillic or Glagolitic, is his. Usually, however, it is believed that what is known as the Glagolitic is attributable to him. As was natural if Constantine performed his task before going north, it was a South Slavonic dialect which he reduced to writing. It may well be, indeed, that, born at Thessalonica in a region where many Slavs had settled, both brothers had known South Slavonic from their youth up. Presumably, however, this form of Slavonic was not then so very different from that of Moravia. For his model Constantine probably looked at least chiefly to the Greek letters, but other alphabets may also have furnished him with suggestions.[37] The achievement was notable, and through the translations prepared by the two brothers and their disciples it was to have lasting consequences for Slavic literature, not only in Central Europe and the Balkans, but also in Russia. Here again is an early instance of a practice which by the twentieth century had made Christian missionaries responsible for having reduced more languages to writing than have been provided with scripts by all other agencies combined.

When, finally, Constantine and Methodius reached Rastislav they were received with honour and began the instruction of pupils who were confided to them. Constantine, too, continued his task of translation and put the liturgy and some of the offices into Slavonic.[38] The brothers seem to have regarded the translation of the liturgy into the vernacular as a normal procedure. It was the custom in the East, where liturgies had developed in a number of tongues. It was otherwise in the West. Here Greek and latterly Latin had been the only tongues employed. In the use of Slavonic, Constantine and Methodius encountered opposition,[39] presumably chiefly from German priests who looked with jaundiced eyes upon a movement which would probably lead to independence of German ecclesiastical and political control.

After a sojourn in Moravia which one tradition declares to have been forty months, and another four and a half years, the two brothers set out for Rome, perhaps, as one account declares, summoned by the Pope, perhaps to gain Papal support for their innovation, and possibly to obtain ordination for some

---

[36] *Vita Constantini,* Chap. 14; *Vita Methodii,* Chap. 5; *Translatio S. Clementi,* Chap. 7.

[37] W. Vondrák, *Altkirchenslavische Grammatik* (Berlin, Weidmannsche Buchhandlung, 2d ed., 1912, pp. 656); M. Spinka, *Slavic Translations of the Scriptures,* in *The Journal of Religion,* Vol. XIII (1933), pp. 417-422; Jagić in *Cambridge Medieval History,* Vol. IV, p. 222; Dvorník, *Les Slavs, Byzance et Rome au IXe Siècle,* pp. 161-163.

[38] *Vita Constantini,* Chap. 15.

[39] *Vita Constantini,* Chap. 16.

of their disciples.[40] Probably it was quite hopeless to expect ordination from the German prelates for clergy who would use the vernacular liturgy. On their way the brothers passed through the domains of Kocel, who was pleased with their Slavonic literature and entrusted pupils to them.[41] On their journey, too, they are said to have faced criticism at Venice for their use of Slavonic.[42] In Rome, tradition declares, the Pope gave them a cordial reception, approved their Slavonic service books, and made arrangements for the ordination of their pupils. The mission of Constantine and Methodius came at a time when the Papacy was in sharp conflict with the Patriarch Photius. It may be that the Papal summons—if it was that which brought the brothers to Rome—arose out of fear of the increase of Greek influence in Central Europe. It has also been suggested that the cordiality toward the Slavonic liturgy and literature was born of a desire to hold the allegiance of the Slavic constituency.[43] While at Rome Constantine assumed the monastic garb and the name of Cyril. Here, too, he fell ill and died (Feb. 14, 869) and was buried in the basilica of St. Clement.[44]

After the death of his scholar brother, Methodius seems to have contemplated returning to Constantinople and withdrawing to a monastery.[45] From this step he appears to have been dissuaded by the dying wish of Constantine that he continue their missionary labours.[46] The traditional account, moreover, maintains that Kocel, who had been so pleased with the brothers, asked of the Pope the services of Methodius and that, in complying, the Holy See wrote to the Slavic princes Kocel, Rastislav, and Svatopluk commending Methodius to them and giving approval to saying mass and administering baptism in the vernacular—with the exception that in the mass the Epistle and the Gospel must be read first in Latin and then in Slavonic.[47] This Svatopluk who here makes his appearance in our story was a nephew of Rastislav[48] and ruled a region in Central Europe.

[40] *Vita Constantini*, Chap. 16; *Translatio S. Clementi*, Chaps. 7, 8.
[41] *Vita Constantini*, Chap. 16.
[42] *Ibid.*
[43] Hauck, *Kirchengeschichte Deutschlands*, Vol. II, p. 721. Over the fashion in which the struggle between Rome and Photius affected the mission of the two brothers, see also Dvorník, *Les Slavs, Byzance et Rome au IXe Siècle*, pp. 174-183.
[44] *Vita Constantini*, Chaps. 17, 18; *Translatio S. Clementi*, Chap. 10. The date is from the Pannonian legendary account. The usual date given is 868, but 869 is probably correct. —Dümmler, *Die pannonische Legende von heiligen Methodius* in *Archiv f. K. öst. Ges.-Quellen*, Vol. XIII, p. 181.
[45] At least this is the conjecture of Jagić in *Cambridge Medieval History*, Vol. IV, p. 225.
[46] *Vita Methodii*, Chap. 7.
[47] *Vita Methodii*, Chap. 8.
[48] *Annales Fuldenses*, an. 870.

Methodius is said to have returned to Kocel, to have been received with honour, and then to have been sent back to Rome with a request from the Prince that the Pope consecrate him Bishop. This petition may have had its origin in a desire of Kocel to render the Church in his realms independent of control by German prelates. Whether in response to this suggestion or for other reasons, Rome revived the ancient archiepiscopal see of Sirmium (now Mitrovica) in Pannonia on the lower course of the Save and appointed Methodius to it.[49]

The Holy See may have welcomed this as an opportunity to extend its influence farther into the Balkans against the Eastern Church. Although Sirmium was remote from Salzburg, the Germans looked with no kindly eye upon the activity of Methodius in what they esteemed the ecclesiastical territory of that See.[50] The year was 869 or 870 and coincided with an expansion of German political power in Central Europe. In 870 Svatopluk allied himself for a time with Carloman, who was the eldest son of Louis the German and after 865 ruled in Bavaria and Carinthia. Rastislav was taken and sent captive to Carloman.[51] In 871 Svatopluk himself was placed in custody and released only on humiliating terms.[52] Kocel probably dared not assume too pronounced a position against the Germans. The German bishops, therefore, were in the ascendant. Methodius was summoned before a synod, was found at fault, presumably for infringing on the territory of Salzburg, and for two and a half years was in Swabia, in confinement in a monastery.[53] However, the action of the German synod constituted a direct challenge to Rome. The Pope intervened, two of the German bishops involved were rebuked, and Methodius was ordered to be freed and reinstated in his diocese.[54] This ecclesiastical defeat of the Germans roughly coincided with military reverses in Moravia. In 874 the Germans were constrained to recognize the autonomy of Moravia in return for an annual tribute.[55]

However, Methodius, although restored to his diocese, did not achieve a complete victory. Apparently Rome found it wise to offer an olive branch to

[49] *Vita Methodii*, Chap. 8; Hauck, *op. cit.*, Vol. II, p. 722. On the See of Sirmium, see Dümmler, *Die pannonische Legende vom heiligen Methodius*, pp. 185-189.

[50] *De Conversione Bagoariorum et Carantanorum Libellus*, Chaps. 12, 14, and *Excerptum de Karentanis*, in *Mon. Germ. Hist., Scriptorum*, Vol. XI, pp. 13-15.

[51] *Annales Fuldenses*, an. 870.

[52] *Annales Fuldenses*, an. 871.

[53] *Vita Methodii*, Chap. 9; Hauck, *op. cit.*, Vol. II, p. 724.

[54] See the Papal letters bearing on the case in *Mon. Germ. Hist., Ep.*, Vol. VIII, pp. 281, 282, 285, 286.

[55] *Annales Fuldenses*, an. 872; Dvorník, *Les Slavs, Byzance et Rome au IXe Siècle*, p. 211.

the Germans. While allowing Methodius to preach in Slavonic, the Pope ordered him to cease using the Slavonic liturgy.[56]

Methodius, released and vindicated, is said to have returned to Moravia. The Moravians drove out the German priests and welcomed him as their Archbishop, and Svatopluk is reported to have turned over to him the administration of the clergy and churches of his territories.[57] Probably the recent victories over the German arms made this natural and popular.

However, Methodius had not yet seen the end of his troubles. The German clergy continued their opposition to the Byzantine missionary and his Slavonic literature. It may have been they who accused him at Rome and aroused the suspicion of the Holy See. In 879 Pope John VIII ordered Methodius to Rome to answer to charges of unorthodoxy and of employing the Slavonic tongue in the mass in defiance of the Papal prohibition.[58] Methodius obeyed the summons and proved so convincing that he not only disproved the indictment of his doctrinal integrity, but obtained permission for the use of Slavonic in the services of the Church—in the mass, in the reading of the Scriptures, and in the canonical hours. Latin, however, might be used in the mass if it seemed best to Methodius and "his judges." The Pope also sought to bring order into the ecclesiastical organization of Moravia. Methodius was appointed the head of the hierarchy. The Swabian Wiching, a favourite with Svatopluk, was placed at the head of the important See of Nitra (Neutra) with the command to obey the Archbishop. Provision was made for the consecration by the Pope of a third bishop, to be chosen by Methodius and Svatopluk. The Archbishop and his two suffragans were then to appoint and consecrate such other bishops as might be needed. All, however, whether priests or bishops, were to give obedience to the Archbishop.[59]

Even with this unequivocal acquittal and endorsement, Methodius was not yet free from the intrigues of his enemies. Bishop Wiching professed to have received from Pope John VIII a letter detracting from the authority of the Archbishop. The Pope wrote to Methodius (March 23, 881) expressing his regrets for the machinations of Wiching and declaring that he had not sent the latter any secret order and that he had not written any epistle except that which he had addressed to Svatopluk.[60]

Our records give us only a few other glimpses of the latter days of the sturdy

[56] Letter of John VIII to Methodius, in 879, in *Mon. Germ. Hist., Ep.,* Vol. VII, p. 161.
[57] *Vita Methodii,* Chap. 10.
[58] Letter of John VIII to Methodius, and letter of John VIII to Svatopluk in 879, in *Mon. Ger. Hist., Ep.,* Vol. VII, pp. 160 ff.
[59] Letter of John VIII to Svatopluk, June, 880 in *Mon. Germ. Hist., Ep.,* Vol. VII, pp. 222-224.
[60] *Mon. Germ. Hist., Ep.,* Vol. VII, Chaps. 243, 244.

missionary, and even these are imperfectly discerned through the mists of legend. We read of a journey to Constantinople at the command of the Emperor and of honours conferred by that monarch. We read, too, that Methodius and two of his disciples translated rapidly from Greek into Slavonic all the Bible except the Books of the Maccabees. His translations are also said to have included the works of the Fathers. Methodius is reported to have had an audience with the King of the Hungarians (Magyars). That pagan monarch is declared to have received him with marked respect and to have asked him to remember him in his prayers.[61] As his days drew to their close Methodius designated as his successor Gorazd, one of his disciples. We do not know the place of his death, but the date seems to have been April 6, 884 or 885.[62]

After the death of Methodius the Christian communities in Moravia which the two brothers had nourished at the cost of so much labour and in the face of such opposition from rival missionaries fell upon troubled days. The new Pope, probably disturbed by unfavourable news from Moravia, sent a bishop and two priests with orders to forbid the Slavonic mass and to require Gorazd to come to Rome under temporary suspension of his episcopal powers. Presumably Bishop Wiching, the old enemy of Methodius, was once more active against the party which favoured the Slavonic liturgy.[63] To this continued division in the Church were added new inroads of pagans. In the year 900 the Magyars, moving in from the East, crossed the Danube and occupied Lower Pannonia. In 906 they destroyed the Moravian state.[64] While the Slavic population was not eliminated and probably retained its Christian faith, the Church must have suffered from the fresh disorder.

In the Slavic lands to which Constantine and Methodius devoted so much of their active missionary years, much of what they had sought to accomplish was frustrated. Their effort to put the services and the sacred books of the Church into the language of the people met with persistent opposition and the wavering Papal support was at last withdrawn. In those regions which acknowledged Rome, the Slavonic liturgy persisted only in a few dioceses of Croatia, Istria, and Dalmatia, and for a time in Bohemia.[65] Barbarian invasions

[61] *Vita Methodii*, Chaps. 13, 15, 16.

[62] *Vita Methodii*, Chap. 17. This gives the date as April 6, the third indiction in the year 6393 from the creation of the world. Dvorník, *Les Legendes de Constantin et de Méthode vues de Byzance*, p. 392, says the year was 884. Jagić, in *Cambridge Medieval History*, Vol. IV, p. 229, says it was 885. Dümmler, *Die pannonische Legende vom heiligen Methodius*, p. 199, believes the date is not later than the beginning of 886.

[63] Jagić, in *Cambridge Medieval History*, Vol. IV, p. 229. Letter of Pope Stephen V to Svatopluk, 885, in *Mon. Germ. Hist., Ep.*, Vol. VI, pp. 354-358.

[64] *Cambridge Medieval History*, Vol. IV, pp. 211, 212; Hauck, *op. cit.*, Vol. II, p. 726.

[65] Jagić, in *Cambridge Medieval History*, Vol. IV, p. 229.

laid waste Moravia, to which the brothers had first been summoned and to which they had devoted most of their energies.

Yet Constantine and Methodius were far from having failed. Their disciples, driven out of Moravia, carried their influence to other Slavic peoples in the Balkans and to the Bulgarians. The tradition which they had established of translating Christian literature into Slavonic persisted. To them all those Slavs who came within the fold of the Eastern Church were indebted. In both the Roman Catholic and the Orthodox Slavic world their memory is revered. If we judge them by the extent of the movements which they set in motion, they deserve to be ranked among the greatest of Christian missionaries.

By the time of the death of Methodius, important groups of the Slavs of Central Europe had adopted Roman Catholic Christianity. Others, as we shall see in the next chapter, were accepting Christianity in its Greek Orthodox form. In the ninth century, while in the West Christianity was recovering from the blows dealt it by the incursions of the Northmen and was beginning to win the invaders to its fold, in Central Europe and the Balkans it was commencing the conversion of large numbers of the Slavs and of the Bulgars.

Strangely enough, the conversion of Bohemia and the Czechs was delayed until the close of the ninth and was not completed until well along in the tenth century. Although geographically Bohemia lay much nearer to the centres of German Christian power than did Moravia and much of Pannonia, its Slavic population was considerably later in entering the Christian fold. This may have been because the German advance was more readily achieved down the Danube Valley than across the protecting curtain of hill and forest into Bohemia. Or it may have been because the German power, being nearer and hence more obviously a menace, was resisted more stoutly. If this latter were so, Christianity, being identified by the Czechs with German dominion and culture, would also be regarded with hostile eyes. Whatever the reason, it is clear that the Bohemian rulers were later in accepting baptism than were those of Moravia, Pannonia, and Carinthia. This inevitably meant that the masses were slower to adopt the faith.

As we have seen, in 845 a group of Bohemian chieftains and their entourage were baptized in Regensburg, but this event seems not to have been followed by any marked extension of the faith among the Czechs. When Christianity finally gained a firm foothold in Bohemia it came first not from the Germans, but from the more recently converted Moravia. This was natural. The Czechs were more inclined to receive it from fellow Slavs than from the German conquerors. Moreover, for a time Bohemia was ruled from Moravia. Svatopluk's father-in-law, Duke Bořivoj of Bohemia, is said to have been baptized, together with his wife, Ludmila, by Methodius[66] (although the accuracy of this report has been vigorously questioned). Presumably priests trained in the tradition of Constantine and Methodius entered Bohemia from Moravia, bringing with them Slavonic service books. At least traces of the Slavonic liturgy as late as the eleventh century appear to argue the presence of such a clergy.[67] The baptism of Bořivoj, if it occurred, and of Ludmila was not followed by the conversion of their subjects. The majority of the Czechs seem to have remained pagan.[68] Yet Bořivoj's two sons, Spytihněv and Vratislav, were regarded as Christians. Spytihněv succeeded to his father's authority, and under him Vratislav ruled a portion of the land.[69]

The death of Svatopluk was followed shortly by the weakening of the Moravian realm. German influence increased in Bohemia. In 895 Spytihněv and some of the Bohemian nobles appeared at Regensburg and recognized the German overlordship. Spytihněv called in German priests who used the Latin liturgy.[70] In 897 a Bohemian embassy sought German help against the Moravians.[71] In 900 a Bohemian army followed by a Bavarian army entered Moravia and laid waste much of the land.[72] This increase of German influence must have made for the strengthening of the Christian connexion of such of the rulers as relied on German help. It reinforced the Latin as against the Slavonic type of Christianity. Presumably, too, groups which sought independence of the Germans, once Christian Moravia had waned, would bid for the support of the non-Christians and constitute a pagan reaction.

Vratislav, as we have seen, was a Christian. His wife, Drahomíř, appears to have been a Christian in name, but not averse to uniting with the pagans

[66] Cosmas, *Chronica Boemorum*, Book I, Chaps. 10, 14, in *Mon. Germ. Hist., Scriptorum*, Vol. IX, pp. 39, 44; Hauck, *op. cit.*, Vol. III, p. 185, n. 1. The historicity of the event is questioned by Moreau in Descamps, *Histoire Générale Comparée des Missions*, p. 248, and in Naegle, *Die Anfänge des Christentums in Böhmen* (*Historisches Jahrbuch*, Vol. XXXII, for the year 1911, pp. 502-510). However, in what is said to be the best history of Bohemia, V. Novotný, *České Dějiny*, Vol. I, p. 383, the historicity is affirmed and is dated *c.* 880-885. Naegle, *loc. cit.*, suggests that Spytihněv was the first Christian prince of Bohemia. Bořivoj is said to have been the builder of the oldest church in Bohemia. Lippert, *Social-Geschichte Böhmens in vorhussitischer Zeit.* (Vienna, F. Tempsky, 2 vols., 1896, 1898), Vol. I, p. 155.

[67] *Monachi Sazavensis Continuatio Cosmae Chronica Boemorum*, in *Mon. Germ. Hist., Scriptorum*, Vol. IX, pp. 149-154; Hauck, *op. cit.*, Vol. III, p. 185.

[68] Dvorník, *The Life of St. Wenceslas*, p. 23.

[69] *Gumpoldi Vita Vencezlavi Ducis*, Chaps. 2, 3, in *Mon. Germ. Hist., Scriptorum*, Vol. IV, p. 214; Dvorník, *op. cit.*, p. 26; Hauck, *op. cit.*, Vol. III, p. 186; Lippert, *op. cit.*, Vol. I, p. 164.

[70] *Annales Fuldenses*, an. 895; Spinka, *The Mediaeval German Church and the Conversion of the Czechoslovaks and the Poles*, p. 11. The Slavic liturgy held its place beside the Latin for about two centuries. Spinka, *op. cit.*, p. 11.

[71] *Annales Fuldenses*, an. 897.

[72] *Annales Fuldenses*, an. 900.

for her own purposes. Václav (better known in Western Europe as Wenceslas), the eldest son of Vratislav, was reared as a convinced Christian and seems to have had almost monkish tastes and ideals. Vratislav died when Václav was still a youth and Drahomíř became dominant, drove out the priests, led a pagan reaction, and did away with her mother-in-law, Ludmila, who seems to have been an earnest Christian.[73] Drahomíř may have been moved as much by hatred of the Germans as by dislike for Christianity. Very possibly, too, she loved power and was jealous of Ludmila. The rough nobility may have been angered by the monkish ways which their young prince was being taught. The tomb of the murdered Ludmila soon became a centre of popular veneration and miracles were ascribed to it.[74]

When, not many years thereafter, probably *c.* 923-924, Václav (Wenceslas) took over the reins of power, he was still only eighteen years of age. For a time he banished from court his mother, the truculent Drahomíř. He recalled the exiled priests. Other priests, hearing of the favourable turn in the fortunes of the faith, entered from Bavaria and Swabia. The Saxon power was beginning to come to the fore. Václav found it advisable to become a tributary to the Saxon German King, Henry I, the Fowler. It may be that he felt the need of foreign support against the opposition. Certainly under him German clerical influence was strong. The accounts which have reached us declare that Václav was not only a builder of churches and a zealous patron of the faith, but that he himself was ardent in his personal religious devotions and was generous to the poor, that under his royal robes he wore a rough shirt, and that he remained a virgin.

Against this ascetic, pro-German prince opposition was certain, on grounds of both patriotism and religion. In 929, while he was still not past his youth, one morning when on his way to mass, Václav was murdered by his own brother, Boleslav.[75] This violent and untimely end, added to the reports of his piety, made of Václav the national saint.

Boleslav succeeded Václav and instituted an anti-German, anti-Christian reaction. Bohemia, however, could not permanently maintain its independence against the growing Saxon power. In 950 Otto I compelled Boleslav to become

[73] *Gumpoldi Vita Vencezlavi Ducis,* Chap. 11, in *Mon. Germ. Hist., Scriptorum,* Vol. IV, pp. 214-217; *Passio S. Ludmillae,* in *Mon. Germ. Hist., Scriptorum,* Vol. XV, Pt. 1, pp. 573, 574.

[74] Dvorník, *The Life of St. Wenceslas,* p. 33.

[75] *Gumpoldi Vita Vencezlavi Ducis,* in *Mon. Germ. Hist., Scriptorum,* Vol. IV, pp. 213-223, and Hauck, *Kirchengeschichte Deutschlands,* Vol. III, p. 192, n. 4, give the date as Sept. 28, 935. With this agrees Pertz, in *Mon. Germ. Hist., Scriptorum,* Vol. IV, p. 221. Dvorník, *The Life of St. Wenceslas,* p. 68, and Moreau in Descamps, *Histoire Générale Comparée des Missions,* p. 249, give the date as Sept. 28, 929. With this latter date agrees Novotný, *České Dějiny,* Vol. I, p. 467.

his tributary[76] and presumably inaugurated a period more favourable to Christianity.

In 967 Boleslav died and was succeeded by his son, another Boleslav, who ruled until 999. Boleslav II appears to have been energetically Christian. It was in his time that the nominal conversion of Bohemia was probably substantially completed. He is credited with having founded and embellished twenty churches and with strengthening the monasteries.[77] It is generally believed that his reign saw the creation of the first Bohemian bishopric, that of Prague, and that this was done at the direction of the German Emperor Otto I. A Saxon who had long lived in Bohemia and knew the language of the country was the first incumbent and the see was placed under the Archbishopric of Mainz.[78] The second Bishop of Prague was a Czech, Vojtěch, best known to history as Adalbert. Adalbert was a scion of a princely Slav family which was related to the then ruling (Saxon) dynasty of Germany. It is said that in days when the majority were still pagan and when the nominal Christians were semi-pagan in practice, his parents were noted for their Christian piety. He was educated at Magdeburg, where in the tenth century an episcopate had been established as a centre for missions among the Northern Slavs. There he came under the influence of the Cluny movement. When he became Bishop of Prague he aroused opposition by attempting to raise the moral standards of his flock, to introduce the Cluny reforms, and to purify of its corruptions the half-heathen faith which went by the name of Christianity. Driven out, he went to Rome. Recalled to Prague, he once more felt constrained to leave. After another period in Rome, in a monastery, he became a missionary, perhaps among the Magyars, and certainly among the Poles and the Prussians. Among these last he suffered martyrdom (997).[79] With him Czech Christianity may be said to have become missionary. However imperfectly the majority may have been practising the faith, the Bohemians were

[76] Widukind, *Res Gestae Saxonicae*, Book III, Chap. 8 (in *Scriptores rerum Germanicarum*, Hanover, 1904).

[77] Cosmas, *Chronica Boemorum*, Book I, Chap. 22, in *Mon. Germ. Hist., Scriptorum*, Vol. IX, pp. 48, 49.

[78] See Hauck, *op. cit.*, Vol. III, pp. 196-199, especially the long discussion of the different traditions of the founding of the See of Prague in footnote 6 of p. 196.

[79] *Passio Sancti Adalperti Martiris*, in *Mon. Germ. Hist., Scriptorum*, Vol. XV, Pt. 2, pp. 706-708 (German translation by W. Wattenbach in *Die Geschichtschreiber der deutschen Vorzeit*, Vol. XXXIV, Leipzig, 1891); two biographies and other documents in *Acta Sanctorum*, April 23; Canaparius, *Vita Adalberti*, in *Mon. Germ. Hist., Scriptorum*, Vol. IV, pp. 581-595 (German translation of Canaparius by H. Hüffer in *Die Geschichtschreiber der deutschen Vorzeit*, Vol. XXXIV, Leipzig, 1891); Bruno, *Passio Sancti Adalberti Episcopi et Martyris*, in *Mon. Germ. Hist., Scriptorum*, Vol. IV, pp. 596-612.

now thought of as Christian and from them emissaries were beginning to reach out to convert the peoples of other lands.

From the story of the winning of the Slavs we must turn aside for a moment to tell of the entrance into the faith of a non-Slavic people, the Magyars, invaders from the East. The origin of the Magyars, or Hungarians, is a matter of dispute. They seem to have been a blend of Finno-Ugrian and Turkish elements, the chief controversy being over which of the two predominated. In the last decade of the ninth century they began forays into Moravia and Pannonia. About 895-896 large bodies of them migrated into the modern Hungary and established permanent colonies, precursors of the later Hungarian state.[80] The Magyar settlement of Hungary coincided with political weakness in the West. The Carolingian Empire was disintegrating from internal dissension and was being hammered by the Northmen. The Saxon monarchs had not yet restored order. Under these circumstances, the doors were open to fresh incursions from the East. From the present Hungary as a base the Magyars repeatedly invaded Italy and Western Europe. Beginning with the close of the ninth century in the annals of the time we often hear of their raids. They laid waste lands as distant as those of the Saxons and penetrated even to the North Sea and the Garonne. They burned churches and plundered monasteries. Some priests they killed before the altars, and others they carried away captive, together with many of the lay parishioners. Nearer at hand, in Pannonia, they seem to have reduced most of the churches to ruins. Later they raided southward into the Balkans.[81]

In the tenth century German power revived under the leadership of the Saxon rulers and the tide of Magyar invasion was rolled back. Again and again the Magyars were repulsed. Finally, in 955, Otto I inflicted on them an overwhelming defeat near Augsburg which brought to an end their threat to the West.[82]

Probably the Magyars were never very numerous and their raids had cost them a heavy toll in life. Divided as they were into tribes, they might have

[80] C. A. Macartney, *The Magyars in the Ninth Century* (Cambridge, 1930), *passim;* Kadlek in *Cambridge Medieval History*, Vol. IV, pp. 194-199; Knatchbull-Hugessen, *The Political Evolution of the Hungarian Nation*, Vol. I, pp. 3-10; Eckhart, *A Short History of the Hungarian People*, pp. 14-17.

[81] Widukind, *Res Gestae Saxonicae,* Book I, Chaps. 17, 18, 20, Book II, Chap. 5; *Annales Hildesheimenses,* an. 906, 911, 915; *Annales Fuldenses,* an. 900; Adam of Bremen, *Gesta Hammaburgensis Ecclesiae Pontificum,* Book I, Chaps. 53, 55; Kadlec in *Cambridge Medieval History*, Vol. IV, p. 212; Hauck, *Kirchengeschichte Deutschlands*, Vol. III, pp. 150-152.

[82] *Annales Hildesheimenses,* an. 955; Hauck, *op. cit.,* Vol. III, pp. 152, 153; Kadlec in *Cambridge Medieval History,* Vol. IV, pp. 199, 200.

disappeared, absorbed by the Slavic majority, as did the Avars. From this fate they were saved by a succession of able leaders who welded them into a nation. The princes who achieved this unification espoused Christianity and utilized that faith and its clergy to assist the creation of a strong state. Moreover, they sought to bring the Magyars into the circle of civilized peoples. Here, too, the Christian Church proved of great assistance.

How early conversions began among the Magyars we do not know. Presumably some of the Slavs who survived in the occupied territories held to their Christian faith. Certainly many of the captives taken on the raids in the West continued to profess the religion of their fatherland. The revival of German political power and German military victories under the Saxons, especially under Otto I, were followed by German migrations eastward into much of the present Austria. This meant the extension of the boundaries of German Christianity. The descendants of the pagan Saxons who had offered such stout resistance to Charlemagne thus became the means of the continued spread of the faith which their fathers had so fiercely opposed. The heads of the frontier sees of Passau and Salzburg, and particularly of Salzburg, were active in supervising the building of churches and the development of an ecclesiastical organization for these German colonies.[83] Here was one of the early instances, to be multiplied many times in later centuries, of the expansion of Christianity through the migrations of its adherents. The advancing German frontier made Christianity increasingly a factor with which the Magyars were compelled to reckon. Moreover, to the south lay Bulgaria and the Christian Byzantine Empire. The former, recently converted and become a powerful state, brought Christianity close to the southern boundary of Hungary. To the north lay Christian Moravia and Poland. As we shall see in a moment, in the latter part of the tenth and the first half of the eleventh century, the faith was gaining in Poland. From three sides, therefore, Hungary was facing an aggressive Christian front. It would have been strange if the Magyars, possessing only a primitive religion, had not conformed.

Missionaries of the Greek Church entered from the south-east and made some converts.[84] Report has it that in 94) two of the Magyar princes, Gyula and Bulosudes, from Transylvania, were baptized, while on a political errand in Constantinople, and that Gyula brought back with him a missionary bishop.[85] Gyula, it is said, remained true to his new faith. His daughter, Sarolta, is declared to have married Geisa (or Geysa).

[83] Hauck, op. cit., Vol. III, pp. 153-179.

[84] Juhász, Das Tschanad-Temesvarer Bistum im Frühen Mittelalter, pp. 30, 35, 57.

[85] Robinson, The Conversion of Europe, p. 304. Robinson does not give his authority for this statement.

Geisa seems to have been the first prince who made progress in consolidating the Magyars into a political unit. With him the marauding period ends and that of a settled, civilized people begins. He seems, too, to have been the first Magyar prince to dream of making all his people Christian. However, for his Christianity he turned not to Constantinople but to the West. Why he did so we do not know. It may have been because the nearest Slavs were of that faith. It may also have been because the Magyar raids westward had brought familiarity with Latin Catholicism. Or it may have been that the revival of German power under the Saxons, and especially under Otto I, had won his respect. Whatever the reasons, Geisa's choice was momentous, for it bound Hungary to the West rather than to the East.

Apparently Geisa made overtures to the great Christian power on the west, for in 973 Hungarian envoys, presumably from him, appeared at the court of Otto I.[86] Under him the way seems to have been opened for German missionaries to enter the Magyar domains. We hear of a German embassy to Hungary, headed by a bishop.[87] Bishop Piligrim of Passau sent priests to Hungary. He himself visited the country and was greatly encouraged by what he saw. Already, so he reported to the Pope, about five thousand Magyars had been baptized and opposition to Christianity had disappeared. He said that he found numerous prisoners of war who were holding to their Christian faith and were baptizing their children, although secretly. They welcomed the coming of the German priests and began to build chapels.[88] Piligrim may have been too sanguine. However, missionary work there was and continued to be. A Swabian, Wolfgang, a monk, went independently to Hungary as a missionary and with one or two companions began to preach. In this he displayed a certain impatience of discipline, for, contrary to ecclesiastical regulations, he left his monastery and went to the Magyars without episcopal authorization. Piligrim, who apparently regarded himself as the head of the Hungarian mission, summoned Wolfgang to Passau. However, Piligrim was so much impressed with the latter's spirit and ability that he recommended him for the head of the See of Regensburg.[89] Other missionaries came. As we have suggested, Bishop Adalbert of Prague seems to have sent missionaries to the Magyars and later for a brief time to have gone

[86] *Annales Hildesheimenses,* an. 973.

[87] See Hauck, *op. cit.,* Vol. III, p. 172, n. 3, for source and a discussion of the date.

[88] Hauck, *op. cit.,* Vol. III, p. 173, citing letter of Piligrim to Benedict in Endlicher, *Monumenta,* pp. 131 ff. On the authenticity of the letter, see Blumberger in *Archiv für öster. Geschichte,* Vol. XLVI, pp. 239 ff.

[89] Arnold de S. Emmer, II, 1 ff. in *Mon. Germ. Hist., Scriptorum,* Vol. IV, pp. 556 ff.; Othlon, *Vita S. Wolfgang* in *Mon. Germ. Hist., Scriptorum,* Vol. IV, pp. 527 ff.; Hauck, *op. cit.,* Vol. III, pp. 174-176.

in person to them.[90] He is said to have baptized the family of Geisa, including Geisa's son Vajk, who is better known in history as Stephen. This, however, has been questioned. It seems probable that he was the founder of the first Benedictine monastery in Hungary.[91]

The progress of Christianity appears to have been furthered by the marriage of Geisa, after the death of his first wife, to a Polish princess, Adelheid.[92] Bishop Piligrim maintained that if the Magyar mission were to be permanent, Hungarian bishoprics would need to be founded.[93] He dreamed of having Passau elevated to archiepiscopal dignity, with the Magyars under its metropolitan jurisdiction. However, his dream failed of realization and the Hungarian bishoprics were not created. For a time, indeed, the mission suffered a reverse. The Emperor Otto II became so engrossed in a quarrel with Henry II, Duke of Bavaria, and in Italian affairs that some of the Magyars renewed their raids. Churches in the German settlements on the frontier were plundered and burned and the colonists were killed or taken captive.[94] Geisa, however, either continued or renewed his friendship with the Christian West. In 995, with the approval of the Emperor Otto III, his son Stephen (Vajk) was married to Gisela, the daughter of Duke Henry II of Bavaria.[95] Geisa, too, used compulsion in bringing his subjects to accept baptism. Some submitted under the threat of armed force and many prominent Magyars who declined to comply were reduced to menial positions.[96]

Under Stephen the work of Geisa was continued and expanded. Stephen energetically carried on the conversion of his people to Christianity and at the same time endeavoured to unify the realm and to make it a state after the pattern of the monarchies of Western Europe. More than any other he was the creator of Hungary. His religious and political policies seem to have been integral parts of a unified program.

Stephen succeeded his father in 997. Almost immediately he ordered his subjects to accept Christianity. He himself toured his domains and preached

[90] Bruno, *Vita Sancti Adalberti,* Chaps. 16, 23, in *Mon. Germ. Hist., Scriptorum,* Vol. IV, pp. 603, 607.

[91] *Stephani Regis Ungariae Vita Maior,* Chaps. 4, 5, in *Mon. Germ. Hist., Scriptorum,* Vol. XI, p. 231. On the baptism of the family of Geisa, see a long discussion in Csuday, *Die Geschichte der Ungarn* (translated by M. Darvai), Vol. I, p. 99, n. 1. See also Voigt, *Brun von Querfurt,* pp. 4-6.

[92] Csuday, *op. cit.,* Vol. I, pp. 97, 98.

[93] Hauck, *op. cit.,* Vol. III, p. 177, citing letter of Piligrim to Pope Benedict.

[94] Hauck, *op. cit.,* pp. 177-182.

[95] Csuday, *op. cit.,* Vol. I, p. 103.

[96] Knatchbull-Hugessen, *The Political Evolution of the Hungarian Nation,* Vol. I, p. 12, citing *Chronicon Dubnicense,* p. 34, and Bonfini, *Rerum Hungaricarum Decades,* Dec. ii, Bk. I.

the new faith.[97] He set the example of liberating his slaves. Only a few years after his accession, in the year 1000, he is said to have asked and received from the Pope the royal title, a crown, and an ecclesiastical organization for his realm, with a metropolitanate and subordinate bishoprics.[98] He founded and endowed a number of monasteries, and instituted two archbishoprics and eight bishoprics. He corresponded with the Abbot of Cluny and thus was in touch with the leading Western Christian reform movement of the age.

Many missionaries entered to share in the task of conversion and in the instruction of the neophytes. A large proportion of these seem to have been Slavs. Part of the evidence for this is the Slavonic origin of much of the ecclesiastical terminology of the Magyars. We hear of Radla, a companion of Bishop Adalbert of Prague, of Anastasius, formerly abbot of a monastery near Prague, later of one in Hungary, and eventually Archbishop of Gran (Esztergom), and of Astrik, who had been a priest under Adalbert, then an abbot in Poland, later an eloquent preacher of the faith in Hungary, and finally Archbishop of Kalocsa.[99] We read of two Polish monks, Zoerard and Benedict, who came as missionaries to the Magyars.[100] Not all the missionaries were Slavs. Others were Germans.[101]

By legal enactments Stephen sought to enforce Christian observances and to give the clergy something of the assured and privileged position which they enjoyed in Western Europe. Respect for Sunday and decorum during religious services were enjoined. Bishops were accorded judicial powers in matrimonial and ecclesiastical matters, and the payment of tithes was commanded.[102] Stephen encouraged the coming of foreign settlers and organized his realm partly on the model of German institutions.[103]

The innovations were not carried through without severe and stubborn resistance. We hear of more than one uprising on behalf of the old religion and the traditional customs.[104] This was to be expected and probably arose as much from opposition to the growth of royal authority as from affection for the hereditary faith.

[97] On Stephen, see two fairly early lives, *Vita Maior* and *Vita Minor S. Stephani* in *Mon. Germ. Hist., Scriptorum*, Vol. XI, pp. 226-242, and a later life in *Acta Sanctorum*, Vol. XLI, pp. 456 ff. (Sept. 2).

[98] Ep. Sylvester II in Migne, *Pat. Lat.*, Vol. CXXXIX, Cols. 274 ff. The authenticity of the letter has been questioned.—Knatchbull-Hugessen, *op. cit.*, Vol. I, p. 13, n. 2; Juhász, *op. cit.*, p. 46.

[99] Kadlec in *Cambridge Medieval History*, Vol. IV, p. 214.

[100] *Acta Sanctorum*, Vol. XXXI, (July, Vol. IV), pp. 326 ff.

[101] Juhász, *op. cit.*, pp. 42, 43, 49, 63.

[102] Knatchbull-Hugessen, *op. cit.*, Vol. I, p. 18, citing Endlicher, *Monumenta*, pp. 310 ff.

[103] Knatchbull-Hugessen, *op. cit.*, Vol. I, pp. 15-19.

[104] Robinson, *The Conversion of Europe*, p. 309; Csuday, *op. cit.*, Vol. I, pp. 131-160.

Stephen was disappointed in a successor from his own loins. His only son, Emeric, lost his life in a bear hunt in 1031. He himself died in 1038. Before the century was out, both father and son had been canonized.

As might have been anticipated, the removal of the strong arm of the king-missionary was followed by a reaction against Christianity and the royal authority. Internal dissensions over the succession, foreign wars, and fresh invasions from abroad troubled the realm. Pagan rites were revived, and Christians, including at least one bishop, were killed.[105] Under Bela I, who reigned 1061-1063, representatives on the royal council asked that they be allowed to stone the bishops, disembowel the priests, hang the collectors of tithes, and destroy the churches.[106] Yet both Christianity and the royal power survived. Toward the close of the eleventh and at the beginning of the twelfth century the strong monarchs Ladislas I (1077-1095) and Koloman (1095-1114) enacted legislation to strengthen Christianity and the Church.[107] The work of Geisa and Stephen was never really undone. The Magyars had come within the circle of Christian peoples and into the family of Latin Christianity.

Almost contemporary with the spread of Christianity among the Magyars was the winning for the faith of a strong position among the Poles. Poland is another of the states, like Norway and Hungary, where the growth of the monarchy appears to have been closely associated with the process of conversion to Christianity. The rulers who created the royal power and extended the territories controlled by the crown were also those who sponsored the introduction of the new faith. The faith entered through both Slavic and German agents.

Just when Christianity first reached the Slavs in the region which later came to be known as Poland we do not know. It is possible that some of the disciples of Constantine and Methodius were responsible for its introduction.[108] What seems to be the first well-authenticated conversion is that of the Duke Mieszka (in various accounts called also Misika and Mieczyslav). Mieszka had close relations with the Scandinavians and one of his daughters may have been married successively to two Scandinavian princes.[109] He ruled over only

[105] Juhász, op. cit., pp. 67-70.

[106] Knatchbull-Hugessen, op. cit., Vol. I, p. 12.

[107] Csuday, op. cit., Vol. I, pp. 163-180; Knatchbull-Hugessen, op. cit., Vol. I, pp. 20, 21; Robinson, op. cit., p. 309.

[108] J. X. Seppelt, Zur Einführung des Christentums in Polen, in Zeitschrift für Missionswissenschaft, Vol. X (1920), p. 88. Some traces of Greek observances are cited as evidence.

[109] Samuel H. Cross, Scandinavian-Polish Relations in the Late Tenth Century (in Studies in Honor of Hermann Collitz, Baltimore, 1930, pp. 114-140).

a portion of the subsequent Poland and in 963 had been forced to recognize
the overlordship of the expanding Saxon Empire.[110] He paid tribute to the
Emperor Otto I and, with Duke Boleslav of Bohemia, appeared at the
imperial court.[111] He was known as a friend of the Emperor.[112] In 965 or
966 Mieszka married Dobrawa (the Czech spelling is Dubrovka), the sister
of Boleslav II of Bohemia. She was a Christian, and it is said to have been
under her influence that Mieszka was baptized (966 or 967).[113] The conjecture seems reasonable that his German connexions predisposed Mieszka to
take this step and that he lent a willing ear to his bride's arguments. Presumably, too, Czech clergy accompanied Dobrawa to her new court.[114] Although Bohemia was probably still in part a mission field, priests from there
may have seen in the favour of Mieszka an opportunity to win still another
people. In 968 a bishopric was created for the Poles and its seat fixed at
Poznań (Posen).[115] It is often said that this bishopric was placed under the
new Archiepiscopal see of Magdeburg which Otto I had planned to supervise
the missions among the Slavs on his north-eastern border. This, however, is
questioned.[116] The first incumbent of the See of Poznań was one Jordan,[117]
a German, and the second was Vunger, also a German, who held the post
from 982 to 1012.[118] After the death of Dobrawa, Mieszka married Oda, of
a Saxon noble family.[119] This tie bound him even closer to the Christian
German Empire. Before his death (992), Mieszka is said to have transferred
the overlordship of his realm to the Holy See.[120] How much progress was
made under Mieszka in the conversion of the masses we do not know. Presumably the Duke was either active in furthering the instruction of his nobles
and people or gave every facility to missionaries.

[110] *Thietmari Merseburgensis Episcopi Chronicon*, Book II, Chap. 14 (*Scriptores rerum Germanicarum*, Hanover, 1889).

[111] Thietmar, *op. cit.*, Book II, Chaps. 29, 31.

[112] Widukind, *Rerum Gestarum Saxonicarum*, Book III, Chap. 69.

[113] Thietmar, *op. cit.*, Book IV, Chap. 55; *Annales Cracoviensis Vetusti* and *Annales Capituli Cracoviensis* (*Mon. Germ. Hist., Scriptorum*, Vol. XIX, pp. 577, 585); P. Kehr, *Das Erzbistum Magdeburg und die erste Organisation der christlichen Kirche in Polen* (*Abhandlungen der preussischen Akademie der Wissenschaften, 1920, phil.-hist. Klasse*); Zeissberg in *Archiv für öster. Geschichte*, Vol. XXXVIII, p. 56; Roepell, *Geschichte Polens*, Vol. I, p. 95.

[114] Hauck, *Kirchengeschichte Deutschlands*, Vol. III, p. 201, so conjectures.

[115] Hauck, *op. cit.*, Vol. III, p. 201, citing *Ann. Bohem.*, an. 968 (Miklosich, *Slav Bibliothek*, Vol. II, p. 301).

[116] See summary of the discussion in Kehr, *op. cit.*, pp. 6 ff.

[117] Thietmar, *op. cit.*, Book II, Chap. 32, Book IV, Chap. 56.

[118] Thietmar, *op. cit.*, Book IV, Chap. 45, Book VII, Chap. 5; Seppelt, *op. cit.*, p. 89; Kehr, *op. cit.*, p. 33.

[119] Seppelt, *op. cit.*, p. 89; Kehr, *op. cit.*, p. 32; Roepell, *op. cit.*, Vol. I, p. 100.

[120] Seppelt, *op. cit.*, p. 90; Kehr, *op. cit.*, pp. 31, 32.

Under Mieszka's son Boleslaw Chrobry ("the Brave"), great progress was registered in the extent of the Polish state, the dignity of its ruler, and the position of the Church. Boleslaw reigned from 992 to 1025. His authority is said to have been recognized from the Baltic to the Carpathians and from the Elbe to the Bug. His realm, therefore, was one of the most extensive of the Europe of his day. On much of it his overlordship must have sat rather lightly, but he was one of the more important European monarchs of his generation. Toward the end of his life he assumed, too, the title of King. Under him the Church in Poland experienced a large growth. He gave active support to missionaries. He held Bishop Adalbert of Prague in high regard and assisted him in his mission. After the latter's martyrdom at the hands of the pagan Prussians (997), Boleslaw brought the body in honour to his realm. He deposited it, not at the episcopal city of Poznań, but about thirty miles away at Gniezno (Gnesen). Here, since the later years of Mieszka, had been the Polish capital.[121]

Three years after the death of Adalbert, in the year 1000, Gniezno (Gnesen), which held the body of the saint, was made an archiepiscopal see. At its head was placed a brother of the martyred Adalbert and under it were created three suffragan bishoprics. These were Kolberg, in Pomerania, Breslau, in Silesia, and Cracow, not far from Moravia. Presumably they give some indication of the regions where Christians were most numerous or where missions were being most actively prosecuted. Poland was thus accorded an ecclesiastical structure of its own.

This important act appears to have been the deed of the Emperor Otto III. That youthful ruler died in 1002, in his twenty-second year, and was only a young man of about twenty when Poland was given its hierarchy. He was the son of the Emperor Otto II and his mother was the daughter of the Byzantine Emperor. Reared to the purple, he entertained grandiose dreams of reviving the glories of the ancient Roman Empire. He had procured the election of his former tutor, the brilliant and learned Gerbert, to the Papal throne as Sylvester II, and it was probably not difficult to obtain the latter's consent to what was done in Poland in 1000. Otto III paid a visit to the tomb of Adalbert, whom he had known and esteemed, and while there he raised Gniezno to its archiepiscopal dignity and created for it the suffragan sees which we have mentioned. This seems to have been a departure from the frontier policy of his house. His grandfather, Otto I, had made Magdeburg the seat of an archbishop and apparently had wished it to have authority

---

[121] Seppelt, *op. cit.,* citing H. C. Voigt, *Adalbert von Prag,* pp. 195 ff.; Roepell, *op. cit.,* Vol. I, pp. 107, 108.

over the Church along the north-eastern Slavic border. The missions among the Slavs could thus be kept under German control and be made to assist German imperialism. By his act Otto III rendered the Polish Church virtually independent of German imperial control—or at least he weakened the ties which bound it to his house. The evidence is insufficient to enable us to determine whether the suggestion was his own or whether it originated in the astute mind of the ambitious Boleslaw. Boleslaw was intent upon building for himself a vast and independent realm and the idea may quite possibly have been his. Certainly an archdiocese independent of the Germans would make for a stronger Poland. Not unnaturally the step met with criticism from Magdeburg. Moreover, the See of Poznań, although only a short distance from Gniezno, was left subject to Magdeburg, perhaps because of the opposition of its bishop.[122] In succeeding years Boleslaw repeatedly fought Otto's successor, the Emperor Henry II, and the latter may more than once have rued the generous imprudence of his boyish predecessor.

Apparently Boleslaw encountered opposition in his attempts to propagate Christianity. We read of the murder of two Italians whom he and Otto III brought from Ravenna.[123]

After the death of Boleslaw, a reaction set in against the royal authority, the associated Christianity, and the German Queen and the foreign clergy. For a time the Polish Kingdom broke apart. Bishops and priests were driven out or killed and churches and monasteries were burned. The Bishoprics of Breslau and Kolberg disappeared. However, the work of Boleslaw was never completely undone. Later monarchs succeeded in restoring some dignity to the royal estate and in according support to the Church.[124] In 1040, with German help, Kazimierz (Casimir) won the Polish throne and gave fresh strength to the distraught Church. Boleslaw II (1058-1079) and Boleslaw III (1102-1139) regained some of the lost territory, notably Silesia and Pomerania. Under the latter, as we shall see, marked progress was made in the conversion of the Pomeranians. Yet it was long before Christianity was as strong in Poland as in Western European lands. In a letter to Boleslaw II, Pope

---

[122] The best source is Thietmar, *op. cit.*, Book IV, Chap. 45, for Thietmar was a contemporary. Representing the view of Magdeburg, he was critical of the legality of the act. See also *Gesta Archiepiscoporum Magdeburgensium* (*Mon. Germ. Hist., Scriptorum*, Vol. XIV, p. 390) and *Annales Magdeburgenses* (*Mon. Germ. Hist., Scriptorum*, Vol. XVI, p. 159). Secondary accounts are Hauck, *op. cit.*, Vol. III, p. 272; Kehr, *op. cit.*, pp. 35 ff.; Seppelt, *op. cit.*, pp. 91, 92; Thompson, *Feudal Germany*, p. 642; Spinka, *The Mediaeval German Church and the Conversion of the Czechoslovaks and the Poles*, pp. 21-23.

[123] Voigt, *Brun von Querfurt*, p. 6.

[124] Seppelt, *op. cit.*, p. 93; Maschke, *Polen und die Berufung des deutschen Ordens nach Preussen*, p. 12; Spinka, *op. cit.*, p. 24.

Gregory VII complained that the bishops, not having a metropolitan with a fixed see, wandered here and there ordaining priests and that the bishops were too few for the population and their territories too large.[125] It is significant, too, that when Boleslaw III set about the conquest and the conversion of Pomerania, he found missionaries, not among the Polish clergy, but among the Germans. As late as the twelfth century, therefore, religious life in Poland must have been at a low ebb.

West of the Poles and north of the Czechs were other Slavic peoples. At the outset of the ninth century they constituted the majority of the population in most of what is now the north-western part of Germany and along the middle and lower courses of the Elbe and Oder and their tributaries. Even so far west and south as the valley of the Saale they were in the majority. Collectively they were known to the Germans as the Wends. Among themselves they were called Slavs. They had taken the lands once occupied by the Germans, when, in the centuries during the collapse of the Roman Empire in the West, those peoples had moved south. Like the Slavs elsewhere, they were subdivided into many groups. Between the Saale and the Mulde were various tribes of the Sorbs. East and north along the Oder to the Haff and the Baltic were, to give them the German or Latin forms of their name, the Wilzi, also called Lutici and Welatabi. On the right bank of the lower course of the Elbe were the Obodrites. The Obodrites in turn were subdivided (again using Germanized or Latinized forms) into the Wagrians in Holstein, the Reregi, the Polabi, and the Warnabi in Lauenburg and Mecklenburg, and the Linoni and the Smeldingi on the banks of the Elbe. The inhabitants of Pomerania were also Wends.

Under Charlemagne some of the Wends most closely in touch with the Christian Germans—in the Hartz Mountains and along the Saale—were converted. That monarch regarded as Christians the Slavs in the valley of the Main and commanded the building of churches there. However, he made no effort to bring within his Empire or into the fold of the Church the great body of Wends north and east of the Elbe.[126]

Nor did the Carolingians after Charlemagne put forth any effort to incorporate the Wends into Christendom. In his Papal commission as Legate, Anskar was sent to the Slavs as well as to other peoples in the North.[127] He

[125] Letter of Gregory VII to Boleslaw (A.D. 1075), in Migne, *Pat. Lat.,* Vol. CXLVIII, Cols. 423-425. See also Seppelt, *op. cit.,* p. 93.

[126] Hauck, *op. cit.,* Vol. II, pp. 351-354, Vol. III, pp. 72, 73. For the work of the English Willehad among the Slavs see *Vita Willehadi* (translation in *Die Geschichtschreiber der deutschen Vorzeit achtes Jahrhundert,* Vol. III, pp. 93 ff.), Chap. 5.

[127] Rimpert, *Vita Anskarii,* Chap. 13.

seems, however, to have devoted his attention chiefly to the Scandinavians. In the earlier decades of its history the Archdiocese of Hamburg-Bremen did little or nothing for the Wends. If converts were made from among them, they must have been sporadic and relatively few. The monks of the Saxon monastery of Corvey are said to have made an effort to win some of the Slavs, but only with limited and temporary success.[128]

It remained for the Saxon rulers to carry Christianity to their Slavic neighbours on their east. When they undertook the task, they employed much the same methods that Charlemagne had used in the conversion of their own ancestors. Whether they were conscious of taking a leaf out of their own history we do not know. Like Charlemagne, however, they combined the methods of force of arms and the establishment of an ecclesiastical organization.

It must be noted that the beginning of the advance of the frontiers of Christianity into the lands of the Wends was roughly contemporaneous with an expansion of Christianity on a number of fronts—in Scandinavia, among the Magyars, and among the Russians. As we shall see, however, the conversion of Wendland required several centuries and then was completed as much or more by the immigration of Christian Germans as by the acceptance of the faith by the Slavic inhabitants.

The conversion of the Wends was complicated by what seems to have been racial friction. Certainly the Germans again and again waged their war of conquest with marked cruelty, and the Slavs, not unnaturally, proved loath to adopt the faith of their hated conquerors.

The Wends were by no means entirely uncivilized. They had fortresses and cities. Their religion was a polytheism with imposing temples and images and a powerful priesthood.[129]

The first of the Saxon monarchs to be active in extending his control over the Wends was Henry I, "The Fowler," who died in 936. It will be recalled that he was successful in war against the Danes and compelled one of their rulers to accept the Christian faith. It is not strange, therefore, that he also employed his arms against the Wends. We hear that he reduced the Obodrites,[130] who were near the Danish border, and the Sorbs, who were farther south, and others of the Slavs.[131] Some of these, we read, he constrained not only to promise tribute to himself, but also to agree to become Christians.[132]

---

[128] Helmold, *Chronica Slavorum,* Book I, Chap. 6. For the work of Anskar for the Slavs see Rimpert, *Vita Anskarii* (in *Scriptores rerum Germanicarum,* Hanover, 1884), Chap. 15.
[129] Hauck, *op. cit.,* Vol. III, pp. 84, 85; Thompson, *Feudal Germany,* pp. 387-392.
[130] Widukind, *Rerum Gestarum Saxonicarum,* Book I, Chap. 36.
[131] Some promised to become Christian.—Adam of Bremen, *Gesta Hammaburgensis Ecclesiæ Pontificum,* Book I, Chap. 56 (58).
[132] *Ibid.*

Apparently, however, in his efforts to convert the Wends Henry was given little support by the German clergy. The Archbishopric of Hamburg-Bremen would have been a logical leader in such a mission, but its energetic head, Unni, was too engrossed in pursuing the dream of Anskar and reaching the Scandinavians to have energy to divert to the Slavs.[133] We hear that Bishop Adalward, of the Saxon Diocese of Verden, preached to the Wends,[134] but with what, if any, results we do not know.

Much greater advance was made under Henry the Fowler's son, Otto I the Great. Every schoolboy knows—or should know—that Otto substantially enlarged the territory and authority of his house and was crowned Roman Emperor. It was to be expected, therefore, that he would seek to extend his borders into the Slavic territories on the east. It was not surprising, moreover, that he employed the Church as a means of consolidating his rule.

Into the details of the story of the wars of Otto the Great and his lieutenants against the Wends we must not take time to go. We must content ourselves with noting that with more or less success Otto gained recognition of his overlordship as far as the Oder.[135] However, it was two centuries or so after his death before the region was fully assimilated to German rule and to the Church.

Otto the Great's achievement gave some opportunity for missionaries. Presumably, however, the sullen hate produced by the conquest made difficult their work. Moreover, we discover little evidence of eagerness among German Christians to undertake the arduous task of winning the Slavs by personal, friendly contact. Yet we hear of at least one missionary. Boso, a monk from a monastery just outside of Regensburg, entered the service of Otto. Among other activities, he undertook a ministry to the Slavs. He is said to have sought to teach the Slavs the *Kyrie Eleison*, but to have been mocked for his pains.[136] German garrisons and fortresses were established in Wendland. For them chaplains were provided, and it is probable that some of these sought to minister not only to their German parishioners but also to the Slavs.[137] Whether many conversions ensued appears doubtful.

However slowly conversion may have proceeded, Otto endeavoured to encourage it and to give strength to the Church in Wend territory by establishing bishoprics. In 948 he founded the sees of Brandenburg and Havelberg. To both were apportioned extensive territories. To both, too, were assigned large

[133] Hauck, *op. cit.*, Vol. III, pp. 72-82.
[134] Adam of Bremen, *op. cit.*, Book II, Chap. 1.
[135] *Cambridge Medieval History*, Vol. III, p. 192, gives a summary.
[136] Thietmar, *Merseburgensis Episcopi Chronicon*, Book II, Chaps. 36, 37.
[137] Hauck, *op. cit.*, Vol. III, pp. 95, 96.

revenues, some of them in the form of tithes.[138] These, particularly the tithes, would be regarded as burdensome by their flocks and would probably retard conversion. The headquarters of one bishop were fixed at Oldenburg,[139] the site of a Slavic holy place, not far from the present Lübeck.

Otto did more. He arranged for an archbishopric to supervise the ecclesiastical organization of Wendland. This he placed at Magdeburg, which was separated from Wendland only by the Elbe, and which from at least the time of Charlemagne had been an important trading-centre. Otto's original plan was to transfer to Magdeburg the seat of the adjacent Saxon Bishopric of Halberstadt. Halberstadt was rich in monasteries and, since some Slavs were scattered through its territory, presumably its clergy were accustomed to deal with them. Delays occurred, due to the opposition of the Archbishop of Mainz, whose jurisdiction would thereby be curtailed, and to the Bishop of Halberstadt. After several years and toward the end of his life, in 968 Otto eventually had his desire—but without the erasure of the Bishopric of Halberstadt. Magdeburg was made the seat of an archbishopric and under it were placed the Bishoprics of Havelberg and Brandenburg and the newly created sees of Meissen, Zeitz, and Merseburg.[140] For the first Archbishop the choice fell on Adalbert. The new prelate had had missionary experience in Russia and so was not unfamiliar with the Slavs.[141] The missionary Boso became Bishop of Merseburg.[142]

Mixed and dubious success followed these elaborate plans of Otto. Archbishop Adalbert is reported to have won to the faith many of the Slavs.[143] Moreover, in the days of a contemporary of Adalbert, Archbishop Adaldag of Hamburg-Bremen, the majority of the Slavs in the jurisdiction of that see are said to have been converted.[144] On the other hand, at least the large majority of the clergy were German and were separated from the Slavs by barriers of language and race and by the distrust of a subject population. It is declared that many of the Saxon nobles were far from eager for the conversion of the Wends, for this might lead to the union of the Slavs with the

---

[138] Hauck, op. cit., Vol. III, pp. 102-104.

[139] Helmoldi Presbyteri Bozoviensis Chronica Slavorum (Scriptores rerum Germanicarum, 1909), Book I, Chaps. 11, 12 (an English translation is by F. J. Tschan, The Chronicle of the Slavs, by Helmold, Priest of Bosau, Columbia University Press, 1935); Hauck, op. cit., Vol. III, pp. 105-108.

[140] Hauck, op. cit., Vol. III, pp. 109-127.

[141] Thietmar, op. cit., Book II, Chap. 22.

[142] Hauck, op. cit., Vol. III, p. 130.

[143] Adam of Bremen, Gesta Hammaburgensis Ecclesiæ Pontificum, Book II, Chap. 15 (13).

[144] Adam of Bremen, op. cit., Book II, Chap. 20 (17); Helmold, op. cit., Book I, Chaps. 11, 12.

crown against their oppressors.[145] We know that more than a century later the majority of the Wends still seem to have been pagan.[146]

In 983, only a decade after the death of Otto, a violent uprising of the Wends broke out in which many of the professing Christians joined. The rage of the insurgents was directed partly against the bishops. In Havelberg the mob destroyed the bishop's throne. Three years before, in Brandenburg, a bishop had been strangled by his people, and now the corpse was dug up and thrown to the dogs.[147]

One of the reasons for the uprising of 983 was the tyranny of the German rulers. Another was probably to be found in the weakening of the power of the immediate successors of Otto the Great on the north-eastern frontier. The Margrave Gero, who had been Otto's strongest lieutenant in the German conquest of the area between the Elbe and the Oder, had died before Otto, in 965.[148] Otto's son, Otto II, became engrossed in Italian affairs. Indeed, before his death (983) he had suffered a severe reverse in Italy. The next Emperor, Otto III, was a minor during most of his reign and the regency did not have the strength of the first Otto. It is not surprising that the work of conversion lagged.

Henry II, who succeeded Otto III and reigned from 1002 to 1024, attempted to restore the royal authority along the eastern frontier, and particularly against the Poles. However, he did not press Christian missions, perhaps because he felt that these would arouse opposition and so jeopardize his rule. To some of the Wends, in return for their recognition of his overlordship and the payment of tribute, he promised autonomy in their internal affairs, presumably including toleration for their pagan faith.[149] He even punished a German soldier for disfiguring a Slavic idol.[150] With this policy, Henry II, canonized though he later was by the Church, could not be expected to give active support to missions among the Wends. If any were conducted it would be either by bishops or by independent missionaries. We do hear of two of the latter. Bruno of Querfurt, who died in the first decade of the eleventh century and who led an active missionary life in several regions, laboured for a time among the Slavs.[151] For a relatively brief period in 1017 and perhaps in the

---

[145] Tout, *The Empire and the Papacy*, p. 23.

[146] Hauck, *op. cit.*, Vol. III, pp. 135-138.

[147] Thietmar, *op. cit.*, Book III, Chap. 17.

[148] *Cambridge Medieval History*, Vol. III, p. 202.

[149] Thietmar, *Merseburgensis Episcopi Chronicon*, Book VI, Chaps. 22, 25, 28, Book VIII, Chap. 59; *Annales Hildesheimensis*, an. 1029; Hauck, *Kirchengeschichte Deutschlands*, Vol. III, pp. 628, 629; Thompson, *Feudal Germany*, p. 406.

[150] Thietmar, *op. cit.*, Book VIII, Chap. 64.

[151] Voigt, *Brun von Querfurt*; Hauck, *op. cit.*, Vol. III, pp. 630, 631.

following two years, the hermit Günther preached among those to the east of the Elbe, but with what results we do not know.[152]

However, the tolerant policy of Henry did not prevent a severe anti-German and anti-Christian uprising. Like the one of 983, it is said to have been provoked by the injustices of the German rulers. It broke out in 1018, or perhaps a few years earlier, and was most severe in the North-west, along the Elbe and the Baltic. Churches were burned, priests were driven out, much of the superficial Christianity disappeared, and paganism revived.[153] As a rule the German secular lords whose domains were on the Slavic frontier seem to have had little interest in missions and to have felt no scruples against appropriating the property of the Church.[154]

The successor of Henry II, the Emperor Conrad II (died 1039), continued the work of Henry in strengthening the realm, and rendered it more powerful along its eastern frontiers. He made war against the Wilzi, and in 1035 and 1036 invaded their lands and wasted their cities and fields. The war was waged with ferocity. A crucifix came into the possession of the Wends and they gouged out its eyes and cut off its hands and feet. In retaliation, Conrad had some Wend prisoners drawn up before the disfigured crucifix, ordered them mutilated after the same fashion, and left them to die.[155] Under such circumstances the Wends could not be expected to have any love for Christians or for the Christian faith.

In the reign of Conrad began a series of events which for a time meant further damage to the Christian cause, but which later had other results. A Wend chieftain, Uto, or Udo, a nominal Christian, was killed by a Saxon. Udo's son Gottschalk was then at school in a monastery. On the news of his father's death he left his books, gathered about him a group of Wends, and raided the Christian Saxons. In time he was taken by a German noble, but his captor deemed it wise to release him and to send him away as an ally. Gottschalk thereupon joined himself to the Danish King Canute and was with that monarch in England. After the death of Canute, Gottschalk returned to his ancestral home and regained his inherited lands and title. Presumably it was during his absence that he had become an adherent of the faith in which he had been nurtured. The Danes were now Christian, and he had married a daughter of the Danish King. It is certain that he aided in propagating

[152] Hauck, op. cit., Vol. III, pp. 631, 632.
[153] Thietmar, op. cit., Book IX (VIII), Chap. 5 (4); Helmold, Chronica Slavorum, Book I, Chap. 16; Adam of Bremen, op. cit., Book II, Chap. 42 (40).
[154] Helmold, op. cit., Book I, Chap. 19.
[155] Wipo, Gesta Chuonradi (in Wiponis Opera, in Scriptores rerum Germanicarum, 3d ed., 1915), Chap. 33.

Christianity among the Slavs. Often he spoke in church, explaining to his people the Christian religion. Many who had relapsed were won back. His activities were in the North-west, in the general region of Schleswig, Holstein, Lübeck, and Mecklenburg.[156]

Fortunately for the cause of Christianity, the area in which Gottschalk ruled was near to Hamburg, and the See of Hamburg-Bremen was at that time occupied by the able and ambitious Adalbert. Adalbert, as we have seen in the preceding chapter, aspired to have his Archbishopric made the Patriarchate of the North, and was zealous in furthering missions and making effective his ecclesiastical jurisdiction over as large an area as possible. He reinforced the missionary labours of Gottschalk and divided the Slavic diocese of Oldenburg into three bishoprics.[157]

From this rapid progress of Christianity a violent and disastrous reaction occurred. Henry III was succeeded by Henry IV, famous for his contest with Pope Gregory VII. During the early part of his reign Henry IV was a minor. Archbishop Adalbert of Hamburg-Bremen was in control, but in 1066 was dismissed by Henry, who had just been declared of age. The youth of Henry and the disgrace of Adalbert made for weakness on the frontier. Added to it was division among the Saxon lords, lay and clerical, who governed the marches. The Duke of Saxony, of the house of Billung, fell upon the estates of the disgraced Adalbert and deprived the Archbishop of two-thirds of his lands. The smouldering hate of the Wends against the oppression of the Saxons took advantage of the situation and in 1066 burst out in an explosion which wrecked both the Church in their midst and Saxon rule. Gottschalk was killed. His wife, the Danish princess, was driven naked out of Mecklenburg. At least one priest was slain before the altar. The aged Bishop John of Mecklenburg was beaten and driven through one Slavic city after another. Then his feet and hands were cut off and his head was presented as an offering to one of the pagan gods. Many other Christians, lay and clerical, suffered for their faith.[158] Here and there some Germans ventured on raids of reprisal. We hear of one Burckhardt, Bishop of Halberstadt, who in 1068 led a party against the Wilzi, who were among the leaders in the revolt, brought devastation and fire, and rode back upon the sacred horse.[159] As late as 1114 it was

[156] Adam of Bremen, *op. cit.*, Book II, Chaps. 66 (64), 79 (75) ; Book III, Chaps. 19-21 (18-20) ; Helmold, *op. cit.*, Book II, Chaps. 19, 20.

[157] Adam of Bremen, *op. cit.*, Book III, Chaps. 21 (20), 49 (48) ; Helmold, *op. cit.*, Book I, Chap. 22 ; Hauck, *op. cit.*, Vol. III, p. 656.

[158] Adam of Bremen, *op. cit.*, Book III, Chaps. 50 (49), 51 (50) ; Helmold, *op. cit.*, Book I, Chaps. 22, 26.

[159] *Annales Augustani*, an. 1068, in *Mon. Germ. Hist., Scriptorum*, Vol. III, p. 128.

said that a Christian could rarely be found beyond the Elbe.[160] It was many decades before the Church recouped its losses in the lands of the Obodrites and the Wilzi.

Through the rest of the land of the Wends the progress of Christianity in the eleventh century was but little greater than among the Obodrites. Between the Saale and the Elbe no such violent fluctuations occurred as in the North. The public observance of the pagan cults ceased. However, outside the towns, which were predominantly German, the Church made little headway. In the twelfth century the region was gradually depopulated of its Slavs by war, the slave trade, and emigration. As the Wends disappeared, their places were taken by German farmers. These were Christian and for them a regular church life was gradually organized, with parishes and monasteries.[161]

East of the Elbe the beginning of the twelfth century saw the Church almost moribund. Only the Bishoprics of Havelberg and Brandenburg were regularly occupied, and their incumbents usually dwelt remote from their dioceses. For decades Christianity registered no gains.[162] Henry IV was too engrossed in his struggles with the Pope and his own nobles to pay much attention to the frontier.

It was not until nearly the close of the eleventh century, almost a generation after the uprising of 1066, that Christianity began to recover beyond the Elbe. Fresh gains were then made in various places. For instance, Henry, a son of Gottschalk, led a group of Christian Obodrites and Germans and in 1093 won a decisive victory over the pagan Wends.[163]

We must now turn for a time from the extreme North-west to a people farther to the east, the Pomeranians. The conversion of the Pomeranians was due to a combination of Danish, Polish, and German factors. Religiously the chief influence was a German Bishop, Otto of Bamberg. It will be recalled that Boleslaw Chrobry, who reigned in Poland from 992 to 1025, greatly expanded the boundaries of his realm and furthered the winning of his subjects to the Christian faith. Boleslaw extended his overlordship to Pomerania. As we

---

[160] *Annales Pegaviensis,* an. 1114, in *Mon. Germ. Hist., Scriptorum,* Vol. XVI, p. 252, line 16.

[161] Hauck, *op. cit.,* Vol. IV, pp. 577-585.

[162] Hauck, *op. cit.,* Vol. IV, p. 585.

[163] Helmold, *op. cit.,* Book I, Chap. 34. Helmold does not give the dates. His account has been challenged. See Tschan, *The Chronicle of the Slavs, by Helmold, Priest of Bosau,* p. 120, n. 1, and Thompson, *Feudal Germany,* p. 421, n. 1. The date and some of the facts appear to be confirmed by *Annales Hildesheimenses* (*Scriptores rerum Germanicarum,* Hanover, 1878), an. 1093, where it is said that Magnus, Duke of the Saxons, subdued the rebellious Slavs, taking fourteen cities. Helmold says that Magnus was related to Henry, was his overlord, and that at Henry's call he came and defeated the Slavs.

have said, one of the dioceses founded during his reign and placed under the new Polish archiepiscopal see of Gniezno (Gnesen) was Kolberg, in Pomerania and on the Baltic.[164] The first Bishop of Kolberg was Reinbern, a German. Well educated according to the standards of his time, earnestly ascetic in his private life and devotions, Reinbern zealously set about combating paganism and burned non-Christian shrines.[165] Whether permanent results attended his efforts we do not know. Nor are we informed that he had a successor.[166] The political and religious reaction which followed the death of Boleslaw may have erased whatever of beginnings of Christianity existed. During the latter half of the eleventh century Pomerania was independent and paganism flourished.

Fairly early in the twelfth century, however, a change began. Christianity was seeping in from Germany. One of the rulers of Pomerania, Vratislav (Wartislaw or Warcislaw), had been carried off captive in his youth, and at Merseburg, a German episcopal see, had been baptized. On returning to his own people he seems not to have continued to live as a Christian, but to have been friendly toward the faith.[167] His wife was of that religion, although lukewarm,[168] and in his entourage were those who had once been Christians but had relapsed.[169] We hear of other prominent Pomeranians who had been baptized in Saxony, but who, on returning home, either fell away or observed their faith only in secret.[170]

The formal conversion of Pomerania took place through a succession of events initiated through the temporary conquest of Pomerania by the Poles. Boleslaw III (1102-1139) did much to revive the central power in Poland and to extend the borders of the realm. Shortly before 1121 he invaded Pomerania, captured some of its cities, led away captive a large number of its inhabitants, and required of those whom he left in their homes on oath that they would become Christians and pay tribute to him. He compelled, too, the captives to renounce paganism and to embrace Christianity. Boleslaw III attempted to persuade the Polish bishops to undertake the task of instructing in the faith

---

[164] Thietmar, *Merseburgensis Episcopi Chronicon*, Book IV, Chap. 45.

[165] Thietmar, *op. cit.*, Book VIII, Chap. 72.

[166] Hauck, *Kirchengeschichte Deutschlands*, Vol. IV, p. 587.

[167] Ebo, *Ottonis Vita*, Book III, Chap. 6 (text in Jaffé, ed., *Bibliotheca rerum Germanicarum*, Vol. V, Berlin, 1869, translation in C. H. Robinson, *The Life of Otto, Apostle of Pomerania, 1060-1139, by Ebo and Herbordus*, London, 1920).

[168] Herbordus Scholasticus Montis St. Michaelis Bambenbergensis, *Dialogus de Vita Ottonis Episcopi Bambenbergensis*, Book II, Chap. 19 (text in Jaffé, ed., *op. cit.*, Vol. V, translation in Robinson, *op. cit.*, p. 53).

[169] Herbordus, *op. cit.*, Book II, Chap. 21.

[170] Ebo, *op. cit.*, Book II, Chaps. 8, 9; Herbordus, *op. cit.*, Book II, Chap. 26.

those whom he had so roughly constrained to accept it. None, however, would assume the difficult mission.[171]

The first to go to the Pomeranians with the authority of Boleslaw was Bernhard, a Spaniard. Bernhard was a monk who is said to have been consecrated Bishop at Rome, but, because of violent opposition in his diocese, to have decided to leave it and to volunteer for the Pomeranian enterprise. Boleslaw, to whom he presented himself, attempted to dissuade him, but since the Bishop persisted, gave him a guide and interpreter and wished him success. Ascetic that he was, Bernhard came to the Pomeranians barefoot and in mean garb. When he announced that he was the messenger of the Creator of heaven and earth he was derided. Possibly fearing the vengeance of Boleslaw, the Pomeranians declined to take him at his word and to test his divine commission by casting him into a burning building to see whether he could escape unscathed. When he attacked a sacred pillar they beat him, but when he attempted to preach they shipped him out of the country. He thereupon returned, indignant and crestfallen, to Boleslaw. He had not even achieved the coveted crown of martyrdom.[172]

His own Polish bishops having failed him and Bernhard's mission having miscarried, Boleslaw turned to Bishop Otto of Bamberg.[173] Although he was a German and his see was in Southern Germany and a long journey from Pomerania, Otto had Polish connections of long standing. In his young manhood he had served in Poland, perhaps at first as a simple teacher, and ap-

[171] Herbordus, *op. cit.,* Book II, Chaps. 4, 5.
[172] Ebo, *op. cit.,* Book II, Chap. 1.
[173] What is probably the oldest biography of Otto is Ebo, or Ebbo, *Vita Ottonis Episcopi Bambergensis,* by a priest-monk in the diocese of Bamberg. Written within a generation after Otto's death, it professes to be based on information from a friend of Otto. Another, and probably a slightly later biography, is Herbordus, *Dialogus de Ottone Episcopi Bambergensis,* also by a priest-monk of the diocese. The Latin texts of both lives, edited by Philip Jaffé, are in *Bibliotheca rerum Germanicarum,* Vol. V (Berlin, Weidmann, 1869), and in *Mon. Germ. Hist., Scriptorum,* Vol. XII, pp. 746-883. Herbordus seems to have drawn both from Ebo and from other sources. English translations of parts of Ebo and Herbordus are in C. H. Robinson, *The Life of Otto, Apostle of Pomerania, 1060-1139, by Ebo and Herbordus* (London, S.P.C.K., 1920). A third biography, by a monk in the Prüfling Monastery, appears to. have been based chiefly on Ebo and Herbordus. The text is in *Mon. Germ. Hist., Scriptorum,* Vol. XII, pp. 883-903, and a German translation is in *Das Leben des Bischofs Otto von Bamberg von einem Prüfeninger Mönch,* by A. Hofmeister (Leipzig, 1928). A brief account of these three and of three other mediæval biographies, with references to the literature, is in Robinson, *op. cit.,* pp. 9 ff. Hauck, *Kirchengeschichte Deutschlands,* Vol. IV, pp. 593-605, has a careful account with extensive references to the sources and later literature. See also Martin Wehrmann, *Geschichte von Pommern* (Gotha, Friedrich Andreas Perthes U.-G., 2 vols., 1906-1919), Vol. I, pp. 59-74; W. Kümmel, *Die Missionsmethode des Bischofs Otto von Bamberg und seiner Vorläufer in Pommern* (Gütersloh, C. Bertelsmann, 1926); Nottrott, *Aus der Wendenmission* (Halle, 1897), pp. 412-425; and Addison, *The Medieval Missionary,* pp. 56-71.

parently later in the court as chaplain to the German wife of the ruler. He seems to have acquired a knowledge of the Polish language, an accomplishment which probably stood him in good stead among the Slavic Pomeranians.[174] He was a man of affairs, an administrator who had been imperial chancellor and had had his share in court life and in the business of diplomacy and government.[175] In his own diocese he was a builder and organizer, a founder and renewer of churches and monasteries.[176] At the time when Boleslaw invited him to undertake the mission, Otto was probably in his sixties,[177] but he seems to have had the physical vigour of robust manhood.

Otto obtained the consent of the Pope and accepted the invitation.[178] Before setting out he is said to have consulted with Bishop Bernhard and to have been advised not to go in humble fashion, but to use enough pomp to impress the Pomeranians.[179] Otto selected helpers from his diocese and proceeded to Poland. Here he was welcomed by Boleslaw. The latter largely financed the mission and sent along three of his chaplains.[180] It was, then, as an agent of Boleslaw that Otto came to the Pomeranians. In accepting baptism from him they were carrying out the terms of their agreement with the Polish conqueror.

Otto was received with honour by Vratislav, who, as we have seen, had been baptized and was one of the Pomeranian rulers. With the support of Vratislav and with the authority of Boleslaw, Otto and his companions began the work for which they had come. They moved from place to place, baptizing and giving instruction to the neophytes. They took care to administer the baptismal rite with decorum and dignity. Often some training preceded baptism. Usually more detailed teaching followed. At best, however, it was only a few days in length. It consisted in such commands as the observance of Sunday, Lent, and the saints' days, attendance at mass, prayers, confessions, alms-giving, and the prohibition of infanticide, of marriage within the prohibited degrees of relationship, of polygamy, and of idolatry and other pagan rites. Otto saw that churches and chapels were built.

Often the Bishop met resistance and even violence. The pagan priests were recalcitrant and numbers of the populace objected to departing from the cus-

[174] Ebo, op. cit., Book I, Chap. 1; Herbordus, op. cit., Book II, Chap. 6, Book III, Chap. 32; Hauck, op. cit., Vol. IV, p. 593, n. 1.

[175] Ebo, op. cit., Book I, Chap. 3.

[176] He had built twenty-four churches and six castles.—Herbordus, op. cit., Book I, Chap. 26. See also Hauck, op. cit., Vol. IV, p. 594.

[177] Ebo, op. cit., Book II, Chap. 3; Herbordus, op. cit., Book I, Chap. 40; Hauck, op. cit., Vol. IV, p. 594, n. 2.

[178] Ebo, op. cit., Book II, Chap. 3.

[179] Ebo, op. cit., Book II, Chap. 2.

[180] Ebo, op. cit., Book II, Chap. 4; Herbodus, op. cit., Book II, Chaps. 9, 10.

toms of their ancestors and adopting the God of the hated foreigners. To overcome the opposition Otto employed not force, but diplomacy. He sought to win the leaders and through them the people. On occasion he threatened the violent with the displeasure of Boleslaw. He appears to have taken pains to make it clear that he personally had no selfish interest to further and that he did not wish any of the property of the Pomeranians. For several months in 1124 and 1125 he was in the region. He was then summoned back to his diocese to settle troubles which had arisen in his absence. In his brief mission by no means all the Pomeranians had been baptized, but in at least some of the main towns Christian communities had been planted. His success was aided by the fear of the yearly raids by the Poles and by the hope that if Christianity were accepted these would cease. Otto's character and methods also had a large share in the result.[181]

It is not surprising that a violent reaction occurred against this rapid departure from the old ways. Before Otto had been many months out of Pomerania paganism revived and wholesale apostasies from Christianity began. The priests of the ancient faith were active and in Stettin persuaded the populace that an epidemic was due to the anger of the slighted gods.[182] Apparently, too, the Pomeranians attempted to throw off the Polish yoke[183] and with it what they regarded as the Polish religion.

Otto heard of the reaction and determined to go to the rescue of the young Church. In 1128, approximately three years after his former visit, he set out. This time he did not go by way of Poland, but obtained the authorization not only of the Pope, but also of the German King (later Holy Roman Emperor) Lothair.[184] It was, therefore, under the protection of the German and not of the Polish realm that he returned. Once more he had the support of Vratislav and under his ægis made his way through the land, reclaiming apostates, destroying pagan shrines, and making fresh converts. He went in person to Boleslaw, the Polish ruler, and induced him to forego his punitive expedition. At Stettin he seems to have met his greatest difficulty. Here, at great risk of their lives, he and his entourage entered the town when many of the populace, stirred up by the priests of the old religion, were clamouring for their blood. Otto addressed the mob and finally won the leaders of the city by threatening to place his curse on the inhabitants if they did not repent. Otto, indeed, had taken up his crozier and put on his stole to proclaim the curse when the city fathers, terrified, asked for a brief time in which to confer,

[181] Ebo, *op. cit.*, Book II ; Herbordus, *op. cit.*, Book II.
[182] Ebo, *op. cit.*, Book III, Chap. 1.
[183] Ebo, *op. cit.*, Book III, Chap. 13.
[184] Ebo, *op. cit.*, Book III, Chap. 3.

came back, and offered their submission. The fear of the Bishop's magic had proved effective. When, in the autumn of 1128, Otto returned to Bamberg, he seems to have left the Church in Pomerania much stronger even than at the close of his first visit.[185]

To give permanency to his work and to complete the organization of the Pomeranian Church, Otto would normally have obtained the creation of an episcopate for the land. Both Vratislav and Otto desired this and Otto suggested as Bishop his interpreter and companion, Adalbert. For some reason, possibly because of the inability of the Archbishops of Magdeburg and Gniezno to agree on which of the two should supervise the new diocese, the step was not carried out.[186] Eventually, in 1140, the year after Otto's death, Pope Innocent II himself consecrated Adalbert and placed the new see under neither Magdeburg nor Gniezno, but directly under Rome.[187] Adalbert's hands were strengthened by the coming of the Premonstratensians. The Premonstratensian Canons had been founded a few years before by Norbert, who died in 1134 as Archbishop of Magdeburg. It was natural that among their earliest efforts should be missions to the Wends and that some of them should come to Pomerania.[188]

In spite of the labours of Otto and those who succeeded him, it was many years before Christianity was really well rooted in the affections of the Pomeranians. In the twelfth and thirteenth centuries German settlers, Christians, entered in large numbers, until they and their descendants constituted the majority of the population. German and Danish monastic communities were founded, and these encouraged the coming of German farmers to till their lands. By the end of the twelfth century the Slavic Pomeranians began to feel at home in the Church. Slavic names appeared in the lists of the clergy, an indication that the priests were no longer exclusively German. By the time of the centenary of Otto's first coming, the assimilation of the Pomeranians to Christianity seems to have been fairly well completed.[189]

From Pomerania we must turn once more to the north-western portion of the land of the Wends and to other Slavic areas between the Elbe and the Oder. Here the process of conversion had a somewhat stormier course. No one with quite the skill and ability of Otto emerged to hasten it and in the first half of the twelfth century it was somewhat retarded. Yet it was com-

---

[185] Ebo, *op. cit.*, Book III; Herbordus, *op. cit.*, Book III.
[186] Hauck, *Kirchengeschichte Deutschlands,* Vol. IV, pp. 604-606.
[187] Hauck, *op. cit.*, Vol. IV, pp. 607-609.
[188] Hauck, *op. cit.*, Vol. IV, p. 610; Workman, *The Evolution of the Monastic Ideal,* pp. 365, 366.
[189] Hauck, *op. cit.*, Vol. IV, pp. 813-815.

pleted by about the same time, and in large part, as in Pomerania, by the influx of German settlers.

Among the Obodrites, as we have seen, under Henry, a son of Gottschalk, recovery from the effects of the revolt of 1066 began before the close of the eleventh century. Yet Henry seems not to have been very active in propagating his inherited faith. Except in Old Lübeck, the town where Henry usually made his headquarters, in all the land of the Slavs there appears to have been neither priest nor church for the Wends.[190] Among the Wilzi, in the later Brandenburg, early in the twelfth century a few Christian chieftains were found, but among the populace there were only a very few Christians.[191] During the first third of the twelfth century in a number of places beyond the Elbe the clergy became more active and a few gains were registered.[192]

The most energetic attempt in the first half of the twelfth century to bring about the conversion of the Obodrites was associated with the name of Vicelin. Vicelin began his labours as missionary among the Obodrites in 1126, the year after the close of Bishop Otto's first sojourn in Pomerania, and continued them until his death, in 1154. In his later years he was Bishop of Oldenburg, the see that had been established by Otto the Great nearly two centuries before.[193] Vicelin was probably a Saxon. As a youth he led a studious and a gradually deepening religious life. He sought ordination of the saintly Norbert, the Archbishop of Magdeburg, and then, being attracted to mission work among the Obodrites, he went to the Archbishop of Hamburg and asked an appointment. The latter was glad to find a volunteer for a task which so few had been willing to undertake, and in 1126 Vicelin and a few companions went to Lübeck, to the Christian Prince Henry. The following year his plans were disrupted by the death of Henry. He laboured among the German settlers on the border, to purify and deepen their nominal Christianity, but missions among the Wends lagged.

As the years passed, an increasing number of settlers entered from Germany and the Low Countries. The region, therefore, began to take on the aspect of a Christian land.

[190] Helmold, *Chronica Slavorum,* Book I, Chap. 34. The same chapter speaks of churches being rebuilt, but this may mean only those of the Germans.

[191] Hauck, *op. cit.,* Vol. IV, p. 620, gives several instances, but it is not clear from the source (Ebo, *Vita Ottoni,* Book III, Chap. 3) that the Wirikind whom he mentions as a Christian really was one.

[192] Hauck, *op. cit.,* Vol. IV, pp. 621, 622.

[193] On Vicelin, see *Versus de Vita Vicelini* and *Sidonis Epistola,* in *Scriptores rerum Germanicarum* (edition of J. M. Luppenberg by B. Schmeidler, Hanover, 1909) in same volume with Helmold, *op. cit.;* Helmold, *op. cit.,* Book I, Chaps. 42-79, and Hauck, *op. cit.,* Vol. IV, pp. 623 ff.

In 1147 a fresh war broke out which brought another great reverse to Christianity. In Germany the Second Crusade was preached by Bernard of Clairvaux. With Bernard's endorsement, several thousands of Saxons, Poles, and Czechs who took the cross directed their arms, not against the Moslems in the Holy Land, but against the Wends. As a result, the progress of the faith among the latter seems to have been hindered and not furthered. One of the leaders of the Wends, alarmed by the threat of invasion, attacked the Christians, and the hatred of the Slavs for the Christian name was accentuated. Some Wends were baptized, but obviously the conversion was only nominal.[194]

By the end of the twelfth century the land between the Elbe and the Oder seems to have become substantially Christian. As in Pomerania, the chief factor in bringing this about was the immigration of Christian Germans.[195] The immigration was hastened by the efforts of Henry the Lion (1129-1195), Duke of Saxony, who was vigorous in extending his authority and in founding German settlements and towns beyond the Elbe. It was he who completed the German conquest of the region. He aided the Church and encouraged the establishments of the Cistercians. The land became more and more German in blood and in culture. The remnants of the Slavs appear gradually to have been assimilated. It may be that at least some of the Wends submitted to baptism to avoid discriminatory imposts and to acquire the privileged status of Germans.[196] The founding of monasteries hastened conversion. Cistercians and Premonstratensians both had a share.

Apparently the last of the Wends to become Christian were in the Island of Rügen, in the Baltic, off the Pomeranian coast. Protected by the sea, they long held to their old gods. The destruction of paganism was achieved by an invasion of the King of Denmark in about 1168 or 1169. Wend pirates, especially from Rügen, had long wasted the Danish coast. About the middle of the twelfth century there came to power in Denmark Absalon, later Archbishop of Lund. Warrior, statesman, diplomat, and zealous and earnest churchman, under his direction and counsel the Danes wiped out the Wend pirates and extended their own control to much of the Baltic coast. Absalon and the Danish King, Valdemar I, invaded Rügen, captured the Wend strongholds, desecrated and destroyed the fanes and the images of the gods (one

---

[194] Helmold, op. cit., Book I, Chaps. 62-66; Hauck, op. cit., Vol. IV, pp. 628-631.

[195] On this process see Helmold, op. cit., Book I, Chaps. 68 ff.; Hauck, op. cit., Vol. IV, pp. 631-651; Thompson, Feudal Germany, pp. 502-528; Cambridge Medieval History, Vol. V, pp. 356 ff.

[196] Helmold, op. cit., Book I, Chap. 84 (83), tells of a Wend chieftain who said that he and his people would willingly become Christians if they could have the rights of the Saxons in respect to property and taxes.

of the most revered images was knocked down, dragged out, and cut up for firewood), and provided means for the erection of churches.[197]

North and east of the lands of the Wends and the Poles were other territories along the Baltic—the later East Prussia, Lithuania, Latvia, Estonia, and Finland. Here the process of conversion was long delayed. Not until the fifteenth century was it even superficially completed. The peoples were of various racial stocks. The chief groups, as the present names of the region indicate, were the Finns, the Estonians or Ests, the Letts, the Prussians, and the Lithuanians. In the conversion of these Baltic peoples to the Roman Catholic type of Christianity, the Danes, the Swedes, the Germans, and the Poles participated. In most of the areas the chief agents were the Germans. In the main, the spread of Christianity was a phase of German expansion.

The first missionary to these Baltic peoples of whom we know was the Slav, Adalbert, the second Bishop of Prague, who in 997 met a martyr's death while attempting to carry the Christian message to the Prussians.[198]

A little more than ten years later, in 1009, Bruno of Querfurt similarly came to a martyr's end among the Prussians. Bruno, also known as Brun and Boniface, was born about 974 of Saxon noble stock and was educated in the frontier city of Magdeburg. The death of Adalbert made a profound impression on him and seems to have kindled an ambition to become a missionary and attain a like crown. Bruno won the favour of the young and visionary Emperor Otto III and went to Italy with him. There, in about 1002, he was appointed Archbishop to the heathen, without a fixed see, by Sylvester II, the former tutor of Otto III, whom the latter had raised to the Papal throne. He later held the title of Bishop of Querfurt. For a time he was a missionary in Hungary. Boleslaw Chrobry of Poland promised him help for a mission to the Prussians, to which he had presumably been attracted by the fate of his hero. Boleslaw was forced by war to postpone the fulfilment of his undertaking. Disappointed but not discouraged, Bruno went to Russia and was there for portions of the years 1007 and 1008. Some of this time he spent in Kiev, and during part of it he was a missionary to a Turkish people with one branch of whom he had become acquainted while in Hungary. Thence

[197] Saxo Grammaticus, *Gesta Danorum*, Book XIV, Holder's ed., pp. 504 ff., especially pp. 573-575; Helmold, *op. cit.*, Book II, Chap. 12. On the date see Tschan, *The Chronicle of the Slavs by Helmold, Priest of Bosau*, p. 274, n. 1. See also R. N. Bain in *Encyc. Brit.*, 14th ed., Vol. I, p. 63.

[198] *Passio Sancti Adalperti Martiris*, in *Mon. Germ. Hist.*, *Scriptorum*, Vol. XV, Pt. 2, pp. 706-708; Canaparius, *Vita Adalberti*, in *Mon. Germ. Hist.*, *Scriptorum*, Vol. XIV, pp. 581-595; Bruno, *Passio Sancti Adalberti, Episcopi et Martyris*, in *Mon. Germ. Hist.*, *Scriptorum*, Vol. IV, pp. 596-612.

he returned to Poland to attempt to carry out his earlier dream. With a group of companions he entered the land of the Prussians. His reception was un-friendly, but he and his band pursued their way, preaching as they had op-portunity, until the martyr's fate overtook them all.[199]

So far as our records tell us, the renewal of efforts to win to Christianity the peoples on the eastern shores of the Baltic was to wait for more than a century after the tragic death of Bruno. Whether, in this interval, some con-versions occurred we do not know. In the eleventh century, as we have seen, the Danes, Norwegians, and Swedes were becoming Christian. They had long been voyaging to the eastern shores of the Baltic and effecting settle-ments. It is possible, therefore, that in the eleventh century some of the Scan-dinavians to the east of the Baltic had become Christians and that a few individuals from non-Scandinavian peoples of that region had received bap-tism. However, only in the twelfth century did Christianity become the faith of the majority in Scandinavia, and not until then could Scandinavians be expected to become active as missionaries to others than their own country-men. Moreover, in the eleventh century Polish Christians seem not to have been disposed to undertake missions beyond their own borders, and between the powerful Christian German peoples and the eastern shores of the Baltic were the Poles and the pagan Wends. It is not surprising that the twelfth century was half spent before serious attempts of which we have record were made to plant Christianity in these lands.

As was to be expected, some of the earliest efforts at conversion of which we hear were by the Scandinavians. Shortly after the middle of the twelfth century, King Eric of Sweden, who later became the patron saint of his realm, led an expedition against the Finns (who are said to have been attack-ing the Swedes) and defeated them. As a result many accepted baptism and churches were founded.[200] With him went an Englishman, Bishop Henry of Upsala, who seems to have remained after Eric departed and later was mar-tyred. He is called the founder of the Finnish Church.[201] Swedish settlements persisted in the south-western part of Finland. Pope Alexander III (1159-1181) took an active interest in the missions in the North, and from one of

---

[199] *Acta Sanctorum,* Feb. 14 (Vol. V, pp. 797 ff.) ; D. H. G. Voigt, *Brun von Querfurt* (Stuttgart, 1907).

[200] *Vita et Miracula Sancti Erici Regis et martyris,* in *Scriptores rerum Suecicarum,* Vol. II, p. 274; Schybergson, *Geschichte Finnlands* (Arnheim's translation), p. 9; Hallen-dorff and Schück, *History of Sweden,* p. 33; Svanström and Palmstierna, *A Short History of Sweden,* p. 27.

[201] *Vita et Miracula Sancti Henrici Episcopi et Martyris,* in *Scriptores rerum Suecicarum,* Vol. II, pp. 331-343; *Finlands Medeltidsurkunder,* Vol. I, p. 11; Schybergson, *op. cit.,* p. 9; Svanström and Palmstierna, *op. cit.,* p. 31.

his letters addressed to the Archbishop of Upsala and the latter's suffragans and to Duke Gutherm, it seems that when a Swedish army appeared the Finns promised to observe the Christian faith and asked for teachers and preachers, but that when the army retired they apostatized and persecuted the missionaries.[202] In 1192 we have mention of a bishopric at Abo.[203] In a letter dated in 1209 Pope Innocent III spoke of the report that conversions had been taking place in Finland and urged that the errors of paganism be extirpated.[204] A Dominican by the name of Thomas was bishop in Finland from 1220 to 1245 and did much to strengthen the Church there.[205] In the wars between the Swedes and Novgorod, the latter sometimes used the pagan peoples to embarrass the former and presumably encouraged them to resist conversion, at least to the Swedish variety of Christianity.[206] In 1249 the Swedish Jarl Birger Magnusson, one of the most prominent figures of mediæval Sweden, organized an expedition which conquered much of Finland and led the majority of the population to an outward acceptance of the Christian faith and of Swedish law and customs.[207] For years the most powerful personage in the land was the Bishop of Abo.[208] Thus, as so often in the history of the spread of religions, conquest, colonization, and the assimilation of the subject peoples to the faith of the conquerors went hand in hand.

In the northern part of Scandinavia, in territory which eventually was divided between Norwegian, Swedish, Finnish, and Russian control, have lived for many centuries those whom the Swedes call the Lapps. Never a numerous people and having to contend with an adverse climate, culturally the Lapps have been backward. How early they were touched by Christianity we do not know. It is said that in the eleventh century, under that Archbishop Adalbert of Hamburg-Bremen who attempted to extend the influence of his see throughout the North, some of them were converted.[209] A Bishop Stephen, or Simon, sent by Adalbert, is reported to have been a missionary among them.[210] In the thirteenth and fourteenth centuries, as the Swedes pushed northward, the Lapps were brought into intimate touch with this now professedly Christian

---

[202] *Finlands Medeltidsurkunder,* Vol. I, p. 12.
[203] *Finlands Medeltidsurkunder,* Vol. I, p. 16.
[204] *Finlands Medeltidsurkunder,* Vol. I, p. 19.
[205] Schybergson, *op. cit.,* p. 12.
[206] Schybergson, *op. cit.,* pp. 12, 13.
[207] Schybergson, *op. cit.,* p. 14.
[208] Schybergson, *op. cit.,* p. 21.
[209] Adam of Bremen, *Gesta Hammaburgensis Ecclesiæ Pontificum,* Book III, Chap. 16 (15). The name which Adam gives to the Lapps is Scritefing.
[210] Adam of Bremen, *op. cit.,* Book III, Chap. 75, Book IV, Chap. 24, Schol. 137 (132, 133).

people. The Archbishops of Upsala took an active interest in them.[211] Especially during the reign of Magnus Ladulaas (1275-1290), a Swedish lord, Birkarle, established his rule over some of the Lapps. The oppression of his followers did not predispose the Lapps to accept Christianity and the few priests who dealt with them knew the language imperfectly. Yet some nominal converts were made. A Lapp woman, Margaret, who lived in Sweden in the latter part of the fourteenth century, interested some in high places in missions to her people. Late in that century we hear that an Archbishop of Lund busied himself in their behalf. In the fifteenth century we read of monks from Bergen having a mission among them.[212]

When, in the course of the twelfth century, the lands of the Wends were being occupied by Germans and assimilated to German culture, it was natural that German interest should increase in the Baltic regions to the east, and that German merchants, missionaries, and settlers should overflow into them, found German colonies, and seek to conquer and to win to their faith the non-German peoples. The Danes, too, were concerned, but not being so politically powerful or so numerous as the Germans, did not leave so deep an impress. In the latter half of the twelfth century, Absalon, the powerful and able Archbishop of Lund, dreamed of bringing into existence in that region a church which would enhance the Danish ecclesiastical sphere of influence. With the support of Pope Alexander III, who, as we have seen, concerned himself with missions in the North, he consecrated Fulco, a French monk, as Bishop for that area. What came of the effort we do not know.[213] We have seen Absalon's success in breaking the power of paganism in the island of Rügen. Archbishop Absalon and King Valdemar I (died 1182) laid the foundations for a brilliant but brief Danish empire on the southern and eastern shores of the Baltic. This came to its apex and began its disastrous decline under Valdemar II (died 1241), the son of Valdemar I. Valdemar II made numerous conquests along the Baltic, most of which had little effect upon the spread of Christianity. However, in Estonia he began an occupation which had lasting results. Bishop Albert, the founder of Riga, of whom we are to hear more in a moment, called to his help Valdemar II.[214] Valdemar obtained from the Pope title for his realm and the Church to whatever lands he might acquire from the

---

[211] Vahl, *Lapperne og den lapske Mission,* Part II, pp. 82, 83.

[212] Vahl, *op. cit.,* Part II, pp. 4, 5.

[213] Bunge, *Liv-, Esth-, und Curländisches Urkundenbuch,* Vol. I, pp. 2, 3, Nos. 2-8; Hauck, *Kirchengeschichte Deutschlands,* Vol. IV, pp. 653, 654.

[214] Bunge, *Das Herzogthum Estland unter den Königen von Dänemark* (Gotha, Friedr. Andr. Perthes, 1877, pp. xv, 391), p. 14, citing *Chronicon Danicum Langebek, Scr. rer. Danicarum,* III, 265.

pagans.[215] In 1219 he came north with a huge fleet. He sailed into the Gulf of Finland and on its south coast began the construction of a castle at Reval. With the King were Archbishop Andrew and three other bishops. The King gave the Ests gifts and the bishops baptized many.[216] In 1220 we hear of the baptism of numbers of others of the Ests, some by Germans and some by Danes.[217] In 1222 the Ests arose and left little of the Danish rule except Reval.[218] Into the subsequent history we must not take the time to go in any detail. Through the Knights of the Sword the Germans took Reval and all Estonia. Eventually, through Rome and the Papal legate, Reval, with two-thirds of Estonia, was returned to Valdemar (1238). Most of the ephemeral empire of Valdemar passed into other hands, but the northern part of Estonia long remained under the control of the Danes. In the earlier years of their occupation we read of Crusades ordered by Rome against the pagans and the Russians. The land proved difficult to hold. Rebellions were frequent and there were foreign foes. About the middle of the fourteenth century (1347) the Danish portion of Estonia came under the Knights of the Sword. Even under the Danes the Germans had been numerous. They now entered into possession. Yet the Danes had had a share in the establishment of the Church in the land and in the conversion of its peoples.[219]

In 1141, with the approval of Rome, Bishop Henry of Olomouc (Olmütz) attempted a mission to the Prussians, but with no success.[220] The earliest German missionary efforts east of the Baltic which led to permanent results are associated with the name of Meinhard. Meinhard was a member of the monastic community at Segeberg, in the land of the Wends, not far from Lübeck, and perhaps had caught some of the missionary spirit of Vicelin, whom he had known. When already well along in years, stirred by tales which merchants and sailors told of the peoples to the east, he joined himself to the trading-ships from Lübeck, went to the lower Dvina, and preached to whomever would hear him. In 1184 he built a church not far from the mouth of the river. In 1186 he visited Bremen and reported on his work. The Arch-

[215] Bunge, *Das Herzogthum Estland unter den Königen von Dänemark,* p. 15, citing bull of Honorius III of Oct. 9, 1218.

[216] Heinrich, *Chronicon Lyvoniae* (ed. G. H. Pertz in *Scriptores rerum Germanicarum,* Hanover, 1874), Book XXIII, Chap. 2.

[217] Heinrich, *op. cit.,* Book XXIV, Chaps. 1, 2.

[218] Heinrich, *op. cit.,* Book XXVI, Chap. 11.

[219] Bunge, *op. cit.,* pp. 35 ff., 195 ff.

[220] *Canonici Wissegrad, Contin. Cosmae Chron. Boemorum,* an. 1141, in *Mon. Germ. Hist., Scriptorum,* Vol. IX, p. 147; *Monachi Sazavensis Contin. Cosmae,* an. 1139, in *Mon. Germ. Hist., Scriptorum,* Vol. IX p. 158; *Annales Gradicenses,* an. 1141, in *Mon. Germ. Hist., Scriptorum,* Vol. XVII, p. 651; *Preussisches Urkundenbuch,* Vol. I, pp. 1, 2, Nos. 1-3; Hauck, *op. cit.,* Vol. IV, p. 670.

bishop, presumably envisaging here an opportunity to enlarge his see and to continue the tradition of Anskar, consecrated Meinhard as Bishop. Meinhard was reinforced by a number of missionaries, and Rome gave him its support. However, some of his converts apostatized, and on his death, in 1196, the future of the enterprise which he had so courageously begun seemed un-promising.[221]

The situation was complicated by the immigration of German settlers. The land was spoken of as well watered, fertile, wooded, and with streams abound-ing in fish. Even in the days of Meinhard, Berthold, an abbot who had left his monastery to join the mission, is said to have preached widely in Germany and to have encouraged rich and poor, clergy and nobles, to go to Lübeck and embark for this new German colony.[222] The earlier inhabitants would natu-rally fear the irruption of these strangers and regard the acceptance of Chris-tianity as an indication of submission. The native population was not so nearly displaced by Germans as in the lands of the Wends. Germans remained in the minority. Eventually, however, they became the dominant, ruling class.

Berthold, who was chosen to succeed Meinhard in the episcopate, felt it ad-visable to have the support of an army of Crusaders. Long before his time, Crusades had caught the imagination of both high and low in Europe and were a favourite way of attempting to spread the faith. They combined warlike ad-venture, the opportunity for new lands and for wealth and fame, and the religious motive. Bishop Berthold fell early in the fighting, in 1198, but the army compelled many of the Livonians to accept baptism. As soon as the Crusaders departed, the involuntary neophytes washed off the baptismal waters and sacrificed some of the Christian priests to the pagan gods.[223]

To replace Bishop Berthold, Archbishop Hartwig of Bremen consecrated his own nephew, the youthful Albert. Albert proved to be as much a territorial magnate and secular conqueror as a missionary. He recruited soldiers through the villages, cities, and castles of Germany, and sent them forth in expedition after expedition. From various lay and clerical lords of Germany he obtained assistance in money, arms, ships, and provisions. We have already noted his experience with Valdemar II of Denmark. Near the mouth of the Dvina he founded a German city, Riga. To assist his Crusade and apparently taking as his models the military orders of the Knights Templars, the Knights Hos-

[221] Arnold, *Chronica Slavorum* (ed. by G. H. Pertz, in *Scriptores rerum Germanicarum*), Book V, Chap. 30; Bunge, *Liv-, Esth-, und Curländisches Urkundenbuch*, Vol. I, pp. 2, 3, Nos. 10, 12, 14; Hauck, *op. cit.*, Vol. IV, pp. 655, 656.

[222] Arnold, *op. cit.*, Book V, Chap. 30.

[223] Bunge, *Liv-, Esth-, und Curländisches Urkundenbuch*, Vol. I, p. 3, No. 13; Arnold, *op. cit.*, Book V, Chap. 30; Hauck, *op. cit.*, Vol. IV, p. 656.

pitallers, and the recently founded Teutonic Knights (some of whose origi-
nators had come from his own region of Bremen and Lübeck), he organized
(1202) the Knights of the Sword (officially *Fratres Militiæ Christi*) and placed
them directly under his own control. The Knights took the vow of celibacy,
and, using the form of the Templars, renounced all and gave themselves to
"the army of Christ."[224]

The Order of the Sword, as we have said, was not responsible only to the
Pope, as were the Templars, but was also under the Bishop, an agent of his
colonizing and missionary program. The organization proved true to its name
and employed its arms actively in subjugating the pagan peoples. In 1207, only
five years after the foundation of the Order, the conquest of much of the Dvina
Valley was completed. By September, 1217, the southern and western portions
of Estonia had been subdued. The northern and eastern sections of Estonia, as
we have seen, became a Danish possession. South and west of the Dvina, in
Courland and Zemgale (or Semgalle), the year 1225 saw the task of occupation practically finished.[225] By a decree of the Emperor Otto IV, in 1212, a
third of the newly seized lands were to go to the Knights.[226]

With conquest went the baptism of the inhabitants. In 1229, for instance,
a treaty with some of the pagans in Courland pledged them to accept baptism,
to observe all the Christian rites, and in other ways to live as Christians.[227]
Repeatedly in the accounts of the wars and of the German occupation we hear
of priests going through the country and baptizing large numbers.[228] By 1207
all of Livonia is said to have been baptized.[229] In 1210 Innocent III[230] and in
1212 the Emperor Otto IV[231] spoke in official documents of the Livonians as
having been won to the Christian faith. In 1213 Innocent III declared that a
large part of Estonia had been converted.[232] It may be that these statements

---

[224] Arnold, *op. cit.*, Book V, Chap. 30; Hauck, *op. cit.*, Vol. IV, p. 657.
[225] Heinrich, *Chronicon Lyvoniae,* Book X, Chaps. 13, 17, Book XI, Chaps. 6 ff., Book
XIX, Chaps. 4, 7, 8, Book XX, Chaps. 2-8, Book XXI, Chaps. 1-5; Bunge, *Das Herzogthum
Estland unter den Königen von Dänemark,* pp. 12, 13; Hauck, *op. cit.,* Vol. IV, p. 659.
Also, on the conquest and conversion of these regions, see Kurd von Schlözer, *Livland und
die Anfänge deutschen Lebens in baltischen Norden* (Berlin, 1850); Erich Chudzinski,
Die Eroberung Kurlands durch den Deutschen Orden im 13. Jahrhundert (Borna-Leipzig,
1917); P. Schwartz, *Kurland im dreizehnten Jahrhundert* (Leipzig, 1875); Ernest
Seraphim, *Geschichte Livland* (Gotha, 1906); Peter Z. Olins, *The Teutonic Knights in
Latvia* (Riga, 1928); H. Hildebrand, *Die Chronik Heinrichs von Lettland* (Berlin, 1865).
[226] Bunge, *Liv-, Est-, und Curländisches Urkundenbuch,* Vol. I, Cols. 32, 33, No. 25.
[227] Bunge, *Liv-, Esth-, und Curländisches Urkundenbuch,* Vol. I, Col. 135, No. 103.
[228] Heinrich, *op. cit.,* Book X, Chap. 14, Book XI, Chap. 7, Book XXIV, Chaps. 1-5;
Bunge, *Liv-, Esth-, und Curländisches Urkundenbuch,* Vol. I, Col. 141, No. 106.
[229] Heinrich, *op. cit.,* Book XI, Chap. 1.
[230] Bunge, *Liv-, Esth-, und Curländisches Urkundenbuch,* Vol. I, Col. 22, No. 16.
[231] Bunge, *op. cit.,* Vol. I, Col. 32, No. 25.
[232] Bunge, *op. cit.,* Vol. I, Col. 43, No. 36.

were exaggerations. Certainly a change of faith brought about under such conditions could not have been accomplished through any understanding of the inward import of what was being accepted.

Sometimes the motive for receiving baptism seems to have been the desire for assistance against enemies. So, in 1219, some of Zemgale sought the aid of the Bishop against the Letts and were promised it on the condition that they be baptized. It is significant, too, that the petitioners declared that the acceptance of the rite would incur such hatred from Letts and fellow Zemgalians that they would comply only if they were assured armed protection.[233] Obviously the Germans were profiting by the divisions among the various peoples. Clearly, too, they were not loved, and Christianity was regarded as a German (or, in Northern Estonia, as a Danish) faith. Baptism meant the acknowledgment of German or Danish rule.

Instruction in things Christian was given. Some of this was conveyed by miracle plays of the kind which were so popular in mediæval Europe and so useful with illiterates.[234]

Reactions were to be expected. These were the more likely to occur because of the financial imposts levied for the support of the Church and the construction of church buildings. Here, as elsewhere in much of Europe, taxes for the maintenance of the Church, in the form of tithes or otherwise, were collected.[235] Naturally these were unpopular and must have added to the unrest.

The situation was further complicated by rivalries among the invaders. The Russians, especially of the two great commercial cities of Pskov and Novgorod, resented the coming of the Germans and the Danes and waged war.[236] They were Greek Orthodox in faith. For a brief time, too, in 1220, the Swedes effected a landing in Estonia, baptizing the population and building churches.[237] The Danes and the Germans, as we have seen, were often at odds. Baptism became a symbol of submission to the authority of the nation whose priests administered the ceremony.[238] We read of competition between Danish and German priests in attempting to baptize the populace. In one instance the Danes punished a local head man for accepting the rite from the Germans.[239] Now, as in later centuries, the peoples on the eastern shores of the Baltic were the prey of the conflicting imperialisms of their neighbours. Then, as later,

[233] Heinrich, *op. cit.*, Book XXIII, Chap. 3.
[234] Heinrich, *op. cit.*, Book IX, Chap. 14.
[235] Bunge, *op. cit.*, Vol. I, Cols. 303, 304, No. 240.
[236] As in Heinrich, *op. cit.*, Book XXV, Chap. 2.
[237] Heinrich, *op. cit.*, Book XXIV, Chap. 3.
[238] Heinrich, *op. cit.*, Book XXIV, Chap. 1.
[239] *Ibid.*

religious propaganda was inextricably mixed with political and commercial policies.

The missionary activities of Bishop Albert were contemporary with the high tide of the mediæval Papacy. The earlier years of his conquests in the Baltic coincided with the pontificate of the masterful Innocent III (1198-1216). For a generation or so after Innocent III, the Papal throne was occupied by strong men. It is not surprising, therefore, that Rome took not only an active interest, but also an energetic part, in the direction of the mission. Numerous documents attest the Papal concern for the region. In 1221 Pope Honorius III appointed William of Modena Legate to Livonia, Prussia, and some adjacent regions.[240] Albert did not fulfil his ambition to become an archbishop, independent of Hamburg-Bremen, in the territories which he had won for the faith, and William of Modena practically took out of his hands the administration of the Church in Livonia.[241] Albert died in 1229, "the last great missionary bishop of Germany" of the middle ages.[242] The Papal Legate, backed by Rome, stepped decisively into the controversy between the Archbishop of Bremen and the cathedral chapter of Riga over his successor. Papal Legates created new dioceses and in other ways directed the Church in the newly acquired areas. Here, as elsewhere in Europe, the Papacy of the first half of the thirteenth century asserted its authority.[243]

South of Livonia lay Lithuania and Prussia. There conversion was much more retarded than in Livonia, Courland, and Estonia. We have seen the tragic end of the attempts of Adalbert of Prague and Bruno of Querfurt to introduce Christianity into Prussia. We have noted, too, the failure of Henry of Olomouc (Olmütz) a generation after Bruno. Subsequent to this last miscarriage two generations elapsed before another effort finds a place in our records. Early in the thirteenth century Gottfried, the abbot of a Polish monastery, became interested through the imprisonment by the Prussians of two of his monks. With the endorsement of Pope Innocent III, in 1205, 1206, or 1207 he crossed the Vistula with a band of missionaries and we read that he won two Prussian chiefs and that one of his companions was martyred.[244] Gottfried soon drops out of the records and may have died before 1211.[245]

---

[240] Bunge, *Liv-, Esth-, und Curländisches Urkundenbuch,* Vol. I, Cols. 73, 74, No. 69.
[241] Heinrich, *Chronicon Lyvoniae,* Book XXIX, Chap. 8; Hauck, *Kirchengeschichte Deutschlands,* Vol. IV, p. 664.
[242] Hauck, *op. cit.,* Vol. IV, p. 666.
[243] Hauck, *op. cit.,* Vol. IV, pp. 661-669. See some instances in C. Schirren, *Fünfundzwanzig Urkunden zur Geschichte Livlands im dreizehnten Jahrhundert* (Dorpat, 1866), Nos. 1, 2, 5-9, 11a, 11b, 12, 13, 15.
[244] *Preussisches Urkundenbuch* (Königsberg i. Pr., 1882), Vol. I, Pt. 1, p. 2, No. 4; Hauck, *op. cit.,* Vol. IV, p. 670; Fritz Blanke, *Die Entscheidungsjahre der Preussenmission* (in *Zeitschrift für Kirchengeschichte,* Vol. XLVII, 1928), p. 24.
[245] Hauck, *op. cit.,* Vol. IV, p. 671, n. 2.

Within a few years a number of other missionaries, most if not all of them Cistercians, were at work in Prussia. We hear of Christian, Philip, and other monks of whom Innocent III spoke in 1210 as labouring in Prussia and whom he placed under the protection of the Polish Primate, the Archbishop of Gniezno.[246] Two years later, in 1212, Innocent III commanded the abbots who made up the general chapter of the Cistercians to place no obstacles in the way of those missionaries—Christian, Philip, and their companions—who had gone to the Prussians.[247] It may be that the exodus of monks to the Prussian mission had caused concern to some of the Cistercian monasteries. By 1216, perhaps in 1215, Christian was consecrated Bishop.[248]

Innocent had the interest of the converts deeply at heart. He admonished the Archbishop of Gniezno (Gnesen) to defend them against oppression and warned the Dukes of Poland and Pomerania not to exploit them.[249] He commanded that the converts be brought together into a Christian village and he exhorted them to live worthy Christian lives.[250] A local prince, Wladislaw, gave the Bishop a village.[251] By 1216, then, the mission of Christian and his colleagues had met with some success.

Apparently the non-Christians resented the defection of their fellow Prussians from the ancestral faith, for in 1217, the year after Innocent's death, Pope Honorius III authorized a Crusade against the pagan enemies of the newly converted Prussians and to those who participated in it or contributed to its expenses were promised spiritual rewards the same as though they had gone to the Holy Land and Jerusalem. However, the Crusaders were forbidden, without the consent of the Bishop, to enter territory occupied by the Christian Prussians.[252]

The Pope and Bishop Christian were under no illusion that true conversions and a vigorous Christian community could come from the use of the sword alone. Even while the Pope was seeking to stimulate Germans to take up the Crusade[253] he was also calling for funds to found schools for the training of Prussian boys to be missionaries to their own people and to purchase girls

[246] *Preussisches Urkundenbuch,* Vol. I, Pt. 1, p. 4, No. 5. On the part of the Poles in the early missions to the Prussians see Maschke, *Polen und die Berufung des deutschen Ordens nach Preussen,* pp. 16-21.

[247] *Preussisches Urkundenbuch,* Vol. I, Pt. 1, p. 5, No. 6.

[248] *Preussisches Urkundenbuch,* Vol. I, Pt. 1, p. 10, No. 14; Hauck, *op. cit.,* Vol. IV, p. 672, n. 1.

[249] *Preussisches Urkundenbuch,* Vol. I, Pt. 1, p. 6, No. 7.

[250] *Preussisches Urkundenbuch,* Vol. I, Pt. 1, pp. 8, 9. Nos. 12, 13.

[251] *Preussisches Urkundenbuch,* Vol. I, Pt. 1, p. 10, No. 14.

[252] *Preussisches Urkundenbuch,* Vol. I, Pt. 1, pp. 11, 12, 14, 15, 18, 22, Nos. 15, 16, 20, 21, 26, 31.

[253] *Preussisches Urkundenbuch,* Vol. I, Pt. 1, pp. 14-16, Nos. 20-22.

of pagan mothers to save them from infanticide and to rear them as Christians.[254] He authorized Bishop Christian to choose other bishops for the Prussians.[255] He commanded the Crusaders to hand over their captives to the Bishop that he might baptize them.[256]

How widely successful Bishop Christian was we do not know. Apparently he and his Crusaders did not make as many converts as did Bishop Albert in Livonia. He did, however, acquire a considerable amount of landed property for the support of the mission. He established himself in Kulm (Chelmno) on the edge of Prussia.[257]

Before long the Prussian mission was given new aspects. In 1224 William of Modena, of whom we have already spoken, was named Papal Legate, not only to Livonia, but also to Prussia and to other lands on the Baltic. In 1225 Pope Honorius III took the neophytes of Livonia and Prussia under the protection of St. Peter.[258] Rome, under the great twelfth and thirteenth century Popes so active and powerful in its control of Europe, was thus evincing an even more direct interest in Prussia. In 1224, moreover, the brilliant Emperor Frederick II declared that the peoples of Livonia, Estonia, Prussia, and neighbouring provinces were under the ægis of the Empire.[259] In 1226 Frederick II formally authorized the Master of the Teutonic Knights to accept lands in Kulm and elsewhere which had been given him on condition that he wage war for the conversion of the Prussians and to occupy other lands which he might conquer.[260] The Duke of Mazowia and Kujawia (Cuyavia) presented the Order with the land of Kulm and a village in Kujawia and in 1230 Bishop Christian deeded them all his territory in Kulmerland.[261] Frederick II soon became too absorbed in his Italian and Sicilian interests, in his struggle with the Pope, and in his own projected Crusade to Jerusalem to pay much attention to the Baltic lands. In the course of the century the Papacy declined in prestige and became less able to give direct supervision to the missions in Prussia. However, the Teutonic Knights entered upon the undertaking, conquered the land, and remained in possession for many generations.

The Teutonic Knights of St. Mary's Hospital at Jerusalem had arisen about a generation before from the efforts of merchants of Bremen and Lübeck to

[254] *Preussisches Urkundenbuch,* Vol. I, Pt. 1, p. 17, Nos. 23, 24.
[255] *Preussisches Urkundenbuch,* Vol. I, Pt. 1, p. 14, No. 19.
[256] *Preussisches Urkundenbuch,* Vol. I, Pt. 1, p. 25, No. 38.
[257] *Preussisches Urkundenbuch,* Vol. I, Pt. 1, pp. 27-38, Nos. 41-51; Hauck, *Kirchengeschichte Deutschlands,* Vol. IV, p. 674.
[258] *Preussisches Urkundenbuch,* Vol. I, Pt. 1, pp. 39-41, Nos. 53-55.
[259] *Preussisches Urkundenbuch,* Vol. I. Pt. 1, p. 38, No. 52.
[260] *Preussisches Urkundenbuch,* Vol. I, Pt. 1, pp. 41-43, No. 56.
[261] *Preussisches Urkundenbuch,* Vol. I, Pt. 1, pp. 47, 53, Nos. 64, 73.

establish a hospital to care for the sick and wounded at the siege of Acre. In 1198 and 1199 had come the formal organization of the Order. The Knights sought opportunity for commerce and conquest and found it first in Transylvania. In 1211 King Andrew II of Hungary invited them into that region, partly to protect it against the pagan Cumans or Comans, a Turkish people who became powerful in South-eastern Europe in the eleventh and twelfth centuries. German settlers entered largely from settlements already established in Transylvania. A beginning was made in reducing the Cumans and in baptizing them. However, the King and the Knights could not agree and, under threat of superior force, the latter withdrew. In the winter of 1225-1226 the Knights received an invitation from the Pole, Conrad of Mazowia and Kujawia, who sought their assistance against a tribe of Prussians.[262] With this began the enterprise for which the Knights are most remembered.

Having its connexions with the North of Germany and with cities interested in the Baltic trade, the Teutonic Order became a natural source of the military force required by the Emperor and the Church for imperialism and Christian missions in Prussia and in other territories on the Baltic. Within less than a century the centre of the Order shifted from the East to its new and larger possessions in the North.[263]

To the assistance of the Knights the Pope summoned members of the recently founded Dominicans. They were to give spiritual care to the Prussians and were to seek recruits for the Crusade in such widely separated districts as Pomerania, Gottland, Poland, and Bohemia.[264] Rome, too, was active in calling to the Crusade aid from other quarters.[265]

The Teutonic Knights set about the reduction of the land. By 1283, or within about half a century, they had completed it.[266] In at least one of the treaties establishing peace between the Knights and the conquered, it was stipulated that all who were not baptized must receive the rite within a month, that those who declined to comply should be banished from the company of Christians, that any who relapsed into paganism should be reduced to slavery, that pagan worship was to cease, that such Christian practices as monogamy were to be adopted, that churches were to be built, that the neophytes must attend church

[262] Maschke, *Polen und die Berufung des deutschen Ordens nach Preussen,* pp. 21 ff; G. Vernadsky, *A History of Russia* (Yale University Press, revised edition, 1930, pp. xix, 413), p. 30, n. 12.

[263] Hauck, *op. cit.,* Vol. IV, pp. 675, 676; John Foisel, *Saxons Through Seventeen Centuries* (Cleveland, 1936—a popular treatise), pp. 47-49.

[264] *Preussisches Urkundenbuch,* Vol. I, Pt. 1, pp. 64-67, 73, 93, Nos. 84, 85, 87, 98, 123. The dates are July 9, 1231, July 18, 1231, Jan. 23, 1232, Oct. 6, 1233, Feb. 22, 1236.

[265] *Preussisches Urkundenbuch,* Vol. I, Pt. 1, p. 67, No. 88.

[266] Hauck, *Kirchengeschichte Deutschlands,* Vol. IV, p. 679.

on Sundays and feast days, that provision must be made for the support of the clergy, and that the converts must observe the Lenten fast, make their confessions to a priest at least once a year, and partake of the communion at Easter.[267]

It was not to be expected that the conquest would proceed smoothly to its consummation. We hear that on one occasion the Prussians, probably by feigning the desire for baptism, succeeded in capturing Bishop Christian.[268] Dissensions broke out among the various forces which were subjugating the country. Pope and Emperor quarrelled. The Knights were not always inclined to respect the wishes of Bishop Christian. Christian complained, indeed, that the Knights hindered the building of churches by the Crusaders who had preceded them. In 1233 the Pope empowered the Order to take directly into its service priests who were not subject to the Bishop. Rome planned to divide the land into a number of dioceses.[269]

Bishop Christian died in 1245 and by so doing removed one of the important factors in the friction. In 1245 an Archbishop was appointed for Prussia and under him were placed the Bishops of Prussia, Livonia, and Estonia. The Pope adopted the general principle of allotting two-thirds of the conquered lands to the Order and one-third to the bishops. Eventually, too, German settlers entered and helped to give stability to the conquest. Prussia was added to the other territories on the Baltic which were incorporated into the sphere of influence of the Germans and into Roman Catholic Christianity.[270]

Last of all the Baltic peoples to be brought into the fold of Latin Christianity were the Lithuanians. Their conversion began late and was long delayed by their antagonism to the Teutonic Knights. For years they were chronically at war with the Order and were of the conviction that since Christianity was the faith of the hated Knights they would have none of it. Finally it was to obtain assistance against the Knights that they accepted baptism.

In a Papal document of 1244 we find mention of Christians in "Lettouia," which may indicate that some Lithuanians had accepted the faith.[271] From a manuscript of the year 1251 we hear that King Mindowe (also known as Mendorg) of Lithuania had become a Christian and had sent an embassy to

---

[267] *Preussisches Urkundenbuch*, Vol. I, Pt. 1, pp. 158-165, No. 218. The date is Feb. 7, 1249.

[268] *Preussisches Urkundenbuch*, Vol. I, Pt. 1, p. 74, No. 100.

[269] *Preussisches Urkundenbuch*, Vol. I, Pt. 1, pp. 100, 101, No. 134; Hauck, *op. cit.*, Vol. IV, pp. 679-682; Blanke, *Die Entscheidungsjahre der Preussenmission* (in *Zeitschrift für Kirchengeschichte*, Vol. XLVII, 1928), p. 33.

[270] *Preussisches Urkundenbuch*, Vol. I, Pt. 1, p. 127, No. 176; Hauck, *op. cit.*, Vol. IV, pp. 682-684.

[271] *Preussisches Urkundenbuch*, Vol. I, Pt. 1, p. 118, No. 157.

Rome. The Pope received him under his protection and claimed all of his territory as the property of the Holy See. The Bishops of Courland and of the Island of Oesel were commanded to care for the completion of the conversion and to unite with the Teutonic Knights in the defense of the neophytes. The Bishop of Kulm was instructed to crown Mindowe and at the same time to take the King's acknowledgment of the suzerainty of the Pope.[272] One suggestion has it that Mindowe became a Roman Catholic to break a coalition of the Teutonic Knights, the Poles, and Daniel of Volynia against him. After his conversion he gained the assistance of the Knights against Daniel.[273] Mindowe is said to have made extensive grants of territory to the Teutonic Knights[274] and he is also reported to have agreed in 1260 to transfer his entire realm to the Order in case he died without heirs.[275] It must be added, however, that the authenticity of the documents purporting to embody these concessions is contested.[276] In 1255, five years or so before the promise of 1260, a document declares that Mindowe's son was to be crowned by a Latin bishop as King of Lithuania.[277] Provision was made for the consecration of a member of the Order as Bishop of Lithuania.[278]

Conflicting reports of the fate of Mindowe have come down to us. A Papal letter dated Jan., 1268, speaks of the King in high terms and declares that he had been killed by "sons of perdition" and authorized the King of Bohemia to wrest the throne from the pagan Lithuanians and the Tartars.[279] Other reports declare that shortly before his death Mindowe broke with the Teutonic Knights and renounced the Christian faith.[280] It is clear that either before or after his

[272] *Preussisches Urkundenbuch*, Vol. I, Pt. 1, p. 181, No. 249.
[273] George Vernadsky, *Political and Diplomatic History of Russia* (Boston, Little, Brown and Co., 1936, pp. ix, 499), pp. 97, 98. See also *Preussisches Urkundenbuch*, Vol. I, Pt. 2, p. 33, No. 39; Schmidlin-Braun, *Catholic Mission History*, p. 220, n. 16, citing Totoraitis, *Die Litauer unter König Mindowe* (Freiburg, 1905).
[274] *Preussisches Urkundenbuch*, Vol. I, Pt. 1, pp. 206, 215, 236, Nos. 274, 284, 324, Pt. 2, pp. 33, 39, 69, Nos, 39, 40, 79.
[275] *Preussisches Urkundenbuch*, Vol. I, Pt. 2, p. 91, No. 105.
[276] *Preussisches Urkundenbuch*, Vol. I, Pt. 2, pp. 38, 94; Schmidlin-Braun, *Catholic Mission History*, p. 220, n. 16, citing Totoraitis, *Die Litauer unter König Mindowe* (Freiburg, 1905).
[277] *Preussisches Urkundenbuch*, Vol. I, Pt. 2, p. 91, No. 105.
[278] *Preussisches Urkundenbuch*, Vol. I, Pt. 1, p. 206, No. 273.
[279] *Preussisches Urkundenbuch*, Vol. I, Pt. 2, p. 197, No. 279.
[280] In Bunge, *Liv-, Esth- und Curländishes Urkundenbuch*, Vol. II, Col. 171, No. 703, is a letter from Pope John XXII, June 1, 1324, to King Gedimin, which declares that Mindowe had abjured Christianity because of the atrocities and the injuries which he had received at the hands of the Teutonic Knights. A similar position is taken by L. Lemmens, *Die Heidenmissionen des Spätmittelalters*, pp. 14, 15. References to a discussion of the question are in B. Altaner, *Die Dominikanermissionen des 13. Jahrhunderts*, p. 184, n. 26.

passing a violent pagan reaction drove the Teutonic Knights from the land.[281] The situation was complicated by the irruption of the Mongols.[282]

All traces of Christianity may have been eliminated, at least for a time. In 1282 the King of Lithuania told an embassy from Riga that he did not wish to become a Christian, for he feared the fate which had overtaken his neighbours in Zemgale.[283] We hear of several Christians fleeing from the country in 1333 and being granted protection and land by the Teutonic Knights.[284] These, however, may not have been descended from thirteenth-century converts, but may have been the products of renewed efforts of missionaries.

In 1324 missions were recommended. The Archbishop and the city of Riga were engaged in a struggle with the Teutonic Knights. Gedimin, King of Lithuania and a pagan, apparently saw here an opportunity for help against the ancient enemy of the realm. There came to the Holy See a letter purporting to be from him and saying that he and his people were ready to accept Christianity and would concede to Dominicans and Franciscans liberty to preach if only the Pope would not grant his support to the Order. The Pope, then at Avignon, sent two prelates, who reached Vilna in 1324.[285] However, when they arrived, the King denied that he had ever authorized any one to promise for him that he and his subjects would be baptized. Yet he continued his friendship with Riga and allowed Franciscans to labour in his realm.[286]

Missionaries were still in danger, and during the reign of Gedimin a number were martyred. Gedimin's son and successor, Kestuit, fought chronically with the Teutonic Knights and remained a pagan. That reign, too, saw martyrdoms of Franciscan missionaries.[287]

In 1382 Kestuit was murdered and was followed on the throne by his nephew Jagiello. Jagiello carried on the war with the Knights. In doing so he sought the aid of the Poles. The Poles consented to an alliance on the condition that he accept baptism and marry the princess, who was heir to the Polish throne. Accordingly, on Feb. 15, 1386, Jagiello was baptized at Cracow. A large number of Polish clergy returned with him and his bride, a Franciscan became the head of the newly founded diocese of Vilna, the pagan temples were destroyed, the holy fire extinguished, the sacred serpent killed, and the consecrated groves

[281] *Preussisches Urkundenbuch,* Vol. I, Pt. 2, pp. 197, 333, Nos. 279, 529.
[282] *Preussisches Urkundenbuch,* Vol. I, Pt. 2, p. 197, No. 279.
[283] Bunge, *op. cit.,* Vol. II, Col. 66, No. 638, art. 34.
[284] *Preussisches Urkundenbuch,* Vol. I, Pt. 2, pp. 488, 489, Nos. 791, 792.
[285] Bunge, *op. cit.,* Vol. II, Cols. 171-186, Nos. 703-705, 707, 708.
[286] Lemmens, *op. cit.,* pp. 15, 16.
[287] Lemmens, *op. cit.,* pp. 16, 17.

cut down. The work of conversion proceeded apace and the land became nominally Christian.[288]

The process of conversion so long delayed and so rapidly carried out proved superficial. As late as the seventeenth century Jesuits in their missionary journeys across Lithuania complained of the survival of pagan practices.[289]

As we suggested at the outset of this chapter, the spread of Christianity in Central Europe and along the Baltic was closely related to the eastward expansion of the Teutonic peoples. It was chiefly associated with German imperialism, German migration, and German commerce. Down into the fourteenth century the Germans were generally the major political power of Western Europe. First came the Frankish state, which, under Charlemagne, revived the name and aspired to the dignity of the Roman Empire. Then the Saxon monarchs again renewed the imperial title and gave it a commanding position. The Franconian Emperors, followed by the Hohenstaufens, continued to uphold the power and the prestige of the German Holy Roman Empire. German settlers moved eastward, filling the present Austria and the territory between the Elbe and the Oder, and constituting an important element of the population in Silesia, Bohemia, Hungary, including Transylvania, and along the Baltic in Pomerania, Prussia, Courland, Livonia, and Estonia. German merchants pressed eastward and in time controlled most of the trade of the Baltic. German adventurers, often in the guise of Crusaders, subjugated the non-German peoples and hewed out estates for themselves.[290] Christian missionaries sometimes constituted the outposts of German power and often played a large part in the assimilation of the non-German peoples to German culture.

It would be an anachronism to read back into these years the intense national feeling of the nineteenth and twentieth centuries. Yet racial and cultural contrasts there were, and these contrasts added bitterness to the struggle between Germans and the non-German peoples to the east and north-east.

For almost the first time in its history, Christianity became a tool of an expanding political and economic imperialism. This had been foreshadowed in the support given by the Frankish monarchs to missions among the Frisians and to Boniface and in the Carolingian conquest of the Saxons. Now for centuries along the eastern German frontier the spread of Christianity and of German dominion went together. It was not a new phenomenon in human

[288] Lemmens, *op. cit.*, p. 17.

[289] Katzenelenbogen, *The Daina. An Anthology of Lithuanian and Latvian Folk-Songs*, p. 9.

[290] An interesting, although not always accurate, account of this eastward expansion of the Germans is in Thompson, *Feudal Germany*, pp. 387-658. See also James Westfall Thompson, *The German Church and the Conversion of the Baltic Slavs* (*American Journal of Theology*, Vol. XX, 1916, pp. 205-230); very critical of the Church.

experience to see religious and political conquest go hand in hand. That had been so frequent as to be almost the rule. During these very centuries it was being paralleled in the extension of Islam and in the reconquest of lands from the Moslems. Later, after 1500, Christianity was to witness it on a grand scale: for more than four centuries the expansion of European peoples and of Christianity were to be intimately associated. Yet never before over so large an area had the spread of Christianity been so closely linked to political and commercial imperialism as in the German East. Even the Crusades in the Near East, while spectacular, had as their major object not the conversion of the Moslems but the capture of the Holy Places and the protection of Christian pilgrims.

To be sure, by no means all the expansion of Christianity recounted in this chapter was a tool of German imperialism. In the conversion of the Moravians and the Bohemians and of the Balkan Slavs, missionaries from the Byzantine Empire had an important share. The winning of the Poles, the Bohemians, the Moravians, and the Balkans, while in large part the achievement of German missionaries, was, like much of that of Western Europe, engineered by the native princes and was not imposed by German conquest. Hungary was led into the Church by its monarchs and the missionaries were Slav as well as German. In Rügen, Northern Estonia, Finland, and among the Lapps conversion was associated with Scandinavian and not German imperialism. The Lithuanians were eventually won by the Poles—although in an effort to offset German aggression. In Estonia, Livonia, Prussia, and to a less extent Lithuania, the Papacy, while usually employing German agents, was prominent in the direction of the missions. Moreover, only infrequently did the German Emperors take the initiative in the active extension of the frontier. Some there were, like Otto the Great, who directed much of their energy to expanding their eastern borders. To most, however, this part of the imperial program was either non-existent or was given little attention. Yet when all these exceptions are enumerated, the fact remains that in most of the spread of Latin Christianity into Central Europe and along the southern and eastern shores of the Baltic, the German element was important and in much of it was dominant.

In many places, as we have suggested, the German conquest was effected with marked cruelty. Often, too, baptism was imposed as a condition of peace. Again and again bloodshed and aggression seem to have been augmented by an appeal to religious conviction and enthusiasm. We have seen that Crusades to win pagans to the faith or to protect Christians against pagans were preached by some of the greatest of the Popes, by some of the most zealous missionary bishops, and even by the saintly Bernard of Clairvaux. To be sure, probably few warriors responded to these Crusading appeals from purely religious motives. Always, presumably, there was the restless thirst for adventure, or for fame, or for new lands. Yet the religious motive, with the spiritual rewards promised by the clergy, initiated some and gave impetus to others of the expeditions which extended the geographical boundaries of German control and of Latin Christianity.

It must be added at once that the age was one of war and oppression. The expansion of Northern European peoples which had given the *coup de grâce* to the old Roman Empire in the West was still in progress. The native glorification of arms had only begun to be tempered by Christian ethics and emotions. The German conquests in the East were not always so cruel as had been the raids of Vikings in the pre-Christian days of the Scandinavians.

It must also be added that many of the German missions among the Slavs were not accompanied by force. That of Otto of Bamberg among the Pomeranians is probably the most noteworthy, but it had many less spectacular counterparts. Often, too, Crusading armies were followed by humble monks, many of them Cistercians, who drained the swamps, cleared away the hampering forests, improved and expanded agriculture, and taught the masses the tenets and practices of the religion which had been so rapidly thrust upon them. The Christianity of the day was not only accentuating German conquests: it was also ameliorating them and making them less inhumane and more civilizing than had been those of Northern European peoples in their pre-Christian days.

Moreover, the motive of German missions was by no means entirely the glory and profit of the German people. It was often predominantly or entirely religious.

We must, however, note the interesting fact that few remonstrances were made in the Christian name, and, of course, none at all in any other name, against the cruelties and atrocities of the exploitation of non-German peoples by the Germans. Some there were. In the time of Charlemagne, as we have seen, Alcuin had the courage to call attention to the futility of attempting to inculcate a knowledge of real Christianity at the point of the sword. We hear of protests against the drastic measures of the Teutonic Knights. One of the most vigorous of them is said to have been made by the scholarly Franciscan, Roger Bacon.[291] Apparently, however, none of these denunciations modified appreciably the deeds of the German conquerors.

As our narrative progresses into its later phases we shall hear a swelling chorus in the name of Christ against the ruthlessness of the exploitation of

---

[291] Thompson, *Economic and Social History of Europe in the Later Middle Ages,* p. 185.

non-Christian, non-European peoples by nominally Christian European masters. It first became notably conspicuous in the sixteenth and seventeenth centuries, particularly in the Spanish conquests in the Americas and the Philippines. Here a Las Casas and others of similarly acute conscience not only raised their voices against the barbarities of the *conquistadores*, but succeeded in having humanitarian legislation placed on the statute-books. More than that, in some areas and over long periods these laws were partially observed. In the nineteenth century devoted reformers, most of them acting consciously from Christian motives, made an end to the commerce in African flesh by European traders and abolished the enslavement of Africans by the white peoples of America and Western Europe. Much, too, of the wide movement to accord better treatment to the millions in Africa, Asia, and the islands of the sea who had been brought under the control of Europeans by the imperialism of the nineteenth and twentieth centuries can be traced to Christianity. Apparently, as Christianity is longer on the earth it has become increasingly effective in alleviating and even in preventing the stark barbarities which usually accompany the subjugation of one people or race by another. In the European Middle Ages, however, in the German imperialism in Central Europe and on the Baltic, this result had only begun to be seen.

To this chapter must be added a feature of the spread of Christianity which at first sight seems but little related to the others which we have been treating —the efforts to win the Jews to the Christian faith. It is not merely literary convenience which appends this section in this particular place. Here, as in most of the preceding portions of the chapter, the expansion of Christianity was complicated by sharp racial differences, and was part of the effort at the mastery and assimilation of one people by another. Here, too, are marked contrasts in cultures.

This is the one portion of the narrative embraced in the last two chapters in which we must record failure to win a people even to a nominal adoption of the Christian faith. As we shall see in a moment, many Jews submitted to baptism and numbers probably accepted it out of religious conviction. Yet, in spite of efforts of Church and state and of private individuals, there remained recalcitrant elements who held stubbornly to their inherited religion.

The Jews were widely scattered in mediæval Europe. This is not the place to enter upon the history of their diffusion. Wherever they were, they tended to remain a people apart. They were town dwellers and did not fit into the system of agricultural feudalism. Indeed, Christians made it difficult for them to own farming lands. Like religious and racial minorities the world over, the Jews were inclined to confine themselves to a limited group of occupations. They were merchants, money-lenders, physicians, and, in their own circles, teachers and scholars. In the Roman world they had held to their own customs and religion and in this respect they were not substantially altered under the heirs of Roman rule, whether those heirs were Moslem or Christian. Seepages there were from among them to Islam and to Christianity. Sometimes, under the threat of compulsion, conversions took place wholesale. In general, however, the Jews remained such in faith and to a large extent in culture.

Toward the Jew the adherents of Latin Christianity displayed a variety of attitudes. Often there was the tolerance of indifference. Many friendships were made across the barriers of creed and race. In a few instances we read of Christians becoming converts to Judaism.[292] Repeatedly efforts were made to win the Jews. Some of these were by persuasion, some were by required attendance upon Christian sermons, and others by physical violence. Persecutions were frequent.

Just how far Christianity and its official exponents, the clergy, shaped the attitudes of monarchs and people is probably impossible to determine. That they were factors is clear. At times they made for moderation and on other occasions for cruel fanaticism. However, the feeling against exclusive minorities which appears in every land and under any faith contributed to the ill will which often was so explosive and which aggravated the tendency of the Jews to keep to themselves. So, too, did the economic factor—the popular dislike for the bargaining merchant and especially for the money-lender.

Whether, in general, the dislike for the Jews and the violence against them increased with time is difficult to determine. Any region which contained many of them witnessed waves of persecution which were often accompanied by attempts at compulsory conversion. In years of high emotional mass tension or fear, the Jews, as a peculiar people, might be singled out for attack. Notable were the outbreaks of violence connected with the First Crusade, with the advent of the mysterious and terrifying Black Death in the fourteenth century, and with the threat of the Mongol invasion. Particularly spectacular were the efforts of the rising Spanish monarchy in the fifteenth century to convert or expel this minority which, like the Moors, stood in the way of the religious and cultural unity of the realm.

[292] Glaber, *Hist. sui Temporis*, Book III, Chap. 6, in Migne, *Pat. Lat.*, Vol. CXLII, Cols. 655-657; Guibert, *De Vita Sua*, Book III, Chap. 16, in Migne, *Pat. Lat.*, Vol. CLVI, Col. 949; Grayzel, *The Church and the Jews in the XIIIth Century*, p. 23; McCulloch, *Medieval Faith and Fable*, p. 232; Katz, *The Jews in the Visigothic and Frankish Kingdoms of Spain and Gaul*, p. 45; Baron, *A Social and Religious History of the Jews*, Vol. II, pp. 40, 43, 57.

We can take time to mention only a few of the attempts at conversion and of the attitudes of the Christian churchmen, secular rulers, and populace towards the Jews. It is not clear that these are typical, for to determine that in any scholarly fashion would involve a full survey of Jewish-Christian relations in these ten centuries. It is certain that not all the most prominent incidents and measures are here enumerated. However, by the mention of a few concrete examples we may be able to give some hint of what a full history would include.

What is said to have been the first recorded case of the compulsory baptism of Jews in Gaul was in the second half of the sixth century in the diocese of Uzes. The bishop, Ferreol, had attempted to win the Jews by conciliatory methods, but was accused to the King of too great friendliness with them. He brought many to baptism, and to the recalcitrants he gave the choice of expulsion or baptism. Many elected the former.[293] In 582 King Chilperic of the Franks ordered the baptism of the Jews and himself stood godfather to many of them.[294] We read that in the second half of the sixth century Avitus, a bishop in Auvergne, sought to convert the Jews in his diocese. He succeeded with one, but in the procession after the baptism he was insulted by another of the race, and in retaliation an angry mob of Christians destroyed the synagogue. Thereupon a number of Jews asked for baptism and the unbaptized left and went to Marseilles.[295]

Through letters of Gregory the Great, written within a generation or so of this time, we catch glimpses of current attitudes. From Arles and Marseilles in Southern Gaul, from Naples and Terracina, and from Palermo, we hear reports of violence by bishops against the Jews, in all but two instances arising in part from efforts to make conversions, and in one growing out of the seizure of the Jewish hospital and synagogue.[296] Gregory himself was eager to win the Jews to his faith, and on the estates of the Church which he controlled in Sicily he offered to reduce the rent of those who would accept baptism.[297] However, he thoroughly disapproved of the use of force to bring about this happy consummation and admonished over-zealous bishops against it.[298]

Roughly contemporary with these events were anti-Jewish measures in Visi-

[293] *Gallia Christiana* (1739), Vol. VI, p. 613.
[294] Gregory of Tours, *Hist. Franc.,* Book VI, Chap. 17.
[295] Gregory of Tours, *Hist. Franc.,* Book V, Chap. 11.
[296] Gregory I, *Ep.* I, 35, 47, *Ep.* IX, 6, 55, *Ep.* XIII, 12, in Migne, *Pat. Lat.*, Vol. LXXVII, Cols. 489, 509-511, 944, 945, 993, 994, 1267, 1268.
[297] Gregory I, *Ep.* II, 32, *Ep.* V, 8, in Migne, *Pat. Lat.*, Vol. LXXVII, Cols. 566, 730.
[298] Gregory I, *Ep.* I, 35, 47, *Ep.* XIII, 12, in Migne, *Pat. Lat.*, Vol. LXXVII, Cols. 489, 509-511, 1267, 1268.

gothic Spain. Recared, who had brought about the triumph of Catholicism over Arianism, enforced existing laws which placed restrictions on the Jews and which went back to Roman times. He also commanded the baptism of the children of mixed marriages. Sisebut, who came to the throne in 612, went much further. He reaffirmed the laws of Recared and ordered that all Jews be baptized, with banishment and the confiscation of goods as the unpleasant alternative. As a result, so it is said, many submitted to the rite and others sought refuge in Gaul and Africa. Why Sisebut took this action we do not know. It is interesting to note that Isidore, the Archbishop of Seville, the leading Spanish prelate and one of the most learned men of his day, disapproved of the King's violence. The Fourth Council of Toledo, over which Isidore presided, declared that Christianity must be accepted voluntarily. Once having become adherents, however, converts could, if necessary, be constrained to hold to it.[299] Isidore, too, wrote a tract to answer the anti-Christian arguments of the Jews.[300]

Apparently the commands of Recared and Sisebut did not effectively lead all Jews into the Church. Some purchased exemption by bribing laymen and clergy.[301] Repeatedly later Councils re-enacted legislation or passed new laws to compel conformity. Here, as elsewhere through Europe during much of the Middle Ages, stringent measures were adopted to end the ownership by Jews of Christian slaves and particularly to prevent the circumcision and conversion to Judaism of such slaves.[302] The Ninth Council of Toledo, in 655, ordered all baptized Jews to spend all Jewish and Christian feast days in the presence of a bishop, to be sure that they did not observe the one and did observe the other.[303] Towards the close of the seventh century new legislation commanded that all Jews in the peninsula be enslaved and that their sons be taken away from them at the age of seven and be reared as Christians.[304]

The first half of the seventh century witnessed energetic measures by the Merovingians. One ecclesiastical enactment, of 615, with the endorsement of the King, forbade a Jew to occupy any military or civil position which placed

[299] R. Altamira in *Cambridge Medieval History*, Vol. II, pp. 173, 174; Milman, *History of the Jews*, Vol. III, pp. 108-114; *IV Concil. Tolet.*, Art. 57, in Migne, *Pat. Lat.*, Vol. LXXXIV, Cols. 379, 380; Katz, *The Jews in the Visigothic and Frankish Kingdoms of Spain and Gaul*, pp. 11, 12.

[300] In Migne, *Pat. Lat.*, Vol. LXXXIII, Cols. 459 ff.

[301] *IV Concil. Tolet.*, Art. 58, in Migne, *Pat. Lat.*, Vol. LXXXIV, Col. 380.

[302] Milman, *op. cit.*, Vol. III, pp. 114-121, citing decrees of the various Councils of Toledo; R. Altamira in *Cambridge Medieval History*, Vol. II, pp. 176-179; Katz, *op. cit.*, pp. 13, 17.

[303] Parkes, *The Conflict of the Church and the Synagogue*, pp. 361-369.

[304] R. Altamira, in *Cambridge Medieval History*, Vol. II, p. 181, citing *Forum Judicum*, Law XVIII, Lib. XII, tit. 2.

him over a Christian. Disobedience had baptism as its penalty.[305] Dagobert I (died 639) is said to have ordered all Jews to accept baptism or leave the realm.[306]

In the early centuries of the Moslem rule in Spain the Jews, in general, enjoyed toleration and became prosperous. They profited, too, by the order and prosperity which Charlemagne brought to much of Western Europe. During the latter part of his reign, Charlemagne was not unfriendly to them, and under the reign of his son, the religious Louis the Pious, toleration was the imperial policy. Yet neither in Moslem Spain nor in the realms of the Christian Franks does prejudice seem entirely to have died out.[307] For instance, it was under Louis the Pious that Agobard, the Archbishop of Lyons, wrote vigorously against the Jews.[308]

When, in 1096, the various bands and armies which composed the First Crusade were on their way to the East, in some places their zeal vented itself on the luckless race. In Germany, for instance, we hear of Crusaders compelling Jews to be baptized and in at least one place we read of an indiscriminate massacre—of men, women, and children. It is not surprising that some of the involuntary converts took an early opportunity to resume their ancestral faith.[309] It is pleasant to record that Bernard of Clairvaux, who preached the Second Crusade from which arose, as we have seen, violent expeditions against the Wends, opposed the persecution of the Jews which attended that Crusade.[310]

Much more chronic than the outburst of anti-Jewish fanaticism which accompanied the excitement of a Crusade was the charge of the ritual crucifixion of a Christian by the Jews, usually at the Passover season. Stories of this kind seem to have enjoyed wide popular currency and credence.[311]

Throughout the Middle Ages, efforts to convert the Jews must have been very numerous and persistent. Nor were they entirely fruitless. For thousands the threat or the direct application of force led to outward conformity. Relapses were frequent and many maintained secretly some of their Jewish rites and beliefs. For others, however, conversion seems to have come as a result of religious conviction. If we may judge from what we know to have been the case in later centuries, still others, the children of converts, were assimilated

[305] Milman, *History of the Jews*, Vol. III, p. 123, citing *Concil. Paris*, can. XV, and giving the Latin text.
[306] *Gesta Dagoberti I, Regis Francorum*, c. 24, in *Mon. Germ. Hist., Script. rer. Merov.*, Vol. II, p. 409. See also on measures under the Merovingians, Katz, *op. cit.*, pp. 22-28.
[307] Milman, *op. cit.*, Vol. III, pp. 140-158.
[308] Migne, *Pat. Lat.*, Vol. CIV, Cols. 70-114.
[309] As in *Annales Hildesheimenses* (*Scriptores rerum Germanicarum*, 1878), an. 1096.
[310] Bernard of Clairvaux, *Ep.* 363, 365, in Migne, *Pat. Lat.*, Vol. CLXXXII, Cols. 563-568, 570.
[311] See instances in Hyamson, *A History of the Jews in England*, pp. 19, 20, 69, 70.

imperceptibly into the Christian population. Thus, when we read that in the Norman domains William Rufus attempted to coerce Christian Jews to return to their original faith,[312] it is obvious that there must have been enough converts to attract the royal attention. Fairly early in the fourteenth century the Dominicans began in Oxford a mission for the Jews and won enough to make advisable the establishment of a House of Converts.[313] We hear, too, of a House of Converts founded in London in 1232 by Henry III and maintained until the expulsion of the Jews from England in 1290. Baptism in England was not easy, for it involved not only obloquy from one's fellow Jews, but the forfeiture of the greater part of the neophyte's possessions. Yet conversions there were, among them that of a former religious head of the English Jewish community.[314]

In France, as in so much of Western Europe, we read of repeated violence against the Jews, probably more often through the dislike of the populace and the frenzy of the mob than through the deliberate policy of the rulers. However, frequently it was stimulated by those in high places. Sometimes this was accompanied by compulsory baptism.[315] From time to time Jewish converts to Christianity, with the ardour of proselytes, instigated measures against those of their former faith. Thus in 1239 one of these is credited with obtaining from the Pope a bull commanding the burning of the Talmud. We hear of another who was responsible for public discussions of the relative truth of the two faiths.[316] In some places it became customary to require Jews to present themselves at church and listen to sermons against Judaism.[317]

Since baptism was so often accepted under duress, it is not strange that many nominally Christian Jews reverted to their ancestral religion. Repeatedly we find records of such defections. They were treated harshly by the populace, by the state, and by the Church.[318] So long as Jews were not baptized, the Church, so such an authority as Thomas Aquinas held, could not constrain them or their children to accept the rite, nor should the Church interfere with their property. The Church should, however, prevent them from corrupting the faith of Christians. Once Jews had been baptized, they were held to have

[312] Hyamson, op. cit., pp. 11, 12.

[313] Hyamson, op. cit., p. 88; Stokes, A Short History of the Jews in England, p. 37.

[314] Stokes, op. cit., pp. 37-39. If his fellow Jews did not prevent a convert from inheriting his patrimony, the King might confiscate it, for the conversion of a Jew meant financial loss to the Crown.—Grayzel, The Church and the Jews in the XIIIth Century, pp. 18, 19.

[315] Milman, op. cit., Vol. III, pp. 213-229.

[316] Abrahams, Jewish Life in the Middle Ages, pp. 440-442.

[317] Abrahams, op. cit., p. 440.

[318] Lea, A History of the Inquisition in the Middle Ages, Vol. II, pp. 63, 273, 284.

placed themselves under the jurisdiction of the Church, and the latter was under obligation to restrain them, forcibly if necessary, from apostatizing.[319]

Numerically the most extensive accessions of Jews to Christianity seem to have been in the Iberian Peninsula. Under both Moslem and Christian rulers the treatment of Jews ranged from friendship and generous toleration to violence and compulsory conversion. Thus under the earlier Moslem overlords the Jews prospered. Then, in the twelfth century, came the fanatical Almohades from Africa and proscribed in their domains the practice of Judaism and Christianity. Many Jews preferred exile to apostasy, and among them were those who found more generous treatment in the Christian states of the peninsula.[320] Indeed, the twelfth, thirteenth, and fourteenth centuries were the golden age of the Jews in Spain. The persecutions which had marked the last years of the Gothic rule seemed to belong only to the past. Jews held high posts in the courts of Christian kings, nobles, and churchmen. The administration of the finances of the Christian states was largely in their hands. By providing the sinews of war they gave important assistance to the reconquest of the peninsula from the Moslems. Formal regulations existed which ostensibly forbade their making converts from Christianity, but in practice toleration was the rule and strict enforcement and persecution, although not unknown, were the exception. Under such favourable conditions, the Jews seem to have multiplied. One estimate places the number of married and adult males near the end of the thirteenth century at about 850,000. This indicates a Jewish population of more than two millions. The kings especially were the protectors of a race whose members proved so useful to them.[321] Such a privileged status could not but breed popular dissatisfaction. The tax collector and the money-lender, however useful they may be to the ruler, are never kindly regarded by the masses.

It is not surprising that as the thirteenth and fourteenth centuries wore on, attitudes began gradually to change. As early as 1242 a royal edict was issued, confirmed by the Pope in 1245, which empowered members of the mendicant orders to enter the Jewish and Moslem quarters and to compel the inhabitants to assemble and listen to sermons presenting Christianity.[322] How many baptisms followed we do not know, but years later, in 1331, we hear of Jews

---

[319] Thomas Aquinas, *Summa,* Part II, 1st No. See Q. X, art. 8-12.

[320] Roth, *A History of the Marranos,* p. 9; Harris, *History of the Mediæval Jews,* pp. 180, 181.

[321] Lea, *A History of the Inquisition of Spain,* Vol. I, pp. 84-90. A smaller estimate of the Jewish population of Spain at about this time places it at half a million.—Robinson, *The Conversion of Europe,* p. 553. See also on this period of Jewish prosperity, Milman, *op. cit.,* Vol. III, pp. 271 ff.

[322] Lea, *A History of the Inquisition of Spain,* Vol. I, p. 91, citing Aquirre, VI, 369.

attacking two Franciscans who were leading away a Jewish youth in an effort to convert him.[323] In the decade between 1260 and 1270 we read of a convert, a Dominican, who was given a royal order commanding the Jews to assemble and accord him a respectful hearing whenever he wished to dispute with them and to defray his expenses out of the tribute due the king.[324] In 1328 a series of massacres wrought havoc among the Jews of Navarre.[325] Peter the Cruel of Castile (1350-1368) showed the Jews favour. They became his ardent supporters, and the revolts against his rule, accordingly, had anti-Jewish phases.[326] In 1391 extensive and fanatical anti-Jewish riots swept over the Christian portions of Spain. Mobs attacked the Jewish residents, destroyed or seized their property, and killed many. A large number were baptized, some forcibly, and others to escape the fate of their fellows. The monarchs for a time sought to stem the tide, probably not from humane feelings, but because any damage to the obnoxious but useful race brought injury to the royal exchequer.[327]

The fateful year of 1391 seems to have marked the end of toleration. Jews by the hundreds continued to seek immunity by submitting to baptism. A Dominican, Vincente Ferrer, whose eloquence is said to have had much to do with arousing the mass hysteria of 1391,[328] between 1408 and 1416 once more moved about the land, preaching to Jews and making converts. Vincente Ferrer was of an aristocratic family, from 1391 to 1395 served as confessor of Queen Yolanda of Aragon, and later was appointed by Pope Benedict XIII as confessor and master of the apostolic palace. He was zealously missionary and to carry out his purpose refused high ecclesiastical preferment, including the cardinalate. Beginning with 1399 he toured much of Southern France and Northern Italy with the authority of a Legate a latere Christi, preaching to great audiences and winning converts from among the Cathari and Waldensees. From 1408 into 1416 he was most of the time south of the Pyrenees. Here he is said by his eloquence and his zeal to have brought thousands of Jews to the Christian faith.[329] A number of the converts rose to high position in the Church

[323] Fritz Baer, Die Juden im christlichen Spanien, Vol. I, p. 264.

[324] Lea, op. cit., Vol. I, pp. 90, 91.

[325] Roth, op. cit., p. 13; Lea, op. cit., Vol. I, p. 100.

[326] Milman, op. cit., Vol. III, pp. 284-288; Roth, op. cit., p. 13; Lea, op. cit., Vol. I, pp. 101, 102.

[327] Some of the documents reflecting the violence and including some of the official efforts at protection are in Fritz Baer, op. cit., Vol. I, pp. 657, 667, 682, 694. See also Lea, A History of the Inquisition of Spain, Vol. I, pp. 105-110; Roth, op. cit., pp. 15-17; Sachar, A History of the Jews, pp. 206-208.

[328] Lea, op. cit., Vol. I, pp. 112, 113.

[329] Vita by Pater Ranzano in Acta Sanctorum, April, Vol. I, pp. 481-510; Catholic Encyclopaedia, Vol. XV, pp. 437, 438. See a royal authorization of Vincente Ferrer's preaching, in Baer, op. cit., Vol. I, p. 793.

and by oral and written argument were active in endeavouring to win their fellows to baptism.[330] Among them were those who intermarried with some of the most highly placed Spanish families.[331] Apparently it was at least partly at the suggestion of Vincente Ferrer and some of the leaders among the *conversos* that additional restrictive Papal legislation was enacted against those who still held to the religion of their fathers. Yet Vincente Ferrer publicly protested against bloodshed as a means of propagating Christianity.[332]

The rapid advent of so many Jews into the Church brought with it new problems. The *conversos* and their descendants, freed from the taxation and other restrictions which had been their lot before baptism, became prominent in Church and state. Popular prejudice against them increased. They were widely accused of secretly observing Jewish rites and of being Christians only in name. So great was the clamour that in 1480, under the authority of a Papal bull of 1478, the Inquisition was established in the domains of Ferdinand and Isabella. This had no jurisdiction over Jews who remained such in religion, but it was for the purpose of detecting heresy and took action against some of the Jewish Christians.[333]

Feeling continued against those Jews who persisted in holding to their hereditary faith. Finally, in 1492, Ferdinand and Isabella ordered them either to be baptized or to leave Spain. Some accepted baptism. More of them chose exile. Some of the latter, appalled by the miseries which met them abroad, returned to Spain and submitted to baptism. Eventually the Spanish government declined to admit them even on that condition. Some fled to Naples and there, to allay popular hostility, were baptized. Others sought refuge in Navarre, but in the ensuing privations many asked for baptism to avoid slavery or death.[334]

Still others entered Portugal, where a not unfriendly regime allowed them to find homes on payment of a tax. Within a few years, however, a change of policy brought great suffering. In 1497 a royal order commanded the baptism of all children between the ages of four and fourteen. A few months earlier an edict had been issued requiring all Jews and Moslems to leave the kingdom before the end of October, 1497. In the process of deportation the majority, under great pressure, submitted to baptism to save their freedom and their lives. As in Spain so in Portugal, baptism, while gaining for them per-

[330] Lea, *op. cit.*, Vol. I, pp. 115, 116.
[331] Lea, *op. cit.*, Vol. I, p. 120.
[332] Lea, *op. cit.*, Vol. I, pp. 118, 119; Baron, *A Social and Religious History of the Jews*, Vol. II, p. 48.
[333] Roth, *op. cit.*, pp. 29-53; Lea, *op. cit.*, Vol. I, pp. 122-134; Sachar, *op. cit.*, pp. 208-213.
[334] Lea, *op. cit.*, Vol. I, pp. 135-144; Sachar, *op. cit.*, pp. 212-216.

mission to remain, did not insure the Jews against popular ill will. Moreover, suddenly forced into the Church as the Jews had been, even more of crypto-Judaism seems to have persisted than in Spain. In the first half of the sixteenth century the Inquisition was introduced into Portugal and was directed to detecting and punishing those who secretly practised the faith of their progenitors.[335]

It must be said that in general the Popes displayed a more moderate Jewish policy than would have been theirs had they heeded the populace. To be sure, Innocent III, after an edict earlier in his pontificate which commanded Christians to respect Jewish property and cemeteries and not to interfere with their festivals, and which condemned compulsory baptism,[336] later expressed his indignation at the preference shown them over Christians by Christian princes and insisted that they had killed the Son of God and were still blasphemers.[337] Under Innocent III, moreover, the Fourth Lateran Council (1215) required Jews to wear a distinctive badge,[338] a custom which may have been derived from the Moslem practice.[339] As a rule, however, the Popes denounced as untrue some of the popular accusations, including that of ritual murder, stood against forcible baptism, and sought to restrain the Crusaders and anti-Jewish mobs.[340] Yet in spite of the official attitude of the See of Peter, repeatedly the rejection of Christ and of the Christian faith was made the excuse for violence by the mob against the non-conforming Jewish communities.

With the end of this chapter we have completed our survey of the main phases of the extension of the borders of Western Christendom between the years 500 and 1500. To be sure, we have yet to recount the successful efforts to regain the ground lost to Islam in Spain and Sicily, the establishment of outposts in the Near Orient by the Crusades, and the far-flung efforts of the Franciscans and Dominicans in Eastern Europe and in Central Asia, India, and the Far East. To these we shall come later. Yet, with these exceptions, we have finished that part of our story.

Generally speaking, in Europe since 1500 the geographic boundaries of Western Christianity have remained substantially as they were in that year. With

[335] Roth, *A History of the Marranos*, pp. 54-73.

[336] Innocent III, *Regestorum*, Book II, No. 302 (1199), in Migne, *Pat. Lat.*, Vol. CCXIV, Cols. 864, 865.

[337] Innocent III, *Regestorum*, Book X, No. 190, in Migne, *Pat. Lat.*, Vol. CCXV, Cols. 1291-1293.

[338] Milman, *op. cit.*, Vol. III, p. 206.

[339] Abraham, *Jewish Life in the Middle Ages* (1932 ed.), p. 318.

[340] Grayzel, *The Church and the Jews in the XIIIth Century*, pp. 14-18, 76-82; F. J. Foakes Jackson in *An Outline of Christianity*, Vol. II, p. 405.

some relatively minor changes, the area in that continent occupied by Latin Christianity and its descendant, Protestantism, has continued for the last nearly four and a half centuries to be identical with that which it had gained by the end of the fifteenth century.

The reasons for this stability of boundaries are, in general, two. First, except in the East, Western Christianity had occupied all the territory up to the seas which hem in Europe. Save for the Jews, all the peoples of Western Europe had become professedly Christian. Second, on the east, the Latin form of Christianity had a common boundary with the Greek form of that faith. By 1500 Islam had entered South-eastern Europe and had gained a foothold against Christianity. However, long before that year, the dominant religion in Eastern Europe was that of the Greek Orthodox Church. Latin and Greek Christianity expanded simultaneously, the one from the western portion of the Roman Empire and the other from the eastern portion. The one looked to Rome for its ecclesiastical direction, the other to Constantinople. The one found in the Teutonic peoples most of its leading champions and the majority of the chief agents of its spread. Especially did it obtain an ally in the succession of Germanic ruling houses which fell heir to the Roman Empire in the West. The other made its largest numerical gains among the Slavs and eventually, as Constantinople declined as a Christian power and then was taken by the Moslem Turks, had as its main political support the outstanding Slavic state, Russia. By the end of the fifteenth century, then, these two types of Christianity faced each other across a common boundary which, with comparatively slight variations, has remained unchanged. The leaders of neither had much love for or fellowship with the other. On occasion each attempted to win adherents from the other. Of the two, in its efforts at proselytizing, Roman Christianity proved the more aggressive and the more successful. In general, however, the contest, in so far as it was a contest, eventuated in a stalemate. To the story of the spread of the Greek form of Christianity we must now turn.

Chapter IV

THE SPREAD OF CHRISTIANITY FROM THE EASTERN POR-
TION OF THE ROMAN EMPIRE, INTRODUCTORY; GAINS
UNDER JUSTINIAN; NORTH AFRICA; NUBIA; ETHIOPIA; THE
JACOBITES; THE BALKANS; THE BULGARS; SERBIA; THE
CAUCASUS; RUSSIA; THE JEWS

IN THE last two chapters we have been recounting the expansion of Christianity from the Western or Latin half of the Roman Empire. We have
seen how, in the fifth and sixth centuries, when, through so much of the West,
the structure of the Empire collapsed, Christianity, far from vanishing with it,
persisted and spread into regions and among peoples which had never acknowledged the control of Rome. By 1500 in Western Europe, Rome, as the
seat of the head of the Latin-using branch of Christianity, held spiritual sway
over a larger area than, in that particular part of the continent, had ever submitted to the rule of the Cæsars. Moreover, as we are to see later, having thus
established itself in Western Europe, from that as a base, Latin Christianity,
together with its major offshoot, Protestantism, eventually expanded into much
of the rest of the world.

On first thought, the normal expectation would have been that a much
more extensive spread of Christianity would have occurred from those portions
of the basin of the Mediterranean where the Roman Empire persisted for
some centuries longer. Until 1453, or up to nearly the close of the thousand
years which constitute the second main stage of our story, there ruled from
Constantinople a succession of monarchs who, although of various houses,
considered themselves the legitimate heirs of the empire which once had its
seat on the seven hills by the Tiber. For generations after the Roman secular
dominion had faded north of the Alps, they continued to control not only the
eastern shores of the Mediterranean, but also large sections of North Africa,
Sicily, and much of Italy and Spain. Indeed, in Italy they made headway
against the Goths and in North Africa put an end to the rule of the Vandals.
During most of the sixth century this truncated but still imposing Roman
Empire shared with Persia the distinction of being the most powerful realm
on the earth. For centuries thereafter it was one of the major powers. By the

223

year 500 Christianity had become the faith of the overwhelming majority of the inhabitants of this state. For nearly two centuries, with the brief interruption under Julian, it had been the avowed religion of the Emperors. If, in spite of the collapse of the rule with which it had been associated, Christianity had spread so extensively in the West, how much more was it to be expected that, supported by the prestige of this Romano-Byzantine state, it would be widely propagated in Africa, Asia, and Eastern Europe.

In contrast with what superficially might have been anticipated, Christianity spread less widely from this eastern perpetuation of the Roman Empire than it did from the politically disorganized West.

The reasons for this comparative failure are many. Some are obvious. Others must be conjectural. It is clear that in geography lay some of the most potent causes. In Africa, except for the Nile Valley, extension southward was blocked by the Sahara. As we are soon to see, a noteworthy expansion of the boundaries of Christianity took place up the Nile. To the south-east stretched Arabia, from which the Moslem movement was soon to break forth. To the east was the Sassanian realm, with its strong espousal of Mazdaism and its chronic antagonism to Rome and to the religion of Rome. From the East, moreover, came wave after wave of invaders. Often these first impinged upon the Byzantine Empire and partly spent their force before pushing on towards Western Europe. They came too rapidly to be completely overcome and assimilated by this eastern champion of the Christianity of the Mediterranean world. Yet the Byzantine bulwark, as we have suggested, partially protected the West. Only in the Balkans and north and east of the Black Sea did the influences from Constantinople have relatively free course among culturally backward peoples. Here the Christianity of the eastern portion of the Roman Empire made notable gains.

Another important factor in restricting the expansion of Christianity from the Byzantine descendant of Rome was the phenomenal spread of Islam. To this, and to the major territorial losses to which it subjected Christianity, we are devoting a later chapter. Being nearer the historic centre of Islam than was the West, Eastern Christianity bore much of the brunt of the Moslem attack. Because of Islam, many of the invaders whom Eastern Christendom had to meet were not crude polytheists, as were most of the barbarians of the West, with a type of religion which succumbed easily to a more advanced religion, but were Moslems, convinced that theirs was a later and higher revelation than Christianity.

A third factor, much more difficult to evaluate, was the close association of Eastern Christianity with the state. The Byzantine Empire, following the example of Rome, esteemed religion ancillary to its political purposes. To a large extent it controlled the Church and made it an organ of the state. In the West, however, with the collapse of the Roman rule, organized Christianity more nearly emancipated itself from the dominion of the temporal powers. In the West the struggle between Church and state was recurrent, but it was more of an equal contest than in the East. The Christian impulse, accordingly, was somewhat less subordinated to political considerations and less trammelled by secular connexions than in the East. Then, too, in the West, in the presence of barbarian kingdoms which it antedated and whose boundaries it greatly overpassed, the Church as such was a decidedly more powerful institution than in the East. To be sure, even in the East the Church was by no means always subservient. To a greater degree than its pre-Christian predecessors among the state religions of Rome, it gave rise to movements which at times criticized and even sought to control the state. Yet, in the main, in the West the Christian impulse enjoyed larger freedom of expression. It is possible that here is to be found one reason, perhaps the most potent one, for the greater vigour displayed by the Western branch of the Christian movement. It is significant that in the East a very large proportion of the major missionary undertakings were initiated or at least actively supported by the Byzantine state. The conversion of non-Christian peoples in North Africa, the introduction of the faith to Nubia, Constantine and Methodius, and the clergy sent to Vladimir in Kiev are but outstanding instances. The West saw somewhat less of this. There missions arose more from the spontaneous efforts of individual Christians and of non-political Christian groups.

A fourth factor, closely related to this last, may have been the smaller place which Christianity had in the life of the eastern as compared with the western section of Europe. To be sure, the East thought of itself as Christian and gloried in its orthodoxy. Yet the old structure of pre-Christian Græco-Roman life persisted in the East with not so much of a break as in the West. Christianity had less opportunity to build and infuse a new culture. In the West the old more nearly disappeared, whether that was the heritage from Rome or the institutions of the barbarians. However imperfectly it may have been moulded, at least more of the new existed which had been shaped under the impulse of Christianity. We have seen that in the West it was chiefly from its geographic frontiers that Christianity spread. Most of these were outside the regions where the influence of pre-Christian Roman culture remained and were where the primitive culture of the barbarians had more nearly disintegrated. When adopted, therefore, what was called Christianity possessed a more dominant place in the life of the people and more nearly determined its ideals than in the East. That being the case, it displayed greater vitality in moving on to new areas.

In the Eastern descendant of the Roman Empire several branches of Christianity were found. The Christianity which spread from it was not all of one kind. By the year 500, except in the Teutonic kingdoms of the West, Arianism had ceased to be very important. The Monophysites were strong and made notable gains in non-Christian territories. On the eastern borders were Nestorians. Chief, however, was what came to be regarded as Greek Orthodox Christianity. Under Hellenistic influence, the prevailing form of Christianity in the East assumed, as we have seen, certain distinctive features. For generations an outward semblance of unity was maintained with the Latin Christianity of the West. For centuries the Popes as Bishops of Rome had official relations with the monarchs who reigned from Constantinople. Indeed, the Popes long sought from the Emperors confirmation of their election. As time passed, the tie which connected Latin Christianity with the Eastern Empire and with the eastern wing of what was called the Catholic Church became more tenuous and relations grew more strained. Repeatedly formal schism between the two great wings of the Church occurred. The final break came in 1054 when the civil authorities closed the Latin churches in Constantinople and Papal legates formally pronounced excommunication against the Eastern Church. Reunions effected by the Council of Lyons (1274) and the Council of Florence (1439) proved abortive and were only of brief duration. To be sure, some Greek-speaking communities, chiefly in Southern Italy and Sicily, remained in communion with Rome.[1] Others were won over to Rome. By and large, however, Roman Catholicism, overwhelmingly Latin in ecclesiastical language, and what came to be known as the Orthodox churches, in which the Hellenistic tradition was dominant and in which the Patriarch of Constantinople enjoyed the primacy, remained apart.

Yet, while in sympathy and in leadership Latin Christianity was separated from the Christianity of the Eastern Empire, in many ways the two were very much alike. In formal creed Roman Catholicism and Greek Orthodoxy were not far removed from each other. Some differences in customs there were. In contrast with the rule of celibacy in the West, many of the lower clergy of the Eastern churches were married. The Western clergy were often shaven and the Easterners bearded. The latter gave to the laity both the bread and the wine of the communion; the former gave only the bread. The East used leavened bread in the Eucharist; the West unleavened. The Latin Church

[1] *Catholic Encyclopedia*, Vol. VI, pp. 763-765; Frank Gavin in *An Outline of Christianity*, Vol. II, pp. 225-227.

added *filioque* to the portion of the Nicene Creed which described the procession of the Holy Spirit. Yet these variations were relatively minor. All branches, whether Roman Catholic, Orthodox, or Monophysite, emphasized monasticism as the highest form of Christian living. In all, moreover, the active missionaries were drawn chiefly from the monks. It was a monastic type of Christianity which was propagated. In the East no Pope existed to give direction to missions or to furnish a centre of reference. In the East as in the West, however, temporal rulers had an outstanding share in the spread of Christianity, both in initiating missions and in leading their people in the acceptance of the faith. As between East and West the missionary methods were, in general, strikingly similar.

In the sixth century, especially under Justinian, what was called the Roman Empire enjoyed a marked if brief revival. Portions of the territories lost to the Germanic invaders were regained and some of the old prestige of the Roman name was restored. Partly as a result, in a number of areas Christianity extended its borders and many new converts were made. In this expansion of the faith more than one branch of the Church participated.

Justinian I began to have an important share in affairs of state during the reign of his all but illiterate uncle and foster father, Justin. From 518 until his uncle's death, in 527, he was the power behind the throne. He himself reigned from 527 until his own death, in 565. His, then, was a long rule. One of his greatest ambitions was to regain the territories lost by the Empire to the barbarians. Through costly wars which laid heavy burdens on the economic structure of the weakened realm he partly succeeded in his purpose. Sicily, some of the islands of the western part of the Mediterranean, and much of North Africa, of Spain, and of Italy were reconquered.

Justinian was both devout and deeply interested in theology. He believed himself to be governing under the protection of the God of the Christians. He was zealous in bringing religious uniformity to his domains by the extirpation of the remnants of paganism and by the overcoming of heresy. He was also eager to further missions beyond the borders of the Empire.

Within the Empire paganism was to be found chiefly at the two extremes of society—among the educated and the aristocracy on the one hand and on the other among peasants and mountaineers in remote districts. To reach the first groups Justinian adopted a number of measures. Early in his reign he reaffirmed existing legislation against pagans and commanded civil officials and bishops to make themselves cognizant of any pagan superstitions within their jurisdictions.[2] Additional legislation named death as the penalty for apostasy and attempted to prevent the contamination of the mind of youth with pagan philosophy by forbidding any "infected with the madness of the unholy Hellenes" from doing any teaching.[3] Justinian instituted a persecution of pagans, working damage to their persons and confiscating their estates. Some, under pressure, nominally conformed but secretly maintained their old rites and sometimes were caught at them.[4] Several in high places were accused of paganism and we hear that on at least one occasion the convicted were turned over to the churches to be instructed in the Christian faith.[5] Much of the Christianity of the time must have been very superficial. We read of one in high favour with Justinian who, when he went to a Christian sanctuary to spend the night in prayer, was said to go garbed like a pagan priest.[6] As we have seen in an earlier chapter, Justinian brought an end to the teaching of the old philosophy in the famous Athenian schools. Precisely what happened we do not know, but we hear that some of the philosophers sought refuge with the hereditary enemy of Rome, Persia, and that, homesick, they returned. In a treaty of 532 the Persian monarch exacted of Justinian the promise that they would not be persecuted or required to accept Christianity.[7]

In western Asia Minor were many pagans, both in the rural areas and in the towns. We know of at least one missionary, John of Ephesus, being sent to win these. He himself claims to have converted many thousands, to have destroyed temples, and, aided by ample funds from Justinian, to have founded churches and monasteries.[8] On the island of Philæ, up the Nile near the imperial border, at the command of Justinian temples were torn down, the priests put under guard, and the images sent to Constantinople.[9] In an oasis of Egypt, in a temple to Ammon the ancient sacrifices were stopped, the population became Christian, and a church was built to the Virgin.[10]

Justinian did not seek to convert the Jews to Christianity.[11] He did, however, institute action against the Samaritans. Some of these, under pressure, took the Christian name. Others became Manichæists. Still others rebelled and were reduced with great slaughter.[12]

---

[2] *Cod. Just.*, i, 11, 9.
[3] *Cod. Just.*, i, 11, 10.
[4] Procopius, *Anecdota*, XI, 31, 32.
[5] Bury, *History of the Later Roman Empire* (1923 ed.), Vol. II, p. 369.
[6] Procopius, *History of the Wars*, I, xxv, 10.
[7] Bury, *op. cit.*, Vol. II, pp. 370, 371.
[8] John of Ephesus, *Eccles. Hist.*, Book III, Chap. 36; Bury, *op. cit.*, Vol. II, p. 371.
[9] Procopius, *History of the Wars*, I, xix, 36, 37.
[10] Procopius, περι κρισμάτων (*de Aed.*), Book VI, Chap. 2.
[11] Bury, *op. cit.*, Vol. II, p. 366.
[12] Procopius, *Anecdota*, xi, 24-30. See a brief modern account in Mercier, *Histoire de L'Afrique Septentrionale*, Vol. I, pp. 156-173.

Even in the heart of the Empire, however, Justinian did not succeed in completely stamping out paganism. We hear of one fortress, Maina, in Laconia in Greece where the cults of the ancient gods were maintained into the ninth century.[13]

In North Africa, the reconquest of the land from the Vandals was followed by marked changes in the religious situation. The Catholic Church triumphed over Arianism and the Donatists, and the process of the conversion of pagan peoples seems to have been resumed. In 533, under the general direction of the famous Belisarius, the fleet and the armies of Justinian began their attack. Within a few months the rule of the Vandals was completely eliminated. The reduction of the older indigenous stock—the Moors or Berbers—required a longer time and was never complete, but within a few years what was called Roman rule was re-established in much of what is now Tunis and Algeria, in a few places in what is now Libya, and on the southern shore of the Strait of Gibraltar.[14] The prosperity of the third and fourth centuries seems never to have been fully restored. Yet for nearly two hundred years the renewed Roman rule was continued. The conquest led to the revival of the Catholic Church. Catholicism had survived under the Vandals, but the latter, being Arians, had favoured their own branch of the faith and the Donatists. In 534 and 535, or as soon as the triumph of his arms warranted the step, Justinian expelled the Arians and the Donatists from the churches and other religious places, and restored to the Catholics the confiscated ecclesiastical property. Arians, Donatists, and Jews were denied graves or any of their religious rites. Synagogues were to be turned into churches and Jews were forbidden to own Christian slaves.[15]

During the Vandal occupation Christianity may have lost ground among the Berber population. As we have seen, the Berbers had never been completely won to the faith. Christianity—particularly Catholic Christianity—had been chiefly the religion of the Latin-speaking population and its spread was, in the main, coextensive with the process of Romanization. It was strongest in the cities and weakest in the rural districts.[16] Naturally, with the collapse of Roman rule it suffered greatly. Certainly at the time of the reoccupation by Justinian many of the Berber tribes normally within the Roman sphere of influence were pagan.[17]

Justinian was very eager that the conquest should make for the extension

[13] Bury, *A History of the Eastern Roman Empire from the Fall of Irene to the Accession of Basil I*, p. 381, citing Constantine, *De Adm. imp.*, 224.
[14] Procopius, *History of the Wars*, Books III, IV.
[15] *Novellae*, 37; Duchesne, *L'Église au VI Siècle*, p. 640.
[16] Mesnage, *Le Christianisme en Afrique. Origines, Développements, Extension*, p. 327.
[17] Diehl, *L'Afrique Byzantine*, pp. 324, 325, citing a number of sources.

ot Christianity. We read that during his reign some of the Berber groups accepted the faith. Of these at least two were in the present Libya, in the vicinity of ruined Roman cities which the Emperor rebuilt.[18]

After Justinian's death conversion continued. It was associated with the expansion of Byzantine rule. At least some of the Berber tribes which made their peace with the Empire apparently sealed the compact by accepting baptism. The acknowledgment of imperial authority and entrance into the body of the faithful seemingly went hand in hand.[19] The Donatists who had fled to the frontier and who persisted to at least the close of the sixth century[20] may have been something of an obstacle to the missions of the Catholics.[21] So, too, on the borders and beyond were a number of peoples who professed Judaism, possibly derived from exiles from the Byzantine rule.[22] Judging by the ruins which remain, the Byzantine period witnessed much building of churches in the cities, and this may indicate an extension of Christianity among the urban population.[23] Certainly when, early in the eighth century, the rule of the Byzantine Christians was violently displaced by that of Moslem conquerors, a large proportion of the population in the northern portions of the present Tunisia and in the north-eastern sections of the present Algeria were Christian. During the Byzantine occupation, moreover, Christians were to be found in cities as far east as the later Tripoli and Lebda and westward beyond the Straits of Gibraltar.[24]

The Christianity under this Roman-Byzantine rule seems not to have displayed anything like the vigour of that of pre-Vandal times. No writers or thinkers appeared who would compare with an Augustine, a Cyprian, or a Tertullian. Pope Gregory the Great took an active interest in the Church of Africa, but the time had passed when it was the chief centre of Latin Christianity. A decline had set in, possibly due in part to the Vandals, and perhaps to the long struggle between Catholics on the one hand and Donatists and Arians on the other. This decay Justinian and his successors were unable to arrest. The non-Latin using portions of the population seem never to have been so thoroughly won by the Church or so fully assimilated to Roman cul-

[18] Procopius, De Aed., Book VI, Chaps. 3, 4.
[19] Diehl, op. cit., pp. 327, 328; Duchesne, op. cit., pp. 650-652.
[20] Gregory the Great, Ep. I, 74, in Migne, Pat. Lat., Vol. LXXVII, Cols. 529, 530.
[21] Diehl, op. cit., p. 328.
[22] Diehl, op. cit., p. 329. Also see map in Mesnage, Le Christianisme en Afrique. Déclin et Extinction, after p. viii, and Mesnage, op. cit., pp. 92 ff.
[23] Mesnage, Le Christianisme en Afrique. Origines, Développements, Extension, p. 328.
[24] Mesnage, Le Christianisme en Afrique. Déclin et Extinction, passim, and especially map after p. viii. For lists of bishops and for maps see Mesnage, L'Afrique Chrétienne Évêches et Ruines Antiques, passim; Leclercq, L'Afrique Chrétienne, Vol. II, p. 286.

ture as were those of Spain and Gaul. In the fourth century, when in Gaul Christianity was making rapid headway among the rural population and the conversion and the Romanization of the countryside were proceeding hand in hand, in North Africa the Church was torn by the Donatist schism. Certainly in North Africa the Church suffered more from the barbarian invasions and the collapse of Roman rule than in Spain or in Gaul. In the sixth and seventh centuries it produced no one equal to Gregory of Tours, Isidore of Seville, Gregory the Great, or Benedict of Nursia, the children of contemporary Latin Christianity in Gaul, Spain, and Italy. Obviously the Church of North Africa was not so nearly in a healthy condition as was that of these other three areas. It is not surprising, therefore, that it suffered so severely from the Moslem invasion and displayed less power of resistance to Islam than did the Church in any other major section of the Mediterranean littoral.

In the Nile Valley the reign of Justinian saw an expansion of Christianity which was followed in later centuries by a wide extension in Nubia, the Sudan, and Ethiopia. As we have suggested in an earlier chapter, the great majority of the Egyptian Christians developed peculiarities of language and national feeling. To these were added, in the fifth and sixth centuries, the entrance of Monophysitism. The struggle between the Orthodox and the Monophysites absorbed much of the time and attention of Justinian. His Empress, the independently minded Theodora, sympathized with the Monophysites. Justinian sought, in vain, to bring about religious unity.[25] In the course of time, the great majority of the Egyptians adhered to Monophysitism and the Orthodox were recruited mainly from those in the cities who were Greek in language and sympathy. Monophysitism, moreover, became the faith of the majority in Palestine and Syria. It was to be expected, therefore, that it would be the Monophysite form of Christianity rather than the Orthodox which would be propagated up the Nile and in Ethiopia.

Nubia, south of what we usually denominate Egypt, early had a fairly high culture. This may have been derived in part from immigrants from Egypt. There was, however, an independent script. More than one state existed in the region.[26] How early Christianity entered we do not know. In A.D. 350 the first Christian King of Axum, in Ethiopia, invaded the region, plundering and destroying,[27] but we do not hear that he made any attempt to win the people to his newly adopted faith. If any Christians were there before the sixth century they must have been very much in the minority. In the last quarter of

[25] For the story of this phase of Justinian's reign, see Bury, *History of the Later Roman Empire*, Vol. II, pp. 364-394.
[26] Kraus, *Die Anfänge des Christentums in Nubien*, pp. 4-28.
[27] *Deutsche Aksum Epedition*, Vol. IV, No. 11, cited in Kraus, *op. cit.*, p. 10.

the fourth century the famous edict of Theodosius I counts the inhabitants as pagans. So does a traveller of the first quarter of the fifth century.[28] We have already seen that pagan cults were maintained on the island of Philæ, near the Egyptian border of Nubia, until Justinian put an end to them. Yet in the fourth century a Christian community with a bishop had appeared on Philæ and by the middle of the fifth century churches on the island had been destroyed by pagans from the South.[29] Cosmas Indicopleustes, writing not far from the middle of the sixth century and in the time of Justinian, declares that there were Christians among the Nubians.[30]

So far as we know, the first serious attempts to introduce Christianity into Nubia were in the reign of Justinian. From sixth-century accounts which are by men who had opportunity to obtain first-hand information we have reports which are not always easy to reconcile.[31] Apparently both Orthodox and Monophysite Christianity entered at approximately the same time. What seems to have happened is about as follows. Theodosius, the Monophysite Patriarch of Alexandria, had a priest Julian, an elderly man who wished to become a missionary to the nomads on the eastern borders of the Thebaïd. Julian approached the Empress Theodora, who, as we have seen, was friendly to Monophysites. She promised him her support. Justinian, however, so the story proceeds, wished the Orthodox to go rather than this heretic and arranged for such a mission, ordering that it be provided with gifts for the ruler and the people. Theodora, with her customary energy, saw to it that Julian reached Nubia first. Julian went to the Nobadæ (or Nobatæ), was well received, and won them to the Christian faith. In spite of his sufferings from the severe heat, he remained there two years and then left, commending the neophytes to the care of the Bishop of Philæ. The Bishop discharged the trust, at least until 551, instructing the new Christians and extending the work of conversion.

[28] Budge, *A History of Ethiopia, Nubia, and Abyssinia*, Vol. I, p. 113.

[29] Kraus, *op. cit.*, pp. 27, 48.

[30] *The Christian Topography of Cosmas, an Egyptian Monk, Translated from the Greek and Edited with Notes and Introduction* by J. W. McCrindle (London, Hakluyt Society, 1897), Book III, p. 120. The text is in Migne, *Pat. Gr.*, Vol. LXXXVIII, Cols. 169, 170.

[31] See the varying accounts summarized and analysed in Kraus, *op. cit.*, pp. 54-93. Kraus, *op. cit.*, pp. 94-134, gives the archæological and epigraphical evidence. The brief accounts in Bury, *History of the Later Roman Empire*, pp. 328-330, Duchesne, *L'Église au VIe Siècle*, pp. 296-303, and Duchesne, *Les Missions Chrétiennes au Sud de l'Empire Romain*, pp. 82-90, are inadequate and are superseded by Kraus. Kraus gives careful references to the sources. Among them are John of Ephesus, *Ecclesiastical History*, Third Part, Book IV, Chap. 5-7 (see William Cureton, *The Third Part of the Ecclesiastical History of John Bishop of Ephesus*, Oxford University Press, 1853, and the translation of the *Third Part of the Ecclesiastical History of John of Ephesus* by R. P. Smith, Oxford University Press, 1860, pp. 250-256); and John of Biclarum, *Chronicon*, in *Mon. Germ. Hist., Auctores Antiquissimi*, Vol. XI, p. 212.

In the meantime the Orthodox missionaries sent by Justinian arrived, found the field pre-empted, were received coldly, but, undiscouraged, went on to another people in Nubia, the Makorites, and won many among these to their branch of the faith. Certainly many surviving gravestones with Greek Byzantine texts bear witness to the presence of Orthodox Christianity in Nubia. It may be, indeed, that during the latter part of the reign of Justinian the Orthodox in Nubia fared better than the Monophysites. The latter's protector, Theodora, died in 547, eighteen years before the Emperor. Justinian, with his usual attention to details, may be supposed to have given some thought to the spiritual care of these converts of his envoys.

The year after Justinian's passing, the Monophysite Patriarch Theodosius, then on his own death bed (566), bethought him of the converts made by Julian two decades before and commissioned Longinus to go there as Bishop. The Empress Theodora, indeed, had long before requested that Longinus be made Bishop in that region. Longinus was delayed by unfriendly Orthodox imperial officials. However, eventually he eluded them and reached his diocese. Here he built a church and reared a native clergy. After a time he was recalled to Alexandria to help settle some ecclesiastical disputes. He was away from Nubia for some time. During his absence his enemies in Alexandria, also Monophysites, sent missionaries to Nubia who attempted unsuccessfully to wean his flock from him and who also failed to make converts of a people in the southern part of Nubia who had asked Longinus to come to them. About 580 Longinus returned to Nubia. From here, through a journey of great peril and hardship, he pushed farther south and won still another people to his faith. How long he was in Nubia we do not know. Nor do we know whether he ever returned to Alexandria.[32]

What later missionaries came to Nubia, or, indeed, whether they came, is not disclosed by our records. However, from the numerous inscriptions which remain, most of them on graves, we know that Christianity spread, that rulers adopted the faith or inherited it, and that temples were transformed into churches. The capital of one of the Christian kingdoms was at Dongola, on the Nile, between the third and fourth cataracts. Since the inscriptions are most of them in Greek or Coptic or both, we gather that close contact with the

---

[32] See the summary in Kraus, *Die Anfänge des Christentums in Nubien,* pp. 138-156. The account of Longinus, with his letters, Kraus cites from J. M. Schönfelder's edition of John of Ephesus, *Ecclesiastical History* (Munich, 1862). An English translation is in R. P. Smith, *The Third Part of the Ecclesiastical History of John of Ephesus* (Oxford, 1860), Book IV, Chaps. 8-11, 22, 49-53, pp. 256-264, 285, 315-327. The theory that the Christianity in Nubia had a Byzantine as well as a Coptic origin finds support in the recent discoveries of Ugo Monneret de Villard, *The New York Times,* March 9, 1931.

Christians in Egypt was maintained.[33] We read, too, of the appointment of bishops for Nubia by the Monophysite Patriarch.[34] As we shall see later, in Nubia and the Sudan, Christian kingdoms ecclesiastically connected with the Coptic Church held out against Islam until the fourteenth and in some places until the sixteenth century.[35]

Adjoining the Sudan is Ethiopia (Abyssinia). We have seen that as early as the first half of the fourth century the historic nucleus of this state, Axum or Aksum, had received Christianity and that its rulers had accepted the faith. We have also noted that by the end of the fifth century the Church there had become Monophysite and that the civil authorities were exercising a kind of protectorate over the Christians on the opposite shores of the Red Sea in Arabia. In the middle of the sixth century Cosmas Indicopleustes speaks of Christians, churches, and monks in Ethiopia, Aksum, "and all the country about it."[36] There are accounts which ascribe the conversion of the country to the age of Justinian. These declare that the King of Ethiopia vowed that he would accept Christianity if he conquered the Homerites or Himyarites on the coast of the Red Sea and that, having won, he sent to Justinian for missionaries and was given a bishop, John, who had been a priest of Alexandria, and who, accompanied by clergy, went to Aksum.[37] It is clear, however, that Christianity had been planted in the land long before this time. However, it seems well established that about 525 Ethiopians intervened in Southern Arabia in behalf of Christians who were being persecuted and it may well be that Justinian encouraged the expedition.[38]

During the sixth and seventh centuries the Ethiopian Church continued to prosper. It was in fairly close touch with the Coptic Church and in its monasteries the literature written by the monks of Egypt was studied.[39] From the

[33] Kraus, *op. cit.,* pp. 96-128; Budge, *The Egyptian Sûdân,* Vol. II, pp. 292-297; Budge, *A History of Ethiopia,* Vol. I, pp. 116, 117.

[34] Eutychius, *Annales,* in Migne, *Pat. Gr.,* Vol. CXI, Cols. 1122, 1123.

[35] Clarke, *Christian Antiquities in the Nile Valley,* p. 12; Budge, *The Egyptian Sûdân,* Vol. I, pp. ix, x, Vol. II, pp. 292-300, 306; Budge, *A History of Ethiopia,* Vol. I, pp. 116-119; report of excavations by Ugo Monneret de Villard in Southern Nubia of Christian churches and monasteries ranging in date from the eighth to the twelfth century, in *The New York Times,* March 14, 1933.

[36] *The Christian Topography of Cosmas* (McCrindle's edition), Book III, p. 120. Text in Migne, *Pat. Gr.,* Vol. LXXXVIII, Cols. 169, 170. See a convenient summary, D. H. Moore, *Christianity in Ethiopia* (in *Church History,* Vol. V, No. 3, Sept., 1936, pp. 271 ff.).

[37] Joannis Malalae, *Chronographia,* in Migne, *Pat. Gr.,* Vol. XCVII, Cols. 639-642; Duchesne, *L'Église au VIe Siècle,* p. 287; Moreau, in Descamps, *Histoire Générale Comparée des Missions,* p. 178.

[38] Moberg, *The Book of the Himyarites, passim,* and especially pp. lxviii, lxxvi, lxxvii; Bell, *The Origin of Islam in Its Christian Environment,* pp. 36, 37.

[39] Budge, *A History of Ethiopia,* Vol. I, pp. 153, 154; Schubert, *Geschichte der christlichen Kirche im Frühmittelalter,* p. 145.

seventh to the thirteenth century the history of the land is almost a blank.[40] It is clear that there were attacks by Arabs and pagans and that in the tenth century Juditta, a princess of the Jewish faith, making herself mistress of the country, destroyed Aksum and every trace of Christianity in it. Her successors were Christians, but of a tradition different from that of Aksum.[41] In these centuries the existing Christian literature was almost wiped out. In the thirteenth century occurred what professed to be the restoration of the ancient line of kings, the Solomonic (which averred that it was descended from Solomon and the Queen of Sheba). Under the change of rulers came fresh contacts with the Coptic Christian communities, then displaying new energy from a reform movement, and with them a revival in the Ethiopian Church. Literature was introduced from Egypt, Coptic monks translated the New Testament into one of the languages of the land, multiplied copies of it, and compiled books of ritual.[42] Yet Ethiopian Christianity seems not to have been stimulated into producing literature of its own.[43] To the manner in which it developed its own peculiarities we will refer in a later chapter.

In the reign of Justinian began a marked eastward expansion of another branch of Monophysitism, the Jacobites. The Jacobites grew partly, as have so many bodies of Christians, by accessions from existing Christian communities and partly by conversions from among non-Christians. However, that story must be told in connexion with the movement of Christianity into the Sassanid Empire and beyond and must be reserved for a later chapter.

We read that in other directions the reign of Justinian encouraged missions, this time supposedly of the Orthodox branch of the Church. In the Caucasus lived the Abasgi, from whom had come many of the eunuchs of the Roman Empire. They became Christian and Justinian had a church built for them. Moreover, it is said that Justinian sent to them one of their own number, a eunuch from the imperial palace, and commanded their rulers to desist from the practice of making eunuchs of the boys.[44] We hear, too, that the Eruli or Heruli, who sometime before had crossed the Danube and settled on Roman territory, were persuaded by Justinian to become Christians.[45] We are told, also, that Justinian sent a bishop to some Goths on the River Don,

[40] Enno Littmann, in *Deutsche Aksum-Expedition*, Vol. I, p. 57.
[41] Budge, *Legends of Our Lady Mary*, pp. xlii, xliii.
[42] Budge, *A History of Ethiopia*, Vol. I, pp. 154 ff.; Budge, *Legends of Our Lady Mary*, pp. xlii, xliii; Enno Littmann, in *op. cit.*, Vol. I, p. 57; Littmann, *Geschichte der äthiopischen Litteratur*, in *Geschichte der christlichen Litteraturen des Orients*, p. 204.
[43] Littmann, *Geschichte der äthiopischen Litteratur*, in *op. cit.*, pp. 189-204; Budge, *A History of Ethiopia*, Vol. II, pp. 562, 563.
[44] Procopius, *A History of the Wars*, VIII, iii, 18-21.
[45] Procopius, *op. cit.*, VI, xiv, 28-34.

not far from the Sea of Azov, but whether they had previously been Arians or pagans seems uncertain.[46]

In 569, shortly after Justinian's death, the Garamanti, in the Arabian desert, asked the Emperor, Justin II, for missionaries.[47]

Justinian had been in his grave scarcely three-quarters of a century when there began the Moslem invasion from Arabia which tore from the Empire which he had taken such pride in restoring some of its fairest provinces and altered profoundly the religious map of the Mediterranean basin and of much of Asia. Again we must reserve for a later chapter the narrative of those events. Here, however, we must note that the Moslem conquests practically put an end to the spread of Christianity from the southern shores of the Mediterranean. For centuries Christianity continued to expand eastward through Asia, but this was not from the Byzantine state. In spite of many efforts, no large numerical or territorial gains were made by Byzantine Christianity against Islam. To the west Latin Catholicism blocked expansion. Even if the Empire had retained control of Syria, Palestine, and Egypt, Monophysitism in its various forms was there the faith of the majority of Christians. Greek Orthodoxy, the state church, here drew chiefly from the imperial officials and the Greek residents. In Persia the majority of Christians were Nestorians. The only missionary field remaining was to the north, in the Balkans and Eastern Europe. It was here, therefore, that Greek Orthodox Christianity had its greatest extension.

For centuries the tide of barbarian invasion surged southward through the Balkan Peninsula and beat upon the frontiers of the Empire. Except for some of the Goths of the fourth century and for the Crusaders, the attacks were by non-Christians and those which came by way of Europe were by pagans. In the quarter of a century after the fateful battle of Hadrianople (378) the Goths ravaged Macedonia and Greece.[48] In the fifth century came the Huns, who raided as far as Thermopylæ.[49] Even under the strong Justinian, in the sixth century, the Balkans and Greece were repeatedly penetrated—by the Huns, the Slavs, and the Bulgars—and on the eve of Justinian's death the Avars became a menace.[50] After the death of Justinian conditions grew much worse. The Empire, pressed by its recurring wars with Persia and, later, by the

[46] Procopius, op. cit., VIII, iv, 10-12; A. A. Vasiliev, The Goths in the Crimea (Cambridge, The Mediaeval Academy of America, 1936, pp. x, 292), pp. 57-69.
[47] Chronicon of John of Biclarum, in Mon. Germ. Hist., Auctores Antiquissimi, Vol. II, p. 212.
[48] Cambridge Medieval History, Vol. I, pp. 250 ff.
[49] Cambridge Medieval History, Vol. I, pp. 362-364.
[50] Cambridge Medieval History, Vol. II, p. 31.

Saracens, could not devote its full strength to the protection of its northern frontiers.

During the latter part of the sixth century and in the seventh century Slavs and Avars again and again invaded the Balkans and Greece.[51] Permanent settlements were effected, largely by the Slavs. It has, indeed, been asserted—and vehemently denied—that the ancient Hellenic stock of Greece died out and was replaced by Slavs who adopted the language of the land. It is clear that large numbers of Slavs settled in the Balkans and in Greece, including the Peloponnesus, and that many were moved into Asia Minor.[52]

In the second half of the seventh century a new barbarian kingdom arose in the Balkans, largely in territory which had been wrested from the Empire. The Bulgars, a people of Hunnic (Turkish) origin, moved in and defeated the Byzantine forces. The Emperor bought peace only on the condition of the cession of territory south of the Danube and the payment of tribute. The bulk of the population over which the conquerors ruled was Slavonic. In time the Bulgars, the dominant minority, were assimilated in blood and in language to the Slavic majority. The process, as we shall see, was interrelated with conversion to Christianity. Repeated wars were waged between the Bulgars and the Empire. Again and again the Bulgars carried the hostilities into the imperial dominions and even pushed their attack up to the walls of Constantinople.[53]

The conversion of these invaders from the north must have begun very early. Most of it occurred as part of the process of assimilation. In Greece, in Asia Minor, and in much of the Balkan Peninsula, the newcomers found themselves in territory which Constantinople regarded as inseparable from the Empire and in the midst of a culture of which Christianity formed an integral part. The immigrants, most of them Slavs and all of them from peoples of a much simpler culture, in time quite naturally fitted into the life about them and accepted baptism. The absorption was not perfect. By most of the barbarians many of the more polished and subtle features of civilized life were missed or ignored. Yet outwardly there was much of conformity. However, even within the territories definitely under imperial control, the process was not completed until the ninth century or even later. Before the ninth century

[51] See instances in John of Biclarum, *Chronicon,* in *Mon. Germ. Hist., Auctores Antiquissimi,* Vol. XI, pp. 214 ff., from the years 576-581.

[52] Vasiliev, *History of the Byzantine Empire,* Vol. I, pp. 207, 213-216, 239, 240, 265, 266-293; Bury, *A History of the Later Roman Empire from Arcadius to Irene* (1889 ed.), Vol. II, pp. 143, 144.

[53] Vasiliev, *op. cit.,* Vol. I, pp. 266-268; Bury, *A History of the Eastern Roman Empire from the Fall of Irene to the Accession of Basil I* (A.D. 802-867), pp. 332 ff.

conversions outside the regions where the Empire was effective must have been relatively few.[54]

Assimilation was hastened by the military organization of the realm. Following the established practice of the Roman Empire, the forces of the Byzantine rulers were recruited largely from barbarian peoples. By the sixth century the armies had long been those of a state which esteemed itself Christian and which tended to regard its wars as waged in behalf of the Orthodox religion and with the support of the Christian God. In the army, feasts were officially observed in honour of the Virgin and the patron saints. It must have been easy, accordingly, for those who bore the imperial arms to adopt the imperial faith.[55]

In Asia Minor assimilation was probably very rapid. The Slavs were here in the midst of a population which was predominantly Christian. Conversion and Hellenization must have gone hand in hand. Yet our records contain only a hint of the process.[56]

In Thrace, Macedonia, Epirus, and Greece absorption into the Hellenistic Christian culture must also have proceeded naturally and unspectacularly. The episcopates which had existed before the invasions presumably largely persisted. In many places, especially in the cities and towns, Christian communities must have survived and church life have continued, diminished, but without much interruption. To be sure, some bishoprics seem to have lapsed, especially in Macedonia, but seldom was the Church entirely wiped out over large areas. In the intervals of peace churches must have been rebuilt and monasteries restored.[57] We hear that a large force of Slavs, mixed with other peoples, was baptized by the monks of the celebrated monastic centre of Mt. Athos.[58] The Patriarch of Constantinople had the custom of appointing inspectors to oversee the work of conversion in the European provinces.[59] Some Slavs rose high in Church and state. We hear of one, Nicetas I, who became Patriarch (766-780), and Slavic blood flowed in the veins of several of the outstanding political figures of the Empire.[60]

Assimilation was not quickly completed, even in Greece. Where the Slavs settled in compact masses, their absorption must have been much slower than

[54] Runciman, *A History of the First Bulgarian Empire*, pp. 281-283.

[55] Dvorník, *Les Slaves, Byzance et Rome au IXe Siècle*, pp. 67, 68.

[56] Dvorník, *op. cit.*, p. 103.

[57] Dvorník, *op. cit.*, pp. 84-99, 103. On the process in Greece see Bury, *A History of the Later Roman Empire from Arcadius to Irene* (London, 1889), Vol. II, pp. 455, 456.

[58] Dvorník, *La Vie de Saint Grégoire le Décapolite et les Slaves Macédoniens au IXe Siècle*, pp. 32, 33.

[59] Spinka, *A History of Christianity in the Balkans*, p. 23.

[60] Bury, *A History of the Later Roman Empire from Arcadius to Irene* (London, 1889), Vol. II, p. 525.

where they mingled as individuals and small groups with a Christian population. Not until the ninth century were the Slavs of the Peloponnesus finally reduced, and the way prepared for their conversion and Hellenization. Probably not until the fifteenth century did the Slavs cease to form distinct groups in Greece.[61]

As we have earlier suggested, in parts of the Balkans, including the Dalmatian coast, competition occurred between the Eastern and Western Churches. We have already narrated what is known of the spread of Roman Catholic Christianity in that region.

In the Balkans as in Moravia, the great period of the conversion of the Slavs was the ninth century. In the ninth century both the Byzantine Empire and its Church experienced a marked revival. The iconoclastic controversies which for over a century had at intervals rent the state and troubled the Church were at an end. The enthusiasm with which the defenders of the saints, their relics, and their images, had fought for their faith had communicated itself to the masses.[62] An intellectual revival broke out and distinguished scholars graced the Empire. The most learned and brilliant of them all, Photius, became Patriarch. Through a career which knew alternations of great power and of political disgrace he conducted himself with dignity and sagacity. His energy and initiative had much to do with furthering the missions of his Church. Bardas, the real power in the Empire during much of the reign of his nephew, Michael III, "the Drunkard" (835-867), was a patron of learning and pursued a vigorous foreign policy.[63] The dissolute Michael III was murdered by his favourite, Basil, who may have been of mixed Armenian and Slavic descent, and who as Basil I (867-886) founded the Macedonian dynasty and proved to be a ruler of marked ability and energy.[64]

It is not surprising that under Bardas Constantine and Methodius received the imperial commission which started them on their momentous missionary labours among the Slavs of Central Europe. Nor is it strange that the latter part of the ninth century witnessed the conversion of the Bulgars to the Byzantine form of the Christian faith.

To connect these events with what was happening in the West, it is interesting to recall that this was towards the close of that expansion of Christianity which took place during the reigns of the great Carolingians and that from

[61] Bury, *A History of the Eastern Roman Empire from the Fall of Irene to the Accession of Basil I,* pp. 379, 380.

[62] Dvorník, *La Vie de Saint Grégoire le Décapolite et les Slaves Macédoniens au IXe Siècle (Paris, Librairie Ancienne Honoré Champion,* 1926, pp. 91), p. 9.

[63] *Cambridge Medieval History,* Vol. IV, pp. 45, 46; Dvorník, *Les Slaves, Byzance et Rome au IXe Siècle,* pp. iii, iv.

[64] On Basil's ancestry see Vasiliev, *History of the Byzantine Empire,* Vol. I, p. 367.

the north-west the Latin form of the faith was penetrating the Central European territories of the Slavs. The advance against the paganism of the Slavs, the Avars, and the Bulgars was being made from two sides. Rivalry and conflict punctuated the relations between the emissaries of the two wings of the Church.

It was in the ninth century that the Greek form of Christianity made marked headway among the Slavic Serbians. Long before, the Emperor Heraclius (575-642) had sent Roman missionaries who had baptized some of the Serbians.[65] How lasting these conversions were we do not know. In the second half of the ninth century the Emperor Basil I reduced the Serbian pirates whose homes were in the Narenta Valley. He not only swept them off the seas, but he also laid waste their homes, sent them a number of priests, and constrained them to accept baptism.[66] Taking timely counsel from the fate of these fellow-Serbians, Mutimir (c. 850-891), probably to make his peace with the powerful Basil and to preserve his authority, sent to Constantinople offering his submission and requesting missionaries. The formal conversion of Mutimir's people followed.[67]

Most influential of the conversions made by the Byzantine Church in the ninth century was that of the Bulgars. In the first half of the ninth century this series of events must have seemed highly improbable. The Bulgars and their Slavic subjects and allies, notably under the leadership of one Krum, inflicted defeat after defeat on the Byzantine forces. The Emperor Nicephorus was killed in battle (811) and his skull was fashioned into a drinking-cup for the victor. The invading armies fought their way to the very walls of Constantinople. Even the death of Krum did not end the Bulgarian menace. Again and again successes were gained over the Byzantine arms. To be sure, the laurels were not all on one side. Nor did war always exist between the two realms. Usually, however, the military advantage was with the Bulgars.[68]

Yet, as we have so often found to be the issue in earlier stages of our story, the barbarian eventually adopted the culture and the religion of the civilized neighbours for whom he was repeatedly more than a match in the open field. Greek was employed in the official documents of the Bulgars, and Byzantine artisans and architects seem to have been used to construct and embellish buildings.[69] At least one Bulgar of high rank who took refuge in Constantinople

[65] Constantine Porphyrogenitus, *De Administrando Imperio*, Chap. 32, in Migne, *Pat. Gr.*, Vol. CXIII, Cols. 289-292; Spinka, *A History of Christianity in the Balkans*, p. 23.
[66] Spinka, *op. cit.*, p. 24.
[67] *Ibid.*
[68] Bury, *A History of the Eastern Roman Empire from the Fall of Irene to the Accession of Basil I*, pp. 332-381.
[69] Bury, *op. cit.*, pp. 333-335.

accepted baptism.[70] It may be that in the domains of the Bulgars Christian communities survived the invasions. It is certain that thousands of Christians were carried captive into Bulgarian lands. Among these were priests. Some of the prisoners laboured for the conversion of their pagan masters and met with a degree of success. An occasional spasm of persecution sought to stem the drift toward the Byzantine faith, perhaps because to the rulers this latter appeared to portend Byzantine political control, but in the third quarter of the ninth century Christianity seems to have been honeycombing the ranks and to have reached the higher classes.[71]

The process of conversion was brought to a dramatic climax by the baptism of the Bulgarian King Boris. This event probably occurred in the year 864 or 865.[72] It was not fortuitous. From two sides the Bulgars were being pressed by Christian powers. To the north-west were the Germans. Boris first fought and then, defeated, supported Louis the German, the recipient of the portions of the Carolingian empire which lay east of the Rhine.[73] In 862 Louis believed that he had persuaded Boris to agree to accept baptism—of course into the Latin form of Christianity.[74] About the same time the Moravian prince, Rastislav, sent the request to Constantinople which resulted in the dispatch of Constantine and Methodius on their memorable mission. Constantinople could not view with equanimity the growing Carolingian influence on its borders. Nor could it be content with the adoption of Roman Christianity by the Bulgars. The Patriarch Photius and the Pope were at odds with each other. In 863 the Pope called upon Photius to resign or be excommunicated. Presumably, therefore, Constantinople was not averse to taking decisive action.

Around so important an occurrence as the baptism of Boris legend has been busy. What seems to have been the order of events is this. While the Bulgarian forces were out of the country assisting Louis the German, the Byzantine army invaded the land. To the absence of much of the army a famine was added. Boris had no alternative but to submit. In return for a concession of territory, he agreed to withdraw from his alliance with Louis, to accept baptism, and to acknowledge the suzerainty of the Emperor Michael III. Envoys of Boris were

---

[70] Bury, *op. cit.*, p. 336.

[71] Theophylactus Archiepiscopus Bulg., *Historia Martyrii XV Martyrum*, in Migne, *Pat. Gr.*, Vol. CXXVI, Cols. 192 ff.; Dvorník, *Les Slaves, Byzance et Rome au IXe Siècle*, p. 100, citing Theop. Cont. V, *De Bas. Mac.*, Chap. 4 (Bonn, pp. 216, 217), IV, Chap. 4 (Bonn, pp. 162, 163); Bonn III, 408 ff.; Bonn II, p. 185; Bury, *op. cit.*, pp. 381, 382; Spinka, *A History of Christianity in the Balkans*, p. 28.

[72] Various dates are given, ranging from 845 to 865, most of them 860-865. See some in Hergenröther, *Photius*, Vol. I, pp. 598, 599.

[73] Spinka, *op. cit.*, pp. 29, 30.

[74] Nicolai Papae I, *Capitula*, in Migne, *Pat. Lat.*, Vol. CXIX, Col. 875, xii; *Hincmari Remensis Annales*, in *Mon. Germ. Hist., Scriptorum*, Vol. I, p. 465.

baptized in Constantinople and a mission of Greek clergy, sent by Photius, went to Bulgaria and baptized Boris himself.[75]

This act of Boris was followed by the rebellion of his nobles. It may be that they objected to Byzantine overlordship. Perhaps they were indignant over the departure from the old ways. They may have been jealous of the royal power. Certainly Boris soon began, as did later the Kings of Norway and King Stephen of Hungary, to use the new faith as a means of curtailing the power of the local magnates and achieving a united monarchy under a ruler with enhanced powers. He may have dreamed of amalgamating the Bulgar ruling minority with the Slavic majority by making Christianity the religion and Slavonic the language of all. To this the Bulgarian magnates quite naturally objected. Whatever the motives of the opposition, Boris won and took summary vengeance.[76]

The conversion of the Bulgarians proceeded apace. The Patriarch Photius sent Boris a long letter setting forth the theological doctrines and the ethical precepts of the Christian faith as interpreted by the Greek Church.[77] Greeks and Armenians poured into the country, baptizing and instructing the people. Among the missionaries were discrepancies in doctrine, and it may be that some of the teachers were of the heretical group called the Paulicians.[78] Inevitably the conversion was very superficial. It is not surprising that the worship of the chief Slavic deity is said to have persisted into the eighteenth century.[79]

Boris was eager to make his realm ecclesiastically as well as politically independent. He wished it not to be an apanage of either the Frankish or the Byzantine Empire. When Photius ignored his request for a Bulgarian episcopate, he turned to the West and sent requests for clergy to the Pope and to Louis the German.[80] Both readily complied. The Pope to whom the invitation came, Nicholas I (858-867), was one of the ablest of the long line who have occupied

---

[75] See a summary of the various accounts and an attempt to untangle them in Spinka, *op. cit.*, pp. 31-33; Bury, *A History of the Eastern Empire from the Fall of Irene to the Accession of Basil I*, pp. 385, 386; Dvorník, *Les Slaves, Byzance et Rome au IXe Siècle*, pp. 186-188. On the date, see Dvorník, *op. cit.*, p. 187, n. 2. See as one of the sources Theophylactus Arch. Bulg., *Historia Martyrii XV Martyrum*, in Migne, *Pat. Gr.*, Vol. CXXVI, Cols. 197-200.

[76] *Annales* Bert. (*Hincmar*) A.D. 866, in *Mon. Germ. Hist., Scriptorum*, Vol. I, pp. 473 ff.; *Nicolaus Responsa*, in Migne, *Pat. Lat.*, Vol. CXIX, Col. 988.

[77] The letter is in Migne, *Pat. Gr.*, Vol. CII, Cols. 628 ff. See a summary in Hergenröther, *Photius*, Vol. I, pp. 602-604.

[78] *Nicolaus Responsa*, in Migne, *Pat. Lat.*, Vol. CXIX, Col. 978 ff., especially Chaps. 78, 104, 106; Bury, *A History of the Eastern Roman Empire from the Fall of Irene to the Accession of Basil I*, pp. 387, 388, citing Snopek, *Konst. Cyr.*, 17.

[79] Spinka, *A History of Christianity in the Balkans*, p. 34, citing L. Niederle, *Slovanské Starožitnosti* (Praba, 1900-1924), II, Pt. I, ed. 2, p. 99.

[80] *Annales Fuldenses*, an. 866 (in *Scriptores rerum Germanicarum*, Hanover, 1891); *Annales Bert.* (*Hincmar*), an. 866, in *Mon. Germ. Hist., Scriptorum*, Vol. I, p. 474.

the Fisherman's chair. He wrote a lengthy epistle to Boris, answering the latter's questions and giving him counsel.[81] He dispatched it by two bishops, Formosus of Porto and Paul of Populonia, together with gifts of sacred vessels and books. After the legates had been presented to Boris, they busied themselves with preaching and baptizing in what must have seemed to them a most amazingly fertile field.[82] When the bishop and the priests and deacons sent by Louis reached Bulgaria, they found the Pope's emissaries already there and obtained the consent of their King to return home.[83]

However, to Boris the Papal connexion proved as disappointing as had that with Photius. Boris wished most of all to have an archbishop appointed to head the Bulgarian Church. He seems to have been a good judge of men, for he asked for the office the Legate, Bishop Formosus, who later became Pope. This request Rome declined, and suggested that one of the priests be elected to the post and be sent to Rome for consecration.[84]

Into the rather complicated details of the ensuing negotiations we must not go.[85] They were inextricably associated with the relations of Rome with Constantinople and with the fortunes of the Patriarch Photius. Here we must content ourselves with noting the outcome. Boris failed to find satisfaction at Rome and turned once more to Constantinople. The Emperor Basil proved conciliatory to a project which promised to embarrass Rome and to strengthen the Byzantine Church and state. In 870, at the behest of what called itself the Eighth Œcumenical Council, the Patriarch Ignatius of Constantinople consecrated a Bulgar, presumably the choice of Boris, as Archbishop for Bulgaria and sent him with ten bishops and many priests to his new see. The Latin clergy recognized the futility of resistance and returned home. Henceforward the Bulgarian Church remained within the sphere of Greek Christianity.[86]

The Papacy was not content to surrender Bulgaria without remonstrance. Pope Hadrian II lodged vigorous protest with the Patriarch Ignatius.[87]

---

[81] The Papal letter, dated Nov. 13, 866, is in Migne, *Pat. Lat.,* Vol. CXIX, Cols. 978-1016.

[82] *Annales Fuldenses,* an. 867.

[83] *Ibid.*

[84] P. Jaffé, *Regesta Pont. Rom.,* Vol. I (Leipzig, 1885), p. 367, No. 2887.

[85] See summary of some of the documents in Jaffé, *op. cit.,* p. 372, Nos. 2916, 2925. See summary accounts in Spinka, *op. cit.,* pp. 40-42; in Dvorník, *Les Slaves, Byzance et Rome au IXe Siècle,* pp. 191-195; and Schubert, *Geschichte der christlichen Kirche im Frühmittelalter,* pp. 511-524.

[86] Anastasius Bibliothecarius, *Vita Adriani,* in *Historia de Vitis Romanorum Pontificorum,* in Migne, *Pat. Lat.,* Vol. CXXVIII, Cols. 1395, 1396; Anastasius Bibliothecarius, *Interpretatio Synodi VIII Generalis,* in Migne, *Pat. Lat.,* Vol. CXXIX, Cols. 20 ff.; Runciman, *A History of the First Bulgarian Empire,* pp. 113, 114; Spinka, *op. cit.,* pp. 42, 43.

[87] Jaffé, *op. cit.,* Vol. I, p. 374, Nos. 2943, 2944.

Hadrian's successor, John VIII, wrote a number of letters to Boris, threatening and admonishing that ruler, but without avail.[88] In 879 a Council in Constantinople under Photius, now restored, referred the question to the Byzantine Emperor and the latter decided in favour of Rome. Boris, however, quietly continued his relations with Constantinople.[89]

Why Boris chose Constantinople rather than Rome is not certain. Possibly the glamour of the former city, so much nearer and more impressive than the latter, had its influence. Presumably, too, Boris wished to control the Church in his territory as effectively as the Emperor dominated that in the Byzantine realms and had learned that in this he had more chance of success in affiliation with Greek than with Roman Christianity.

The decision to adhere to the Greek form of Christianity having been finally made, Boris gave every facility for the increase of the influence of that branch of the faith. Undoubtedly with his cognizance and perhaps with his encouragement, the Bulgarian magnates sent their sons to Constantinople to be educated under the general direction of Photius.[90] Photius and the Emperor Basil seem to have founded a Slavonic school in Constantinople, presumably for the purpose of assisting in strengthening the tie with Bulgaria.[91] Boris dispatched a younger son, Simeon, to that city to be educated as a monk, very possibly with the purpose of having him return to head the national church.[92]

To Boris, intent upon building a Bulgarian Church for a population predominantly Slavonic, opportune assistance came from an unexpected quarter. In the very years when Boris had been bringing about the conversion of his people, Constantine and Methodius, labouring among the Slavs of Central Europe, had been developing a Christian literature in Slavonic. Methodius, as we have seen, survived his brother by a number of years, took the leading part in developing and organizing the Church in Moravia, and reared a body of disciples who were at home in Slavonic and who employed the Slavonic liturgy and the Slavonic translations of the sacred books.

Methodius, it will be recalled, met stubborn and at times virulent opposition from German missionaries to whom his use of Slavonic in liturgy and literature was anathema. After the death of Methodius, the enemies of the

[88] Jaffé, op. cit., Vol. I, p. 377, Nos. 2962, 2964; p. 382, No. 2996; p. 383, No. 2999; p. 388, No. 3040; p. 397, No. 3130; p. 408, No. 3246; p. 410, No. 3261; Mon. Germ. Hist., Ep., Vol. VII, pp. 58 ff., 60 ff., 153 ff., 158 ff., 260, 266; Spinka, op. cit., pp. 43-45.
[89] Runciman, A History of the First Bulgarian Empire, pp. 114-121.
[90] Photius, Ep. 95, in Migne, Pat. Gr., Vol. CII, Cols. 904, 905.
[91] Runciman, op. cit., p. 124.
[92] Liudprandus Cremonensis, Antapodosis (ed. Bekker, Hanover, 1915), Book III, Chap. 29.

great apostle brought about the expulsion of the clergy whom he had trained. Some of these were sold as slaves to the Venetians. Others, including Gorazd, whom Methodius had chosen to succeed him, were escorted out of the country and then allowed to fend for themselves.

Several of the enslaved clergy who had been put on the market in Venice attracted the attention of an envoy of the Emperor Basil, were redeemed and were sent to Constantinople. There some of them were rewarded with benefices. Others, perhaps with Basil's encouragement, went to Bulgaria.[93] Those who had been exiled from Moravia made their way into Bulgarian territory and received a cordial welcome from Boris. At least one of these, Clement of Ohrid (Ochrid), was sent by Boris to Macedonia to bring the Slavs of that region into the faith. There he established a famous school for the clerical life and for translating sacred books. Clement, himself probably a Byzantine Slav, later became what seems to have been the first Bishop "of the Bulgarian tongue."[94]

The disciples of Methodius, in monasteries and as missionaries, trained hundreds in the tradition established by that apostle and his brother, and translated more of the literature of the Church into Slavonic. In 889 Boris himself resigned his throne and entered the monastery of St. Panteleimon, which he had founded near his capital as a centre of Slavic Christian culture, and furthered the literary and religious labours of that institution.[95] Through the support of the powerful Boris, the dream of Constantine and Methodius had at last found realization and in their followers Boris had discovered a means of fulfilling his objective.

The work which Boris had begun was carried to its consummation by his son Simeon. It was a startling but quite understandable chain of events which put a younger son and a monk on the Bulgarian throne. Boris was at first succeeded by his eldest son, Vladimir. Vladimir led a reaction. Around him rallied the elements who were aggrieved by the new policies. The Bulgarian nobles who opposed the centralizing tendencies of Boris and who clung to paganism as a feature of the old ways which were being displaced by the innovations now had the upper hand at court. An effort was made to revive the time-honoured religious customs. After a few years, Boris, thoroughly aroused, emerged from his monastic retirement, deposed Vladimir, had him blinded and placed in confinement, called a national

---

[93] Runciman, *op. cit.*, p. 125; Spinka, *op. cit.*, p. 47.

[94] *Vita S. Clementi*, in Migne, *Pat. Gr.*, Vol. CXXVI, Cols. 1194 ff.; Runciman, *op. cit.*, pp. 125-127; Spinka, *op. cit.*, pp. 47-49; Dvorník, *Les Slaves, Byzance et Rome au IXe Siècle*, pp. 312-316.

[95] Spinka, *A History of Christianity in the Balkans*, pp. 47-49.

assembly, and had Simeon chosen for the vacancy.[96] At the same time Boris induced the assembly to substitute Slavonic for Greek as the language of the Bulgarian Church.[97] That done, he again retired to his monastery and there lived on until 907.[98]

Thus placed at the head of the nation, Simeon renounced the monastic life.[99] He retained, however, his religious interest and the zeal for letters which he had acquired during his years in Constantinople. He encouraged the translation of works from the Greek and hastened the creation, already in progress, of a Bulgarian literature. This literature, to be sure, was composed chiefly of translations and not of original works, but it served to put his people, so recently without a written form of their own speech, into touch with the learning of the Greek Christian world.[100] It was from Bulgaria rather than from Moravia that the Christian Slavonic literature spread to other Slavic peoples.

In other ways Simeon proved an ambitious and able monarch. He introduced to his court and capital something of the splendour to which he had become accustomed in Constantinople. He expanded the territories of his realm. In an attempt to equal the ruler of the Byzantine Empire, he made himself in title an Emperor, "the Tsar and Autocrat of all Bulgarians." He brought together the Bulgarian bishops and had them declare the Bulgarian Church autocephalous and then place at the head of that Church a Patriarch. The new Patriarch formally and officially crowned Simeon, hailing him with the imperial title. The Patriarch of Constantinople denounced these acts as usurpations, but Simeon seems to have obtained from Rome the recognition of the changes.[101]

With Simeon (died 927) the formal completion of the conversion of the Bulgarians may be said to have been completed. Bulgaria, with a unified monarchy and an autocephalous Church, had officially entered the ranks of professedly Christian nations. Boris, originally forced into the acceptance of the faith, had used it as a tool for a political and cultural revolution. In a little over a generation the nation had been largely transformed.

[96] *Reginonis Chronicon*, in *Mon. Germ. Hist., Scriptorum*, Vol. I, p. 580; Theophylactus Bulg., *Historia Martyrii XV Martyrum*, in Migne, *Pat. Gr.*, Vol. CXXVI, Cols. 213, 214; Runciman, *A History of the First Bulgarian Empire*, pp. 133, 134.

[97] Runciman, *op. cit.*, p. 135. The change may have been gradual.

[98] Runciman, *op. cit.*, p. 152.

[99] Liudprandus Cremonensis, *Antapodosis*, Book III, Chap. 29.

[100] Runciman, *op. cit.*, pp. 138-141. The Cyrillic rather than the Glagolitic form of writing Slavonic was rapidly adopted. Runciman, *op. cit.*, p. 140, declares that both scripts were the invention of Constantine (Cyril). Spinka, *op. cit.*, p. 53, says that the Cyrillic script was evolved by the court scholars of Simeon and was not the invention of either Constantine or Methodius.

[101] Spinka, *op. cit.*, pp. 52, 53.

The ninth century, so noteworthy for the rapid extension of Christianity among the Slavs, witnessed the dissemination of the faith among still another Balkan nation, the Serbs. We have already noted that the Emperor Basil I sent missionaries at the request of Mutimir, the Serbian ruler. Basil, by the prowess of his navy and army, had augmented the prestige of the Byzantine Empire in the Adriatic and along the Dalmatian shore, and this was one of the results.[102]

The Serbs had on their borders states adhering to different types of Christianity. In time Roman Catholicism predominated in Croatia and in Hungary. On the south the Byzantine Empire made itself felt from the sea and overland through Macedonia and, on occasion, through Bulgaria. It, of course, was Greek Orthodox and encouraged Hellenizing tendencies. To the southeast was Bulgaria. Under Simeon it became the major Balkan power and exercised a profound influence upon the Serbs. In general, it was Greek Orthodox, but it made for the spread of the Slavonic liturgy and literature. The Slavonic tradition also entered from Macedonia, where Clement (died 916), who, as we have seen, was a loyal disciple of Methodius, became powerful in the Church.

The complexion of the Serbs' religious life reflected the shift in the fortunes of these various neighbours. Into the confusing details of that record we must not attempt to go. While Simeon was bringing glory to Bulgaria, Slavonic features were prominent. When, after his death, the Byzantine Empire once more became ascendant, Hellenizing influences gained. At other periods Roman Catholicism made headway. As a rule, Latin Christianity was represented by continuing, strong episcopal sees, centres of the Latin rite. At one of its periods of prestige, Rome, in 1077, accorded the royal dignity to Serbia's ruler on the condition that the Pope be acknowledged the overlord of the land. In general, whatever its varying ecclesiastical allegiances, Christianity continued to spread and the Serbs became professedly Christian.[103]

It was not until the early part of the twelfth century that Christianity became thoroughly naturalized in Serbia and assumed a distinctly national complexion. This it did under Greek Orthodox auspices and thus Serbia entered finally within the orbit of that branch of the faith. As in Bulgaria, this was due to a scion of the royal family. Rastko, better known under his monastic

---

[102] Constantine Porphyrogenitus, *De Administrando Imperio*, Chap. 32, in Migne, *Pat. Gr.,* Vol. CXIII, Cols. 289-292; Dvorník, *Les Slaves, Byzance et Rome au IXe Siècle,* p. 217; Jireček, *Geschichte der Serben,* Vol. I, p. 173.

[103] Jireček, *op. cit.,* Vol. I, pp. 178 ff.; Spinka, *A History of Christianity in the Balkans,* pp. 73 ff. See also Constantine Porphyrogenitus, *op. cit.,* Chap. 32, in Migne, *Pat. Gr.,* Vol. CXIII, Cols. 287-298.

name of Sava, was the youngest son of one of the Serbian rulers. He was born in 1174 and was educated at his father's court. There, at about the age of eighteen, he was won to the monastic life by a Russian from the great centre of Greek Orthodox monasticism, Mt. Athos. Fearing the opposition of his parents, he left home secretly, fled to Mt. Athos, and there, in a Russian monastery, assumed the monastic vows. Within a few years, in 1195, the young prince-monk's father abdicated his throne and donned the monastic habit. Together father and son took over a decayed foundation, and on it with princely munificence built a monastery which gained official recognition by the Synod of Mt. Athos and the Byzantine Emperor as a Serbian centre. Sava became the head of the new institution and made it the training-school for most of the future leaders of the Serbian Church. Later Sava traversed his native land, teaching the Orthodox doctrines and liturgy which he had learned on Mt. Athos and of which he had become so convinced a champion.

In the early part of the thirteenth century, with the enhanced power of the Papacy under the great pontiffs of that generation and with the capture of Constantinople by the Crusaders (1204), the prestige of Greek Orthodoxy was for the moment in eclipse and that of Roman Catholicism in the ascendant. Sava's brother Stephen was then ruling in Serbia. In light of the predominance of the West, he felt it politic to face in that direction. He divorced his wife, married the Roman Catholic daughter of the Doge of Venice, and he and his new spouse were crowned by the Papal Legate. The Papal Legate thereupon set about Romanizing the Church in Serbia. The clergy, thoroughly impregnated with Orthodoxy by Sava, resisted.

Apparently it was because he was aroused by the danger of Latinizing the Serbian Church that Sava sought and obtained from the Byzantine Emperor, Patriarch, and Holy Synod the right of the bishops of Serbia to elect and consecrate their own Archbishop. This made the Serbian Church autocephalous.

To the new post Sava himself was appointed. He returned to his native land and was cordially welcomed by his royal brother and the populace. As the first head of the Serbian Church, Sava thoroughly drilled it in Eastern Orthodox beliefs and customs and left upon it an impress which has never since been effaced. The Latin authorities might protest and continue to have a following, but the bulk of the people remained loyal to the Orthodox national faith. Sava, too, established schools for the training of the clergy. He is said to have fought the remnants of pagan customs, but to have tolerated those which were not too obviously out of accord with Christianity. As his brother Stephan gave definitive form to the Serbian Kingdom politically, so, to an even greater extent, Sava determined the religious future of the Serbs.[104]

From the Balkans we turn to another region into which the Christianity of the Eastern Empire expanded—the lands east and north of the Black Sea. From ancient times the Greeks had been commercially important in the Black Sea and had established posts from which their culture spread. It was not surprising that Constantinople, placed at the exit from the Euxine, fell heir to that heritage. For centuries the Byzantine Empire played an important rôle in the area about the Black Sea. Constantinople as the commercial metropolis and the largest city became the chief centre from which culture penetrated to the rude but vigorous peoples who from time to time invaded the borders of the Euxine. It was to be expected that since Constantinople was known as a Christian city, Christianity shared in its prestige, won many of the invaders, and became the predominant religion of the region.

We have seen how even before the close of the fifth century Christianity had made converts in the Caucasus and had been planted among the Goths in the Crimea. Conversion continued after that century, at times with accelerated pace.

Just when and how some of the Christian peoples of the Caucasus adopted the faith we do not know. We have seen that the traditional date of the conversion of the Georgians is early in the fourth century. We have also seen that about the time of Justinian the Abasgi in the Caucasus accepted Christianity. A tenth-century Moslem writer speaks of several peoples in the Caucasus who in his time were or had been partly or entirely Christian in name. Thus the Goumiks were reported to be Christians, the Zerikerans to have among them Christians, Jews, and Moslems, and Serir to have a Christian king.[105] The same writer declares that in the eighth century the Alans had become Christian, but that about the middle of the tenth century they had abjured the faith and driven out the clergy whom the Byzantine Emperor had sent them.[106] The time reported for the conversion of the Alans may be inaccurate. Moreover, the apostasy, if it occurred, must have been only temporary, for later we find the Alans classed as Christians. From other

[104] See a translation of a late (at least sixteenth or seventeenth century) biography of Sava in V. Yanich and C. P. Hankey, *Lives of the Serbian Saints*, pp. 12-30. See chiefly on these two paragraphs Spinka, *op. cit.*, pp. 76-90.

[105] Maçoudi, *Les Prairies d'Or*, Vol. II, p. 40.

[106] Maçoudi, *op. cit.*, Vol. II, pp. 42, 43; Runciman, *The Emperor Romanus Lecapenus and His Reign*, pp. 172, 173. However, the Alans were said still to be pagan in the ninth century.—Bury, *A History of the Eastern Roman Empire from the Fall of Irene to the Accession of Basil I*, p. 409, n. 2.

sources we hear of at least three other peoples of the Caucasus who in the tenth century contained Christians. In creed and affiliation one of these was Armenian rather than Greek Orthodox.[107]

The most notable of the gains of Byzantine Christianity, not only north of the Black Sea but in any geographic area, was in what is now Russia. This was to be expected, for here that branch of the faith faced its only really open door to an extensive region occupied by peoples with relatively primitive faiths. Elsewhere on the borders of the Eastern Empire, as we have seen, territory was restricted or the land was pre-empted by religions against which Greek Orthodox Christianity could make little or no headway. On the west was Latin Christianity, on the east Armenian and Nestorian Christianity, Zoroastrianism, and, from the seventh century onward, Islam. On the south were still other branches of the Christian faith and, beginning with the seventh century, Islam. Only on the plains north of the Euxine had these rival systems as yet few or no representatives. There the existing religions were mostly polytheistic and animistic and offered little resistance to an advanced religion. Moreover, as the Moslems and the Italian cities increasingly shut Constantinople out of the commerce of the eastern part of the Mediterranean, the merchants and monarchs of that metropolis looked more and more to the Euxine. In the ninth and tenth centuries the exports to the Black Sea rose to renewed importance.[108] During parts of these centuries the Empire was governed by able and aggressive rulers. Constantinople, as the largest and wealthiest city which the peoples of the Black Sea knew, must have given enormous prestige to the faith which it professed. It is, therefore, not surprising that in these decades Byzantine Christianity made significant gains in what we now call Russia.

Into the complicated ethnographic history of what at present is termed the Ukraine we must not go. On these plains and broad valleys lived for longer or shorter intervals numbers of the peoples whom we have had occasion to mention in our story—Goths, Huns, Avars, and Slavs. From the end of the sixth to the beginning of the ninth century the Eastern Slavs occupied much of the land from the north-western corner of the Black Sea on the south to Lake Ladoga on the north, and from the Danube on the west to the Don on the east.[109] Divided into many tribes and without political unity, they fell victims to conquering invaders. In the sixth century came the Avars and remained the dominant power until the ninth century, when they were crushed by the Franks. In the seventh century a Turkish folk, the Khazars,

[107] Runciman, *op. cit.*, p. 171.
[108] Thompson, *Economic and Social History of the Middle Ages*, p. 338.
[109] Vernadsky, *A History of Russia*, p. 15.

appeared and established a powerful state with its chief centre north of the Caspian, not far from the present Astrakhan. Their domain extended as far west as the Dnieper and they controlled much of the trade between the Far East—where the T'ang Dynasty then ruled over one of the largest empires which mankind had yet seen—and the Black Sea and between the Moslem states and the Slavonic peoples.[110]

When, in the ninth century, came the great irruptions from Scandinavia, Northmen, presumably mostly Swedes, made their way along the plains and river valleys of what is now the western part of Russia and became masters of the Slavic population. Never perhaps more than one hundred thousand in number, eventually, as in so many other parts of Europe, they were absorbed by the subject majority. Their chief city in the North was Novgorod. They pushed on south and not far from the middle of the ninth century became the rulers at Kiev.[111] These Scandinavians were known as Varangians and Rus, both of them names whose origin and earliest designation have been hotly debated. In the course of time Rus or Russ was applied to the state which centred about Kiev and later was extended to cover all the eastern Slavonic nation.

Some of the Scandinavians became residents of Constantinople and included members of the imperial guard.[112] In 860, when the Emperor was away fighting the Saracens and the fleet was absent, Northmen swooped down on Constantinople itself, plundered the suburbs, and threatened the city. In the emergency the Patriarch Photius did much to restore the shaken morale of the populace.[113] This proved to be only one of several conflicts between the Eastern Empire and the Varangians.

Christianity had long been penetrating into the region of South Russia. Audius, reported as having been exiled there by the Emperor Constantine the Great, seems to have made converts in that area.[114] We have seen that before the year 500 Catholic Goths were found there. Efforts were made from South Russia to win to the Christian faith the Khazars. As we have already recorded, the scholar-missionary Constantine, later distinguished for his labours among the Slavs of Central Europe, is said to have served a missionary apprenticeship among the Khazars. The story as reported is that Khazars sent to the imperial court for a Christian teacher and that Constantine, already well

---

[110] Bury, *op. cit.*, pp. 402 ff.; Vernadsky, *op. cit.*, p. 16.

[111] Mawer, in *Cambridge Medieval History*, Vol. III, p. 327.

[112] Vernadsky, *A History of Russia*, pp. 17, 18; Mawer, in *Cambridge Medieval History*, Vol. III, pp. 327, 328; Hallendorff and Schück, *History of Sweden*, pp. 16-20.

[113] Bury, *op. cit.*, pp. 411-423.

[114] *Epiphanii Adv. Haeres.*, Book LXX, Chap. 14, in Migne, *Pat. Gr.*, Vol. XLII, Col. 371.

known as a lecturer and philosopher, was dispatched to them and instructed them in his faith.[115] It appears that Islam, Christianity, and Judaism all competed for the allegiance of the Khazars and that the majority of the rulers adopted Judaism.[116] Most of the Khazars, then, did not become Christians, at least not in the days of their might.

However, the Khazars proved to be a waning power. The future lay with the state which arose around Kiev and of which the Scandinavian Rus became the princes. It was the conversion of its leaders which paved the way for the final success of Greek Christianity in Russia.[117] It may be that the vigorous and able Patriarch Photius, whom we have already had occasion to mention in connexion with the conversion of the Bulgars, helped to make a beginning. At least in a letter written in the decade of the 860's he declared that he had organized a mission among the Russians and that it had so far succeeded that the Russians had asked for a bishop.[118] We are also informed that a bishop was sent as a missionary to the Russians by the Emperor Basil I (867-886), who did so much to extend Byzantine power, and by the Patriarch Ignatius, and that he made many converts.[119]

Whatever the truth back of these accounts, it is clear that by the middle of the tenth century a number of Christians were to be found in Kiev. Some of the Varangians had been employed in Constantinople by the Byzantine state. Others had been there as merchants. It seems probable that of these, especially among those in government service, a number accepted the Byzantine religion. By whatever means they had become Christians, by the middle of the tenth century some of the Russians in the state of Kiev were adherents of the faith. In a treaty signed in 944 between Kiev and the Eastern Empire the Rus are several times described as consisting of baptized and unbaptized.[120] Although the ruler, Igor (913-945), was a pagan, the Christians among his

---

[115] *Vita Cum Translatione S. Clemente,* in *Acta Sanctorum,* March 9, Chaps. 1, 6.

[116] Bury, *op. cit.,* pp. 405-408; Lübeck, *Die Christianisierung Russlands,* p. 15; Dubnow, *History of the Jews in Russia and Poland,* Vol. I, pp. 19-28; Dvorník, *Les Slaves, Byzance et Rome au IXe Siècle,* pp. 133-136.

[117] Many accounts exist of the beginnings of Christianity in Russia and the conversion of Kiev. Probably the best is in Golubinsky, *Istoriya Russkoi Tserkvi (A History of the Russian Church),* Vol. I, Pt. 1. Good summaries based largely upon Golubinsky are M. Spinka, *The Conversion of Russia,* in *The Journal of Religion,* Vol. VI (1926), pp. 41-57, and Koncevičius, *Russia's Attitude towards Union with Rome,* pp. 16 ff. Traditional accounts, now partly discredited and superseded, are in Adeney, *The Greek and Eastern Churches,* pp. 356-370, and Robinson, *The Conversion of Europe,* pp. 485 ff .

[118] Photius, Letter in Migne, *Pat. Gr.,* Vol. CII, Cols. 735-738; Dvorník, *op. cit.,* p. 143. Hergenröther, *Photius,* Vol. II, p. 597.

[119] Adeney, *The Greek and Eastern Churches,* p. 357, citing Constantine Porphyrogenitus (but not giving the exact reference).

[120] Spinka, *The Conversion of Russia,* in *The Journal of Religion,* Vol. VI, p. 43.

subjects evidently enjoyed toleration.[121] It is clear that in his day at least one church existed in Kiev.[122]

Whether Igor ever made a public or a secret profession of the Christian faith we do not know. It is probable that he did not. It is clear, however, that his wife, Olga, became a Christian. When she took this step and what led her to do so we may never be able to determine. We are not even sure of the place or the date of her baptism. What appears to be the best conjecture fixes the year as 954, nearly a decade after the death of Igor. She visited Constantinople in 957, and then is said to have had her own priest with her. Probably her baptism had occurred before that time and was not, as a later account declared, celebrated while she was in the city.[123]

Olga was a woman of consequence. Her husband's early death left her the dominant figure at Kiev. During the minority of her infant son she was regent. Presumably with her assistance the Christian community at Kiev increased in numbers and prestige. We hear that she sent to the Emperor Otto I asking for a bishop and priests to convert her people. One Libertius is reported to have been consecrated bishop in response to her request, but to have died before he could begin his mission. The Archbishop of Mainz thereupon consecrated in his place Adalbert. Adalbert had no very great success and, returning to Germany, became the first incumbent of the frontier see of Magdeburg.[124]

Olga seems to have been unable to win to her faith her son Svyatoslav for whom she had acted as regent. Svyatoslav (died 972) proved a typical Viking ruler and spent most of his reign away from home fighting. He warred successfully against the Khazars on the east and the Bulgars on the west and greatly enlarged the territory of Kiev. While not prohibiting his subjects from accepting baptism, he did not look with favour upon those who took that step. He died as he had lived, by the sword.[125]

Svyatoslav was succeeded by his eldest son, Yaropolk, who in turn came to a violent end—at the hands of the troops of Vladimir, another son of Svyatoslav. Vladimir enjoyed a long reign and it was under him that the Russian state officially made the transition from paganism to Christianity.

[121] *Ibid.*
[122] Golubinsky, *op. cit.,* Vol. I, Pt. I, pp. 63, 64, 95.
[123] Golubinsky, *op. cit.,* Vol. I, Pt. I, pp. 74-84, gives a detailed discussion of the problem of the baptism of Olga. See also Spinka, *op. cit.,* pp. 44, 45; Koncevičius, *Russia's Attitude towards Union with Rome,* p. 18; and Vernadsky, *Political and Diplomatic History of Russia,* pp. 40, 41.
[124] Koncevičius, *op. cit.,* p. 19; Vernadsky, *Political and Diplomatic History of Russia,* p. 41.
[125] Golubinsky, *op. cit.,* Vol. I, Pt. I, p. 86; Spinka, *The Conversion of Russia,* in *The Journal of Religion,* Vol. VI, p. 46; Vernadsky, *A History of Russia,* pp. 19-21.

The traditional and oft-narrated account of this momentous step says that Vladimir was visited by representatives of Islam, Judaism, Roman Catholicism, and Greek Christianity, each of whom sought to win him. It declares that of the various missions the Greek made upon him the deepest impression and that he took the decisive step after a delegation sent by him reported the effect on them of a service in the Cathedral of St. Sophia, in Constantinople.

The account is almost certainly a later fabrication.[126] It does, however, reflect the choice which probably confronted Vladimir as he faced the disintegration of the hereditary paganism and the necessity of adopting the religion of one of his civilized neighbours. The decision for the Greek form of Christianity was natural, for that was the faith of the strongest of the near-by states and of the city of which Vladimir had most to expect commercially. Probably more of his subjects were of the Greek belief than of any other of the three.[127]

Vladimir may have come to power in Kiev with the support of the antiChristian elements. When his formal conversion and baptism occurred we cannot certainly prove. One hypothesis puts it in the year 987. The place is even more debatable.[128] That Vladimir allied himself with the Greek form of Christianity is indubitable. He received delegates from the Pope and sent representatives to Rome, but for what reason is not clear.[129] He added to his large array of wives and concubines Anna, a princess of the Byzantine imperial house, and with her introduced Greek clergy. This marriage he obtained by capturing the Byzantine town of Korsun in the Crimean Peninsula and exacting it at the price of peace. It was not as a vassal or a tributary of Constantinople that he adopted the faith of that metropolis.[130]

On his return from Korsun to Kiev Vladimir appears to have undertaken actively the conversion of his people. That he immediately destroyed all the idols in the city and required the populace to betake themselves to the river for mass baptism, as some of the older accounts aver, has been questioned—although for one of Viking descent this would not have been an impossible procedure.[131] It is clear that he at least actively encouraged conversion, built churches, and founded monasteries. To other centres he sent clergy to extend to them the work begun at Kiev. We hear, for example, of the baptism of

---

[126] Golubinsky, *op. cit.*, Vol. I Pt. I, pp. 120, 121; Lübeck, *Die Christianisierung Russlands*, p. 10.
[127] See a brief treatment of this in Vernadsky, *A History of Russia*, pp. 24, 25.
[128] Spinka, *op. cit.*, pp. 50-52; Koncevičius, *op. cit.*, p. 25; Vernadsky, *Political and Diplomatic History of Russia*, p. 47.
[129] Golubinsky, *op. cit.*, Vol. I, Pt. I, pp. 220, 593.
[130] Spinka, *op. cit.*, pp. 53, 54; Vernadsky, *A History of Russia*, p. 25.
[131] Spinka, *op. cit.*, pp. 54, 55.

the population of Novgorod in 991 by the Bishop of Korsun. By the end of Vladimir's reign Russia contained three bishoprics. Vladimir was unwilling to agree to ecclesiastical control from Constantinople.[132] We also hear of a brief mission by the German Bruno, a representative of Latin Christianity.[133]

As a matter of chronological comparison it is interesting to note that while Vladimir, of Scandinavian descent, was bringing about the conversion of his state in Russia to Greek Christianity, the conversion of the Danes, the Norwegians, and the Swedes to Latin Christianity was occurring. The two major forms of Christianity were advancing simultaneously in overcoming the Scandinavian menace.

Following the death of Vladimir (1015), the succession was contested. One son, Svyatopolk, had the aid of his father-in-law, Boleslaw the Brave of Poland (reigned 992-1025), who, as we have seen, had built up an extensive but ephemeral empire and was active in the spread of Latin Christianity among his subjects.[134] Had Svyatopolk succeeded in holding the power which at first he managed to seize, it is conceivable that Russia might have come permanently within the orbit of Rome. However, the victory rested not with Svyatopolk but with his brother Yaroslav. The latter's adherence to the Greek form of Christianity was probably confirmed by the Roman Catholic inclinations of his rival. Yaroslav took an active interest in ecclesiastical affairs. He furthered the translation of literature from Greek into Slavonic, built churches, schools, and monasteries, and through singers from Constantinople is said to have laid the foundations for the distinctively Russian church music.[135] Under him, moreover, a synod of the bishops within his realm elected as Metropolitan Hilarion, the first of Russian origin to hold that post.[136]

Christianity continued to spread. The centres from which missionary efforts radiated were usually the various episcopal sees. In general the active agents were monks.[137] For example, in the twelfth century hermits from Novgorod introduced the faith into the region of Vyatka, west of Perm.[138]

Even more than in Western Europe the conversion, especially of the masses, seems to have been merely nominal. Some of the upper classes appear outwardly to have conformed. Many decades elapsed, however, before

[132] Lübeck, op. cit., p. 12; Spinka, op. cit., pp. 55-57; Vernadsky, *Political and Diplomatic History of Russia*, p. 48.

[133] Thietmar, *Merseburgensis Episcopi Chronicon* (in *Scriptores rerum Germanicarum*, Hanover, 1889), Book VII, Chap. 34.

[134] Vernadsky, *A History of Russia*, pp. 25, 26.

[135] Lübeck, op. cit., p. 13.

[136] Vernadsky, *A History of Russia*, p. 27; Koncevičius, *Russia's Attitude towards Union with Rome*, p. 33.

[137] Lübeck, op. cit., p. 14.

[138] Lübeck, op. cit., p. 24.

the majority of the population were willing to adopt even such outward observances as attendance at the services of the Church and the reception of the
sacraments. We hear of two bishops forced out of their sees by popular
clamour because of their efforts to induce their people to keep a few of the
fast days of the Christian year.[139] It is not surprising that the populace expected of their Christian pastors and monks what tradition had taught them
to be the function of professional experts in religion—the exorcism of
demons.[140]

The superficiality of the Christianity of the land is attributable to a number
of factors. Fully as much as in the West, the Christianity preached was
ascetic. The ideal Christian was held to be the monk. This may have been
accentuated by the dualism which made so strong an appeal to the Hellenistic mind and which in Eastern Christianity took not only the chronic form
of monasticism and the hermit, as in the West, but also from time to time
broke out in such sects as the Paulicians and, in the Balkans, the Bogomils.
In Russia the immediate effect religiously was to divide the population into
two unequal parts—on the one hand the monks, to whom was left the perfect
practice of the Christian life, and on the other hand the vast majority, of
whom the most that could be expected was the observance of a few of the
rites of the Church and a slight conformity to some of the Christian virtues.
To this factor were added others. The higher clergy were to a large extent
foreigners. The head of the Russian Church was usually appointed by the
Patriarch of Constantinople. In two and a half centuries only two Metropolitans were native Russians. Although a majority of the bishops were
Russians, many were Greeks. For a much longer period than in most lands
in Western Europe, a proportion of the higher clergy were from abroad and
understood little either of the customs or the language of their flocks. Moreover, dioceses were large and their size made difficult their adequate supervision by the bishops. The clergy were too few in number for the huge areas
of Russia. The parish priests tended to be chosen by their flocks. They were
inadequately trained and poorly paid, little was expected of them beyond the
correct performance of the rites of the Church, and, once they had ordained
them, the bishops exercised little effective control over them.[141] Then, too,
the bishops tended to be the appointees of the local lay princes, although they
were still consecrated by the Metropolitan.[142]

[139] Milukow, *Skizzen russischer Kulturgeschichte,* Vol. II, p. 8.
[140] Milukow, *op. cit.,* Vol. II, p. 9.
[141] Milukow, *op. cit.,* Vol. II, pp. 11-13, 16-18; Conybeare, *Russian Dissenters,* pp. 15,
17, 70, 71.
[142] Eck, *Le Moyen Age Russe,* p. 124.

The superficiality of much of the conversion and of the resulting effect upon the life of the people must not be exaggerated. The first literary work in Russia was by the monks and clergy. Some books were translated directly from the Greek. Others came by way of Bulgaria in translations already made into Slavonic. The Slavonic employed in Bulgaria was not so different from the language of the Russians as to make its use in the liturgy utterly unintelligible. Sermons and lives of Russian saints and monks were written, and the first chronicles were compiled within monastic walls. Ecclesiastical architecture and painting, largely on Byzantine models, helped to shape Russian artistic life.[143]

In the first half of the thirteenth century the land was conquered by the Mongols. For more than a hundred years these invaders from Asia remained dominant politically. From their capital at Sarai on the Volga the Golden Horde ruled most of the Russians. The Mongol dominion had profound effects upon all phases of Russian life and led, quite unintentionally, so far as the Mongols were concerned, to a deepening of the religious life of the Russians and to the geographic extension of the Christian faith.

The immediate result of the Mongol conquest was to weaken the Church. Clergy and monks shared in the sufferings of the war. Many perished. Numerous church buildings were laid in ruins and service books and vestments and vessels used in worship were destroyed.[144]

However, ultimately the Mongol conquest greatly strengthened the Church and deepened its hold upon the affections and loyalty of the Russian people. As elsewhere in the early stages of their rule, the Mongols were religiously tolerant. At the outset they themselves adhered loosely to a form of shamanism. Toward the middle of the thirteenth century the son of one of the Mongol rulers of Russia was baptized.[145] Later the dominant groups among the Golden Horde embraced Islam. In general, however, whatever their faith, in Russia the Mongols were friendly to the Church. Even after they accepted Islam we hear of one Metropolitan who commanded their respect and to whose prayers was attributed the recovery of the sight of a wife of one of the Khans.[146] They did not force even part of the Russian people to change their faith. They granted full recognition to the civil rights of the clergy.[147] The Church was permitted to preserve its judicial autonomy in matters moral

---

[143] Vernadsky, *A History of Russia*, pp. 34-36.

[144] Golubinsky, *Istoriya Russkoi Tserkvi*, Vol. II, Pt. I, pp. 14-16.

[145] Eck, *op. cit.*, p. 149.

[146] Theophilus, *A Short History of the Christian Church*, p. 23; Vernadsky, *Political and Diplomatic History of Russia*, p. 112.

[147] Golubinsky, *op. cit.*, Vol. II, Pt. I, pp. 14, 17.

and religious, particularly in questions of marriage, of sexual offences, of inheritance, and of the duties of children to parents.[148] It enjoyed immunity from certain kinds of taxation. It acquired wealth and its Metropolitan became a great temporal lord.[149] In the uncertainties and disorders of the times many sought the solace of religion. Directed by its Metropolitan, the Church remained the only institution which embraced the majority of the Russians in which the Slavs had an active voice. Shortly before the Mongol conquest, the tie of the Russian Church with Constantinople had been weakened by the capture of that city by the Crusaders and by the short-lived Latin Empire. The seat of the Metropolitan was eventually moved to Moscow, much farther from Constantinople and hence less under the influence of the Œcumenical Patriarch than when it was at Kiev.[150] In Russia, therefore, the Orthodox Church came to be looked upon as the one institution in which all who were ruled by the Mongols could unite. For the Russian, the word Christian held a national significance. Just as elsewhere in the East the various regional churches came to be centres of community consciousness and the preservers of national culture and traditions against the Moslem conquerors, so in Russia the Church became the one expression of Russian unity.[151] However superficial the conversion of their forefathers, and however limited their own knowledge of the tenets of their faith might be, under Mongol rule the Russians increased in the intensity of their allegiance to the Church. The average peasant probably did not know the Lord's Prayer, the Creed, or the Ten Commandments. Yet peasant and noble took pride in the names "Orthodox" and "Christian," and Russia became "Holy Russia."[152] When in 1453 Constantinople passed into the hands of the Turks, the Russian Church and princes felt themselves to have succeeded the Byzantine Empire as the champions of Orthodox Christianity. Moscow had become the "third Rome."[153]

Moreover, as we have suggested, the Mongol period witnessed the territorial extension of Russian Christianity. In the third quarter of the thirteenth century a bishopric was established at Sarai, the capital of the Golden Horde. Relatively few converts were made from the Mongols, however, and the episcopate was primarily not for missionary purposes, but for the care of

[148] Eck, op. cit., pp. 132, 133, 147-149; Lübeck, Die Christianisierung Russlands, p. 26.
[149] Eck, op. cit., pp. 160, 176-184.
[150] Adeney, The Greek and Eastern Churches, pp. 380-384; Milukow, op. cit., Vol. II, pp. 16-18.
[151] Eck, op. cit., pp. 122, 126.
[152] Milukow, Skizzen russischer Kulturgeschichte, Vol. II, p. 14.
[153] Eck, op. cit., pp. 425, 426; Theophilus, op. cit., p. 23.

Russian Christians.[154] It was in the North that the chief expansion of the faith took place. On many the Mongol rule rested heavily. Numbers sought escape by abandoning the world and adopting the monastic life. Hermits made their way to the forests of the North, far removed from the centres of Mongol power, and there built themselves cells. In some places communities of monks assembled. One estimate declares that from the thirteenth to the sixteenth century two hundred and ninety-four new monasteries, one hundred and sixty of them originally hermitages, arose on the frontiers.[155] Around many of these monasteries towns sprang up. Settlers were attracted by the sanctity of some hermit and wished to be under the protection of one so obviously a favourite of God. The monasteries became schools in the Christian faith and in agriculture. Under their tutelage pagans were converted, lands cleared, roads and canals built, marshes drained, and improved methods of cultivating the soil and breeding cattle introduced.[156] Through them, too, the Russian language was spread and various Finnish tribes were assimilated to Russian culture.[157]

The most famous of the missionaries on the frontier was Stephen of Perm. Born between 1330 and 1346 of humble parents, he early formed the purpose of going as a missionary to the Zyrians, a Finnish people who lived between the Northern Dvina and Pechora Rivers, north-east of Moscow. From merchants he learned something of their tongue. He became a monk, studied Greek, and, devising an alphabet for that purpose, he translated the service books into Zyrianian. He went as a missionary to the people of his choice and displayed high courage in destroying a representation of one of the native deities and by accepting the challenge of a pagan sorcerer to undergo the test of fire and water. He is said to have passed the ordeal unscathed and, when the challenger drew back, to have gained in prestige among the populace. He baptized many, established monasteries, taught the converts the Psalter and the Gospels, and began training a native clergy. In time he was consecrated Bishop for the new domain he had won for the Church. As chief pastor, he fed his flock in time of famine, protected them against rapacious officials in Moscow and Novgorod, and at least once headed them to repulse an attack of an enemy tribe. Before his death (1396) he had the satisfaction of seeing a large proportion of the Zyrians baptized.[158] His work was continued. In 1463, for example, a Bishop John baptized the ruler and

[154] Lübeck, op. cit., p. 26; Eck, op. cit., p. 37.
[155] Eck, op. cit., pp. 28, 29.
[156] Eck, op. cit., pp. 133-135.
[157] Smirnoff, A Short Account of the Historical Development and Present Position of Russian Orthodox Missions, pp. 1-3.
[158] Lübeck, op. cit., pp. 20-24.

people of the district of Perm.[159] Yet more than a century after Stephen's death we still hear of pagans in the region of Perm, in a portion of which he had lived.[160]

We hear that in the fourteenth century at least one missionary monk of Novgorod attempted to win converts from among the Lapps. Some of his disciples carried on his labours. After the middle of the fifteenth century the mission was extended and had headquarters on an island in the White Sea.[161] We read of missions in the fourteenth century much nearer to Novgorod, to islanders in Lake Ladoga.[162] At its inception near the beginning of the thirteenth century the diocese of Ryazan, only a little over a hundred miles south-east of Moscow, had many pagans in its bounds. In the fifteenth century an incumbent of that see was active as a missionary—until 1447, when he was made Metropolitan of Moscow.[163]

From time to time leaders of Latin Christianity endeavoured to bring the Russians within the orbit of Rome. In the latter part of the twelfth century Pope Clement III attempted to induce the Russians to join in the Third Crusade.[164] Pope Innocent IV offered to assist against the Mongols by raising a Crusade on condition that the Russians come into union with Rome.[165] In the thirteenth century, after the Mongol conquest, Franciscans arrived at Kiev and were welcomed, perhaps because of hope of aid from the West against the invaders.[166] Dominicans also came to Kiev, but about 1238 were driven out.[167] In the fourteenth and fifteenth centuries Roman Catholic influence entered by way of Lithuania. As we have seen, in the latter part of the fourteenth century the rulers of that state were converted to the Latin form of Christianity through the Polish connexion. Since Lithuania controlled many of the Russians in the West, some of the upper classes among the latter became Roman Catholics. However, the majority of the masses adhered to Greek Christianity.[168] In the second quarter of the fifteenth century, Isidore, a monk of Constantinople who had been made Metropolitan of Russia, assented to a union of Latin and Greek Christianity, and was appointed Cardinal and Papal Legate to Lithuania, Russia, Livonia, and Poland.

[159] Koncevičius, *Russia's Attitude towards Union with Rome*, p. 28.
[160] Lübeck, *op. cit.*, pp. 23, 24.
[161] Lübeck, *op. cit.*, pp. 18, 19.
[162] Lübeck, *op. cit.*, p. 18.
[163] Lübeck, *op. cit.*, p. 32.
[164] Lübeck, *op. cit.*, pp. 15-18.
[165] Adeney, *The Greek and Eastern Churches*, pp. 385-387.
[166] Koncevičius, *op. cit.*, p. 100, citing Wadding, *Ann. Minorum*, Vol. III, p. 124.
[167] Altaner, *Die Dominikanermissionen des 13 Jahrhunderts*, pp. 196-225.
[168] Vernadsky, *A History of Russia*, p. 44.

However, he proved unable to carry the Russian Church with him, a bishop who would have none of Rome was substituted for him in the Metropolitanate, and he had no recourse but to return, unsuccessful, to Rome. Although the Pope gave him the title of Patriarch of Constantinople and for some time a succession of Latin Metropolitans of Kiev was maintained, the vast majority of Russian Christians remained resolutely aloof from the Papal connexion.[169] They became the self-appointed champions of Orthodoxy.

One last topic remains to be mentioned in the spread of the Greek form of Christianity—the attempts to convert the Jews. Probably in a combination of religious zeal and of a desire to enforce religious unity, a number of Eastern Emperors sought to bring into the Christian faith the Jews in their domains. Thus the Justinian code left unchanged the death penalty for those who attacked Jewish converts to Christianity,[170] ordained exile and confiscation of goods to a Jew who circumcised a Christian,[171] and contained a prohibition against building new synagogues.[172] Early in the seventh century an attempt of the Emperor Phocas to coerce the Jews of Antioch to accept baptism goaded the unhappy people to a revolt which was met by slaughter and banishment.[173] The Emperor Heraclius is said to have wished Dagobert, King of the Franks, to baptize all the Jews in the latter's realm.[174] It is not strange that when, in the seventh century, the Persians invaded Palestine, the Jews sided with them against the Christians.[175] In the first quarter of the eighth century Leo III ordered Jews baptized.[176] Many, to escape, fled to Syria. In the ninth century Basil the Macedonian forcibly brought numbers to baptism and wrought devastation in Jewish communities.[177] Whether under Roman Catholic or Greek Orthodox, under Christian or Moslem, the Jews were subject to disabilities and periodic persecution. On the other hand,

[169] Koncevičius, op. cit., pp. 115-126; Adeney, op. cit., pp. 390-392.
[170] Cod. Just., I, 9, 3 = Cod. Theod., XVI, 8, 1.
[171] Cod. Just., I, 9, 16.
[172] Cod. Just., I, 9, 18.
[173] Kraeling, The Jewish Community at Antioch, p. 160. In the reign of Phocas the Jews in Mesopotamia are said to have planned to kill the Christians, and the latter, in retaliation, killed many of the Jews.—Kitab Al-'Unvan, Histoire Universalle écrite par Agapius (Mahboub) de Menbidj, edited and translated by A. Vasiliev, in Patrologia Orientalis, Vol. VIII (Paris, 1912), p. 449.
[174] Fredegarius, Chronicum, in Migne, Pat. Lat., Vol. LXXI, Col. 646.
[175] Vasiliev, History of the Byzantine Empire, Vol. I, p. 237.
[176] Dvorník, Les Slaves, Byzance et Rome au IXe Siècle, p. 67; The Chronography of . . . Bar Hebræus, translation by Budge (Oxford University Press, 2 vols., 1932), Section 118 (Vol. I, p. 109).
[177] Dubnow, History of the Jews in Russia and Poland, Vol. I, p. 23; Vasiliev, op. cit., Vol. I, p. 404.

in the second half of the fifteenth century Judaism exercised a profound influence upon a number of important members of the Russian Church.[178]

Considering the obstacles which it faced, Greek Christianity was not unsuccessful in propagating itself. It was assisted by the prestige of the Roman name and by the awe which the Byzantine Empire, long one of the most imposing and cultivated of the states of its day, inspired in barbarian breasts. Wherever it confronted only animism or polytheism, ultimately it prevailed, as did Latin Christianity in the West. That it spread no farther was due chiefly to the fact that on so much of its border it faced advanced faiths—Zoroastrianism, Islam, and rival forms of Christianity—all of them either supported by strong political structures or by ardent racial and national loyalties.

[178] G. Vernadsky, *The Heresy of the Judaizers and Ivan III* (in *Speculum*, Vol. VIII, 1933, pp. 436-454).

Chapter V

THE SPREAD OF CHRISTIANITY TO THE EAST OF THE BYZANTINE EMPIRE, ESPECIALLY THROUGH THE JACOBITES AND THE NESTORIANS, TO THE MONGOL CONQUEST. THE PERSIAN EMPIRE; ARABIA; CENTRAL ASIA; CHINA; INDIA

IN THE thousand years between the fifth and the sixteenth century Christianity was propagated not only by representatives of its Latin and Greek forms, but by adherents of other types, notably by Monophysites and Nestorians. We have already seen that the Christianity which spread southward from Egypt was mainly Coptic Monophysitism. We are now to narrate the story of the expansion of the faith, chiefly by Nestorians and Monophysites, through much of Asia east of the borders of the Byzantine Empire.

Here, in contrast with the situation in Europe and the Mediterranean basin, Christianity seldom enjoyed the endorsement of a government. Often it obtained toleration. Frequently its adherents rose high in the service of the state. Now and then a prince received baptism. Generally, however, Christians constituted minority groups. Their chief centres were in highly civilized communities in which other religions were espoused by the rulers and by the majority of the populace. When, as in the case of some of the Turks and the Mongols, Christianity seemed to be making promising headway among a people of relatively primitive culture and against a yielding animism or polytheism, ultimately it was abandoned for a faith possessed of more political prestige and supported by a powerful ruling house. The heads of the churches were always under the control of non-Christian rulers, at first the Zoroastrian Sassanids and then the Moslem Caliphs. This was in striking contrast with the position of the Pope in the West and even with that of the Patriarch in Constantinople. Up to 1453 the latter was at least under a professedly Christian ruler. This subordination to non-Christian civil authorities made at times for a deterioration in the character of the leadership. It might also impede the spread of the faith.

Such gains as Christianity achieved were largely in conjunction with the commercial and cultural contacts of groups which it had been fortunate

263

enough to win and to help weld into communities. Its strongholds were among
the Syriac-using peoples of the Tigris-Euphrates Valley. It was because it was
powerful here, and had the support of influential and educated mercantile
and professional elements in the political and commercial metropolises of the
region—Seleucia-Ctesiphon and then Baghdad—that it registered most of such
advances as it did. When, in the thirteenth and fourteenth centuries, Mesopotamia and Baghdad suffered severely and permanently at the hands of
Mongol conquerors, the Christian communities there and in Central Asia
were dealt blows from which they never recovered.

In the present chapter the story will be told down to the irruption of the
Mongols. Then, after a chapter devoted to the advance of Islam, we will
return to the narrative, recounting the marked but temporary expansion of
Christianity in Asia in the thirteenth century and the collapse in the fourteenth and fifteenth centuries.

As we have said in an earlier volume, to a not inconsiderable degree the
comparatively meagre gains east of the Euphrates were the price which Christianity paid for its success in the Roman Empire. It was largely because
Christianity became the religion of the Roman state that it was persecuted
by Rome's hereditary enemies, the Persian monarchs. Eventually the Zoroastrian state was eliminated. However, the destroyer was not Rome, but the
Moslem Arab. Whether, had Rome conquered Persia or had Persia accepted
Christianity, the ultimate fate of Christianity in Mesopotamia, Persia, and
Central Asia would have been different is an interesting but an unanswerable
and tantalizingly fruitless question. It seems probable that the Persians were
not as open to a new religion as were the peoples of the Roman Empire, and
that even had political conditions been different Christianity would not have
made serious headway among them. Certainly no widespread dissatisfaction
with the official Zoroastrianism appears to have existed, and no such decay
of the state cult or hunger for a saviour god was evident as that which
seems to have helped prepare the way for Christianity in the Mediterranean
world. It is one of the commonplaces of history that the long and indecisive
wars between Rome and Persia weakened both combatants and prepared the
way for the relatively easy Arab conquest and the expansion of Islam. Had
Rome in the third and fourth centuries conquered Persia and held it long
enough to enable Christianity to become the prevailing religion there, it may
well have been that the Arab irruption would have been checked near the
border and Islam confined to Arabia, and that Christianity would have assumed the place now held by Islam in Central Asia. Or had Christianity won

Persia as it did Armenia, before it had become identified with the Roman Empire, the future might have been vastly different.

We have already recorded the manner in which the Christianity in the Sassanian realms, by adopting Nestorianism and developing its own hierarchy, became permanently differentiated from that of the Roman Empire. It was this Nestorianism which had the major share in the spread of the faith in Central Asia, India, and China.

To Nestorianism was added, in the sixth century, another form of the faith, the Jacobites. Into the long intricacies of the theological disputations and the civil and ecclesiastical politics out of which came the various branches of the Monophysites we must not go. Here was one of the many effects of the environment on what is inclusively called Christianity. The convictions and ambitions of ecclesiastics and emperors, and racial and regional prejudices and loyalties had quite as much to do with the division between Orthodox and Monophysites and between the various branches of Monophysites as had theological differences concerning the relation of the divine and the human in Jesus. After the Council of Chalcedon (A.D. 451) the discussions ended finally in separation. In the sixth century Justin and his successor Justinian took action against the Monophysites. These rulers drove many beyond the borders of the Empire. The number of Monophysite bishops declined. Through the initiative of an Arab Monophysite chieftain and through the good offices of the Empress Theodora, who championed the heretics against her orthodox but devoted spouse, two Monophysite bishops were consecrated for the Christian Arabs. Probably these border allies against the Persians were too useful to risk alienating over a difference in creeds.

One of the new bishops proved so effective a missionary that he injected new life into the Syrian branch of Monophysitism and helped to give it permanence. Jacob Burda'na or Baradæus was born about 490, of fairly well-to-do parents. He was well educated and had fluent use of Greek, Arabic, and Syriac. From his early youth he devoted himself to the ascetic life. As bishop he was given a roving commission to organize the Monophysites and provide them with bishops and clergy. He displayed amazing powers of physical endurance. During an episcopate which lasted a generation (542-577) he travelled from Nisibis to Alexandria, usually on foot and garbed only in a ragged horse cloth, and is said to have consecrated two patriarchs, eighty-nine bishops, and a hundred thousand priests.[1] The word Jacobite

[1] Schubert, *Geschichte der christlichen Kirche im Frühmittelalter*, p. 144; Wigram, *The Separation of the Monophysites*, pp. 132-137; Bell, *The Origin of Islam in its Christian Environment*, p. 21.

applied to his co-religionists perpetuates his memory, but it had been employed by them before his time to indicate their claim to be the true Church, the custodians of the faith of Jacob or James, the brother of the Lord.[2]

The fact that the Jacobites were persecuted in the Roman Empire assured them a certain amount of welcome in the Sassanian realms. Headquarters were established on the Tigris. The great monastic establishment at Mar Mattai, on a mountain fastness north of Mosul, was in their hands. Missionaries were sent out who concentrated especially on Christian prisoners in Persia from Roman domains, and many of whom were of their branch of the faith. They also won converts from among non-Christians. One of the earliest Jacobite metropolitans in Sassanian territory was martyred for missionary efforts among Zoroastrians.[3] The very name of a distinguished leader, Bar Hebræus, attests a Jewish origin.[4] In 629 the Jacobites set up in Persia a special organization. Their Bishop of Takrite became a metropolitan with twelve bishops under him.[5] The Persian state gave them recognition as a distinct religious community.[6] They were never as numerous as the Nestorians, but they became widely disseminated.

In the millennium between the year 500 and the year 1500 Jacobites and Nestorians were not the only divisions of Christians represented in the vast reaches of Asia which lay east of the Euphrates. In a later chapter we shall see that in the thirteenth and fourteenth centuries and to a less extent in the fifteenth century Roman Catholic missionaries traversed much of the huge area and penetrated to the eastern coasts of Asia. Armenian Christians were widely scattered, some of them by invasions and many of them as merchants. As a rule they seem to have preserved their language, their nationality, and their religion—much like a Jewish diaspora.[7] In the thirteenth and fourteenth centuries Christian Alans from the Caucasus—of whose conversion, it will be recalled, we know almost nothing—formed part of the armed forces which upheld the Mongol rule in China.[8] We hear of Marcionites, apparently out-

[2] Wigram, op. cit., pp. 132-137.

[3] Wigram, An Introduction to the History of the Assyrian Church, p. 241.

[4] The Chronography of . . . Bar Hebræus, translation by Budge, Vol. I, pp. xv, xvi.

[5] Browne, The Eclipse of Christianity in Asia, pp. 10-11; Wigram, An Introduction to the History of the Assyrian Church, p. 241; Labourt, Le Christianisme dans l'Empire Perse sous la dynastie Sassanide, pp. 212-220.

[6] Wigram, An Introduction to the History of the Assyrian Church, p. 241. Labourt, De Timotheo I Nestorianorum Patriarcha (728-823) et Christianorum Orientalium Condicione sub Chaliphis Abbasidis, p. 15.

[7] L. Duchesne, Christian Worship (London, Society for Promoting Christian Knowledge, fifth edition, 1931, pp. xx, 593), p. 74.

[8] See various references to them in Moule, Christians in China before the Year 1550, pp. 140, 141, 196, 208, 252-254, 260-264.

side of Persian territories.[9] Adherents of the Greek Orthodox form of Christianity, or Melchites, as they are often called, were widely disseminated through Asia. Under the Sassanids, because of the traditional enmity between the Roman and Persian Empires, they were not welcome in the Persian domains. With the Arab conquest and the setting up of the rule of the Caliphs at Baghdad, much of the objection to their presence was removed and their numbers seem to have increased. Conflicts between the various schools of Christians annoyed the Caliphate and in the eleventh century it ordered Jacobite and Melchite bishops placed under the Catholicos of the Nestorians and commanded them to obey his edicts.[10] We hear of an Orthodox (Melchite) Metropolitan at Merv.[11] The Melchites had a Catholicos at Baghdad who was said to be under the Patriarch of Antioch.[12] We read, too, of landed proprietors who called themselves Christians, but who maintained that Jesus was only an ordinary man, said that he was one of the prophets, and resisted the efforts of bishops to win them to another position.[13]

In addition to these distinctively Christian groups, other cults in which Christian influences appeared were represented. There were the Mandæans. The Manichæans, too, were scattered through much of Central Asia and into China. Through Islam a certain amount of information concerning Jesus was propagated. In one form or another, then, some knowledge of Christianity was very widely spread through Mesopotamia, Persia, Central Asia, Arabia, and even in China and India. Christianity was strongest in Mesopotamia, near to its original seat and where it had been represented since at least the third century. At one time or another large Christian communities existed much farther east. Yet it was the general decline of population and cities and the massacres of Christians in Mesopotamia which eventually dealt the most severe blows from which Christianity suffered in that region.

Of all the branches of Christianity east of the Euphrates, as we have said, the Nestorians were the most numerous. Into the Nestorian fellowship went the descendants of most of the early Christian communities of the region. The hierarchy of the Nestorians seems to have been more widely extended east of the Euphrates than that of any other of the Churches. Theirs was the

[9] Thomas of Marga, *The Book of Governors,* translation by Budge, Vol. II, p. 481; Barthold, *Zur Geschichte des Christentums in Mittel-Asien bis zur mongolischen Eroberung,* pp. 14-16.

[10] Barthold, *op. cit.,* pp. 24, 25, citing Assemani, *Bibl. Or,* III, II, p. IC f. See also *The Chronography of . . . Bar Hebræus,* translation by Budge, section 139 (Vol. I, p. 127), and Labourt, *De Timotheo I Nestorianorum Patriarcha (728-823) et Christianorum Orientalium Condicione sub Chaliphis Abbasidis,* p. 17.

[11] Albîrûnî, *Chronology of Ancient Nations,* translation by Sachau, p. 283.

[12] Albîrûnî, *op. cit.,* ed. Sachau, p. 284.

[13] Thomas of Marga, *The Book of Governors,* translation by Budge, Vol. II, pp. 309-312.

community first officially recognized by the Sassanids, and the Moslem caliphs appear to have thought of them as the normal and dominant Christian group of their Mesopotamian domains.

This is not the place for an extended description of the theology, the organization, or the other characteristics of that Church. In general, as in other Churches of the period with which we are dealing, monasticism was prominent and highly esteemed. For a generation or more at the close of the fifth and the beginning of the sixth century a strong reaction was felt against celibacy. Some of the ascetics had given the profession a bad name. Wanderers, mendicants, often immoral, they brought annoyance and scandal.[14] In 485 a Synod of Seleucia permitted priests and monks who found that they could not remain continent to marry. Toward the close of the century a council allowed marriage for the lower clergy and monks and even for the Catholicos.[15] However, by the middle of the sixth century the rule of celibacy was revived and in 544 or 545 a Synod forbade any married priest to be either bishop or Catholicos.[16] As elsewhere, the Christianity propagated exalted the monastic ideal. The missionaries appear usually to have been monks.

It must also be noted that, although the dominant Church, in general Nestorians seem to have been more tolerant of other Christian bodies, at least by Mongol times, than were the Orthodox in the Byzantine Empire or than were the Roman Catholics in the West.[17] The official statements of faith were usually not so baldly Nestorian in nature as might have been expected. Often in Persian Nestorian literature it is impossible to discover peculiarly Nestorian earmarks.[18]

As with the Popes in Rome and with the Œcumenical Patriarchs in Constantinople, so with the Nestorian Patriarch or Catholicos, it was only the exceptionally energetic and able holder of the office who took an active part in the initiation of missions. Sometimes, as in the West and in the Byzantine Empire, a metropolitan was aggressively missionary. Presumably, however, as elsewhere, the majority of the members of the hierarchy were lukewarm toward the propagation of the faith.

[14] Labourt, *Le Christianisme dans l'Empire Perse sous la Dynastie Sassanide*, pp. 212-220.
[15] Assemanus, *Bibliotheca Orientalis*, Vol. III, Pt. II; Chabot, *Synodicon Orientale*, p. 312; Barthold, *Zur Geschichte des Christentums in Mittel-Asien bis zur mongolischen Eroberung*, p. 28.
[16] Barthold, *op. cit.*, p. 28; Assemanus, *loc. cit.*; Labourt, *Le Christianisme dans l'Empire Perse sous la Dynastie Sassanide*, pp. 302-321.
[17] Barthold, *op. cit.*, pp. 24, 25. A Nestorian bishop who died in 1256 declared that "the Gospel calls to love. And love includes the believer and the unbeliever, the near and the far, the friend and the enemy."—Browne, *The Eclipse of Christianity in Asia*, p. 66.
[18] Labourt, *Le Christianisme dans l'Empire Perse sous la Dynastie Sassanide*, pp. 247-287; Wigram, *An Introduction to the History of the Assyrian Church*, p. 164.

Because of the disappearance of so many of these Christian communities in the thirteenth, fourteenth, and fifteenth centuries, our knowledge of the expansion of Christianity east of the Euphrates is very fragmentary and maddeningly inadequate. We must content ourselves with moving from country to country and summarizing the scattering information which is ours.

We begin, as is proper, with the Persian Empire itself and with Mesopotamia. Under the Sassanids Christianity continued to face occasional persecution. From time to time the priests of the Zoroastrian state cult or local officials initiated the destruction of churches.[19] As heretofore, the lot of the Christians was closely related to the condition of the relations between the Persian and the Roman Empire. When, for instance, shortly before the middle of the sixth century war broke out between the two states, the Zoroastrian priests succeeded in obtaining official support for a persecution.[20] On the other hand, toward the latter part of the sixth century, Chosroes II, who owed his throne to Byzantine assistance, had a Christian wife, showed favour to Christian churches, and proclaimed liberty of conscience. There is even a report that his grandfather was secretly a Christian and had been baptized.[21] Yet he displayed preference for the Jacobites and was hostile to the Nestorians because the Catholicos of the latter sided with his rivals in the struggle for the succession.[22] Early in the seventh century this same Chosroes made his famous invasion of the Roman domains in which, among other cities, Jerusalem and Alexandria fell into Persian hands, the former with great destruction of churches and of the lives of Christians. Then, in one of the most remarkable recoveries of history, the Emperor Heraclius led the Byzantine forces in a war which had many of the features of a crusade and which rolled back the Persian tide. When victorious, Chosroes assumed an attitude of unfriendly neutrality to the Christians in his realm. But while he was being defeated by armies recruited by gold from Byzantine churches, he persecuted both Jacobites and Nestorians.[23]

Under the Sassanian rule, some converts were made from Persian Zoroastrians. Thus one of the bishops consecrated by Jacob Baradæus is said to have

---

[19] Labourt, *op. cit.*, pp. 347, 348.

[20] Labourt, *op. cit.*, pp. 176-190.

[21] Evagrius, *Eccles. Hist.*, Book VI, Chaps. 19, 21 (London, Samuel Bagster and Sons, 1846, pp. xvi, 318) ; Labourt, *op. cit.*, pp. 208, 209; Butler, *The Arab Conquest of Egypt* (Oxford, The Clarendon Press, 1902, pp. xxxiv, 563), pp. 54, 55, 66.

[22] Labourt, *op. cit.*, pp. 202-206.

[23] Labourt, *op. cit.*, pp. 232-238.

baptized a son of Chosroes I.[24] Some of the most important heads of the Nestorian Church had Persian names and up to the time that they accepted the Christian faith two of them had been Magi.[25] One of these, Mar Aba, did much to reform the Nestorian community and to raise the standards of its monastic life. To him the office of Catholicos meant danger of capital punishment for his apostasy from the state faith. Yet in that position he braved the wrath of Chosroes I and preached openly against Zoroastrianism.[26] We hear, too, of one Dadišo, the son of an official of high rank, who with his sister was converted and embraced the ascetic life and who was crucified for his departure from his ancestral religion.[27] If Persian Zoroastrians of prominence became Christians, it is likely that some of lesser station did so. Yet Christians were probably very much in the minority among Persians of Iranian stock. As before the sixth century, Christians within the Sassanian realms seem chiefly to have been from Syriac-using portions of the population. In Mesopotamia most physicians, the larger proportion of the mercantile and artisan classes, and many members of the civil bureaucracy appear to have been Christians.[28] In the seventh century, at the time of the Moslem conquest, the Christian and Jewish population is said to have numbered about a million and a half. Of these the larger part were probably Christians.[29]

The conquest of Persia by the Moslem Arabs in the seventh century, followed by the establishment of the rule of the Abbasid Caliphs at Baghdad in the eighth century, brought changed surroundings to the Christians in Persia. As a state cult Zoroastrianism was replaced by Islam. The Christian communities were continued as bodies with their own organization and special civil status. The Nestorian Catholicos, as heretofore, depended largely upon the non-Christian head of the state for his office. During the hundred years or so of conquest and disorder which separated the overthrow of the Sassanids from the establishment of order under the Abbasids, the Christians suffered severely. This, however, was not because of persecution by the invaders, but through the general effect of the wars and of civil dissensions. In some respects the Arab conquest improved the lot of the Christians. The latter came to an agreement with the Arabs by which they were assured protection from their

[24] Labourt, *op. cit.*, pp. 198-200.
[25] Barthold, *Zur Geschichte des Christentums in Mittel-Asien bis zur mongolischen Eroberung*, pp. 26, 27.
[26] Labourt, *op. cit.*, pp. 163-191; Chabot, *L'Ecole de Nisibis, son Histoire, ses Statuts* (Paris, Imprimerie Nationale, 1896, pp. 55), p. 10; Wigram, *An Introduction to the History of the Assyrian Church*, pp. 183-209.
[27] Labourt, *op. cit.*, pp. 225-229.
[28] Wigram, *op. cit.*, p. 230.
[29] A. Mez, *Die Renaissance des Islâms* (Heidelberg, Carl Winters, pp. iv, 492), p. 34.

foes, toleration for their religion, and assistance in the repair of their churches.[30] The Arabs, rude at the outset, leaned heavily on Christians for those offices supplied by the educated. Christians held more high places at court than under the Sassanids and taught their masters much of Greek philosophy and many of the arts of peace. Christians, too, as merchants and artisans, profited by the prosperity of the land and especially of Baghdad under Abbasid rule.[31] Missionaries sometimes accompanied the merchants and the flourishing state of commerce aided the spread of the faith. Yet the morale of Christians was not helped by the custom by which the heads of the churches were subject to the whims of Moslem rulers.[32] Moreover, the law against apostasy from Islam seems to have been enforced much more effectively than had been the earlier one against apostasy from Zoroastrianism. So far as we have record, the flow of converts from Islam into Christianity was very much less than had been that from the earlier official religion. Occasionally persecutions broke out. None of these, however, was as severe as the worst of those under the Sassanids.

Christians in the Sassanian and Abbasid realms were more active as missionaries than were Christians from any other land from the fifth to the sixteenth century in which the civil rulers were non-Christian. This seems to have been due to two conditions. In the first place, more than elsewhere the Christians were among the mercantile classes and, even more than in Constantinople and Alexandria, were assisted by a position in Seleucia-Ctesiphon and then Baghdad which gave them extensive contacts along the land trade routes of Asia. In the second place, these commercial contacts brought them into touch with more pagan peoples—as contrasted with Moslems—than were merchants of any other set of Christian communities. Merchants from Mesopotamia and from Christian groups in cities in Central Asia journeyed to China and India and passed through many pagan peoples on their way to the Far East. Added to this were the monastic schools for which the Nestorians were famous and in which many missionaries were recruited and trained.[33]

We have already recounted what is known of the early stages of the spread of Christianity in Arabia. We have seen that by the close of the fifth century most of the borders of the vast peninsula had been touched and that in many places Christian communities existed. Both from the Roman and from the

[30] E. A. Wallis Budge, *The Monks of Kublai Khan* (London, The Religious Tract Society, 1928, pp. xvi, 335), p. 30. See also on the attitude of Christians in the Persian domains toward the Arab conquest, Labourt, *op. cit.*, p. 345.

[31] Labourt, *Le Christianisme dans l'Empire Perse sous la Dynastie Sassanide*, p. 33; Shedd, *Islam and the Oriental Churches*, p. 158.

[32] Barthold, *op. cit.*, p. 27.

[33] Labourt, *op. cit.*, pp. 288-301.

Persian Empire Christian emissaries had come. In the North, along the Roman borders, Christians were found in several of the Arab tribes and states. At Hira, near the Mesopotamian frontier, was a Christian community with a bishop. There were Christians along the Arabian side of the Persian Gulf. In Southern Arabia, where commercial contacts with the Mediterranean and Mesopotamian cities appear to have been frequent, Christians were fairly numerous— in Yemen and among the Himyarites.

In the seventh century Islam put a stop to the growth of Christianity in Arabia and slowly eliminated most of such churches as existed. In the sixth century, however, before the appearance of Mohammed, the spread of Christianity seems to have continued. Hira may have had a Christian prince in the third quarter of the sixth century. It appears clear that near the end of the century its ruler became a Christian, a Nestorian, although some Jacobites were included in the population.[34] As late as 676, after Islam had been expanding for more than a generation, an important synod of the Nestorian Church was held in the land of the Katars in South-eastern Arabia, and among those attending were six bishops from the region, one of them a metropolitan.[35] In the first quarter of the sixth century, perhaps in 523, a severe persecution of Christians in Najran in South-western Arabia occurred, seemingly the work of rulers who were adherents of Judaism. The Christian prince of Ethiopia, as we have seen, engaged in a punitive expedition shortly after 525 and did much to restore Christianity.[36] Presumably, because of the Ethiopian connexion, this Christianity was Monophysite. About half a century later a military expedition from Persia is said to have killed or driven out the Ethiopians and to have set up rulers tributary to the Sassanids. The change in the political atmosphere was not favourable to Christianity, but the churches remained. It is also said that in the eighth century many of the remaining Christians were driven out by the Moslems and removed to the lower courses of the Euphrates.[37]

Just when or how Christianity won the island of Socotra, not far from the entrance to the Gulf of Aden, we do not know. The population seems to have been of mixed origin, drawn there probably because the island was near one of the sea highways. In the sixth century it was Greek-speaking and then

[34] Duchesne, Les Missions Chrétiennes au Sud de l'Empire Romain, p. 121; Evagrius, Eccles. Hist., Book VI, Chap. 22; Guidi, L'Arabe Antéislamique, pp. 33-36; Chabot, L'Ecole de Nisibis, son Histoire, ses Statuts, p. 17.
[35] Mingana, The Early Spread of Christianity in India (Manchester University Press, 1926, pp. 82), pp. 7, 8.
[36] Moberg, The Book of the Himyarites, passim; Bell, The Origin of Islam in Its Christian Environment, pp. 36-39.
[37] Duchesne, op. cit., pp. 90-112.

contained many Christians. The ninth-century Arabs declared that the people had become Christian when the rest of the "Greeks" had done so. Whether the Christians were Jacobites or Nestorians or were divided between the two communions is in doubt. In the fifteenth century they were said to be mostly Nestorians. Their later use of circumcision appears to point to an association with Ethiopian Christianity. From what we know of the influence of Ethiopia in the Christian communities of Southern Arabia, the connexion seems not unlikely. In the sixteenth and seventeenth centuries the populace still clung to Christianity—which was then reported to be of a debased and ignorant type.[38]

In Central Asia to the north of Persia, east of the Caspian and west and east of the Oxus River, Christianity had an extensive spread. For a thousand years and more it was represented, although in varying degrees of strength. It may be that some Christians took refuge there to escape from the Sassanian persecutions.[39] In 334 Merv had a bishop.[40] In the fifth and sixth centuries Merv was still the seat of a bishop and from the sixth or seventh into the eleventh century it was the headquarters of a metropolitan.[41] In the fifth century Herat had a bishop, and in the sixth, tenth, and eleventh centuries possessed a metropolitan.[42] In the eleventh century Samarqand was the centre of a Nestorian ecclesiastical province. It may have been such from several centuries before then.[43] This, of course, implies bishops and Christian communities subordinate to a metropolitan. Toward the close of the fifth century Christians are reported from the lands of the Hephthalite Huns and Turks.[44] From the middle of the sixth century comes the information that among the Turks were Byzantine Christian captives, and that in response to the command of an angel a Nestorian bishop went to the Turks, baptized many, and taught them the art of writing.[45] In 549, at the request of the Hephthalite Huns on both banks of the Oxus, the Nestorian Patriarch sent a bishop for the Christians of that region.[46] About the middle of the seventh century the Metropolitan of Merv

[38] Yule, *The Book of Ser Marco Polo* (Cordier's revision), Vol. II, pp. 406-410; Yule, *Cathay and the Way Thither* (Cordier's revision), Vol. III, pp. 7-9. For the fifteenth-century report see *The Travels of Nicolo Conti* in R. H. Major, editor, *India in the Fifteenth Century* (London, Hakluyt Society, 1857), ii, 20.

[39] Barthold, *Zur Geschichte des Christentums in Mittel-Asien bis zur mongolischen Eroberung*, pp. 14-16.

[40] *Ibid.;* Chabot, *Synodicon Orientale*, p. 310.

[41] Sachau, *Zur Ausbreitung des Christentums in Asien*, pp. 21, 64; Chabot, *op. cit.*, p. 423.

[42] Sachau, *op. cit.*, pp. 21, 64; Barthold, *op. cit.*, pp. 21-23.

[43] Barthold, *op. cit.*, pp. 21-23; Sachau, *op. cit.*, p. 21; Mingana, *The Early Spread of Christianity in Central Asia and the Far East*, p. 29.

[44] Mingana, *op. cit.*, pp. 8-10.

[45] Mingana, *op. cit.*, p. 9.

[46] Mingana, *op. cit.*, pp. 10, 11.

is said to have won many Turks on a river which was possibly the Oxus.[47] Christianity was by no means the only religion in the area. The Oxus Valley seems also to have been a refuge for several of the dualistic faiths, including, notably, Manichæism.[48]

About 781 the Nestorian Patriarch Timotheus wrote that a King of the Turks had become a Christian and that he, Timotheus, had appointed a metropolitan for them.[49] The same Patriarch says that he sent bishops who won to the faith a number of peoples, whom he names, south and east of the Caspian. Apparently it was one of these missionaries, Shûbhâl-îshû, whom the Patriarch Timotheus consecrated Bishop for a mission in some of these districts. As Otto of Bamberg was to do later, Shûbhâl-îshû went with considerable pomp to impress the "barbarians," preached, baptized, built churches, and installed priests. After a number of years of labour, he was killed by robbers on his way back to his home monastery.[50] When reports arrived of his successes, Timotheus appointed Yabalâhâ and Kardagh Metropolitans to different portions of the region. Yabalâhâ wrote Timotheus that he had brought many to the "true faith" and had placed over them bishops whom he had consecrated from among the monks who had accompanied him.[51] We also hear of one Elijah whom the Patriarch Timotheus appointed Bishop of Mûkân. Mûkân was a city, apparently in the region of the Caspian, and when Elijah reached it seems to have been pagan, without Christians, Jews, or Moslems. Elijah preached, is said to have performed miracles, and eventually cut down the huge sacred tree, baptized many, ordained priests and deacons, and taught the neophytes the responses for the services.[52]

For two centuries or more it may have appeared possible that Christianity would become the dominant faith in the region between the Caspian and what later became Chinese Turkestan or Sinkiang. The majority of the population seem to have inherited types of polytheism which usually offer ineffectual opposition to a faith such as Christianity or Islam. In the eighth century Islam began to penetrate the region through Moslem armies. For some reason, however, it made comparatively slow progress.[53] The chief rival of Chris-

[47] *Ibid.;* Labourt, *De Timotheo I Nestorianorum Patriarcha (728-823) et Christianorum Orientalium Condicione sub Caliphis Abbasidis,* pp. 41-44.
[48] Barthold, *op. cit.,* pp. 13, 29-32.
[49] Mingana, *op. cit.,* p. 12.
[50] Thomas of Marga, *The Book of Governors (Historia Monastica)* (translation by Budge), Vol. II, p. 468, 478 ff.; Assemanus, *Bibilotheca Orientalis,* Vol. III, Pt. II, p. 478.
[51] Assemanus, *op. cit.,* Vol. III, Pt. II, p. 478; Thomas of Marga, *op. cit.,* Vol. II, pp. 486-494. See also Shedd, *Islam and the Oriental Churches,* pp. 162, 163.
[52] Thomas of Marga, *op. cit.,* Vol. II, pp. 504-520.
[53] Barthold, *Zur Geschichte des Christentums in Mittel-Asien bis zur mongolischen Eroberung,* pp. 16-20.

tianity was Manichæism.[54] For a time the latter had headquarters at Samarqand.[55] Manichæism lost, perhaps in part because Moslem rulers opposed it more strongly than they did Christianity.[56] In the ninth, tenth, and eleventh centuries Christianity appears to have been very strong. South of Lake Balkash several hundred inscribed gravestones dating from the ninth to the fourteenth century and which obviously record the burial of Christians are evidence of flourishing Christian communities.[57] A Moslem writer of the end of the tenth and the first half of the eleventh century declared that Nestorians formed the majority of the population of Syria, Iraq, and Khurasan—the latter being a region lying south of the Oxus.[58]

The victory of Islam was probably due primarily to the political and numerical predominance of that faith in Persia and to the fact that the rulers of the valleys of the Oxus and Jaxartes, catching the contagion from Persia, eventually became Moslems. A mass conversion to Islam of Turks east of the Oxus seems to have taken place in the eleventh century.[59] Yet at the end of the twelfth century so many Turks in Persia and Mesopotamia were Christian that it seemed necessary to prepare Christian literature for them.[60] The final decision of the issue between Islam and Christianity in Central Asia did not come until the thirteenth and fourteenth centuries.

When Christianity had once reached the cities in the valleys of the Oxus and the Jaxartes and had become strong in them, almost inevitably it was carried farther eastward across the mountains into the basin of the Tarim River, into the region north of the T'ien Shan, and then into China.

China was one of the most populous centres of civilized mankind. For centuries commerce between its millions and Central and Western Asia had been carried on by way not only of the sea, but also by overland routes across what is now Sinkiang and through the oases of the Oxus Valley. Since so many of the Mesopotamian Christians were merchants, Christianity was especially strong among the mercantile communities in such caravan centres as Merv and Samarqand, and many of the traders who traversed the land routes to the Far East and settled in the cities of China were probably Christian. So, too, in

[54] Barthold, *op. cit.*, pp. 29-32; Browne, *The Eclipse of Christianity in Asia*, pp. 93-95.
[55] Barthold, *op. cit.*, pp. 29-32.
[56] Browne, *op. cit.*, pp. 93, 95.
[57] Barthold, *op. cit.*, p. 1; Mingana, *The Early Spread of Christianity in Central Asia and the Far East*, pp. 39-42.
[58] Albîrûnî, *Chronology of Ancient Nations*, translation by Sachau, p. 282.
[59] Barthold, *op. cit.*, p. 50; Mingana, *op. cit.*, pp. 14-17.
[60] Mingana, *op. cit.*, p. 48.

the coast cities of China Christian merchants who had come by the sea from Mesopotamia and Syria might be expected. These Christian merchants were not necessarily active missionaries. Unless they were very different from the vast majority of their occupation elsewhere, whether Christian or of some other religion, most of them were not greatly interested in propagating their professed faith. However, loyalty to their community and its traditions would induce them to support churches, clergy, and monasteries. Some, whether of lay folk, clergy, or monks, would be zealous in spreading their religion. A few non-Christians might be attracted even without such activity.

Whatever the process which accounts for their presence, whether migration or conversion, from Moslem and Chinese texts we know of Christians in what is now Sinkiang or Chinese Turkestan in the ninth century. They seem largely to have been in the towns and oases and not to have been among the nomads.[61]

Toward the beginning of the eleventh century we hear of the faith spreading to some of the nomads or semi-nomads of Chinese Turkestan. About the year 1009 the Metropolitan of Merv wrote to the Catholicos reporting that the ruler of the Keraits, a Turkish people, while hunting in the mountains, was overtaken by a blinding snowstorm. Lost and despairing of life, he saw a vision of a saint who promised that if the prince would become a Christian he would guide him safely home. The chieftain agreed, and once back in his encampment he made inquiries of Christian merchants who were there and was told that he must be baptized. The traders gave him a Gospel which he worshipped daily. He sent to the Metropolitan asking for a priest to baptize him, inquiring about rules of fasting, and asserting that two hundred thousand believed with him. The Catholicos instructed the Metropolitan to send to the Keraits a priest and a deacon to baptize them and to instruct them in Christian rites.[62] Another account of the same incident declares that before he had sent to the Metropolitan, the Kerait prince had been taught Christian prayers or hymns, including the Lord's Prayer, that he had prepared a pavilion with a cross and the Gospel, and that in front of these he placed mare's milk, prayed over it the prayers he had learned, crossed himself, and then, with his company, took a mouthful of the milk.[63] How accurately the details have been

[61] Pelliot, *La Haute Asie*, p. 19.

[62] What purports to be an extract from this letter or at least a summary of it is in Bar Hebræus, *Chron. Eccles.*, II, Col. 279, and the translation here used is in Browne, *The Eclipse of Christianity in Asia*, pp. 101, 102. See also Mingana, *The Early Spread of Christianity in Central Asia and the Far East*, pp. 14-19. Bar Hebræus was a Jacobite.

[63] This account is by a Nestorian, Mari, and an English translation is given in Browne, *op. cit.*, pp. 102, 103. See also Mingana, *op. cit.*, pp. 14-19.

reported we do not know, but we do know that in the thirteenth century the Keraits professed to be Christian.[64]

We know, too, that in the thirteenth century the Onguts, a Tartar folk who then dwelt to the north of the great northern bend of the Yellow River, were Christians[65] and that in that same century some of the Uighurs, a people long prominent in Chinese Turkestan, were of that faith.[66] How or when Christianity entered these two last groups we are not informed. In the Keraits, Onguts, and Uighurs Christianity had moved outside of the towns and into the tents of widely scattered populations. What little information survives as to its further fate among them we are to summarize in a later chapter.

Tibet may have known Christian missionaries. About 781 Timotheus, the Nestorian Patriarch whom we have already noted for his activity in directing missions to the Turks, wrote that he was preparing to appoint a metropolitan for the Tibetans.[67] Whether that was ever done or whether it implies that Christians were already present on that vast plateau we are not informed.

For China we cannot prove the presence of Christianity earlier than the year 635. The reports that the Apostle Thomas introduced the faith to the land are not to be given credence.[68]

The fullest account of what we know of the introduction of Christianity to China is the famous inscription on a monument set up in 781 in or near Ch'angan, then the capital of China, and represented now by the city of Hsianfu.[69] The stone was erected to commemorate the munificence of a

[64] Yule, *Book of Ser Marco Polo* (Cordier's revision), Vol. I, pp. 231-237; Yule, *Cathay and the Way Thither* (Cordier's revision), Vol. III, pp. 15-27; Rockhill, *William of Rubruck,* pp. 106-115.

[65] Moule, *Christians in China before the Year 1550,* pp. 93, 94, 99, 103, 135.

[66] Rockhill, *op. cit.,* p. 140; Bretschneider, *Medieval Researches from Eastern Asiatic Sources,* Vol. I, p. 262.

[67] Mingana, *op. cit.,* pp. 10-14; Labourt, *De Timotheo I Nestorianorum Patriarcha (728-823) et Christianorum Orientalium Condicione sub Caliphis Abbasidis,* p. 45.

[68] Moule, *Christians in China before the Year 1550,* pp. 10-26, gives the references in which the assertion is made that the Apostle Thomas introduced Christianity to China, together with other early references which argue for the coming of the faith to China before the seventh century, declares them unreliable, and suggests a possible manner in which some of them arose. See also some of these references, with other interesting theories, summarized, with appropriate footnotes, in Latourette, *A History of Christian Missions in China,* pp. 48-51.

[69] The literature on this "Nestorian monument of Hsianfu" is very extensive. See the footnotes in Latourette, *op. cit.,* pp. 51-54. The best brief account, with an excellent translation, is in Moule, *op. cit.,* pp. 27-52. Moule's footnotes contain references to other discussions and pertinent information in Chinese and Western writers. A full older treatise is Henri Havret, *La Stèle Chrétienne a Si-ngan-fou,* 3 parts (*Variétés Sinologiques,* Nos. 7, 12, 20), Shanghai, 1895-1897, 1902. P. Y. Saeki, *The Nestorian Monument in China* (London, Society for Promoting Christian Knowledge, 1916, pp. x, 342) is full but not always trustworthy. The place where the monument was found is debated.—See A. C. Moule in *Journal of the Royal Asiatic Society of Great Britain and Ireland,* Jan. 1933,

Christian who had come from Balkh, in the ancient Bactria, in the vicinity of the Oxus, had risen to high favour in the Chinese government, and had been generous in the use of his wealth in caring for the poor and in restoring and enlarging monasteries and churches. The inscription declares that in the year 635 one A-lo-pên had come from Ta Ch'in, bringing the Scriptures. Ta Ch'in was a term employed by Chinese writers to designate the Near East, and especially Syria.[70] A-lo-pên, so the inscription goes on to say, was welcomed by the Emperor, who was none other than the famous T'ai Tsung, the outstanding figure in the founding of the T'ang Dynasty and one of the strongest monarchs in Chinese history. The sacred books are said to have been translated, presumably by imperial command, and to have been examined by T'ai Tsung, who thereupon gave them his approval and ordered their preaching and transmission. T'ai Tsung also directed that the local officials build in Ch'angan a monastery for twenty-one monks. The inscription claims that Christianity enjoyed the patronage of T'ai Tsung's successor, the Emperor Kao Tsung, and that Kao Tsung founded monasteries in each of the *chou* (departments) of the realm. In the later years of Kao Tsung and in succession to him the Empress Wu Hou, an ardent Buddhist, controlled the Empire, and Christianity evidently fared badly. However, shortly after her, the Emperor Hsüan Tsung (Ming Huang), patron of arts and letters (reigned 712-756), under whom the T'ang Dynasty reached its zenith and began its decline, was a patron of the faith.

The conditions of the period favoured the introduction of new foreign cults to China but not their wide popularity. Under the T'ang China shared with the Moslem Arab empire the distinction of being the most powerful and extensive of the realms of its day. The land was prosperous, foreign commerce flourished, and merchants and other residents from abroad were attracted in large numbers. Islam, Judaism, Christianity, Zoroastrianism, and Manichæism were found in the T'ang domains, each associated with its particular groups of foreign adherents.[71] Yet none of them seems to have acquired any extensive following among the Chinese. The religious field had been pre-empted by the native systems of Confucianism and Taoism, and by the Indian-born Buddhism. All of these three, and especially Confucianism, enjoyed official support. With

---

pp. 118-120. See also P. Y. Saeki, *Old Problems Concerning the Nestorian Monument in China Re-examined in the Light of Newly Discovered Facts* in *Journal of the North China Branch of the Royal Asiatic Society*, Vol. LXVII (1936), pp. 81-99.

[70] F. Hirth and W. W. Rockhill, *Chau-ju-kua* (St. Petersburg, Imperial Academy of Sciences, 1912, pp. x, 288), pp. 104, 105.

[71] Yule, *Cathay and the Way Thither* (Cordier's revision), Vol. I, pp. 62, 89, 90, 92; Chavannes and Pelliot, *Un Traité Manichéen Retrouvé en Chine*, pp. 4, 137.

its ritual, asceticism, and ethics, and with its promise of heavenly joys, Buddhism must have seemed to offer much that the newly introduced Christianity could hold out to its followers. It had been in China about six centuries before the T'ang, had attained wide popularity, and in the early years of the T'ang reached the height of its prosperity in the Middle Kingdom. Moreover, as even the Buddhists found to their sorrow, any religion which seemed seriously to threaten the established Confucian culture would be firmly checked by the state, more and more wedded as the latter was to Confucian ideology.

The evidences of the presence of Christianity in China under the T'ang are numerous and continue to accumulate. Chinese books have references to the faith.[72] Imperial edicts mention it.[73] We gather that monasteries were built in a number of different parts of the land, including the important western city of Ch'êngtu.[74] Some Chinese manuscripts discovered in the present century in Tunhuang on the western border prove to be Christian documents.[75] Early in the eighth century a metropolitanate is said to have been created for China. We hear of it again in the ninth century.[76] It is clear that a Christian literature existed in Chinese. The Hsianfu inscription displays a grace of style and contains literary allusions and phraseology which indicate competence in the Chinese language and familiarity with Taoism and Buddhism.[77] One of the Tunhuang Christian documents begins as does a Buddhist sutra and has a Buddhist colouring.[78]

Yet Christianity seems to have remained largely and probably predominantly foreign in membership and leadership.[79] The number of its monasteries, even together with the houses of the Manichæans and the Zoroastrians, is said by a contemporary never to have equalled the number of Buddhist monasteries in one small city.[80] Under such circumstances it is not surprising that a single imperial edict accomplished its ruin. In 845 the Emperor Wu Tsung, a devotee of Taoism, ordered Buddhist monks to return to private life and included Christians in his sweeping proscription.[81] From this blow Christianity did not

[72] See translations of these in Moule, *Christians in China before the Year 1550*, pp. 65-72.
[73] Moule, *op. cit.*, pp. 65, 67.
[74] Chavannes and Pelliot, *op. cit.*, p. 270; Cordier in *T'oung Pao* (1917), p. 63.
[75] Moule, *op. cit.*, pp. 52-64.
[76] Moule, *op. cit.*, p. 20; Thomas of Marga, *The Book of Governors*, translation by Budge, Vol. II, p. 448.
[77] Moule, *op. cit.*, pp. 39, 47; Laufer in *Open Court*, Vol. XXV (1911), pp. 449-454.
[78] Moule, *op. cit.*, pp. 59, 60.
[79] Moule, in *International Review of Missions*, Vol. XX (1931), pp. 456-459.
[80] Moule, *Christians in China before the Year 1550*, p. 69, citing *Ch'üan T'ang Wên*, c. 727, fol. 271°. Yet this is from an inscription in a Buddhist monastery and is not based upon an unbiassed statistical survey.
[81] Moule, *op. cit.*, p. 70.

recover. Probably its decay was hastened by the domestic disorder which accompanied the decline of the T'ang Dynasty and by the growing insecurity to foreign life and property. In 877-878 we hear of Christians in one of the ports, but, significantly, as perishing in the capture of the city by rebels.[82] In 987 a monk who with five colleagues had been sent to China seven years before to put the Church in order told an Arab in Baghdad that he had found no Christians in that realm.[83]

In the eleventh and twelfth centuries Christianity seems to have been all but unknown in most of China.[84] Yet on the northern and eastern borders Christians were found among non-Chinese peoples and, as we have suggested, their numbers were multiplying. Some of them seem even to have moved into North China and Manchuria and to have become sinicized.[85] As we shall see later, in Mongol times Christians once more appeared in China, but only again to disappear and more completely than before.

Whether in the time of the T'ang any Christians or Christian influences moved on to the eastern cultural satellites of China, Korea, and Japan, we cannot certainly prove. That many Koreans and Japanese came to Ch'angan we know. It may be that in that cosmopolitan city they met some of the Christians who sojourned there and carried home the impress of their teachings. That, however, seems yet to be demonstrated. It is also possible that some of the Christian merchants may have come to the ports in the north of Indo-China, but this also we are unable to affirm.

Nor do we know that the Christianity of the T'ang era left any permanent deposit in the religious ideas of the Chinese themselves. In view of the ready syncretism so characteristic of China, this may well have occurred, but we can neither prove nor disprove it.

In India the Christianity of the pre-sixteenth century period had more success than in China. We have seen that the faith was almost certainly present in that land before the close of the fifth century. In the succeeding thousand years Christian communities existed, some of whose descendants have kept to their ances-

[82] Reinaud, *Relation des Voyages Faits par les Arabes et les Persans dans l'Inde et à la Chine dans le IXe Siècle de l'Ère Chrétienne* (Paris, 1845), p. 64. The book contains the Arabic text and a French translation. See also Moule, *op. cit.,* p. 76, which gives an English translation and further bibliographical notes.

[83] Moule, *op. cit.,* pp. 75, 76, gives an English translation of the passage by Abu'l Faradj, who had talked with the monk.

[84] Moule, *op. cit.,* p. 73. Paul Pelliot, in *Journal of the Royal Asiatic Society for Great Britain and Ireland,* Jan., 1933, pp. 15, 16, suggests evidence of at least a persisting slight knowledge of Christianity.

[85] Pelliot, cited in Moule, *op. cit.,* p. 24.

tral faith until our own day—although they have changed their affiliation from one communion to another, a large proportion of them more than once. In spite of the fact that it was represented by minority groups, Christianity became permanently a part of the Indian scene. Yet, walled off by the prevailing social organization into what in effect was a distinct caste, Christians apparently exercised very little if any influence upon the thought and the religious life of their fellow Indians. Christianity was in India, but infiltrated slightly if at all into the prevailing Hinduism.

The greater success of Christianity in India than in China was due primarily to geography. India was much nearer the most populous Christian centres and had more intimate commercial relations with them. Sea and caravan routes led to both Alexandria and Mesopotamia. It seems to have been through them that the Indian Christian communities had their origin.

Of the history of the planting and growth of this Christianity in India we know very little. Although the communities of "Syrian Christians" now found in South India obviously have had a continuous existence stretching over centuries, until the sixteenth century, when they came into contact with the Portuguese, we possess only slight fragments of information concerning them. In the earliest literary references to Christians in India, as we have seen, we are usually unable to tell whether the region designated by that name is what we now call India, or whether by it Southern Arabia is meant. Probably Christianity entered North-west India by land from Persia, and South India by sea, chiefly from Mesopotamia and from ports on both sides of the Persian Gulf and from Southern Arabia.

Archæological evidence, although scanty enough, points to a Persian connexion. In the sixteenth century a cross was found at Mailapur, near the present Madras.[86] The inscription on it was in Pahlavi, or Middle Persian, and the date assigned it is the seventh, eighth, or ninth century.[87] A similar cross in Travancore is said to date from the tenth century,[88] and a second one there is said to be later.[89] Inscriptions on metal plates, perhaps of the eighth and ninth centuries, too, have been reported, partly in Tamil and partly in more than one type of Pahlavi. One records a grant to the head of the Christians

[86] Adeney, *The Greek and Eastern Churches*, pp. 510-522; A. C. Burnell in *The Indian Antiquary*, Vol. III (1874), p. 313; C. P. T. Winckworth in *The Journal of Theological Studies*, Vol. XXX (Apr., 1929), pp. 237-244.

[87] Adeney, *loc. cit.;* Winckworth, *loc. cit.;* Richter, *Indische Missionsgeschichte,* pp. 31-42; W. Germann, *Die Kirche der Thomaschristen* (Gütersloh, C. Bertelsmann, 1877, pp. x, 792), pp. 286, 287; G. M. Rae, *The Syrian Church in India* (Edinburgh, William Blackwood and Sons, 1892, pp. xii, 388), pp. 119 ff.; Yule, *Marco Polo* (Cordier's revision), Vol. II, pp. 358, 359.

[88] Richter, *loc. cit.;* Adeney, *loc. cit.;* Rae, *op. cit.,* p. 120.

[89] Richter, *loc. cit.;* Adeney, *loc. cit.*

of Cranganore (on the south-west coast) of the lordship of a city. Another is the deed of a piece of land with several families of non-Christians to a specified church and congregation. Another is a mortgage, although in this Christians are not certainly involved.[90] These crosses and tablets seem to indicate that Christians of Persian provenance were in South India, on both the east and west coasts. The tablets indicate that at least some of the Christians were persons of wealth and political influence. A tradition has also come down that in the ninth century two Persian clergymen landed on the Malabar coast and received from the King permission to build churches on sites donated by himself and liberty to win converts.[91] It has been suggested that certain characteristics of the Syrian Christians of India may indicate that one or more castes rather high in the Hindu social scale accepted Christianity *en masse*.[92] Certainly in the nineteenth century the ancient Christian communities in South India displayed some of the features of caste. Perhaps this came about through gradual conformity to the Indian social organization by the descendants of immigrants. These may at an earlier time have intermarried with some of the peoples of the land. It may be, too, that if the Christians owned land some of the non-Christians on the soil accepted the religion of their landlords.

Whatever admixture of Indian blood modified its foreign nature, the Indian Christian community preserved outside connexions and retained something of an alien aspect. From a Nestorian author of the seventh century we learn that India had a hierarchy under the jurisdiction of the Nestorian Patriarch in Ctesiphon.[93] The ecclesiastical languages seem not to have been any of the tongues of India, but Syriac or Pahlavi. Yet, largely foreign though it was, this Christianity appears not to have remained as exclusively alien as has another Indian religious group of Persian origin, the Parsees.

With its roots chiefly in Mesopotamia and Persia, Indian Christianity must in part have shared the fortunes of the commerce of the non-Arab elements of that region. After the rise of the Moslem Arab power and of Moslem Arab trade in India and Ceylon, presumably the commerce of the non-Moslem portions of the population of Mesopotamia and Persia suffered from the competition.[94] It may be that here is to be found one reason for the lack of mention of Christian communities in Ceylon by mediæval Arab and European

[90] Richter, *loc. cit.;* Adeney, *loc. cit.;* Rae, *op. cit.,* pp. 154 ff.; Germann, *op. cit.,* pp. 226 ff.
[91] Ayyar, *Anthropology of the Syrian Christians,* p. xvi.
[92] Pickett, *Christian Mass Movements in India* (Cincinnati, The Abingdon Press, 1933, pp. 382), p. 37.
[93] Mingana, *The Early Spread of Christianity in India,* pp. 30-36.
[94] Prakasar, *A History of the Catholic Church in Ceylon,* pp. 8-10.

travellers. If the Island of Taprobana on which in the sixth century Cosmas Indiocopleustes mentions the presence of Christians was really Ceylon, these communities seem to have died out or to have sunk into insignificance. Travellers who would presumably have mentioned them had they existed apparently knew nothing of them.[95]

Europeans who passed through India in the latter part of the thirteenth and in the fourteenth century record the presence of Christians. Thus in the last decade of the thirteenth century Marco Polo mentions Christians in charge of a church at the shrine of St. Thomas at Mailapur, on the east coast.[96] He also found Christians on the west coast, at Quilon.[97] In the first half of the fourteenth century, Jordan, a Dominican who lived in India for a number of years, declared that those who bore the name Christian were widely scattered, but were not baptized, were ignorant of the faith, and confused the Apostle Thomas with Christ.[98] About the middle of the fourteenth century, John of Marignolli, a Papal Legate who journeyed to China and back, reported that in one place in India Christians, by ancient right, had charge of the official measure for pepper and other spices,[99] and that in one place they owned the pepper.[100] However, not far from the time that Marco Polo was in India, Menentillus, a Dominican, reported that the "Saracens" had great influence on the coast of India, and said that there were very few Christians and that these were persecuted.[101] In the fifteenth century Nestorians were said to be scattered over all of India, much as were Jews in Europe.[102] We hear, too, in that century of a Christian high in the service of a prince.[103] Christians appear to have belonged to groups which inherited certain privileges but which long before 1500 had become a slowly waning power. More and more they were found only in the South, where their early commercial communities seem to have been strongest. Yet they survived, as their contemporary Christian communities in China did not.

Whether these widely disseminated Christians made any impression upon

[95] Prakasar, *op. cit.*, p. 10.

[96] Yule, *Marco Polo* (Cordier's revision), Vol. II, pp. 353-355.

[97] Yule, *op. cit.*, Vol. II, p. 375.

[98] Jordan, translated by Yule in *The Wonders of the East by Friar Jordanus* (London, Hakluyt Society, 1863), p. 23.

[99] See a translation of the text in Yule, *Cathay and the Way Thither* (Cordier's revision), Vol. III, pp. 252-254.

[100] Translation of the text in Yule, *Cathay and the Way Thither* (Cordier's revision), Vol. III, p. 257.

[101] Translation in Yule, *Cathay and the Way Thither* (Cordier's revision), Vol. III, p. 63.

[102] *The Travels of Nicolo Conti in the East*, pp. 7, 23, in translation by J. W. Jones in R. H. Major, editor, *India in the Fifteenth Century* (London Hakluyt Society, 1857).

[103] Journey of Abd-er-Razzak, in R. H. Major, *op. cit.*, i, 41.

the content of the non-Christian faiths of India is difficult to determine. The prevailing Hinduism was and is strikingly syncretistic, finding room for ideas and practices from many diverse sources. The suggestion has been made that the Mahabharata and the Bhagavadgita, particularly the latter, while not of Christian provenance, show Christian influence in their development, that some of the stories told of Krishna may have a Christian origin, and that *Bhakti* may owe something to Christianity.[104] All this, however, is admittedly difficult to establish and quite likely is without substantial foundation.

As we have suggested, what normally goes under the name of Christianity was not the only channel by which Christian ideas entered Asia east of the Euphrates. Manichæism, particularly, was widely spread. While it adapted itself freely to different environments and in the Mediterranean world, where churches were strong, displayed more likeness to Christianity than farther east, where churches were weak or absent, wherever it went it must have carried something of the stamp which Christianity appears to have placed upon it at its birth.

This is not the place to recount what is known of the eastward expansion of Manichæism. We have found Manichæism in Central Asia. There, among other peoples who were attracted to it, many of the Uighurs accepted it. The China of the T'ang knew it, largely because of Uighur influence. It lived on long after the collapse of the Uighur power and was found in Fukien as late as the seventeenth century.[105] In the ninth century a Moslem traveller speaks of observing it in Ceylon.[106]

Precisely to what extent the Christianity which spread east of the Euphrates was Nestorian and to what extent Jacobite, Greek Orthodox, and Armenian, the evidence does not enable us to say. That the Melchites and the Armenians were inconsiderable minorities is fairly certain. That the Nestorians were in the large majority is clear. The unknown factor is the influence of the minorities, and especially of the Jacobite minority, upon the Nestorian majority. It may be that in some places the various groups coalesced. The comparative ease with which, in later centuries, members of some of these groups became

[104] See this developed, with appropriate references to the literature, in Clemens, *Der Einfluss des Christentums auf andere Religionen*, pp. 81-91. See also Ayyar, *Anthropology of the Syrian Christians*, p. xvi; Grierson in Hastings' *Ency. of Religion and Ethics*, Vol. II, p. 539; L. J. Sedgwick in *Journal of the Royal Asiatic Society, Bombay Branch*, Vol. XXIII, pp. 109-134.

[105] Pelliot, *La Haute Asie*, p. 17; E. Chavannes and P. Pelliot, *Un Traité Manichéen Retrouvé en Chine;* Pelliot, *Les Traditions Manichéennes au Foukien* (*T'oung Pao*, 1923, pp. 193-214).

[106] Prakasar, *A History of the Catholic Church in Ceylon*, p. 10.

Roman Catholics and with which many of the Syrian Christians of India passed over to the Jacobites may reflect an earlier lack of rigidity of affiliation with particular communions. Certainly we are not always safe in concluding that the Christianity which spread east of the Euphrates was Nestorian. Often we know it to have been such. Occasionally we are not sure.

Whatever the type of Christianity which moved eastward, comparatively little of it can be said to have become deeply rooted. In this it presented a striking contrast with that which in the same period was extending its borders in Western and Eastern Europe. Except possibly in the case of the Syriac-using population of Mesopotamia and its colonies, never does Christianity east of the Euphrates seem to have become an integral element of the culture of any one people. Occasionally a tribe, such as the Keraits, accepted it, but never, apparently, in such fashion as to permit it to become part of the bone and sinew of their life. Its main strength was in groups in Mesopotamia, which, while often wealthy and educated, politically were always subject to a non-Christian government. Seldom, if ever, was the kind of systematic conversion possible which in Europe and the basin of the Mediterranean was so generally accomplished through the co-operation of the state. Outside of Mesopotamia, in region after region and city after city, Christianity was represented by merchant communities. Such groups, like many others of their kind throughout the centuries, probably usually tended to become closed enclaves, in the country but not of it, guarding their own peculiar culture but not consciously reaching out to alter that about them. This was not always the case. Missionaries there were, and zealous and active ones. Yet their successes were sporadic and not of the kind which eventuate in the enduring conversion of peoples and nations.

Chapter VI

THE FIRST GREAT LOSSES OF TERRITORY.
THE RISE AND SPREAD OF ISLAM

IN THE seventh century began great losses to Islam. Indeed, for extensive portions of the Christian world the sharp and important dividing line between the first and second major periods of the spread of Christianity is not the year 500, but the year 622, the *hegira*, the beginning of the Moslem era. In the first six centuries of its history Christianity experienced no major reverse and made no permanent surrender of territory. Persecutions it knew, and severe ones. Some of these proved costly in enrolment. Many of them retarded the spread of Christianity. In some places, as in the Persian Empire, a non-Christian government offered obstacles which never were finally overcome and which set lasting bonds upon the extension of the faith. In other places, as in the Sahara, a natural obstacle opposed an impassable barrier. In Europe the collapse of Roman rule along its northern borders and the irruption of non-Christian invaders brought a destruction to churches and an erasure of Christian communities which for the moment appeared disastrous. In general, however, not only were the lands forfeited through the decay of Roman political rule regained, but Christianity spread northward, far beyond the former boundaries of the Roman Empire, and won peoples who had never known the political sway of Rome. In the West the Church which inherited the name of Rome, and in the East the Church which was closely intertwined with the continuation of the Roman state, brought under the control of Christianity many a people who had never acknowledged and some who never had even heard of the Cæsars.

In the seventh century, however, came a reverse of another kind. In one respect it was like the other invasions which had dealt such severe blows to the decaying Roman Empire: it was an incursion of relatively rude and uncultivated peoples from the fringes of the Mediterranean world. In another and highly important respect it was very different. These Arab invaders were the carriers of a new and vigorous religion which, while paying honour to Jesus, claimed to have a later revelation. In theory this religion tolerated Christianity, but placed the latter's adherents under social and financial disabilities which led many upon whom that faith sat lightly as a conventional

286

inheritance to abandon it for the more profitable creed of the conquerors. The invaders from the North had polytheistic religions which could not stand permanently before the advance of Christianity, or, indeed, of any faith which was actively missionary and, presumably, of a more profound type. Here was an invader whose religion was younger than Christianity and claimed to correct the latter's errors. This faith was aggressive against all religions except Judaism, Christianity, and Zoroastrianism, and at times, in practice, persecuted even these. It had stern laws against apostasy from its own ranks, and as a rule, although not always, welcomed accessions from other systems.

The threat proved the most serious which Christianity had yet faced. By it were lost wider areas than were to be sacrificed until the advent of Russian Communism in the twentieth century. Indeed, in the nine hundred years between the opening of the seventh and the beginning of the sixteenth century, Islam won from Christianity a larger proportion of the latter's adherents and territory than any other rival ever has succeeded in doing. Eighteenth, nineteenth, and twentieth century scepticism and the fascist, socialist, and communist totalitarian states of the twentieth century have not yet cost Christianity nearly so large a percentage of its professed followers as did Islam from the seventh through the fifteenth century. Moreover, Islam was the last religion to emerge after the birth of Jesus which has had an extensive spread or which has proved a major rival to Christianity.

These losses to Islam were in the traditional strongholds and in some of the most highly civilized centres of Christianity. By the year 1500 Islam was dominant in the land of Christianity's birth and Moslem rulers controlled the sacred sites in Bethlehem, Nazareth, and Jerusalem. It was supplanting Christianity in Asia Minor, the area, except possibly Armenia, in which Christians seem first to have been numerically in the majority. In North Africa, early so prominent in Latin Christianity, it had eliminated Christianity except for a few foreign captive slaves. In Egypt and Syria, where Christianity had once been the prevailing religion, the churches had become minority groups, on the defensive and slowly yielding ground. The extensive Christian communities on the upper reaches of the Nile had dwindled to almost nothing. The Ethiopian Church survived, protected by its mountain fastnesses. East of the Euphrates the wide-flung Nestorian and Jacobite communities had shrunk to a few encysted remnants, and numerous peoples among whom Christianity had once made converts had become solidly Moslem. Constantinople, the capital of Greek Christianity, had fallen into Moslem hands, the Œcumenical Patriarchate could be filled only with the approval of a Moslem monarch, and Islam was making headway in the Balkans and in Southern Russia.

In spite of its vast gains in Northern Europe, in 1500 Christianity controlled little, if any, more territory than it had a thousand years before. It had lost to Islam about as much as it had won from paganism.

The advance of Islam against Christianity was not constant. For centuries it all but paused and the boundaries between the two faiths were altered little. Nor were Christians always passive in their resistance. Islam did not permanently retain all the land which it conquered. In the Iberian Peninsula and in Sicily, Christianity regained territory and peoples who had become partially Moslem.

In general the main successes of Islam against Christianity fall into two periods which are separated by several centuries.

The first was in the seventh and eighth centuries, when Islam, in the early flush of its youth and carried on the wave of Arab conquest, achieved a political dominance in Arabia, Syria, Mesopotamia, Persia, Palestine, Egypt, North Africa, and the Iberian Peninsula which was usually followed, often somewhat more slowly, by numerical preponderance.

Then came an interval of nearly five hundred years after the Arab drive slowed down and stopped, when Christianity and Islam seemed to have settled down to a kind of stalemate. Each made some gains as against the other. For example, in the eleventh century the Seljuq Turks, recent converts to Islam, took provinces from the Byzantine Empire and by the middle of the twelfth century Turks had spread over much of Asia Minor. In general the advantage seemed to be with Christianity. That faith was strengthening its base by continued expansion in Northern Europe at the expense of paganism. Against Islam it launched Crusades which for a time wrested from the Crescent territory in Syria and Palestine. A great popular religious awakening in Europe led by the Franciscans and Dominicans carried missionaries of Latin Christianity not only into Moslem lands, but also on the eastern borders of Islam into Central Asia and the Far East. In a new advance, Nestorian Christianity won some of the Turks and Mongols of Central Asia and penetrated once more into China. For a time Christianity seemed about to outflank Islam and to check its further spread in Asia.

Then followed the second period of Moslem victories. These were brought about, not by the Arabs, but by fresh invaders from Central Asia, Turkish and Mongol converts to Islam. At the end of the thirteenth and the beginning of the fourteenth century, after two or three generations of hesitation between the two faiths, the Mongols east of Chinese Turkestan adopted Islam. This sealed the fate of Christianity east of the Euphrates. In the destructive wars of the period Christian communities suffered along with their neighbours. Tribes which had been hesitating between Islam and Christianity became Moslem. Central Asiatic peoples who had formerly been Christian became either Buddhist or Moslem. The Christian minorities once scattered from the Euphrates to the China Sea dwindled or disappeared. Then came the Ottoman Turks, also Moslems, and made Islam dominant politically in Constantinople and the Balkans. Migrations of Moslems and conversions to Islam followed.

Beginning with the eleventh century the gains of Islam at the expense of Christianity were in consequence of the conversion to Islam of the nomads and semi-nomads of Asia. Christianity owed its dominant position in Europe to its missions among the barbarians who fringed the Mediterranean on the north. Islam acquired its territories partly because of the failure of Christianity to win first the peoples of Arabia and then the Turks and Mongols of Asia. In Central Asia the success of Islam was due to the effective barrier which the Zoroastrian Persian Empire placed against the eastward extension of Christianity and to the failure of the Christian Roman Empire to erase the Zoroastrian Sassanids. The Moslem Arabs, arriving on the scene just after the two traditional rivals had been weakened by a peculiarly exhausting renewal of their hereditary warfare, eliminated the Sassanids and their faith and wrested from the Roman Empire some of its fairest domains. Once Islam was established as the ruling power and the dominant faith in Mesopotamia and Persia, its subsequent spread among the peoples of Central and Western Asia was to be expected.

In the sixteenth century Christianity began once more an advance in Asia. In the sixteenth and succeeding centuries both Christianity and Islam won converts in that continent. Neither, however, made extensive gains at the expense of the other. After 1500, neither Islam nor Christianity, as religions, acquired much ground or many converts from the other. The annexation of Moslem territory by professedly Christian powers was not followed by mass movements from Islam to the faith of the new rulers.

As between Christianity and Islam, the former possessed striking advantages. Its ecclesiastical organization and its facilities for missions were more highly developed. In its Church, with its formal admission through baptism and confirmation and its hierarchy, as distinct from civil society, it had a resource which stood it in good stead both for advance into new territory and in defence against an aggressive faith. In its monasteries and, in later centuries, in its missionary societies it produced far more elaborate and specialized agencies for propagating itself than did Islam.

In the present chapter are recounted the gains of Islam from Christianity in the first period and to about the middle of the eleventh century. In some areas the narrative will be carried slightly further. In the succeeding chapter will be told the story of the counter spread of Christianity and of the second era of extensive loss of territory and populations by Christianity to Islam.

Two generalizations must be made which apply to most of the Moslem advances at the expense of Christianity. In the first place, they followed the conquests by Moslem rulers and were confined almost entirely to territories under the control of Moslem governments. Beyond its political borders Islam made only a few scattered converts from Christianity. When Islam expanded, as it often did, outside the territories of Moslem states, nearly always it was at the cost of non-Christian religions and not of Christianity. In the second place, it must be said that forcible conversions from Christianity to Islam were the exception and not the rule. To be sure, such conversions occurred often and in large numbers. Yet the majority of the accessions of Christians to Islam must be attributed to other causes. The most powerful and frequent were, at the outset, a loss of faith in Christianity wrought by the military victories of Islam and the conviction that the divine favour must be with the latter, followed later by the desire to escape the discriminatory taxation and the inferior social status which were the lot of Christians under Moslem rulers. Added to these factors were the migrations of Moslem peoples into territories previously Christian but now under Moslem rulers.

Against faiths other than Judaism and Christianity Islam made freer use of the sword. It is an open question, however, whether in the thousand years between 500 to 1500 force had a larger share in effecting conversion to Islam than to Christianity. No such systematic missionary work was undertaken in the name of Islam as we have seen used to propagate Christianity. Professional missionaries played a much smaller part in the spread of the former than of the latter. Christian monks and monasteries performed a function for the extension of Christianity which Moslem ascetics did not parallel. Yet in the thousand years which we are spanning in this volume the sword seems to have been used as freely to advance the religion of the Cross as it was to propagate that of the Crescent.

From its inception Islam bore something of a Christian stamp. It was not an offshoot of Christianity and should not be classified as a variant of it. In its origin, impulses derived from Jesus did not play nearly so large a part as they did in the rise of the various forms of Gnosticism or even in the inception of Manichæism. The decisive factor in the birth of Islam was Mohammed. Here was a religious genius and leader. So far as outside influences from historic faiths played upon him, these were chiefly Judaism, and from the pre-Islamic faiths of Arabia. Yet Christianity left its impress upon the teachings of

Mohammed and modified profoundly some of the later developments in Islam.

As we have seen, Christianity was widely spread in Arabia on the eve of the rise of Islam. It was particularly strong in the North and in the South. How far Christian ideas had penetrated Arabia is debatable. On the one hand it has been claimed that pre-Islamic Arabia was profoundly influenced by Christianity. It is said that a good deal of knowledge of the Old and New Testaments had spread among the Arabs, that hundreds of traditions attributed to Mohammed were derived from the lives of Christian saints, that the architecture, the painting, the sculpture, and the music of Arabia at the time of Mohammed had Christian origins, that pre-Islamic Arabian poets were either Christians or wrote under Christian influence,[1] and that Christians were the first to make Arabic a literary language.[2] The idea of monotheism is said to have been an importation with Judaism and Christianity as its sources.[3] On the other hand, it is maintained that all of the so-called pre-Islamic poetry may be a later fabrication.[4] It is said that even if the surviving fragments are genuine, while they reflect a superficial knowledge of Christianity, no very great impression was made on them by Christian ideas.[5]

Even though Christian conceptions had spread through parts of Arabia, it is not at all clear that at the outset of his career Mohammed was aware of them or that he ever possessed any great familiarity with them. Mecca, the city of Mohammed's youth and early manhood, seems not to have been a strong Christian centre. The adherents of that faith there appear to have been few in number and poor in quality.[6] Even a casual reading of the Koran quickly discloses a number of passages on Jesus and on Christianity.[7] However, references

---

[1] Cheikho, *Le Christianisme et la Littérature Chrétienne en Arabie avant l'Islam, passim,* and especially Part II, pp. iii, iv.

[2] J. Wellhausen, *Reste arabischen Heidentumes,* in *Skizzen und Vorarbeiten,* Vol. III, p. 201. On pp. 197-203 Wellhausen summarizes what he maintains to have been strong pre-Islamic Christian influence in Arabia. Schubert, *Geschichte der christlichen Kirche im Frühmittelalter,* p. 223, follows Wellhausen in claiming that Christian influences were stronger than Judaism in the rise of Islam.

[3] Torrey, *The Jewish Foundations of Islam,* p. 54, suggests that Arabian monotheism may in its ultimate origin be neither Hebrew nor Christian.

[4] D. S. Margoliouth, *The Origins of Arabic Poetry,* in *The Journal of the Royal Asiatic Society,* 1925, pp. 417-449.

[5] Bell, *The Origin of Islam in its Christian Environment,* pp. 43-49.

[6] Lammens, *L'Arabie Occidentale avant l'Hégire,* pp. 1-49, especially p. 22. In this passage Lammens admits the possibility of a few Christians at Mecca or passing through it, but representing a lay, imperfectly instructed Christianity. See also Clemen, *Der Einfluss des Christentums auf andere Religionen,* pp. 53-81, on this point and on the entire question of the influence of Christianity on Islam.

[7] Koran, ii, 59; iii, 30-50; iv, 168-170; v, 76, 79, 109-118; xvii, 112; xviii, 1-36; xliii, 56-64; lvii, 27; lxi, 6. For a list of passages relating to Jesus, with full translations, see Zwemer, *The Moslem Christ,* pp. 43-53.

to Judaism and to Old Testament characters and narratives are much more frequent and extensive. While the assertion has been made that Mohammed's knowledge of the Old Testament came in part from the Christians,[8] this is unproved and is not generally accepted. The difficulty of effecting a chronological arrangement of the various sections of the Koran makes it difficult to trace accurately the development of Mohammed's thought. Nor are we always sure that the text as we have it is an accurate transcription of Mohammed's words. We have, however, the assertion that at the outset of his career the Prophet possessed no intimate knowledge of either Judaism or Christianity, but that as time passed the amount of material in the Koran relating to the two faiths increased.[9] It is also argued that while Mohammed must early have known something of Christianity,[10] the name of 'Īsā by which he designated Jesus first occurs in the Koran rather late,[11] that only a very few passages seem to reflect a possible dependence on the text of the New Testament, that it is quite unlikely that the Prophet had ever seen the Christian Scriptures,[12] and that Mohammed knew nothing of the basic convictions of Christianity or even of such of its features as were of chief popular interest.[13]

That before his death Mohammed had some information concerning Jesus and Christians is indubitable. It is even said that he knew more of Jesus than of any other religious figure of the past.[14] He emphatically denied that God could have a son,[15] for this seemed to him derogatory to the greatness and the uniqueness of God, but he maintained that Jesus was a prophet, an apostle, and a servant to whom God had been gracious.[16] In one strange passage he seems to believe that the Christian doctrine of the Trinity placed Jesus and Mary as additional gods besides the one god.[17] He gave evidence of knowing little of the events of the life of Jesus and even less of the teachings of the New Testament. He recounted garbled versions of the New Testament account of the angelic salutation to Mary and of the birth of Jesus,[18] he spoke of

[8] Clemen, loc. cit., citing Ahrens, Christliches in Qoran, in Zeitschrift der deutschen morgenländischen Gesellschaft, 1930. See also Bell, op. cit., pp. 66, 67.

[9] Bell, op. cit., pp. 67, 113, 136.

[10] Torrey, op. cit., p. 60.

[11] Torrey, op. cit., pp. 72, 74.

[12] Torrey, op. cit., p. 57.

[13] Torrey, op. cit., p. 60. Torrey advances the thesis that even such knowledge of Christianity as Mohammed possessed may have come through Jewish media.

[14] D. B. Macdonald in Encyc. of Islam, Vol. II, pp. 524-526. On the knowledge of Jesus shown in the Koran, with pertinent passages and an excellent bibliography, see Zwemer, op. cit., pp. 7-56.

[15] Koran, xvii, 112; xviii, 1-4, 36.

[16] Koran, iv, 168-170; v, 76; xviii, 1-36; xliii, 56-64; lxi, 6.

[17] Koran, v, 109-118.

[18] Koran, iii, 30-50; xviii, 1-36.

some of the miracles of Jesus,[19] he mentioned the rejection by the Jews,[20] but he did not include the crucifixion and made only vague references to the resurrection and to the ascension.[21] He had kind things to say of the Christians,[22] as well as severe ones.[23] Some of the very words which he used in the Koran may have come into Arabia through Christianity—although this need not imply that Mohammed was conscious of their derivation.[24]

Judaism and Christianity possibly prepared the way for Islam by weakening the traditional Arabian religions and introducing some of the convictions which Mohammed later incorporated in his teachings. As in Scandinavia the gradual infiltration of Christian ideas led to the disintegration of the old faith and brought familiarity with Christian conceptions, so in Arabia some of the Christian ideology was permeating parts of the land and assisting in the disintegration of the inherited cults.[25] Unlike Scandinavia, however, the adoption of Christianity did not follow, but a religious genius founded a new religion. It is interesting to note that nowhere in Northern Europe did the coming of Christianity prepare the way for the birth and triumph of a new religion. The nearest parallels elsewhere in Christian history are the Gnostics and Mani in the first five centuries and cults which arose in the nineteenth and twentieth centuries among the Maoris, the North American Indians, and the African Negroes subsequent to the coming of the Christian missionary.

The influence of Christianity upon Islam was augmented after the death of Mohammed. The new faith continued to develop and to take on fresh forms and theologies. Upon this growth Christianity had marked effect. As the Moslems conquered Christian populations and as many Christians became converts to Islam, familiarity with Christianity increased, and practices, stories, and concepts entered from the older faith.[26] Many of the Christians conquered by the Moslem Arabs were more cultured than their masters. They instructed their Moslem rulers in the philosophy, the astronomy, the physics, and the

[19] Koran, iii, 30-50; v, 109-118.
[20] Koran, xliii, 56-64.
[21] Koran, iii, 30-50; xviii 1-36.
[22] Koran, ii, 59; iii, 30-50.
[23] Koran, v. 76; xviii, 1-4.
[24] Bell, *op. cit.,* pp. 51, 90.
[25] Bell, *op. cit.,* pp. 55-57; R. A. Nicholson in *The Koran* (Oxford University Press, c. 1928), p. ix.
[26] For a list of quotations from Moslem writers giving Moslem accounts of Jesus see Robson, *Christ in Islam, passim.* See also E. J. Jenkinson, *Jesus in Moslem Tradition* in *Moslem World,* Vol. XVIII (July, 1928), pp. 263-269, and Clemen, *Der Einfluss des Christentums auf andere Religionen,* pp. 53-81. Clemen has an excellent bibliography. Zwemer, *The Moslem Christ,* pp. 79 ff., contains some of the references to Jesus in Moslem tradition.

medicine of the Greeks. Some of the translators of Greek philosophic, scientific, and medical works into Arabic were Christians. Since the garb in which these branches of knowledge reached the Moslems was in part Christian, many Christian ideas were taken over by Moslem scholars. Sometimes, as in Egypt, leading Moslems formed intimate friendships with Christians, including members of the higher clergy, and in this intercourse were influenced by Christianity.[27] Moslem traditions contain many stories which are evidently of Christian origin.[28] It has been suggested that the belief in an Imam-Mahdi and in his second coming which plays so prominent a part in the Shia form of Islam is of Christian provenance,[29] but this is questioned.[30] The early Sunni tradition of the second coming of 'Isā, or Christ, is obviously from the Christians.[31] Several of the Mutazilites, a school of Moslem rationalists, gave a very high place to Christ.[32] Some elements of Christian morality were accepted and put in the form of traditions which were asserted to come from Mohammed himself.[33] It has also been claimed that much of Moslem theology derived its method from the Christian fathers.[34]

It seems fairly well established that the form of Islamic mysticism known as Sufism is deeply indebted to the Christian monasticism which was so prominent in lands first conquered by the Arabs, especially on the northern fringes of Arabia, in Palestine, Syria, and Egypt. The very name of Sufi is from Sūf (wool) and was applied to Moslem ascetics who, imitating the Christian hermits, adopted a coarse woollen garb.[35] Al-Ghazālī (died A.D. 1111), the greatest exponent of Sufi mysticism and asceticism, frequently appealed to the

[27] Smith, *Studies in Early Mysticism in the Near and Middle East, passim;* Browne, *The Eclipse of Christianity in Asia,* p. 51; Bell, *The Origin of Islam in its Christian Environment,* p. 214.

[28] Bell, *op. cit.,* p. 190.

[29] Lammens, *Islam, Beliefs and Institutions* (London, Methuen and Co., 1929, pp. ix, 256), pp. 149-151; Bell, *op. cit.,* p. 206.

[30] Shedd, *Islam and the Oriental Churches* (Philadelphia Presbyterian Board of Publication and Sabbath-School Work, 1904), p. 77.

[31] Lammens, *loc. cit.;* Vasiliev, *History of the Byzantine Empire,* Vol. I, p. 290.

[32] Browne, *op. cit.,* pp. 131, 132.

[33] Browne, *op. cit.,* p. 126.

[34] So the mediæval Jewish scholar Maimonides declared.—Zeitlin, *Maimonides, A Biography* (New York, Bloch Publishing Co., 1935, pp. xi, 234), p. 111.

[35] Bell, *op. cit.,* pp. 200, 201; Nicholson, *The Mystics of Islam,* p. 3. On the part of Christianity in the formation of Sufism, see especially Smith, *op. cit., passim.* Mingana, *Woodbrooke Studies. Christian Documents in Syriac, Arabic,* etc., Vol. III, p. v, says: "Sufism is wholly based on the teaching and practices of the Christian monks and ascetics who inhabited the numerous monasteries strewn in the way of the Arab warriors." This is an extreme view. R. A. Nicholson, in his chapter on *Mysticism* in T. Arnold and A. Guillaume, *The Legacy of Islam* (Oxford, The Clarendon Press, 1931, pp. xvi, 406), pp. 210-238, though allowing some Christian influence, would not go that far.

authority of Christ and to the Gospels, quoting the text in use among the Christians.[36]

We must hasten to add that Sufism was by no means exclusively the product of Christianity in a Moslem environment. Its roots were in primitive Islam. Into it entered many elements, some Neoplatonic, but transmitted through Christians, and some of them Buddhist with no Christian intermediary.[37] The example of Christian mysticism and asceticism was, however, an important factor.

Yet Islam remained Islam. Marked though the influence of Christianity upon it was, in the large majority of its exponents and of its many forms Islam did not become a variant of Christianity. It honoured as its central teacher not the prophet of Nazareth but the prophet of Mecca. The Koran and not the New Testament was its sacred book.

The story of the Arab conquests has often been told, and except in the briefest possible summary needs here no repetition.

It is not at all certain that Mohammed dreamed of the conquest of the Roman and Persian Empires. Nor for the first few years after his death do his immediate successors seem to have done so. Arabs had long been pressing against the defences which the Romans and Persians had set up to protect their borders. In a number of raids the Moslem Arabs proved so successful that conquest and permanent occupation were determined upon. Several conditions favoured their plans. As we have suggested, the Persian and Byzantine realms were weakened by their long and indecisive struggle, and especially by the exhausting wars which they had recently waged with each other. Syria was restive under Byzantine rule and, like the Arabs, was largely Semitic. The disaffection had been accentuated by the efforts of Emperors who adhered to the Greek Orthodox faith to enforce religious uniformity against the Monophysites who were numerically strong in Syria. A similar and drastic effort to reduce the Monophysite Coptic Church to conformity had deepened the gulf between Copt and Greek. Once in Egypt, the Arabs pressed on into North Africa and then, aided by the Berbers, into Spain.

In an amazingly short time, and in spite of dissensions among themselves which retarded the conquest, the Arabs made themselves masters of the southern and eastern shores of the Mediterranean and of the Sassanian domains. Mohammed died in 632. In 636 the conquest of Syria and Palestine seemed certain. The last two Byzantine strongholds in that region, Jerusalem and

[36] Lammens, *Islam, Beliefs and Institutions,* pp. 118-121
[37] Bell, *op. cit.,* pp. 200, 201.

Cæsarea, fell in 638 and 640. By the occupation of Alexandria, in 642, the Arabs had become assured of the speedy possession of all Egypt. By 646 Mesopotamia was conquered, and in 649-650 Fars, the heart of Persia, was overrun. In 697 Carthage, the capital of North Africa, was taken. For a time the Berbers proved a knotty problem, but by 715, with the assistance of Berber forces, the Visigothic rule had been eliminated and practically all of Spain was in Moslem hands. By that year, too, the Arabs had penetrated to the Punjab and far into Central Asia.[38]

More slowly came the Saracen advance into Sicily and Italy. In the ninth century Moslem raids proved serious. At least one of the Popes was constrained to purchase peace by the payment of tribute. By an intermittent warfare lasting seventy-five years, from 827 to 902, Sicily was subjugated. Strongholds were acquired in Southern Italy. Not until 1061 did the Normans begin the Christian reconquest of Sicily, and not until 1091 did they complete it.[39]

In general, as we have suggested, the Arab conquests were not accompanied by forcible conversions from Christianity to Islam. Christians were compelled to pay a special tribute or tax. As a rule they were required to wear a distinguishing mark or garb to indicate their faith.[40] Theoretically they could build no new churches nor could they obtrude their faith on Moslem eyes or ears in public processions or by loud bells. In practice these restrictions were often relaxed, but leniency alternated with attempts at enforcement and with active persecution.[41] At the outset the Arab rulers, far from seeking to win Christians to their faith, often took alarm at conversions: since the special tax levied on Christians was voided by the acceptance of Islam, these meant loss of revenue. Spasmodic attempts were even made to prevent the loss by decreeing that Christians on becoming Moslems must forfeit their landed possessions and retain only their movable property.[42] For a time, the lot of Monophysites was easier under Arab than it had been under Byzantine rule, for no efforts were made, as they had been by the Orthodox, to stamp out these heresies.

[38] See a convenient summary by C. H. Becker, in *Cambridge Medieval History*, Vol. II, pp. 329-378.

[39] Becker, in *op. cit.*, Vol. II, pp. 383-390. Lynn White, Jr., *The Byzantinization of Sicily*, in *The American Historical Review* (Oct., 1936), Vol. XLII, pp. 1-21, shows that Greek refugees from the Persian and Arab invasions in the East and in North Africa helped to strengthen the Greek influence in the Christianity in Italy and Sicily.

[40] The principle of a distinctive garb for Christians may not have been a Moslem invention. It seems to have existed in Persia under the Sassanids.—W. A. Wigram, *An Introduction to the History of the Assyrian Church* (London, Society for Promoting Christian Knowledge, 1910, p. 318), pp. 230, 231.

[41] Bell, *The Origin of Islam in its Christian Environment*, pp. 179, 185-188; Tritton, *Caliphs and Their Non-Muslim Subjects*, pp. 113-136; Arnold, *The Preaching of Islam*, pp. 55 ff.

[42] Tritton, *op. cit.*, pp. 127-136.

So, too, in the former Sassanian realms, the Nestorians fared better under the Caliphs.[43]

Yet slowly or rapidly, under Moslem rule the Christian churches declined in numbers and probably in vitality. They suffered from leakages to Islam. Sometimes religious conviction, sometimes economic and social advantage, and occasionally active persecution made for losses to the dominant faith. The movement was almost entirely in one direction, for, as we have suggested, Moslem law made death the penalty for unrepentant apostasy from Islam,[44] and it was the rare individual who had the conviction and the courage to make the break. Debates there were between Moslems and Christians, and many Christian apologies against Islam were composed. It is doubtful, however, whether these won many converts. They may rather have been chiefly defensive, to strengthen the morale of Christians against Moslem propaganda.[45] Only when territory passed into the hands of Christian rulers could any large numbers of Moslems be expected to go over to the Church. More and more Christianity became identified with particular minority enclaves. It may be, too, that by natural increase as well as by conversions the Moslem elements in the population outstripped the Christians. Polygamy may have made for this result, particularly since so many of the wives were taken from the Christians as captives or slaves.[46]

The fate of the churches was not the same in every land. We must proceed to sketch it country by country. Usually our information is fragmentary and imperfect. We catch only glimpses, generally confused, of the process by which Islam became dominant numerically in so many of the regions where Christianity had prevailed.

In Arabia itself Christianity did not immediately disappear. Some Christian Arabs early embraced Islam.[47] Within a few years after the death of Mohammed, Omar, in response to what was believed to be a saying of the Prophet that two religions could not be at the same time in the peninsula, expelled at least some of the Jews and Christians from Arabia.[48] Yet Mohammed himself is said to have granted protection to the Christians of Najran, and it was in spite of his promise that many of them were removed to Iraq. The number of Christians in Najran is said to have declined in eighty years from forty

---

[43] Schubert, *Geschichte der christlichen Kirche im Frühmittelalter*, pp. 228, 229.

[44] Zwemer, *The Law of Apostasy in Islam*, pp. 33-54; Tritton, *op. cit.*, p. 181.

[45] Browne, *The Eclipse of Christianity in Asia*, pp. 109 ff.; Mingana, *Woodbrooke Studies*, Vol. II, pp. 1-162.

[46] J. W. Thompson, *Economic and Social History of the Middle Ages (300-1300)* (New York, The Century Co., 1928, pp. ix, 900), p. 194.

[47] Bell, *op. cit.*, pp. 181-183; Arnold, *The Preaching of Islam*, p. 47.

[48] Browne, *op. cit.*, pp. 34, 35.

thousand to eight thousand.[49] The Christian communities in Yemen seem long to have survived, for we hear of a bishop of that region in the second quarter of the ninth century.[50] In Hira, on the edge of Mesopotamia, which we have seen to be a strong Christian centre, the population are reported to have insisted that they were Arabs, but to have chosen to pay the discriminatory tax levied on Christians to the acceptance of Islam.[51] In the fourth quarter of the eighth century, Arabs, the Banū Tanūkh, near Aleppo, were Christians. The Caliph compelled them to become Moslems to the number of about five thousand men.[52] Yet as late as 823 some of this tribe remained Christian.[53] We hear, too, of another Arab Christian tribe, the Banū Taghlib, some of whom aided in the Arab conquest, but many of whom for half a century or more held to their Christian faith.[54] In the nineteenth century some Arabs still recalled that their ancestors had been Christians, and one tribe, which was neither Moslem nor Christian, was alleged to have had a Christian past.[55]

In Syria the Arabs appear not to have been unwelcome. Some of the Monophysites preferred Moslem Arab to Greek Orthodox Byzantine rule,[56] but this does not mean that they therefore were inclined to accept the new faith. As we have seen in an earlier volume, many among the non-Greek population in Syria were late in becoming Christians. Even in the latter part of the sixth century, paganism survived in Phœnicia and Philistia.[57] Probably Christianity sat rather lightly upon the descendants of those who had been so recently converted, especially when this had been done by force. It is not impossible that fairly soon after the Arab conquest numbers of the rural population of Syria, out of harmony as they were with the Greek-speaking towns, became Moslems.[58] We hear that among the converts were many of the lower clergy, several of the bishops, and eventually two Jacobite Patriarchs.[59] We read of the

---

[49] Browne, *op. cit.*, pp. 34-36.

[50] Thomas of Marga, *The Book of Governors,* translation by Budge, Vol. II, p. 448. For the date see Vol. I, p. xxvi. For other hints of the late survival of Christianity in Yemen, see Browne, *op. cit.*, pp. 12, 35.

[51] Arnold, *op. cit.*, pp. 50, 51; Browne, *op. cit.*, p. 31.

[52] *The Chronography of . . . Bar Hebræus,* translations by Budge, Vol. I, p. 117.

[53] Browne, *op. cit.*, p. 59.

[54] Browne, *op. cit.*, pp. 32-34; Arnold, *op. cit.*, p. 49.

[55] Palgrave, *Narrative of a Year's Journey through Central and Eastern Arabia (1862-1863)* (London, Macmillan and Co., 2 vols., 1865), Vol. I, pp. 61, 118, 119, 150.

[56] Arnold, *op. cit.*, pp. 54, 55.

[57] Schultze, *Geschichte des Untergangs des griechisch-römischen Heidentums* (Jena, Hermann Costenable, 2 vols., 1887, 1892), Vol. II, p. 251.

[58] Bouchier, *A Short History of Antioch* (Oxford, Basil Blackwell, 1921, pp. xii, 324), p. 203.

[59] Shedd, *Islam and the Oriental Churches,* p. 152.

Nosairis, a religious group who originated in the tenth century and who are ostensibly a Moslem sect, who present a bizarre mixture of Christian, pagan, and Moslem elements. However, they may never have been Christians, but may have passed over directly from paganism to Islam.[60] We hear, too, of crypto-Christians among the heterodox tribes of Asia Minor,[61] former Christians who outwardly had accepted Islam.

The boundary between the Byzantine Empire and the Caliphate was not constant. In the latter half of the tenth century, for instance, the former regained Cilicia and occupied parts of Syria. In the captured areas the Moslem population was taxed, the Christians were released from imposts, and freedom of conversion in either direction between Islam and Christianity was guaranteed.[62] Whether the Church regained any of its lost children is, however, not clear.

In the Caucasus the Christian state of Georgia repeatedly suffered from Moslem attacks. In the seventh century Arabs acquired the overlordship of the land and in the ninth and eleventh centuries Turks wasted the country. How far Georgians embraced Islam is not certain. Again and again native rulers threw off the foreign yoke, and Christianity seems to have been associated with the national spirit.[63]

In the ninth century the Moslems established a strong foothold in Crete[64] and compelled part of the Christian populace to accept Islam, but in the third quarter of the following century Nicephorus Phocas reconquered the island for the Eastern Empire.[65] The Arabs repeatedly raided Cyprus and carried away many of the population. Nicephorus Phocas recovered the island and it remained in the hands of the Empire until the latter part of the twelfth century, when it passed to the Western Crusaders.[66] In neither Crete nor Cyprus does the Moslem occupation of these early centuries seem to have brought any large proportion of the population to accept Islam.

In the former Persian Empire, it will be recalled, Christians at first fared rather better under Arab Moslem rule than they had under the Sassanids. To

---

[60] Lammens, *Islam, Beliefs and Institutions,* pp. 169-176.

[61] Hasluck, *Christianity and Islam under the Sultans,* Vol. II, pp. 469-473.

[62] Vasiliev, *History of the Byzantine Empire,* Vol. I, pp. 374, 375.

[63] Tamarati, *L'Eglise Géorgienne,* pp. 70-79; S. C. Malan, *A Short History of the Georgian Church,* pp. 82 ff.

[64] J. B. Bury, *A History of the Eastern Roman Empire from the Fall of Irene to the Accession of Basil I* (London, Macmillan and Co., 1912, pp. xv, 530), pp. 288-290. A. A. Vasiliev, *Byzance et les Arabes,* Vol. I (Brussels, Institut de Philologie et d'Histoire Orientales, 1935), pp. 49-57.

[65] Vasiliev, *History of the Byzantine Empire,* Vol. I, p. 374.

[66] Hackett, *A History of the Orthodox Church of Cyprus . . . A.D. 45-A.D. 878* (London, Methuen and Co., 1901, pp. xviii, 720), p. 50.

be sure, they were placed under disabilities. Some of these, such as the wearing of a distinctive dress and the payment of a special tax in lieu of military service, appear not to have been unlike those which they had formerly known.[67] Others, such as the prohibition of the construction of new church buildings,[68] seem to have been more restrictive than the regulations of the Sassanids. Yet, as we have suggested, at the outset the educated Christians were more highly cultivated than their Arab masters; some of them held high places at court,[69] and through Christian teachers the Arabs were introduced to much of the learning which had in turn been derived from the Greeks.[70] Moreover, while its Mesopotamian centres were under the Abbasid Caliphs, this trans-Euphrates Christianity seems to have a much greater extension in Central and Eastern Asia than it had enjoyed under the Sassanids.

In spite of the partial improvement in their situation, the Christian communities under Moslem Arab rule in the Tigris-Euphrates Valley, in Persia, and in Central Asia suffered losses and remained minority groups. Thus, on the testimony of a contemporary Nestorian Patriarch, although they had not been persecuted, many Christians of Persia, and especially in Merv, accepted Islam soon after the Arab conquest.[71] The Caliph Omar II (717-720) was zealous in encouraging missions, granted converts remission from the special poll tax levied on non-Moslems, and was rewarded by seeing a large number come over to Islam.[72] In the course of the centuries several bishops and metropolitans were converted. Some of them seem to have taken the step because they were disgruntled in the Church or had been disciplined. In most instances, however, we cannot be sure of their motives.[73] From time to time a Caliph or a governor instituted persecutions. These usually took the form of enforcing the existing statutes by requiring a distinguishing mark for Christians and tearing down new churches.[74] Occasionally anti-Christian mobs wrought destruction. Altercations among the Christians themselves made for

[67] Browne, *The Eclipse of Christianity in Asia,* p. 44; Wigram, *An Introduction to the History of the Assyrian Church,* pp. 63, 190, 230, 231.

[68] Browne, *op. cit.,* p. 45.

[69] Bell, *The Origin of Islam in its Christian Environment,* pp. 180, 181. *The Chronography of . . . Bar Hebræus,* translation by Budge, Vol. I, p. 115, speaks of a Christian physician who in the eighth century was in high favour with the Caliph.

[70] Bell, *loc. cit.*

[71] Arnold, *The Preaching of Islam,* pp. 81, 82, giving a translation of the text. The text is cited from Assemanus, *Bibliotheca Orientalis Clementino-Vaticana,* Vol. III, Pt. I, pp. 130, 131.

[72] Arnold, *op. cit.,* pp. 82, 83.

[73] Arnold, *op. cit.,* pp. 86, 87.

[74] *The Chronography of . . . Bar Hebræus,* translation by Budge, Vol. I, pp. 127, 141; Browne, *op. cit.,* pp. 58-60.

weakness.[75] We know, too, that in at least one instance the decay of a monastery was brought about in part by the heavy taxes exacted by Moslem governors.[76] Christianity fared better than Zoroastrianism, perhaps because it displayed greater vitality, and possibly because it was in less disfavour with the Arabs. The collapse of Zoroastrianism, however, seems to have brought few if any new converts to the Church. One state faith displaced another, and the new, Islam, became the heir of the old. In Persia Islam developed characteristics peculiar to that country and to a larger extent than Christianity ever had done became identified with the genius of the race.[77] This was not necessarily from greater adaptability, but was probably because of its position as the official religion.

In Egypt at the time of the Arab conquest, as we have said, the churches were weakened by prolonged strife and were poorly prepared to resist the coming of a new religion. For many years the Byzantine Emperors had intermittently been attempting to coerce the Monophysite Copts to conform to the Orthodox faith. The struggle was intensified by racial differences and nationalist sentiment. On the one hand the Copts were the native Egyptian element. On the other the Orthodox, or Melchites, were drawn chiefly from the Greek-speaking sections of the populations and were identified with Byzantine imperialism. As in Syria and Palestine, so in Egypt, on the eve of the Arab invasion the churches had suffered, along with the rest of the life of the community, from the brief Persian occupation—even though the Persians had been religiously tolerant.[78] Then, after the Persians had been expelled, the Emperor Heraclius appointed one Cyrus as Patriarch and civil Governor of Egypt, with the commission to bring the Copts into line with the imperial Church. Cyrus employed severe measures, the Coptic Patriarch, Benjamin, went into hiding, and the Coptic Church became very disorganized.[79]

Cyrus was still at his post when the Arab invasion began. For some reason he offered a weak resistance, assented to Arab terms, and made a treaty which Heraclius would not ratify. Then after the death of Heraclius and his own reappointment to Egypt, Cyrus surrendered Alexandria to the Arabs—and that in spite of the fact that the defences of the city were supposed to be all but impregnable.[80] Thus what was one of the largest cities in the world of its day passed into Moslem hands. In possession of the key positions in the Delta,

[75] Browne, op. cit., pp. 53-58.
[76] Thomas of Marga, Book of Governors, translation by Budge, Vol. I, p. lxvi.
[77] Shedd, Islam and the Oriental Churches, p. 166.
[78] Butler, The Arab Conquest of Egypt, pp. 87, 88, 91.
[79] Butler, The Arab Conquest of Egypt, pp. 155, 174-193.
[80] Butler, op. cit., pp. 259-357.

the Arabs easily completed the subjugation of the rest of the land. It is quite unproved that the Copts assisted the Arabs. Rather it was Cyrus, the Melchite Patriarch and Governor, who facilitated their triumph and who by his persecution left the Coptic Church seriously crippled. Yet in the main the leaders of the Copts seem to have looked upon the Arab conquest with relief and as preferable to Byzantine religious persecution.[81]

As in Syria and Palestine, in Egypt the restrictions imposed by the Arabs upon the Monophysites were less onerous than those of the Orthodox Byzantine rule. The usual discriminatory tax was placed on Christians, and by at least the tenth century Christians were commanded not to attempt to win a Moslem from his faith, to marry Moslem women, to speak disparagingly of the Prophet or the Koran, to display crosses, to mourn their dead publicly, to sound their bells or play their music in such a manner as to force them on Moslem ears, to build houses higher than those of the Moslems, to ride thoroughbred horses, to drink wine in public, or to allow swine to be seen. They were, too, to wear a distinctive garb.[82]

Under the relatively mild Arab rule, the Coptic Church revived. The Patriarch Benjamin came out of hiding and gave the Church strong leadership. The Arabs prevented the Copts from taking revenge on their enemies and the Melchite Church survived.[83] Since most of the Byzantine officials had left after the conquest and at first the Arabs were in need of non-Arab officials, Copts were widely employed in the government.[84] Christian artists and architects, too, were used, and did much to develop the forms which are associated with the Arab name.[85] The monasteries were the strongholds of the Coptic faith and often friendly relations existed between their abbots and the Moslem rulers.[86]

Yet under the Arabs, tolerant though they were at first, the Coptic Church permanently lost ground as it had never done under the Byzantine régime. At the very outset many Christians, both Copts and Melchites, went over to Islam.[87] The fall of revenue derived from taxation, more than fifty per cent by the time the conquest was a generation old, seems to indicate a mass apostasy from Christianity.[88]

As time passed, the lot of the Copts became harder. Early in the eighth

[81] Lynn White, Jr., in *The American Historical Review* (Oct., 1936), Vol. XLII, p. 10.
[82] Butler, *op. cit.*, pp. 447-456.
[83] Butler, *op. cit.*, pp. 439-443, 447.
[84] Butler, *op. cit.*, pp. 447-456.
[85] Butcher, *The Story of the Church of Egypt*, Vol. I, p. 372.
[86] Butler, *op. cit.*, pp. 469-492.
[87] Butler, *op. cit.*, p. 363; Arnold, *The Preaching of Islam*, pp. 103-106.
[88] Arnold, *op. cit.*, p. 103.

century heavy financial burdens were placed on Christians, and in despair many became Moslems.[89] About the middle of the same century four successive Caliphs so persecuted the Christians that several bishops forsook their sees and numbers of Christians turned Moslem.[90] Often in that century the Copts rose in revolt and as often were suppressed.[91] In the first quarter of the eleventh century Hakim, the mad Caliph, instituted a severe persecution and demolished churches.[92] Some conversions there were from Islam, but these were visited with severe penalties. In the latter part of the tenth century, for instance, two prominent Moslems became Christians. Both were persecuted and one met a martyr's death.[93] Yet, against all obstacles, the Coptic Church persisted, the most vigorous of all the Christian churches of Africa.

In Egypt, Syria, Palestine, and Mesopotamia, as Arabic became the dominant language, a Christian literature in that tongue proved necessary if the churches were to hold and instruct their constituencies. It speaks well for the vitality of these churches that this literature was prepared. In the eighth century an Arabic translation of the Psalms appeared, and there were other translations of portions of the Bible. In producing this literature Jacobites, Nestorians, and Copts were all active.[94]

In Nubia the Church founded in the sixth century survived for many centuries. To be sure, about the middle of the seventh century, in connexion with their conquest of Egypt, the Arabs invaded Nubia and took Dongola, its capital. Yet Nubian Christianity continued to flourish and had close connexions with the Copts. In the eighth century a Nubian army marched into Lower Egypt to relieve its persecuted fellow Christians. Early in the eleventh century a King of Nubia built churches and monasteries, and in the twelfth century Dongola was reported to be a large city with several churches.[95] Recent archæology has disclosed the remains of many churches in the region.[96] Beginning in the thirteenth century, we begin to hear of the decay of Chris-

[89] Butcher, op. cit., Vol. I, pp. 395, 396.
[90] Butcher, op. cit., Vol. I, p. 407.
[91] Butcher, op. cit., Vol. I, pp. 412-439; Tritton, The Caliphs and Their Non-Muslim Subjects, p. 144.
[92] Butcher, op. cit., Vol. II, pp. 23-33.
[93] Butcher, op. cit., Vol. II, pp. 8-19.
[94] Brockelmann, Die syrische und die christlich-arabische Litteratur, in Geschichte der christlichen Litteraturen des Orients (Leipzig, C. F. Amelangs Verlag, 1907), p. 67.
[95] Budge, A History of Ethiopia, Vol. I, pp. 117-119; Budge, The Egyptian Sûdân, Vol. I, pp. ix, x, Vol. II, pp. 185-187, 298-300; Adeney, The Greek and Eastern Churches, p. 620; Budge, Legends of Our Lady the Perpetual Virgin and her Mother Hannâ, p. xlii.
[96] New York Times, March 17, 1933, p. 17.

tianity and of the building of mosques.[97] Yet Christianity was to persist for centuries longer.

In North Africa the Christian communities disappeared more quickly and completely than in any other of the major regions on the Mediterranean littoral. Probably the reason is to be found in their character. While some converts had been made among them, most of the Berbers seem to have remained non-Christian.[98] It was in the cities, among the population of immigrant descent, that the Church was strongest. This was in striking contrast with Egypt and Spain and even with Syria and Palestine.

When the Arabs invaded Egypt, many Christians fled to North Africa. Among the refugees were priests, monks, and nuns, some of whom began an active propaganda for their own schools of Christianity and so led to dissensions.[99] When the Arabs moved on to North Africa and took it, a large proportion of the Christian population seems to have migrated to Spain, Italy, Greece, Gaul, and even Germany. The migration was hastened by the hard choice offered by the Caliph Omar II of apostasy or exile.[100] Some of the Christians went over to Islam, perhaps to save their possessions.[101] Numbers of Christians were killed in the conquest.[102] However, some of the clergy and the faithful survived and stayed on. In Carthage the Archbishop remained and watched over the bones of Cyprian. In the eleventh century there were still five bishops. Yet the few Christians were divided and we hear of an Archbishop imprisoned by the Arabs at the instigation of members of his own flock.[103] In the eleventh century Pope Leo IX, an advocate of the Cluny movement, sought to revive the Church in Africa.[104] In 1074 in the city of Ipona the Christians elected an Archbishop, and, since the three bishops necessary for consecration could not be found, the Moslem ruler sent him to Rome for the rite. Pope Gregory VII dispatched letters by him lamenting the condition of the Church in North Africa and endeavouring to strengthen it. Christians were still to be found there, although

---

[97] Budge, *The Egyptian Sûdân*, Vol. I, pp. ix, x.

[98] Iselin, *Der Untergang der christlichen Kirche in Nordafrika*, pp. 58-60.

[99] Leclercq, *L'Afrique Chrétienne*, Vol. II, pp. 300-314.

[100] Leclercq, *op. cit.*, Vol. II, p. 314; Da Civezza, *Storia delle Missioni Francescane*, Vol. VI, pp. 49-51; Lynn White, Jr., in *The American Historical Review* (Oct., 1936), Vol. XLII, p. 11, n. 52, p. 12.

[101] Mesnage, *Le Christianisme en Afrique*, Vol. II, pp. 133-138.

[102] Da Civezza, *loc. cit.*

[103] Da Civezza, *loc. cit.*; Bouchier, *Life and Letters in Roman Africa*, pp. 116, 117. On surviving Christians and sees towards the end of the ninth century, see Mesnage, *L'Afrique Chrétienne. Evêches et Ruines Antiques*, pp. 367, 379; Da Civezza, *op. cit.*, Vol. VI, pp. 49-51.

[104] Letter of Leo IX in Migne, *Pat. Lat.*, Vol. CXLIII, Cols. 729-731.

many of them were captives and not native born.[105] In 1160 Christians, persecuted in Africa, fled to Sicily.[106] We hear of a bishop in Morocco in 1246[107] and of Christians in North Africa as late as the fourteenth century.[108] Until the eighteenth century or early in the nineteenth Christianity was represented by captives taken by North African corsairs, but indigenous Christianity seems to have perished long before 1500. Modern travellers and missionaries believe that among some tribes of North Africa and the Sahara, notably the Kabils and the Tuaregs, they discover customs and beliefs derived from a Christianity which the ancestors of these peoples once professed.[109]

In the conquest of Spain, only a very few martyrdoms are recorded.[110] The restrictions placed on Christians seem to have been lighter than in almost any other section of the Arab empire.[111] Christians, while regarded with a certain scorn, were allowed to practise their faith undisturbed. Clergy and monks could appear in public in their professional garb.[112] Only under the Berber dynasties (the Almoravides and the Almohades) of the eleventh and twelfth centuries was there much anti-Christian fanaticism,[113] and this may have been partly a reaction against the growing Christian political power in the North. Yet a large number of professed Christians seem to have gone over to Islam. Slaves on whom the Christianity of their old masters had slight hold appear quickly to have taken up the faith of the new conquerors. Many also of the middle classes and of the nobility became Moslems.[114] Even some of the clergy, including one archbishop, apostatized.[115] Christian wives of Arab and Berber Moslems were common and their off-

---

[105] Letters of Gregory VII in Migne, *Pat. Lat.*, Vol. CXLVIII, Cols. 449-451.

[106] Leclercq, *op. cit.*, Vol. II, p. 314.

[107] Arnold, *The Preaching of Islam*, p. 127.

[108] Arnold, *op. cit.*, p. 129.

[109] Mesnage, *Le Christianisme en Afrique: Déclin et Extinction*, p. 192; D. Campbell, *Tuareg Trails* (London, Pickering and Inglis, c. 1913, pp. 39), p. 5; *Wanderings in Widest Africa* (London, The Religious Tract Society, 1930), p. 76; J. Bouniol, editor, *The White Fathers and Their Missions* (London, Sands and Co., 1929, pp. 334), pp. 140, 141. Moslems sent missionaries to the Kabils after 1492 to convert them to Islam, claiming that they were without God or religion and might have some traces of their former Christianity.—Arnold, *op. cit.*, pp. 127, 128.

[110] Haines, *Christianity and Islam in Spain*, A.D. 756-1031, pp. 29-31. An older account of the Moslem conquest of Spain is to be found in R. Dozy, *Geschichte der Mauren in Spanien . . . 711-1110* (German edition, Vols. 1, 2, Leipzig, 1874, French edition, Vols. 3, 4, Leyden, E. J. Brill, 1861).

[111] Haines, *op. cit.*, p. 18; Arnold, *The Preaching of Islam*, p. 135.

[112] Haines, *op. cit.*, pp. 60-62, 93, 94; Arnold, *op. cit.*, p. 135.

[113] Arnold, *op. cit.*, pp. 142, 143; R. Altamira in *Cambridge Medieval History*, Vol. VI, pp. 398, 399; J. B. Trend in Arnold and Guillaume, *The Legacy of Islam*, p. 10.

[114] Haines, *op. cit.*, pp. 21, 26, 27; Arnold, *op. cit.*, pp. 132, 140.

[115] Arnold, *op. cit.*, pp. 133, 134.

spring were reared as Moslems.[116] It may have been that some remnant of the Arian attitude, with its tendency towards a Christology more nearly akin to that of the Moslems, facilitated conversions.[117] These converts from Christianity and their descendants—Muwallahs they were called—may have formed the largest group of the population.[118] They were often looked at askance by Berbers and Arabs,[119] much as in later centuries Jewish and Moslem converts to Christianity were regarded with jaundiced eyes by other Christians in Spain.

Those who remained Christian were modified by their contacts with Moslems. We hear of Christians, and even clergy, submitting to circumcision. The morale of the Church declined. Councils were summoned by Moslem rulers and sometimes Jews and Moslems sat in them. Many of the clergy, including the bishops, owed their offices to Moslem rulers, and some are said to have purchased their posts and others to have been little better than atheists.[120] Latin, the language of the Church and of Christian theology, began to give place to Arabic, and with its decline came a growing lack of familiarity with Christian literature.[121] A form of the adoptionist heresy which for a time spread in Spain and which regarded Jesus as by birth simply man, may have been the product of contact with Islam.[122] About the middle of the ninth century a few monks brought martyrdom on themselves by reviling Islam and Mohammed, but the majority of Christians deemed their zeal indiscreet.[123] At least one effort was made to amalgamate Christianity and Islam to form a new religious sect.[124] But for the reconquest by the Christian states of the North, Christianity seemed in process of losing its vitality and eventually of disappearing from Spain.

For a time in the eighth century Islam penetrated north of the Pyrenees and for about half a century the call to prayer of the *muezzin* was heard in Southern Gaul.[125]

In the seventh and eighth centuries, due partly to Greek refugees from Persian and Arab invasions in the East and in North Africa, Latin Chris-

[116] Trend in *op. cit.*, p. 6.

[117] Arnold, *op. cit.*, p. 134.

[118] Haines, *op. cit.*, pp. 99-106.

[119] *Ibid.*

[120] Haines, *op. cit.*, pp. 33, 74-86, 149-156.

[121] P. G. Bridge, *Ramon Lull* (Madras, Christian Literature Society for India, 1932, pp. 107), p. 23; Haines, *op. cit.*, pp. 74-77; Arnold, *op. cit.*, pp. 137, 138.

[122] Haines, *op. cit.*, pp. 107-114.

[123] Arnold, *op. cit.*, pp. 141, 142; Haines, *op. cit.*, pp. 32-54, 58-73.

[124] Haines, *op. cit.*, pp. 115, 116.

[125] T. Hodgkin, *Italy and Her Invaders* (Oxford, The Clarendon Press, 8 vols., 1892-1899), Vol. VI, p. 419.

tianity had been supplanted in Sicily by that of the Greek type.[126] In the ninth century the Moslems began their conquest of Sicily from the Byzantine Empire.[127] Dissensions among the invaders and stubborn resistance by the defenders retarded the progress of Moslem arms, and not until the latter half of the tenth century did the last Christian stronghold fall. Many of the conquered turned Moslem, but Christianity and the Greek tongue persisted even though adhered to by diminished numbers.[128]

The Europe which remained ostensibly Christian felt Islamic influence. For instance, some thirteenth-century sects declared Islam to be as true as Christianity.[129]

In the second half of the ninth century and early in the tenth century the outlook for Christianity seemed darker than at any time since the persecution of Diocletian and more doubtful than it was ever again to be. Islam, carried on the wave of Arab conquest, was politically supreme on fully half of the shores of the Mediterranean, and in its territories the churches, while tolerated, were progressively suffering huge numerical losses. Italy was being raided and the Pope constrained to pay tribute. Most of the centres of ancient culture were in Moslem hands, and the Arabs, apt pupils under their Christian instructors, were becoming the leaders in civilization. Out of the material given them by the classical and Christian past they were creating a brilliant culture. Only in the Byzantine Empire did a Christian culture exist which could be deemed at all equal to the culture led by the Moslem Arabs. In Italy, Gaul, and Germany the torch of Christian civilization, after flaming up for a brief moment under the great Carolingians, was flickering and burning low. The pagan Northmen were threatening its extinction. In the Christianity of the British Isles decline had set in, relieved only temporarily by Alfred. Pressed from the south by the youthful Islam championed by the victorious Arabs, and threatened from the north by the ruthless Scandinavians, Christianity, like the remnants of the Roman name and rule with which it had been so long and so closely asociated, may well have seemed doomed. The future appeared to lie not with it but with Islam. Only in Central Europe and the Balkans among the Slavs and the Bulgars was Christianity making headway against the forces which threatened to engulf it.

[126] Lynn White, Jr., *The Byzantinization of Sicily,* in *The American Historical Review* (Oct., 1936), Vol. XLII, pp. 1-21.
[127] A. A. Vasiliev, *Byzance et les Arabes* (Brussels, 1935), Vol. I, *passim*.
[128] *Cambridge Medieval History*, Vol. IV, p. 147.
[129] J. A. McCulloch, *Medieval Faith and Fable* (Boston, Marshall Jones Co., 1933, pp. 345), p. 239.

Chapter VII

THE COUNTER-ADVANCE AGAINST ISLAM (BY FORCE IN SPAIN AND SICILY AND THROUGH THE CRUSADES AND BY PERSUASION THROUGH THE MISSIONS OF THE THIRTEENTH, FOURTEENTH, AND FIFTEENTH CENTURIES) FOLLOWED BY THE SECOND GREAT LOSSES OF TERRITORY (THROUGH THE MONGOLS AND TURKS)

FROM the fate of slow extinction which towards the end of the ninth century seemed impending, deliverance came to Christianity through a variety of channels. The Arab advance slowed down and finally stopped. Internal dissensions and rising tribal, personal, family, and regional differences brought to an end the always fragile unity of the Arab Empire. Confronted by the hard realities of human nature, of human society, and of geography, the ideal of an inclusive brotherhood proved as elusive among the followers of the Prophet as it had among those of the Christ. The Arab conquerors, as had others before and after them, succumbed to the fruits of their successes. Intermarriage with non-Arab stocks, the softening and debilitating consequences of luxury, and internecine feuds brought disintegration and decay. Except for the Berbers and, later, the Seljuq Turks, for the moment no new converts came into the fold who proved capable of carrying forward into fresh territory the banners which had halted in the hands of the now prosperous but satiated Arabs.

Moreover, Christianity displayed remarkable powers of recuperation. The Church of the Byzantine Empire, which in the seventh and eighth centuries had lost so heavily to the Arabs and Islam and several of whose home provinces had been overrun by non-Christian Slavs, Avars, Magyars, and Bulgars, revived, and in the ninth and tenth centuries assimilated the invaders within its borders and extended its frontiers far northward. In the tenth and eleventh centuries Latin Christianity won the Northmen—not only those in lands hitherto Christian but also in Scandinavia itself. The Byzantine Empire regained some of the territory which it had lost to the Arabs. From Western Christendom arose movements which sought to retake part of the ground forfeited to Islam. First came the use of armed force—reconquests in the

Iberian Peninsula, in Italy and Sicily, and the Crusades. Next came the way of persuasion—through a missionary movement which in geographic extent was unprecedented in Christian history. The Nestorians, too, once more moved their outposts into the Far East. For a time Islam seemed outflanked.

Then, in the fourteenth and fifteenth centuries, fresh reverses arrived. The Mongols of Persia, after hesitating between Christianity and Islam, became ardent and aggressive Moslems. The Ottoman Turks, also loyal Moslems, wiped out the shaken remnants of the Byzantine Empire and carried the Crescent into Greece and the Balkans. The Christian communities east of the Euphrates disappeared or dwindled to feeble shadows of their former selves. Disasters, dissensions, and decay of religious conviction in Western Christendom brought weakness and apathy to the once promising missionary enterprise. In 1500 the outlook for Christianity, although not quite so dark as six centuries before, was far from encouraging.

To a fuller summary of the events and movements outlined so briefly in these introductory paragraphs—except those which have been covered in previous chapters—we must now address ourselves.

The first of these movements, the break-up of the Arab Empire and the slowing down of the advance of the frontiers of Islam, need be no more than mentioned. Divisions among the Arabs had been chronic since the death of the Prophet. However, until 750 some semblance of a united realm had been preserved. Then, when the Umayyad Caliphate came to an end, the inclusive Moslem Arab state perished with it. In Persia ruled the Abbasids, and in other sections of the Moslem world independent realms emerged. In most of these, non-Arab elements mixed with the Arabs. The force of the Arab advance was spent and for centuries gains of new territory by the successor states were local and relatively few.

Of the Christian achievements in winning the Scandinavians, the Slavs, the Magyars, and the Bulgars we have told in previous chapters. These were advances against polytheism, not against Islam, and need be mentioned only to call attention to the fact that while in the name of Christianity prolonged, energetic, and, in some sectors, successful campaigns were being waged to retrieve the ground lost to Islam, in Northern Europe the frontiers of Christianity were also being pushed forward. In 1500 Latin Christianity had only recently completed its nominal conversion of Western Europe, and in Eastern Europe Orthodox Christianity was still being extended in the Russian domains. Obviously this persistent missionary effort was an indication of vigour. With the exception of some of the Russians, it was carried on only by those peoples whose rulers were Christian.

Another of the movements of these centuries was the advance of the Christian frontiers by the Christian states of the East. Of the various Christian states of the East, the Byzantine Empire was the largest. Politically the Armenians were never able to do more than preserve their independence. Usually they could not accomplish even that. Generally they were a subject people. Sassanids, Greeks, Arabs, Seljuqs, Mamluks, Tartars, and Ottoman Turks in succession subdued the land. At irregular periods, sometimes extending over centuries, an Armenian house succeeded in maintaining its independence and its domain over larger or smaller portions of the Armenian people. Always the jealousies of local princes offered obstacles to union. Always the Church was the chief centre of Armenian national consciousness. When, in the ninth, tenth, and eleventh centuries, Armenian culture came to a luxuriant blooming, it was predominantly religious in its art and its literature. Yet never does the Armenian Church seem to have been strong enough to reach out for converts against Islam, and seldom does it seem to have won adherents from paganism or from other branches of Christianity.[1] The Georgians, too, were usually under the suzerainty of some foreign power and neither in their days of independence nor in their periods of subjection does their Church seem to have sent missionaries to other peoples.

The Byzantine Empire had better fortune in pushing back the borders of Islam and in winning converts from that faith. In the latter part of the tenth and in the first half of the eleventh century the Byzantine forces were able to take advantage of the waning strength of the Abbasids to establish their authority in Cilicia and Syria. Antioch and Aleppo, the two chief centres in Syria, passed to Byzantine control. In 975 Damascus, Tiberias, Nazareth, and Cæsarea submitted to John Tzimisces. Even though some of these successes were ephemeral, during two generations the Byzantines were dominant in regions which for more than three centuries had been in Moslem hands. It is not surprising that under these circumstances a number came over from Islam to Christianity. Even before this period of Byzantine advance, about 865, some Moslems taken prisoners by the Byzantines were baptized, and the Emperor Michael III, "the Drunkard," ordered them conveyed to the border and allowed to choose whether they would remain by the faith whose symbol had been imposed upon them.[2] In the year 982 an Arab tribe in the vicinity of Nisibis, to the number of about twelve thousand men, irked by the financial exactions of their Moslem rulers, moved into Byzantine territory and

---

[1] F. Macler, in Cambridge Medieval History, Vol. IV, Chap. VI.
[2] The Chronography of . . . Bar Hebræus, translation by Budge, Vol. I, p. 144.

accepted the Christian faith.[3] It seems not unlikely that since these two instances of mass conversion have come down to us in the very fragmentary records of the time, there were others of which we have no report. These Byzantine victories were only temporary. As we shall see in a moment, in the eleventh century fresh vigour came to Islam through the Seljuq Turks, and the frontier of Islam was carried forward into Asia Minor beyond its former borders.

It was from Latin Christendom that the most energetic and fruitful efforts were made to roll back the Moslem tide. Why this should have been is undetermined. It is closely akin to the question of why the Christianity which had its stronghold among Western European peoples spread more widely and exercised more influence upon mankind than has any other branch of the faith.

The first form which the advance of Western Christendom took was the use of military force. This was employed in three series of campaigns. The earliest to begin, the most prolonged, and, measured by the territory taken, the most significant was that which drove the Moslems south of the Pyrenees and eventually expelled them from the Iberian Peninsula. The second, much briefer, was that which retook Sicily. The third is what we generally denominate the Crusades.

The reconquest of the Iberian Peninsula and the elimination of Islam was a process which covered nearly eight centuries. Spanning as it did so long a stretch of time, in it were utilized all the various kinds of measures which Western Christians employed against Islam—war, Crusades, Crusading orders, compulsory baptism, exile, toleration, and persuasion by teaching and preaching.

The eighth century saw both the high tide of the Arab conquest and the beginning of the Christian counter-advance. The defeat of the Arabs and Berbers at the battle of Tours (or Poitiers) in 732 was followed in 759 by the loss of Narbonne, the last Arab base north of the Pyrenees. In 793 the Arabs made a raid across the Pyrenees, but in 801 Barcelona surrendered to the forces of Charlemagne.[4]

Even earlier, centres of Christian resistance had shown themselves in the North of Spain. Asturias is said never to have been brought into subjection, and a victory there of the Christian forces in 718 is the traditional date of

[3] Kremer, *Culturgeschichte des Orients,* Vol. II, pp. 495, 496.
[4] See a brief summary by C. H. Becker in *Cambridge Medieval History,* Vol. II, pp. 373-375, and by G. Seeliger in the same volume, pp. 604-606.

the beginning of the reconquest. Another centre was in Aragon and still others were in León, Navarre, Castile, Galicia, and Catalonia. Gradually, in spite of wars among themselves, the Christian rulers gained ground at the expense of the Moslems. Not always did the tide of battle run in their favour. For instance, in the latter part of the tenth century, Almanzor, the great minister and general of the Caliph of Cordova, inflicted on them defeat after defeat. Yet in 1034, only a generation or so after the death of Almanzor, the Caliphate of Cordova came to an end and from then on leadership in Spanish life was usually and increasingly in the hands of the Christian states.[5]

The disappearance of the Caliphate of Cordova deprived the Moslems of Spain of a unifying leadership. They were divided into a number of states. Even the reinforcement given by fresh Berber forces from Africa, first the Almoravides and then the Almohades, brought only temporary reprieve and failed to achieve coherence. Moreover, in the Moslem domains were Christians living under their own bishops and occasionally under independent Christian lords. Some of these were prepared to co-operate with the Christian invaders.[6] It was not a solid mass of Moslems who were to be mastered. To be sure, the Christian advance was not without reverses. Some strongholds were taken, lost, and retaken more than once. The Christian states did not act as a unit, and the struggles between them and within them made for delays. However, by about the middle of the thirteenth century, the territories in the hands of Moslems had been reduced to the state of Granada. Here the reconquest paused for more than two centuries. Granada was not a serious menace to the Christian kingdoms, and for a variety of reasons almost no important efforts were made to eliminate it. Then, when the union of Ferdinand and Isabella brought together all the Christian forces except Portugal and Navarre, the advance was resumed. The capitulation of Granada to these Catholic monarchs, in 1492, made an end to Islam as a political power in the Iberian Peninsula.[7]

Inevitably the prolonged warfare against the Moor left a deep mark upon the national character of the Spaniards and the Portuguese. In effect it was a series of Crusades. Early in the thirteenth century, at the request of King Alfonso VIII of Castile, the Pope ordered a general Crusade preached and some foreign adventurers came to the assistance of the Spaniards.[8] This aid,

[5] R. Altamira in *Cambridge Medieval History*, Vol. III, pp. 409-428.
[6] Pidal, *The Cid and his Spain*, pp. 40-42.
[7] R. Altamira in *Cambridge Medieval History*, Vol. VI, pp. 393-416, Vol. VII, pp. 567, 572, 574, Vol. VIII, pp. 487-490. See also R. Dozy, *Histoire des Musulmans d'Espagne* (Leyden E. J. Brill, 1861), Vol. III, pp. 209 ff.
[8] Altamira in *Cambridge Medieval History*, Vol. VI, p. 409.

however, proved illusory. In general the Spaniards and Portuguese had little help from abroad.[9] The Crusading attitude, so deeply ingrained, persisted and bore fruit later in conquests and missions in Africa, the Americas, and Asia. Out of the struggle, too, emerged military orders, like those which arose from the Crusades in the East. They were of help in effecting the reconquest. For instance, in 1249-1250 they subdued part of Algarve for Portugal.[10] At least one of them, the Order of Christ, which was founded in 1319 and fell heir to the confiscated property of the Templars,[11] was involved in the early stages of the explorations and conquests in Africa and the East.

Many were the heroes who by their prowess and their knightly virtues became the models for later generations of warriors. Of these the most famous was Rodrigo or Ruy Diaz de Vivar, better known as the Cid, who lived in the latter half of the eleventh century. He was a scion of the nobility of Castile, but much of his life was spent in exile from his native kingdom. At times he was an ally of one or another of the Moslem princes, and on other occasions he fought the Moslems. It was he who in 1095 captured Valencia for the Christians—although it had to be abandoned not long after his death.[12]

As may be gathered from even this brief summary of the career of the Cid, the reconquest was not always marked by religious intolerance. Indeed, Christian monarchs seem usually to have granted entire liberty of conscience to the Moslems in the captured territories. Sometimes this was guaranteed by the formal terms of the capitulation. Thus when the Cid took possession of Valencia he left to the Moslems their mosques, houses, and estates.[13] It is even said that Moslems were treated with more forbearance than the Christians had been in the days of the Arab-Berber conquest. Usually the Moslems were promised the enjoyment of their religion and their laws and, for a time, magistrates of their own race.[14] In Valencia they were so free that they attempted to convert the Christians. They were, however, required to live in segregated districts and to pay tithes to the Church and a special tribute to

[9] We hear, for instance, of Normans from France assisting in the capture of Monzón on the river Cinca in c. 1065.—Altamira in op. cit., Vol. VI, p. 395. In 1147 a Crusading fleet carrying Anglo-Normans, Germans, and Flemings aided in the capture of Lisbon from the Moslems.—E. Prestage in Cambridge Medieval History, Vol. VIII, p. 509.

[10] Prestage in op. cit., Vol. VIII, p. 515.

[11] Prestage in op. cit., Vol. VIII, p. 515; Jann, Die katholischen Missionen in Indien, China und Japan, pp. 3-25. The oldest of these military orders, the Knights of Santiago de Calatrava, was founded by 1158 by a Cistercian and followed the Cistercian modification of the Benedictine rule.—Jann, op. cit., p. 16.

[12] Altamira in Cambridge Medieval History, Vol. VI, pp. 401-403; Pidal, op. cit., pp. 71 ff.

[13] Pidal, op. cit., p. 368.

[14] Lea, A History of the Inquisition in Spain, Vol. I, pp. 56-62.

the state.[15] In other words, the Christian rulers adopted much the same policy towards the Moslems that Moslem princes had applied to Christians.

In spite of tolerance and the persistence of Moslems in the Christian kingdoms, the elimination of Islam from Spanish and Portuguese domains followed the reconquest. Some Moslems chose to leave the country and took refuge with their fellow believers in North Africa. Others, quite as voluntarily, felt it expedient to adopt the faith of their new masters. Moreover, active missionary work accompanied the military advance, especially in its later stages. Monasteries were founded in the conquered territories, and they and the military orders reduced to cultivation lands wasted by war, encouraged the immigration of Christian colonists, and aided in the work of conversion.[16] In the first part of the thirteenth century, before Moslem territory had been reduced to the Kingdom of Granada, came the great burst of missionary enthusiasm accompanying the birth and early days of the Franciscans and Dominicans. It is not surprising that in both orders active missionaries arose. The last Moslem ruler of Valencia, Abu Said, was converted and his palace given to the Franciscans.[17] The Dominican Raymond of Penaforte (died 1275) with the support of the Kings of Castile and Aragon founded schools for the study of Arabic and Hebrew to prepare missionaries for the Moslems and the Jews. At his request Thomas Aquinas wrote a handbook for missionaries, *Summa contra Gentiles*. Raymond himself baptized many Moslems. In this period quite a large number of books of apologetics and polemics were composed.[18] Early in the fifteenth century the Dominican Vincente Ferrer, whom we have already noticed as winning many Jews, is said to have been the means of the conversion of a large number of Moslems.[19] Often in later centuries the labours of the friars were facilitated by legislation which directed royal officials to require attendance of Moslems and Jews at the preaching of the missionaries and by the favours officially shown to converts.[20] Down to nearly the close of the fifteenth century greater leniency was shown to Moslems than to Jews.[21]

Not always did tolerance prevail. Thus in 1085, after the capture of the city by Alfonso VI of Castile and León, Bernard, a French monk, was made

[15] Bridge, *Ramon Lull*, p. 26.

[16] Altamira in *Cambridge Medieval History*, Vol. VII, p. 593; Prestage in *op. cit.*, Vol. VIII, p. 510.

[17] Schmidlin, *Katholische Missionsgeschichte*, pp. 190, 191.

[18] Lemmens, *Die Heidenmissionen des Spätmittelalters*, pp. 95-102; Moreau in Descamps, *Histoire Générale Comparée des Missions* (Paris, Librairie Plon, 1932, pp. viii, 760), p. 293; Altaner, *Die Dominikanermissionen des 13 Jahrhunderts*, pp. 89-98.

[19] Peter Ranzano, *Vita S. Vincenti Ferrerii* in *Acta Sanctorum*, Apr. 5, Vol. I, p. 493.

[20] Lea, *A History of the Inquisition in Spain*, Vol. I, pp. 56-62.

[21] Lea, *The Moriscos in Spain*, pp. 12-15.

Bishop of Toledo. By the provisions of the capitulation certain mosques had been reserved to the Moslems, but Bernard, disregarding the royal pledge, said mass in the chief of these. Alfonso was indignant, but in politic fashion the Moslems asked that the Bishop be pardoned and gave the mosque for a church.[22] The Inquisition, established in Spain in 1480 by Ferdinand and Isabella, was employed to ferret out those Jews and Moslems who, while ostensibly Christians, were secretly adhering to their former faith.[23]

As time passed, intolerance increased. It culminated after the conquest of Granada. By the terms of the surrender, Moslem religion and law were to be preserved and Moslems were guaranteed protection for themselves and their property.[24] The first Archbishop, Hernando de Talavera, respected these provisions and sought the conversion of the populace by persuasion and tact. He ordered his clergy to learn Arabic and he himself studied the language and said prayers in it.[25] Partly as a result, thousands of Moslems were baptized.[26] However, the powerful Cardinal Ximenes de Cisneros believed the policy to be too lenient and employed more energetic measures. He began using force. The result was a revolt whose suppression proved costly and sanguinary and a royal decree which gave the Moslems the choice of emigration or baptism.[27] The latter was enforced not only in Granada but also throughout Castile and León. From it, however, Aragon was excepted. Many chose baptism. The sincerity of their profession was naturally suspect. In the sixteenth century attempts to assimilate the converts, or *Moriscos,* by compelling them to wear Spanish dress and to speak the Spanish language, were followed by revolt. In a later volume the story will be told more in detail. Here we must content ourselves with saying that in 1609 and 1610 the remnants of these nominally Christian but partially Moslem Moriscos were expelled.[28] The Spanish monarchs had at last obtained outward religious uniformity. Islam had been finally eliminated.

The Norman conquest of Sicily (begun in 1061 and completed in 1091) seems not to have been undertaken from religious motives. The Normans were Roman Catholics, but their original migrations into South Italy and

[22] Haines, *Christianity and Islam in Spain, A.D. 756-1031* (New York, The Bruce Publishing Co., 1932, pp. viii, 119), p. 93.
[23] E. Ryan, *The Church in the South American Republics,* p. 27.
[24] Lea, *The Moriscos in Spain,* pp. 18-23.
[25] Lea, *op. cit.,* p. 25.
[26] Lea, *op. cit.,* p. 31.
[27] Lea, *op. cit.,* pp. 33-45; Reginald Merton, *Cardinal Ximenes and the Making of Spain* (London, Kegan Paul, Trench, Trübner and Co., 1934, pp. xiv, 279), pp. 76-85.
[28] Lea, *op. cit.,* pp. 345 ff.; Altamira in *Cambridge Medieval History,* Vol. VIII, p. 490; C. H. Robinson, *The Conversion of Europe* (New York, Longmans, Green and Co., 1917, pp. xxiii, 640), pp. 280-282.

their subsequent acquisition of Sicily appear to have been from the love of
adventure and power and the desire for estates. Essentially their purposes
were the same as those which led their pagan ancestors to establish themselves in Normandy. Even had they wished to impose their faith on the
non-Roman Catholic and non-Christian elements among their subjects, their
numbers were too few to make this advisable. Their policy, then, was one of
religious tolerance. Jews, Moslems, Greek Orthodox, and Roman Catholics
enjoyed equal rights.[29] Moslems had their own laws and judges. Moors held
high places at the Norman court.[30] Toward the end of the twelfth century
Moslems were still numerous and influential, especially in Palermo.[31] Yet
Count Roger I, who completed the conquest, gave much attention to re-
organizing and reinforcing the Church, for it had suffered severely under
Moslem rule. After sharp controversy, Roger obtained from the Pope the title
of Legate Apostolic and several bishoprics were founded.[32] In the chaos which
at the close of the twelfth century followed the decay of the Norman rule and
preceded the tolerant administration of the sceptical Emperor Frederick II (in
whom were united Norman and Hohenstaufen), we hear of Moslems who
from fear accepted baptism. We read, too, of Moslem revolts, and of their
suppression by the young Frederick when he assumed the reins of power.[33]
Yet Frederick himself was friend of Moslem and Christian. In spite of their
rule of nearly two centuries, Moslems seem never to have been in the majority in Sicily. Inevitably under Christian rule their numbers declined. In 1233
Frederick II said that a part of the Saracens had long been converted. Ten
years or so earlier the Dominicans had obtained Papal permission to work
among some of his troops. Later it was ordered that no Christian should
prevent his Moslem slaves from being baptized.[34] The eventual extinction
of Islam was certain. After the middle of the thirteenth century the Arabs
disappeared as a distinct race.[35]

The Crusades form one of the most striking features of European history.
Their very name proclaims their connexion with Christianity. From the
memorable sermon of Urban II in November, 1095, which had so much to
do with the launching of the first of the series, the Popes again and again

[29] C. H. Haskins, *The Normans in European History* (Boston, Houghton Mifflin Company, 1915, pp. viii, 258), p. 225.

[30] F. Chalandon in *Cambridge Medieval History*, Vol. V, Chap. IV.

[31] Curtis, *Roger of Sicily and the Normans in Lower Italy,* pp. 420-424.

[32] Chalandon, *Histoire de la Domination Normande en Italie et en Sicile,* Vol. I, pp.
342-347.

[33] M. Schipa in *Cambridge Medieval History*, Vol. VI, pp. 132, 142.

[34] Altaner, *Die Dominikanermissionen des 13 Jahrhunderts,* pp. 113, 114.

[35] Curtis, *op. cit.,* p. 420.

summoned the faithful to join in them. The Crusades entered into the texture of the life of Mediæval Europe. For at least four hundred years they constituted part of the idealism of Western Christendom. Never has any other religion—unless it be Islam—or any other section of the Christian Church given birth to such a prolonged succession of holy wars. Certainly no other branch of the Church and no other religion has given rise to such a long line of expeditions to recover and to hold the sites sacred to its faith.

It is a commonplace that the Crusades had the religious motive as only one of their causes. Essentially they were a continuation of that migration of Teutonic peoples which had formed so important a factor in the collapse of the Roman Empire. They constituted, too, an early stage of that expansion of Western European peoples which from the close of the fifteenth century has been one of the outstanding features of the world's history, and which, in the past four centuries, has penetrated all the globe and has transformed mankind. As we shall see again and again, Christianity was only one of the factors which brought about this expansion. As we shall also repeatedly see, always Christianity has modified it. Whether without Christianity it would have occurred is one of the unanswered and probably unanswerable questions which tantalize the historian.

As originally conceived, the Crusades were not intended as instruments for spreading Christianity or for regaining the populations lost to Islam. Pope Urban II declared the objective to be the rescue of the holy places in Palestine, the defence of the Christians of the East against the Moslem, and the rolling back of the tide of Mohammedan conquest.[36] In a certain sense the Crusades were an outgrowth of the Cluny movement, for Gregory VII, who was a champion of that dream, had planned an expedition to aid the Byzantine Empire against the advancing Seljuqs and to bring the Eastern Christians once for all under the unifying sway of Rome.[37]

By no means all of the expeditions termed Crusades had the same objective as the first of the series. A number had as their purpose the defence of footholds in the East obtained by earlier Crusades or, after that city again fell into the hands of the Moslems, the recovery of Jerusalem. One was directed against Constantinople. Crusades were preached against the Slavs north and east of the Elbe, against the Moslems in Spain, against the Albigenses, and against various enemies of the Pope. Of these only a minority

---

[36] W. B. Stevenson in *Cambridge Medieval History,* Vol. V, p. 265. See also, among the vast literature on the causes and motives of the Crusades, Munro, *The Kingdom of the Crusaders,* pp. 30, 31; Powicke, *The Christian Life in the Middle Ages,* pp. 39, 57.

[37] W. B. Stevenson in *op. cit.,* Vol. V, p. 270.

had as even an incidental aim the conversion of non-Christians and still fewer sought the baptism of Moslems.

The Crusades both hindered and facilitated the advance of Islam and proved both a help and an obstacle to the spread of Christianity. The First Crusade aided in stemming the Seljuqs and in winning a reprieve for the Eastern Empire and the Greek Church. On the other hand, the Fourth Crusade, through the capture of Constantinople and the consequent ephemeral Latin Empire, dealt the Byzantine Empire a blow from which that realm never fully recovered and may have contributed to the ultimate fall before the Ottoman Turks and so to the disastrous weakening of the Greek Church.[38] The Crusades were the means of obtaining territorial footholds in the East for Latin Christianity. From the towns and fortresses in the hands of the Franks missionaries went forth. The Crusades assisted the formation of those mercantile colonies of Western Christians in the Eastern Mediterranean which even without their aid would presumably have arisen from the commerce of the Italian cities. Yet the missions from these centres won very few Moslems.[39] They succeeded only in bringing into communion with Rome portions of the constituencies of the various Eastern churches and in Cyprus in effecting through the long Latin occupation a partial fusion of the Greek and Latin clergy and congregations.[40] Moreover, the Crusades probably accentuated the bitterness between Moslems and Christians[41] and led the former more than ever to identify Christianity with military and imperialistic ambitions. At the same time the Crusaders who resided long in the East often grew tolerant of Islam and became disinclined to win converts from it.[42] What the Moslems saw of the lives of most of the Crusaders and of the garrisons which the Latin Christians established in the East, including those of the Hospitalers and the Templars, probably heightened their disdain for Christian character. Usually the Crusaders and the garrisons tended to give themselves to the luxury of the East[43] rather than to the transformation of Eastern morals and religion. Only in the Teutonic Knights and the consequent conversion of the

[38] Adeney, The Greek and Eastern Churches, pp. 259, 260; F. J. Foakes Jackson in An Outline of Christianity, Vol. II, pp. 257 ff.

[39] We hear that Moslem parents brought their children to Christian priests for baptism because they thought thus to make their offspring strong and healthy (Munro, op. cit., pp. 124, 125), but this does not mean that those baptized were reared as Christians.

[40] J. Hackett, A History of the Orthodox Church of Cyprus (London, Methuen and Co., 1901), p. 152.

[41] Browne, The Eclipse of Christianity in Asia, pp. 174, 175. Yet often there was fraternizing between Franks and Moslems, the use of common sites of worship, and the Templars protected Moslems in the free exercise of Islam.—Munro, op. cit., pp. 124, 125.

[42] Munro, op. cit., pp. 119, 120, 124, 125.

[43] Munro, op. cit., pp. 119, 120; J. W. Thompson, Economic and Social History of the Middle Ages (New York, The Century Co., 1928, pp. ix, 900), p. 434.

Prussians did the Crusades make a substantial contribution to the permanent spread of Christianity—and that was as a by-product and not among Moslems.

The use of force was not the only means employed by Christians to meet the advance of Islam, to keep their fellow believers from apostasy, and to win converts from Islam. In the East debates between Moslems and Christians appear to have been common. We hear of them and of a controversial and apologetic Christian literature. The Christians sought to substantiate their contentions about Jesus and their Christology by appeals to the miracles and to Old Testament prophecy, and the Moslems replied by claiming that the Christians had tampered with the text of the Scriptures to make it fit their purposes.[44]

In the West arose a conviction that a better way than the Crusades should be found for dealing with the Moslem. The traditional view had been that Christendom must be perpetually at war against Islam and its adherents. By the middle of the thirteenth century came a modification of this attitude. Thus Thomas Aquinas maintained that the infidel has rights, as the heretic does not, that war can be waged against him only to prevent him from hindering the faith or persecuting Christians, and that he cannot be forced to believe. Roger Bacon held Crusades to be a cruel and useless waste of time, and declared that the infidel should be converted, not attacked.[45] He said that Orientals and Arabs had not been converted because they had not been taught the Catholic doctrine in their mother tongue and declared that pagans would become Christians very gladly if the Christian princes who laboured for their conversion did not seek to enslave them and if the Church would permit them to retain their liberty and their possessions.[46] In many quarters enthusiasm for the Crusades waned and the ideal of the peaceful winning of Moslems by missions grew.[47] So Pope Honorius IV (died 1287) wished to see the Moslems converted and to this end encouraged the study of Arabic at the University of Paris. In consequence of a decision of the Council of Vienne early in the fourteenth century, several of the universities

[44] Browne, op. cit., pp. 109-125; A. Mingana, An Ancient Syriac Translation of the Kur'ān (Manchester University Press, 1925, pp. 50), p. 3.

[45] Powicke, The Christian Life in the Middle Ages and Other Essays, p. 42. For the views of Thomas Aquinas, see his Summa Theologica, translated by the Fathers of the English Dominican Province (London, R. and T. Washbourne, 21 vols., 1912-1922), Part II, 1st No., q. 10, art. 8.

[46] The Opus Major of Roger Bacon, translated by R. B. Burke (Philadelphia, University of Pennsylvania Press, 2 vols., 1928), Vol. II, p. 797. Lemmens, Geschichte der Franziskanermissionen, p. 4.

[47] Brehier, L'Église et l'Orient au Moyen Age, pp. 211-214.

established chairs of Oriental languages to prepare missionaries.[48] In accordance with this growing purpose an apologetic literature was brought into existence.[49]

Closely integrated with the new desire of Latin Christians to convert the Moslems through missions were the activities of the Franciscans and the Dominicans. Upon them, indeed, fell the burden of the missions of the thirteenth, fourteenth, and fifteenth centuries. The older orders were primarily organizations of ascetics interested in the salvation of their own souls and living apart from the world. Only incidentally were they missionary. In contrast, the Franciscans and Dominicans, while religious orders and, especially some of the Franciscans, displaying strong strains of asceticism, were primarily missionary organizations. To be sure, the older orders had often provided missionaries. In 1221 Pope Honorius III addressed all the archbishops, directing each to send two, three, or four men as missionaries and mentioning the Cistercians especially as a source for recruits.[50] Speedily, however, the Franciscans and Dominicans became the chief support of the Roman Catholic Church in extending its frontiers. Through all the succeeding centuries they have had prominent places in the spread of the Christian faith.[51]

These two orders arose in the first quarter of the thirteenth century. They at once stimulated and were the outgrowth of a remarkable religious revival which swept across Latin Christendom. The thirteenth century witnessed a great burst of life in Europe—the rise of universities, the building of cathedrals, and the expansion of commerce in Asia. Italian merchants penetrated even to China. As so often in the history of Western Europe, this new life had as one of its features religious awakenings, some of them outside the existing ecclesiastical structure and branded as heresies, and some within the organized Church. As always thereafter in the history of Western Europe, commercial expansion was followed by missionaries who were the products of these awakenings and who were challenged by the broadening geographic horizons to go with the Gospel to the lands to which merchants were penetrating.

At the outset, the major work of the Dominicans and Franciscans was among their fellow Christians, deepening the religious life of the masses. However, the Dominicans came into existence partly out of an effort to win

[48] Wadding, *Annales Minorum*, Vol. V, pp. 156, 157.
[49] L. Berg, *Die katholische Heidenmission als Kulturträger* (second edition, Aachener Missionsdruckerei, 3 vols., 1927), Vol. II, p. 348.
[50] Altaner, *Die Dominikanermissionen des 12 Jahrhunderts*, p. 1.
[51] On the contrast between the purposes of the older orders and those of the Dominicans and Franciscans, see G. R. Galbraith, *The Constitution of the Dominican Order, 1216 to 1360* (Manchester University Press, 1925, pp. xv, 286), pp. 175-191.

back to the Church the Albigenses and early in their careers both orders extended their efforts to pagans and Moslems.

Francis of Assisi himself went on three missions to the Moslems. He believed that the Saracens would rapidly be converted if only the Gospel were announced to them in its simplicity. It was probably in 1212 that he started on the first of these expeditions, only to be deflected from it by shipwreck.[52] In 1212 the Kings of Aragon, Navarre, and Castile inflicted a defeat on the Almohades. Francis felt that the victory, if it were really to reap fruit among the Moors, should be followed by the presentation of the Gospel. He therefore went to Spain in 1214 or 1215, but because of illness returned home.[53] In 1219 he accompanied Crusaders to the East and made his way to Egypt. The moral condition of the troops which represented the Christian name caused him agony of soul. With some members of the army he had great influence. He preached to the Moslems with but scanty success—although he and his companions were shown marked respect by the Sultan.[54] Within the lifetime of Francis, members of his ardent company in the first fervour of the new movement journeyed to various lands. Some went to Syria. Others proceeded to Tunis but were constrained to leave by Christian residents who feared the consequences for themselves of the mob which might be aroused by a display of missionary zeal. In 1219 a group went to Morocco and there suffered martyrdom.[55]

Dominic, too, believed that he had received a commission to undertake the world-wide proclamation of the Gospel.[56] The general chapter of the Order which met at Bologna in 1221 decided that the members should go through the world, preaching to every creature.[57] In the company of the Dominicans great missionaries were early found. We have already mentioned Raymond of Penaforte, a confessor of kings and Popes, who won many Moslems in Spain and advocated careful preparation for missions among them. We shall meet many others.

One of the most notable missionaries of the thirteenth and fourteenth centuries, Raymond Lull, at one time or another in his life had relations with both the Dominicans and the Franciscans. However, a mystic and an individualist, he never fitted fully into either Order. Lull was born about the

---

[52] Sabatier, *Life of St. Francis of Assisi,* pp. 170, 171; Schlund, *St. Franziskus und sein Orden in der Heidenmission, passim.*

[53] Sabatier, *op. cit.,* p. 173; Schlund, *loc. cit.*

[54] Sabatier, *op. cit.,* pp. 226-233; Schlund, *loc. cit.*

[55] Sabatier, *op. cit.,* pp. 204, 205, 224-226; Civezza, *Storia Universale delle Missioni Francescane,* Vol. I, pp. 82-122.

[56] Altaner, *Die Dominikanermissionen des 13 Jahrhunderts,* p. 2.

[57] Schmidlin, *Katholische Missionsgeschichte,* pp. 182-184.

year 1232, in Majorca, the son of a wealthy resident who had come to the island soon after its reconquest by the Christians.[58] As a boy he was a page at the court of the King of Aragon, and as he grew to manhood he led the dissolute life of a courtier. Although married and the father of a son and a daughter, he was absorbed in the many amours to which his highly emotional nature impelled him. While inditing some amorous verses he was four times smitten by a vision of Christ in agony on the cross. This brought him remorse and (1263) to a full dedication of himself to the Christian life. Residing as he did on an island which only shortly before his birth had been retaken from the Moslems, it was natural that he should think of missions to the Islamic world. Gradually there grew within him the desire to stir kings and Popes to send missionaries. Crusades, he felt, had failed, and the Holy Land was to be gained only by love, prayer, and tears. Yet he believed that Crusades should be continued as an auxiliary to missions and he helped promote the one which captured the Island of Rhodes. He had a desire, too, to preach in Africa and there to attain the martyr's crown.

Setting aside some of his property for his wife and children, Lull sold the remainder and gave the proceeds for the poor. He studied extensively, familiarized himself with Arabic, and with the aid of the King established on Majorca a school for the training of missionaries. He wrote voluminously. More than one of his works was an attempt to use the philosophy and the knowledge of his day to present the Christian faith in a manner which would prove convincing to non-Christians. The teaching of this system was part of the missionary method which he advocated. He was a mystic and some of his writings were in that field. The question has been ardently debated as to whether in his mysticism he was influenced by the Sufis.[59] While he did not write exclusively in it, he did much to give Catalan the dignity of a literary language.

Lull travelled widely and again and again attempted to persuade Popes and Cardinals to found monastic institutions for the study of languages as a means of preparing missionaries. In pursuit of his purpose of creating interest in the type of the training of missionaries to which he had given himself and of presenting his system of apologetics, more than once he visited the University of Paris, the great centre of theological studies of his day. He lectured, too, at the University of Montpellier. He presented his plan before

[58] The fullest recent account of Lull in English, and a very careful piece of work, is E. A. Peers, *Ramon Lull, A Biography* (London, Society for Promoting Christian Knowledge, 1929, pp. xviii, 454). Briefer and based largely on Peers is P. G. Bridge, *Ramon Lull, a Medieval Bakta* (Madras, Christian Literature Society for India, 1932, pp. 107).

[59] Bridge, *op. cit.*, p. 30.

the general chapter of the Dominicans. The Dominicans seem not to have done as he wished. The Franciscans proved more friendly. More and more his relations were with them and eventually he became a tertiate of that order. Dominicans later were among his bitterest critics.

Lull wished to see the Church reformed—to have it free itself of luxury and pluralism, set aside its best preachers as missionaries and equip them with the various languages of the world, and devote a tenth of its wealth to the Crusades and missions until the Holy Land should be conquered and the world won to the Christian faith. He rightly saw in the Mongols a great opportunity and a major crisis for the future of Christianity. Their faith, he held, was rudimentary and they should be converted before they accepted Islam or Judaism. He wished to bring into communion with Rome the churches of the East, for these, he believed, were in a better positon than the Christians of the West to win the Moslems and the Mongols.

Lull was not content with promoting an interest in missions. In Aragon he obtained royal permission to enter all synagogues and mosques in the realm and preach the Christian faith. More than once he himself went as a missionary to Moslem lands. At Genoa on one occasion he engaged passage to North Africa, and then, filled with forebodings of the persecution that would certainly confront him, allowed the ship to sail without him. He fell ill of remorse, but, sick though he was, insisted on being placed on a ship bound for Tunis. Once on board and the inner conflict resolved, he quickly recovered. In Tunis he debated with Moslems, but was arrested and deported and stoned by the mob on his way to the boat (1292). In 1307, although then probably in his middle seventies, he went to Bugia, east of Algiers. There he publicly offered to debate the truth of the Christian faith, was imprisoned, but was treated with moderation, was allowed to dispute with some of the Moors, and then was deported. In 1314, now probably past eighty years of age, he was again in North Africa. In Tunis, protected by fellow Aragonese and a friendly monarch, he is said to have made some converts. However, at Bugia, late in 1315 or early in 1316, he was stoned so severely that he died.

Lull is important, not because of the converts he made, for these were few, not primarily because of his place in literature and in the history of thought, although that is significant, and not even for his devotion and his character, but because he is typical of many of his generation who were moved by the religious currents and the widening geographic horizons of the time to new endeavours to spread the Christian faith and who, without entirely discarding the Crusades, emphasized preaching and intellectual argument as a way of winning converts.

Active and persistent though Lull was in seeking to awaken a missionary interest in the universities, the Church, and among the leading statesmen and ecclesiastics, most of the Roman Catholic missions of the thirteenth, fourteenth, and fifteenth centuries, as we have said, were not by him or by spirits kindled by him, but were by Dominicans and Franciscans. In spite of their origin in the same generation, their influence upon each other, and the early suggestion that they be combined,[60] the two orders embodied different ideals and pursued somewhat different methods. In some of their branches the Franciscans clung to their early dream of poverty—not only as individuals, but as a community—and of lay preaching. The Dominicans, true to their official title, the Order of Preachers, emphasized scholarship and preaching by the clergy.[61] Dominic did not regard martyrdom as the act of greatest perfection, while Bonaventura defended his fellow Franciscans for seeking martyrdom on the ground that it, like the death of Christ, was an act of perfect love. The Brothers Minor were, accordingly, more inclined to go forward in the face of danger when prudence might lead the Dominicans to draw back.[62] Both orders, we must hasten to add, could boast heroic souls. Toward the end of the thirteenth century the Dominicans developed within their order for the conduct of foreign missions the *Societas fratrum peregrinantium propter Christum*, an instrument which, with one interval after the Black Death, endured until 1456. It was composed of two, then of three, and finally of four monasteries in the Near East which were missionary centres and which each province of the Order was under obligation to supply with a fixed number of missionaries.[63] The Franciscans organized their missions into six vicariates, three of which were among the Mongols and one each in Morocco, in the northern part of the Balkans, and in the region of Walachia, Podolia, and Ruthenia. At the head of each was a vicar, a special representative of the General of the Order. Taking a leaf out of the Dominican notebook, the Franciscans formed a *Societas peregrinantium* with the same name as the other, but with different methods and territories.[64]

From the beginning, the Papacy supported the missionary activities of both Franciscans and Dominicans, writing Moslem monarchs on their behalf and granting them special privileges and exemptions.[65]

Between them the two orders covered most of the Moslem world. In North

---

[60] Sabatier, *Life of St. Francis of Assisi,* pp. 215, 216.

[61] *Ibid.*

[62] Lemmens, *Die Heidenmissionen des Spätmittelalters,* p. 106.

[63] Lemmens, *op. cit.,* pp. 3, 4; Altaner, *Die Dominikanermissionen des 13 Jahrhunderts,* pp. 227-229; Moreau in Descamps, *Histoire Générale Comparée des Missions,* pp. 271, 272.

[64] Lemmens, *op. cit.,* pp. 4-7.

[65] Lemmens, *op. cit.,* p. 2; Lemmens, *Geschichte der Franziskanermissionen,* pp. 11, 12.

Africa both were represented. Seldom, of course, was active work among Moslems possible. Yet in 1228 or 1229 an Almohadean prince in Morocco, to gain the aid of Ferdinand III of Castile, promised that the Christian soldiers sent him should have the free exercise of their religion, granted permission to build a church, and consented to the baptism of Moslems.[66] Even before this, in 1219, Franciscans had reached Morocco, in 1225 Pope Honorius III had sent both Dominicans and Franciscans to Morocco and had authorized the appointment of a Dominican as bishop, and in 1226 the Pope had commanded the Archbishop of Toledo to send members of both orders to that region and had granted him power to ordain two as bishops.[67] In 1233 we hear of a Franciscan Bishop of Fez and in 1246 of another Franciscan bishop.[68] Christian soldiers and merchants and Christian captives were in North Africa and required clerical ministrations. In the fourteenth century we meet Bishops of Morocco, Tangiers, and Bugia.[69] In the fifteenth century we hear of Franciscan monasteries in Tangiers and Ceuta, ports on the south side of the Straits of Gibraltar.[70] In Tunis were Christian merchants who within the quarter assigned them enjoyed religious liberty—sometimes exacted by European princes by force—and in spite of a hostile population churches were built and clergy served in them.[71]

We must add that the two Mendicant Orders were not alone in North Africa. Through raids by corsairs, many Christian captives were brought to that region. For the physical and spiritual care of these and for assistance in their release, the Order Hospitaler of the Holy Spirit and of Captives, better known as the Trinitarians, was founded toward the close of the twelfth century. As a pledge that the promised ransoms would be forthcoming, Trinitarians themselves sometimes became prisoners. About 1223 the Order Sacred and Military of Our Lady of Mercy, or the Mercedarians, was founded for a similar purpose. In the course of the centuries the two Orders are said to have obtained the release of nearly a million and a half captives.[72]

In "Libya" Conrad of Ascoli, a Franciscan, is said to have won sixty-four hundred to the faith.[73]

[66] Lemmens, *Geschichte des Franziskanermissionen,* p. 10, citing E. Tisserant and G. Wiet, *Lettre de l'Almohade Mortada au Pope Innocent IV* in *Hespéris,* Paris, 1926, p. 48.

[67] Altaner, *op. cit.,* pp. 98-103.

[68] Lemmens, *Geschichte der Franziskanermissionen,* pp. 12, 13.

[69] Altaner, *op. cit.,* pp. 98-103.

[70] Lemmens, *Geschichte der Franziskanermissionen,* pp. 12, 13; Schmidlin, *Katholische Missionsgeschichte,* pp. 191, 192.

[71] Altaner, *op. cit.,* pp. 103-113.

[72] Marie, *Histoire des Instituts Religieux et Missionnaires,* pp. 68-75.

[73] Lemmens, *Die Heidenmissionen des Spätmittelalters,* p. 101.

Egypt, in which their founder had preached, had a marked attraction for Franciscans. When the end of the Crusades somewhat relaxed the feeling against Western peoples, the Franciscans came, chiefly to care for European merchants and prisoners. The fourteenth century saw at least seven martyrs of that order in that land. Some effort was made to attract the Copts, and the Patriarch was persuaded to send representatives to that Council of Florence which in 1439 effected a fleeting union between the Roman and Greek Churches.[74]

Very early after the inception of their orders, both Franciscans and Dominicans made their way to Syria and Palestine. They established themselves in the cities which still remained in the hands of Western Christians, the fruits of the Crusades. Some not only cared for the Christians, but also made efforts to reach the Moslems. Where the political situation was favourable they sometimes met a friendly reception and even won converts. Thus, in territory controlled by the Crusaders, in the middle of the thirteenth century the Dominican William of Tripolis is said to have baptized over a thousand Moslems.[75] Some of the Moslem princes who hoped for help from the West against their enemies, whether Moslem or Mongol, were also friendly, although no one of them seems actually to have been baptized.[76] After Baghdad was taken by the Mongols we hear of at least one Dominican there trying to reach the Mongols.[77]

When in 1291 the Crusaders lost Acre, their last stronghold in Syria and Palestine, the lot of missionaries became harder. The friars confined themselves chiefly to pilgrims and merchants. Later the Franciscans were given by the Pope the care of the Holy Places.[78] In the fourteenth century most of the Bishops of Bethlehem were Dominicans.[79] Martyrdoms were numerous and sometimes followed attempts to convert Moslems.[80]

One of the main objectives of Roman Catholic missions in the Near Orient, including those of the Franciscans and the Dominicans, was the union of the various Christian bodies of those regions under the ægis of the Pope. It has been characteristic of Christians that many of the various bodies into

[74] Lemmens, *Die Heidenmissionen des Spätmittelalters*, pp. 95-102; Lemmens, *Geschichte der Franziskanermissionen*, pp. 18-20.

[75] Schmidlin, *Katholische Missionsgeschichte*, pp. 180-184.

[76] Altaner, *op. cit.*, pp. 72-88.

[77] *Ibid.*

[78] R. Huber in *Commentarium Ordinis Fratrum Minorum S. Francisci Conventualium* (Jan. 1934), Vol. XXXI, pp. 21-29; Lemmens, *Geschichte der Franziskanermissionen*, pp. 25, 61-66; Lemmens, *Die Franziskaner im Hl. Lande, 1 Teil, Die Franziskaner auf dem Sion (1335-1552)* (Münster im Westf., Aschendorff, 2d ed., 1925, pp. xi, 208).

[79] Altaner, *op. cit.*, pp. 19-41.

[80] Lemmens, *Geschichte der Franziskanermissionen*, p. 75.

which they have been divided have sought to attract other Christians to
fellowship, and hence to partial or complete conformity with themselves. The
story of most of these multiform efforts is only incidental to the history of
the expansion of Christianity as a whole. It is chiefly important in determining the kind of Christianity which has spread. It has, therefore, but a relatively
minor part in our narrative.

The successes of the efforts of Latin Christians to draw the churches of
the East into communion with Rome varied both with the time and with
the particular church. More than once the Greek and Roman Churches seemed
to have been brought together. For instance, the conquest of Constantinople
by the Fourth Crusade in the thirteenth century for a while strengthened
the Church of Rome in the Greek East and in the Balkans. More than once
in the twelfth and thirteenth centuries progress appeared to be made toward
ending the schism between the Armenians and Rome. Some leaders of the
Jacobites came over to Rome. About the middle of the fifteenth century
formal constitutions were promulgated by Pope Eugenius IV for the Maronites
and for such of the Jacobites and Nestorians as were in communion with
Rome. From practically all the Eastern churches groups were won. Usually
these became Uniates, bodies which preserved their ancient rites and customs
but which recognized the primacy of the Pope and in creed conformed with
Rome. Only in the case of the Maronites, however, did an entire church come
over. From the other churches only minorities were gained.[81]

The Franciscans and Dominicans did not confine to Moslems their efforts
for non-Christians. As we have seen, they were active in the conversion of
the Prussians and the Lithuanians.[82] They assisted in the completion of the
conversion of Livonia, Courland, and Estonia.[83] Dominicans were prominent
in the spread of the faith and the growth of the Church in Finland.[84]

Especially noteworthy were the efforts of the two orders to outflank Islam
and to hem it in by a ring of Christian peoples in Southern Europe and in
Asia. Not that the missions in these regions had the encirclement of Islam
as their conscious objective. They were, rather, attempts to bring about the
conversion of non-Christians wherever these were found, and particularly

[81] Adrian Fortescue, edited by George D. Smith, *The Uniate Churches. The Byzantine
Rite in Italy, Sicily, Syria and Egypt* (London, Burns Oates and Washbourne, 1923, pp.
xxi, 244): scholarly, by a Roman Catholic; Civezza, *Storia Universale delle Missioni
Francescane*, Vol. III, p. 582; Lemmens, *Geschichte der Franziskanermissionen*, pp. 31-35;
Altaner, *op. cit.*, pp. 41-72, 155-160; L. Bréhier in *Cambridge Medieval History*, Vol. IV,
pp. 619-623; Tamarati, *L'Eglise Géorgienne*, pp. 416, 438-450.

[82] Altaner, *Die Dominikanermissionen des 13 Jahrhunderts*, pp. 160-186; Schlund, *St.
Franziskus und sein Orden in der Heidenmission*, p. 25.

[83] Altaner, *op. cit.*, pp. 186-192; Schlund, *loc. cit.*

[84] Altaner, *op. cit.*, pp. 192-196.

where these threatened the Christian states of the West. Yet in effect they constituted a movement to reach peoples in Asia or of Asiatic origin before they were absorbed by Islam. In a very few sections which, significantly, bordered on Western Christendom, they were successful. In the major parts of the area covered they failed—and that in spite of the fact (or perhaps because of it) that they were scattered over a larger territory than ever before had seen missions of any other branch of the Church at any one time.

Franciscans and Dominicans vigorously prosecuted missions among the Cumans. The Cumans were a Turkish-speaking folk who in the eleventh century appeared on the southern steppes between the Dnieper and the Urals. One more of those migrations from Asia which for centuries threatened Western and Southern Europe, they proved both a menace and (at least once) useful allies to the Byzantine Empire. They were numerous north of the Danube in Walachia and Moldavia and troubled the monarchs of Hungary. From them, incidentally, came a large proportion of those troops who founded the Mamluk Dynasty in Egypt.[85] It was against the Cumans that in 1211 the King of Hungary had summoned the Teutonic Knights. The latter were expelled about 1225, but before then a bishopric had been established for the invaders.[86] In 1221 the Dominicans began a mission among the Cumans and soon had won two princes and a number of the latters' followers. In 1228 a Hungarian Dominican was appointed to a bishopric for them.[87] To allay a possible suspicion that the missionaries were political agents of the King of Hungary, in 1229 Pope Gregory IX placed the Cumanian neophytes under the protection of the Holy See and commanded that no secular prince should force on them his overlordship or enslave them.[88] Within a very few years, before the middle of the thirteenth century, the Mongol storm killed many of the Cumans and about ninety of the Dominicans. Numbers of the Cumans sought refuge in Hungary, and upon at least some of them the condition was placed that they become Christians. Both Dominicans and Franciscans laboured among the settlers in the Hungarian realms. Converts were made, but as late as 1348 a considerable part of the Cumans in Hungary were still pagan.[89] In 1303 a German Franciscan compiled what is said to have been the first

[85] A. A. Vasiliev, *History of the Byzantine Empire* (Madison, Wis., 2 vols., 1928, 1929), Vol. I, p. 393, Vol. II, pp. 24, 290.

[86] Augustus Potthast, *Regesta Pontificum Romanorum* (Berlin, Rudolph de Decker, 2 vols., 1874, 1875), Vol. I, p. 515, Nos. 5863, 5864 (in the year 1218).

[87] *Mon. Germ. Hist., Scriptorum,* Vol. XXIII, p. 921.

[88] Altaner, *op. cit.,* p. 145.

[89] Altaner, *op. cit.,* p. 151, citing Theiner, *Vetera Monumenta Historica Hungariam sacram illustrantia,* Vol. I, n. 1149.

dictionary in the Cumanian tongue.[90] Eventually the Cumans took on the religious complexion of the lands in which they were. The easternmost became Moslems, others became Greek Orthodox, and those in the West, especially in Hungary, became Roman Catholics.[91]

Some of the Dominicans in the Cumanian mission learned of the existence of Magyars farther east, descendants of those who centuries before had halted on the great westward migration. Several efforts were made to establish missions among them, but the Mongol invasion brought them to an end.[92]

The Mongol irruption, as we have already seen, profoundly affected the spread of Christianity in Eastern Europe and in Asia. During approximately its first fifty years, down to about the middle of the thirteenth century, it dealt Christianity many blows. Most of the Mongols were neither Christian nor Moslem, but in their conquests they put many thousands to the sword and Christians suffered along with the others. Peoples in Central Asia among whom were many Christians—Naimans,[93] Keraits, Uighurs, and Onguts— were conquered. We have recorded something of the destruction wrought in Russia and to the missions among the Cumans.

However, in the second stage of the Mongol domination, extending roughly over the latter half of the thirteenth century and the first quarter and in places the first half of the fourteenth century, conditions favoured the propagation of the Christian faith. Most of the Mongol rulers of the time were at least neutral in matters religious, and some were friendly to Christians. For a time the Mongols in Persia seemed inclined to unite with the Christian states of the West against the Moslems. Except on a few of the borders, the wars of conquest had ceased. Over the vast realm which stretched from the China Sea into Southern Europe and to the Euphrates the trade routes were probably safer than ever they had been. Coinciding as it did with the burst of missionary enthusiasm which expressed itself through the Franciscans and Dominicans, it is not surprising that the period witnessed a rapid multiplication of Roman Catholic missions in the Mongol dominions. Nor is it strange that Nestorians were widely scattered and prominent. For about two generations the fate of Christianity in China seemed to hang in the balance, with a very good chance that some large portions of the Mongols, like other conquering barbarians before them in Europe, would ask for baptism and establish strong Christian states.

[90] Lemmens, *Geschichte der Franziskanermissionen*, p. 4.
[91] Lemmens, *Die Heidenmissionen des Spätmittelalters*, pp. 18-21. On the Cumanian missions see also Civezza, *op. cit.*, Vol. I, pp. 348-372.
[92] Altaner, *op. cit.*, pp. 151-155.
[93] Yule, *Cathay and the Way Thither* (Cordier's revision), Vol. III, p. 20, note 3.

Many among the Roman Catholics recognized the gravity of the crisis, even though not always clearly, and sought to take advantage of the opportunity. What was probably, at least in part, a diplomatic mission to the Mongols, but of which we know little, was led by a Friar Lawrence of Portugal.[94] The Council of Lyons in 1245 decided to send two missions to the Mongol princes, one of Dominicans and one of Franciscans, to endeavour to convert them and to induce them to shed less Christian blood. One of these, headed by the Franciscan John of Plano Carpini, left Lyons in 1245, came to the court of the Great Khan at Karakorum in the summer of 1246, and, dismissed with a terse and somewhat haughty answer, reported to the Pope.[95] The other, in charge of the Dominican Anselm of Lombardy, reached the camp of a Mongol general much nearer Europe and was treated with scornful indignity.[96] Louis IX of France sent the Franciscan, William of Rubruquis (or Rubruck), who reached the Black Sea in 1253, made his way to the court of the Great Khan near Karakorum, and in 1255 arrived at Antioch on his return trip.[97]

A picturesque and heroic effort was made to establish Christianity firmly in China. China had been conquered by the Mongols and was the most populous and the richest portion of the Mongol domains. Here, at Cambaluc (later Peking and then Peiping), Khubilai Khan, a grandson of Jenghiz Khan and acknowledged as the head of the vast empire of the Mongols, fixed his capital and was the first ruler of a new Chinese dynasty, the Yüan. Khubilai, wishing the support of whatever supernatural powers might exist, showed respect to Christianity, as he did to several other religions.[98] Under the Mongols foreigners came to China, some of them as officials, some as soldiers, and others as merchants. Among the foreigners were many Christians. We have seen that at the time of the Mongol conquest Christians were numerous among peoples on the borders of what we now think of as China Proper. Under the Mongol rule some of these moved into China. The mother of Khubilai was a Nestorian Christian, a Kerait princess.[99] The Onguts, north of the Yellow River, were Nestorians.[100] A native of Cambaluc, a Nestorian monk, Rabban Sauma, who may have been an Uighur, and a younger companion, Mark, born in 1245 in North China, the son of an archdeacon and possibly an Ongut, journeyed

[94] Rockhill, *William of Rubruck*, pp. xxi-xxvi.

[95] *Ibid.;* Yule, *Cathay and the Way Thither* (Cordier's revision), Vol. I, p. 156; Howorth, *History of the Mongols,* Part II, pp. 68-75.

[96] Rockhill, *loc. cit.;* Howorth, *op. cit.,* Part III, pp. 72-75; Altaner, *Die Dominikaner-missionen des 13 Jahrhunderts,* pp. 120-128.

[97] Rockhill, *op. cit., passim;* Yule, *op. cit.,* Vol. I, p. 158.

[98] Yule, *Marco Polo* (Cordier's revision), Vol. I, pp. 343, 344, 348, 349.

[99] Cordier, in *Catholic Encyclopedia,* Vol. III, p. 669.

[100] Pelliot in Moule, *Christians in China before the Year 1550,* p. 235

westward on pilgrimage. Eventually Mark was raised to the Nestorian Patriarchate as Mar Jabalaha III. In 1287 and 1288 Rabban Sauma visited Rome, Bordeaux, and Paris on a diplomatic mission through which the Mongols of Persia were attempting to make contacts with the Christian powers of Western Europe.[101] Christians were so important in the China of the Mongols that a government bureau was established to supervise their monasteries and rites.[102] From a variety of contemporary sources, Chinese and European, we discover that Nestorians were widely scattered.[103] They seem to have been mostly non-Chinese and chiefly in the cities. We hear, for example, of Nestorian churches in Chinkiang,[104] Yangchow,[105] and Hangchow.[106] One European account of the fourteenth century declares that the Nestorians in Cathay numbered thirty thousand and were very rich[107]—but such round numbers are to be distrusted. The prosperity of Nestorianism in Chinkiang seems to have been due to the Christian Mar Sergius or Sargis, a physician of Samarqand, who was made governor of the city in 1277 or 1278 and who built seven monasteries in or near it.[108] Christian Alans from the Caucasus formed part of the Mongol military contingent in China.[109] How much these various non-Chinese Christians of Asia endeavoured to win Chinese to their faith we do not know. Presumably active missionary effort was the exception.

At the end of the thirteenth and in the fourteenth century, however, Franciscans came to China with the avowed purpose of making converts. European merchants were fairly numerous in China under the Mongols[110] and it is not strange that Franciscans followed them.

[101] See translations of the Syriac text of the pertinent source in J. A. Montgomery, *The History of Yaballaha III . . . and of Bar Sauma* (New York, Columbia University Press, 1927, pp. 82), and in E. A. Wallis Budge, *The Monks of Kûblai Khan*, etc. (London, Religious Tract Society, 1928, pp. xvi, 335). Montgomery translates less than half the work. Extracts and a summary, with useful notes, are in Moule, *op. cit.*, pp. 94-127. See also Mingana, *The Early Spread of Christianity in Central Asia and the Far East*, pp. 19, 20 and Yule, *Cathay and the Way Thither* (Cordier's revision), Vol. I, pp. 119-121. On the nationality of the two see Moule, *op. cit.*, p. 94, n. 1, and Pelliot in *T'oung Pao*, 1914, p. 630.

[102] Pelliot in *T'oung Pao*, Dec., 1914, p. 637; Moule, *op. cit.*, pp. 225-228.

[103] See some of these in Moule, *op. cit.*, pp. 128-165, 216-240; Ch'ên Yüan, *Yüan Yeh-li-k'o-wên K'ao, passim;* Yule, *Book of Ser Marco Polo* (Cordier's revision), Vol. II, pp. 66, 132; Henri Bernard, *Notes sur l'Histoire Ancienne du Christianisme en Extrême-Orient* (*Monumenta Serica*, Peking, 1935, Vol. I, Fasc. 2, pp. 478-486).

[104] Moule, *op. cit.*, pp. 14-165; Yule, *Marco Polo* (Cordier's revision), Vol. II, pp. 176-178.

[105] Pelliot in *T'oung Pao*, 1914, pp. 623-644.

[106] Yule, *Marco Polo* (Cordier's revision), Vol. II, p. 192.

[107] Yule, *Cathay and the Way Thither* (Cordier's revision), Vol. III, p. 102.

[108] Pelliot in *T'oung Pao*, 1914, pp. 623-644; Moule, *op. cit.*, pp. 145-157.

[109] Moule, *op. cit.*, pp. 260-264.

[110] Odoric of Pordenone says that he found many persons in Venice who had been in Hangchow.—Translation in Moule, *op. cit.*, p. 242.

Roman Catholic missionaries were about a generation later in reaching China than were Roman Catholic merchants. In 1269 two of the latter, Maffeo and Nicolo Polo, arrived at Acre bearing letters from Khubilai to the Pope asking for teachers in the science and religion of Europe. After a delay, two Dominicans, one of them the William of Tripolis whom we have already met, were appointed to accompany the Polos. Before they were far on the long journey, the two friars took alarm at the dangers and allowed the Polos (the two older and the young Marco, now with them) to go on alone.[111] A rumour that Khubilai had been baptized led the Pope in 1278 to start a group of five Franciscans toward China.[112] What happened to them we do not know.

So far as we are informed, the first Roman Catholic missionary to reach China was John of Montecorvino, a Franciscan. He had been in the Near East for some years, and in 1291, when in his middle forties, he left Tauris on a journey which in 1294 brought him to Cambaluc, bearing a letter from the Pope to Khubilai. The latter had recently died, but his successor received John and the Papal letter. John met bitter opposition from the Nestorians, who were established there before him and were powerful at court. However, he remained at Cambaluc, and by 1305 had completed a church, had translated the New Testament and the Psalter into "the language and character which is in most general use among the Tartars," and had won about six thousand converts. He had brought over to the Roman Catholic faith many of the Onguts, including a Prince George. About 1303 he had been joined by another friar.[113] By 1306 he had completed a second church in Cambaluc.[114]

When the news of John's success reached Europe, reinforcements were started toward him. John was appointed Archbishop of Cambaluc and seven members of his order were named as bishops to serve under him. Of the seven, three died on the way to Cathay and a fourth apparently either did not go at all or turned back before completing the journey. From time to time other Franciscans came to China. In 1311 three more were appointed bishops, of whom only one arrived at his destination. John died about 1328 or 1329.[115] A successor was appointed, but seems to have died before reaching Cambaluc.[116] Centres were established in several cities, among them Hangchow,[117]

[111] Yule, *Marco Polo* (Cordier's revision), Vol. I, pp. 13-23.

[112] Yule, *Cathay and the Way Thither* (Cordier's revision), Vol. III, p. 5; Lemmens, *Die Heidenmissionen des Spätmittelalters*, pp. 64-79.

[113] See translation of the letter of John from Cambaluc, Jan. 8, 1305, in Moule, *Christians in China before the Year 1550*, pp. 171-177.

[114] See translation of letter of John from Cambaluc, 1306, in Moule, *op. cit.*, pp. 177-180.

[115] On the date see Moule, *op. cit.*, pp. 196, n. 56, 253.

[116] Lemmens, *op. cit.*, pp. 64-79; J. de Moidrey, *La Hiérarchie Catholique en Chine, en Corée et au Japon (1307-1914)* (Shanghai, *Variétés Sinologiques*, No. 38), p. 3.

[117] Odoric of Pordenone, text in Yule, *Cathay and the Way Thither* (Cordier's revision), Vol. II, pp. 312, 313; and translated in Moule, *op. cit.*, pp. 241-244.

only a few years previously the capital of the Sung dynasty, at the port called Zaitun (probably Ch'üanchow in Fukien),[118] at Yangchow,[119] and possibly at Nanking.[120] A large number were baptized, none of them Jews or Moslems, and one of the friars lamented that the converts did "not walk straight in the path of Christianity."[121] In 1336 the Alans, who had been won to affiliation with the Roman Catholic Church, complained in a letter to the Pope that since the death of John they had been left without spiritual direction.[122] In reply to this plea a party of clergy were sent to Cathay, came to Cambaluc in 1342, and arrived at Avignon on the return trip in 1353.[123] An account by John of Marignolli, a Papal legate and one of their number, speaks of the cordial reception accorded them at Cambaluc. He also said that in Cambaluc the Franciscans had a cathedral and several churches and lived at the Emperor's table.[124] At least in Cambaluc the missionaries were supported by the state.[125]

Our information concerning this Franciscan mission to Mongol China is at best fragmentary. Very possibly other centres existed of which we have not yet learned and missionaries may have arrived whose names have not come down to us.

Whether any knowledge of this Christianity in the China of the Mongols penetrated to Korea, Japan, Indo-China, or the Philippines we are unable to say. It has been suggested that two or three centuries later the Spaniards found in the Philippines images which gave indications of a Christian origin,[126] but this is unproved.

The larger part of India was untouched by the Mongol armies. It was at least partly for this reason that in the thirteenth and fourteenth centuries no such extensive influx of Christians was witnessed as in China. We have seen that Christian communities connected with those in Mesopotamia and Persia existed in India in these centuries. Of their history at this time, however, and as to whether they were growing or declining in numbers, we possess no certain information. A number of Roman Catholic missionaries on their way to or from China passed through India and some remained there for a year

[118] Letter of Andrew of Perugia, translated in Moule, *op. cit.,* pp. 192-194; letter of Peregrine in Moule, *op. cit.,* pp. 207-210; Odoric of Pordenone in Yule, *Cathay and the Way Thither* (Cordier's revision), Vol. II, pp. 310, 311.

[119] Odoric of Pordenone, text in Yule, *Cathay and the Way Thither* (Cordier's revision), Vol. II, p. 317; translation in Moule, *op. cit.,* p. 245.

[120] What may be a Franciscan church at Nanking has been described by J. Prip-Möller in an article in *Artes,* Vol. III, summarized in *The Chinese Recorder,* Nov., 1935, Vol. LXVI, pp. 654-656.

[121] Letter of Andrew of Perugia in Moule, *op. cit.,* p. 191.

[122] Letter transplanted in Moule, *op. cit.,* pp. 252-254.

[123] Moule, *op. cit.,* p. 252.

[124] John of Marignolli, translated in Moule, *op. cit.,* p. 258.

[125] Moule, *op. cit.,* pp. 192, 258.

[126] Lorenzo Pérez in *Revista de la Exposición Misional Española,* Dec., 1928, pp. 97-103.

or more. Thus John of Montecorvino was in India about thirteen months and there baptized about a hundred.[127] Some few Dominicans and Franciscans made India their major mission field. Writing in 1324, Jordan Catalani says that he, a Dominican, left Tabriz with four Franciscans, intending to go to Cathay. The Franciscans were martyred by the Moslems at Tana, on the island of Salsette, not far from the present Bombay, and Jordan took their relics and buried them in a church.[128] He himself remained in India, speaks of baptizing about three hundred, of whom many were pagans and Moslems, and found no opposition to preaching or baptism.[129] In 1330 he is mentioned as Bishop of Columbum or Columben (Quilon, on the south-west coast), the chief mart of the pepper trade.[130] Beginning in 1346 or 1347 John of Marignolli spent over a year at Columbum, dwelling in the Latin Church of St. George. He speaks of an Indian slave of a Genoese merchant who had been baptized, and of baptizing the father of this boy, apparently a devout Hindu who professed to have been led to the missionary by a dream.[131] These few glimpses are about all that we have and indicate a Roman Catholic mission much less extensive than that in China.

In Russia, as we have suggested, after the conquest the Mongols were for a time tolerant of the Church and even friendly to it. It is said—although this is disputed—that Sertak, the son and for a brief time the successor of Batu, that grandson of Jenghis Khan under whom much of the Mongol occupation had been achieved, was a Christian.[132] Bereke, who followed (c. 1256-1265), became a convert to Islam, the first of the ruling Mongols to become a Moslem.[133] The next Khan, Mangu Timur, held to the Mongol faith of shamanism, and not until Uzbek, who ruled from 1314 to 1341, was a Moslem again at the head of the Golden Horde.[134] Yet Uzbek was not generally anti-Christian and was tolerant of the Church.[135]

[127] Letter of John from Cambaluc, translated in Moule, op. cit., p. 171.
[128] Letter of Jordan, dated 1324, summarized in Henry Yule, *Mirabilia Descripta. The Wonders of the East by Friar Jordanus* (London, Hakluyt Society, 1863, pp. xvii, 68), p. vi.
[129] Jordan translated in Yule, op. cit., p. 23.
[130] Yule, op. cit., p. vii. On Jordan see also J. Richter, *Indische Missionsgeschichte* (second edition, Gütersloh, 1924), pp. 42-49; Lemmens, *Die Heidenmissionen des Spätmittelalters*, pp. 80-86; The Capuchin Mission Unit, *India and Its Missions* (New York, The Macmillan Company, 1923), pp. 84-86.
[131] John of Marignolli, translated in Yule, *Cathay and the Way Thither* (Cordier's revision), Vol. III, pp. 218, 257, 258. On the date see Yule, op. cit., Vol. III, p. 216, n. 3.
[132] Howorth, *History of the Mongols*, Vol. II, p. 92; Altaner, *Die Dominikanermissionen des 13 Jahrhunderts*, pp. 138-141.
[133] Howorth, op. cit., Vol. II, p. 105.
[134] G. Vernadsky, *A History of Russia* (New Haven, Yale University Press, revised edition, 1930), p. 42.
[135] Howorth, op. cit., Vol. II, p. 154.

In the realms of the Golden Horde Roman Catholic missions prospered for more than two generations. Southern Russia was nearer to Europe than was any other main division of the Mongol Empire, and on the Black Sea the establishments of Italian merchants offered convenient footholds. The tolerance of the Khans made missions possible. In general the Pope assigned the region to the Franciscans, but Dominicans were also present. At the beginning of the fourteenth century the Brothers Minor had seventeen stations in the area. We read of a monastery in the Mongol capital, Sarai, and we hear that the friars accompanied the nomads on their wanderings, preaching and administering the sacraments. Converts were made, among them members of the royal family. Several bishoprics were created and two archbishoprics. After the middle of the century the Black Death almost wiped out the missionaries, but reinforcements were sent, and at the end of the fourteenth century an increasing number of the Christians in the Caucasus were being brought into fellowship with Rome.[136]

In Persia and Mesopotamia where the shamanist Mongols overthrew the Moslem Abbasid Caliphate and ruled in its stead, for a time the cause of Christianity seemed to prosper.[137] The Nestorian element among the conquerors which entered partly through the Keraits was strong. Hulagu, who captured Baghdad and founded the dynasty of the Il-khans which headed the Mongol rule in Persia, had as mother the Kerait Christian princess who was also the mother of Khubilai.[138] His favourite wife was a Christian.[139] Perhaps because the Abbasids, whom he was eliminating, were Moslem, Hulagu showed favour to the Christians when he captured Baghdad and in the wholesale slaughter which followed the fall of the city spared those whom the Catholicos had gathered under his protection in a church. The Mongols deemed it wise to win the support of the Christian peoples of Western Asia as a means of undercutting the Moslem powers dominant in that area. Of Mangu, a brother of Hulagu and Grand Khan from 1251 to 1259, it is reported that he and his retinue were baptized by an Armenian bishop.[140] However, if this

---

[136] Lemmens, *Die Heidenmissionen des Spätmittelalters,* pp. 51-64; Civezza, *Storia Universale delle Missioni Francescane,* Vol. II, p. 626; Schmidlin, *Katholische Missionsgeschichte,* pp. 189, 190.

[137] On a general survey of the history of the relation of the Persian Mongols to Christianity, see René Grousset, *Histoire de l'Asie* (Paris, G. Crés et Cie, 3 vols., 1922), Vol. III, pp. 99-111.

[138] Howorth, *op. cit.,* Vol. III, p. 90.

[139] *The Chronography of . . . Bar Hebræus,* translation by Budge, Vol. I, p. 431; J. Labourt, *Le Christianisme dans l'Empire Perse sous la Dynastie Sassanide (224-632)* (Paris, Victor Lecoffre, 1904), p. 350.

[140] Browne, *The Eclipse of Christianity in Asia,* p. 149, citing from Assemani. Vol. III, Pt. II, p. cvi, the Armenian historian Haithon.

actually occurred, it was undoubtedly a political move to obtain the aid of the Armenians and in the mind of Mangu probably possessed no religious significance. Christians were prominent in the service of at least some of the Il-khans and many of the Christians now became arrogant toward the Moslems.[141] There are coins of the Il-khans which bear the Christian legend, "In the name of the Father, the Son, and the Holy Ghost, one God."[142] Hulagu's successor, Abaga, had for wife a Christian, the daughter of the Byzantine Emperor Michael Palæologus.[143]

Then, too, for a time the Mongols looked with friendly eye upon the Christian states of Western Europe as possible allies against the Moslem powers in the Near East. Embassies came and went between the Mongols and the West.[144] Compared with the vast Mongol Empire, the kingdoms of thirteenth- and fourteenth-century Europe were petty principalities. Probably the Mongols regarded them with a certain amount of disdain. Yet they might prove useful. To men as indifferent religiously as were the first few generations of Mongol conquerors, whose hereditary shamanism, like its associated culture, was rapidly disintegrating through their contacts with other religions and cultures, Christians, if politically of potential assistance, were worth conciliating.

The fall (1291) of Acre, the last stronghold of the Crusaders in Palestine and Syria, and the progressive military weakness of Christianity in Western Asia probably chilled the Mongol enthusiasm for Christian alliances. Perhaps the issue was never really uncertain. The Il-khans and their followers naturally adopted the faith of the majority of their subjects. Ahmad, who reigned from 1280 to 1284, may have been baptized as a boy, but became a Moslem.[145] He persecuted the Christians.[146] Ahmad's successor, Arghun, was friendly to the Christians.[147] It was by him that Rabban Sauma was sent to solicit the aid of the Christians of Europe against Syria and Palestine.[148] The next two rulers, Gaikhatu[149] and Baidu, were also well disposed toward the Christians,[150] but in 1295, only four years after the fall of Acre, what seems to have been a pro-Islamic movement made the Moslem Ghazan Khan.[151] It appears to have

[141] Howorth, op. cit., Vol. III, pp. 141, 150; Mingana, The Early Spread of Christianity in Central Asia, pp. 8-19.
[142] Mingana, op. cit., p. 48.
[143] Grousset, op. cit., Vol. III, p. 105.
[144] Wadding, Annales Minorum, Vol. V, pp. 35-42; Altaner, op. cit., pp. 128-138.
[145] Howorth, History of the Mongols, Vol. III, pp. 285, 286.
[146] Budge, The Monks of Kûblai Khân, p. 158.
[147] Howorth, op. cit., Vol. III, p. 313; Budge, op. cit., p. 163.
[148] Budge, op. cit., pp. 165 ff.
[149] Montgomery, The History of Mar Yaballaha III, p. 80.
[150] Budge, op. cit., p. 206.
[151] Howorth, op. cit., Vol. III, p. 396.

been the pressure of the Moslem majority which led Ghazan to persecute the Christians at the outset of his reign,[152] for in general he was tolerant.[153] The need for help against Egypt probably dictated a friendly policy toward Christian princes and peoples in the Near East. Ghazan was succeeded (1304-1316) by a brother who is known as Uljaitu and who, although he is said to have had a Kerait Christian mother and to have been baptized, was a Moslem, possibly through his wife's influence.[154] Under Uljaitu persecutions of Nestorians occurred,[155] but he cultivated friendly relations with the monarchs of Western Europe in hope of their help against Egypt.[156] Perhaps for this reason Roman Catholic missionaries—so long as they confined their efforts to non-Moslems—were comparatively secure. Under the next monarch, Abu Said, the power of the Il-khans disintegrated[157] and in the disorder the lives of missionaries must have been imperilled.

During the Mongol rule in Persia and down to the disintegration of the Il-khan dynasty, Franciscans and Dominicans came to the realm. In general, the Papacy favoured the sending of Dominicans to the region, but some Brothers Minor were also there. In 1240 Dominicans settled at Tiflis. In 1318 Sultania, which the Il-khan Uljaitu did much to build and which he made one of the finest cities in Persia, was created the seat of a Latin archbishopric and entrusted to the Dominicans. Under it were placed a number of bishops. No bishopric was established in Mesopotamia, for there the Nestorians were still powerful and very hostile. About the middle of the century the Dominicans and Franciscans appear each to have had about fifteen stations in the Persian realms. Most of the efforts of the missionaries were directed toward winning the Nestorians, Jacobites, Orthodox, Armenians, and Georgians to communion with Rome.[158]

Missions, too, were established in Central Asia beyond the domains of the Il-khans. In 1339 a bishop and six other Brothers Minor were martyred at Almaliq, a Mongol capital in Ili, and the following year John of Marignolli preached there, baptized several, and built a church.[159] The last news of

---

[152] Howorth, op. cit., Vol. III, p. 397; Budge, op. cit., pp. 210 ff.

[153] Budge, op. cit., pp. 220, 221, 249.

[154] Howorth, op. cit., Vol. III, p. 535.

[155] Budge, The Monks of Kûblai Khân, pp. 260 ff.; Browne, The Eclipse of Christianity in Asia, pp. 168-170.

[156] Howorth, op. cit., Vol. III, pp. 573-579.

[157] Howorth, op. cit., Vol. III, p. 585.

[158] Lemmens, Die Heidenmissionen des Spätmittelalters, pp. 26-51. Jordan says that in Tabriz in his day there was a Roman Catholic church with about a thousand converted "schismatics."—Yule, The Wonders of the East by Friar Jordanus, p. 8.

[159] John of Marignolli, translated in Yule, Cathay and the Way Thither (Cordier's revision), Vol. III, p. 212.

mediæval Roman Catholic missionaries in that region was in 1362, and is of martyrdoms.[160]

To the decline of Christianity in Asia, to the fresh expansion of Islam, and to the collapse of the widespread Roman Catholic missions a number of causes contributed.

First of all was the fact that the invaders who emerged from Central Asia in successive waves became Moslems rather than Christians. This, as we have seen, was largely because, through the Arab conquest of the Sassanian Empire, the dominant political power and culture which the invaders met as they pushed westward was Moslem. This, in turn, as we have said, goes back to the failure of Christianity to win the first Sassanids and this to the fact that Christianity had become the faith of the Roman Empire.

The earliest of the waves of Moslem invaders from Central Asia was the Seljuq Turks. About the tenth century they moved from the steppes into Transoxiana and in the eleventh century accepted Islam through Mahmud of Ghaznah (998-1030), a vigorous and zealous Moslem under whose suzerainty they lived. It has been suggested that some of the group out of which the Seljuqs came had been Christians before the mass conversion of Islam.[161] In the eleventh century the Seljuqs continued to move south and west and clashed with the Byzantine Empire. Some established themselves in Asia Minor.[162] In Asia Minor the Seljuqs seem to have been very tolerant with the Christians. We hear, indeed, of a Seljuq sultan of the thirteenth century wishing to use a bath belonging to the Church and to have the sacrament given to his unbaptized children—a request which the Œcumenical Patriarch (of Constantinople) deemed it wise to grant.[163] Little or no compulsion appears to have been employed to bring over the population to Islam. Some Christians actually preferred the Seljuq rule to that of the Byzantine Emperors.[164] Yet gradually Christianity disappeared. Thus Laodicea, which in 1210 seems to have had only Christians, before 1333 had become largely Moslem.[165] Probably this was due partly to Turkish immigration and partly to conversion. Christian shrines and sacred places were taken over by the Moslems and were held sacred to Islam, much as earlier pagan ones had become Christian.[166]

---

[160] Lemmens, op. cit., pp. 80-86.

[161] Barthold, Zur Geschichte des Christentums in Mittel-Asien, pp. 42-50.

[162] H. M. J. Loewe in Cambridge Medieval History, Vol. IV, pp. 299 ff.

[163] S. Runciman, Byzantine Civilization (New York, Longmans, Green and Co., 1923, pp. 320), p. 131.

[164] Ramsay, The Cities and Bishoprics of Phrygia, Vol. I, p. 16.

[165] Ramsay, op. cit., Vol. I, pp. 27, 28.

[166] Ramsay, op. cit., Vol. I, p. 242; Hasluck, Christianity and Islam under the Sultans, Vol. I, p. 57.

The second great wave of invasion was that of the Mongols. The slaughter attending their first incursions had depleted both Christian and Moslem populations. Then, as the Mongols in Persia became Moslems, persecutions of Christians broke out. As we have seen, these were not constant, but they appear to have been fairly severe.

A second cause of the recession of Christianity in Asia was the break-up of the Mongol Empire. In the third quarter of the fourteenth century the Mongols were driven from China and were replaced by a native dynasty, the Ming. So far as we are aware, no active persecution of Christians was undertaken, but most of the Christians seem to have been non-Chinese[167] who had come in under the Mongols and many of whom held office or in other ways were dependent on Mongol rule. Missionaries could no longer rely upon the state for support. The overland trade routes became more unsafe and communication with Europe was increasingly uncertain. Peoples among whom Christians had been found, such as the Onguts, Keraits, and Uighurs, disappeared or became Moslems or Buddhists. Efforts to reinforce the Roman Catholic missions proved unsuccessful. At least we know of parties of missionaries who started for Cathay and of whose fate we cannot learn.[168] By 1600, when Christian missionaries once more were penetrating China, only vague memories of earlier Christians survived. Apparently at least one community had persisted until well along in the Ming, but under threat of persecution its church had been turned into a temple and its members joined the Jews or the Moslems or became pagans.[169] A few physical relics and fragmentary literary references and documents are all that remain to tell us of the once widely scattered Christians.[170] The Christianity which had been in China or near the borders for eight centuries or more had vanished.

In Persia during the disorder which accompanied and followed the decline of the Il-khans the Christians suffered. The see of the Nestorian Catholicos is said to have been vacant nearly ten years (1369-1378), and from 1379 to 1404 the see of the Jacobite Maphrianus was unfilled.[171]

---

[167] Moule, *Christians in China before the Year 1550*, p. 150, n. 17, knows of only two, or at most three, passages which show the existence of Chinese Christians before 1550.

[168] Moidrey, *La Hiérarchie Catholique en Chine, en Corée et au Japon*, pp. 1-3, 426; H. Cordier, *Histoire Générale de la Chine* (Paris, Paul Geuthner, 4 vols., 1920, 1921), Vol. II, pp. 426.

[169] Moule, *op. cit.*, pp. 1-5; Moule in *International Review of Missions*, Vol. XX (July, 1931), pp. 456-459.

[170] See Moule, *Christians in China before the Year 1550*, pp. 78-93; M. W. Brown in *Chinese Recorder*, Vol. LXIV, p. 77. On the strange and numerous bronze crosses— whose Christian connexion is not finally proved—see M. W. Brown in *Chinese Recorder*, Vol. LXIV, pp. 76-82.

[171] Browne, *The Eclipse of Christianity in Asia*, p. 172.

A third cause of Christian losses in Asia was Timur or Tamerlane (1336-1405). His conquests in Central Asia, Persia, and the Caucasus were accompanied by incredible slaughter. He was, too, an ardent Moslem. Under him what survived of the Christian communities must have dwindled rapidly.[172]

A fourth factor contributing to the decline of Christianity in the East was the appearance of fresh Moslem invaders. In the thirteenth and fourteenth centuries, while the Mongol power was reaching its apex and declining, the Ottoman Turks were becoming powerful in Asia Minor. They arose out of those Turks who for centuries had been filtering into Western Asia. The first of them in Asia Minor are said to have arrived in the thirteenth century, seeking refuge from the Mongols. About the middle of the fourteenth century they began acquiring territory in Europe. In 1453 Constantinople fell to them, and the Byzantine Empire, so long the bulwark of Christianity against Islam, came to an end. Their domains included Greece and the Balkans. Western Europe trembled for its safety.

During their conquest the Ottoman Turks seem not always to have engaged in active persecution of Christians. Christians and Turks had long been living side by side in Asia Minor and often a good deal of reciprocal toleration existed.[173] Mohammed II, who took Constantinople, forbade any persecution of Christians, made himself the protector of the Greek Church, and gave to Christians the status of a separate community under its Patriarch akin to that of the Nestorians under the Sassanids and the Abbasids.[174]

Yet the Ottoman advance altered profoundly the religious complexion of Asia Minor, the Caucasus, Greece, the Ægean, the Balkans, and much of the territory on the lower Danube. Islam and not Christianity was now the state religion. The head of the Greek Church became subject to a Moslem sultan. Moslem Turks moved into areas which for centuries had been exclusively Christian. Thousands of Christians came over to Islam.[175] Some of these conversions were voluntary. In the case of many, systematic and compulsory conversion was practised. For instance, sons of Christians were torn from their parents, reared as Moslems, and enrolled in military service. Out of the choicest of them were drawn the members of a picked standing corps, the Janizaries.[176] Roman Catholic missions suffered.[177] The Christian

[172] Bréhier, L'Église et l'Orient au Moyen Age, p. 312.

[173] F. W. Hasluck, Christianity and Islam under the Sultans (Oxford, The Clarendon Press, 2 vols., 1929), Vol. II, pp. 370-372.

[174] Arnold, The Preaching of Islam, pp. 145, 146.

[175] As in Georgia and the Caucasus.—Lübeck, Die Christianisierung Russlands, pp. 32, 61.

[176] Lord Eversley and Valentine Chirol, The Turkish Empire from 1288 to 1914 (London, T. Fisher Unwin, second edition, 1923, pp. 456), pp. 16, 23, 24, 41-43; A. H.

communities continued, but on the defensive. The churches became the conservers of various Eastern nationalities within the Moslem Ottoman Empire.

In Egypt, the Sudan, and Ethiopia (Abyssinia), Christianity was slowly losing ground. In Egypt in the fourteenth century persecutions of the Copts broke out, perhaps because of jealousy of the high positions held by Christians in government service and their disregard of the traditional restrictions. Many Copts became Moslem converts.[178] In the Sudan the morale of the Church declined. In 1500 churches still existed, but the population was drifting into Islam.[179] In Ethiopia Islam was penetrating the country, partly from the coast of the Red Sea where Moslem rulers had established states.[180]

A fifth set of causes of the recession of Christianity before Islam in the fourteenth and fifteenth centuries was to be found in conditions in Western Europe. The Black Death wrought havoc in the monasteries of Europe and badly depleted the missionary staff in Asia.[181] In Western Europe, too, came a decay of missionary enthusiasm. In the latter part of the fourteenth and in the early part of the fifteenth century the Great Schism divided the Roman Catholic Church and brought scandal to Western Christianity. The Renaissance chilled Christian conviction in the hearts of many, and during much of the fifteenth century churchmen occupied the See of Peter who were more intent upon art and literature or upon creating principalities for their relatives than upon quickening and deepening the religious life of Europe. It is not surprising that in the fifteenth century, after attempts to revive them, the special organizations for missions in the Franciscan and Dominican Orders came to an end.[182]

Beset by an advancing Islam in the East, having lost the larger proportion of its wide-flung communities in Asia, and suffering from corruption and indifference in the Church which represented it in the West, in 1500 Chris-

---

Lybyer, *The Government of the Ottoman Empire in the Time of Suleiman the Magnificant* (Harvard University Press, 1913, pp. x, 349), pp. 15-18; Arnold, *op. cit.*, p. 150; Adeney, *The Greek and Eastern Churches*, pp. 309-320; A. Toynbee, *A Study of History* (Oxford University Press, 1934), Vol. III, pp. 36-43, quoting at length from Busbecq, a Flemish resident in the Ottoman Empire in the sixteenth century, in *A. Gislenii Busbequii Omnia quae extant* (Leyden, 1633, pp. 99-102, 432-439).

[177] Civezza, *Storia Universale delle Missioni Francescane*, Vol. V, p. 210.

[178] A. S. Tritton, *The Caliphs and Their Non-Muslim Subjects* (Oxford University Press, 1930, pp. 240), pp. 18-36, 61-77; E. L. Butcher, *The Story of the Church in Egypt* (London, Smith, Elder and Co., 2 vols., 1897), Vol. II, pp. 183-218; E. A. W. Budge, *The Egyptian Sûdân* (London, Kegan Paul, Trench, Trübner and Co., 2 vols., 1897), Vol. II, p. 306.

[179] Arnold, *op. cit.*, pp. 109-112.

[180] Arnold, *op. cit.*, pp. 113, 114.

[181] Lemmens, *Die Heidenmissionen des Spätmittelalters*, pp. 61, 62.

[182] Lemmens, *op. cit.*, pp. 3, 4; Moreau in Descamps, *Histoire Générale Comparée des Missions*, pp. 271, 272.

tianity did not seem to face a promising future. The coming centuries might well have appeared to belong to Islam. In the Mediterranean world Islam was dominant in all the ancient centres of civilization except Italy, Spain, and Southern France. It controlled Mesopotamia and Persia. It was strong in Central Asia and was represented by communities in India and China which were still to experience a sturdy growth. Moslem merchants were in possession of most of the trade between the Far East and the West, and Islam was spreading along the sea routes to the Malay Peninsula and the islands of the East. Christianity was slowly yielding its remaining footholds in Asia and was confined almost entirely to Europe. Even in Europe, in the South-east it was threatened by Moslem Turks, flushed with victory, and in the West was torn by internal strife and menaced by scepticism.

These dark shadows were not the entire picture. Within the Church in the West were many protests against the prevailing corruption. Some who sought to stir their fellow Christians to a new and better life—a Hus, a Savonarola—paid for their temerity with their lives. Yet many reformers were not ejected by the official Church. On some fronts Christianity was making gains in territory. In Russia peoples in the North were being won and a great state was arising which was to take the place of the Byzantine Empire as the champion of Greek Orthodoxy. The close of the fifteenth century saw the final erasure of the political power of Islam in Spain. Moreover, the fifteenth century witnessed the beginning of that expansion of Spain and Portugal which in succeeding centuries was to add vast territories to the Roman Catholic Church. In the fifteenth century took place the conquest and conversion (projected in the fourteenth century) of the Canary Islands. The occupation was begun in the first decade of the fifteenth century under grant from the King of Castile and the encouragement of the Pope. By 1436 conversion had made decided progress. As a foretaste of what was to happen in the New World, some of the conquerors sold numbers of the natives into slavery, and the Church, through the Popes, protested and attempted to prevent it.[183] In the fifteenth century, too, came the occupation of Madeira and the Azores (both previously uninhabited) and the beginning of the Portuguese explorations along the west coast of Africa. These were accompanied by clergy to hold the settlers to the Christian faith and, in Africa, to win the natives.[184] While in the fifteenth century Christianity had met with many reverses, a new day of unprecedented life and expansion was about to dawn.

[183] Moreau in Descamps, *op. cit.*, p. 292; Civezza, *op. cit.*, Vol. V, Chap. 7; M. Bishop, *The Odyssey of Cabeza de Vaca* (New York, D. Appleton-Century Co., 1933, pp. vii, 306), p. 5; Schmidlin, *Katholische Missionsgeschichte*, pp. 192, 193.
[184] Schmidlin, *op. cit.*, p. 193; Lemmens, *op. cit.*, pp. 92-94.

Chapter VIII

THE EFFECT OF CHRISTIANITY UPON ITS ENVIRONMENT, 500–1500

WHAT effect did Christianity have upon its environment in the thousand years between the year 500 and the year 1500? How far and in what ways did it shape the many and varied peoples whom it won to its fold? What part did it have in moulding the portions of mankind which had accepted it before the sixth century?

These questions cannot be satisfied by facile and simple replies. To answer them we need to know what the Christianity was which produced the results that we are endeavouring to discover. It varied from place to place and from generation to generation. Then, too, the environment was by no means uniform. It also differed from region to region and from century to century. Moreover, our records are fragmentary: huge gaps exist which make impossible the determination of the answers to important phases of the queries. Yet the surviving material is so extensive that to cover it all is the task of at least one lifetime and involves a knowledge of many languages. To add to the difficulty, the queries often carry us into the realm of intangibles which defy measurement and even at times escape observation. Moreover, it is frequently impossible to determine how far a particular institution or idea or custom is to be assigned to Christianity and how far to some other factor.

In spite of the difficulties, the questions are so important that they demand attempts at answers. In many an instance at least partial replies are possible. We must take care, however, not to venture on too dogmatic generalizations and be willing again and again to confess ignorance and to offer our conclusions as tentative.

While it underwent many changes in detail and in the last three or four centuries of the thousand years displayed a few markedly new variants, in its main features the Christianity of the period remained true to the types which had been developed before the close of the fifth century. In these respects the effect of Christianity upon its environment was much greater than the effect of the environment upon Christianity. The peoples who inherited Christianity professed zeal in adhering to what had come to them from their fathers. The peoples who in this period adopted Christianity for the most part were barbarians who regarded with awe or desire the cultures of the peoples whom they conquered and were disposed to esteem as authoritative the faith in the guise in which it was taught them. In general, orthodoxy was at a premium and dissent and obvious variations were violently detested. Heresy was a major crime. Public opinion, the state, and the organized Church agreed in warring against it.

The main features common to the forms of Christianity to which the majority of Christians belonged during these thousand years can be quickly and briefly summarized. Most of the creeds by which Christians standardized their beliefs remained those which had been formulated before the year 500. They constituted an important part of the instruction given to neophytes and to successive generations of the children of Christians. In essence, the sacraments, too, remained as they had been. Assent to the creeds and reception of the sacraments, especially those of baptism and the eucharist, were still regarded as of primary importance. For the most part, the monasticism which had been developed before the close of the fifth century continued to be valued as the highest Christian living. Additional orders and new forms of the monastic life appeared, particularly in the Latin Church, but complete chastity, the renunciation of all personal possessions, and the cultivation of the devotional life either in hermitages or in communities now as formerly characterized the monastic ideal. Nor did the ethical standards officially taught by Christian organizations alter greatly—although their applications varied, sometimes markedly so. Miracles were still thought of as normal results of Christianity and were believed to occur in large numbers. Then, too, the goal of Christianity was, as before, the attainment of a blissful immortality.

Christianity was not, of course, identical with the Church. However, the visible Church would not have come into existence but for the impulse which came from Jesus. When, therefore, we are able to trace a movement, an institution, or a cultural characteristic to the Church, we are safe in seeing in it a result of Christianity, even though other factors may have joined in producing it.

The intensity of the effects of Christianity varied from region to region. In general they were more striking and profound in Western Europe, were less so in the Eastern continuation of the Roman Empire, and were still less so in society in general under Moslem rule and east of the Euphrates.

The cause or causes of this difference in the effects of Christianity, as we have more than once suggested, are debatable and probably were varied.

One reason seems to have been that in the West the structure of the Roman Empire and of Græco-Roman life disintegrated more fully than in the East, and that the Church, as the institution which did most to tutor the peoples of the West in civilization, suffered less restraint than it did in the East. Since the Church as an institution supposedly stood more exclusively for the Christian faith than did the state, Christianity presumably had freer course in the West.

Obviously, under Moslem rulers and east of the Euphrates, where in most sections Christians were in the minority, their faith made less impression upon life as a whole than in the Eastern Empire and in the West, where they were in the overwhelming majority.

Still another factor was geography. The Church in the Eastern Empire and across the Euphrates had again and again to stand the shock of invasions of non-Christian peoples from still farther east and, in the seventh century, from Arabia. In the West distance and the Eastern Empire formed buffers against invasion from Asia: once the peoples of the North had been won, the perils from non-Christian folk were greatly lessened. Christianity could, therefore, be more aggressive and less on the defensive. More of its energies could be directed to the transformation of the individuals and the communities which adhered to it.

Another possible factor was race—although this would be hard to establish.

Then, too, for some reason Eastern and especially Greek Christianity was more contemplative, mystical, and other-worldly than was that of the Latin West. This may have been due to the greater influence of Neoplatonism and the mystery religions in the Hellenistic East than in the Roman West. The activist features of Western Christianity may have been a legacy from the practical Roman spirit. It may be, too, that the West caught more of the spirit of Jesus, with its care for the maimed and the underprivileged. Latin Christianity, to be sure, was other-worldly and made much of heaven and of the beatific vision of God. Yet it was less passive and gave more incentive to moulding this present life than did that of the East.

Whatever the reasons, the differences between regions in the effects of Christianity were marked, and we must divide our study accordingly. We will first address ourselves to the fruits of Christianity in the West and devote to that the largest proportion of our space. Then we will say something of the Eastern Empire and of Greek Christianity there and in Russia. Finally we must notice briefly the effects of the other churches of the East. Obviously we must not take the time to cover even the first of these regions in detail. Our survey must be a summary and an interpretation.

In Western Europe after the year 500 Christianity influenced profoundly more phases of life than it had in the Roman Empire before that time.

This was for several reasons. At the inception of the Christian movement, as we have seen, its members made no effort to transform society as a whole. They abstained from many of the customs and practices in the communities about them. Within their societies they attempted, with considerable success, to lead lives different from those of the world without. Yet they seem not to have planned to revolutionize the existing social, economic, and political order. When in the third century the Church grew rapidly and when in the fourth and fifth centuries the vast majority of the citizens of the Roman Empire became professedly Christian, Emperors and the leaders of the ecclesiastical hierarchy sought to make the Church a bulwark of the existing order. As a whole, the official Church co-operated with the state in attempting to save society from the impending chaos. To be sure, as we have seen, the impulse derived from Christianity, either singly or in conjunction with other factors, wrought some changes—as in amusements, in marriage and the family, and in the laws. In the main, however, the more earnestly Christian spirits adopted the monastic life and so far as possible separated themselves from society. The monastic communities were meant to embody the Christian ideal. Little or no thought was given to inducing society as a whole to do so.

In the West, on the other hand, after the fifth century the train of events gave the Church a position more commanding than it had previously held or than it possessed in the East or beyond the Euphrates. Placed in that situation, the Church, through the ablest of its leaders, sought to make Christianity a force throughout society. The disintegration of the Empire in so much of the West, as we have suggested, left the Church the main custodian of Roman culture, and, indeed, of civilization itself. In sixth-century Gaul, for example, when the civil authority of the Roman world was crumbling and the barbarian kingdoms were being established, the episcopate was largely recruited from the old Gallo-Roman aristocracy and included many men eminent for learning, virtue, and ability. The bishops, accordingly, exercised some of the functions and enjoyed much of the prestige which once had belonged to Roman officialdom. They became the protectors of their dioceses against invaders and constituted a stable factor in a kaleidoscopic society.[1] Pope Gregory the Great, to safeguard the vast possessions of the Roman See and to procure justice for the ordinary Christian in a chaotic time, was forced to deal with the Lombards and was led greatly to extend the latent powers of his office. As the barbarians of Western Europe were won to the faith, it was to Latin Christianity that they gave their allegiance. They regarded Rome as the headquarters of their religion, made pilgrimages to it, and accorded its Bishop a place higher and powers

[1] Dill, *Roman Society in Gaul in the Merovingian Age,* pp. 272, 502.

more extensive than were given elsewhere to any Patriarch. To be sure, under Moslem rule the various Patriarchs in the East became the civil as well as the ecclesiastical heads of their respective communities, but they were never so nearly independent of the state as were the Roman pontiffs. Certainly they never dreamed of controlling the Moslem princes as did the abler of the Popes some of the Christian princes of Western Europe. In the West the Latin Church became jointly, with the Holy Roman Empire, the heir of the Roman imperial tradition. However, its authority extended over a larger area than did that of even the greatest of the Germans who held the imperial dignity. Through Europe as a whole it was much more effective than the Teutonic continuation of the Roman Empire.

The Roman Catholic Church was the agency which tutored the barbarians of the West in the arts of civilization. Through missionaries and princes in communion with it the non-Christian peoples of the West were, as we have seen, led to accept the Christian faith. Through monks, priests, and bishops, and through monarchs who looked to the clergy for advice, such cultures as they had were transformed. These converts and their immediate descendants regarded the Church with an awe which was bred partly by the Roman name and partly by religious sanctions. The Church spoke with an authority which was generally conceded. Before its punishments—the interdict and excommunication—both king and peasant trembled. The Church entered every phase of life. As a result, the Christianity of which it professed to be the expression and the custodian had a profound effect. The Church transmitted much of Græco-Roman culture. But it did more. Through it came an impulse which made of the new culture of Western Europe not a pale copy of the past, but a new creation which in every phase bore the impress of Christianity.[2]

It is interesting to compare the events which were happening almost simultaneously in China and in Western Europe. In China the structure of the Confucian state had crumbled in the third century. Barbarians came in from the North. A new religion, Buddhism, was rapidly growing in popularity. Yet in China recovery took place more quickly. Buddhism had no such extensive effect upon Chinese culture as had Christianity upon Western Europe, and when order and unity were re-established, the Confucian tradition, slightly modified, but essentially the same, reasserted itself.

Through the Church which at once embodied the Roman dream of a visible empire and the Catholic vision of a spiritual community embracing all Christians, the tradition was inculcated in the West of Christendom, a society

[2] Here see among others D. C. Munro in *An Outline of Christianity*, Vol. II, pp. 1, 2; G. G. Coulton in *op. cit.*, Vol. II, p. 299.

embracing all Christians and conforming in its life to Christian principles. It was a society into which men came through baptism, but baptism was administered to all infant children of Christians. It was not, therefore, a community which men entered by conscious choice, one by one, unless they had been born of non-Christian parents. Eventually, too, this Christendom, so it was held, although usually vaguely, should expand until it included all mankind. To be sure, pagans, Jews, and Moslems were not in it, and many Christians were outwardly separated from it—in "schism." Heretics there were, too, with whom Christian society must reckon and either win to the Catholic faith or eliminate. Yet in Western Europe this ideal of Christendom, of a society living according to Christian principles, was pervasive.

In association with this concept of Christendom arose a culture which, while inheriting much from the Græco-Roman past, incorporated, even though very imperfectly, features of Christian provenance. To be sure, in many of its aspects this culture was a glaring contradiction of Christianity. Monasticism flourished, and while also often patently in practice the denial of Christian virtues, attracted many who sought the perfect Christian life which they could not find in "the world." Yet in the West monasticism was often active in moulding society. Especially was this the case as the centuries advanced and new ascetic communities arose. The Franciscans and Dominicans were much more aggressive in entering into the world about them than had been the earliest Benedictines. But many Benedictines had also sought to transform the world. Indeed, the Cluny movement, originating among Benedictine monks, sought to bring all nominally Christian Europe to a better observance of Christian principles and to have the Church as the guardian and embodiment of Christianity control every phase of life. In the West, then, even monasticism contributed toward making all society Christian.[3]

The conception of Western Europe as a community upon which Christianity had made an indelible impression was persistent. Increasingly as the Middle Ages advanced, non-ecclesiastical bodies, such as cities and the state, took over functions once performed by the Church. Sometimes the transfer was effected only through conflict between the Church and the state. More and more indi-

---

[3] This development of the idea of Christendom has been repeatedly described. As a few of the references, see Jarrett, *Social Theories of the Middle Ages*, p. 4; Taylor, *The Mediaeval Mind*, Vol. I, pp. 11, 13, 170; Troeltsch, *The Social Teaching of the Christian Churches*, pp. 201-207, 308-328; McIlwain, *The Growth of Political Thought in the West*, pp. 308-313; Dawson, *Progress and Religion*, pp. 167, 169; H. B. Workman in Paton, Bunting, and Garvie, *Christ and Civilization*, pp. 292-294; Cunningham, *Christianity and Economic Science*, p. 80. On the authority of the Pope over all non-Christians as well as Christians, see McIlwain, *op. cit.*, p. 234.

vidual states controlled the Church within their domains. After 1500 the Roman Catholic Church lost its hold on great sections of the West. In the nineteenth and especially in the twentieth century thousands had no connexion with organized Christianity. Yet the tradition of a community embracing all mankind continued, and upon the culture of that community the influence of Christianity did not diminish, but increased.

In the realm of religion it was to be expected that the influence of Christianity upon Western Europe would be marked. As in the Roman Empire, Christianity wiped out the cults and the gods which had preceded it. Also as in the Roman Empire, the elimination was not complete. It will be recalled that the initial adoption of Christianity was usually by groups, some of them very large, and with a minimum of preliminary instruction. The result was a most superficial acquaintance with the new faith and the persistence of many customs and attitudes of mind associated with pre-Christian religions. In addition to giving assurance of salvation in a future life of bliss, Christianity was expected to do for its followers what the preceding religions had promised, only more effectively. Many ways which formerly had been used to attain these ends were preserved, in some instances in greatly modified forms, and generally under a Christian name. In this way, as we are to say more at length in a later chapter, popular Christianity was transformed. In creeds and in the main outlines of its organization and sacraments it was substantially unchanged, but as regarded by the majority of its adherents and as practised it was markedly altered. In the main it continued the development which had begun when in the fourth and fifth centuries the population of the Roman Empire flocked into the Church.

Even at the outset, the adoption of Christianity brought striking innovations. The bright aspect of early Scandinavian Christianity was the opposite of the grim inescapable fate which characterized pre-Christian Northern religion. The mighty Christ, his triumphant resurrection, and his gleaming kingdom in heaven were now dominant.[4] In Merovingian times, after the formal conversion of the Franks, even with all the murders and adulteries which marked that robustious age, the outward forms of the new faith were widely observed—prayer before eating, the sign of the cross over the cup of water before it was drunk, weddings and burials in charge of the clergy, attendance at public worship, the celebration of Christian festivals, and gifts to the poor and to churches.[5] The Christian saints revered by the newly converted Germans dif-

[4] A. Olrik, *Viking Civilization* (New York, W. W. Norton and Co., 1930, pp. 246), p. 149; Jorgenson, *History of Norwegian Literature*, pp. 90-92.
[5] Hauck, *Kirchengeschichte Deutschlands*, Vol. I, pp. 157-223.

fered decidedly from the gods and the spirits whom they displaced.[6] In the minds of the early converts, too,[7] as of their descendants, heaven and hell were very vivid.

The Church did not allow the remnants of paganism to survive without an effort to stamp them out. Repeatedly councils and synods proscribed them. Thus a council in 692 forbade feasts in honour of Pan and of Bacchus, the use of the pagan oath, and the building of fires and leaping over them at the time of the new moon.[8] The first council called by Carloman and Boniface (April, 742) took action against such pagan heritages as feasts for the dead, offering animals before a church in honour of the dead, and forecasting the future.[9] A sermon ascribed to Eligius, who in the seventh century was a missionary in what is now Belgium, urged Christians not to put their trust in amulets or to consult soothsayers or fortune-tellers, or to resort to auguries, or to note the day on which they left or returned home.[10] If the sermon is not authentic, it at least represents the attitude of some of the clergy of the Middle Ages.

Efforts were made, too, to instruct the masses in the Christian faith. The nominal conversion of the Anglo-Saxons had scarcely been completed when Bede urged the young Archbishop of York to see that those who did not know Latin were drilled in the Apostles' Creed and the Lord's Prayer in their native tongue and said that he himself had often translated these for uneducated priests.[11] In the regions under his charge, Boniface directed that each priest give annually to his bishop an account of his ministry and had every bishop go through his diocese once a year, teaching his flock and prohibiting pagan practices, divinations, the drawing of lots, auguries, and the like.[12] Bishop Otto of Bamberg taught his Pomeranian neophytes to observe Sundays, saints' days, and Lent, and to come to mass and confession.[13]

Both the parish and the diocese were instruments for the eradication of non-Christian customs and the inculcation of Christian tenets. Thus one of the

[6] H. Timerding (editor), *Die christliche Frühzeit Deutschlands* (Jena, Eugen Diederichs, 1929, pp. 276, 226; a collection of lives of missionaries, with a preliminary essay and notes), Vol. I, p. 7.

[7] See, for instance, the story told by Boniface in Kylie, *The English Correspondence of St. Boniface,* pp. 78-89.

[8] J. B. Bury, *A History of the Later Roman Empire from Arcadius to Irene* (London, Macmillan and Co., 1889, 2 vols.), Vol. II, p. 395.

[9] Hauck, *op. cit.,* Vol. I, p. 488.

[10] Migne, *Pat. Lat.,* Vol. LXXXVII, Cols. 527, 528.

[11] G. F. Browne, *The Venerable Bede* (London, Society for Promoting Christian Knowledge, 1930, pp. xiii, 327), pp. 191-195.

[12] Boniface to Cuthbert, in Kylie, *The English Correspondence of St. Boniface,* pp. 176-191.

[13] Ebo, *Vita Ottonis* (in *Mon. Bambergensia* ed. by P. Jaffe, Berlin, Weidmann, 1869), Book II, Chap. 12.

measures of Charlemagne was to establish the parish system more firmly and to endow parish churches.[14] As the population increased, parishes multiplied, at least in Germany. Preaching ceased to be primarily a function of the bishop and was done by the parish clergy.[15] As the centuries progressed, it was regarded as part of the duty of the parish priest to see that every child was taught the Apostles' Creed and the Lord's Prayer.[16] Later in the Middle Ages the Franciscans and Dominicans by their preaching did much for the instruction of the masses. Repeatedly, at least in the later Middle Ages, English bishops and archbishops charged the parish clergy to instruct their flocks in the articles of faith, the Ten Commandments, the seven deadly sins, the seven virtues, and the sacraments. Admittedly many of the clergy did not do this, but instances were not unknown, or so we hear from Germany, where a faithful priest took his duty seriously.[17] Portions of the Bible were put in the vernacular.[18] For the illiterate majority there were the services of the Church, preaching, the miracle plays, and the pictures of Biblical stories in which the stained-glass windows, the sculptures, and the frescoed walls were rich. Christian themes made their way into the songs, the stories, and the poetry which became the common property of all. The growth of auricular confession multiplied the opportunity of the priesthood for individual instruction. Care was taken to acquaint the laity with the meaning of the ritual of the mass.[19]

If this education of the masses was to be carried out, an informed and devoted body of clergy was essential. Many efforts were made to recruit and to prepare such a clergy. In the eighth century, for instance, a Bishop of Metz was responsible for a custom which spread widely through Gaul by which the bishop and his canons lived and ate together and brought in young men and trained them for the clerical life.[20]

Monasteries, too, were a means of religious education and of exalting standards of what they believed to be a thoroughgoing Christian life. Sometimes monasteries made provision for the spiritual care of the lay population about them. Especially did some of the Benedictine foundations and, in the twelfth and thirteenth centuries, the Augustinians and Premonstratensians engage in

---

[14] Ratzinger, *Geschichte der kirchlichen Armenpflege*, pp. 198-200.

[15] Hauck, *op. cit.*, Vol. IV, pp. 3-113.

[16] Powicke, *The Christian Life in the Middle Ages*, p. 82; Stead, *The Story of Social Christianity*, Vol. II, p. 14.

[17] G. G. Coulton, *Social Life in Britain from the Conquest to the Reformation* (Cambridge University Press, 1919, pp. xx, 566; a compilation of sources).

[18] Robinson, *The Conversion of Europe*, pp. 17-22, gives a list of part of these translations.

[19] Cutts, *Parish Priests and Their People in the Middle Ages in England*, p. 243.

[20] Ratzinger, *op. cit.*, p. 209.

the cure of souls.[21] Always (at least in theory) they gave instruction to those who took the monastic habit. While many fell into a sad state of decay in manners and morals, as a whole monasteries held before those outside their walls the ideal of a complete commitment, and through their teaching and their services they familiarized their members with Christian tenets, the Psalter, and with many other portions of the Scriptures.

That these efforts at instructing the masses and rearing a worthy body of clergy and monks were partly successful is abundantly clear. The attempts at monastic reform, from Columban through the Cluniac, Carthusian, Cistercian, Premonstratensian, and many other movements, down through the Franciscans and Dominicans, were possible only because a large body of public opinion supported them as expressions of the Christian life. Moreover, the friars drew their livelihood, not from endowments made once for all by the wealthy, as did the monasteries before them, but from the daily gifts of the many. The popular religious movements of the thirteenth, fourteenth, and fifteenth centuries show how widely and deeply Christianity had penetrated Western Europe. The mendicant friars, the followers of Peter Waldo, of Wyclif, and of Hus, the Brethren of the Common Life, and many another set of groups were expressions of religious conviction which, as the centuries passed, spread to more and more people. Even had the other revivals not come to birth, the preaching of the Franciscans and the Dominicans would alone have given the masses a knowledge of Christianity such as they had not before possessed. In Germany the thirteenth century saw a flowering of lay piety outside monasteries,[22] and in the fourteenth century the Friends of God continued to spread Christian beliefs and practices among the laity. The German mystics (many of whom were included in the Friends of God) and the Brethren of the Common Life are only a few of the indications of the fact that before 1500 Christianity was affecting profoundly the life of Europe and stirring it to fresh and creative religious expression.[23]

As we have suggested, Christianity spread from the top down. Kings and

[21] Hauck, op. cit., Vol. IV, pp. 326-427.

[22] Hauck, op. cit., Vol. IV, pp. 924-933.

[23] The literature on thirteenth, fourteenth, and fifteenth century mysticism is extensive. See among others Anna G. Seesholtz, Friends of God, Practical Mystics of the Fourteenth Century (New York, Columbia University Press, pp. viii, 247); E. Underhill in Cambridge Medieval History, Vol. VII, Chap. 26; W. R. Inge, Christian Mysticism (London, Methuen and Co., 6th ed., 1925, pp. xv, 379), Lectures 4 and 5; E. Underhill, The Mystics of the Church (New York, George H. Doran Co., no date, pp. 260), Chaps. 5-7; R. M. Jones, Studies in Mystical Religion (London, Macmillan and Co., 1923, pp. xxxviii, 512), Chaps. 9-14. A convenient translation of one of the most famous of the books growing out of the movement is Theologia Germanica, translated from the German by Susanna Winkworth (London, Macmillan and Co., 1874, pp. lxvii, 213).

princes usually led the way in accepting the faith, and their nobles and the common folk followed. It seems significant that until the twelfth or thirteenth century the leaders of monastic reform (which embraced a large proportion of the most deeply religious) were often from the upper classes. Thus Berno, the first abbot of Cluny, Dunstan, who led in reform in England, Robert, who began the Cistercian Order, Bruno, to whom the inception of the Carthusians was due, Stephen, the founder of the Good Men of Grammont, and Norbert, the creator of the Premonstratensians, were of noble blood. So, too, was Bernard of Clairvaux, the most influential Latin Christian of the first half of the twelfth century. In contrast, Francis of Assisi, who was the ideal Christian of the thirteenth century, was from the *bourgeoisie*. Christianity was working its way downward. Chaucer's picture of the parson[24] is an indication that the ideal of the pastor, a peculiarly Christian profession whose objective is the cure of souls, had found its way into literature.

The formal conversion of Western Europe was, then, only the beginning of a process which went on for centuries and through which Christianity more and more penetrated the populace, was consciously appropriated by it, and gave rise to new movements. As we are to see in later volumes, that process continued long after 1500.

On the other hand, the evidence is extensive of widespread and repeated failures to attain the ideals of making earnest and intelligent Christians of the descendants of those who had come into the Church *en masse*. In the next chapter we shall see the manner in which pre-Christian religious beliefs and attitudes mingled with the religion which supposedly was being adopted to constitute a new amalgam of popular convictions and practices. Bede lamented the neglect of confirmation, the excessive size of dioceses, and the numerous localities which had no one to teach the people the difference between good and evil.[25] Many of the clergy and monks were far from embodying the ideals of the faith they professed. Numbers of priests, monks, and nuns violated their vows of chastity.[26] Clerical drunkenness, venality, and simony were common. Services were hastily and carelessly performed.[27] Mass was said over wax images as a curse against an enemy, or was celebrated ten times or more in a day that an adversary might die on the third day.[28] Bishops as secular magnates became

---

[24] Chaucer, *Prologue to the Canterbury Tales.*

[25] Browne, *The Venerable Bede,* pp. 280-281.

[26] In one archdiocese in the thirteenth century about fifteen per cent of the parish priests were habitually incontinent.—Coulton, *Life in the Middle Ages,* Vol. I, pp. 79-84.

[27] Coulton, *op. cit.,* Vol. I, pp. 36-38.

[28] Petrus Cantor, *Verbum Abbreviatum,* in Migne, *Pat. Lat.,* Vol. CCV, Chap. 29, Col. 106.

so absorbed in affairs of state that they neglected the spiritual care of their dioceses. The clergy were held in chronic contempt—even while the sacerdotal office was respected.[29] The many efforts at reform of the clergy and monasteries and of the Church as a whole are at once an indication of a religious life which could not remain content with abuses or with anything short of the perfection set forth in the Gospels, and of patent and chronic departures from that standard. The introduction of Christianity brought a tension between the ideal and the actual. Many were attracted, yet many were content to find a more or less comfortable living in the endowments and other emoluments provided by the faithful.

Moreover, these centuries saw much scepticism. It is a mistake to denominate the mediæval period of Western Europe the "age of faith." Conformity to the established religion was enforced by Church and state. "Heresy" was combated as a public menace. Traditionally in human history religion had been a community rather than an individual concern. In every land the tribe or the nation was held to be endangered if the cults peculiar to it were not observed. In the process of conversion, the various peoples of Western Europe had made Christianity the faith of their particular groups. As a matter of policy, therefore, outward acquiescence in the Roman Catholic form of the faith was insisted upon. Privately, however, thousands took Christianity very lightly or denied it entirely, and publicly it was often derided. Large numbers believed just enough in the Christian God to insult him. A mob might beat the image of a saint in revenge for his failure to grant their petitions.[30] The sacraments were burlesqued.[31] Many preferred the love of women to a hypothetical paradise. Warrior lords chose fighting and this present world rather than a heaven of whose existence they were doubtful.[32] Numbers of the laity did not believe enough in the hell portrayed so luridly by the priests to fear it—unless on their deathbeds.[33] In the twelfth and thirteenth centuries, when the tides of religious life ran strong and many popular movements gave evidence of the manner in which Christianity had gripped both the humble and the mighty, by a strange contrast which was often seen in later centuries, much scepticism was abroad. It flourished at the court of the brilliant Emperor Frederick II. Many

[29] Huizinga, *The Waning of the Middle Ages*, p. 160; L. Pastor, *History of the Popes*, edited by F. I. Antrobus and R. F. Kerr (St. Louis, B. Herder; London, Kegan Paul, Trench, Trubner and Co., 20 vols., 1902-1930), Vol. I, pp. 31, 32. The literature on the corruption in the church is enormous. See as samples of many possible quotations, Pastor, *op. cit.*, Vol. I, pp. 38, 62, 72, 90, 241.

[30] Coulton, *Five Centuries of Religion*, Vol. I, pp. 186-188.

[31] McCulloch, *Medieval Faith and Fable*, p. 236.

[32] McCulloch, *op. cit.*, p. 233.

[33] Coulton, *op. cit.*, Vol. I, pp. 67-73.

held the Scriptures to be fables and derided the belief in future punishments.[34] In the twelfth and thirteenth centuries, in contrast with the friars, among the Goliards, wandering scholars, were some who were frankly pagan and who parodied sacred songs.[35] In France in the thirteenth century, after the failure of the Sixth Crusade, were those who, disillusioned by the collapse of an enterprise blessed by the Church, declared that God was on the side of the Saracens, and gave up their belief in Christ.[36] Dante tells of Epicureans who did not believe in a future life.[37]

In morals as well as in religion the effect of Christianity was marked. Indeed, since in Christianity morals and religion are theoretically inseparable, this was to be expected. Very early after conversion, peoples began to bear the ethical impress of the newly adopted religion. Among the Anglo-Saxons, many, even from the ruling families, entered the monastic life and submitted to its demands.[38] Theodore, the famous missionary Archbishop of Canterbury of the seventh century, in his penitential spoke out against drunkenness, sexual offences, theft, murder, and perjury.[39] Presumably these standards, backed by his authority, had some effect. The laws of the Olaf Haraldsson, who had so much to do with the conversion of Norway, forbade the exposure of infants (except monstrosities) and provided that at the opening of the *thing* a slave should not be sacrificed, as heretofore, but freed.[40]

The means by which the ethical standards of Christianity were inculcated and enforced were many. From them, too, are to be seen the ideals enjoined. Long before the sixth century or the conversion of Northern European peoples the Church had developed penance for the moral discipline and spiritual renewal of its members. After the year 500 this principle was continued and elaborated. Penitentials were widely employed. In their origin they owed much to the Irish monks and, on the Continent, especially to Columban. Archbishop Theodore of Canterbury also helped give them currency.[41] Penitentials were

[34] McCulloch, *op. cit.*, p. 230.
[35] McCulloch, *op. cit.*, pp. 265-286.
[36] McCulloch, *op. cit.*, p. 236.
[37] Dante, *Inferno*, X, 14 ff.
[38] Bede, *Eccles. Hist.*, Book V, Chap. 19.
[39] Haddan and Stubbs, *Councils and Ecclesiastical Documents Relating to Great Britain and Ireland* (Oxford, The Clarendon Press, 1859-1878, 3 vols.), Vol. III, pp. 176 ff.; Howorth, *The Golden Age of the Early English Church* (New York, E. P. Dutton and Co., 1927, 3 vols.: a standard work), Vol. III, pp. 238 ff.
[40] T. B. Willson, *History of the Church and State in Norway* (Westminster, Archibald Constable and Co., 1903, pp. xii, 367), pp. 73, 74.
[41] Oakley, *English Penitential Discipline and Anglo-Saxon Law in Their Joint Influence*, p. 37; Workman, *The Evolution of the Monastic Ideal*, pp. 212-214; J. L. G. Meissner in Phillips, *A History of the Church of Ireland*, Vol. I, pp. 196-199; Watkins, *A History of Penance*, Vol. II, pp. 587 ff., 756-768.

manuals for priests and contained lists of penances for various offences. In Western Europe their use was often required.[42] The attitudes and acts inveighed against included pride, envy, unchastity, anger, bitterness, gluttony, avarice, murder, perjury, usury, the promiscuous bathing of men and women, and the consumption of animals dying a natural death.[43] With penance, too, grew the custom of private confession to the priest. At first voluntary, the practice grew until, in 1215-1216, the Lateran Council made it compulsory.[44] While, as time passed, penance became more and more lax and the penalties imposed almost nominal,[45] in the earlier centuries when the barbarians had first entered the Christian fold, penance and the penitentials must have proved powerful in holding before the consciences of the newly converted and their immediate descendants ideals of forgiveness, kindness to the underprivileged, and self-control.[46]

Preaching was extensive. Sometimes the sermons were to the lower clergy and sometimes by them. As the centuries wore on, the homiletical habit seems to have increased. The Cluniac and the Cistercian revivals brought a growing use of the pulpit[47] and the mendicant orders gave it even greater currency. Crowds thronged the more eloquent of the friars.[48] Bishops preached to their clergy and parish priests, and curates to their parishioners.[49] By no means all sermons dealt with ethics. They were on a wide variety of subjects. Many, however, were on morals and still more had a moral tendency. Among the sins denounced in sermons were the use of oaths in conversation, greed, lust, anger, drunkenness, gambling, the lack of respect for parents, gossiping, vanity, luxury, and covetousness. Among the virtues extolled were generosity, temperance, chastity, patience, gladness, perseverance, love, and humility.[50] Deeds were declared to speak more loudly than words. We hear of one English preacher who, in addition to declaiming against the pride and the frailties of women, berated merchants and the rich and declared that a rich man could

---

[42] Oakley, *op. cit.,* p. 14.

[43] Oakley, *op. cit.,* pp. 43-63, 64-88; Lea, *A History of Auricular Confession and Indulgences,* Vol. II, pp. 102-107.

[44] Lea, *op. cit.,* Vol. I, pp. 183-229; Watkins, *op. cit.,* Vol. II, pp. 748, 749.

[45] Lea, *op. cit.,* Vol. II, pp. 169-232.

[46] Lea, *op. cit.,* Vol. II, pp. 102-112.

[47] Owst, *Preaching in Medieval England,* pp. 48-95.

[48] Huizinga, *The Waning of the Middle Ages,* pp. 4-6; Zawart, *The History of Franciscan Preaching and of Franciscan Preachers, Passim.*

[49] Owst, *op. cit.,* pp. 1-47.

[50] Owst, *Literature and Pulpit in Medieval England,* pp. 234, 236, 376-413; Owen, *Preaching in Medieval England,* p. 249; J. R. Sala, *Preaching in the Anglo-Saxon Church* (Chicago, private edition, 1934, pp. 80-144), pp. 108, 110; Zawart, *op. cit.,* pp. 244 ff.

not enter the Kingdom of Heaven.[51] Time and again the wealth of the clergy was denounced.[52] A manual of Archbishop Peckham issued in 1281 to guide the clergy in the preaching of the faith and which seems to have had a wide circulation, emphasized the moral duties of Christians.[53]

Stories and legends which passed from mouth to mouth also inculcated Christian virtues. Thus one which, with variations, was told for centuries, held up for praise a knight for pardoning his father's murderer when the latter clung to a wayside cross whereon Christ had died for man's redemption.[54] The point of the stories was usually ethical, but the incidents were generally miraculous. Many of these were narrated to give point to sermons, but seldom were they incidents drawn from common life. Various legends showed God as punishing pride, greed, selfishness, and laziness, and as rewarding kindness. They also extolled charity, self-sacrifice, repentance, humility, and forgiveness.[55]

Not all the virtues praised in the Middle Ages were of purely or even distinctly Christian origin. It seems significant, for instance, that in the building of the Bankers' Guild in Perugia prudence, justice, temperance, and strength were typified by pagan personages, and faith, hope, and love by figures of Christian origin.

The question immediately arises as to how far the precepts extolled by the Church were obeyed. Even a slight acquaintance with the Middle Ages discloses appalling and wholesale departures from them. The Merovingians, descended from the first Christian king of the Franks, had a record notorious for cruelty and treachery, and their nobles were no better. Barbarians who, in adopting a smattering of Gallo-Roman culture, had broken with their inherited moral standards, were as yet but slightly touched by the ethics of their new faith.[56] In the Inquisition the Church gave secular courts examples of cruelty.[57] We have already noted the decline in religious enthusiasm which the fourteenth and fifteenth centuries witnessed. This seems to have been accompanied by a decay in morals among many of the clergy and laity which Christianity was unable to prevent. To the havoc wrought by the repeated epidemics of the Black Death in the fourteenth century is ascribed part of the

[51] James Gairdner, Lollardy and the Reformation in England (London, Macmillan and Co., 1908-1911, 3 vols.; standard), Vol. I, pp. 28-36.
[52] Ibid.; Stead, The Story of Social Christianity, Vol. I, pp. 194-196.
[53] Cutts, Parish Priests and Their People in England in the Middle Ages, pp. 216-222.
[54] Coulton, Life in the Middle Ages, Vol. I, pp. 75-78.
[55] Rappaport, Medieval Legends of Christ, passim, especially p. 12.
[56] Taylor, The Mediæval Mind, Vol. I, p. 195.
[57] Coulton in An Outline of Christianity, Vol. II, p. 290.

responsibility for this demoralization.[58] The Hundred Years' War must have led to the lowering of morals in France.[59]

Yet the picture is not so simple as this would indicate. We need to recall that under the Carolingians an improvement was registered. This may have been due in part to the fact that by then Christianity had had a longer time to mould the Franks than under the Merovingians. It is doubtful whether in England the moral condition of the clergy was as adversely affected by the Black Death as some have supposed.[60] We must remember, too, that the fourteenth and fifteenth centuries, which displayed so much lack of religious zeal and such moral slackness, out of which came a Boccaccio and a Machiavelli (who wrote in the sixteenth but came to manhood in the fifteenth century), witnessed also the later years of Eckhart, the work of his followers, the Brethren of the Common Life, Bridget and the birth of the Order which she founded, Savonarola, the *Imitatio Christi*, the *Theologia Germanica*, and the German mysticism which partly expressed itself through the Friends of God.[61] We should likewise remind ourselves that the author of the *Imitatio Christi* and at least some of the great German mystics were interested not only in an inward fellowship with God, but also in a religion which issued in action in life with one's fellows. Apparently as the centuries passed and the full implication of the ethics of the New Testament became better understood by the multitudes of professing Christians, some flatly rejected them and went to the other extreme, while others took them seriously and put them more fully into practice.

One way of determining the effect of Christianity upon any age or people is to observe individuals who were regarded by their contemporaries as outstanding as Christians and to inquire into the manner in which their faith moulded their lives. This, to be sure, cannot be entirely satisfactory. Those who have been revered as saints were probably not typical. Presumably they bore the impress of Christianity more deeply than did the vast majority of their contemporaries. Moreover, it is impossible to determine accurately the exact extent to which their characters were the result of that religion and how far they were the product of other factors. Precise scientific measurements are out of the question.

Yet generalizations can often be made which clearly are not far from the

[58] Coulton, *op. cit.*, Vol. II, p. 174 ff., 397; Stead, *op. cit.*, Vol. II, p. 13; Lea, *A History of Auricular Confession and Indulgences*, Vol. I, p. 383.

[59] A. H. Thompson in *Cambridge Medieval History*, Vol. V, p. 692.

[60] Wood-Legh, *Studies in Church Life in England under Edward III*, p. 161.

[61] On these mystics and their works see E. Underhill in *Cambridge Medieval History*, Vol. VII, pp. 796 ff.

exact truth. For instance, while Francis of Assisi carried to the end traces of his early admiration for the troubadours, obviously the dominant influence in his life was his Christian faith. Moreover, he is a striking evidence of the extent to which Christianity had spread to the masses. Apparently the religious impressions which shaped his life were received in his native city, and religiously before its most famous native son brought it distinction Assisi seems to have been much like many another town in Italy. It was not a community marked by unusual fervour or by a level of religious instruction higher than the average from which came the impulses that started Francis upon his career. Francis was a layman and without the special instruction given the clergy. It was his exceptional response to what had become the common property of Western Europe which made him notable.

We must recall that never, apparently, was Christianity the only factor in the making of an individual. Thus the Christian King Alfred and the pre-Christian world seen in Beowulf have similarities which are drawn from their common Anglo-Saxon heritage, and the Irish saints were as irascible as the Irish bards.[62] Yet both Alfred and the Irish saints differ from their pre-Christian predecessors in ways which are traceable to their faith. Eckhart in his mysticism had much of Neoplatonism,[63] but he displayed traits which were due to elements in Christianity which were not of Neoplatonic origin and his Neoplatonism must have been transmitted to him in one way or another through Christian channels.

A large tome could be filled with the names and brief biographical sketches of more or less celebrated men and women of the European Middle Ages who in one way or another were the product of Christianity. Some of them would have been prominent entirely apart from their Christian faith. Others clearly owed to Christianity the qualities which have saved them from obscurity. Among the former were men like Charlemagne and Louis IX. Among the latter one thinks at once of such women as Catherine of Siena and Bridget, the most remarkable woman of mediæval Sweden, of the missionaries we have met—Columban, Columba, Augustine, Boniface, Anskar, and many another—and of such others as Bernard of Clairvaux, Pope Gregory VII, Peter Waldo, Dominic, Anselm, Hus, Savonarola, and Thomas Aquinas, some of them pillars of the official church, and some of them branded by it as heretics. There was a power in Christianity which moulded men and women and lifted some of them out of mediocrity.

[62] Taylor, op. cit., Vol. I, pp. 133, 144.
[63] See a summary and a bibliography of Eckhart in A. C. McGiffert, A History of Christian Thought (New York, Charles Scribner's Sons, 1932, 1933, 2 vols.), Vol. II, pp. 359-377.

Just what did Christianity do to all of these? To answer that question is to elaborate the topic of this chapter, for they were largely products of their age and that in turn was partly the result of Christianity.

Was there something distinctive common to all these which can be traced to Christianity? Always the accredited standard of the Christian life was what men believed Jesus had said and done and what men held was the significance of his birth, life, teachings, death, and resurrection. As a rule, those most highly esteemed as Christians by their contemporaries and by succeeding generations, and therefore those regarded as exemplars of Christian living, were they who were thought of as embodying most nearly the ideals of the New Testament and especially of the Gospels and as reproducing most closely the life of Christ. It may be that this devotion to Jesus increased as the centuries passed. Certainly it was potent in the twelfth century in Bernard of Clairvaux and even stronger in Francis of Assisi a hundred years or so later. In popular belief Jesus might share his honour with his mother. Mary might even be preferred as an intercessor. However, she was revered because she was the mother of Jesus. Jesus as presented to the Gospels and in the teaching of the Church was the authority. It was through him, so Christians were taught, that man's salvation had been wrought. The pre-Christian Jewish Psalter by its part in the services of the Church must have exerted a powerful influence, but the Gospels and the Epistles were given an even more central place. It was, we must repeat, the virtues praised and exemplified in the New Testament which to a greater or less extent were personified in those whom the people of Mediæval Europe regarded as Christian saints. If a Louis XI was popularly rated below Thomas á Kempis in character, it was because he fell so much farther short of the standard set by Jesus.

Upon marriage, the family, and the relations of the sexes the influence of Christianity was varied. Marriage was one of the sacraments and was controlled by the Church. The Church forbade polygamy, specified the degrees of relationship within which marriage might not take place, and reserved to itself the decision as to whether a marriage had been valid. It did not always succeed. In Ireland and Wales, for instance, pagan marriage practices were long prevalent.[64] Through its penitential discipline the Church inculcated prenuptial chastity and prohibited sexual intercourse outside the marriage bond. On the one hand, the prevailing asceticism which was stressed as the highest standard of Christian living tended to look upon woman as a temptation and an evil and by the difficulty of its attainment encouraged irregular sex connexions for clergy, monks, and nuns. A crass attitude towards women and

[64] McNeill, *The Celtic Penitentials*, p. 104.

towards marriage was widespread. Romance and wedlock were probably more frequently divorced than united. On the other hand, the cult of the Virgin Mary which was so prominent in both the Greek East and the Latin West and which owed so much to the ascetic ideal, exalted womanhood and chastity.[65]

Presumably the Christmas festival and the carols which arose out of it promoted a high regard for the dignity of child-bearing and for infancy and childhood. Certainly to Christian influence can be traced much of the sentiment against infanticide and the growth of foundling hospitals.[66]

Holidays and festivals were largely those of the Church and either were associated with some event in the Christian year or had been taken over by the Church and marked by religious ceremonies. Thus in Merovingian times the Church attempted to enforce among the peasants the keeping of Sunday, and many miracles were reported in which offenders against the day had been punished.[67] In Saxon England the observance of Sunday was often enjoined in the royal laws.[68] Holy days were repeatedly celebrated by high and low with drunkenness, licence, and crime, and many remained outside the church while the priests said mass,[69] but the religious significance of the festival was not always forgotten.

With its emphasis upon the future life, Christianity naturally wrought changes in the customs associated with death and burial. In Scandinavia, for instance, pagan interments had been near the village. Under the influence of Christianity they were made in the churchyard. By masses for the dead the Church professed to follow the soul beyond the grave. Masses endowed for this purpose and chantry priests to say them constituted a familiar feature of mediæval society.[70]

Many forms of association carried the impress of Christianity. The monastery

[65] On these points, so frequently developed, see among other references Ebo, *Vita Ottonis*, Book II, Chap. 12; Herbordus, *Dialogus de Ottone Episcopi Bambergensis*, Book II, Chap. 22 (both the latter in *Mon. Bambergensis*, P. Jaffe, ed., Berlin, Weidmann, 1869); Heinrich Finke, *Die Frau im Mittelalter* (Kempfen and Munich, Jos. Kösel'schen Buchhandlung, 1913, pp. xii, 190), pp. 49-77; Richard von Koebner, *Die Eheauffassung des ausgehenden deutschen Mittelalters* (*Archiv für Kulturgeschichte*, Vol. IX, Leipzig, B. G. Teubner, 1911, pp. 136-198, 279-318), *passim*; Lecky, *History of European Morals*, Vol. II, pp. 317, 318, 337-387; Troeltsch, *The Social Teaching of the Christian Churches*, pp. 129-132; Huizinga, *The Waning of the Middle Ages*, p. 176; H. B. Workman in Paton, Bunting, and Garvie, *Christ and Civilization*, pp. 304-306; Coulton, *Five Centuries of Religion*, Vol. I, pp. 176-182.

[66] Workman in *op. cit.*, pp. 296-299; Larson in *Church History*, Vol. IV, p. 164.

[67] Dill, *Roman Society in Gaul in the Merovingian Age*, p. 253.

[68] Cutts, *Parish Priests and Their People in the Middle Ages in England*, pp. 79, 80.

[69] Coulton, *op. cit.*, Vol. II, pp. 74, 75.

[70] See, for example, Wood-Legh, *Studies in Church Life in England under Edward III*, pp. 90-126.

was prominent and in theory was a thoroughly Christian unit. As we shall have occasion repeatedly to see again and again, and probably increasingly as the years have passed, Christianity has given birth to efforts to organize communities on purely Christian principles. In the Middle Ages the monasteries were the usual expressions of this impulse. However, in the West monasticism underwent a change. As the centuries passed, the new movements which arose, notably the Crusading orders, those engaged in redeeming captives, and especially the friars, were absorbed not in their own communities, but in assisting the suffering and underprivileged about them. Perhaps the example of Jesus and of his zest for bringing a more abundant life to those whom he touched may have operated to modify the self-centred character of much of early monasticism. By the end of the period, moreover, various experiments were made in other forms of organization which apparently had the objective of realizing a completely Christian community. Thus in the thirteenth century groups existed, chiefly of labourers in the towns, who called themselves simply "The Brethren." The official Church regarded them as heretics, and they had no use for priests, studied the Scriptures, were members of praying bands, educated their children, were kind to the poor and crippled, and kept in touch with one another by visitors and correspondence.[71]

The parish was distinctly of ecclesiastical origin and, widely spread as it was, had a marked effect on society, especially in rural sections.[72]

Many organizations arose which made no attempt to embrace the entire life of their members, but were in close fellowship with the Church. Some of them are known as confraternities. Numbers of them were guilds which undertook to fulfil for their members the functions of burial clubs, hospitals, and insurance. Each had a patron saint and might maintain a special chapel in a parish church and would at least see that a light was burned on special days in honour of its saint.[73] Some guilds provided masses for the dead. Others were for the purpose of increasing the number of services, or of preparing the accessories which added dignity to the services. Still others had the care of the poor or the maintenance of bridges as an object.[74] As towns grew, the number of such organizations multiplied.[75]

Unlike the monasteries, the towns were not the creation of Christianity.

[71] Stead, *The Story of Social Christianity*, Vol. II, p. 23.
[72] For a description of the parish in England, see Gasquet, *Parish Life in Mediæval England*, and Cutts, *Parish Priests and Their People in the Middle Ages in England*.
[73] Workman in Paton, Bunting, and Garvie, *Christ and Civilization*, pp. 310-312; Westlake, *The Parish Guilds of Medieval England*, pp. 2-5, 11-16, 60-65; Gasquet, *op. cit.*, pp. 253 ff.
[74] Westlake, *op. cit.*, pp. 26-48.
[75] Lallemand, *Histoire de la Charité*, Vol. III, p. 57.

Many of them, however, arose around monasteries and cathedrals.[76] Christianity helped order the life of the towns and gave it many of its distinctive features.

From the outset the Christian communities had cared for their own poor, widows, and orphans. When the Church and society became almost coterminous and especially in the West after the structure of the Roman state disappeared, ecclesiastical organizations largely took over the functions of poor relief and of care for the orphaned, the aged, and the sick. These charitable activities had their rise in acts and commands attributed to Jesus himself and found confirmation throughout the New Testament. In the same category came care for travellers and strangers and for captives. The Middle Ages esteemed one of the marks of an ideal Christian selfless devotion to the poor, the prisoners, and the sick. Mediæval churchmen, while upholding the right of private property, declared it to be the duty of those possessing this world's goods to relieve the necessities of the destitute.[77]

The examples are numerous, and large works have been compiled on this single phase of European life. Here we can mention only a few of the features and instances. After the weakening of the civil government in Rome, the church of that metropolis through its bishops and by means of its vast estates took over the care of the city's poor.[78] In the Gaul of the fourth and fifth centuries the bishops made provision for the poor of their dioceses. These bishops were often from wealthy families and gave liberally from their own property and from the goods of the Church.[79] In the sixth century the possessions of the Church greatly increased and some decentralization in their administration became necessary. The bishop more and more delegated that phase of his functions to agents.[80] In Carolingian times poor relief was carried on by bishops and abbots and was made a charge upon the property and the tithes of the churches, but it also was deemed obligatory on all Christians.[81] By a growing

---

[76] P. H. Ditchfield, *The Church in the Netherlands* (London, Wells Gardner, Darton and Co., 1893, pp. xii, 396: semi-popular), p. 36, points out that this was true in the Low Countries. John Evans, *Life in Mediæval France* (Oxford University Press, 1925, pp. 234: semi-popular), p. 65, says that the Truce of God, which made abbeys and churches sacrosanct, was a means of attracting settlers around these institutions. See also Boissonnade, *Life and Work in Medieval Europe*, p. 113.

[77] Bede Jarrett, *Mediaeval Socialism*, pp. 80-90.

[78] Liese, *Geschichte der Caritas*, Vol. I, p. 126; H. H. Howorth, *Saint Gregory the Great* (New York, E. P. Dutton and Co., 1912, pp. lv, 340), pp. 196-203; F. H. Dudden, *Gregory the Great* (London, Longmans, Green and Co., 2 vols., 1905); Vol. I, pp. 247-250.

[79] Uhlhorn, *Die christliche Liebesthätigkeit*, Vol. II, pp. 15, 16.

[80] Ratzinger, *Geschichte der kirchlichen Armenpflege*, pp. 180-185.

[81] *Cap. Mis. Gen.* 802, in *Mon. Germ. Hist., Cap. Reg. Franc.*, Vol. I, p. 94, Chap. 14, p. 96, Chap. 27; Uhlhorn, *op. cit.*, Vol. II, pp. 54-56; Chadwick, *The Church, the State, and the Poor*, p. 35; Liese, *op. cit.*, Vol. I, pp. 141, 143; Ratzinger, *op. cit.*, pp. 211-215.

custom, penance could be performed by providing for the indigent or for aliens or by freeing prisoners.[82] Charlemagne said that he was responsible to God and the saints as the protector of widows, orphans, and strangers.[83] Monasteries, too, as they increased in number and wealth, gave attention to the poor, the sick, and travellers. For several centuries after the Carolingians, they bore the brunt of the care of the underprivileged.[84] As we have more than once suggested, it is interesting that these institutions, originally self-centred and existing exclusively for the salvation of their own members, should, especially in the West, come to feel it their Christian duty to assume certain functions for those outside their membership.

Brotherhoods and orders arose to serve in hospitals. One of the first of which we know began late in the ninth century in Siena. In the eleventh century many cathedrals and parish churches had hospitals.[85] By the thirteenth century most of the hospitals were not under the bishops, but in charge of monasteries and of hospital orders.[86] A large proportion, perhaps a majority of monasteries seem to have had hospitals attached to them, several gave training in medicine, and many abbots became expert physicians.[87] Hospitals cared not only for the sick, but also for the orphaned and the poor, and in the cities many of them fed prisoners.[88] In the tenth century, Bernard of Menthon, archdeacon in the diocese of Aosta, did much to revive solicitude for the poor in Northern Italy, organized many groups for the aid of charity, and founded two hospices, the Great and the Little St. Bernard, for the comfort and relief of travellers through the Alpine passes.[89] In the twelfth century, out of a hospital begun by a citizen of Montpellier, grew the Order of the Holy Ghost of Montpellier, which in time possessed many houses. Partly under the encouragement and regulation of churchmen, the study of medicine flourished at the University of Montpellier.[90]

In the thirteenth century and possibly earlier, homes arose where unmarried

[82] Ratzinger, op. cit., p. 220; Uhlhorn, op. cit., Vol. II, p. 49.

[83] Cap. Mis. Gen. 802, in Mon. Germ. Hist., Cap. Reg. Franc., Vol. I, p. 93, sec. 5. See also Capit. of 794, Mon. Germ. Hist., Cap. Reg. Franc., Vol. I, p. 77 (Chap. 40).

[84] Ratzinger, op. cit., pp. 305, 306; Riesman, The Story of Medicine in the Middle Ages, p. 19.

[85] Lallemand, Histoire de la Charité, Vol. III, p. 40; Meffert, Caritas und Krankenwesen, pp. 164 ff.

[86] Ratzinger, op. cit., pp. 318-338.

[87] Liese, op. cit., Vol. I, p. 150; Riesman, op. cit., pp. 19-22.

[88] Ratzinger, op. cit., p. 316. On the care for orphans by Christians in Western Europe see Léon Lallemand, Histoire des Enfants Abandonnés et Délaissés (Paris, Alphonse Picard, 1885, pp. vii, 791), pp. 88-130.

[89] Ratzinger, op. cit., p. 261.

[90] Lallemand, op. cit., Vol. III, pp. 141-144; Riesman, op. cit., pp. 125 ff.; Meffert, op. cit., pp. 214 ff.

women and widows lived together in community life under a mistress. The inmates did not beg, but earned their living by working, sometimes in private families. Many of them added the care of the sick as an unpaid labour of mercy and some of them joined the Franciscans as tertiates.[91]

Late in the Middle Ages, perhaps at the beginning of the fourteenth century, the Cellites or Alexians came into existence. They liked the name *fratres voluntarii pauperes*. Usually they were uneducated artisans who lived in groups of four to six, held their possessions in common, and lived by gifts. They were lay brotherhoods for the care of the sick and the burial of the dead.[92]

The Brethren of the Common Life conducted schools and ministered to the poor.[93] The mysticism which was so strong in Germany in the fourteenth and fifteenth centuries expressed itself partly in active philanthropy.[94] This attempt of mysticism to find an outlet in service for the unfortunate seems to take its inspiration from the example of Jesus. Although not always present in what is called Christian mysticism, it seems to be characteristically Christian. In few if any forms of mysticism untouched by Christianity has it been so prominent.

Many efforts were made to rescue the prostitutes who abounded in the Middle Ages. In the thirteenth century an Order of St. Mary Magdalene existed for them, and in the fourteenth century numbers of cities contained houses of *sorores de penitentia*.[95]

Extensive provision was made for what was called leprosy. Whether all of what went by this name would come under the modern medical definition of that disease is uncertain. Leprosy was very prevalent and was regarded with dread and loathing. For one proclaimed a leper a special service was often held, with mass and the communion, and a formal separation from society decreed.[96] This custom and the casting out of the leper may have been derived from Old Testament regulations.[97] With the solicitude for sufferers from the malady seen in the pages of the Gospels, it is not surprising that the Christians of Western Europe were energetic in establishing hospitals for them. Many a monastery had a special house for lepers, and thousands of hospitals were arranged specifically for them. In the thirteenth century the Crucigeri had charge of many of the leper asylums.[98]

[91] Uhlhorn, *op. cit.*, Vol. II, pp. 377-389.
[92] Uhlhorn, *op. cit.*, Vol. II, pp. 390-394.
[93] Uhlhorn, *op. cit.*, Vol. II, pp. 368-375.
[94] Uhlhorn, *op. cit.*, Vol. II, pp. 350-375.
[95] Uhlhorn, *op. cit.*, Vol. II, pp. 298-302.
[96] Uhlhorn, *op. cit.*, Vol. II, pp. 251-260.
[97] Lev. xiii, 45, 46.
[98] Lallemand, *op. cit.*, Vol. III, pp. 239-244; Uhlhorn, *op. cit.*, Vol. II, pp. 251-260;

In the eleventh century the Order of St. Anthony was founded to care for those afflicted by a disease known as *ignis occultus*.[99]

Out of the crusading movement came orders to protect the pilgrims and to serve the ill among men. Of these the most famous were the Knights Templars and the Knights of St. John of Jerusalem. The latter, who were first primarily for the care of hospitals, are popularly known as the Hospitallers or the Johannites. The Lazarites were also famous. Houses of sisters arose to supplement the Hospitallers and the Lazarites.[100]

As we have suggested, orders were formed to ransom Christians taken captive by Moslems. The Johannites were active and the Trinitarians and the Order of Mercy were founded especially for this purpose.[101]

In the name of its faith the Church stretched its protection over the shipwrecked. In 1179 the Third Lateran Council decreed the penalty of excommunication for all who robbed these unfortunates.[102]

Not all the care of the poor and the sick was in the hands of specifically religious organizations. The manor looked after many.[103] As they increased in number and prominence, cities more and more made provision for their indigent and ill citizens. It became a matter of civic pride to possess large and well-equipped hospitals. Yet even these lay undertakings often had as at least part of their impelling motive that of Christian charity, and some were brought under the control of the bishops.[104]

Mediæval charity was not without its serious defects. For instance, not until very late do special houses seem to have been arranged for the insane. Repeatedly these unfortunates were simply driven out of the cities.[105] Then, too, little thought appears to have been given to remedying the conditions which gave rise to poverty and illness. The majority accepted as inevitable a social and economic order in which poor existed and attempts at public hygiene were usually rudimentary or entirely absent.

Paul Sabatier, *Life of St. Francis of Assisi* (trans. by L. S. Houghton, New York, Charles Scribner's Sons, 1909, pp. xxxv, 448), p. 142; C. S. Dutton, *The Samaritans of Molokai* (New York, Dodd, Mead and Co., 1932, pp. xiv, 286), pp. 8-38.

[99] Lallemand, *op. cit.*, Vol. IV, Pt. I, p. 32.

[100] Schnürer, *Kirche und Kultur im Mittelalter*, Vol. II, pp. 294 ff.; Uhlhorn, *op. cit.*, Vol. II, pp. 165-170; Meffert, *Caritas und Krankenwesen*, pp. 164 ff.

[101] Uhlhorn, *op. cit.*, Vol. II, pp. 162, 285-293; Marie, *Histoire des Instituts Religieux et Missionaires*, pp. 68-75.

[102] Kennedy, *Influence of Christianity upon International Law*, p. 45.

[103] Chadwick, *The Church, the State, and the Poor*, p. 33.

[104] Ratzinger, *op. cit.*, pp. 374 ff.; Liese, *op. cit.*, Vol. I, pp. 231 ff.; Uhlhorn, *op. cit.*, Vol. II, pp. 201, 202.

[105] Uhlhorn, *op. cit.*, Vol. II, pp. 294-298. A few separate establishments were, however, set up for the insane, some by priests and monks—H. C. Burdett, *Hospitals and Asylums of the World* (London, J. and A. Churchill, 4 vols., 1891-1893), Vol. I, pp. 53-56.

However, criticisms were not lacking of a structure of society which permitted striking inequalities in wealth, with prosperity for the few and stark indigence and hard labour for the many. At least some of these seem to have found their inspiration in the New Testament. Certainly protests were made in the name of the Christian faith. Among the legends of Christ which enjoyed popular currency were ones which told of him, as he wandered, being refused hospitality by the rich and punishing them, and being received by the poor and rewarding them.[106] In the later part of the twelfth century, in response to a reputed command of the Virgin, a confraternity of the lowly was formed in France which fought against the brigands and then turned against the lords, demanding better treatment.[107] Through much of the Middle Ages, from the twelfth century on, numbers of preachers and of religious bodies, many of them obscure and some of them regarded as heretical, denounced the private ownership of property and insisted that no rich man could be saved.[108] The Peasants' Revolt in England in 1381, while by no means entirely the result of the preaching of the priest John Ball, was coloured by it. For twenty years or more John Ball had been going up and down the land proclaiming the natural equality of man—declaring that all were descended from Adam and Eve.[109] The insurgent peasants are said to have insisted that they were men formed after the same likeness as the lords who treated them as beasts.[110] Back of this was more than a generation of popular preaching by the friars. Especially had the Spiritual Franciscans been condemning the wealth of the Church. Preachers high and low had long been satirizing public wrongs.[111] In the latter half of the twelfth century the Humiliati arose in the Po Valley. They were made up largely of labourers and social outcasts, and appealed to the simplicity of life prescribed by Jesus and the Apostles. In the twelfth century Arnold of Brescia fulminated against the possession of property by the Church, the clergy, and the monks, and had many followers, especially among labourers in the cities of Lombardy. The Apostolic Brethren of the thirteenth and fourteenth centuries preached the near approach of the Kingdom of God, of justice, equality, and peace. In the twelfth century, Peter Waldo, a rich merchant, adopted a life of poverty and attracted supporters who dubbed themselves "the poor men of Lyons." In the Low Countries, the Beghards, or

[106] Rappaport, *Mediæval Legends of Christ*, pp. 144-147.
[107] Evans, *Life in Mediæval France*, p. 66.
[108] Bede Jarrett, *Mediæval Socialism*, pp. 29, 30, 32.
[109] Gairdner, *Lollardy and the Reformation in England*, Vol. I, pp. 15, 16.
[110] John Froissart, *Chronicles of England, France, and Spain*, Vol. II, Chap. 73.
[111] H. B. Workman, *John Wyclif* (Oxford, The Clarendon Press, 2 vols., 1926), p. 239; Owst, *Literature and Pulpit in Medieval England*, p. 220.

Beguins, were groups of men and women, labourers in the cities of Flanders, who held property in common or adopted apostolic poverty. They were also strong in Provence and Southern France. Some of these movements spread widely and were persecuted by the supporters of the established order in Church and state.[112] Underneath all this unrest was in part a conviction widely taught by Christian scholars of the nature of property—ideas of *dominium* and *usus*. Christian eschatology, too, was at times a contributing factor.

By no means all those in Mediæval Europe who declaimed against the injustice of the hard lot of the poor were from the lower strata of society. Many scions of the rich and powerful found their consciences stirred to champion the underprivileged.[113]

Within Christianity was an impulse which stirred individuals, some of them of lowly birth, to go to the stake rather than to depart from a principle which they believed it their duty to hold.[114] In later centuries .this placing of the law of God as interpreted by the conscience of the individual above the commands of court or bishop was to have important and widespread effects in Western society.

Often the protests were unaccompanied by constructive proposals for the thoroughgoing reconstruction of human society or of Western Europe, or even of a particular community. Yet Christians in the Middle Ages were not without projects for a society governed by Christian principles. Indeed, these were very numerous. The Christian impulse seems to have stimulated them. Certainly it was responsible for some of them. In the minds of the most vigorous of the Popes, notably a Gregory VII and an Innocent III, the Church, directed by the inspired occupant of the See of Peter, was the divine instrument toward achieving a Christian society. Many a Pope struggled to make the dream effective. A radical like Marsiglio of Padua in his *Defensor Pacis* proposed what appeared to him an ideal structure for the Christian world. Dante in his *Monarchia* put forward a plan for the government of the world— one in which Pope and Emperor were to be the leaders. Thomas Aquinas dealt with the ethical bases of society. Savonarola endeavoured to induce the Florentines to conform fully to their Christian profession. Many another friar held up in his preaching standards of Christian perfection. However, for all of these

---

[112] See a brief description of a number of these movements in Beer, *Social Struggles in the Middle Ages,* pp. 160 ff. See also E. S. Davison, *Forerunners of Saint Francis* (Boston, Houghton Mifflin, 1927, pp. xvi, 425), pp. 171-200; D. L. Douie, *The Nature and the Effect of the Heresy of the Fraticelli* (Manchester University Press, 1932, pp. xix, 292), p. 248; E. Benz, *Ecclesia Spiritualis* (Stuttgart, W. Kohlhammer, 1934, pp. xv, 481), pp. 256, 349.

[113] Grundmann, *Religiöse Bewegungen im Mittelalter,* pp. 157 ff.

[114] See two instances in Gairdner, *op. cit.,* Vol. I, pp. 67, 174.

earth was but the preliminary stage to the life after death, and it is doubtful whether any of them contemplated the elimination of all injustices and suffering in this present life. For a this-worldly Utopia we must wait for a Christian of a later age.

Toward the institution of slavery and toward the half-free serfs the attitudes of Christians varied. In general, slavery was regarded as a normal phase of human society. By the thirteenth century, however, conditions had long been gradually improving.[115] Manumission was frequent and was often given just before the death of the master as an acceptable service which would count toward the salvation of the enfranchiser's soul. The motives assigned in the formal documents which granted freedom were the brotherhood of man, the example of Christ, love for God, and the hope of redemption.[116] Saxon laws prohibited, on Christian grounds, the sale of Christians out of the country or to pagans. In Anglo-Saxon England a council made provision for the liberation of English slaves held by a diocese on the death of its bishop.[117] The Third Lateran Council (1179) declared that all Christians ought to be exempted from slavery. In 1335 King Magnus Ericson of Sweden decreed that henceforth no one born on his territories of Christian parents should be a slave.[118] Even before this act serfdom had largely disappeared in Sweden.[119] The Council of London in 1102 forbade the slave trade.[120] Slaves, it was held, had souls and equally with their masters could be heirs of eternal salvation. Slavery did not obstruct the effect of God's grace.[121] Again and again the Church attempted to prevent the sale of Christian slaves to Jews or pagans. It decreed excommunication for the master who killed his slave and forbade a slave to be taken from a church in which he had sought sanctuary.[122] Gregory the Great stepped in to threaten punishment to the Bishop of Messina for permitting a vassal of the diocese to sell the young wife of a serf.[123] In the thirteenth century Bologna in emancipating its serfs, and in the fourteenth century the Count of Valois in performing a similar act, professed motives derived from Christianity.[124]

Yet it must also be said that, while Christianity did much to temper the lot

---

[115] See a discussion of this in Bede Jarrett, *Social Theories of the Middle Ages*, pp. 94-121.

[116] Kennedy, *The Influence of Christianity upon International Law*, p. 41.

[117] Cutts, *Parish Priests and Their People in the Middle Ages in England*, p. 82.

[118] Kennedy, *op. cit.*, p. 42.

[119] C. Hallendorff and A. Schück, *History of Sweden* (London, Cassell and Co., 1929, pp. xxiv, 446), p. 45.

[120] Ratzinger, *Geschichte der kirchlichen Armenpflege*, p. 267.

[121] McIlwain, *The Growth of Political Thought in the West*, p. 160.

[122] Lallemand, *Histoire de la Charité*, Vol. II, pp. 157, 158.

[123] Lallemand, *op. cit.*, Vol. II, p. 159.

[124] Brace, *Gesta Christia*, p. 238.

of the slave and of the serf, no campaign was waged against slavery as an institution as was to be done centuries later by Christian folk. Emancipation came slowly and from a variety of causes. In places, too, the Church is said to have perpetuated serfdom on its lands long after that status had disappeared elsewhere.[125]

It was to be expected that the effect of Christianity upon the political structure of Western Europe would be great.

Sometimes Christianity assisted political unification. We have seen how Charlemagne employed Christianity as a means of subjugating the Saxons and how Germans later used it as a tool towards the mastery and assimilation of the Slavs. We have watched princes in Norway, Poland, and Hungary utilize it as an instrument towards the construction of a centralized monarchy. Repeatedly the conversion of a people seems to have reinforced the power of the prince—partly because so often he insisted upon controlling the Church. Joan of Arc, strengthened by her religious fervour, aided in throwing off English rule and in quickening the national spirit of France.

Yet Christianity sometimes made for political division. The conflict between Church and state, between monarch and Pope or monarch and archbishop, weakened the king or emperor and furthered decentralization and the freedom of cities or nobles. The question as to which should be supreme in human society, the Christian community as represented by the hierarchy or the secular state, was one of the chronic issues of mediæval times. Both powers were held to be ordained by God. After a time in the early part of the period when the kings largely controlled the Church, under the Cluniac movement culminating in Gregory VII and Innocent III the Church dictated to the secular princes. The contest between Popes and emperors was one of the factors which produced the political disunion of Germany and Italy. The struggle for hegemony between the Patriarchates of Rome and Constantinople was a major cause of the political and cultural divisions of the Balkan peoples.

Many of the leading statesmen of the Middle Ages were ecclesiastics. Archbishops and bishops often ruled vast estates and exercised functions which are usually regarded as secular. They were also often prominent as royal officials. On the one hand this tended to bring into high office in the Church those who had only a perfunctory concern for their religious duties and on the other it gave the state a religious tinge and introduced a Christian element into legislation and political theory.

Into the political theories of the Middle Ages many factors entered. Some were rationalizations of the existing political organization. Others were derived

[125] Cutts, *op. cit.*, p. 332.

directly or indirectly from Aristotle. Still others were probably of Stoic provenance. The concept of natural law, so familiar in the Roman world, was powerful. To the mediæval thinker, the Roman Empire continued in both East and West, in a Christianized form, and Roman ideas were strong. The New Testament had its effect. The Old Testament, transmitted through Christian channels, made itself felt. Numbers of the Græco-Roman conceptions came through ecclesiastical intermediaries. Augustine's *City of God* strongly influenced many. The theory of divine law which was above the whims of rulers was partly from Christianity. Partly, too, from Christianity was the dream of a single community comprehensive of all mankind. To the mediæval mind the two orders of life, the spiritual represented by the Church and the temporal embodied in the state, were from the eternal counsel of God.[126] In principle, Christendom should constitute a Christian society with Church and state its two complementary parts, both deriving their authority from God. The dream of an empire embracing much of civilized mankind was largely Roman in origin, but the conception of that society as Christendom, held together by the Christian bond and conforming to Christian standards, and the presence of the Church, sharing with the state the rule of that society, had Christian roots. The prominence of the Church and the not unsuccessful effort of many ecclesiastics to give the Church supremacy over the state was, as we have so often pointed out, due to conditions peculiar to Western Europe. Moreover, belief that all mankind is an organism whose mystical head is Christ, and that the Pope, as the vicegerent of Christ, possesses peculiar rights and duties from God and has jurisdiction over all men, was much more comprehensive than the theory of the Roman state. The conviction acquired especial significance in the period beginning with the close of the fifteenth century, when the expansion of Roman Catholic peoples over so much of the earth's surface made possible its geographically wider practical application.

The prefix Holy before the term Roman Empire hints at the change wrought by Christianity in the theory of that rule which in the West claimed to be in the succession of the Cæsars.

Largely from Christian sources, too (although it was foreshadowed by Stoic teaching and by such a Hebrew seer as Ezekiel) came a conception of the sanctity and dignity of the individual which developed in Western Europe in the Middle Ages[127] and which in a later day was to have momentous political and economic consequences. The individual, so it was held, because he is a

---

[126] Among the many statements of this situation, see Gierke, *Political Theories of the Middle Ages,* pp. 10-16; Taylor, *The Medieval Mind,* Vol. II, pp. 275-280.

[127] Carlyle, *A History of Mediæval Political Thought in the West,* Vol. III, p. 3.

man, has an immortal soul, with an infinite future of either tragic suffering or of eternal and radiantly blissful fellowship with God. Whatever his present status, therefore, he has a worth which transcends that of any transient social structure such as the state.

Three of the major political concepts of the Middle Ages seem in part to be due to ideas introduced by a Church which was believed by right to embrace all Christians and to be the representative of civilization among barbarous peoples. These were (1) the conviction that the function of the state is moral, the maintenance of righteousness, and that while the state is a divine concession to human sinfulness it is a remedy for sin; (2) the supreme place of law as the embodiment of justice, so that there is a law which is above the king and by which the king must rule; (3) the relation between king and people as founded on reciprocal obligation and on an agreement to maintain law and justice.[128]

Probably it was at least in part an impulse of Christian origin which led Thomas Aquinas to hold that a ruler exercises his power not irresponsibly, but as a divine trust, and to declare that a king who has betrayed his trust has lost his right to the obedience of his subjects.[129] From a Christian source, too, or at least bulwarked by arguments derived from the New Testament, came the insistence of Occam that all authority, including that of the Pope himself, should be *non dominativus sed ministrativus*.[130] Marsiglio of Padua maintained that the Pope is but the instrument who executes the will of the Universal Church, that the sole legislator of the community is the people, and that it is from the people that the ruler derives his authority.[131] It is significant that both Occam and Marsiglio were supporters of the Spiritual Franciscans[132] and that these latter represented the effort to carry on in its purity and entirety the thoroughgoing Christian life as conceived by Francis of Assisi.

Upon the systems of law of the West Christianity made its impress. It

---

[128] Carlyle, *op. cit.*, Vol. III, pp. 181-185.

[129] Gooch and Laski, *English Democratic Ideas in the Seventeenth Century*, p. 18; H. B. Workman in Paton, Bunting and Garvie, *Christ and Civilization*, pp. 306, 307.

[130] C. K. Brampton, editor, The *De Imperatorum et Pontificum Potestate of William of Ockham* (Oxford, The Clarendon Press, 1927, pp. xxviii, 108), pp. 12-17; Osborne, *Christian Ideas in Political Theory*, p. 108.

[131] H. J. Laski in *Cambridge Medieval History*, Vol. VIII, pp. 627 ff.; S. C. Tornay in *Church History*, Vol. IV, pp. 214-223; Gierke, *The Political Theories of the Middle Ages*, pp. 46-54; McIlwain, *The Growth of Political Thought in the West*, pp. 297 ff. On similar theories by other mediæval thinkers, see Gierke, *loc. cit.*, and Stead, *The Story of Social Christianity*, Vol. I, p. 177.

[132] Laski in *op. cit.*, Vol. VIII, p. 626. On the Spiritual Franciscans see Ernst Benz, *Ecclesia Spiritualis* (Stuttgart, W. Kohlhammer, 1934, pp. xv, 481), and D. L. Douie, *The Nature and the Effect of the Heresy of the Fraticelli* (Manchester University Press, 1932, pp. xix, 292).

would be a mistake to suppose that the legal conceptions and codes of law of Mediæval Europe were entirely or even predominantly Christian in origin. Here, as in other phases of the life of the Mediæval West, the Christian element was only one of many. Roman law, the larger proportion of it reflecting forms developed before the conversion of the Empire, legal ideas from the Teutonic and other peoples which went back to pagan days, and contemporary conditions and developments modified only partly if at all by Christianity had their part. Even canon law—the law of the Church— was not of purely Christian provenance. Many of the churchmen who contributed to it had Roman law as part of the framework of their thinking. Even in those contributions which came through Christian channels pre-Christian elements are prominent. The Old Testament exerted a large influence. Often, too, it is impossible to disentangle the various threads and to affirm confidently of any one that it is from purely Christian roots.

When every proper *caveat* has been entered, however, the fact remains that on the growth of the laws of Western Europe Christianity had a marked effect and that in some specific instances this can clearly be seen. Canon law was developed by those who, while utilizing Roman and other contributions, attempted to make the whole the embodiment of Christian ideals. Partly because many of those who shared in their evolution were churchmen or were trained in canon law, most of the legal systems of Mediæval Europe had Christian features. Much of the Roman law in the form in which it was studied had been codified, reworked, or interpreted by Christians. For instance, the code which bears the name of Justinian owed its compilation and modification to Christians. Moreover, the very introduction of Roman law into some areas was by churchmen who would not have been there but for Christianity.[133] Under Christian influence the meaning of several of the terms in Roman law underwent modification. Thus the very word *justitia* might be employed where the purpose was the salvation of the soul and not the ownership of tangible property.[134]

A few of the many concrete examples of the effort to modify existing law and custom to make them accord with Christian ideals may be singled out somewhat at random. In the ninth century an Archbishop of Lyons argued against trial by fire and water and by battle[135]—even though a contemporary

[133] H. D. Hazeltine, *Roman and Canon Law in the Middle Ages,* Chap. 21 in *Cambridge Medieval History,* Vol. V; McIlwain, *The Growth of Political Thought in the West,* p. 149; H. B. Workman in Paton, Bunting and Garvie, *Christ and Civilization,* p. 280; Schubert, *Geschichte der christlichen Kirche im Frühmittelalter,* pp. 148-152.
[134] Taylor, *The Mediæval Mind,* Vol. II, p. 268.
[135] Agobard in Migne, *Pat. Lat.,* Vol. CIV, Cols. 250-268.

in the archiepiscopate defended the *judicum aquæ frigidæ*.[136] Repeatedly Popes and Councils condemned ordeal by fire, by red hot iron, and by the eucharist.[137] In the first half of the eighth century Liutprand, King of the Lombards, enacted laws which show more humanitarianism and a greater respect for human life than did earlier Lombard laws, and the difference seems clearly attributable to Christianity and perhaps to the priest or priests who did the drafting.[138] Again and again church councils sought to end trial by battle,[139] and, in later centuries, duelling.[140]

What did Christianity accomplish in the promotion of peace, both within states and between them? With the emphasis placed by the New Testament upon love, especially between Christians, the natural expectation would be that in a region professedly Christian, as was Western Europe by the year 1500, the frequency of wars would be reduced, particularly between members of Christendom.

At first glance the record seems quite the contrary. Far from preventing war, Christianity often was urged as a reason for it. The Crusades, wars blessed by the Church and many of them undertaken at the urgent behest of the Pope, were waged in the name of the Christian faith. Even when, as was usually the case, other factors entered, that of religion remained as a cause of the many wars which bore the Crusading name. The profession of arms, far from being deemed inconsistent with the Christian faith, was combined with Christian monasticism in the various military orders. In general, Christian theologians allowed wars if they were "just" and attempted to define circumstances in which that appellation could reasonably be given.[141] To be sure, Crusades were generally, although by no means exclusively, waged against non-Christians and heretics, but even within Christendom itself war was chronic. We must also remember and later recur to the fact that after 1800 within Christendom arose the most powerful armaments which the world has ever seen. In bringing to realization its ideal of love, of peace on earth and good-will among men, Christianity has seemed to be singularly ineffective.

However, the picture has other angles. It must be noted that the thousand

[136] Hincmar in Migne, *Pat. Lat.*, Vol. CXXVI, Cols. 161-171.

[137] Brace, *Gesta Christi*, pp. 168, 174-176.

[138] Thomas Hodgkin, *Italy and Her Invaders* (Oxford, The Clarendon Press, 2d ed., 1892-1899, 8 vols.), Vol. VI, p. 394.

[139] Oliver, *The Social Achievements of the Christian Church*, p. 99.

[140] Brace, *Gesta Christi*, p. 393.

[141] Jarrett, *Social Theories of the Middle Ages*, pp. 181 ff.; A. Vanderpol, *La Doctrine Scholastique du Droit de Guerre* (Paris, A. Pedone, 1919, pp. xxviii, 534), pp. 29-75, 215-238, 300-320.

years included in the period which we are now considering were peculiarly difficult ones in which to give actuality to the dream of peace. The break-down of the Roman Empire, the barbarian invasions, the migrations of peoples, and the disintegration of Europe into petty principalities and city states made for wars. They were occurring outside Christendom. Some of those waged by non-Christians, notably those by the Mongols, were even more destructive than those carried on by Christians.

We must also note that through the Christian impulse much was accom-plished for the alleviation and even the prevention of war. In Europe the day of sovereign states had not yet arrived. Wars within Europe were chiefly "private." If the word state is used in its modern sense it could be applied, if at all, only to the Church. The Latin Church, with the Pope as its head, was in theory and often in fact the ruler and arbiter of Western Europe. The Councils of the Latin Church were a kind of mediæval league of na-tions. In a real sense the canon law of the Church constituted a common law for Western Christendom. If some of the Popes stirred up wars, some were active in preventing them. Thus Pope Benedict XII attempted, although usually without success, to prevent wars between the princes of Europe, em-ploying the somewhat contradictory expedient of attempting to divert the energies of belligerent Europeans to Crusades against Moslems and heretics.[142] Bishop Isleif led Iceland out of the feuds of the saga period to a peaceful social life.[143] It would be interesting to know whether the conversion of the Scandinavians was to any degree responsible for the cessation of the Viking raids which had devastated Western Europe. Certainly Viking expeditions ceased not far from the period of conversion. Such conquests as were made by Scandinavians after their conversion—as by the Normans in England, Italy, and Sicily—although rough and cruel enough, seem not to have been accompanied by as much ruthless destruction of life and property or to have been as adverse to civilization as were the activities of the pre-Christian Vikings. While Catherine of Siena gave her support to a Crusade, she also healed family and civic feuds.[144] At least one writer condemned all wars between Christians.[145] Francis of Assisi helped to compose quarrels which might have led to open strife. Indeed, the abhorrence of war shown by

[142] Wright, *Medieval Internationalism*, pp. 15, 18, 51; J. N. Figgis, *Studies of Political Thought from Gerson to Grotius* (Cambridge University Press, 2d ed., 1931, pp. vii, 224), pp. 13-15; Helen Jenkins, *Papal Efforts for Peace under Benedict XII, 1334-1342* (Philadelphia, 1933, pp. 88; a doctoral dissertation at the University of Pennsylvania), *passim*.

[143] Olrik, *Viking Civilization*, p. 141.

[144] Stead, *The Story of Social Christianity*, Vol. I, p. 215.

[145] Jarrett, *Social Theories of the Middle Ages*, p. 185.

the Franciscan movement was but a culmination of a growing antagonism, prolonged over many centuries, between Christian monasticism and the rude warfare of the Middle Ages.[146] In the first half of the thirteenth century, Friar John of Vicenza traversed much of Italy, reconciling towns and individuals, but later invoked force and, defeated, faded from public notice.[147] The Servants of the Blessed Virgin Mary, or Servites, date from the thirteenth century and arose in Tuscany to oppose the violence and injustice of that region.[148] By their rule, Franciscan tertiates were not to carry offensive arms except in defence of the Church, the Christian faith, or their country.[149] The Council of Rheims (1119) enjoined chaplains of châteaux to suspend religious services in those to which booty from unjust wars was carried.[150] Purvey, Wyclif's assistant in translating the Bible, protested against all Crusades, even when waged against non-Christians.[151]

Comprehensive plans were not lacking for the elimination of at least some of the conflicts which wracked Europe. Various efforts were made to restrict the many private wars which marked the feudal period. In the latter half of the tenth century the Peace of God—initiated by the Archbishop of Bordeaux and given the support of synods—was an attempt to safeguard noncombatants and their property, particularly unarmed peasants, women, merchants, clergy, and the Church, against the chronic fighting. The Truce of God came into being in the following century and was given the support of synods and councils. It forbade warlike acts at certain seasons, generally from every Thursday to Sunday, inclusive, in memory of Christ's sufferings, and at two other periods of the ecclesiastical year—from Advent to eight days after the Epiphany and from Septuagesima to eight days after Easter —later to Pentecost. The Peace of God varied in the persons and goods protected and the Truce of God did not always cover precisely the same days. The two tended to merge. Both were most prevalent in France and Burgundy. It is significant that they were given the support of the Cluny movement, into which went much of the passion for religious reform and revival of the tenth and eleventh centuries. How effective they proved is debatable. The effort persisted into the thirteenth century. Presumably it must have had some success or it would not have continued that long.

---

[146] Sabatier, *Life of St. Francis of Assisi*, p. 328; J. T. McNeill, *Asceticism versus Militarism in the Middle Ages*, in *Church History*, Vol. V (1936), pp. 3-28.
[147] Kennedy, *Influence of Christianity upon International Law*, p. 34; Jarrett, *op. cit.*, pp. 186, 187.
[148] Marie, *Histoire des Instituts Religieux et Missionaires*, pp. 126-129.
[149] Lallemand, *Histoire de la Charité*, Vol. III, p. 8.
[150] Lallemand, *op. cit.*, Vol. III, p. 6.
[151] H. B. Workman in Paton, Bunting and Garvie, *Christ and Civilization*, p. 330.

Whether it contributed at all to the decay of feudalism and to the permanent disappearance of the conditions which it endeavoured to remedy is impossible to determine. It was taken up by some of the secular princes and probably such success as it achieved was due partly to the obvious utility of the measures proposed.[152]

Another effort of briefer duration was that of the Emperor Henry III, who on the "Day of Indulgence" in October, 1043, announced from the pulpit in Constance that he had renounced every thought of vengeance on those who had done him wrong and urged his vassals and subjects to forget all offences to themselves.[153]

At least in England the penitentials imposed penalties for carrying on feuds, thus proscribing a practice which had been sanctioned by pre-Christian standards.[154] Officially, too, the Church was hostile to tournaments and again and again prohibited them, because of the passions which the games aroused.[155]

In the twelfth century Gerohus of Regensburg came out in advocacy of a plan for a Papal prohibition of all war between princes, for Papal arbitration in all disputes, for the penalty of excommunication and deposition for any party to a dispute who violated a judgment once rendered, for the aid of clergy and all princes in the war of defence waged by the party who, having submitted to the Papal decision, had been attacked, and for the deposition of any prince who refused to obey the summons to assist in such a defensive war.[156]

Chivalry and orders of knighthood tended to induce the leaders of the warrior class of Western Europe to conform their ideals and their practice in part to Christian standards. The military orders—the Templars, the Hospitallers, the Teutonic Knights, and the various similar bodies in Spain and Portugal—which did so much to promote chivalry, blended military service with Christian monasticism. From Bernard of Clairvaux, often deemed the embodiment of the twelfth century's ideal Christian, came the initial suggestion for the rule adopted by the Templars. That Christian mystic and missionary, Raymond Lull, wrote a treatise on chivalry which was adopted by or imposed upon many knights as a model and was widely approved by

[152] Stead, *op. cit.*, Vol. I, p. 178; Thompson, *Economic and Social History of the Middle Ages*, pp. 668, 669; Kennedy, *op. cit.*, pp. 30, 31; Evans, *Life in Mediæval France*, pp. 57, 58; Lallemand, *op. cit.*, Vol. III, pp. 7, 8; *Cambridge Medieval History*, Vol. III, pp. 281, 282, 457, 465; Wright, *Medieval Internationalism*, pp. 149-154.

[153] *Cambridge Medieval History*, Vol. III, p. 281.

[154] Oakley, *English Penitential Discipline and Anglo-Saxon Law in Their Joint Influence*, pp. 168-196.

[155] Huizinga, *The Waning of the Middle Ages*, p. 71; Wright, *Medieval Internationalism*, p. 143.

[156] Kennedy, *op. cit.*, pp. 18, 19.

public opinion. Some knightly standards had no necessary connexion with Christianity—valour, adherence to one's plighted word, and generosity. Particular features may have come from Islam through contact with Moslem warriors. Others, however, such as humility, the denunciation of pride and boasting, voluntary poverty, the protection of the weak, love for one's neighbour, and perhaps the respect for women, seem to have entered through Christianity. The rites by which the knight was introduced to his profession contained a mixture of Christian and non-Christian elements.[157]

It is important to note that in these efforts to control war in the name of Christianity there seems to have been little absolute pacifism. The condemnation of all war which some Christians of earlier centuries seem to have felt and which a number of extreme Christian groups adopted in the sixteenth century and later appears to have been rare. It seems usually to have been found, when at all, among a few heretical sects. The *Theologia Germanica* (Chap. 46) declared against withstanding "any creature or thing by force of war, in either will or works." Yet defensive war was generally allowed and not until late was much dissent voiced from aggressive war against the Moslem. In the Middle Ages, however, and largely through the Christian impulse, was prepared the foundation for the later movements to regulate and abolish war—the sense of a family of nations accepting uniform standards of justice, rules for the amelioration of war, and machinery for the peaceable adjustment of international disputes. The Europe of the nineteenth and twentieth centuries with its contradictory combination of highly organized militarism and frequent wars on the one hand, with the dream of peace and extensive machinery for the alleviation and prevention of war on the other, is the legitimate offspring of the Western Europe of the Middle Ages. Here, as in so many other phases of Western life, Christianity has been chiefly responsible for opposing to inherited ideals of self-seeking and the glorification of successful physical force the standards of active good-will, of unselfishness and of humility. Neither has been able to eliminate the other. The result has been, and was in the Middle Ages, a culture marked by illogical and violently contradictory features.

We must add that the failure of the Latin Church in the Middle Ages fully to integrate Western Europe prepared the way for the nation states to which, from the sixteenth century to the present, have been due most of the

---

[157] Huizinga, *The Waning of the Middle Ages,* pp. 66-68, 74; Taylor, *The Mediæval Mind,* Vol. I, p. 529; Troeltsch, *The Social Teaching of the Christian Churches,* p. 399; Brace, *Gesta Christi,* p. 256; McNeill in *Church History,* Vol. V, p. 22; A. H. Thompson in *Cambridge Medieval History,* Vol. V, pp. 682, 683; A. Abram in *Cambridge Medieval History,* Vol. VI, Chap. 24; Walter C. Clifford, *A Knight's Life in the Days of Chivalry* (London, T. Werner Laurie, 1924, pp. xv, 300).

wars of Europe and the frequent approach to international anarchy. If international law and the League of Nations are in some degree a product of Christianity, the state system of the Occident is a symptom of the incomplete success of the mediæval Church in its creation of Christendom.

On the economic life of the Western Europe of the Middle Ages, Christianity had a number of effects. Here, too, Christianity gave rise to somewhat differing results. The Church, the outgrowth and official custodian of the Christian faith, became very wealthy. Many ecclesiastical positions carried large financial emoluments. Simony, the purchase and sale of ecclesiastical office, was an established practice, and the protests of reformers were unable fully to stamp it out. Monasticism enjoined upon all who professed it poverty as one of the conditions of the perfect Christian, but monasteries acquired property and many of them became enormously wealthy. Indeed, even without the many benefactions which were lavished on monasteries, the Benedictine rule, with its ideal of labour for all who followed it and its obligation of individual poverty, made the accumulation of collective wealth by the monastery normal. Now and again radicals urged the secularization of the possessions of the Church and apostolic poverty for Pope and priest,[158] but this was never achieved—except in part in later centuries by rapacious princes acting from other than Christian motives.

The Benedictine rule and the many derived from it probably helped to give dignity to labour, including manual labour in the fields.[159] This was in striking contrast with the aristocratic conviction of the servile status of manual work which prevailed in much of ancient society and which was also the attitude of the warriors and non-monastic ecclesiastics who constituted the upper classes of the Middle Ages. Many of aristocratic birth, in renouncing the world and entering the monasteries, especially the Carthusian and Cistercian houses, undertook manual labour as part of the prescribed routine. Yet it would be hard to prove that their example led their lay relatives to greater respect for those who tilled the soil of their manors.

The monastic organization was a kind of Christian communism, but it would also be difficult to demonstrate that this led to a similar system in non-monastic society.

To the monasteries, however, was obviously due much clearing of land and improvement in methods of agriculture. In the midst of barbarism, the monas-

[158] H. B. Workman in Paton, Bunting and Garvie, *Christ and Civilization,* pp. 325, 326; Gairdner, *Lollardy and the Reformation in England,* Vol. I, p. 11.
[159] Ratzinger, *Geschichte der kirchlichen Armenpflege,* p. 228; Workman, *The Evolution of the Monastic Ideal,* pp. 157-160; Cunningham, *Christianity and Economic Science,* pp. 26, 27.

teries were centres of orderly and settled life and examples of the skilful
management of the soil.[160] Under the Carolingians monks were assigned the
duty of road-building and road repair. Until the rise of the towns in the
eleventh century, they were pioneers in industry and commerce.[161] The shops
of the monasteries preserved the industries of Roman times. Monasteries
cultivated grapes and produced wine. The earliest use of marl in improving
the soil is attributed to them.[162] The great French monastic orders led in
the agricultural colonization of Western Europe.[163] Especially did the Cistercians make their houses centres of agriculture and contribute to improvements in that occupation. With their lay brothers and their hired labourers,
they became great landed proprietors.[164] In Hungary and on the German
frontier the Cistercians were particularly important in reducing the soil to
cultivation and in furthering colonization.[165] In Poland, too, the German
monasteries set advanced standards in agriculture and introduced artisans
and craftsmen.[166]

In their theory of property, mediæval Christian thinkers tended to follow
the Fathers in regarding the natural condition as common ownership and
individual use. God was declared to be the supreme owner. The world, they
held, is for the common benefit of mankind, and all should receive from it
what they really need. Yet, since human nature is sinful, community of
ownership is impossible and private property is permissible, but as a concession to human frailty. Here and there were those who, like the spiritual
Franciscans, denounced all private property.[167]

On some specific economic issues the Church attempted to enforce what it
deemed Christian principles. It prohibited all taking of interest as a mortal
sin. To receive interest was considered worse than theft, and absolution could
be had only through complete restitution of all sums thus acquired.[168] The
unrepentant who exacted interest were pictured as finding their place in
hell.[169] The Jew believed it legitimate to require interest, at least from a

[160] Cunningham, *op. cit.*, p. 21.

[161] Evans, *Life in Mediæval France*, p. 80.

[162] Thompson, *Economic and Social History of the Middle Ages*, pp. 145, 146.

[163] Boissonnade, *Life and Work in Medieval Europe*, pp. 157, 227, 230.

[164] Hauck, *Kirchengeschichte Deutschlands*, Vol. IV, pp. 326, 327; Stead, *The Story of Social Christianity*, Vol. I, p. 187.

[165] Thompson, *op. cit.*, pp. 533, 611-618.

[166] Thompson, *op. cit.*, p. 537.

[167] McIlwain, *The Growth of Political Thought in the West*, pp. 161-163; Cunningham, *Christianity and Economic Science*, p. 10; Jarrett, *Social Theories of the Middle Ages*, pp. 122-149.

[168] Lea, *A History of Auricular Confession and Indulgences in the Latin Church*, Vol. II, pp. 385, 386; Jarrett, *op. cit.*, pp. 162 ff.

[169] Coulton, *Life in the Middle Ages*, Vol. I, pp. 58-61.

Christian, and this accentuated the dislike of Christians for Jews.[170] Yet the Church was the first to accumulate reserves of capital, to begin the system of deposits, credit, and banking, and to advocate a stable coinage.[171] The Templars were famous as bankers.[172] Moreover, some specialists in canon law allowed a return on capital invested in enterprises which involved risk.[173] The Church, too, inculcated the theory of the "just price." This was widely held in Mediaeval Europe and included not only the amount to be asked for goods, but also the wage level. Active attempts were made to establish the factors which determined a just price and to fix the price itself.[174]

In general, Christianity seems to have had more influence upon agriculture than upon industry and commerce, upon rural life than upon the cities. It must be remembered, however, that the guilds by which mediaeval industry and commerce, and even some towns, were organized possessed religious features. They were religious confraternities.[175] Often they provided for masses for the souls of their deceased members. Presumably they would make some effort, even though perfunctory, to govern their affairs according to Christian principles. Of the towns themselves, as we have suggested, many arose in the shadow of a cathedral or of a monastery. Some of the fairs which formed so important a feature of mediaeval commerce were blessed by the Church and given her protection.[176]

The contribution of Christianity to art is so well known as to require no more than the briefest mention. In architecture the face of Europe still bears evidence of the creative stimulus of that religion. Monasteries, parish churches, and cathedrals are the most striking and numerous of the remains of the buildings of the Middle Ages. Forms inherited from Roman antiquity were developed into the Romanesque. The Gothic in its various phases was produced.

From the standpoint of the influence of Christianity, the importance of religious architecture lay not so much in the particular style, for that was shared with secular structures, but in the manner in which brick and stone and the successive fashions in architecture were made to give tangible expression to Christian conceptions. The church building was primarily to en-

---

[170] Cunningham, op. cit., Vol. I, p. 63.
[171] Boissonnade, Life and Work in Medieval Europe, p. 158.
[172] Boissonnade, op. cit., p. 167.
[173] Boissonnade, op. cit., p. 166.
[174] Cunningham, op. cit., p. 43; W. J. Ashley, An Introduction to English Economic History and Theory (New York, G. P. Putnam's Sons, 4th ed., 2 vols., 1910), Vol. I, Pt. I, pp. 133-141; Thompson, Economic and Social History of the Middle Ages, p. 697; Jarrett, Social Theories of the Middle Ages, pp. 160-162.
[175] Evans, Life in Mediæval France, p. 71.
[176] Boissonnade, op. cit., p. 170.

shrine and give visible dignity to the mass. It was centred about the altar, with its daily recurring mystery wrought for man's salvation.

It is important, too, that over much of Western Europe in the earlier of the centuries between the years 500 and 1500 it was largely through the Church that the fine arts were kept alive and developed. The monasteries as havens of peace in disordered times were especially centres of the arts. In them architects, sculptors, skilled penmen, painters, and musicians were trained and found occupation.[177] The manuscripts which were copied in such abundance gave impulse and scope to calligraphy and illumination. Irish monasteries, for instance, were prolific in beautiful examples of the illuminator's skill. Churches for the secular clergy, too, evoked the artistic genius. Upon the vestments and the vessels used in the churches, whether connected or unconnected with monasteries, much care and wealth were lavished. In times when only the small minority could read, and when the services of the Church were in a tongue unintelligible to the masses, religious instruction had largely to be given and the quickening of the devotional attitude had chiefly to be stimulated through the arts. The elaborate sculptures, especially on the Gothic churches, and the mosaics, particularly in structures influenced by the Byzantine tradition, must decidedly have supplemented sermons, miracle plays, and processions. The dominant subjects in sculpture and painting were associated with the Christian faith. In general, through the earlier part of the period, the major interest of the artist and of those who directed him was in the religious aspects of his theme. The human form was not loved for its own sake, but as an instrument for conveying ideas and feelings. The contrast is striking between the art of Greece and Rome, with its emphasis upon the physical beauty of the human body and the visible, and that of the Middle Ages which sought to express through the visible the invisible power and grace of God.[178] Inevitably, however, joy in the sensuous broke through conventions and guided the sculptor's tools, and the results are still seen on many a Gothic structure.

As the generations passed, art ceased to be so exclusively dependent upon the Church. Secular princes and towns became its patrons. The religious interest was less dominant. Yet to the end of the fifteenth century and beyond, the themes treated by painters and sculptors were still drawn largely from Christianity.

Music constituted an important part of the services of the Church, and by this channel continued without a break from the old to the new.[179] For

---

[177] Didron, *Christian Iconography*, Vol. I, pp. 1-7.
[178] Taylor, *The Medieval Mind*, Vol. II, p. 85.
[179] Schubert, *Geschichte der christlichen Kirche im Frühmittelalter*, p. 760.

instance, Charlemagne wished to introduce in his realms north of the Alps the music he had heard at Rome and at his request the Pope sent experts who founded schools of music at Metz and at St. Gall's.[180] The organ was brought into Northern Europe and developed through its use in the churches.

The liturgy of the Church was, too, in one sense, an expression of the artistic sense. Much of it was evoked and dominated by the deepest and most poignant emotions that Christianity knows. The liturgies which developed in the Europe of this period took their inspiration and part of their form from much earlier ones, but indicate the continued power of Christianity to create symbolism to express the beliefs, the hopes, and the aspirations of the Christian faith.

Christianity left its stamp broad and deep upon the literature of the Europe of the Middle Ages. Like so many others of the phases of culture treated here, this can only be hinted at and represented by a few scattered instances. The place of the monasteries in preserving the classics of pagan antiquity is obvious. They were the refuges of books and scholarship during much of the disorder of the sixth to the eleventh century.[181] The humanist Popes of the Renaissance, too, collected in the Vatican the manuscripts of the Greek and Roman past. Throughout much of the period, especially in the earlier part, those who could write were largely trained in monasteries or in schools under the auspices of the Church. It was to be expected that their works would show the influence of the Christian religion. Moreover, the medium of scholarship and much of that of religious and of other literature was Latin, and this was chiefly because it was the official language of the Church of the West. It would be interesting to know how far the Latin style of the Middle Ages was affected by that of the Vulgate, the standard Latin translation of the Bible.

Of religious literature, which constituted so large a proportion of what was written in these centuries, we need not speak. Obviously it was under the control of Christian ideas. It may be well to note that much of it was in the vernacular. For instance, in the ninth century, at Fulda, a translation was made of the Latin harmony of the Gospels.[182]

Of philosophy and what is thought of as the product of scholarship we are to say something in a moment. Here we must rather note the literature in the vernacular. Much although by no means all of this was further removed

---

[180] Joynt, *The Life of St. Gall,* p. 45.

[181] St. Gall's, with its missionary background, had a fragment of Virgil, one of the earliest known extant copies of that poet.—Joynt, *op. cit.,* pp. 48 ff. But for the Mother Benedictine monastery on Monte Cassino, we would not now have the *Histories* of Tacitus, or Apuleius, or Varro.—Haskins, *The Renaissance of the Twelfth Century,* p. 37.

[182] Schnürer, *Kirche und Kultur im Mittelalter,* Vol. II, p. 91.

from ecclesiastical control or inspiration than was the larger part of that in Latin, and more nearly reflected the lay mind.

Some of the poetry of pre-Christian times was given its present forms by Christians and probably displays evidences of the Christian medium through which it has come. That is possibly the case in several of the Scandinavian Eddas.[183]

Caedmon, whose name holds such an important place in the literature of Old English, followed the pre-Christian tradition of his race of improvising popular poems to be sung to music, but, under the inspiration of the newly accepted faith, used Biblical themes.[184] Folk songs show the influence of the partly Christian atmosphere in which they were sung. The Song of Roland is a secular fabric shot through with ideas derived from Christianity. The Arthurian cycle, while embodying much which cannot be called Christian, was obviously worked and reworked under Christian auspices. Whatever its origin and earliest significance, the Grail came to be associated with the Last Supper, and the tale of Parzival, with its note of ultimate redemption and forgiveness, has Christian colouring.[185] The Scandinavian Sagas came largely through a Christian medium, but were chiefly pagan in morality and in their grim outlook.[186] Later came Christian poetry, reflecting clearly the hope which the new faith had brought.[187] William Langland would have been very different had he not lived in a Christian environment. Chaucer's *Canterbury Tales* chose as their occasion a pilgrimage to a Christian shrine, and several of them have distinctly Christian ingredients. Francis of Assisi's *Canticle to the Sun* is in the rhymed Italian prose of the period and is one of the oldest surviving examples—perhaps the oldest—of Italian poetry.[188] The early Franciscans did much to create or give currency to Italian rhymes.[189] Dante is obviously the product of the Christianity of the Middle Ages.

The Middle Ages saw the emergence of much verse in Latin. Some of this was religious and some secular. Much of the latter was by members of the clergy. A large proportion of the religious poetry sprang from the sequences

---

[183] Clemen, *Der Einfluss des Christentums auf andere Religionen*, pp. 31-50; Schubert, *Geschichte der christlichen Kirche im Frühmittelalter*, p. 4; Jorgenson, *History of Norwegian Literature*, p. 19, says that the tendency of present day scholarship is to discount such influences.

[184] Bede, *Eccles: Hist.*, Book IV, Chap. 24.

[185] Taylor, *The Mediæval Mind*, Vol. I, p. 610, contrasts *Parsifal*, with its Christian note of repentance, hope, forgiveness, mercy, and redemption for the sinner, with *Œdipus* and the submission of the unwitting sinner to the necessary consequences of his act.

[186] Jorgenson, *History of Norwegian Literature*, pp. 63 ff.

[187] Jorgenson, *op. cit.*, pp. 90 ff.

[188] Sedgwick, *Italy in the Thirteenth Century*, Vol. I, p. 146.

[189] F. C. Burkitt in *An Outline of Christianity*, Vol. II, p. 327.

of the chanted mass and was composed to be sung to tunes derived from this part of the liturgy.[190] The Gospel story was a centre of much of the emotional life of the Middle Ages and naturally gave rise to verse, some of it in Latin and some in the vernaculars. Church festivals became at once the occasion and the inspiration for popular song and verse.[191]

Drama was deeply indebted to Christianity. The liturgy itself possessed the dramatic element. Usually apart from it and in connexion with the festivals of the Christian year, special plays came into existence. Their development occupied several centuries and they were prominent in the life of the people.[192]

The writing of history was largely by churchmen. The chronicles which constitute the source of much of our information for the events of the period were composed in monasteries.

In no phase of the life of Western Europe, unless it may be religion, was the influence of Christianity so marked as in education and scholarship. North of the Alps, for centuries practically all formal education was carried on through ecclesiastical agencies or in institutions which were the outgrowth of such agencies. Almost all the learning derived from books was transmitted through the clergy—if one makes that term broad enough, as did the Middle Ages, to include some who were not even in minor orders, but whom the Church regarded as being in her service and especially under her protection. This was because of the disappearance in the fifth and sixth centuries of those secular schools and teachers in whose hands had been much of the education in Roman times. In Italy, where the collapse of the old order was not so extensive as in Gaul and where the connexion with Constantinople gave support to some of the earlier traditions, lay schools and schoolmasters continued, although in attenuated numbers.[193] Yet even in Italy the old educational machinery largely broke down. The gap thus left was filled by monasteries, bishops, and, at times, by secular parish priests. The monastery and the bishop found it necessary to have education, the one for its novices and the other for his younger clergy, if the Scriptures and the Fathers were to continue to be read and if the services and the organization of the Church were

[190] Taylor, op. cit., Vol. II, pp. 201 ff.; F. J. E. Raby, A History of Christian-Latin Poetry from the Beginnings to the Close of the Middle Ages (Oxford, The Clarendon Press, 1927, pp. vii, 491), pp. 121 ff.

[191] Taylor, op. cit., Vol. I, p. 19; F. J. E. Raby, A History of Secular Latin Poetry in the Middle Ages (Oxford, The Clarendon Press, 2 vols., 1934).

[192] A standard work giving an account of these dramas, together with many of the texts, is Karl Young, The Drama of the Medieval Church (Oxford, The Clarendon Press, 1933, 2 vols.). See also Edith A. Wright, The Dissemination of the Liturgical Drama in France (Bryn Mawr, Pa. [privately printed], 1936 pp. 201).

[193] M. Deanesly in Cambridge Medieval History, Vol. V, p. 766; Taylor, op. cit., Vol. I, pp. 248-261.

to be maintained. The monasteries, too, were islands of comparative quiet in the troubled seas of the Dark Ages. The Benedictine rule, whose emphasis upon work was often satisfied by literary labours, encouraged them in their maintenance of learning.

Some churchmen looked askance at the study of the non-Christian literature of antiquity and at the continuation of the curriculum of the old secular schools: the taint of paganism still made these suspect to Christians who wished to break completely with pre-Christian faiths.[194] Another cause of the neglect of the traditional learning was the disorder and the disappearance of the old which followed the invasions. Yet some of the Christian schools preserved the old curriculum in a modified form.[195] The Irish monasteries, it will be recalled, while in their scholarship primarily concerned with the documents of the Christian faith, perpetuated some acquaintance with classical literature.

The education given in monasteries and episcopal schools was not always confined to the clergy. In some instances provision was made for those, usually scions of the nobility, who had no thought of entering the service of the Church.[196] Later in the Middle Ages secular agencies, especially in the cities, organized schools. However, the vast majority of the outstanding scholars of mediæval times were from the clergy. North of the Alps the earliest universities were ecclesiastical institutions. Even in Italy the universities often had intimate relations with the Church, and in Northern Europe when schools began to appear in the cities under other than ecclesiastical auspices, usually they followed the curricula handed down through the church schools and made a place for instruction in religious subjects.[197]

Cathedral churches and monasteries were, too, the chief preservers of literature. The libraries of the ancient world were destroyed or dispersed and in the Christian West only ecclesiastical institutions conserved and copied books.

In the extent to which it was done in Western Europe, this wedding of Christianity and learning was unique. To be sure, it had been foreshadowed in the catechetical school in Alexandria under Clement and Origen. Yet before the collapse of the Roman Empire in the West the Church did not find it necessary to undertake much of general education. Strictly religious education was all that seemed to fall within its functions. Other agencies were at hand to conduct the other. That condition persisted in the Byzantine realms.

[194] Rashdall, *Universities of Europe in the Middle Ages*, Vol. I, pp. 26, 27, 36; McGiffert, *A History of Christian Thought*, Vol. II, p. 149.
[195] Rashdall, *op. cit.*, Vol. I, pp. 33, 34.
[196] Joynt, *The Life of St. Gall*, p. 15.
[197] Powicke, *The Christian Life in the Middle Ages*, p. 89.

To be sure, as the Empire became Christian, education was supposed not to be anti-Christian. Still, the Greek Church did not officially undertake it to any such extent as did the Latin Church in the West. This meant that in the Byzantine Empire education was not so dominated by the Christian purpose. Scholarship was not so exclusively the possession of the clergy and education in the monasteries and by church officials was more technically religious and less general in character. East of the Euphrates, Christians, being always a minority group, were never so able to dominate education as they were in the West—although they did instruct their Moslem Arab masters in much of the lore of the civilized world. In the West, however, and notably North of the Alps, as in so many other phases of orderly life, the Church took up the load which had been dropped as other vehicles of civilization disappeared. Something inherent in the Christian faith seems to have led it to do so. At least we shall find organized Christianity assuming the burden of general education in many other periods and areas where no other agency was at hand to carry it.

In taking over the task of general education the Church partly transformed both education and scholarship. While preserving much from the Græco-Roman world, and while assimilating more which came to them later from the Eastern Churches partly by way of the Moslems, Christian teachers and thinkers of the West worked over and thought through afresh that which reached them from the past in light of what they believed to be the Christian revelation. The result was systems of theology and philosophy, and attitudes toward learning which in some ways differed from what had been known before. Often it is difficult to know how much the features peculiar to Western scholarship are to be ascribed to Christianity and how much to other factors. This is especially so after we pass the year 1500. In later volumes we will recur to the question and inquire, even when we cannot determine, how far the spirit which has created the science of modern Europe is of Christian and how far of other origin. Yet distinctive features Western education and scholarship have, and some of them are palpably due to Christianity.

We must now partly fill in with a few specific illustrations the outline and the generalizations with which these last few paragraphs have dealt.

Benedict in his famous monastic rule really worked out a new type of education and applied it to training for the life peculiar to the monastery. The Benedictine rule had in it the element of manual labour and, although not by design, promoted both a scholarship dependent on the written page and improvements in agriculture. Benedict and the monasteries which conformed to his rule, indeed, are said to have effected the first successful revival of agriculture in Italy since the wars of Hannibal had dealt fatal blows to the old peasant economy.[198]

In the sixth and seventh centuries flourished Isidore, Archbishop of Seville. A man of scholarly tastes, he did much to transmit to later generations the learning of the Græco-Roman world.

Early after the conversion of the Anglo-Saxons, schools arose in connexion with the monasteries and the cathedrals. In them were educated such scholars as Bede, now remembered chiefly for his *Ecclesiastical History of the English Nation* but also the author of many other works and himself a teacher; Aldhelm, who acquired a wide knowledge of Christian and ancient pagan literature and learning; and Alcuin, who contributed to the brilliance of the scholarly revival which marked the reign of Charlemagne.[199]

In the ninth century Hrabanus Maurus, successively Abbot of Fulda and Archbishop of Mainz, fought the popular superstitions associated with the eclipse of the moon by teaching that the moon, lighted by the sun, was darkened by passing through the earth's shadow.[200]

Charlemagne added stimulus and gave direction to an intellectual revival. It was to ecclesiastics, however, to whom he turned for teachers and, aside from the palace school, it was to cathedrals and monasteries that he looked for centres of education. Education was to be chiefly to obtain a better prepared body of clergy,[201] presumably as a means toward an improvement in the quality of the Christianity of the population at large.

Among the features of the monastic revival and reform in England in the tenth century associated with the names of Dunstan, Ethelwold, and Oswald were an intellectual awakening at the great monasteries and the production of an extensive religious literature in the vernacular. The Norman conquest was followed by an improvement in the intellectual life in the monasteries, for many of the Norman churchmen were highly educated. Lanfranc and Anselm, successively Archbishops of Canterbury, had been connected with the famous monastic school at Bec.[202] In England, in addition to the universities and the well-known grammar schools, were a large number of other schools taught by the clergy.[203]

[198] Toynbee, *A Study of History*, Vol. III, pp. 265, 266.

[199] Ernest Brehaut, *An Encyclopedist of the Dark Ages. Isidore of Seville* (New York, Columbia University, 1912, p. 274); Bede, *Eccles. Hist.*, conclusion; Browne, *The Venerable Bede*, pp. 1, 2, 6, 7; Hauck, *Kirchengeschichte Deutschlands*, Vol. I, p. 422.

[200] Migne, *Pat. Lat.*, Vol. CX, Cols. 78-80.

[201] G. G. Coulton in *An Outline of Christianity*, Vol. II, pp. 230, 231; Deanesly, in *Cambridge Medieval History*, Vol. V, pp. 772, 773.

[202] Graham, *English Ecclesiastical Studies*, pp. 146-187.

[203] Gasquet, *Parish Life in Mediaeval England*, pp. 73, 118.

In Germany the brilliant reigns of the first three Ottos were accompanied by a quickening in the intellectual life which radiated from the Saxon monasteries and the cathedral schools.[204] In Germany the eleventh century was also marked by intellectual activity. Teaching became more of a specialized profession, but the teachers were still connected with ecclesiastical foundations.[205]

Throughout much of Europe cathedrals often were the chief centres of literary and intellectual productivity.[206]

In the twelfth and thirteenth centuries came a great awakening which registered a new stage in the intellectual history of Europe. It was associated with such a purely secular movement as the growth of towns and commerce, and to it contacts with Moslem scholarship and the rediscovery and appropriation of Aristotle contributed and helped to give form and direction. However, religious features also constituted an integral part of it. One of its most marked manifestations was the rise of universities. In Northern Europe these were largely religious in origin. The prototype of many and the most influential of them all was the University of Paris, which grew out of the cathedral school, and whose major subject was theology. It was at this cathedral school, on the eve of the development of the university, that the famous Abelard studied and taught.[207] However, the form of the universities and the tradition of independence (seldom fully achieved) which is one of the most jealously guarded guarantees of freedom of thought seem to be derived not from Christianity, but from the guild system.

The older monastic foundations and orders had little immediate active part in this awakening. They had a smaller share in the general education of the community. The rising civic spirit founded many schools which were less under ecclesiastical direction than most schools had once been.

However, it is significant that the newer ascetic orders, the Dominicans and the Franciscans, which attracted and stimulated so much of the revived religious life of the thirteenth century, made major contributions to the universities in this their formative period, and that in the ranks of these mendicant orders were to be found some of the most notable scholars of the Middle Ages—Roger Bacon, Thomas Aquinas, Bonaventura, Albertus Magnus,

---

[204] Hauck, *Kirchengeschichte Deutschlands,* Vol. III, pp. 274-342.

[205] Hauck, *op. cit.,* Vol. III, pp. 924-980.

[206] Haskins, *The Renaissance of the Twelfth Century,* pp. 47-54.

[207] On the universities see Hastings Rashdall, *The Universities of Europe in the Middle Ages,* and, by the same author, *Cambridge Medieval History,* Vol. VI, Chap. XVII. See also Stephen d'Irsay, *Histoire des Universités Françaises et Étrangères des Origines à Nos Jours* (Paris, Auguste Picard, 2 vols., 1933, 1935); carefully documented, with an account in the first volume of mediæval universities through the Renaissance.

Alexander of Hales, Duns Scotus, and, later, William of Occam. In the contributions of these men native ability and the intellectual ferment of the times must have played a large part. From their inception the Dominicans emphasized scholarship. The Franciscans early developed it.[208] Presumably, too, the mendicant orders, just because they were new, in their fresh enthusiasm attracted much of the talent of their day. However, it also seems probable that but for the religious dynamic back of these orders and the inspiration which came from their determination to give a renewed demonstration of what it meant to follow Jesus without reservation, these first-class minds would not have been stirred to the intellectual achievements which have made their names memorable. Thus the impulse back of the scholarship of one of the most original and creative intellects of the Middle Ages, Roger Bacon, was at least in part his Christian faith. Scholarship, he maintained, should be useful and the ultimate test of utility was the promotion of such a knowledge of God as would save men. As his culminating argument for the pursuit of scientific knowledge by observation and experiment, Bacon pled that thus Christian theology would be supported and the conversion of non-Christians be advanced. The enemies of the faith, he held, would be destroyed much more by the discoveries of science than by force of arms.[209] Bacon's interest in the conversion of non-Christians was not perfunctory, but comes out again and again in his writings. He insisted that it was to be achieved by acquainting men with the broad range of learning, for all of that was integrated with the divine truth as seen in the Christian revelation.[210] He found joy in knowledge—which he believed God had given to men.[211]

It is significant that from these Northern universities in which the Christian tradition was so strong came some of the outstanding leaders of religious awakenings. Wyclif, Hus, and, later, Luther, Calvin, Loyola, and, still later, Wesley, studied in them. Not all these caught from the universities the spark which kindled them, but the movements which they started owed much to their university connexions.

The union of Christianity with scholarship accomplished through this tradition of higher learning and established in the universities of Northern Europe

[208] On the development of scholarship among the Franciscans see Gratien, *Histoire de la Fondation et de l'Évolution de l'Ordre des Frères Mineurs au XIIIe Siècle* (Paris, Société et Librairie S. François d'Assise, 1928, pp. xxiv, 699), pp. 125-135.

[209] Taylor, *The Mediæval Mind*, Vol. II, p. 507; *The Opus Majus of Roger Bacon*, translated by Robert Belle Burke (Philadelphia, University of Pennsylvania Press, 1928), Vol. II, pp. 631-633.

[210] As in *The Opus Majus of Roger Bacon*, translated by Burke, Vol. II, p. 797. *Part of the Opus Tertium of Roger Bacon*, ed. by A. G. Little, pp. 11, 19, 41.

[211] *The Opus Tertium of Roger Bacon*, ed. by Little, p. 60.

has had momentous consequences for both. To the one it has given the corrective and guidance of trained minds. In the latter it has probably helped to foster that daring and courage which come from a sense of serving the divine and of responsibility to God and not to man, and the conviction that learning must not be for the selfish advancement of its possessors but of use to the highest welfare of man.

Certainly the intellectual life and outlook of the Middle Ages were dominated by a conviction concerning the meaning of life and the nature of the universe which came through Christianity and were held to be distinctively Christian. All of existence, animate and inanimate, was believed to be a universe, created and dominated by God. Human history was thought of not as a series of cycles, as the Greeks had conceived it, but as having a culmination. Man had been created sinless, but had fallen. Through the incarnation, the life, the death, and the resurrection of Jesus, God had wrought a work of redemption by which those who shared in its blessings were to attain a beatific life, and those who missed its beneficent work were to suffer in hell. The divine-human drama on this present earth was to culminate in the second coming of Christ and the Grand Assize.[212]

Much of this, including its apocalypticism, was of pre-Christian Jewish provenance. However, the conception of the drama as focusing about Jesus was uniquely Christian.[213] This view of the universe and of human history dominated scholarship, especially in Northern Europe, where theology held primacy in the subjects of university study. Even in Bologna and Salerno, the oldest Italian centres of university education, where law and medicine had respectively been the dominant interests, theoretically it would not have been challenged.

Moreover, this thirteenth-century movement, by accepting Greek philosophy and using it to interpret the Christian faith afresh, asserted in essence that no incompatibility need exist between human reason and what was declared to be the Christian revelation. The latter might be, as some held, unprovable by the former, but at least the two were not reciprocally contradictory. By many all truth was held to be one. Such a scholar as Roger Bacon could see in science based on experiment an enlargement of the knowledge of the universe of God. Thus freedom was given to reason and the way was prepared

[212] This was stated in an extreme form by Joachim of Floris (c. 1130-c. 1202), who taught that God had divided the world into three ages—that of the Father who ruled His children by force, that of the Son who reigned by wisdom and discipline, and that of the Holy Spirit, when love, freedom, and happiness are to prevail.—Beer, *Social Struggles of the Middle Ages*, pp. 97-100.

[213] Bury, *The Idea of Progress*, pp. 20 ff.

for later intellectual advance. The spread of Aristotelean philosophy helped to stimulate thirteenth-century scholarship and to give form to thought, but the central object or problem of philosophy was believed to be God and his revelation through Christ.

It is a temptation to pause and to describe the theology and philosophy of the Western Europe of the Middle Ages—to attempt to trace the manner in which Christian, pre-Christian, and non-Christian elements entered into the shaping of the intellectual systems and into what is termed Scholasticism. Even a cursory examination, however, would entail so long a section that this chapter would need to be extended beyond all reasonable limits. It would involve a study of such figures as Johannes Scotus Erigena, Anselm, Abelard, Thomas Aquinas, Duns Scotus, William of Occam, Bonaventura, Alexander of Hales, Peter Lombard, Hugo of St. Victor, and Albertus Magnus. It would include a discussion of nominalism and realism, universals, the place of Augustinianism, the relation of faith to knowledge, and many another subject which engaged the intellects of Mediæval Europe. This much, however, we must take time to say. Into philosophy and theology Christianity entered as a prominent and often a dominant element. Persistent efforts were made to formulate a system of thought which would take account of all knowledge, including what was believed to be the Christian revelation. If the conclusions sometimes reached, notably by Occam, made for the separation of faith and reason and declared God to be undiscoverable and unprovable by the human intellect, at least Christianity had provoked thought. Christianity was the major factor in giving birth to the world view of so much of the Middle Ages that the mind and will of God give order to the world. Upon this belief in a dependable world order, thus buttressed, rested much of the science of later centuries.[214]

In the history of thought and of education, as in art, letters, and politics, the series of movements which are usually termed the Renaissance registered a new era. To say that the roots of the Renaissance were many is a banality. Partly because of the variety of the contributing causes, the manifestations were also numerous. Some of them were reciprocally contradictory. That

[214] Of the huge bibliography in this field the following works may be mentioned: McGiffert, *A History of Christian Thought*, Vol. II; A. Harnack, *History of Dogma* translated from the third German edition by Neil Buchanan (London, Williams and Norgate, 7 vols., 1894-1899), Vol. VI; E. Gilson, *L'Esprit de la Philosophie Médiévale* (Paris, Librairie Philosophie J. Vrin, 1932, pp. viii, 329. English translation, New York, Charles Scribner's Sons, 1936, pp. ix, 490) ; D. E. Sharp, *Franciscan Philosophy at Oxford in the Thirteenth Century* (Oxford University Press, 1930, pp. viii, 419); *Beiträge zur Geschichte der Philosophie und Theologie des Mittelalters Texte und Untersuchungen,* founded by C. Baeumker (Münster i.W., Aschendorffsche Verlagsbuchhandlung).

Christianity was one of the roots is fairly obvious.[215] For instance, a large proportion of the subjects treated by the artists of the Renaissance were Christian and the deep religious feeling and insight which many of the greatest of the paintings and sculptures disclose are evidence that their authors were not moved merely by a desire to treat traditional themes in a new way or purely by the command of ecclesiastical patrons. On the other hand, in some of its aspects the Renaissance was obviously non-Christian and even anti-Christian. The admiration for pre-Christian classical culture and ideals did not bring about a revival of classical religious cults, but it encouraged the spread of pagan ideals. The exuberant, self-centred individualism contradicted Christian ethics. Some features of humanism in their glorification of man left little or no room for God.

Yet it is one of the commonplaces of history that in places the Renaissance and humanism showed distinctly Christian features. This was particularly the situation in Northern Europe, perhaps because there the chief subject of the universities and the main object of scholarship had so long been theology, and because, more than in Italy, schools owed their origin to men who professed to act from a Christian impulse. It is significant that Erasmus, the leading representative of humanistic studies in Northern Europe, in his impressionable years was trained by the Brethren of the Common Life. The Brethren, moved by a deeply religious purpose and by the desire to give to their pupils a Christian rearing, were progressive educators, produced some of the best teachers, and conducted some of the most noteworthy schools of the fifteenth century. They taught a Latin which, judged by classical standards, was purer and better than that which had been current.[216] Reared in such an environment, it is not surprising that Erasmus was interested in the Church and its faith.

The Renaissance, then, had both anti-Christian and Christian manifestations. On the one hand it was marked by unspoken or overt scepticism and was accompanied by much denial, in act and in thought, of Christian concepts and ethics. On the other, it had as exponents deeply religious men, and was followed by a quickening of the religious life, the Protestant movement, and the Catholic Reformation, through which Christianity became more vigorous than it had ever previously been in Western Europe.

[215] Konrad Burdach, *Die seelischen und geistigen Quellen der Renaissancebewegung* in *Historische Zeitschrift*, Vol. CXLIX (1933-1934), pp. 477-521, maintains that a source of the Renaissance was the eschatological-apocalyptical writings of Joachim of Floris and the Spiritual Franciscans.

[216] McGiffert, *A History of Christian Thought*, Vol. II, p. 381; G. R. Potter in *Cambridge Medieval History*, Vol. VIII, pp. 711, 712.

The Renaissance was a stage in the development which came to clearer fruition in the eighteenth, nineteenth, and twentieth centuries, by which an open repudiation of Christianity by thousands in the Occident whose fore-fathers had professed that faith paralleled awakenings in which Christianity in the West displayed greater vitality and was more widely influential than ever before in its history.

In Western Europe, then, we have seen emerging between the fifth and the sixteenth century a culture which was in part the product of Christianity. The Roman political order collapsed in much of the territory it had formerly controlled and with it went a large proportion of the associated Græco-Roman culture. Over much of the area the Christian Church was the chief agency for the transmission of what was preserved from the past. It transformed this legacy with the spirit peculiar to itself. Moreover, it won new peoples to the faith and built a spiritual empire in the North-west which extended far be-yond the borders of the former realms of the Cæsars. Partly under the tutelage of the Church a culture emerged which, while inheriting a large amount from the past, was a fresh creation and had Christianity as one of its impulses and formative factors.

In the portion of the Mediterranean world in the hands of the Byzantine Empire, as we have more than once suggested, Christianity occupied a posi-tion different from that which was its in the West. Here politically no abrupt break occurred with the past and the Roman Empire persisted in name until, reduced to a central nucleus of Greek-speaking peoples with fringes composed in part but by no means entirely of barbarians, it became by almost insensible stages a Greek state. Long before the sixth century Christianity had been the official religion. Yet, as had been its predecessors, it was always ancillary to the state. Or, rather, its organized representative, the Church, was controlled by the Emperors. The old culture did not suddenly collapse. It was simply continued under changing conditions which gradually altered it. The Church did not hold the commanding place that it possessed in the West. It did not create so many institutions which directly affected so many phases of life. Yet, through slightly different channels, Christianity was influential and had much to do with what came to be known as Byzantine culture. Especially did the rulers profess to be Christian. Some of them were religious zealots and through the agencies of both state and Church modified their realm accord-ingly. In its way Byzantine culture became almost as different from that of the Greece of the first Christian centuries as was that of Western Europe from the Roman culture of the first four or five Christian centuries. While it did not have so large a part in shaping the future course of human history as did that of Western Europe, it was a major achievement and through much of the Middle Ages was on a higher level of refinement and sophistication than that of the West. We must devote, therefore, a few moments to inquiring the extent to which Christianity moulded it.

First of all, and quite obviously, Christianity profoundly affected the religious phases of Byzantine culture. It was the faith of the state and to it the Emperors gave their support. As we have seen, within the bounds of the Empire some non-Christian cults long survived from pre-Christian days. Again and again peoples professing non-Christian faiths invaded the imperial territories and even effected permanent settlements. Yet, to no small extent with the help of the state, most of those who remained for any great length of time in the Empire became professedly Christian.

By no means all Christians in the Byzantine Empire were adherents of the form of the faith which had official endorsement. Like the Roman Emperors whose heirs they were, the Byzantine Emperors ruled over peoples of several cultures and races. In Spain, North Africa, Italy, and Sicily were many Latin Christians. In Egypt, Palestine, and Syria, Monophysites of different kinds were numerically important. Even in Asia Minor there were Paulicians and in the Balkans the Bogomils. From time to time attempts were made to bring about uniformity, but it was largely because the Empire shrank by losing the territories in which the nonconformists lived that Greek Orthodoxy became increasingly dominant.

Greek Orthodoxy was closely akin to Roman Catholicism. Through many decades and at more than one time during the thousand years between the years 500 and 1500 the two were in communion. In spirit, however, they differed markedly. The Roman Catholics stressed the supremacy of the Pope: the Greek Orthodox permitted, albeit reluctantly, autocephalous churches. Both made much of their creeds and of orthodoxy of doctrine. Probably, however, Greek Orthodoxy placed even greater stress there than did the Latin Church. Both possessed their mystics, but in the main that element seems to have been more prominent in the Greek Church. It may be indicative of the difference between the two that the greatest internal controversy which vexed the Greek Church in this period was over a method of worship, the use or non-use of images, while the Great Schism of the Latin Church was over the question of papal elections and ultimately brought to the fore the issue of the form of church government—the position of a council in relation to the Pope. Presumably the features peculiar to Greek Christianity were due to the effect upon Christianity of the Greek mind and of the

Hellenistic religious spirit, especially of Neoplatonism and of the various Oriental and Greek elements which that embraced.

Having once been given these characteristics, Greek Christianity continued to mould to that pattern the religious faith of successive generations. It must be noted, too, that the mysticism of the Greek Orthodox, while strongly influenced by Neoplatonism, was not merely its continuation. In the seventh century, for instance, Maximus Confessor attempted to free from their Neoplatonic elements that famous set of writings bearing the name of Dionysius the Areopagite which contributed so much to Christian mysticism, and to reconcile them with the doctrines of Greek Orthodoxy. The influence of Maximus persisted for many centuries.[217]

How far Christianity shaped the ethics of the Byzantine Empire is difficult to determine. Greek Orthodoxy is usually held to stress morals less than does its Latin sister. Yet ascetic monasticism was as highly esteemed as in the West. To be sure, Greek monasticism was not as activistic as was that of Western Europe. It had no Benedictine rule with its emphasis upon work, and it knew no Franciscan and Dominican movement with its widespread evangelism of the masses. However, many of the virtues emphasized were the same. On more than one occasion, moreover, in spite of their supposed subservience to the Emperor, highly placed ecclesiastical officials had the courage to denounce what they believed to be evil, even in the occupant of the throne. For instance, in the ninth century the Patriarch Ignatius refused the communion to Bardas (who for a time was all powerful under the Emperor Michael III) because of the profligacy of that magnate, and although he was deposed for his pains, refused to recede from his position.[218] In the thirteenth century the Patriarch Arsenius called a council of bishops and excommunicated the Emperor Michael Palæologus because the latter had cleared his way to the throne by putting out the eyes of his rival, a child of tender years. Although the Emperor had Arsenius deposed, even the man whom he placed in the Patriarchal chair did not grant him absolution until he had cast himself before the Patriarch, confessed his sin, and asked for pardon.[219] Probably personal and political factors as well as righteous indignation entered into the action of Arsenius and the repentance of the Emperor, but obviously here was also a sense of right and wrong of which the standard was Christianity and the judge was the Church through the Patriarch.

In stimulating care for the unfortunate and underprivileged, Christianity

---

[217] Vasiliev, *History of the Byzantine Empire,* Vol. II, p. 414.

[218] Runciman, *Byzantine Civilization,* p. 133; L. Bréhier in *Cambridge Medieval History,* Vol. IV, p. 248; Adeney, *The Greek and Eastern Churches,* p. 234.

[219] Vasiliev, *op. cit.,* Vol. II, p. 366; Adeney, *op. cit.,* p. 260.

seems to have been potent. Thus the Empress Theodora, who was by no means a model Christian but was religiously zealous, perhaps mindful of her own early lot, gathered more than five hundred harlots and in an effort to bring them to a different life confined them in what was appropriately called the Convent of Repentance.[220]

Christianity did not erase the highly stratified social system of the Empire. As in the West, however, the Church provided a channel by which one of lowly birth might rise—even to the Patriarchate.[221]

Upon the political structure of the Empire Christianity had varied effects. It helped to exalt the already absolute power of the Emperor by making him the elect of God and the equal of the Apostles.[222] It strengthened the arms of the soldiers of the Empire by giving them assurance that in fighting they were defending the orthodox faith.[223] On the other hand, more than once it weakened the realm by creating or accentuating internal dissensions. In Syria and Egypt dissatisfaction with imperial rule was heightened by differences between Orthodoxy and Monophysitism. The Iconoclastic controversy which brought turmoil and civil war had zealots on each side who believed that they were contending for Christian truth. Often the monks became important in internal politics. They were spiritual directors of the pious in high places.[224] They had large influence with the populace and sometimes could sway it to their will.

The Greek Orthodox form of Christianity assisted the unification of the Empire. It furthered the process of Hellenization. In many of the conquered territories, particularly where these were peopled by adherents of other kinds of Christianity, numerous Greek Orthodox bishoprics were established. Greek monks went in and became centres for the spread of the Greek language. This was true in Armenia, and in portions of Italy and Asia Minor when these were retaken for the Empire.[225] The extensive migration to Southern Italy and Sicily of Greek Orthodox, some of whom came because they were opposed to iconoclasm, some because they were seeking refuge from the Persians and the Moslems, and others out of antagonism to the Monothelitism of the Emperor Heraclius, strengthened the Greek element in those regions.[226] In the third quarter of the tenth century the devout Emperor Nicephoras Phocas pro-

[220] Procopius, *Anecdota* (H. B. Deming's edition), xvii, 5, 6.
[221] Runciman, *op. cit.*, p. 133.
[222] C. Diehl in *Cambridge Medieval History*, Vol. IV, p. 726.
[223] C. Diehl in *op. cit.*, Vol. IV, p. 739.
[224] Diehl in *Cambridge Medieval History*, Vol. IV, p. 751.
[225] Diehl in *op. cit.*, Vol. IV, p. 737.
[226] Bury, *A History of the Later Roman Empire from Arcadius to Irene* (1889 edition), Vol. II, p. 448; Lynn White, *The Byzantinization of Sicily,* in *The American Historical Review,* Oct., 1936, Vol. XLII, pp. 1 ff.

scribed Latin in church services in Apulia and Calabria and commanded the use of the Greek ceremonial.[227] As we have seen, conversion to Christianity formed an integral part of the assimilation of the Slavic invaders of Macedonia and Greece. Acceptance of Greek Christianity by no means always issued in political annexation. It was, however, followed by the penetration of Byzantine culture.

Upon the Byzantine laws Christianity had some effect. The codes, of course, were built upon the Roman legislation of pagan times. However, the Institutes of the Christian Justinian when compared with those of the non-Christian Gaius of the second century display alterations in the law of marriage, of succession, in respect to chastity, concerning the exposure of infants, and in other details which reflect a greater spirit of humanity. These changes appear to be due, at least in part, to Christianity.[228] The *Ecloga*, promulgated in the first half of the eighth century, about two centuries after the *Institutes* were published and after Christianity had had that much more time to make itself felt, shows more markedly the influence of that faith. Confirmation for legal principles was sought in numerous references to the Scriptures. In the law of marriage the *Ecloga* made every concubine a wife and forbade marriage between Orthodox and heretics. It instituted punishment for fornification, earlier left to the Church. Possibly, too, to Christianity should be ascribed the frequent substitution of maiming the body for the death penalty, and the equal punishment for rich and poor, noble and commoner, in contrast with the varying punishments of the Justinian code.[229] In the *Basilics*, issued in the latter part of the ninth century, and of great importance in Byzantine law, the first book is devoted to the Holy Trinity and the Catholic faith, and three books are given to ecclesiastical law.[230]

Upon Byzantine art Christianity laid a strong hand. Much that was most typical of that art, indeed, while indebted to earlier traditions, owed to the Christian faith its inspiration and many of its forms. Byzantine ecclesiastical architecture, which has as its outstanding achievement the Church of St. Sophia, erected under Justinian, appears to have had one of its roots in the architecture developed for the churches in Syria, Mesopotamia, and Armenia, and was fully as much a creation of the Christianity of the East as was the Gothic church and cathedral of that of the West. The Byzantine church was designed expressly for the purposes of Christian worship as practised by the

[227] Vasiliev, *op. cit.*, Vol. I, p. 409.
[228] Kennedy, *Influence of Christianity upon International Law*, p. 70. See, for example, *Novellae*, XXII, CLIII.
[229] Bury, *op. cit.*, Vol. II, pp. 412-418; Vasiliev, *op. cit.*, Vol. I, pp. 294-298.
[230] P. Collinet in *Cambridge Medieval History*, Vol. IV, p. 713.

Greek Orthodox. At the same time it helped to give form to that worship.[231] The mosaics, too, which are so characteristic of Byzantine art, in their rich flowering were largely a Christian product. So, as well, were the icons. It must also be noted that Christian Byzantine art extended beyond the bounds of Greek Christianity, into the Latin West.

The magnificence with which the rites of the Greek Church were celebrated reflected the pomp and the ornate luxury of Byzantine life. It is almost needless to say, however, that the Greek liturgy was evolved under the inspiration of Christianity.

Upon Byzantine literature the effect of Christianity was profound.[232] To be sure, the study of the authors of Greek pagan antiquity was continued, and with less of a break and probably with fewer qualms of conscience among the educated than was true of pagan Latin literature in the West. Nor does the preservation of classical literature owe as great a debt to the Greek Church as it does to the Latin Church. Secular scholarship went on in the Greek East with far less interruption than in the Latin West. Yet a very large proportion of Byzantine literature was primarily the creation of the Christian spirit. That was obviously true of the vast body of religious literature—on theology, on the devotional life, on the lives of the saints, and on subjects which awakened controversy in the Greek Church. Many sermons were published, and many commentaries on the Scriptures were composed. Epic poetry was largely divorced from classical traditions and bore the stamp of the Byzantine spirit which in turn had been largely shaped by Christianity. Religious poetry flourished, and there were notable writers of Christian hymns. The hymns of Romanos (perhaps of the sixth century) and of Andrew of Crete of the seventh and eighth centuries are especially memorable.[233] Although Greek Christianity was more active than Latin Christianity in encouraging the use of the vernacular tongues in the services of the Church, it assisted in the perpetuation and the spread of the Greek language.

In education and scholarship Christianity was not so potent an influence as it was in Northern Europe. Secular agencies had far more part in establishing

[231] On Byzantine art, see Thomas Graham Jackson, *Byzantine and Romanesque Architecture* (Cambridge University Press, 2 vols., 1913); Charles Diehl, *Manuel d'Art Byzantine* (second edition, Paris, Auguste Picard, 2 vols., 1925); O. M. Dalton, *Byzantine Art and Archæology* (Oxford, The Clarendon Press, 1911, p. xix, 727); André Grabar, *L'Empereur dans l'Art Byzantin. Recherches sur l'Art Officiel de l'Empire d'Orient* (Paris, En Dépot à la Librairie les Belles Lettres, 1936, pp. viii, 296).

[232] On Byzantine literature, see Karl Krumbacher, *Geschichte der byzantinischen Litteratur von Justinian bis zum Ende des oströmischen Reiches* (in *Handbuch der klassischen Altertums-Wissenschaft*, Munich, C. H. Beck, second edition, 1897, pp. xx, 1193).

[233] C. Diehl in *Cambridge Medieval History*, Vol. IV, pp. 764-767; Vasiliev, *op. cit.*. Vol. I, pp. 225, 283, Vol. II, p. 409.

and maintaining schools, and the educational tradition of Græco-Roman times persisted with less of a sharp break than was the case north of the Alps. It is not surprising that some of the greatest minds made efforts to combine all knowledge and to effect a synthesis between it and Christianity, thus displaying the effects both of that faith and of non-Christian factors. The Patriarch Photius, probably the most learned Christian of his generation, sought to promote friendly relations between secular knowledge and the study and teaching of theology.[234]

As we have seen, Greek Christianity, like its Latin sister, did much to spread the faith among the barbarians on the northern frontiers. In the Balkans, as in Northern Europe, the new faith did not quickly erase what had gone before, not even all the pre-Christian religious beliefs. In Serbia, Sava so far as possible adapted to the Christian genius the ancient folkways of his people.[235] Christian marriage was long in prevailing.[236] Among the Slavic peoples of the Balkans the worship of the god Perun is said to have persisted into the eighteenth century,[237] and even today some of the popular customs connected with sowing, reaping, the breeding of cattle, weddings, funerals, and the dead, appear to be of pagan origin.[238] However, upon the Balkan peoples Greek Christianity made a deep impression. Here, like the Roman Catholicism on its borders, it became the vehicle for much of civilization. We have seen that Byzantine missionaries first gave written form to the Slavonic speech and that, under the influence of Christianity, a Slavonic literature was created. In many ways the life of the people was profoundly altered.

From the fifteenth century on, after the Moslem Turkish conquest, the various Orthodox churches became the conservers and the chief representatives of the various nationalities of the Balkans.

From the standpoint of their place in later history the Russians were the most important converts of Greek Christianity. They developed their culture largely under the influence of the imported faith. We have seen that, as in so much of North-western Europe, conversion began with the ruling classes and was very superficial among the masses. Only slowly was Christianity really appropriated by the majority and knit into the fabric of their lives. The cities were the centres of the new faith and early were supplied with churches, monasteries, libraries, and schools. For centuries the widely extended rural areas were Christian chiefly in name. As in so many others parts of the world where

[234] Vasiliev, *op. cit.,* Vol. I, p. 360.
[235] Spinka, *A History of Christianity in the Balkans,* p. 90.
[236] Spinka, *op. cit.,* p. 146.
[237] Spinka, *op. cit.,* p. 34.
[238] Spinka, *op. cit.,* p. 35.

Christianity or some other religion has replaced another, the old gods lived on in the popular mind, but as devils or demons. In spite of the opposition of the clergy, many pagan customs and beliefs persisted.[239] The rural clergy were scarcely fitted to do much to improve the religious knowledge and zeal of their flocks. In spite of the fact that the priests were chosen by the local community, no close tie existed between them and their parishioners. The priests were married and constituted a kind of hereditary class, whose members entered the profession not out of religious conviction, but by the inertia of custom or to make a living. When the clerical office was open to all applicants, many went into it to escape taxation. The majority of the rural village priests seem to have been poorly trained. For a large proportion the only preliminary education was obtained in the two weeks or so spent at the court of the bishop immediately before ordination.[240] Under these circumstances, it is not surprising that outside of the relatively few cities Christianity was long in gaining more than a superficial and formal hold.[241] It was much later than it was in Western Europe in arousing indigenous religious movements such as the followers of Peter Waldo and the mendicant orders. Indeed, none seem to have appeared until after 1500. Until then the Russians were content to abide by religious patterns received from abroad.

Following the Mongol conquest, as we have seen, Christianity made much more rapid headway. Monasteries and hermits were a potent means of spread, for even when these ascetics did not go out among the people the fame of their sanctity often attracted lay folk.

Eventually, then, in Russia, although much more slowly and several centuries later than in Western Europe, Christianity became the conscious possession of the majority. In the larger churches, the services, gorgeous and impressive in the Byzantine tradition, with their candles, incense, vestments, and music, nourished a kind of mysticism and offered a temporary escape from sordid conditions of life.[242] Christian ethics, too, made themselves felt. Love and sympathy for one's neighbour became theoretically accepted standards.[243] Christian legends which became current as folklore attacked drunkenness, and the popular poem often had as its hero a drunkard who gave up his vice and entered a monastery.[244]

As in Western Europe, monasteries cared for the sick and the poor.[245]

[239] Milioukov, Seignobos and Eisenmann, *Histoire de Russie,* Vol. I, p. 108.
[240] Milukow, *Skizzen russischer Kulturgeschichte,* Vol. II, pp. 161-165.
[241] Milukow, *op. cit.,* Vol. II, pp. 192, 193.
[242] Buxton, *Russian Mediæval Architecture,* p. 9.
[243] Milukow, *op. cit.,* Vol. II, pp. 1-7.
[244] Milukow, *op. cit.,* Vol. II, pp. 200, 201.
[245] Eck, *Le Moyen Age Russe,* pp. 133-135.

Through its teaching the Church modified marriage and family relation-ships.[246]

The attitude toward property varied. By 1500 some ecclesiastical writers wished the Church to gain wealth. Others condemned it. Many legends repre-sented Christ as a wanderer whom the rich refused to take in and who pun-ished them, and who, given the best that their hovels could afford, rewarded the poor.[247]

Apparently one of the immediate effects of Christianity upon Russia was an improvement in the condition of the slaves. Under the sons of Yaroslav the old custom was abolished which permitted a free man to kill a slave with impunity, and only corporal punishment was allowed or a claim of compensa-tion from his master.[248] In the eyes of the Church a slave had a soul to be saved. In their sermons and admonitions members of the heirarchy endeav-oured to soften the lot of the slave and recommended moderation and instruc-tion in the faith, rebuked the abuse of the master's power, sought to protect the morality of slaves by encouraging their marriage at adolescence, and recom-mended emancipation for the old. Yet the Church did not combat slavery as such and the clergy, the bishops, and the monasteries possessed slaves.[249]

Christianity aided in the economic development of Russia. Some of its mon-asteries attracted settlers and formed the nuclei of cities and towns. Many of its monasteries, especially on the northern frontier, performed agricultural functions similar to those of the corresponding institutions in parts of West-ern Europe. They cleared virgin lands, built roads and canals, drained swamps, and introduced improved cattle and better methods of tillage.[250]

In the North, as we have seen, Russian monks pressed forward the frontier of Russian culture by their work as missionaries. As we have also suggested, they taught their converts Russian methods of agriculture and of fishing, and instructed them in the construction of houses.[251]

The political structure of Russia was partly moulded by Christianity. Closely in touch with Byzantine ideals as many of them were, the clergy became channels for the introduction of Byzantine legal ideas and of the canon law of the Greek Church.[252] Often prelates and heads of monasteries mixed in the

[246] Milioukov, Seignobos and Eisenmann, *op. cit.,* Vol. I, p. 92.
[247] Rappaport, *Mediæval Legends of Christ,* pp. 144-147; Eck, *op. cit.,* pp. 139-141.
[248] Milioukov, Seignobos and Eisenmann, *op. cit.,* Vol. I, p. 107.
[249] Eck, *Le Moyen Age Russe,* pp. 144, 388-391.
[250] Eck, *op. cit.,* pp. 133-135.
[251] Konrad Lübeck, *Die Christianisierung Russlands* (Aachen, Xaveriusverlagsbuch-handlung, 1922, pp. 118), pp. 20-23; Eugene Smirnoff, *A Short Account of . . . Russian Orthodox Missions* (London, Rivingtons, 1903, pp. xii, 83), pp. 1-3.
[252] Milioukov, Seignobos and Eisenmann, *Histoire de Russie,* Vol. I, p. 92; Eck, *op. cit.,* p. 128.

conflicts between secular magnates, sometimes as partisans, at other times as mediators.[253] In the main the Church made for political unity. With its clergy in every village and with its hierarchy heading up in its one metropolitan, the Russian Church tended to bring the country together. Thus in the tenth century the Church was an instrument of political unity, and centuries later, after the Mongol conquest, it was the one institution which comprised all Russians. Still later its heads favoured the princes of Moscow as they built up a centralized political power.[254]

Culturally Christianity strengthened the Byzantine connexion and formed a barrier against importations from Western Europe. As time passed, especially after Constantinople came into the hands of the Turks, Russians believed themselves the champions of Orthodoxy against the errant Latin West and spurned whatever came from that region of heretics.[255]

An ecclesiastical architecture was developed, at first by Byzantine artisans and on strictly Byzantine models, but later modified by the use of wood and by styles developed on the frontier.[256] Influences on church architecture also entered from Georgia and Armenia.[257] Icons and frescoes were of Byzantine provenance, some of the former being actual importations.[258] Russian church music long remained as it had been transmitted from the South Slavs and the Byzantine Empire.[259]

To Christianity the Russians were indebted for their alphabet. Their first literature was translations of church ritual and canon law, some of them made directly from the Greek in Russia and some brought from Bulgaria. The ecclesiastical Slavonic of Bulgaria, gradually modified to bring it nearer to the Russian speech, was that in use in the Russian Church. Sermons of bishops and lives of saints were composed in Russian. Chronicles strongly impregnated with religious ideas were written by monks.[260] Under Christian influence popular religious poetry was produced.[261] Some monks distrusted learning as a temptation of the devil,[262] but more than one monastery became a centre of scholarship and for years the clergy had a monopoly of the schools.[263] As again

[253] Eck, op. cit., pp. 128, 129.

[254] Eck, op. cit., pp. 10, 132, 133; Milukow, Skizzen russischer Kulturgeschichte, Vol. II, p. 166.

[255] Lübeck, op. cit., p. 13; Buxton, Russian Mediæval Architecture, p. 2.

[256] Buxton, op. cit., pp. 2, 4, 13; Eck, op. cit., pp. 21, 22; Milukow, op. cit., Vol. II, pp. 235, 236.

[257] Vernadsky, A History of Russia, p. 36.

[258] Vernadsky, op. cit., p. 36; Milukow, op. cit., Vol. II, pp. 243-249.

[259] Milukow, op. cit., Vol. II, p. 262.

[260] Vernadsky, op. cit., pp. 33-35; Eck, op. cit., p. 20.

[261] Milukow, op. cit., Vol. II, p. 199.

[262] Milukow, op. cit., Vol. II, p. 6.

[263] Eck, op. cit., p. 10.

and again in many lands and climes, the visible Church, the organized expression of Christianity, became the tutor of a backward people in the arts of a more advanced culture.

Of the effect of Christianity as represented by the Eastern churches other than the Greek Orthodox we must take time to say only a few words, partly because by the close of the fifteenth century it had long been declining.

As we have suggested, Islam brought a succession of grave crises to the Christian communities in the lands where it became politically dominant. For a time Nestorianism flourished more under the Moslem Arabs than under the Zoroastrian Sassanids. To the other Christian groups the Moslem conquests quickly meant dwindling numbers. Eventually that same fate overtook the Nestorians. Christianity was on the defensive.

Under these circumstances, Christians, like Jews in Christian and Moslem lands, and like the Parsees in India, tended to gather into communities, self-contained in their social life and somewhat specialized in their occupations. These Christian communities were in groups, separated by creedal, racial, linguistic, and cultural differences. Monophysite Copts, Syrian Jacobite Monophysites, Armenians, and Nestorians were distinct and sometimes hated one another quite as cordially as they did the Moslems. While it seems unlikely that any of these Christian groups gave active assistance to the Arabs at the time of the conquest, the divisions among them and the controversies over the attempts of the Emperors to enforce religious uniformity undoubtedly weakened the Byzantine realms and facilitated the Moslem victories.

For each group, however, Christianity in the particular form professed by it proved a bond which prevented assimilation into the Moslem majority. The continued existence of non-Moslem enclaves on the eastern borders of the Mediterranean was due partly to race and to language, but chiefly to Christianity.

The extent to which the internal life of these professedly Christian minorities was shaped by Christianity is another question. The religious rites traditionally associated with Christianity were maintained, sometimes with scrupulous zeal. Marriage and the family seem largely to have been governed by standards deemed Christian. However, the ethics of the New Testament did not have so great an effect as might at first thought be supposed. The hereditary position of a minority under social and, at times, financial disabilities made for cunning and trickery, and, on occasion, fawning servility. Venality and intrigue in high places were encouraged by the fact that the ecclesiastical heads of the various churches owed their position to Moslem rulers. To groups so continuously on the defensive and slowly losing in numbers, creative cultural life was difficult if not impossible.

However, these Christian minorities made cultural contributions, especially in the centuries before their numbers had so sadly dwindled. We hear that an Armenian bishop taught some Christian Turks to plant vegetables and sow corn—a work akin to that of Christian missionaries in many other climes and portions of the world.[264] Some impression was made upon the non-Christian religions. We have already seen that Islam was modified by Christianity. How far Buddhism, through possible contacts in Central Asia, was altered is in dispute. Thus far no effect upon it has been proved.[265] It is possible that Christianity in its long existence in India left its stamp on Hinduism. It has been suggested that the Mahabharata, especially the Bhagavadgita, Bhakti mysticism, several of the stories connected with Krishna, and part of the poetry connected with Shiva, may possibly show traces of direct or indirect contact with Christianity. It is also said that Ramanuja, a Hindu religious teacher of the eleventh century, may have been influenced by the Christians. Most of this, however, is at least highly debatable.[266] Missionaries are reported to have taught some of the Turks the art of writing.[267] It is asserted that the Uighur script was derived from the Syriac used by the Nestorians and that through the influence of Uighur literature the Mongolian and Manchu alphabets owe a debt to Christian missionaries.[268] It is, however, just as vigorously declared that the Uighur goes back to recent Sogdian, which, like ancient

[264] Mingana, *The Early Spread of Christianity in Central Asia and the Far East*, p. 47.

[265] The literature is extensive and the subject highly controversial. Some of the literature is Clemen, *Der Einfluss des Christentums auf andere Religionen*, pp. 100 ff.; Schomerus, *Indien und das Christentum*, Vol. II, pp. 15-18, 31-36.

[266] Clemen, *op. cit.*, pp. 81-91; Ayyar, *Anthropology of the Syrian Christians*, p. xvi; G. A. Grierson (who is inclined to stress Christian influence), *Encyc. of Religion and Ethics*, Vol. II, pp. 548-550, Vol. VIII, pp. 234, 235; R. W. Fraser in *Encyc. of Rel. and Ethics*, Vol. V, p. 22; Schomerus, *Indien und das Christentum*, Vol. II, pp. 18-31, 35-48. Charles Eliot, *Hinduism and Buddhism, an Historical Sketch* (London, Edward Arnold and Co., 3 vols., 1921), Vol. II, pp. 217-219, thinks Christian influence doubtful. G. A. Grierson, *Modern Hinduism and Its Debt to the Nestorians*, in *Journal of the Royal Asiatic Society of Great Britain and Ireland*, 1907, pp. 311-328, argues for a strong Christian impulse, especially in the origin of *bhakti*. J. Kennedy in *Journal of the Royal Asiatic Society of Great Britain and Ireland*, 1907, pp. 477-487, discusses Grierson and on pp. 951-991 thinks it possible that some echo of Christian stories of the Nativity is heard in the Gujaras' accounts of the child Krishna. L. J. Sedgwick, *Bhakti in The Journal of the Bombay Branch of the Royal Asiatic Society*, 1911, pp. 109-134, is cautious.

[267] Mingana, *op. cit.*, p. 9.

[268] Mingana, *op. cit.*, p. 47; Bretschneider, *Medieval Researches from Eastern Asiatic Sources* (London, Kegan Paul, Trench, Trübner and Co., 1910, 2 vols.), Vol. I, p. 262.

Sogdian, is asserted to be derived not from the Syriac used by the Nestorians, but from its first cousin, Aramaic.[269]

More certain is the important contribution of Christians to Arab culture. A large portion of what is known as Islamic Arab art and architecture is said to have been developed by Egyptian Christian engineers and artisans. Mosques are declared to have been planned by Greek architects and their detailed decoration to have been the work of Coptic craftsmen.[270] Saracenic art, therefore, seems under obligation to Christians. We have already seen that the Arabs of Mesopotamia owed much of their philosophy, mathematics, and science to Christians who put into Arabic the Syriac versions of Greek literature in these fields.[271] At their famous school at Edessa the Nestorians studied not only theology, but logic, philosophy, rhetoric and grammar, and medicine as taught by the Greeks.[272] They were, therefore, prepared to introduce their Arab masters to these fields of learning. The Nestorian medical school at Jundaisabur in Susiana is reported to have been one of the sources of the beginnings of Arab medicine. It was Nestorians who translated into Arabic the great body of Greek medical writings, which had already been put into Syriac.[273] Thus the Arab medicine to which Western Europe was so deeply indebted was due in part to Nestorians. Much of the lore of Greek antiquity, then, which reached Western Europe through the Moslem Arabs had come to the latter through Nestorian channels.

It is interesting to speculate whether a causal connexion existed between the decline in creative art and thought in the Islamic world and the dwindling of the Christian communities which that world embraced. Certainly the great period of Moslem culture was in the first few centuries after the Arab conquest of so much of the Christian world, and the flowering was most marked in Mesopotamia, Egypt, and Spain, where the surviving Christian communities were more vigorous than any others under Arab rule. Not a large amount of fresh Moslem cultural contributions, except possibly some poetry, originated in Arabia itself, where Christianity was numerically relatively weak and early disappeared, or in North Africa where the churches quickly shrank almost to

[269] P. Pelliot, *La Haute Asie* (no date or publisher, pp. 37), p. 14.

[270] E. L. Butcher, *The Story of the Church of Egypt* (London, Smith, Elder and Co., 1897, 2 vols.), Vol. I, p. 372; Adeney, *The Greek and Eastern Churches*, p. 586.

[271] Richard Bell, *The Origin of Islam in Its Christian Environment* (London, Macmillan and Co., 1926, pp. vii, 224), p. 214.

[272] E. A. W. Budge, *The Monks of Kûblâi Khân* (London, The Religious Tract Society, 1928, pp. xvi, 335), p. 31.

[273] L. E. Browne, *The Eclipse of Christianity in Asia* (Cambridge University Press, 1933, pp. 198), p. 8; Donald Campbell, *Arabian Medicine and Its Influence on the Middle Ages* (London, Kegan Paul, Trench, Trübner and Co., 2 vols., 1926), Vol. I, p. 13; Meffert, *Caritas und Krankenwesen*, 96.

the vanishing point. Obviously, the Greek and Hellenistic heritage did not have as prolonged an effect in a Moslem environment in leading to new cultural achievements as it did in the Christian *milieu* of Western Europe. Clearly, too, after the Mongol and Turkish irruptions wiped out so much of Mesopotamian Christianity and dealt serious blows to the Greek Orthodox, no such fresh blooming took place as after the Arab conquests. It may be that without the stimulus of strong Christian communities possessing a vitality which Islam had not yet curbed, the latter faith, because of inherent defects, could not do what Christianity did in Northern Europe, arouse barbarians to cultural creativity. To be sure, the difference may be one of race. Mongols and Turks may have been less capable of producing an advanced culture than were the Arabs. Yet against this hypothesis is the fact that the greatest Arab cultural achievements, except in poetry, were not in Arabia but, as we have said, in Mesopotamia, Persia, Egypt, and Spain, with their large Christian communities, and that in Europe Christianity proved potent among races as diverse as Celts, Teutons, and Slavs. Perhaps climate was responsible. That, however, seems neither proved nor disproved. In the present stage of our knowledge we cannot give a final answer to the question, but the suggestion of the historic impotence of Islam to develop a high new culture apart from Christianity is one which cannot lightly be dismissed.

Necessarily this chapter has had to cover much ground and most of it very hurriedly. So rapid a survey, however, if accurate, may have the advantage of perspective. From it several conclusions must be apparent.

First of all, the Christians of the sixth to the sixteenth century had no more purpose of working a complete transformation in human society to make it conform fully to the principles of the New Testament than did those of the first five centuries. Because, however, the vast majority in certain areas had become professing Christians, the feeling was abroad that in these regions standards of social morality more nearly in accord with Christianity must be generally adopted than in the old pagan days.

In the second place, efforts were put forth in numerous communities, most of them monastic, to organize societies which would be thoroughly Christian. Again and again through reforms and new types of movements attempts were made to realize this ideal.

In the third place, in general, and outside those Christian groups which were partially submerged by Islam, the effect of Christianity deepened with the passing centuries. It was more marked in that continuation of the Roman Empire which is known as Byzantine than it was in the Rome of the first five centuries of the Christian era. Upon the newly converted peoples of Northern Europe, whether in Russia or the West, the growth and intensification of the influence of Christianity are even more obvious. Progressively Christianity became an integral part of these nations and affected every phase of their lives. No people and no community was entirely the product of Christianity. Into many, however, that faith entered as an important factor. Whether it made for good or for ill we must not here attempt to decide. To do so would entail the difficult and prolonged task of establishing ultimate standards of judgment and means of measurement. It is, however, clear that, in spite of marked geographic reverses, what is termed Christianity—the movement which had its inception in Jesus—was making an increasingly deeper impress on what was known as Christendom and, through Islam especially, outside Christendom.

If it can be put in a paragraph, in what direction or directions did Christianity modify civilization? It tended to eradicate rival religions. It worked toward the adoption of its own cult and of its ethics. It made for monogamy, care of the underprivileged, and greater mercy, humility, and control of the passions (except when, as frequently, it contributed to stirring up war). It fostered certain types of mysticism. It provided channels for the transmission of the literature, philosophy, law, and science of Greece and Rome. It stimulated creative activity in the realms of the intellect, of art, of music, and of literature. By insisting that man's existence on this planet is a decisive prelude to a future of unimaginable length and that God, through the redemption wrought in Christ, has made possible for those who accept that redemption an eternal fellowship with Him, it gave a meaning and direction to human life, and a dignity which the latter had never before known. Much which Christianity presented ran counter to current ideals and emotions. It brought a sharp conflict, especially in Western Europe—a conflict which has not yet been resolved. Never did it fully have its way. Yet again and again it was making changes and its influence was spreading and deepening. Whether these contributions were good or bad, helpful or harmful, is another question. About the fact of the contributions there can be, in general, no reasonable doubt.

Chapter IX

THE EFFECT OF THE ENVIRONMENT UPON CHRISTIANITY
500–1500

IN THE thousand years between the sixth and the sixteenth century, what
effect did the environment have upon Christianity? Presumably very great
changes could be expected. The period was long, twice the preceding one,
and that latter had witnessed extensive developments in the organizational and
intellectual structure of the faith. It was marked by more than one revolution
in the world in which Christianity was set. Over much of the area won in the
first five centuries the political and social structure with which Christianity
had become closely associated disappeared. Successive irruptions of barbarians
altered the culture of most of Europe and North Africa. Borne by invaders
first from Arabia and then from Central and Western Asia, a fresh religion,
Islam, became a new and aggressive neighbour which dispossessed Christianity
of much of its territory and gave rise to distinctive cultures with which some
Christians had intimate relations. Most of the peoples who accepted Christianity in the course of the thousand years had, at the time of their conversion,
been on a level of civilization very different from that of the Roman Empire
in which pre-sixth-century Christianity had taken form. The new cultures
which emerged in Western Europe, partly under the influence of the faith, were
still different. Presumably, therefore, surrounded by such a shifting environment, the Christianity inherited from the ancient world would, by the year
1500, emerge profoundly altered.

The changes, however, while marked, were not so extensive as might have
been anticipated. Many were outgrowths of previously existing features. As
we suggested near the beginning of the preceding chapter, among the large
majority of those who professed the faith, the main outlines of the Christianity
of the year 500, even though altered in details, continued to be the chief characteristics of the Christianity of the year 1500. The Church was still administered by bishops. The priestly office was, in general, what it had been. For
the majority of Christians the Nicene and Apostles' Creeds remained the outstanding authoritative intellectual formulations of the faith. For even more
Christians the canon of Scriptures which had been fixed before the end of the

fifth century was still revered. Monasticism remained prominent. The sacraments continued to be esteemed essential.

The contrast with the earlier period is marked. In its first five and especially in its initial three centuries, when it was making its way in the Græco-Roman world, the converts placed the stamp of their backgrounds and individual experiences upon their new faith. Christianity took on many diverse forms. Only slowly did a few of these become dominant. In contrast, in the thousand years after the fifth century the converts made few revolutionary changes in what they had accepted.

On second thought this persistence of outstanding features of Christianity is not strange. At the outset of its history Christianity had still to create its organization, its creeds, and its canons. The original impulse, impinging on different environments, gave rise to a number of forms. By the year 500, what was called Christianity had acquired a garb which claimed the sanctity of antiquity and of Apostolic endorsement. It had ceased to be fluid, had crystallized, and was not readily remodelled. Then, too, most of the peoples won to Christianity after the year 500 were barbarians who, when once they had taken the step of baptism, were inclined to accept as final the forms in which the faith had been brought to them. In their eyes it came with divine authority and was unchanged from the time of the Apostles. For the barbarian peoples of Western Europe, too, the Christianity which they accepted came with the endorsement of Rome, and the name of the Eternal City, associated as it was with empire and civilization and hallowed by the tomb of the Prince of the Apostles, inspired awe. To alter what had been given on such authority was thought to jeopardize the salvation to attain which the faith had been adopted. In the Balkans and Russia, Greek Christianity bore the endorsement of the Byzantine Empire, the strongest, richest, and most highly civilized state of that region. The rulers of the Eastern Empire prided themselves on being orthodox, champions of the true faith. Most of them, therefore, opposed all which seemed to them to smack of novelty. Moreover, in both East and West conversion was by large groups. Individual religious experience was less prominent than in the first two centuries. Only the minority penetrated to the inward meaning of the faith and still fewer sought to put on what they had received the impress peculiar to a personal experience.

In the West it was not until the twelfth and thirteenth centuries, when the thousand years were more than half over, that important movements emerged which professed to be Christian but which departed markedly from traditional standards. In the Balkans the variants arrived earlier, but may have taken their rise from an impulse which came from Asia. In Russia, not until after 1500 did prominent modifications emerge. Apparently it was centuries before the barbarian peoples reached a stage of cultural development in which radical original innovations were ventured in what had been transmitted from the high culture of antiquity. Even then many of the innovators claimed not to be bringing anything new, but to be returning to the pure faith of Christ and his Apostles.

While it is true that for the majority of Christians outwardly the structure of the religion which they professed retained the main outlines with which it had entered the sixth century, the environment wrought many modifications. Especially is this seen to be the case if the word environment be made to include, as in the previous period, the racial, regional, cultural, and political setting, and the strong leaders who emerged with distinct and striking religious convictions.

The first modification to be noted is the disappearance of one of the types of Christianity, Arianism, which in the year 500 was still strong. As we have seen, Arianism was largely identified with the Goths and with the Germanic peoples influenced by them. The bulk of the descendants of the Roman provincials remained true to the Roman Catholic form of the faith. As the Goths, always a minority, coalesced with those whom they ruled, they adopted the creed of the majority. In some regions the process was hastened by the conversion of the Franks to Roman Catholic and not to Arian Christianity.

A second modification was the solidification of the regional differences in Christianity. This was a natural sequel of the break-up of the Roman Empire, or, to put it more accurately, it accompanied and followed the dwindling of the areas controlled by the eastern heirs of the Roman name. In Egypt and in Syria the adherence to Monophysitism was at once a cause and a consequence of the rising tide of feeling against Greek Byzantine rule. Both the Emperors and their subjects associated conformity to the Greek type of Christianity with submission to the imperial rule. By slow stages Latin and Greek Christianity moved apart. With this cleavage the waning of Byzantine imperial authority in Italy and the growing independence of the Bishops of Rome had much to do.

Because of this regional division of what in the fifth century had once been embraced by the Catholic Church of the Empire, it is convenient to follow the precedent set in earlier chapters and pursue our topic area by area.

We proceed, then, to the section of Europe occupied by the Church which looked to the Bishop of Rome as its head.

One of the outstanding developments in the West was the accentuation of the position of the Pope. The exalted place which the Papacy occupied during much of the Middle Ages was due to a number of factors. Traditions established before the beginning of the sixth century provided a foundation. The decline of the power of the Emperors of Constantinople in Italy, especially under the blows of the Lombards, freed the Popes from the imperial control which had heretofore been their lot. The Papal missions in Great Britain established the power of the Roman pontiff among the Anglo-Saxons. The labours of Boniface carried on under Papal authorization extended the spiritual empire of Rome in Germany. The support of the Carolingians gave added strength. In the disorders that overtook Western Europe in the latter part of the ninth and at the beginning of the tenth century, the Papacy suffered in the moral quality of its occupants, but the political disintegration in Western Europe provided an opportunity for the assertion of the claims of a centre of unity whose administrators could boast superhuman prerogatives. In the eleventh century the Cluny movement made itself felt and Gregory VII brought the See of Peter to a new height of power. At the close of the twelfth and the beginning of the thirteenth century the able Innocent III marked the apex of the might of the mediæval Papacy. When, in the latter part of our period, the Holy See suffered in prestige, it was in part because of the emergence of strong states and of their attempts to control the head of the Church.[1]

In the course of the ten centuries the area touched by the Papacy had greatly expanded. At one time or another its farthest Western limits had been in Greenland, its northern limits in Scandinavia, its southern limits on the west coast of Africa, and its eastern limits Cambaluc, Hangchow, and Zaitun in China. To be sure, by no means all the intervening territory owned, even vaguely, the authority of the Roman pontiff, but no secular dynasty or other head of a religious body had ever before exerted an influence to such widely extended limits.

The enhanced position of the Pope and the staunch adherence to the creeds and the main forms of the organization inherited from the first five centuries did not prevent the subtle infiltration of the popular religion of Western Europe by the remnants of the pre-Christian faiths.

As a rule it was attitudes rather than specific beliefs and customs which

[1] On the Papacy in this period, see the standard work by Ludwig Pastor, *The History of the Popes from the Close of the Middle Ages* (edited by F. I. Antrobus, St. Louis, B. Herder, 2d ed., 1902-1930, 20 vols.), but which, unfortunately, begins only as far back as 1305. Joseph McCabe, *Crises in the History of the Papacy* (New York, G. P. Putnam's Sons, 1916, pp. xiv, 459), is a good popular account. See, too, *Cambridge Medieval History*, Vol. II, Chap. 22; Vol. V, Chaps. 1, 2; Vol. VI, Chap. 1; Vol. VII, Chap. 10; Vol. VIII, Chaps. 1, 5. F. Gregorovius, *Geschichte der Stadt Rom im Mittelalter* (Stuttgart, 8 vols., 1859-1872), really contains a history of the Popes from the fifth to the sixteenth century. H. K. Mann, *The Lives of the Popes in the Middle Ages* (London, Kegan Paul, Trench, Trubner and Co., 18 vols., 1925-1932), carries the story from 590 to 1304.

persisted from paganism.[2] Yet some direct continuation there was. Wells held sacred by pagan cults were placed under the protection of Christian saints. The ritual connected with the wells and the acts of healing assigned to their waters remained unchanged and were ascribed to the new patrons.[3] Sometimes the myths and the rites connected with the ancient gods were transferred to the saints.[4] In Norway, after conversion, the old community ale feasts were continued to insure peace and good harvests, but the ale was now drunk to Christ and the Virgin Mary. The ale feast given by an heir as a sign that he had entered into his inheritance was kept up, but gradually came to be looked upon as given for the benefit of the soul of the departed. The Christian priest, too, blessed the ale.[5] In the latter half of the sixth century a Synod of Tours banned a blending of paganism and Christianity by which offerings were made to the dead on the feast of St. Peter's chair, and a Synod of Auxerre recorded that on Christian holy days, and especially on St. Martin's day, evening banquets were held in the churches, apparently a continuation of an earlier sacrificial meal.[6] The Feast of Souls which followed the Feast of All Saints was consecrated to the memory of the dead. Pagan customs in honour of the departed were transferred to that day, some of them with very little change.[7] In Germany the fire which at the winter solstice had been lighted to Donar became connected with the name of St. John. Horses and cattle formerly under the protection of the gods of earth and fruitfulness were entrusted to St. Leonard.[8] In Saxony some pagan attitudes were carried over; the Creed and the Lord's Prayer, memorized as they were in a foreign tongue, were employed as magic formulæ.[9] Columba in his missions in Scotland is said to have substituted for the wands, finger, and charms of the pagans the Christian blessing and the sign of the Cross and thus to have expelled demons.[10] In pre-Christian days in Norway Thor was supposed to wage war against the Throlds, spirits of the mountains and forests. After the adoption of Christianity the canonized

[2] In the mass of material given in MacCulloch, *Medieval Faith and Fable,* only relatively few instances are found which are conclusively transferences of specific religious practices into Christian times.

[3] MacCulloch, *op. cit.,* p. 27; Mackenzie, *Scottish Folklore and Folk Life,* p. 268.

[4] MacCulloch, *op. cit.,* p. 27; Robinson, *The Conversion of Europe,* p. 466.

[5] Larson in *Church History,* Vol. IV, pp. 159-172.

[6] Hauck, *Kirchengeschichte Deutschlands,* Vol. I, p. 117.

[7] Hanna Rydh in *Bulletin No. 3 of the Museum of Far Eastern Antiquities, Stockholm,* pp. 69-98.

[8] Timerding, *Die christliche Frühzeit Deutschlands,* Vol. I, p. 17. See also on surviving pre-Christian customs and beliefs in Germany, Julius Lippert, *Christentum, Volkglaube und Volksbrauch. Geschichtliche Entwicklung ihres Vorstellungs inhaltes* (Berlin, Theodor Hofmann, 1882), pp. 379 ff.

[9] Hauck, *op. cit.,* Vol. II, p. 408

[10] Mackenzie, *op. cit.,* p. 232

Olaf was substituted for Thor as their opponent.[11] The legends told of Freya were applied to the Virgin Mary[12] and to the latter were given the functions of the former as the ruler of the animals of the forest and of the divine midwife who assisted at the birth of children.[13] In Sweden in pagan days the image of Frey had been conveyed in procession around the fields to insure good harvests; in mediæval times the shrine of St. Eric was brought to the same fields for the same purpose.[14] As late as the eighteenth century in one of the highland regions of Norway the farmers carried an image, called St. Nicholas, three times round a lake and then washed it, a custom which may well be of pre-Christian descent.[15] It has been suggested that an ancient goddess persisted in Christian Scotland as Bride or Bridget.[16] In Brittany many ancient *mores*, some of them apparently of pagan provenance, have survived, woven into the texture of popular Christianity.[17] In France the pagan custom of pouring a libation on the altar where the sacred fire was born may have lived on in some peasant Christmas celebrations.[18]

The continuation under Christianity of sites sacred to paganism was very common. Thus converted Germans liked to pray in the places held holy in their pre-Christian days, and the Celts as Christians often perpetuated the regard which as pagans they had shown for particular spots.[19] In Scandinavia, Christian churches were frequently built on the sites of pagan temples.[20] However, this did not necessarily involve the persistence of the beliefs and customs which were once associated with these spots. The erection of the Christian shrine might even be a symbol of the triumph of the new over the old.

In the Middle Ages the belief in miracles flourished. In some instances it seems clear that of the Christian faith was expected the same kind of superhuman acts which had been associated with paganism, and, in addition, it was contended that Christianity was even more potent in their performance. In early Irish Christian literature, when the saints conflict with the druids they are represented as succeeding by performing miracles of the same kind as

---

[11] Willson, *History of the Church and State in Norway from the 10th to the 16th Century*, p. 4.

[12] Rappoport, *Mediæval Legends of Christ*, p. 56.

[13] Gjerset, *History of the Norwegian People*, Vol. I, p. 257.

[14] Hallendorf and Schück, *History of Sweden*, p. 29.

[15] Larson, in *Church History*, Vol. IV, p. 164.

[16] Mackenzie, *op. cit.*, pp. 187-192.

[17] Thomas Taylor, *The Life of St. Samson of Dol* (London, Society for Promoting Christian Knowledge, 1925, pp. xli, 82), p. xxxvii.

[18] Alexander Bertrand, *Nos Origines. La Religion des Gaulois. Les Druides et le Druidisme* (Paris, Ernest Leroux, 1897, pp. ix, 436), pp. 110, 111.

[19] Leo Ueding, *Geschichte der Klostergründungen der früher Merowingerzeit* (Berlin, Dr. Emil Ebering, 1935, pp. vii, 288), pp. 136-143.

[20] Willson, *op. cit.*, p. 121.

their rivals, only greater.[21] Thus a druid declared that he could make winds unfavourable to Columba and prevent the latter from sailing. The early Christian record declares that, when Columba embarked, the wind was indeed contrary, but that he successfully sailed against it and that it soon turned and went with him.[22]

However, it is not possible to prove that the belief in miracles is simply a survival from paganism. It is in the Gospels, and while not much of it appears in the writings of the Church Fathers of the first three centuries, it must have been fairly continuously present in the faith of a large proportion of the Christians. So, at least, the stories which circulated among Christians seem to show. It may well be that the miraculous element which abounds in mediæval religion was fully as much the product of Christianity as of paganism. Thus Gregory of Tours, who was of old Gallo-Roman senatorial stock and was not a convert from either Germanic or Roman paganism, plentifully sprinkles his history with miracles in which he obviously believes.[23] Moreover, not only in the first few generations of converts, as in Bede's narrative,[24] do we find a confidence in the miraculous, but the belief flourished fully as luxuriantly and perhaps more so as the centuries passed and paganism faded more and more into the limbo of things forgotten.[25]

Much of magic existed, closely related to this belief in the miraculous. Thus the host was used for such diverse ends as to stay mortality among bees, to sprinkle over cabbages as a remedy for caterpillars, and by an unchaste priest to seduce a woman.[26] An image of St. Sebastian with a prayer, if carried always, was supposed to be an infallible protection against the plague.[27]

Relics abounded and were believed to be potent in working miracles.[28] Relics, indeed, had a large place in the popular religion of the period.

The cults of the saints, too, were prominent. Saints, through their relics or in other ways, were confidently regarded as effective agents for miracles in behalf of their devotees.

It is by no means clear, however, that magic, relics, and cults of the saints were legacies from Teutonic, Celtic, or Græco-Roman paganism. Even though some of the stories connected with them, notably with the saints, were from

[21] McNeill, The Celtic Penitentials, p. 100.

[22] Adamnan, Life of St. Columba, Book II, Chap. 35.

[23] See, for instance, Gregory of Tours, Hist. of the Franks, Book VIII, Chaps. 14, 15, 16. See also Brehaut, History of the Franks by Gregory of Tours, pp. x, xi, xix.

[24] In Bede, Eccles. Hist., Book V, Chaps. 12-14, is an example of this. There the imagery and ethical conceptions seem to be of Christian and not pagan provenance.

[25] As in Coulton, Life in the Middle Ages, Vol. I, pp. 8-14, 22-24, Vol. III, p. 127.

[26] Coulton, Five Centuries of Religion, Vol. I, pp. 112-114.

[27] MacCulloch, Medieval Faith and Fable, p. 127.

[28] MacCulloch, op. cit., pp. 137-153.

the mythology of other faiths,[29] the nucleus may well have been an indigenous Christian growth.

None of these—miracles, magic, relics, or the cult of the saints—was new in this period. They were developments of what had begun before the year 500.

Greek and Roman non-Christian antiquity continued to have effects, some of them of little consequence and some very powerful. For instance, in the Cathedral of Chartres are statues of fourteen virtues. Of these the ones which can be deciphered are "libertas, honour, velocitas, fortitudo, concordia, amicicia, majestas, sanitas, securitas."[30] Several of these obviously have a pagan as well as a Christian ancestry. Some of the literature of classical antiquity was studied in the schools conducted under the ægis of the Church, and the attitudes it reflected must have made an impression on the succession of educated minds. We hear of one Vilgardus who cherished a warm admiration for the pagan Latin poets and, holding that their words were authoritative, is said to have taught much that was contrary to the accepted Christian faith. Apparently he had many followers in Italy and Spain.[31] The Christian Dante revered Virgil. In the Italian Renaissance, magnates of the Church, including some of the Popes, were leaders in attempts to resurrect Greek and Roman antiquity.[32] To be sure, that revival could not be an exact reproduction of the pre-Christian past. The indelible stamp of Christianity remained. Renaissance sculptors used the new techniques to treat Christian themes. Yet the admiration for classical culture helped to form the temper of the Church and made an impression which in some phases was more than transient.

Most notable of all the influences of antiquity upon Christian thought and practice was that of Greek philosophy. The Church Fathers who had borne the impress of the Greek schools were studied and revered, notably Augustine. Through them generations of churchmen and theologians imbibed of Greek thought. Platonism had its effect. The writings associated with the name of Dionysius the Areopagite, saturated as they were with Neoplatonism, made a decided impression upon some of the mediæval and Renaissance mystics and thinkers.[33] The twelfth and thirteenth century revival of the study of Aristotle threatened a revolution in Western theology. Ecclesiastical authorities were alarmed and for a time sought to prohibit at the University of Paris instruction in Aristotle's physics and metaphysics. Their concern was not without

---

[29] MacCulloch, op. cit., p. 134.

[30] Didron, Christian Iconography, Vol. I, p. 84.

[31] Rudolph Glaber, Hist. sui Temporis, Book II, Chap. 12, in Migne, Pat. Lat., Vol. CXLII, Col. 644.

[32] See a popular treatment of this by W. H. Hutton, in An Outline of Christianity, Vol. II, p. 434.

[33] Whittaker, The Neo-Platonists, p. 189.

warrant, for some prominent Christian scholars, under the influence of Aristotle and of Averroes, his Arab interpreter, denied divine providence and fore-knowledge of contingent events and even rejected immortality. On the other hand, eminent Christian minds rethought Christian theology in the light of Aristotle and were esteemed orthodox by the Church. Most distinguished of these was Thomas Aquinas. In him the inherited Christian beliefs were placed in the forefront, but Aristotle helped to shape their formulation and through him left a permanent stamp on Roman Catholic theology.[34] The result was not Aristotelianism: it was a theology in which historic Christian elements were dominant but integrated with many of the convictions of that philosophy.

Canon law, the law of the Church, was moulded both by early Christian principles and by ideas inherited from Roman law. Thus the conception of the "law of nature," so general in the ancient world, is to be found not only in the secular legal conceptions of Mediæval Europe but also in canon law.[35]

Contemporary non-Christian neighbours of Christianity had an influence. Although Jews were widely scattered through Europe, they seem to have had little effect upon the beliefs of the majority of Christians about them. However, the writings of Maimonides, the famous Jewish scholar of the Middle Ages, made an impression on such important Christian thinkers as Alexander of Hales, Albertus Magnus, and Thomas Aquinas.[36]

Islam was more potent than Judaism. It was, indeed, from the Moslems that the Christians of the West seem to have derived the use of the compulsory badge by which they distinguished Jews for all to see.[37] Some thirteenth-century sects held Islam to be as true as Christianity,[38] and, as we have suggested, much of the materialistic scepticism among Christian thinkers of that century was from the study of Moslem philosophy. One of the commonplaces of the history of the philosophy and theology of Mediæval Europe is the influence of Moslem upon Christian thought. Notable were the effects of the great Eastern Moslem scholar, Avicenna (A.D. 979-1037), who became available in Latin translation in the early part of the thirteenth century, and of the greatest of the Spanish Arabian thinkers, Averroes (A.D. 1126-1198). Both were familiar with Greek philosophy, notably with Aristotle. Avicenna was also moulded in

[34] See a convenient summary in McGiffert, *A History of Christian Thought*, Vol. II, pp. 257 ff. See also Etienne Gilson, *The Philosophy of St. Thomas Aquinas* (translation from the third edition), Cambridge, W. Heffer and Sons, 2d ed., 1924, pp. xv, 372.

[35] Carlyle, *A History of Mediæval Political Theory in the West*, Vol. I, pp. 102-110.

[36] Zeitlin, *Maimonides. A Biography*, p. 209, citing Guttmann, *Der Einfluss der maimonidischen Philosophie . . . Moses ben Maimon*, pp. 135-230. On Jewish philosophy see Isaac Husik, *A History of Mediæval Jewish Philosophy* (New York, The Macmillan Company, 1916, pp. 1, 462).

[37] *Cambridge Medieval History*, Vol. VII, p. 642.

[38] MacCulloch, *Medieval Faith and Fable*, p. 239.

part by Neoplatonism and by Jewish ideas. Both Averroes and Avicenna were studied by the Christian Schoolmen. Many of the latter were deeply affected by them. Some tended to accept much of this imported Moslem thought. Others reacted against it, but were stimulated by it to fresh intellectual creativity. The more prominent of the resulting philosophies were not reproductions either of Arabian or of Greek thought. They displayed concepts which were quite alien to Averroes and to Avicenna, to Plato and to Aristotle. Stimulated by their Christian faith, Western European intellects were constructing something like and yet unlike Moslem and Greek philosophy.[39]

From the long and intimate contact there of the two faiths, it might have been expected that the Christianity of Spain would be especially influenced by Islam. However, the evidence for such a modification is slight. Some Spanish heresies may just possibly have sprung from Islam. In sections where Moslems were in political control, numbers of Christians were circumcised and some abstained from meats proscribed by Moslem law. The hypothesis has been advanced that the military orders of Spanish Christians were suggested by similar bodies among Moslems and that chivalry had Moslem roots. Yet most of these connexions are highly doubtful. Indeed, in some respects the effect of Islam seems to have been to make many Christians greater sticklers for the distinctive features of their own religion.[40]

It was not only religions which modified the Christianity of the Western Europe of the Middle Ages. A great variety of other factors which defy logical arrangement made their impress. Before its disappearance Arianism had been altered by its Germanic environment. As we have seen, Arianism eventually was abandoned by the Græco-Roman population and became the religion of the Goths, the Vandals, and a few others of the Teutonic invaders. In this Germanic Arianism the speculative problem of the nature of the Trinity, the original focus of controversy, passed into the background. The liturgy was in the vernacular and the Bible was prized in its translation by Ulfilas. Monasticism was not tolerated and the clergy were married. While the traditional orders of bishops, priests, and deacons were preserved, the ecclesiastical structure was in part assimilated to the military and agricultural organization of the German invaders. The churches tended to become tribal and national and were official cults. For them no such inclusive centre of unity existed as their rivals, the Roman Catholics, possessed in the Papacy.[41]

[39] MacCulloch, op. cit., p. 241; E. Gilson, The Spirit of Mediæval Philosophy (New York, Charles Scribner's Sons, 1936, pp. ix, 490), pp. 80, 178-182, 255, 266, 397, 398, 408-410; W. H. V. Reade in Cambridge Medieval History, Vol. V, pp. 814-829.

[40] C. R. Haines, Christianity and Islam in Spain A.D. 756-1031 (London, Kegan Paul, Trench and Co., 1889, pp. 114-136, 149-156).

[41] Schubert, Geschichte der christlichen Kirche im Frühmittelalter, pp. 22-30.

A good deal of danger existed that the Roman Catholic Church, like Arianism, would be broken up into a number of tribal or state churches subordinate to the monarch or to the local princes. This peril was accentuated by the mass movements dominated by the rulers through which the large majority of conversions had been wrought. Traditionally, as we have more than once reminded ourselves, religion has been fully as much a group as an individual matter. Each tribe or people has had its god or gods and its cult. When Christianity was substituted for the earlier faiths, the old attitudes toward religion tended to persist. The monarchs of the territorial states which succeeded the Roman Empire in Western Europe or which formed outside the borders of what had been the Roman Empire usually attempted to control the Church within their domains.[42] Thus the Merovingians and then the Carolingians largely dominated the Frankish Church and each of the strong Scandinavian monarchs sought to control the Church in his own realm.

This tendency to break up the united Church of the Roman Empire was aided by several other circumstances. The transition from an urban to an agrarian economy furthered it. The Roman Empire had been a congeries of cities. As the Empire became Christian, each city had a monarchical bishop who possessed marked authority. With the barbarian invasions, cities declined and economic life went back to a crude kind of agriculture. The Church became agrarianized.[43] Rural parishes came into being and the actual power of the bishop declined or was modified. The archpriest and the archdeacon developed and tended to weaken the authority of the bishop.[44] North of the bounds of the former Empire large cities had never existed, and the scanty population was scattered in small groups. In consequence, many parishes had to be erected and ecclesiastical decentralization followed.[45] Monasteries, too, tended to become independent of the bishops and the heads of monasteries became princes much as did the bishops.[46]

In time the Church accumulated great wealth. Most of it, as was usual with riches in the early Middle Ages, was in the form of land. Under the late Merovingians, for instance, the Church gradually became the largest landowner in the Frankish state.[47] Elsewhere it had a similar fate.[48] Bishops and monasteries controlled vast properties. These proved too great a temptation

[42] Schubert, *op. cit.*, pp. 34-41, 159; Troeltsch, *The Social Teaching of the Christian Churches*, pp. 207-219.

[43] Schubert, *op. cit.*, p. 540.

[44] Schubert, *op. cit.*, pp. 579, 580.

[45] George Ratzinger, *Geschichte der kirchlichen Armenpflege* (Freiburg im Breisgau, Herder, 2d ed., 1884, pp. xiv, 616), p. 189.

[46] Hauck, *Kirchengeschichte Deutschlands*, Vol. III, pp. 443-447.

[47] Hauck, *op. cit.*, Vol. I, pp. 364-388.

[48] Troeltsch, *op. cit.*, pp. 220-224.

and secular princes sought to put their sons or their favourites in episcopal sees and in abbacies. By the eighth century, these leading positions in the Church had become largely secularized. The lower clergy, taking their cue from the higher, were no better.[49] In England the Crown used ecclesiastical income and offices to support diplomatic, judicial, and other officials engaged in the civil administration. Men were appointed to benefices who were not qualified religiously to fulfil the duties of their offices.[50]

Indeed, the Church was in peril of being largely secularized and absorbed into the feudal system—that decentralized type of political and economic organization which prevailed through much of Mediæval Europe.[51]

From the fate of division and complete subordination to the state and from full feudalization the Church was rescued by the Papacy and by the movement associated with the name of Cluny.[52] The Papacy proved a centre of unity and the political divisions of Europe gave to the abler of the pontiffs an opportunity to enhance their office. By striving for sacerdotal celibacy the Cluny movement helped to keep the clergy from becoming an hereditary caste handing down their dignities from father to son.[53] While the idealists did not completely succeed in enforcing monastic celibacy upon the secular clergy, theirs was a measure of attainment sufficient to have the priests' unions regarded as concubinage and not legal marriage.[54] The struggles between Holy Roman Emperors and Popes over investiture and between the Crown and the Church in England are notable instances of the effort of Popes and bishops to assert the independence of the Church of the secular arm and, at times, even its supremacy over temporal princes.[55]

The Papacy and the reformers prevented the secularization of the Church and its complete division into regional religious bodies subordinate to the state. Yet in various areas Christianity took on features peculiar to the locality and going back to pre-Christian cultures. A full description of this process would expand these paragraphs into a volume. Only a few examples can here be ventured.

[49] Hauck, op. cit., Vol. I, pp. 364-388.
[50] Cutts, Parish Priests and Their People in the Middle Ages in England, pp. 321, 324 ff.
[51] Thompson, Economic and Social History of the Middle Ages, pp. 678, 679; Lea, History of Sacerdotal Celibacy, Vol. I, pp. 167-169.
[52] D. C. Munro in An Outline of Christianity, Vol. II, p. 5; Schubert, op. cit., pp. 46, 47; Troeltsch, op. cit., pp. 229, 233, 235.
[53] Lea, op. cit., Vol. I, pp. 270 ff., 287, 342.
[54] Lea, op. cit., Vol. I, pp. 247, 296, Vol. II, pp. 1-30.
[55] As one reference from the immense literature on this subject, see McIlwain, The Growth of Political Thought in the West from the Greeks to the End of the Middle Ages, pp. 201-216.

We have earlier seen how large a part Irish Christianity played in Western Europe. Some of its peculiarities seem to have been due to the persistence of earlier customs and attitudes of mind. It is possible that the Irish form of the tonsure, which was one cause of contention with the Roman customs, was derived from the druids or from some other Celtic source.[56] A system of penitentials and of penances which spread widely through Western Europe was largely a contribution of Celtic Christianity.[57] Fasting as a means of obtaining boons from supernatural beings and exile as a punishment may have been common in pre-Christian Celtic times. Both are prominent in the penitentials.[58] The Celtic Church, reflecting its environment, was organized by tribes rather than by the type of territorial divisions which had characterized the Roman Empire. Christianity as it was adopted took the place of the previous religion of the tribe, and some of the old tribal religious customs persisted.[59] It is said, for instance, that, contrary to the rule in Latin Christianity by which the priest could be the judge as to whether he would administer the sacraments to any person, in the Celtic Church, because of his tribal connexion every individual was entitled to the services of the priest and the latter had no discretion in the matter.[60]

In an earlier chapter we have seen that the bishop occupied a peculiar position in Irish Christianity. As elsewhere, he had the power to ordain. However, he was not the head of a territorial hierarchy, as he had been in the settled Roman world and as he became elsewhere. In practice he was administratively subordinate to the head of the monastic community. Often he was without a fixed diocese. The primary importance of the monastic life in the Irish Church had altered the traditional episcopal organization. In the Roman Empire the territorial monarchical episcopate had been well developed before the appearance of monasticism. In the West in general it was perpetuated, even though with some modifications. Only in this early Irish form of the Church did it suffer a profound alteration.

It is said to have been the custom of pre-Christian Celtic bards to utter curses against those who offended them. The irate maledictions invoked by the Irish clergy seem to have been a continuation of the same habit.[61] It may be that

[56] Louis Gougaud, *Christianity in Celtic Lands* (London, Sheed and Ward, 1932, pp. lxii, 458), p. 204; McNeill, *The Celtic Penitentials,* p. 102.

[57] McNeill, *op. cit.,* pp. 2, 120 ff.

[58] McNeill, *op. cit.,* pp. 130-133.

[59] Bund, *The Celtic Church in Wales,* pp. 19, 49; McNaught, *The Celtic Church and the See of Peter,* p. 107.

[60] Bund, *op. cit.,* p. 38.

[61] Taylor, *The Mediæval Mind,* Vol. I, p. 133.

something in the Celtic character accounts for the activist note in the monasticism which Columbanus brought to the Continent.[62]

A huge collection of Sicilian folklore made in the nineteenth and twentieth centuries shows many features of popular religion which may go back to the Middle Ages or even earlier and which may indicate that in what now passes for Christianity are to be found deposits from Greek and Roman faiths and from the Islam that was later so powerful on the island.[63]

In Spain the extensive control of the Church by the rulers which prevailed while the Goths were Arians may be one of the sources of the later authority over the Roman Catholic Church in their domains which was exercised by the Spanish princes.[64]

In Anglo-Saxon writings Christianity often takes on martial and emotional notes, presumably from the cultural background. A warlike tone is heard in the paraphrases of Scripture—in that of Genesis, for instance. Christ is often represented as a young hero who vanquishes evil and conquers his enemies, rather than as a suffering Saviour. Yet Latin remained the prevailing language in which the Scriptures were utilized by the Anglo-Saxon Church. Anglo-Saxon adaptations of devotional Latin literature display appreciation of Christian feeling and admiration for the asceticism of Latin monasticism. There is little in what we know of Anglo-Saxon preaching which is purely Anglo-Saxon: the homilists drew from sources common to all Western Christians—the Bible, the patristic writings, and the lives of the saints.[65]

It would be interesting to know how early in English Christianity are to be found those emphases upon the practical and ethical phases of Christianity which are so marked in post-Reformation times. To judge from some of the sermons and other surviving writings, they go back in part to the mediæval period.

Among all the Germanic peoples Christ seems to have been pictured as the mighty God of heaven, with a retinue of Apostles in the days of his flesh and of angels after he had reascended to his heavenly stronghold.[66] Some of the early Teutonic monasticism shows traces of the German law of association.[67]

We have already noted how in Scandinavia several pagan customs, modified,

[62] Schubert, *Geschichte der christlichen Kirche im Frühmittelalter*, p. 100 ff.
[63] Giuseppe Pitre, *Biblioteca delle Tradizioni Popolari Siciliane*, Palermo, 25 vols., 1871-1913.
[64] J. L. Mecham, *Church and State in Latin America* (University of North Carolina Press, 1934, pp. viii, 550), p. 5.
[65] Taylor, *op. cit.*, Vol. I, p. 183; Gjerset, *History of the Norwegian People*, Vol. I, pp. 183, 184; J. S. Sala, *Preaching in the Anglo-Saxon Church* (Chicago, private edition, 1934, pp. 80-144), pp. 95, 97.
[66] Olrik, *Viking Civilization*, p. 142.
[67] Schubert, *op. cit.*, p. 600.

passed over into Christianity. In Norway the three first episcopal sees corresponded to the centres where the old *Things* had been held and the laws promulgated.[68] In Sweden the mediæval bishops were warrior chiefs and like the "lawmen" were primarily leaders of the people. The laity joined in their nomination. The lower clergy were elected by the people.[69] After their conversion the Scandinavians continued the ancient minni-drinking—memorial toasts at the sacrificial feasts. Now, however, the toasts were in honour of Christ, Mary, the Holy Ghost, the saints, or the Archangel Michael.[70] In the years immediately after the conversion of the Scandinavian peoples, priests were few and often barely ably to translate the Latin text of the mass. The new faith was disseminated largely by trusted men of experience and by the song of the skald. Under these circumstances it is not strange that the imported religion took on some features of native garb. God the Father almost disappeared and to the masses Christ and God became synonymous. Christ was thought of as the creator of the world and the ruler of the heavens. His sufferings were incomprehensible but his splendour was stressed.[71]

Local customs developed which probably cannot be ascribed to any particular cultural heritage. Thus in England on the feast of the Holy Innocents a boy bishop was elected by his fellows, and his ministers sang the first vespers of the saint and went around the parish making collections for a feast for themselves.[72]

Pilgrimages were a constant and prominent factor in the religious life. Some were to shrines within the country and others to shrines in foreign lands, especially to Rome and to the sacred sites in Palestine. They combined an act of devotion with relief from the monotony of life at home.[73]

We have said that, in general, the sacraments were an inheritance from the period before the sixth century. However, before the year 500 the exact nature of the sacraments had not been given clear authoritative interpretation, nor had the number been fixed. What there was in the Middle Ages which led to more precise official definition is not certain. Perhaps it was the prominence given the miraculous. After a discussion which lasted for several centuries, the number was officially decreed to be seven—by the Council of Florence in 1439.[74]

[68] Willson, *History of Church and State in Norway*, pp. 118-120.

[69] Hallendorff and Schück, *History of Sweden*, p. 40.

[70] Williams, *Social Scandinavia in the Viking Age*, p. 388.

[71] Olrik, *Viking Civilization*, p. 146.

[72] Gasquet, *Parish Life in Mediæval England*, pp. 165-167.

[73] For a brief description of what pilgrimages meant to the English, see Cutts, *Parish Priests and Their People in the Middle Ages in England*, pp. 308 ff.

[74] McGiffert, *A History of Christian Thought*, Vol. II, pp. 313-331.

The sacrament given central place was the eucharist. It is said that the belief in the change of the substance of the elements into the body and blood of Christ was first clearly stated by Paschasius Radbertus in 844,[75] but the doctrine had a more ancient lineage and Gregory the Great gave his powerful endorsement to a very similar position. The Lateran Council in 1215 declared that Christ's "body and blood are truly contained in the sacrament of the altar under the form of bread and wine, the bread being changed into body and the wine into blood by divine power."[76] With this belief in transubstantiation and with the mediæval confidence in the miraculous, it is not surprising that stories of the host displaying actual blood became common.[77] Nor is it strange that the Feast of Corpus Christi, instituted in the thirteenth century and centring about the eucharist, became popular and was celebrated with much pomp.[78]

With the emphasis upon the mass and upon the benefits procured through it for the dead as well as for the living, there arose chantries. These were very popular in England in the fourteenth and fifteenth centuries. They were endowed and through them masses were said for the benefit of the souls of the founders. At least some of the clergy who served them, "the chantry priests," also assisted the priest in charge of the parish in visiting the sick and looking after the poor.[79]

As we have seen in the preceding chapter, the liturgy, a term which in time came to be identified with the service of the mass, further developed in the Middle Ages. We need not go into the history of the various liturgies, or of the process, a very natural one, by which the rite of the Roman Church eventually prevailed—modified by an early rival, the so-called Gallican rite.[80]

One prominent feature of both the Latin and Greek Churches was the Virgin. Already in the fourth century her perpetual virginity was being affirmed and she was being honoured above all the saints.[81] In Western Europe in the Middle Ages her cult attained still greater prominence. By the beginning of the thirteenth century all churches of the first rank and many others

---

[75] MacCulloch, *Medieval Faith and Fable,* p. 156.

[76] McGiffert, *op. cit.,* Vol. II, pp. 313-331.

[77] MacCulloch, *op. cit.,* p. 160.

[78] H. F. Westlake, *The Parish Guilds of Mediæval England* (London, Society for Promoting Christian Knowledge, 1919, pp. viii, 242), pp. 49-59; *The Catholic Encyclopedia,* Vol. IV, p. 390.

[79] Gasquet, *Parish Life in Mediæval England,* pp. 95, 96; Cutts, *Parish Priests and Their People in the Middle Ages in England,* p. 438.

[80] See Karl Young, *The Drama of the Medieval Church* (The Clarendon Press, 2 vols., 1933); *The Catholic Encyclopedia,* Vol. IX, pp. 296-313.

[81] MacCulloch, *Medieval Faith and Fable,* p. 102.

had lady chapels.[82] Why the Virgin was given such prominence must be a matter of conjecture. It has been suggested that it was because of a popular undefined hunger for an embodiment of female virtues in the Deity. Another hypothesis is that it was in part an outgrowth of the need of monks for compensation for their unmarried state and their lack of female companionship. Whatever the source, many a tale which circulated from mouth to mouth or found its way into a manuscript had as its point the mercy and kindness of the Virgin and her power as an intercessor with her Son. Hymns and poems in her honour abounded. To her were attributed some of the characteristics of the noble dame of the time and she was pictured as subject to moods and caprices.[83]

The popular conception of Christ varied somewhat from land to land and from century to century. In the tenth century, for instance, he was still depicted, as he had long been, as a beardless, adolescent youth. Before the eleventh century he was no longer portrayed as the Good Shepherd—the form that had been so common in early Christian iconography—and instead he was represented as a man of severe aspect, melancholy, and in the scenes of the Great Assize as the inexorable Judge.[84] Yet Bernard of Clairvaux had a warm personal devotion to him, as did many another in the latter part of the Middle Ages.

So, too, with the conceptions of God. They varied and in part reflected the institutions of the age. When Gregory the Great called God Father he meant by father what that term had connoted to the Roman world—one who is kind to the obedient, stern with the wayward, and exacting from all his children the strictest discipline.[85] Later, when feudalism developed, God had in popular religion something of the cruelty, the capriciousness, and the unconscious ignorance of a feudal lord.[86] Anselm, in his theory of the atonement, in *Cur Deus Homo*, seems to have thought of God as being somewhat like an overlord whose honour has been outraged by human sinfulness and demands reparation.[87]

We have pointed out that the Crusades were one of the mediæval fruits of Christianity. The obverse of this is probably also true. They were part of the effect of the warlike spirit of Europe upon Christianity. Men who inherited war from pagan forefathers as the most honourable of occupations saw nothing

[82] Coulton, *Five Centuries of Religion*, Vol. I, p. 142.

[83] MacCulloch, *op. cit.*, p. 108; Coulton, *op. cit.*, p. 145; Henry Adams, *Mont-Saint-Michel and Chartres* (Boston, Houghton Mifflin Co., 1905, pp. viii, 401), pp. 250-284.

[84] Didron, *Christian Iconography*, Vol. I, p. 253.

[85] McGiffert, *A History of Christian Thought*, Vol. II, p. 150.

[86] Coulton, *op. cit.*, Vol. I, p. 189.

[87] Anselm, *Cur Deus Homo*, in Migne, *Pat. Lat.*, Vol. CLVIII, Cols. 361-431.

inconsistent in dedicating their arms to the Christ and striving by the mailed fist to attain Christian ends.

By no means all these many influences of environment upon Christianity were self-conscious adaptations. Some may have been deliberate. Others were doubtless quite unconscious. Probably many of them arose gradually without anyone being aware of what was happening. Presumably still others were planned, but usually with an eye to the solution of an immediate problem, not with any doctrinaire theory of making an alien faith at home. Only a few times, as from Pope Gregory the Great or by a Bishop of Winchester in a letter to Boniface, do we have records of formulated schemes of adaptation. It is noteworthy that neither of these was by actual missionaries, but by men, able, no doubt, but far removed from the task of the missionary. Not until the twentieth century, in a world full of sensitive rival nationalisms and by missionaries and some native Christians in lands resentful of Western tutelage, do we have extensive conscious efforts to make Christianity seem "indigenous."

What can be classified either as the effects of its environment upon Christianity or the effects of Christianity upon its environment are the many new religious movements of these thousand years which partly came out of a Christian background and most of which professed to be Christian. We are not here concerned with their detailed description or history. We are, rather, interested in pointing out certain trends in their origin and in their characteristics.

As we have suggested, most of them were late in emerging. To be sure, several variants began to appear early. We have seen how in most regions Christianity tended to take on features peculiar to the pre-Christian culture of each area. Irish Christianity developed many of its unique characteristics either before or not long after the beginning of our period and was markedly aggressive. In Scandinavia Christianity long had customs which dated from the period of conversion. In some areas, perhaps in all, for generations after the era of formal conversion, ecclesiastical officials or synods found it necessary to take steps to eradicate practices of pagan origin and significance. In spite of all efforts, some customs and attitudes from pre-Christian times persisted.

Yet as a rule these regional variants remained within the ample fold of the great Latin Church. At times the connexion with Rome might be very tenuous or almost non-existent, but conscious schism was rare. Celtic Christianity was the most particularistic, but no evidence seems to exist that its leaders thought of it as distinct in essential doctrine from the rest of the Christianity of the West. In Britain a cleavage occurred between the Celtic bishops and those directly appointed by Rome, and Bede makes it clear that no love was lost between British and Anglo-Saxon Christians. However, the difference seems to have been racial and not creedal. The distinctions did not approach in magnitude the gulf which existed between Monophysites and Orthodox or between Armenians and other Christians, or between Nestorians and Monophysites. Apparently the differences between these Western varieties were not great enough to prevent intercommunion—the formal test which traditionally has been considered crucial in determining the existence of unity among Christians. Indeed, the Christianity of the Irish succeeded in modifying that of the rest of Western Europe. To it is due much of the system of penance as later practised by the Roman Catholic Church.[88] The Irish Columban encountered opposition on the Continent, but it was not on doctrinal grounds. His preaching and that of Luxeuil appear to have been practical, an appeal to live more consistently the type of life which in theory most Christians accepted as ideal.[89] It was chiefly because of his individualism and his sturdy denunciation of sin in high places that he made enemies.

To be sure, as early as the eighth century we hear of a few marked divergences which almost became sects. An opponent of the English Boniface, a Celtic Bishop Clemens, in Austrasia, in addition to marrying and permitting others of the clergy to marry, taught that the Lord had freed all those bound in Hades, the believing and the unbelieving, the worshippers of God and those who prayed to idols.[90] Boniface also encountered one Adalbert, a Frank of humble birth, who called himself a bishop and an intermediary between God and man, who claimed to have a letter from Christ, to perform miracles, and to know the secret sins of all. He preached widely and gained a large but ephemeral popular following. In 745 a synod called by Boniface deposed him from the bishop's office, and the verdict was confirmed by Rome.[91] However, neither of these men, apparently, thought of himself as a heretic, nor do we know that either began a movement which endured for any great length of time.

Before the twelfth century most of the new religious movements in Western Christendom directed their energies toward a reformed and stricter monasticism or toward purging the Church of obvious moral evils. They attempted nothing basically original. In the Christianity which the peoples of Northern Europe had adopted, monasticism was the conventional path for pursuing the perfect Christian life. The rule generally accepted for the monastic communi-

[88] McNeill, *The Celtic Penitentials*, pp. 150 ff.
[89] Hauck, *Kirchengeschichte Deutschlands*, Vol. I, pp. 293-298.
[90] Hauck, *op. cit.*, Vol. I, pp. 518-525.
[91] Hauck, *op. cit.*, Vol. I, pp. 515-517, 522, 525.

ties was that of Benedict, formulated about the time of the conversion of the Franks and before the conversion of Anglo-Saxons, the Germans and the Scandinavians, the Slavs, or the Magyars. To these converts, then, it was one of the established features of the faith. The majority of the attempts at monastic reform were enforcements of that rule with more or less important modifications or revisions. Throughout most of the period, religious awakenings took the form of a revived monasticism. So, too, until the twelfth and thirteenth centuries the efforts to cleanse the Church as a whole of moral corruption did not question the creeds or the sacraments or the clerical office, but simply sought to make actual the standards which it was believed the Church had always taught. The basic convictions of the faith and the organization of the Church as they had been transmitted from the past by the missionaries were not challenged.

One variety of monasticism, said to have been originally an attempt at reform, was the Culdees. They were found in Ireland and especially in Scotland. Their history is obscure, but they seem to have appeared in Ireland toward the close of the eighth century under the name of Céli-Dé. Their aim is reported to have been the restoration of purity of life and austerity of discipline. They combined the ideal of the hermit with a certain amount of community life and dwelt together under a rule with a spiritual superior. The first recorded mention of them in Scotland was in 843. They appear for years to have constituted the clergy of much of Scotland and to have chosen such bishops as existed. In time they degenerated and by the twelfth century some of them married, held property, and transmitted ecclesiastical endowments to their children. They fell into bad odour and disappeared.[92]

By the beginning of the tenth century the observance of the Benedictine rule had almost entirely lapsed in the monasteries of France. To this decay the ravages of the Northmen had contributed. Even without such external misfortune, monastic communities tended to grow lax in the pursuit of their ideal. In much of Germany the monastic life had fallen into evil somnolence since the days of Boniface, and here, too, invasions of barbarians—Scandinavians and Magyars—had wrought havoc. Reactions came. In 910 a monastery was founded in Cluny which embodied an energetic revival of the enforcement of the original Benedictine principles but in modified form. Monasteries observing the Cluny rule multiplied. Here was a religious awakening, a fresh zeal to take seriously the Christian profession which was now nominally universal

[92] Duke, *The Columban Church,* pp. 165-170; Macewen, *A History of the Church of Scotland,* Vol. I, pp. 121-131.

in so much of Western Europe, and to follow whole-heartedly the evangelical and apostolic life.

In course of time the Cluny movement spread through much of Western Christendom.[93] Hildebrand, officially Pope Gregory VII, although he himself was not a monk and had never resided at Cluny, embodied the ideals of the awakening and sought to purge the entire Roman Catholic Church of its chronic abuses of simony and nepotism and to constrain all the clergy to become celibate.[94]

The tide of revival continued to rise and under various leaders made itself felt through most of the Church. At the end of the tenth and in the eleventh century other religious awakenings took form and were propagated through various new monastic movements—the Cistercians, the Good Men of Grammont, the Camaldulians, the Vallombrosians, and the Carthusians. Early in the twelfth century came the Premonstratensians.[95] They were all probably in part reactions against the current disorder, attempts to escape from the murder and rapine, the robbery and anarchy of the times, and to lead a quiet life in which repentance could be effective and peace with God be found.[96] The Knights Templars and the other military orders which arose out of the Crusades were a fresh expression of monasticism—the military spirit of Western Europe consecrated to what was believed to be a Christian objective.

The new life which gave birth to this reformed monasticism remained within the fold of the official Church and did not question the creeds. Yet in practice it introduced novel emphases and altered popular religion. In Germany, for instance, the Cistercians, who felt that their order belonged in a special sense to Mary, did much to spread the cult of the Virgin.[97] Bernard of Clairvaux helped in bringing a fresh personal enthusiasm for Jesus, a passionate type of religious faith which was both activistic and contemplative. It is interesting, too, that Hugo, the first Master of the Temple, was an intimate friend of Bernard.[98]

The Crusades were themselves in part expressions and contributory factors of religious awakenings. It is significant that they began in 1096, in the latter

[93] Hauck, *Kirchengeschichte Deutschlands*, Vol. III, pp. 343-388, 499-515; Workman, *The Evolution of the Monastic Ideal*, pp. 225-251.

[94] Workman, *op. cit.*, pp. 225-251.

[95] *Ibid.*; Davison, *Forerunners of Saint Francis*, pp. 38-69, 76-95. On Bernard of Clairvaux, probably the most famous of the Cistercians, see W. Williams, *Saint Bernard of Clairvaux* (Manchester University Press, 1935, pp. xxxviii, 423).

[96] A. H. Thompson, in *Cambridge Medieval History*, Vol. V, p. 687.

[97] Hauck, *Kirchengeschichte Deutschlands*, Vol. IV, p. 354.

[98] W. Williams, *Saint Bernard of Clairvaux* (Manchester University Press, 1935, pp. xxxviii, 423), *passim;* Taylor, *The Mediæval Mind*, Vol. I, p. 531.

part of a century which had witnessed so many new monastic movements, and that Bernard of Clairvaux gave them his ardent support. Like the orders which arose out of them, they were the outgrowth of a martial tradition which was older than Christianity but directed toward what the official spokesmen of the faith and popular opinion declared to be Christian ends.

The Crusades had singular accompaniments. There were the famous "Children's Crusades." Then, in the middle of the thirteenth century, a movement which was partly religious and partly a result of social unrest spread from Flanders over France. The Sixth Crusade had failed and Louis IX was a prisoner of the Moslems. This shook men's faith and led many to murmur against a Church which by its corruption and its failure to improve the lot of the peasants and serfs was accused of bringing about the calamity. The unrest found a leader in "the Hungarian" who appeared with what he called a letter from the Virgin and in town after town upbraided the clergy, the friars, and even the Pope for allowing the capture of the Holy Land. He declared that the Virgin had ordered an army of poor folk and shepherds to take the Cross and rescue Louis. Many from these groups followed him. At Bourges he was received with open arms, but on his failure to work promised miracles a butcher killed him. The authorities then dispersed his followers.[99] About 1320 France experienced another appearance of these *Pastoureaux*. The peasantry were restless under the exactions of Philip the Fair, and a priest who is said to have been degraded taught them that only overseas could they gain relief and that they must retake the Holy Sepulchre. The crowds who responded worked havoc on the luckless Jews and the clergy. They were excommunicated by the Pope and were dispersed by the civil authorities.[100]

Up to the twelfth century, as we have said, the religious awakenings in Western Europe made no very marked changes in the inherited patterns of organized Christianity. The Crusades were the widest departure, and they did not commence until nearly the beginning of that century. It will be recalled that in an earlier chapter we pointed out that most of these revivals were initiated by scions of the landed aristocracy and drew a large proportion of their leaders from that class. They arose in a predominantly agricultural, feudalized society in which the military and the Church controlled most of the wealth. It was natural that leadership in the Church should be drawn largely from the aristocracy, and that religious movements, when they occurred, to be effective and command attention, should be inspired and domi-

[99] MacCulloch, *Mediæval Faith and Fable*, pp. 259-262.

[100] MacCulloch, *op. cit.*, p. 262, citing E. Baluze, *Capitul. Reg. Franc.* (Paris, 1677), Vol. VII, p. 129, and Muratori, *rer. Ital. Scrip.*, Vol. III, pp. 475, 485, 499 ff.

nated by members of that class. Perhaps it is not straining an hypothesis too far to suggest that awakenings led by aristocrats would be fundamentally conservative. Members of the nobility, proud of their birth, would not wish to upset the existing ecclesiastical order. They would rather seek to purify it and to recall it to its original purpose. They would not wish to overthrow religious institutions, but, rather, to purge them of their abuses.

Now, in the twelfth and thirteenth centuries, a new order began to appear. Towns and cities grew in wealth and size. An urban population composed chiefly of merchants and artisans gained prominence. Feudalism showed signs of decay. Rural land values declined. Many of the peasantry drifted to the towns, and in the country the status of the cultivators of the soil gave indica-tions of change. By the end of the fifteenth century a new Europe had come into being, with wealthy cities, extensive commerce, monarchies of growing power, and with the progressive disappearance of serfdom and of other re-straints on the freedom of the peasant population. In such a Europe the leader-ship no longer rested so fully with the landed aristocracy. In towns and even among the peasants the old order was challenged and changes of many kinds were in the air.

In Europe beginning with the twelfth century, then, it is not surprising that many religious movements broke out led by city dwellers and even peasants, or that these movements departed farther from the established patterns than did the earlier ones led by the aristocracy. Some there were, to be sure, in-itiated by the latter. Many, although at times suspect, succeeded in remaining within the official Church. Others were too far from the accepted system to be thus assimilated and were declared heterodox. From one angle, all were part and parcel of the effect of Christianity on their environment. But for that faith they would not have come into being, or, if born at all, would have exhibited a very different complexion. Yet they also bear the impress of their environ-ment. It is significant that in Russia religious revivals took a quite different form and that among some peoples professedly Christian for centuries no com-parable awakenings have occurred.

The names of these movements are legion and we must not here undertake even a catalogue of them. Only a few can be mentioned, some of them as samples and some because of their prominence. In the eleventh century the Patarini, led by a scion of the lesser nobility but made up chiefly of artisans, peasants, and merchants, arose at Milan and sought to purge the Church of corruption and from its civil powers. About 1115 in the Diocese of Treves groups among the clergy and the laity denied the reality of transubstantiation, rejected infant baptism, and refused to acknowledge other important beliefs and practices of the Church.[101] About 1135 a sect in the Diocese of Liège contended for adult baptism, opposed marriage, and held masses for the dead unnecessary.[102] Not far from the same time Peter of Bruys, a priest in an Alpine village, began a movement which eventually had its centre in Toulouse, but was quite widespread. He professed to base his teaching upon the Bible, rejected the baptism of infants, denied transubstantiation, and, according to an opponent from whom our knowledge of his teachings comes, declared that since God can hear prayer anywhere, church buildings were not needed, said that crosses should be burned because that by which Christ suffered deserved destruction rather than veneration, held that God was mocked by church music, and protested against prayers and alms for the dead on the ground that conduct before death determined one's destiny after that event.[103] Peter's followers were reinforced by Henry, a deacon and monk of Cluny, who, distressed by clerical laxity, in 1116 began an itinerant mission in which he attacked clerical vices, advocated strict clerical celibacy, and preached repentance. He is said to have had great influence with the populace and with the lower clergy. He was opposed by Bernard of Clairvaux, was arrested in 1146, and was condemned to perpetual imprisonment. To the twelfth century belong Arnold of Brescia and his followers. They protested against the corruption of the clergy and advocated that the Church be stripped of its wealth and of political power, and that the clergy confine themselves to spiritual functions.[104]

One of the most prominent of the mediæval religious movements and very far removed from the main stream of Christianity was the Cathari. Their origin is debatable. It has been suggested that they may have been descended spiritually from the Manichæans. It seems clear that they had contacts with the Paulicians and Bogomils of Bulgaria and Thrace. In the tenth century they were already in France; in the eleventh century they were found in Italy and France; and in the twelfth century their views had spread to Germany, Flanders, and Hungary. Their stronghold was in Provence. They were dualists and are reminiscent of the dualistic sects of the early Christian centuries. They rejected the mass, the resurrection of the body, infant baptism, and, indeed, all water baptism, and transubstantiation. They considered marriage sinful and divided their members into two divisions, the *Perfecti* and the

[101] Davison, *Forerunners of Saint Francis,* pp. 100-106; MacCulloch, *Medieval Faith and Fable,* p. 211; *Volpe, Movimenti Religiosi e Sette Ereticali nella Società Medievale Italiana (Secoli XI-XIV),* pp. 1-13.

[102] MacCulloch, *op. cit.,* p. 211.

[103] MacCulloch, *op. cit.,* pp. 208, 209, citing Peter of Cluny, *Ep. adv. Petrobrusianos;* Davison, *op. cit.,* pp. 214-222.

[104] MacCulloch, *op. cit.,* pp. 209, 210, citing J. Mabillon, *Vetera Analecta*(e), 312, Bernard, *Ep.* 241, and Gaufridus, *Vita Bern.,* iii, 6; Davison, *op. cit.,* pp. 107-167.

Credentes. Doctrinally they differed among themselves. Other groups, too, arose who resembled the Cathari but who were not always from the same roots. Eventually they were all stamped out by war and persecution.[105]

Joachim of Floris, who died early in the thirteenth century and whose expositions of prophecy had widespread influence, taught that the age of the Father had ended before the coming of Christ, that the age of the Son was drawing to a close, and that a new age, that of the Holy Spirit, was to begin in 1260. He helped to stimulate the expectation of the early arrival of a new era in which the old would be done away. He himself founded an order, to him the Spiritual Franciscans owed some of the convictions peculiar to them, and his teachings contributed to the ideas of the Roman Tribune, Cola di Rienzi.[106]

The Poor Men of Lyons, also known as the Waldensees, took their rise from Peter Waldo, a rich merchant who in the twelfth century distributed his wealth among the poor and began preaching. For a time they obtained ecclesiastical permission (1179) to use their translation of the Scriptures in the vernacular, but soon were proscribed as heretics. Yet they were widely disseminated from Hungary and Germany to Spain. They did not oppose the Church as such and held to the importance of confession, absolution, and penance. Their emphasis was ethical, and they made much of the Scriptures. They stressed lay preaching and after they were cast out by the Church they became zealous as proselytizers.[107]

There were many groups, some regarded as heretics, included in the comprehensive designation of Fraticelli. Often the term is confined to several movements which grew out of the Franciscans, and notably out of the Spiritual Franciscans. They were strongest in the fourteenth century, but persisted into the fifteenth century.[108]

[105] G. D. Mansi, *Sacrorum Conciliorum nova et amplissima Collectio* (Venice, 32 vols., 1759-1798), Vol. XIX, Col. 376; R. Glaber, *Hist. sui Temporis,* Book III, Chap. 8, in Migne, *Pat. Lat.,* Vol. CXLII, Cols. 659-664; MacCulloch, *op. cit.,* pp. 221-225; *Lettres de Gerbert (983-997)* . . . *par Julien Havet* (Paris, Alphonse Picard, 1889), pp. 161, 162; Hauck, *Kirchengeschichte Deutschlands,* Vol. IV, pp. 887-924; Davison, *Forerunners of Saint Francis,* pp. 201-214, 223, 228; Volpe, *Movimenti Religiosi e Sette Ereticali nella Società Medievale Italiana (Secoli XI-XIV),* pp. 13-19.

[106] H. D. Sedgwick, *Italy in the Thirteenth Century* (Boston, Houghton Mifflin Co., 2 vols., 1912), Vol. I, pp. 36-47; Paul Sabatier, *Life of St. Francis of Assisi* (New York, Charles Scribner's Sons, 1909, pp. xxxv, 448), pp. 28-52; Benz, *Ecclesia Spiritualis,* pp. 1-48, 175 ff.; Decima L. Douie, *The Nature and the Effect of the Heresy of the Fraticelli* (Manchester University Press, 1932, pp. xix, 292), pp. 22-48.

[107] For brief accounts see *Cambridge Medieval History,* Vol. VI, pp. 706, 707; Davison, *Forerunners of Saint Francis,* p. 237-275. For their spread in Germany see Hauck, *op. cit.,* Vol. IV, pp. 887-924. For their activities in Italy see Volpe, *op. cit.,* pp. 48 ff.

[108] Douie, *op. cit.,* pp. 209 ff.; Gratien, *Histoire de la Fondation et de l'Évolution et l'Ordre des Frères Mineurs au XIIIe Siècle* (Paris, Société et Librairie S. François d'Assise, 1928, pp. xxiv, 699), pp. 378-499; *Cambridge Medieval History,* Vol. VI, pp. 709, 710.

The Franciscan and Dominican movements are too well known to require more than the barest mention. They were at once the expression and the agents of a popular, religious revival. Francis of Assisi was a townsman, the son of a merchant, and both orders were particularly strong in the cities. While they had some of the features of traditional monasticism, in many ways they differed greatly from it. Their members did not, as a rule, as was the tendency of the older monastic houses and orders, seek seclusion in communities in rural districts, there to pursue the salvation of their souls. They were, rather, missionaries to both Christians and non-Christians, preachers who were most numerous in the centres of population. The Franciscans had a stormy career. Out of them came a number of descendants, among them the Spirituals, who strove to preserve the emphasis of Francis of Assisi upon poverty.

In the thirteenth, fourteenth, and fifteenth centuries the Flagellants spread over much of Western Europe. Apparently they were stimulated in part by the Plague—the devastating pestilence which again and again wasted Europe. To their minds this Black Death was a judgment of God and a call to repentance to avert the divine vengeance. Under the emotional excitement men restored wrongfully taken goods, murderers asked to be slain, and enemies were reconciled.[109] We hear how in 1349, the year of the Plague, Flagellants came to London, most of them from Holland and Zealand, and twice a day publicly scourged themselves.[110]

Wycliffe and the Lollards in England, and the related movement of Hus and his followers in Bohemia are famous. In both instances men with profound convictions sowed seed which fell on fallow ground. In Bohemia a contributing factor was the irritation of the Czechs against the German foreigners.[111]

In the fourteenth century arose the German mystics, among them Eckhart (born c. 1260), Ruysbroek, Suso, and Tauler, and out of them came the *Theologia Germanica*.[112] How far these were due to a few contagious spirits and how far to a strain in the German nature which three centuries later found an expression through Pietism must be a matter of conjecture. The

[109] MacCulloch, *Medieval Faith and Fable,* pp. 246-256; Seesholtz, *Friends of God,* p. 11.

[110] Coulton, *Social Life in Britain from the Conquest to the Reformation,* p. 259.

[111] James Gairdner, *Lollardy and the Reformation in England* (London, Macmillan and Co., 3 vols., 1908-1911), Vol. I, *passim;* G. M. Trevelyan, *England in the Age of Wycliffe* (London, Longmans, Green & Co., 1909, pp. xvii, 380); H. B. Workman, *John Wyclif* (Oxford, Clarendon Press, 2 vols., 1926); On Hus see K. Kroffa in *Cambridge Medieval History,* Vol. VIII, Chap. II.

[112] Inge, *Christian Mysticism,* pp. 167-194; Seesholtz, *Friends of God, passim.* Huizinga, *The Waning of the Middle Ages,* p. 182.

Brethren of the Common Life, with their stronghold in the Low Countries, combined mysticism with ethical practice and excellent schools.[113]

This swelling tide of popular religion did not cease with the fifteenth century. In the sixteenth century, as we are to remind ourselves in the next volume, it swept on into the Protestant Reformation on the one hand and into the Catholic Reformation on the other. Again historic Christianity was the exciting cause and helped to give form to the results. With it, however, interacted an environment to which Christianity was only one of many contributing factors.

Through many, perhaps most, of the religious movements of the West runs a strain of activism—often in marked contrast with the quietism of Eastern monasticism. This strain becomes more pronounced as the centuries pass, not only before, but also especially after, the fifteenth century. Presumably it goes back to the earliest days of Christianity as pictured in the New Testament. To it, as well, the practical, active Roman spirit may have contributed. Certainly in monasticism it becomes apparent in the first great rule formulated in the West, that of Benedict. It has been a distinguishing and characteristic feature of Western Christianity as a whole.

By 1500, thanks partly to the gradual penetration of the masses by the faith, and partly to the surroundings in which that faith had been set, the Christianity of Western Europe was substantially different from that of the year 500. Creeds might be unchanged, the traditional clerical orders might persist, the sacraments, while further developed, might be in essence what they had been in the fifth century. Monasticism, even though modified by new orders, might still be prominent. Yet the religion of the masses had altered. Christianity, once adopted under the leadership of secular rulers, had permeated the warp and woof of life. Many of the laity, as well as of the clergy, were unwilling to accept uncritically what was given them by the official spokesmen of the ecclesiastical hierarchy. In some places scepticism was rife. In others demands were vocal for a higher type of Christian living than that exemplified by most of the monks and the clergy. New movements of many kinds were changing the religious complexion of the land. Particularly in Europe north of the Alps, where lived the descendants of the barbarians converted since the fifth century, people were ceasing to view with awe a faith which came with the sanction of the Roman name and were beginning to insist upon making that express their own Christian experience. Personal mysticism and practical application of Christian ethics were growing, even though limited to particular circles. Monasticism, while in some of its expressions little changed, had taken on

[113] Seesholtz, *op. cit.*, p. 198; Huizinga, *op. cit.*, pp. 174, 175.

forms which would have seemed utterly strange to churchmen of the fifth century. Hymns and works of devotion had been written. The Christianity of Western Europe of the year 1500 was much more variegated and complex than that of the year 500.

Of all the new movements of these thousand years, only the minority were active in the spread of the faith into new regions. Some of the new monastic orders, of the Crusading orders the Teutonic Knights and the Knights of the Sword, and of the fruits of the ferment of the twelfth and thirteenth centuries the Franciscans and Dominicans, produced missionaries to non-Christians. The vast majority confined their efforts to Christians. Of those which the Church labelled "heresies" not one of the pre-sixteenth-century movements sought to do more than purge Western Christendom of its ills. Perhaps this was because they were so engrossed in winning a place for themselves at home against the force of ecclesiastical restraint that they had no surplus energy for pagans and Moslems. Whatever the reasons, Christianity was presented to non-Christians by the orthodox and, if that term be made to include the friars, almost entirely by representatives of monasticism.

We have seen repeatedly that before the sixth century the official church of the Roman Empire had begun to develop regional characteristics—to take on features peculiar to the culture of the peoples of each major area. Around the greater patriarchal sees of Rome, Constantinople, Antioch, and Alexandria there grew up sectional loyalties. The Emperors were intent upon maintaining unity. Division would bring political weakness. So long as the Empire remained strong the state was usually able to maintain a semblance of ecclesiastical cohesion. When, however, the domains of the Emperors who inherited the Roman name shrank, the various regional churches broke apart. Monophysitism became the slogan for tearing away from the fellowship of the Greek section of the Church the majority of the Christians of Syria and Egypt.

The Latin and Greek Churches maintained, at intervals over a much longer period, a semblance of formal fellowship. The creedal differences between them were relatively minor—chiefly the *filioque* which the Latins had added to the Nicene Creed in describing the procession of the Holy Spirit. The causes both of separation and of the recurring reunions were partly political. So long as the Byzantine Emperors exercised control over Italy, the Bishops of Rome usually sought confirmation of their election from them. The Emperors were thus able to keep the two wings of the Church together. When the Lombards shattered the imperial rule in Italy, the independence of the Papacy increased and the tie with Constantinople became more tenuous. Even while the Emperors still ruled Italy, Europe north of the Alps had escaped from their supervision, but, so far as it was Christian, looked to Rome as the centre of its faith. Peoples thus politically independent of Constantinople were not disposed to be conscious of a religious tie with the Christians subservient to the Patriarch of that city. Added to the political factor was the jealousy between the Pope of Rome and the Patriarch of Constantinople. The former insisted that he was the rightful head of the entire Church. The latter was usually reluctant to concede that standing, at least in practice. Particularly when Rome as a city dwindled almost to insignificance and Constantinople became, as it remained for centuries, the largest, wealthiest, and most highly cultivated city of Europe, it would have been asking too much of human nature to expect the bishops of the latter centre to grant priority to those of the former. Moreover, the Byzantine Emperors, autocrats that they were, could scarcely rest content with granting to an ecclesiastical potentate who was outside their political control a ranking jurisdiction, no matter how slight, over their subjects. It is significant that some, perhaps most, of the successful efforts at what proved transient reunion had political occasions—the last of them being from the desire of the rulers of Constantinople, desperate under the relentless pressure from the Ottoman Turks, to obtain military aid from the West.

Added to other differences were those which arose from contrasting emphases and attitudes of the Latin and Greek Churches. True to the Roman temperament, the former tended to think of Christianity in legal terms, as requiring conformity to law and offering man the chance to escape from the consequences of disobedience by sacrifices and good works. The latter, perpetuating the view of life which expressed itself in the mystery religions of antiquity, regarded salvation as the union of man with God which transformed a mortal into an immortal being.[114] The Latin tended to emphasize the juridical character of the faith: the Greek stressed the mystical.[115] The Latin emphasized the cross, grace, the atonement, and Christ and his work: the Greek prized the incarnation and the resurrection which made possible the union of man with God, and the Holy Spirit.[116] The Greek, inheriting the philosophic tradition, stressed intellectual orthodoxy. There may be a general significance in the name of the chief church structure of Greek Christianity—St. Sophia, St. "Wisdom." The monasticism of the Greek Church tended to quietism.[117] Western monasticism moved toward activism: as illustrations one needs only

[114] McGiffert, *A History of Christian Thought,* Vol. II, p. 161.

[115] Michael Williams, *The Catholic Church in Action* (New York, The Macmillan Company, 1934, pp. 358), p. 266.

[116] N. Zernov in *The International Review of Missions,* Vol. XXIII, pp. 539-546; Christopher Dawson, *Mediæval Religion and Other Essays* (New York, Sheed and Ward, 1934, pp. 195), p. 36; Runciman, *Byzantine Civilization,* p. 129.

[117] Runciman, *op. cit.,* p. 129.

to recall the Cistercians with their emphasis upon manual labour, the Crusading orders with their premium on fighting, and then, late in the period, the Dominicans and Franciscans with their preaching and their service to the poor. Because of the early collapse of the imperial power in the West and the other circumstances we have noticed, the Roman Catholic Church tended to be independent of the civil power and through the Papacy at its height set up and put down princes. In the Byzantine realms, where the imperial power persisted and as an absolutism, the Church was kept subordinate to the state and, in part, as an instrument for governmental purposes.[118] This was probably a survival of attitudes of pagan days both in Rome and elsewhere, for then religion had been regarded as ancillary to society as expressed in the state.

This close association between the Greek Church and the state made eventually for division in the former. As we have seen, the Bulgarian rulers early insisted upon an autocephalous church for their realm independent of control from Constantinople. Sooner or later a similar development took place in most of the major states in which the Greek form of Christianity became the official faith.

Of the influence of pre-Christian religions and philosophies upon Greek Christianity before A.D. 500 we have spoken in the preceding volume. Presumably this effect did not increase after that year, for by then the old paganism as a formal cult had ceased to exist. The philosophies were still taught and studied, but by professed Christians and not by those who gave to them their exclusive allegiance. A few contributions came in from the East. For instance, the romance *Barlaam and Josaphat*, which was put into many languages, enjoyed wide popularity, and in the Greek Church occupied almost the prominence that the Shepherd of Hermas held in the Church in earlier centuries, was a version of the life of the Buddha adapted to Christian purposes.[119] Strangely enough, in spite of the long contact of Greek Christianity with Islam, it seems difficult to prove any significant influence of the latter upon the former.

Much the same belief in miracles and in the potency of the intervention of the saints existed in the Greek as in the Latin Church.[120] For the one as for the other, however, this cannot be proved to be of non-Christian origin.

Among the peoples who became converts to Greek Christianity between the fifth and sixteenth centuries, the supplanted religions made some impression upon the victor. Many of the ancient gods of the Slavs persisted as Christian saints. Perun, the god of lightning, continued to fling his thunderbolts, but as

[118] Runciman, *op. cit.*, p. 111.
[119] Vasiliev, *A History of the Byzantine Empire*, Vol. I, p. 137; Adeney, *The Greek and Eastern Churches*, pp. 282, 283.
[120] For one instance of this see Adeney, *op. cit.*, p. 206.

St. Elijah.[121] Volos (or Veles), the god of flocks, as St. Blasius still performed his customary functions. The goddess who presided over the destiny of new born children had her task and some of her rites transferred to the Virgin Mary. Her day became sacred to the Virgin and the offerings once made in her honour were now dedicated to the Theotokos. Animal sacrifices were offered on the days set apart for St. George and St. Elijah.[122] In Russia, as in so many other lands, the superficially converted masses demanded of the priests of the new faith what they had expected of those of the old. For instance, we hear of people coming to the monastery to ask the abbot to expel demons.[123] Often when one religion supplants another, the gods formerly revered are considered as still existing, but as malevolent and as enemies of the new. So in Russia the ancient gods lived on, but as evil spirits.[124]

In the thousand years with which this volume deals, fewer variants developed from Greek than from Western Christianity. Why this was so is uncertain. It may have been because in the Byzantine Empire religion was so under the control of the state and supported by it that anything smacking of dissent was discouraged. It may have been because of the long resistance against Islam. A religious community consciously on the defensive is usually less tolerant of possible internal divisions, particularly on matters of doctrine, than one which fears little from the outside. In Russia the original process of conversion had been so superficial that centuries elapsed before the faith became the cherished conscious possession of the masses. Not until after 1500 did the Russians develop dissenting sects of any importance.

Yet variations there were, some of them the product of the environment, and some both of the environment and of the inherited Christianity. Within the Byzantine Empire proper the most marked of these was what gave rise to the iconoclastic controversy. This sprang out of attempts to remove the images from the churches and thus to alter the religion which had been developing for centuries. The efforts to eliminate images were led by two strong Emperors, Leo the Isaurian in the eighth century and Leo the Armenian in the ninth. It is said that Jewish and Moslem influences, with their abhorrence of anything that smacked of image worship, were at least partly responsible for the reform. John the Grammarian, the leader of the group of intellectuals who urged Leo the Armenian to action, seems to have been familiar with the science which came through the Arabs and may well have felt the sting of the Moslem scorn for the Christian "idolatry." Whether or not any of the impulse came

[121] Rappoport, *Mediæval Legends of Christ*, p. 143.
[122] Spinka, *A History of Christianity in the Balkans*, p. 35.
[123] Milukow, *Skizzen russischer Kulturgeschichte*, Vol. II, pp. 9, 13.
[124] Milukow, *op. cit.*, p. 9.

from the outside, for several generations the controversy was a major disturbance in the Byzantine Empire.

Like most struggles of its kind, the ostensible issue was involved with others. Both the Leos were strong men who insisted upon dominating the Church, and the question of the independence of the Church from the state was prominent. The leaders of the opposition and the restorers of image worship were both women—Irene and then Theodora—and it is possible that feminine religious attitudes were involved. The monks gave backing to these women, perhaps because of a non-intellectual, fanatical mysticism which had traditionally identified its emotions with the images, and perhaps because of a rebellious resentment against the attempts of the Leos to browbeat the Church.

The struggle ended with the restoration of the images, but in the process the Church was even more firmly subordinated to the state.[125]

Prominent, but less disturbing to the religious life of the Byzantine Empire as a whole, were the Paulicians. Of the origin of the sect we are not entirely sure. They may have been in lineal descent from some of the dualistic Christian bodies of the first centuries. It has often been asserted, but without adequate foundation, that the Paulicians were an offshoot of Manichæism. Probably they were not. Their Christology was adoptionist, and they may have been the spiritual offspring of those Christians of the early centuries who took that view—that Jesus was a mere man until his baptism, when he became the Messiah, the second Adam, the elect Son of God, to the end that all men, by repentance, faith, and baptism, should become sons of God. The Paulicians professed to base their teachings upon the New Testament, all of which they accepted. They also apparently valued at least parts of the Old Testament. Admission to the Church, they held, could be only by adult baptism. After baptism the Holy Spirit was said to enter the believer. Their only sacraments were repentance, baptism, and the eucharist, the latter celebrated at night. They abhorred monasticism. They did not accept the intercession of the saints or the kind of honours paid by the Orthodox to Mary. They repudiated the use of images, crosses, relics, incense, and candles, and did not resort to sacred springs. They celebrated on January 6th the baptism and spiritual birth of Jesus. Their first leader of whom we know and their reputed founder was one Constantine from Mananalis in the region of the upper Euphrates. Set on fire by the Gospels and Paul's letters, in c. 657 he began preaching and founding churches and continued for about a quarter of a century. His missionary jour-

[125] Adeney, *The Greek and Eastern Churches*, pp. 173, 202, 207-209, 213, 214; Vasiliev, *History of the Byzantine Empire*, Vol. I, p. 310; *Cambridge Medieval History*, Vol. IV, pp. 5-45.

neys were up the Euphrates and across the Taurus into Asia Minor. He called himself Silvanus, after Paul's missionary companion. A new leader came at the beginning of the ninth century in the person of the gifted Sergius, who had been referred by a member of the sect to the Gospels and Pauline epistles and through them had entered on a new life. For more than thirty years he preached throughout the central plateaus of Asia Minor, supporting himself as a carpenter. The iconoclastic Emperors tolerated the Paulicians, but the Orthodox rulers persecuted them. When the iconoclastic movement was finally broken, the persecution became more severe. Some of the sect rose in a revolt which was crushed in c. 874. In the eighth and tenth centuries many were transported to Thrace and there were accorded a certain degree of home rule. While outwardly conforming to the established Church, they sent missionaries to Bulgaria—at the time when Christianity was in its early stages among the Bulgars and their subject Slavs. At intervals for several centuries we hear of Paulicians or of those much like them in belief. Even in the nineteenth century some were found in Armenia.[126]

A very persistent sect which spread to Western Europe, but which had its stronghold in the Balkans, was Bogomilism. The sources of the movement are obscure. It is often declared to be an offshoot of Manichæism.[127] Manichæans are said to have been transported from Armenia to Thrace by the Emperor John Zimiskes (969-989) and there to have endured for some time.[128] Bogomilism has also been ascribed to contact with the Paulicians.[129] Neither of these origins seems clearly established. The movement may have been a quite independent development. It is also suggested that Bogomilism fitted into a primitive Slavic dualism and it is asserted that it adopted and adapted old Slavonic festivals, customs, and songs. The Bogomils are reputed to have been opposed to Byzantine culture as well as to the Byzantine Church and to have been a popular nationalistic movement.[130] The alleged founder was a priest called Bogomil, who lived in the tenth century, but that may not have been

[126] Fred C. Conybeare, *The Key of Truth, A Manual of the Paulician Church of Armenia. The Armenian Text, Edited and Translated with Illustrative Documents and Introduction* (Oxford, The Clarendon Press, 1898, pp. cxcvi, 201); Gibbon, *The Decline and Fall of the Roman Empire,* Chap. LIV (Bury's edition, London, Methuen and Co., 1907, Vol. VI, pp. 110-128); Adeney, *op. cit.,* pp. 216-228; J. B. Bury, *A History of the Later Roman Empire from Arcadius to Irene* (London, Macmillan and Co., 2 vols., 1889), Vol. II, p. 396; Vasiliev, *op. cit.,* Vol. II, pp. 21, 22.

[127] As in Sharenkoff, *A Study of Manichæism,* p. 36.

[128] Anna Comnena, *Alexiadis,* Book XIV, in Migne, *Pat. Gr.,* Vol. CXXXI, Cols. 1099, 1100.

[129] Steven Runciman, *A History of the First Bulgarian Empire* (London, G. Bell and Sons, 1930, pp. xii, 337), pp. 190-194. Spinka, *Christianity in the Balkans,* pp. 61-64, leans toward a Paulician-Manichæan origin.

[130] Sharenkoff, *op. cit.,* pp. 37, 38.

his real name: the derivation of the term Bogomil is in dispute.[131] Whatever its possible foreign sources, Bogomilism was clearly in part a nationalistic Bulgarian reaction against Byzantine imperialism, culture, and faith. It was also in part a protest against the morals of the Orthodox clergy. While no similar sect of any consequence arose in the early stages of Christianity among the peoples of North-western Europe, parallels can be found in primitive peoples among whom Christianity entered in the nineteenth and twentieth centuries. We shall find them among the Maoris of New Zealand and in several places among the Negroes of Africa.

Bogomilism divided into more than one stream. In general, however, it was frankly dualistic. It regarded matter as evil and as the creation of the devil, looked askance at marriage, fasted, held that the death and resurrection of Jesus were only apparent, and that the body and blood of Christ were not real. It taught that the true Mother of God was not Mary, but the New Jerusalem from which Christ emerged and to which he returned. It attached great importance to prayer, especially to the Lord's Prayer. It rejected the sacraments and ikons of the Greek Church and criticized the Orthodox clergy. It honoured the Old but rejected the New Testament. Its adherents were divided into the "hearers" and the "perfect."[132] Bogomilism was persecuted by both Greek Orthodox and Roman Catholics. However, it persisted for centuries. For a time it was strong in Serbia. At least in the twelfth century it was present in Hum, the later Herzegovina. In Bosnia in the twelfth century it was favoured by the state, perhaps as a foil against the political menace of powerful neighbours—Roman Catholic Hungary on the one hand and Eastern Orthodox powers on the other. From Bosnia Bogomilism spread to Croatia, Dalmatia, Hungary, and Slavonia. Indeed, until the fifteenth century Bogomilism remained the national faith of Bosnia. After the Turkish conquest in the fifteenth century many Bogomils, preferring Islam to the Roman Catholicism which the Hungarians had tried to force on them, turned Moslem. The last of the Bogomils are said to have been converted to Roman Catholic Christianity in the seventeenth century.[133]

In the fourteenth century two councils of the Greek Church were called to pass on a dispute over what seems to us a slight variation in the mystical experience. Monks on Mt. Athos practised a type of self-hypnosis by fixing their eyes on their navels and holding their breath as long as possible. A state of ecstasy followed in which each saw himself surrounded by a halo of light and

[131] Sharenkoff, *op. cit.,* p. 36.
[132] Sharenkoff, *op. cit.,* pp. 43, 52, 63-65, 81; Adeney, *The Greek and Eastern Churches,* pp. 225-228; Spinka, *op. cit.,* pp. 64-66, 94, 95.
[133] Sharenkoff, *op. cit.,* pp. 40, 41; Spinka, *op. cit.,* pp. 157-183.

felt himself carried into the presence of Christ. The question at issue was whether this light was the same as that which shone around Christ at the Transfiguration. The councils decided in the affirmative.[134]

Other developments there were in Greek Christianity, but none so spectacular as those we have mentioned. The church services of Constantinople were famous for their splendour. It may be that this was in part a result of the wealth and luxury which characterized the city through much of the Middle Ages and that the customs so established in the capital were copied in the entire region in which this type of Christianity spread. The hymns that arose out of individual experience and devotion were both a product of Christianity and assisted in shaping it. Many of them were written on Mt. Athos[135] and possibly helped to confirm the quietistic, mystical emphasis of the Greek Church.

How far if at all the most extensive conquest of the Greek Church, Russia, modified the faith in this period is not certain. As we have suggested, the Mongol domination made a deep impression on the Russians. It may have led them to accentuate the quietistic, ascetic tendency in what had come to them. It may have deepened their religious feeling and have led to a more heartfelt acceptance of the faith. Before 1500, however, as we have said, no strains of the imported religion were evolved which were markedly peculiar to the country.

Of the other churches of the East we must not say much, although some changes within them are of great interest. The sharp cleavage of the Monophysites from the Orthodox and the attempts of the Empire to enforce uniformity were both causes and effects of the progressive disintegration of the state which the Byzantine rulers had inherited from the Romans. With the coming of Islam the churches in the regions conquered by Moslems were placed on the defensive. In each of these Christian bodies, community and religion became identified. The churches tended to ossify and to cling with grim desperation to the traditions and beliefs inherited from a more expansive past. Their members began to display characteristics which are not infrequently found in minority religious communities elsewhere—a reliance upon wits rather than upon physical strength, intellectual acumen, a skill in trade, and pride offset at times by fawning servility.

On the fringes of some of these churches the faith tended to lose its distinctive features and to merge with other religions. Thus some Nestorians in India

[134] Adeney, *op. cit.*, p. 286.
[135] Adeney, *op. cit.*, p. 286.

are said by the fourteenth century to have carried on a form of worship which was a mixture of Christian, Moslem, and Hindu elements.[136]

Ethiopia was one of the most distant outposts of Monophysitism. In time it was almost surrounded by Islam and paganism. Relations with the Coptic Church, to which it looked for ecclesiastical leadership and fellowship, were often slight. It is not strange, therefore, that the Christianity of the land displayed striking peculiarities, some of them probably imported and others largely or entirely indigenous. Thus the use of magic was prominent and one set of magical prayers attributed to Christ, Mary, and some of the Apostles is said to resemble the spells and formulæ of the Egyptian Book of the Dead.[137] In the country are church buildings of two shapes, round and rectangular. It has been suggested that the round ones are successors of the huts in which Ethiopians in pre-Christian times kept their gods or the sacred symbols of their cult.[138] As in so many other branches of the Christian Church, the Virgin has been venerated and many stories have been told of the miracles performed by her. Even two Arabs were said to have been saved from death in shipwreck by calling on her for help.[139] Some of the miracles attributed to the Virgin were common to several other churches, but some were derived from purely Egyptian or native sources and were products of the magic, demonology, and witchcraft of these regions.[140] Whether the circumcision of children[141] was of Jewish or of other non-Christian origin is uncertain.

As we have had occasion to say again and again, of all the regions into which Christianity spread, it was in Western Europe that the greatest number of variations developed. In Western Europe, too, the faith showed more persistent and vigorous vitality than elsewhere. Much of this was obviously due to Christianity itself. A very large part of it, however, must have been because of environment. Some of it was racial. Some was geographic—the relative isolation from the aggressive Islam and from the destructive waves of invasion from Central Asia. Perhaps some was climatic. Some was almost certainly due to the political organization of the region. It was from this Christianity of Western Europe, so full of vitality, and with a progressively larger number

---

[136] G. A. Grierson in *Journal of the Royal Asiatic Society of Great Britain and Ireland,* 1907, p. 312.

[137] Budge, *A History of Ethiopia,* Vol. II, pp. 581ff. Also on the use of magic, see Walker, *The Abyssinian at Home,* pp. 10-115.

[138] Budge, *op. cit.,* Vol. I, p. 159.

[139] E. A. W. Budge, *One Hundred and Ten Miracles of Our Lady Mary* (Oxford University Press, 1933, pp. lvii, 355), *passim.*

[140] Budge, *One Hundred and Ten Miracles of Our Lady Mary,* pp. vi-ix, xiii.

[141] Walker, *op. cit.,* pp. 2, 4.

of variations, that most of the expansion of the faith henceforth came. Russian Christianity, that child of the Greek Church, was the only other form which after 1500 occupied fresh territory by conversion.

It is significant for the future of Christianity that in Western Europe more than elsewhere an active struggle was carried on to lift the practice of professed Christians to the original Christian ideals. Between these ideals and the society in which they are set a tension always exists. In the period which we have been studying, by various processes the tension was partially resolved.

One method was the conformation of the Christian religion to the society about it. What passed for Christianity, the popular and official religion which was called by that name, was to some degree transformed. It compromised its original principles as set forth in its earliest documents. Ethical standards and religious concepts quite alien to its primitive genius crept in or were formally tolerated. Such were pride of place and position, magic, the ecclesiastical promotion of war, the Church's blessing upon the profession of the warrior in the processes by which a youth entered knighthood and, more especially, in the military orders, those interesting efforts to combine the complete renunciation of the world demanded by monasticism with that life of the warrior which was traditionally held foremost in honour among Western European peoples.

Another method of resolving the tension was to flee from the world into monastic communities where, in theory, the primitive Christian ideal could be wholeheartedly pursued. To be sure, the sincere monks found that they brought the conflict with them. The records of their inner struggles and of the recurring battle for monastic reform show how futile was the hope, even within the shelter of monastic walls, of escaping the tension. Yet there the issues were somewhat clarified and simplified.

The monastic way was, in general, that of the Eastern churches. It is interesting but quite useless to speculate whether this may have been because of the lingering influence of the dualistic despair of the flesh which surrounded Christianity in its early spread in the Hellenistic world. Few or only half-hearted efforts were made to bring the entire Christian community to the level of New Testament standards.

In Western Europe, however, the situation was different. Through the centuries and increasingly so as the generations passed, the endeavour was again and again made to end the tension by leading all professing Christians, lay as well as clerical, those outside as well as those inside the monasteries, fully to follow Jesus and his Apostles. To be sure, monasticism was popular, but the increasing tendency was for those who had taken the vows to extend their influence outside the walls of their monasteries. The steps in the transition from the early Benedictines in the sixth century to the Franciscans and Dominicans in the thirteenth are most illuminating. Increasingly sects and movements arose to attempt to bring all Christians to the high standards of the founder of their faith. Such, in essence, was the direction in which Hildebrand struggled. Thither, too, tended Francis of Assisi, Wycliffe, and many another. In the Western type of Christianity was a restless conscience which was not content to resolve the tension either by compromise or by flight. It is significant for the later complexion of the faith that it was Western Christianity through which most of the future expansion was accomplished.

Chapter X

BY WAY OF SUMMARY AND ANTICIPATION

ONLY the briefest of summaries is required. Nor need the forward look use many words. The initial chapter of this volume was in part also an anticipatory summary and more than once in the later chapters we have looked into the future and have sought to show the transition by which it connects with the past that we have here recounted. Yet, even though short, summary and forecast there must be. Without the one the main trends of these thousand years may be obscured by the multiplicity of details. Without the latter the place of this millennium in the stream of history may be missed.

The period opened with a major crisis in the history of Christianity. In the course of its first five centuries that faith, beginning as an obscure Jewish sect, had become the official religion of the Roman Empire. This was a major achievement, especially so since even after the disasters of the fourth century that state was still the most powerful and the basin of the Mediterranean the most important centre of culture on the planet. However, in the fifth century the decay of the Empire and the impending collapse of its culture had become apparent. In the succeeding four centuries the *débâcle* was all but completed. A succession of invasions beginning with the Goths and ending with the Arabs and the Northmen reduced the political boundaries of the Byzantine continuation of the Empire chiefly to Greece, a southern portion of the Balkan Peninsula, the Ægean, and Asia Minor. Over much of the lost territory the old Græco-Roman culture had dwindled or disappeared. A younger religion, Islam, vigorous and still malleable, was dominant in most of the Mediterranean littoral. Would Christianity continue to expand? Could it even survive? Would it not go down with the wreck of the world with which it had become so closely identified? Was it not fated to be the faith of merely the vanishing remnants of the old order?

The outcome of the crisis was not quickly apparent. Indeed, not until more than the thousand years had passed was the answer clear. To be sure, Christianity, coming with the prestige of the Roman or Byzantine name and of Mediterranean culture, very slowly made its way among the peoples of Northern Europe and by 1500 had won the majority of them to a formal allegiance.

Yet as late as the fourteenth and fifteenth centuries it lost most of its out-posts in Persia, Central Asia, and the Far East, and in the fifteenth century the Moslem Ottoman Turks overwhelmed the last remnants of that Byzantine Empire which for centuries had served as its eastern bulwark and planted Islam in Greece and the Balkans as the politically dominant religion. Long before the close of the fifteenth century Christianity had assisted in bringing into being and nurturing a new and energetic culture in Western Europe. In 1500—if one excepts the somewhat dubious prospect in Russia—any hope of a further expansion of Christianity appeared to be identified with the future of the peoples of that region. Yet here the faith seemed threatened with internal disintegration. In Italy the Renaissance had brought a dry rot of scepticism. Even the Popes appeared in morals and aspirations more pagan than Christian. Criticism of the Church and of the clergy was rife. Most of the thirteenth- and fourteenth-century movements which had given such evidence of vitality had lost their first enthusiasms, had died out, or had been crushed by persecution. To be sure, devout souls there were, and such a movement as the Brethren of the Common Life quietly inculcated exacting ideals. Much of the very criticism was proof of vigour. Yet the horoscope was by no means clear. If anything, in 1500 it seemed against any growing future for the now ancient faith.

However, shortly before and after 1500 new and unpredictable movements brought Christianity the greatest expansion it or any other religion had yet known. In the Americas, Western Europeans discovered and conquered vast lands of whose existence the peoples of the Eastern Hemisphere had not been aware. Around Africa they opened up a new sea route to Southern and Eastern Asia. Adventurous Russians moved eastward across Siberia. The Moslem, only recently so threatening, was not so much defeated by head-on op-position—although even that came eventually—as he was outflanked. Almost simultaneously came a new burst of life in Western Christianity. The Protestant movement in its various aspects was not only a protest, but also and chiefly a series of fresh awakenings. Parallel with it and merely in part as a "counter"-reformation came a religious quickening among the peoples who remained true to the Roman Catholic faith. Never in all its history had Christianity known such a revival, such a widespread series of efforts to induce both laity and clergy to live up to the professed standards of their faith. This new life transformed the geographic discoveries and conquests of Western European peoples into fields for the extension of Christianity. Within a hundred years the totally unexpected had happened. Professedly Christian peoples had ceased to be on the defensive and in a great explosion had mastered more widely distributed areas than ever any group of peoples or cultures had previously even known. Western Christianity, recently so inwardly distraught and moribund, had suddenly shown unprecedented vigour.

The movements so begun were not ephemeral. Toward the close of the eighteenth century something of a lull occurred, particularly in religious conviction. It may be that events after 1914 indicate another lull. Yet the nineteenth and the first two decades of the twentieth century witnessed a much more extensive expansion of European peoples and cultures and of Christianity than did even the sixteenth, seventeenth, and eighteenth centuries. To this post-fifteenth century expansion of Christianity the preceding millennium and a half had been only a prelude. To it the succeeding volumes will be devoted.

BIBLIOGRAPHIES

IN THE ensuing bibliographies the arrangement, as will quickly be seen, is by chapters and by topics under those chapters. As a rule a title is mentioned only once in the bibliography of a given chapter, and titles are listed in the order in which they are first mentioned in the footnotes. As a rule, too, only those titles are listed in the bibliographies which are cited more than once in the footnotes. For titles cited only once in the footnotes, the necessary bibliographical information is given with the citation. This, it will be noted, is a procedure different from that employed in the first volume. There the bibliographies included a complete list of all books used—except for some well-known sources. In this present volume for a complete bibliography on any given topic it is necessary to go to the footnotes under that topic. This, however, should prove fully as convenient as the other arrangement.

CHAPTER II

General Books. In no single book is there to be found an adequate account of the entire period and area covered in this chapter. George Frederick Maclear, *A History of Christian Missions during the Middle Ages* (Cambridge and London, Macmillan and Co., 1863, pp. xxi, 466), was excellent in its day, but in many places is now out of date. Charles Henry Robinson, *The Conversion of Europe* (London, Longmans, Green, and Co., 1917, pp. xxi, 640), is more recent but in some places has not gone as thoroughly into the sources as has Maclear. It is useful, but must be employed with care. James Thayer Addison, *The Medieval Missionary, A Study in the Conversion of Northern Europe A.D. 500-1300* (New York, International Missionary Council, 1936, pp. xiv, 176), is a careful and accurate study of missionary methods. J. Schmidlin, *Katholische Missionsgeschichte* (Steyl, Missionsdruckerei, 1924, pp. xi, 598) and Moreau, *Les Missions Médiévales,* which is Chapter IV (pp. 141-232) of Descamps, *Histoire Générale Comparée des Missions* (Paris, Librairie Plon, 1932), are both excellent and contain valuable bibliographies, but are necessarily brief summaries. The English translation of Schmidlin, edited by Matthias Braun under the title *Catholic Mission History* (Techny, Mission Press, pp. xiv, 862, of which pp. 126-199 are on the topics treated in this chapter), has some additions to the text and bibliographies of the German edition. Brief but good on the subject of this chapter are certain sections of Hans von Schubert, *Geschichte der christlichen Kirche im Frühmittelalter* (Tübingen, J. C. B. Mohr, 1921, pp. xxiv, 808). Several of the chapters of *The Cambridge Medieval History* (Cambridge University Press, 1911 ff.), are of assistance. Wherever, as is often, Albert Hauck, *Kirchengeschichte Deutschlands* (Leipzig, J. C. Hinrichs'sche Buchhandlung, 5 vols., 1922-1929), deals with subjects which fall within the range of our story, it is invaluable, both in its judicious and accurate treatment and in its extensive footnotes and references to the sources. The *Monumenta Germaniæ Historica*, whose successive volumes have now been appearing for over a century, is a mine of standard texts of original sources. The *Acta Sanctorum* and J. P. Migne, *Patrologiæ cursus completus . . . in qua prodeunt patres, doctores scriptoresque ecclesiæ Latinæ* (Paris, 221 vols., 1844-1864) and usually referred to as *Patrologiæ Latinæ* (abbreviated to *Pat. Lat.*), are also thesauri of sources.

* *Italy. Gregorii Magni Dialogi,* edited by Umberto Moricca (Rome, Tipografia de Senato, 1924, pp. xcv, 347), in its second book contains our earliest account of Benedict of Nursia. Margaret Stokes, *Six Months in the Apennines, or a Pilgrimage in Search of the Irish Saints in Italy* (London, George Bell and Sons, 1892, pp. xiv, 313); based upon travel and upon research in the pertinent sources and literature. Thomas Hodgkin, *Italy and Her Invaders* (Oxford, The Clarendon Press, 8 vols., 1892-1899); a standard book. Pasquale Villari, *The Barbarian Invasions of Italy,* translated by Linda Villari (New York, Charles Scribner's Sons, 2 vols., 1902). Thomas Hodgkin, *Theodoric the Goth. The Barbarian Champion of Civilization* (New York, G. P. Putnam's Sons, 1896, pp. xvi, 442); by an outstanding authority on the period. Paulus Diaconus, or Paul the Deacon, *Historia gentis Langobardorum* (edited by L. Bethmann and G. Waitz in *Monumenta Germaniæ Historica, Scriptores rerum Langobardorum,* pp. 12-187, Hanover, 1878), is by an eighth-century Lombard patriot and tells the story from 568 to 747. Paul the Deacon, *History of the Langobards,* translated by William Dudley Foulke (Philadelphia, The Department of History, University of Pennsylvania, 1907, pp. xlii, 437), contains excellent notes. Jonas, *Life of St. Columban by the Monk Jonas,* edited by Dana Carlton Munro (Philadelphia, Department of History of the University of Pennsylvania, 1902, pp. 36).

The Iberian Peninsula. Victor Schultze, *Geschichte des Untergangs des griechisch-römischen Heidentums* (Jena, Hermann Costenoble, 2 vols., 1887-1892); scholarly and based largely on the sources. H. Leclercq, *L'Espagne Chrétienne* (Paris, Libraire Victor Lecoffre, 1906, pp. xxxv, 396); carefully done by a Roman Catholic scholar, bringing the story down to the fall of the Visigothic monarchy.

Gaul and the Franks. Gregory of Tours, *Historia Francorum* (best modern edition, W. Arndt and B. Krusch in *Monumenta Germaniæ Historica, Scriptores rerum Merovingicarum,* Vol. I, 1885, pp. 1-450); a famous account by a sixth-century bishop of distinguished family. An English edition is *Gregory, Bishop of Tours, History of the Franks, Selections, Translated with Notes* by Ernest Brehaut (New York, Columbia University Press, 1916, pp. xxv, 284). An English translation of Salvian, *On the Government of God,* is by Eva M. Sanford (New York, Columbia University Press, 1930, pp. viii, 241). Samuel Dill, *Roman Society in Gaul in the Merovingian Age* (London, Macmillan and Co., 1926, pp. xiii, 566), is well written and scholarly. Thomas Taylor, *The Life of St. Samson of Dol* (London, Society for Promoting Christian Knowledge, 1925, pp. xli, 82). Auguste Dupouy, *Histoire de Bretagne* (Paris, Boivin et Cie, 1932, pp. vi, 424); a semi-popular account.

Ireland and Irish Missions. Arnold J. Toynbee, *A Study of History* (Oxford

University Press, Vols. 1-3, 1934); a monumental work of correlation and interpretation. John Campbell McNaught, *The Celtic Church and the See of Peter* (Oxford, Basil Blackwell, 1932, pp. xv, 118). John A. Duke, *The Columban Church* (Oxford University Press, 1932, pp. xii, 200); based upon an extended examination of the sources and of the pertinent literature. Walter Alison Phillips, *A History of the Church of Ireland from the Earliest Times to the Present Day* (Oxford University Press, 3 vols., 1933-1934); by several members of the clergy. Alexandre Bertrand, *Nos Origines. La Religion des Gaulois. Le Druides et le Druidisme* (Paris, Ernest Leroux, 1897, pp. ix, 436). J. W. Willis Bund, *The Celtic Church of Wales* (London, D. Nutt, 1897, pp. vii, 530); based upon the sources; taking positive positions on some controversial issues. Louis Gougaud, *Christianity in Celtic Lands* (London, Sheed and Ward, 1932, pp. lxii, 458), translated from the author's manuscript by Maud Joynt, is *Les Chrétientes Celtiques* revised and enlarged. It is by a Benedictine and is the best one-volume comprehensive account. It contains excellent footnotes. Louis Gougaud, *Gaelic Pioneers of Christianity*, translated from the French by Victor Collins (New York, Benziger Brothers, 1923, pp. xxiii, 166); a briefer and more popular account. Margaret Stokes, *Three Months in the Forests of France. A Pilgrimage in Search of Vestiges of the Irish Saints of France* (London, George Bell and Sons, 1895, pp. li, 291); based upon travel and upon research in the sources. The Count de Montalembert, *The Monks of the West from St. Benedict to St. Bernard* (Edinburgh, William Blackwood and sons, 7 vols., 1861-1876); ardently appreciative of the monks and of Christianity. Maud Joynt, *The Life of St. Gall* (London, Society for Promoting Christian Knowledge, 1927, pp. 168). George T. Stokes, *Ireland and the Celtic Church. A History of Ireland from St. Patrick to the English Conquest in 1172* (London, Society for Promoting Christian Knowledge, 6th edition, 1907, pp. xvi, 382). H. J. Lawlor, *St. Bernard of Clairvaux's Life of St. Malachy of Armagh* (London, Society for Promoting Christian Knowledge, 1920, pp. lxvi, 183). John Thomas McNeill, *The Celtic Penitentials and Their Influence on Continental Christianity* (Paris, Edouard Champion, 1923, pp. vi, 199); a doctoral dissertation.

Great Britain. G. F. Browne, *The Conversion of the Heptarchy* (London, Society for Promoting Christian Knowledge, revised edition, 1906, pp. 236); semi-popular lectures, with an anti-Roman Catholic bias tending to minimize the part of the missionaries sent from Rome. Arthur West Haddan and William Stubbs, *Councils and Ecclesiastical Documents Relating to Great Britain and Ireland*; edited, after Spelman and Wilkins (Oxford, The Clarendon Press, 3 vols., 1859-1878); a standard collection of documents. Edward Foord, *The Last Age of Roman Britain* (London, George G. Harrup and Co., 1925, pp. 294); based upon fairly careful research. G. F. Browne, *The Christian Church in These Islands before the Coming of Augustine* (London, Society for Promoting Christian Knowledge, 1895, pp. 156); popular lectures by an expert. W. Douglas Simpson, *The Celtic Church in Scotland. A Study of Penetration Lines and Art Relationships* (Aberdeen University Press, 1935, pp. 120). Bede, *Historia Ecclesiastica,* is by a monk of the seventh and eighth centuries who was at pains to collect accurate information concerning the "Ecclesiastical History of the English Nation," and is the chief source for the introduction and early development of Christianity among the English. A standard edition is by Charles Plummer (Oxford, The Clarendon Press, 1896). Another is J. A. Giles, *Bede's Ecclesiastical History of England; also the Anglo-Saxon Chronicle* (London, George Bell and Sons, 1907, pp. xliv, 515); a new edition of a work whose preface is dated 1847. An excellent translation, based on Plummer's Latin text, is A. M. Sellar, *Bede's Ecclesiastical History* (London, George Bell and Sons, 1907, pp. xliv, 439). G. F. Browne, *The Venerable Bede. His Life and Writings* (London, Society for Promoting Christian Knowledge, revised edition, 1930, pp. xiii, 327). C. E. Whiting, *The Life of the Venerable Bede* and Wilhelm Levison, *Bede as Historian,* in A. Hamilton Thompson, editor, *Bede, His Life, Times and Writings* (Oxford, The Clarendon Press, 1935, pp. xvi, 277), pp. 1-38, 111-151. Archibald Scott, *The Pictish Nation, Its People and Its Church* (Edinburgh, T. N. Foulis, 1918, pp. xiv, 561); emphasizes the work of Ninian. William F. Skene, *Celtic Scotland. A History of Ancient Alban* (Edinburgh, David Douglas, 3 vols., 1876-1880). Thomas Taylor, *The Life of St. Samson of Dol* (London, Society for Promoting Christian Knowledge, 1925, pp. xli, 82). A. W. Wade-Evans, *Life of St. David* (London, Society for Promoting Christian Knowledge, 1923, pp. xx, 124); careful, scholarly. Alan Orr Anderson, *Early Sources of Scottish History, A.D. 500 to 1286* (Edinburgh, Oliver and Boyd, 2 vols., 1922); translations from selected passages, chiefly from Scottish and Irish sources. W. Douglas Simpson, *The Historical Saint Columba* (Aberdeen, Milne and Hutchison, 1927, pp. xiii, 177); gives to Columba a much less prominent place in the conversion of Scotland than is usual. Henry Osborn Taylor, *The Mediæval Mind. A History of the Development of Thought and Emotion in the Middle Ages* (London, Macmillan and Co., 2 vols., 1911); a standard work. Adamnan, *Life of Saint Columba, Founder of Hy,* edited by William Reeves, in *The Historians of Scotland,* Vol. VI (Edinburgh, Edmonston and Douglas, 1874, pp. clxxxiv, 385). Bertram Colgrave, *The Life of Bishop Wilfrid by Eddius and Stephanus* (Cambridge University Press, 1927, pp. xvii, 192); text, translation, and notes. Henry H. Howorth, *The Golden Days of the Early English Church* (New York, E. P. Dutton and Co., 3 vols., 1917); a standard work. William Bright, *Chapters of Early English Church History* (Oxford, The Clarendon Press, third edition, 1897, pp. xx, 525); carefully done with extensive footnotes. Alex. R. Macewen, *A History of the Church of Scotland* (London, Hodder and Stoughton, Vol. I, 397-1546, 1913, pp. xv, 487). Pierre Batiffol, *Saint Gregory the Great,* translated from the French by John L. Stoddard (London, Burns, Oates and Washbourne, 1929, pp. vi, 292); semi-popular, scholarly, by a Roman Catholic. F. Hornes Dudden, *Gregory the Great. His Place in History and Thought* (New York, Longmans, Green and Co., 2 vols., 1905); a standard work. Henry H. Howorth, *Saint Gregory the Great* (London, John Murray, 1912, pp. li, 340); excellent. Paul the Deacon, *Vita Gregorii* (text in Migne, *Pat. Lat.,* Vol. LXXV); Paul the Deacon seems to have written a Life of Gregory, but great doubt exists as to whether the present text ascribed to him is really his (Howorth, *op. cit.,* pp. xlv, xlvi). John the Deacon, *Vita Gregorii* (text in Migne, *Pat. Lat.,* Vol. LXXV), was written in the last quarter of the ninth century and must be used with care. Henry H. Howorth, *Saint Augustine of Canterbury* (London, John Murray, 1913, pp. cxix, 451); with careful references to the sources; the back title is *Augustine the Missionary.* Arthur James Mason, *The Mission of*

St. Augustine to England according to the Original Documents (Cambridge University Press, 1897, pp. xix, 252); the Latin texts and the English translation. Charles Hole, *Early Missions to and within the British Islands* (London, Society for Promoting Christian Knowledge, pp. xi, 244). Edward L. Cutts, *Augustine of Canterbury* (London, Methuen and Co., 1895, pp. xii, 207). G. F. Browne, *Augustine and His Companions* (London, Society for Promoting Christian Knowledge, 1910, pp. vi, 205). Thomas of Elmham, *Historia Monasterii S. Augustini Cantuariensis,* edited by Charles Hardwick (in *Chronicles and Memorials of Great Britain and Ireland during the Middle Ages,* London, 1858, pp. xxxv, 541). John L. Gough Meissner, *The Celtic Church in England after the Synod of Whitby* (London, Martin Hopkinson, 1929, pp. xii, 240); based upon fairly wide reading. Charles Creighton, *A History of Epidemics in Britain from A.D. 664 to the Extinction of the Plague* (Cambridge University Press, 1891, pp. xii, 706). *Remains of the Late Rev. Arthur West Haddan*, edited by A. P. Forbes (Oxford and London, James Parker and Co., 1876, pp. xxv, 528); a collection of articles, largely of reviews. Fernand Cabrol, *L'Angleterre Chrétienne avant les Normands* (Paris, Victor Lecoffre, 1909, pp. xxiii, 341); by a Roman Catholic Scholar.

The Frisians. H. Pirenne, *Histoire de Belgique* (Brussels, Henri Lamertin, 7 vols., 1902-1932); a standard work. Édouard de Moreau, *Saint Amand Apotre de la Belgique et du Nord de la France* (Louvain, Éditions du Museum Lessianum, 1927, pp. x, 367); by a Jesuit, based upon extensive and careful research. P. H. Ditchfield, *The Church in the Netherlands* (London, Wells Gardner Darton and Co., 1893, pp. xii, 396); semi-popular, with little reference to the sources. Bertram Colgrave, *The Life of Bishop Wilfrid by Eddius Stephanus. Text, Translation, and Notes* (Cambridge University Press, 1927, pp. xvii, 192). Josef Jung-Diefenbach, *Die Friesenbekehrung bis zum Martertode des hl. Bonifatius* (Missionsdruckerei St. Gabriel, Post Mödling bei Wien, 1931, pp. viii, 118); carefully documented. Alcuin, *Vita Willibrordi*, in *Monumenta Germaniæ Historica, Scriptores rerum Merovingicarum*, Vol. VII, pp. 81-141. Alexander Grieve, *Willibrord. Missionary to the Netherlands, 691-739. Including a Translation of the Vita Willibrordi by Alcuin of York* (Westminster, The Society for the Propagation of the Gospel in Foreign Parts, 1923, pp. 139). Franz Flaskamp, *Die Anfänge friesischen und sächsischen Christentums* (Hildesheim, Franz Borgmeyer, 1929, pp. xvi, 81); of value chiefly for its elaborate footnote references to sources and literature. H. A. Wilson, *The Calendar of St. Willibrord from Ms. Paris Lat. 10837. A Facsimile with Transcription, Introduction, and Notes* (London, Harrison and Sons, 1918, pp. xxiv, xiii, 49. Henry Bradshaw Society, Vol. LV). Franz Flaskamp, *Suidbercht, Apostel der Brukterer, Gründer von Kaiserwerth* (Duderstadt, Aloys Mecke, 1930, pp. 30); scholarly.

Boniface. See bibliography in footnote 371. In addition, see Heinrich Timerding (editor), *Die christliche Frühzeit Deutschlands in den Berichten über die Bekehrer* (Jena, Eugen Diederichs, 1929); a collection of lives of leading missionaries, with preliminary essay and notes; Franz Flaskamp, *Auf hessischen Bonifatiuspfaden* (Münster in W., Aschendorffsche Verlangsbuchhandlung, 1924, pp. 29); Wilhelm Neuss, *Die Anfänge des Christentums im Rheinlande* (Bonn, Kurt Schroeder, 1923, pp. 90); especially important for the evidence from inscriptions, utensils, and the like; Charles Joseph Hefele, *A History of the Christian Councils,* translated and edited by W. R. Clark and H. N. Oxenham (Edinburgh, T. and T. Clark, 5 vols., 1871-1896); Ferdinand Gregorovius, *Geschichte der Stadt Rom im Mittelalter vom fünften Jahrhundert bis zum sechzehntes Jahrhundert* (Stuttgart, J. G. Cotta'scher Verlag, 1859-1872).

The Saxons. Heinrich Böttger, *Die Einführung des Christenthums in Sachsen durch den Frankenkönig Karl von 775 bis 786 insbesondre zur Vertheidigung der Aechtheit der Urkunde desselben über Vergrösserung und Begrenzung der Diöcese Bremen von 14. Juli, 788* (Hanover, F. Klindworth, 1859, pp. 100).

The Scandinavians. C. T. Keary, *The Vikings in Western Christendom A.D. 789 to A.D. 888* (London, T. Fisher Unwin, 1891, pp. xv, 511). Ragnar Svanström and Carl Fredrik Palmstierna, *A Short History of Sweden,* translated by Joan Bulman (Oxford, The Clarendon Press, 1934, pp. xx, 443); a scholarly summary in a readable style. Carl Hallendorff and Adolf Schück, *History of Sweden* (London, Cassel and Co., 1929, pp. xxiv, 446), translated from the Swedish by Mrs. Lajle Yapp. Knut Gjerset, *History of the Norwegian People* (New York, The Macmillan Company, 2 vols., 1915); based upon the sources and pertinent monographs in various languages. *The Anglo-Saxon Chronicle,* edited, with a translation, by Benjamin Thorpe (in *Rerum Britannicarum Medii Aevi Scriptores,* London, Longman, Green, Longman, and Roberts, 2 vols., 1861). T. D. Kendrick, *A History of the Vikings* (London, Methuen and Co., 1930, pp. xi, 412); scholarly. M. W. Patterson, *A History of the Church of England* (London, Longmans, Green and Co., 1929, pp. viii, 457). William Hunt, *The English Church from Its Foundation to the Norman Conquest (597-1066)* (London, Macmillan and Co., 1899, pp. xix, 444). G. W. Kitchin, *A History of France* (Oxford, The Clarendon Press, 4th ed., Vol. I, B.C. 58-A.D. 1453, 1899, pp. xxii, 614). Konrad Maurer, *Die Bekehrung des norwegische Stammes zum Christenthume in ihrem geschichlichen Verlaufe quellenmässig geschildert* (Munich, Christian Kaiser, 2 vols., 1855, 1856; old, but standard; centres on Norway, but also includes Denmark, Sweden and Iceland. Axel Olrik, *Viking Civilization* (New York, W. W. Norton and Co., 1930, pp. 246); popularly presented results of the findings of a distinguished specialist. Snorre Sturlason, *Heimskringla, or the Lives of the Norse Kings,* edited with notes by Erling Monsen and translated into English with the assistance of A. H. Smith (New York, D. Appleton and Co., 1932, pp. xxxvii, 770); the author, a prominent man of Iceland in the twelfth and thirteenth centuries, based this famous work upon earlier accounts and legends, and made some effort at a critical evaluation of his sources. See another edition, with the text, in *Heimskringla. Nóregs Konunga Sǫgur af Snorri Sturluson udgivne for samfund til udgivelse af gammel nordisk litteratur ved Finnur Jónsson* (Copenhagen, L. Møllers Bogtrykkeri, 4 vols., 1893-1901). Mary Wilhelmine Williams, *Social Scandinavia in the Viking Age* (New York, The Macmillan Company, 1920, pp. x, 451); excellent, Thomas B. Willson, *History of the Church and State in Norway from the Tenth to the Sixteenth Century* (Westminster, Archibald Constable and Co., 1903, pp. xii, 382); in semipopular style, based upon fairly wide reading. For a bibliography of Anskar, see footnote 515. What is referred to as *Ann. Einh.* is *Annales Regni Francorum inde ab a. 741 usque ad a. 829. Qui dicuntur Annales Laurissenses Maiores et Einhardi* (edition of G. H. Pertz by F. Kurze, Hanover, 1895, pp. xx, 204, in *Scriptores rerum Germanicarum*). Adam of Bremen, *Gesta Hammaburgensis Ecclesiæ Pontificum* (edited by Bernhard Schmeidler in *Scriptores rerum Germanicarum*, Hanover, third edition, 1917, pp. lxvii, 353); written in the second half of the eleventh century by one who knew the See of Hamburg-Bremen intimately in the days of the great Archbishop Adalbert; a major source for the history of North-western Europe. *Saxonis Grammatici Gesta Danorum,* edited by Alfred Holder (Strassburg, Karl J. Trübner, 1886, pp. lxxxviii, 724); a standard edition of an uncritical but famous history composed at the instance of the distinguished Archbishop Absalon of Denmark by an author who lived late in the twelfth and early in the thirteenth century. A later edition is *Saxonis Gesta Danorum primum A. C. Knabe et P. Hermann recensita, recognoverunt et ediderunt J. Olrik et H. Raeder* (Hauniae, Levin, et Munksgaard, 2 vols., 1931. Widukind, *Rerum Gestarum Saxonicarum* (ed. of G. Waitz by K. A. Kohr, Hanover, 1904, fourth edition, pp. xxxiii, 161, in *Scriptores rerum Germanicarum*); by a monk who died about 1004 and who was a member of the Corvey community, the leading monastery of Saxony of his day. Erik Arup, *Danmarks Historie* (Copenhagen, H. Hagerups, Vol. I, to 1282, 1925, pp. 344). Lawrence M. Larson, *Canute the Great 995 (circ)—1035 and the Rise of Danish Imperialism during the Viking Age* (New York, G. P. Putnam's Sons, 1912, pp. xviii, 375). Henry Goddard Leach, *Angevin Britain and Scandinavia* (Cambridge, Harvard University Press, 1921, pp. xi, 432); semi-popular and scholarly. Sigrid Undset, *Saga of Saints,* translated by E. C. Ramsden (New York, Longmans, Green and Co., 1934, pp. xii, 321); popularly written account of Norwegian saints, most of whom lived before the fourteenth century. Charles Plummer, *Two Saxon Chronicles . . . on the basis of an edition by John Earle* (Oxford, The Clarendon Press, 2 vols., 1892, 1899). Magnus Olsen, *Farms and Fanes of Ancient Norway* (Oslo, H. Aschehoug and Co., 1928, pp. xv, 349); scholarly. *Fagrskinna. Nóregs Kònonga Tal udgivet for samfund til udgivelse af gammel nordisk litteratur ved Finnur Jónsson* (Copenhagen, S. L. Møllers Bogtrykkeri, 1902-1903, pp. xxix, 415). Ari Thorgilsson, *The Book of the Icelanders (Islendingabók), edited and translated with an introductory essay and notes by Halldór Hermannsson* (Ithaca, Cornell University Library, 1930, pp. vii, 89); excellent. *Kristni-Saga, sive Historia Religionis Christianae in Iselandiam introductae nec non pattr af Isleifi Biskupi sive Narratio de Isleifo Episcopus* (Hafniae, 1773; text, with Latin translation. Knut Gjerset, *History of Iceland* (New York, The Macmillan Co., 1924, pp. vi, 482). Arthur Middleton Reeves (editor and translator), *The Finding of Wineland the Good: the History of the Icelandic Discovery of America* (London, Henry Frowde, 1895, pp. lxxiii, 205). William Hovgaard, *The Voyages of the Norsemen to America* (New York, The American-Scandinavian Foundation, 1914, pp. xxi, 304). John Wordsworth, *The National Church of Sweden* (London, A. R. Mowbray and Co., 1911, pp. xix, 459); the attempt of an Anglican bishop to understand and portray the Church of Sweden.

CHAPTER III

No one general work covers in any satisfactory way all those phases of the spread of Christianity which we have attempted to tell in this chapter. G. F. Maclear,

A History of Christian Missions during the Middle Ages (Cambridge and London, Macmillan and Co., 1863, pp. xxi, 466), is now partly out of date, and C. H. Robinson, *The Conversion of Europe* (London, Longmans, Green and Co., 1917, pp. xxiii, 640), while useful, has not gone with sufficient thoroughness into the pertinent sources and literature. J. Schmidlin, *Katholische Missionsgeschichte* (Steyl, Missionsdruckerei, 1924, pp. xi, 598)—in its English edition, Joseph Schmidlin, a translation edited by Matthias Braun, *Catholic Mission History* (Techny, Ill., 1933, pp. xiv, 862), somewhat enlarged—and Moreau, *Les Missions Médiévales,* pp. 141-293 in Descamps, *Histoire Générale Comparée des Missions* (Paris, Librairie Plon, 1932), are excellent summaries and are particularly valuable for their bibliographies. Yet both are sketches rather than full accounts. The chapters in Volumes III and IV of Albert Hauck, *Kirchengeschichte Deutschlands* (Leipzig, J. C. Hinrichs'sche Buchhandlung, 5 vols., 1922-1929) which fall within the period and the area dealt with in this chapter are the most nearly satisfactory of any account, both for their treatment of the subject and for their elaborate footnotes. Yet even they do not attempt to cover all the story. Especially are they not concerned with Scandinavian missions on the Baltic and the conversion of Lithuania. They deal with the conversion of the Magyars only in so far as that was effected by Germans. *The Cambridge Medieval History* has some excellent chapters which are of great help. James Thayer Addison, *The Medieval Missionary. A Study of the Conversion of Northern Europe* (New York, International Missionary Council, 1936, pp. xiv, 176) is also useful.

We must now enumerate in the order of the topics treated and in the sequence in which the books which require mention appear under these topics the other works which we have cited more than once.

The Avars. Evagrius, *Ecclesiastical History. A History of the Church in Six Books from* A.D. *431 to* A.D. *594* (English translation, London, Samuel Bagster and Sons, 1846, pp. xvi, 318), is by a sixth-century author who spent most of his life in Antioch. *Annales Laurissenses Maiores et Einhardi,* also called *Annales Regni Francorum inde ab a. 741 usque ad a. 829* (after the edition of G. H. Pertz by Frederick Kurze, in *Scriptores rerum Germanicarum,* Hanover, 1895).

The Slavs of Central Europe and along the Adriatic, including Slovenes, Moravians, and Czechs. Matthew Spinka, *A History of Christianity in the Balkans* (Chicago, The American Society of Church History, 1933, pp. 202), is a thoroughly good piece of work, based upon the sources. F. Dvorník, *Les Slaves Byzance et Rome au IXe Siècle* (Paris, Librairie Ancienne Honoré Champion, 1926, pp. v, 360), is also carefully done. Václav Novotný, *České Dějiny* (Praha, Nákladem Jana Laichtera na Král Vinohradech, 3 vols., 1912-1930); the standard history of the Czechs. *Les Légendes de Constantin et de Méthode Vues de Byzance* (Prague, Imprimerie de l'État à Prague, 1933, pp. 443), by the same author, is also good. J. W. Thompson, *East German Colonization in the Middle Ages,* in *Annual Report of the American Historical Association for 1915,* pp. 123-150, is written from a point of view which is further expanded in the second half of *Feudal Germany* (University of Chicago Press, 1928, pp. xxiii, 710), by the same author. *Annales Fuldenses,* after the edition of G. H. Pertz, by Frederick Kurze, are printed in *Scriptores rerum Germanicarum* (Hanover, 1891). For a brief bibliography of Constantine (Cyril) and Methodius, see footnote 33. Matthew Spinka, *The Mediæval German Church and the Con-*

version of the Czechoslovaks and the Poles (Ms., Chicago, 1919, pp. vi, 73); an M.A. dissertation, helpful especially for its use of Czech and Polish works.

The Magyars. C. A. Macartney, *The Magyars in the Ninth Century* (Cambridge University Press, 1930, pp. 241), seems fairly carefully done, but see a severe and somewhat adverse review by S. H. Cross and A. Steiner in *Speculum*, Vol. VII (Jan., 1932), pp. 142-146. General accounts of the Magyars which include briefer references to this period are Eugene Csuday, *Die Geschichte der Ungarn* (second edition, translated by M. Varvai, Pesth, Vol. I, pp. 506, 1900); Ferenc Eckhart, *A Short History of the Hungarian People* (London, Grant Richards, 1931, pp. 244), and C. M. Knatchbull-Hugessen, *The Political Evolution of the Hungarian Nation* (London, The National Review Office, Vol. I, pp. viii, 354, 1908). *Res Gestae Saxonicae,* by Widukind (edition of G. Waitz by K. A. Kehr, in *Scriptores rerum Germanicarum*, Hanover, 1904, pp. xxiii, 161), is by a monk who died about 1004 and who was a member of the community of Corvey, the leading monastery of Saxony of his day. For contemporary events he possessed much first-hand information. Adam of Bremen, *Gesta Hammaburgensis Ecclesiæ Pontificum* (third edition, by Bernhard Schmeidler, in *Scriptores rerum Germanicarum*, Hanover, 1917, pp. lxvii, 353), written in the second half of the eleventh century, is one of the standard sources for the history of North-eastern Europe. George Pray, *Historia Regum Hungariae* (Buda, Pt. 1, 1801, pp. cliv, 333). *Annales Hildesheimenses* (edited by G. Waitz, in *Scriptores rerum Germanicarum*, Hanover, 1878, pp. viii, 69), is a monastic chronicle which comes down to 1137. Coloman Juhasz, *Das Tschanad-Temesvarer Bistum im frühen Mittelalter 1030-1307. Einfügung des Banats in die westeuropäische germanisch-christliche Kulturgemeinschaft* (Münster-in-W., Aschendorffsche Verlagsbuchhandlung, 1930, pp. x, 368), is a scholarly, detailed account of the early days of Christianity in an area on the south-eastern border of Hungary.

Poland. J. X. Seppelt, *Zur Einführung des Christentums in Polen,* in *Zeitschrift für Missionswissenschaft*, Vol. X, 1920, pp. 86-93, is an excellent summary. *Thietmari Merseburgensis Episcopi Chronicon* (edition of J. M. Lappenbergh by Frederick Kurze in *Scriptores rerum Germanicarum*, Hanover, 1889), covers the years 908-1018 and is by an author who lived 975-1018, who during the later years of his life was Bishop of Merseberg, and who, when he writes of contemporary events, often does so from personal knowledge and from the bias of one in his position. Richard Roepell and Jacob Caro, *Geschichte Polens* (Hamburg and Gotha, Friedrich Perthes, 5 vols., 1840-1888); volume one by Roepell; old but good. Erich Maschke, *Polen und die Berufung des deutschen Ordens nach Preussen* (Danzig, Danzigger Verlags-Gesellschaft, 1934, pp. 84); contains a brief summary. For the rest of the bibliography on Poland see footnotes under that topic.

The Wends. A standard source for much of the conversion of the Wends is Helmold, *Chronica Slavorum* (edition of J. M. Lappenberg by Bernhard Schmeidler, in *Scriptores rerum Germanicarum*, Hanover, 1909). An English translation with an extensive and valuable introduction and notes is Francis Joseph Tschan, *The Chronicle of the Slavs by Helmold, Priest of Bosau* (New York, Columbia University Press, 1935, pp. xii, 321). Helmold, who served as a missionary in the land of the Wends, much of the time not far from Lübeck, lived in the twelfth century and wrote in large part from personal knowledge and from the reports of his contemporaries. His viewpoint is that of a missionary. T. F. Tout, *The Empire and the Papacy* (918-1273) (London, Rivingtons, 1909, pp. vii, 526), is a competent handbook, without footnotes or extensive bibliography. James Westfall Thompson, *Feudal Germany* (University of Chicago Press, 1928, pp. xxiii, 710), specializes on the expansion of the German people and culture on the northern and eastern frontiers, and so is useful. It is, however, possible to take exception to some of the interpretations given to the sources cited, and the book must be used with care. D. H. G. Voigt, *Brun von Querfurt, Mönch, Eremit, Erzbischof der Heiden und Märtyrer* (Stuttgart, J. F. Steinkopf, 1907, pp. xii, 525), by a professor of Church History at Halle. L. Nottrott, *Aus Wendenmission* (Halle, C. V. Kaemmerer und Co., 1897, pp. vii, 579), lacks adequate footnotes.

For a bibliography of Otto of Bamberg see note 173.

Scandinavian Expansion on the Baltic. Saxo Grammaticus, *Gesta Danorum* (edited by Alfred Holder, Strassburg, Karl J. Trübner, 1886, pp. lxxxviii, 724), the first nine books of which are translated into German by Hermann Jantzen, in *Saxo Grammaticus, Die ersten neun Bücher der dänischen Geschichte* (Berlin, Emil Felber, 1900, pp. xix, 533), was composed, at the instance of Archbishop Absalon, in the last quarter of the twelfth and first quarter of the thirteenth century. The author was not a critical historian, but is least undependable when he deals with events of his own day. J. Vahl, *Lapperne og den lapske Mission* (Copenhagen, G. E. C. Gads Voghandel, 1866, pp. 174, 189), has extensive references to the sources and to pertinent literature. Friedrich Georg von Bunge, *Das Herzogthum Estland unter den Königen von Dänemark* (Gotha, Fried. Andr. Perthes, 1877, pp. xv, 391), is by an outstanding authority and has extensive footnotes. M. G. Schybergson, *Geschichte Finnlands,* translated into German by Fritz Arnheim (Gotha, Friedrich Andreas Perthes, 1896, pp. xxiv, 663), is a standard work with references to the sources. *Scriptores rerum Suecicarum Medii Aevi* (Upsala, 3 vols., 1818-1876). *Finlands Medeltidsurkunden Samlade och i tryck utgifna af Finlands Statsarkiv genom. Reinh. Hausen* (Helsingfors, Kejserliga Senatens Tryckeri, 1910, Vol. I, to 1400, pp. 594). Carl Hallendorff and Adolf Schück, *History of Sweden,* translated from the Swedish by Mrs. Lajla Yapp (London, Cassell and Co., 1929, pp. xxiv, 446). Ragnar Svanström and Carl Fredrik Palmstierna, *A Short History of Sweden,* translated by Joan Bulman (Oxford, The Clarendon Press, 1934, pp. x, 443).

German Expansion in Estonia, Livonia, and Prussia. Friedrich Georg von Bunge (editor), *Liv-, Esth-, und Curländisches Urkundenbuch nebst Regesten* (Reval, Kluge und Ströhm, Vol. I, 1093-1300, 1853; Vol. II, 1301-1367, 1855); a standard collection of sources. *Preussisches Urkundenbuch* (Königsberg, 2 vols., 1882-1935); another standard collection of sources. Arnold, *Chronica Slavorum* (edition of I. M. Lappenberg by G. H. Pertz, in *Scriptores rerum Germanicarum*, Hanover, 1868, pp. 265), is by a monk of Lübeck of the twelfth and thirteenth centuries. Heinrich, *Chronicon Lyvoniae* (edition of W. Arndt by G. H. Pertz, Hanover, 1874, pp. xxiv, 223), by a priest of the thirteenth century who writes of events in Livonia from first-hand information. C. Schirren (editor), *Fünfundzwanzig Urkunden zur Geschichte Livlands im dreizehnten Jahrhundert* (Dorpat, E. J. Karow, 1866, pp. 25). *Scriptores rerum Prussicarum, oder die Geschichtsquellen der preussischen Vorzeit,* edited by T. Hirsch, M. Töppen, and E. Strehlke (5 vols., Leipzig,

1861-1874). B. Altaner, *Die Dominikanermission des 13. Jahrhundert* (Habelschwerdt, Schles., Frankes Buchhandlung, 1924, pp. xxiii, 247); very carefully done, with extensive footnotes. Leonhard Lemmens, *Die Heidenmission des Spätmittelalters* (Munster i.W., Aschendorffsche Verlagsbuchhandlung, 1919, pp. x, 112); primarily concerned with Franciscan missions. F. Blanke, *Die Entscheidungsjahre der Preussen mission (1206-1274),* in *Zeitschrift für Kirchengeschichte,* Vol. XLVII (1928), pp. 18-40. James Westfall Thompson, *Economic and Social History of Europe in the Later Middle Ages* (New York, The Century Co., 1931, pp. vii, 545).

Lithuania. Aside from the authorities already described, Uriah Katzenelenbogen, *The Daina, An Anthology of Lithuanian and Latvian Folk-Songs* (Chicago, Lithuanian News Publishing Co., 1935, pp. xii, 165).

The Jews. Solomon Grayzel, *The Church and the Jews in the XIIIth Century. A Study of Their Relations during the Years 1198-1254, Based on the Papal Letters and the Conciliar Decrees of the Period* (Philadelphia, The Dropsie College for Hebrew and Cognate Learning, 1933, pp. lx, 377); made up largely of documents and their translations. J. A. MacCulloch, *Medieval Faith and Fable* (Boston, Marshall Jones Co., 1933, pp. 345); a scholarly collection of incidents with references to the sources. Solomon Katz, *The Jews in the Visigothic and Frankish Kingdoms of Spain and Gaul* (Cambridge, Mass., The Mediæval Academy of America, 1937, pp. xi, 182, vi); well documented. Salo Wittmayer Baron, *A Social and Religious History of the Jews* (New York, Columbia University Press, 3 vols., 1937); objective, extensively documented. Henry Hart Milman, *The History of the Jews, from the Earliest Period down to Modern Times* (New York, Vol. III, W. J. Widdleton, 1877, pp. vii, 479), while old, is still useful, especially for its references to the sources. James Parkes, *The Conflict of the Church and the Synagogue. A Study in the Origins of Anti-semitism* (London, The Socino Press, 1934, pp. xxvi, 430); well documented, arguing the thesis that the restrictions placed upon the Jews in the Middle Ages were due to the conflict between the Church and the Synagogue and not to the hostility of the Roman world to the Jews. Albert M. Hyamson, *A History of the Jews in England* (London, Methuen and Co., second edition, revised, 1928, pp. xxi, 327); a popular account with excellent bibliographies. H. P. Stokes, *A Short History of the Jews in England* (London, Central Board of Missions. The Society for Promoting Christian Knowledge, 1921, pp. vi, 122); for a popular audience by an expert. Israel Abrahams, *Jewish Life in the Middle Ages* (London, Edward Goldston, Ltd., 1932, pp. xx, 478); a posthumous revised edition of a standard work. Fritz Baer, *Die Juden im christlichen Spanien. Erster Teil. Urkunden und Regesten.* (Berlin, Akademie für die Wissenschaft des Judentums, 2 vols., 1929, 1936): very important, a collection of Latin, Spanish, and Hebrew documents with German summaries. S. M. Dubnow, *History of the Jews in Russia and Poland from the Earliest Times until the Present Day,* translated from the Russian by D. Friedlaender (Philadelphia, The Jewish Publication Society of America, Vol. I, to 1825, 1916, pp. 413); without references to the sources. Maurice H. Harris, *History of the Mediæval Jews from the Moslem Conquest of Spain to the Discovery of America* (New York, Bloch Publishing Co., second edition, 1916, pp. 384); a pro-Jewish textbook. Henry Charles Lea, *A History of the Inquisition of Spain* (New York, The Macmillan Co., 4 vols., 1906, 1907) and *A History of the Inquisition of the*

Middle Ages (New York, Harper & Brothers, 3 vols., 1888); both based upon extensive and careful research, and with a marked bias against the Church. Cecil Roth, *A History of the Marranos* (Philadelphia, The Jewish Publication Society of America, 1932, pp. 422); apparently founded upon wide reading and research, but without references to the sources. Abram Leon Sachar, *A History of the Jews* (New York, Alfred A. Knopf, 1931, pp. xv, 408, xxiv); in semi-popular form, by a Jew.

CHAPTER IV

Procopius was a Byzantine historian who wrote in the sixth century. A standard edition of his works with an English translation, by H. B. Dewing, is being published in London by William Heineman, 1914ff. His *Anecdota* is vigorous in its dislike of Justinian and Theodora. Another edition of his works, *Opera Omnia*, is published at Leipzig, by Tuebner. See also *Of the Buildings of Justinian by Procopius (circ. 560 A.D.)*, translated by Aubrey Stewart and annotated by C. W. Wilson and Hayter Lewis (London, Adelphi, 1886, pp. viii, 178). J. B. Bury, *History of the Later Roman Empire from Arcadius to Irene (395 A.D. to 800 A.D.)* (London, Macmillan and Co., 2 vols., 1889), is a standard work, but for its earlier sections is superseded by J. B. Bury, *History of the Later Roman Empire from the Death of Theodosius I to the Death of Justinian (A.D. 395 to A.D. 565)* (London, Macmillan and Co., 2 vols., 1923). Excellent, too, is J. B. Bury, *A History of the Eastern Roman Empire from the Fall of Irene to the Accession of Basil I* (A.D. 802-867) (London, Macmillan and Co., 1912, pp. xv, 530). For the history of the sixth century writer, John of Ephesus, a Monophysite, see the Syriac text in *The Third Part of the Ecclesiastical History of John Bishop of Ephesus*, edited by William Cureton (Oxford University Press, 1853, pp. viii, 418) and a translation by R. Payne Smith in *The Third Part of the Ecclesiastical History of John of Ephesus* (Oxford University Press, 1860, pp. xlv, 463).

North Africa. Ernest Mercier, *Histoire de l'Afrique Septentrionale (Berbérie) depuis les Temps les plus Reculés jusqu'a la Conquête Française (1830)* (Paris, Ernest Leroux, 3 vols., 1888-1891); excellent. J. Mesnage, *Le Christianisme en Afrique* (Algiers, Adolphe Jourdon, 3 vols., 1914, 1915) and *L'Afrique Chrétienne. Evêches et Ruines Antiques* (Paris, Ernest Leroux, 1912, pp. xii, 592), carefully done, by one of the White Fathers. L. Duchesne, *L'Église au VIe Siècle* (Paris, E. de Boccard, 1925, pp. viii, 663); standard. Charles Diehl, *L'Afrique Byzantine. Histoire de la Domination Byzantine en Afrique (533-709)* (Paris, Ernest Leroux, 1896, pp. xiv, 644). H. Leclercq, *L'Afrique Chrétienne* (Paris, Victor Lecoffre, 2 vols., 1904); based upon extensive research.

Nubia. Johann Kraus, *Die Anfänge des Christentums in Nubien* (Mödling bei Wien, Missionsdruckerei St. Gabriel, 1931, pp. viii, 158); thorough, by a Roman Catholic. E. A. Wallis Budge, *A History of Ethiopia, Nubia and Abyssinia* (London, Methuen and Co., 1928, pp. xxx, viii, 675); by a distinguished scholar. E. A. Wallis Budge, *The Egyptian Sûdân, Its History and Monuments* (London, Kegan Paul, Trench, Trübner and Co., 2 vols., 1907); based partly upon the author's own archæological researches in that region. E. A. Wallis Budge, *Legends of Our Lady Mary the Perpetual Virgin and Her Mother Hanna, Translated from the Ethiopic*

Manuscripts (London, The Medici Society, 1932, pp. lxxv, 317). L. Duchesne, *Les Missions Chrétiennes au Sud de l'Empire Romain* (*École Française de Rome, Mélanges d'Archéologie et d'Histoire,* 1896, pp. 79-122). *Deutsche Aksum Expedition* (Berlin, Georg Reimer, 4 vols., 1913).

Arabia. Axel Moberg, *The Book of the Himyarites. Fragments of a Hitherto Unknown Syriac Work* (Lund, C. W. K. Gleerup, 1924, pp. clxxii, 61); introduction, translation, and text.

The Slavs in the Balkans; the Bulgars; the Serbs. A. A. Vasiliev, *History of the Byzantine Empire* (Madison, Wis., University of Wisconsin Studies in the Social Sciences and History, 2 vols., 1928, 1929); by a competent Russian. Steven Runciman, *A History of the First Bulgarian Empire* (London, G. Bell and Sons, 1930, pp. xii, 337); readable and in general competent, but in places must be used with care. F. Dvorník, *Les Slaves, Byzance et Rome au IXe Siècle* (Paris, Librairie Ancienne Honoré Champion, 1926, pp. v, 360); based on a careful study of the sources. Matthew Spinka, *A History of Christianity in the Balkans. A Study of the Spread of Byzantine Culture among the Slavs* (Chicago, The American Society of Church History, 1933, pp. 202); thorough and competent. Constantin Jireček, *Geschichte der Serben* (first vol., to 1371, Gotha, Friedrich Andreas Perth, 1911, pp. xx, 442); a standard work. Voyeslav Yanich and C. Patrick Hankey, *Lives of the Serbian Saints* (London, Society for Promoting Christian Knowledge, 1921, pp. xx, 108); translations without critical notes or indications of dates and authorship.

The Caucasus. Maçoudi, *Les Prairies d'Or,* text and translation by C. Barbier de Meynard and Pavet de Courtelle (Paris, l'Imprimerie Impériale, 10 vols., 1861-1869). Steven Runciman, *The Emperor Romanus Lecapenus and His Reign. A Study of Tenth-Century Byzantium* (Cambridge University Press, 1929, pp. vi, 275).

Russia. James Westfall Thompson, *Economic and Social History of the Middle Ages (300-1300)* (New York, The Century Co., 1928, pp. ix, 900). George Vernadsky, *A History of Russia* (New Haven, Yale University Press, revised edition, 1930, pp. xix, 413); a summary by a thoroughly competent scholar. George Vernadsky, *Political and Diplomatic History of Russia* (Boston, Little, Brown and Co., 1936, pp. ix, 499). Konrad Lübeck, *Die Christianisierung Russlands* (Aachen, Xaveriusverlagsbuchhandlung, 1922, pp. 118); objective, scholarly, by a Roman Catholic, using Russian and Western European material. S. M. Dubnow, *History of the Jews in Russia and Poland,* translated from the Russian by I. Friedlaender (Philadelphia, The Jewish Publication Society of America, Vol. I, to 1825, 1916, pp. 413); no references to sources. Golubinskii, *Istoria Russkoi Tserkvi* (Moscow); a standard, critical work. Joseph B. Koncevičius, *Russia's Attitude towards Union with Rome (9th-16th Centuries)* (Washington, The Catholic University of America, 1927, pp. xxix, 197); a doctoral dissertation whose footnote references are not always easy to confirm. J. Hergenröther, *Photius, Patriarch von Constantinopel* (Regensburg, Georg Joseph Manz, 3 vols., 1867-1869). Walter F. Adeney, *The Greek and Eastern Churches* (New York, Charles Scribner's Sons, 1928 [preface, 1908], pp. xiv, 634); a scholarly summary, now superseded in certain sections. Paul Milukow, *Skizzen russischer Kulturgeschichte deutsche von Verfasser durchgesehene Ausgabe von E. Davidson* (Leipzig, Otto Wigand, 2 vols., 1898, 1901). Alexander Eck, *Le Moyen Age Russe* (Paris, Maison du Livre Étranger, 1933, pp. xiv, 570).

Theophilus, *A Short History of the Christian Church* (San Francisco, Douglass Brothers, 1934, pp. 46); an official statement by an Orthodox bishop for a popular audience. Eugene Smirnoff, *A Short Account of the Historical Development and Present Position of Russian Orthodox Missions* (London, Rivingtons, 1903, pp. xii, 83); by the chaplain of the Russian Embassy in London.

The Jews. Carl H. Kraeling, *The Jewish Community at Antioch* (New Haven, Antioch Index Publications, No. 1, 1932, pp. 31); competent.

CHAPTER V

In general: varieties of Christianity east of the Euphrates. Hans von Schubert, *Geschichte der christlichen Kirche im Frühmittelalter* (Tübingen, J. C. B. Mohr, 1921, pp. xxiv, 808); excellent. W. A. Wigram, *The Separation of the Monophysites* (London, The Faith Press, 1923, pp. xviii, 208). Richard Bell, *The Origin of Islam in Its Christian Environment* (London, Macmillan and Co., 1926, pp. vii, 224); semi-popular lectures by an expert. Laurence E. Browne, *The Eclipse of Christianity in Asia from the Time of Muhammed till the Fourteenth Century* (Cambridge University Press, 1933, pp. 198); an excellent survey, based on wide reading in the sources and pertinent literature, by an Anglican missionary. J. Labourt, *Le Christianisme dans l'Empire Perse sous la Dynastie Sassanide* (Paris, Librairie Victor Lecoffre, 1904, pp. xix, 372); standard. J. Labourt, *De Timotheo I Nestorianorum Patriarcha (728-823) et Christianorum Orientalium Condicione sub Chaliphis Abbasidis* (Paris, Librairie Victory Lecoffre, 1904, pp. xv, 86). W. A. Wigram, *An Introduction to the History of the Assyrian Church or the Church of the Sassanid Persian Empire 100-640 A.D.* (London, Society for Promoting Christian Knowledge, 1910, pp. 318); by an English missionary. *The Book of Governors. The Historica Monastica of Thomas Bishop of Marga, A.D. 840,* edited and translated by E. A. Wallis Budge (London, Kegan Paul, Trench, Trübner and Co., 2 vols., 1893). Bar Hebræus, *The Chronography of Gregory Abû'l Faraj, the Son of Aaron, the Hebrew Physician Commonly Known as Bar Hebræus, being the First Part of His Political History of the World,* translated from the Syriac by Ernest A. Wallis Budge (Oxford University Press, 2 vols., 1932). W. Barthold, *Zur Geschichte des Christentums in Mittel-Asien bis zur mongolischen Eroberung. Berichtigte und vermehrte deutsche Bearbeitung nach dem russischen Original herausgegeben von Dr. Rudolf Stübe* (Tübingen, J. C. B. Mohr, 1901, pp. vii, 74); excellent. Joseph Simonius Assemanus, *Bibliotheca Orientalis Clementino-Vaticana* (Rome, Typis Sacræ Congregationis de Propaganda Fide, 3 vols., 1719-1728). Albîrûnî, *The Chronology of Ancient Nations: an English Version of the Arabic Text of the Alhârul-Bâķiya of Albîrûnî on "Vestiges of the Past" Collected and Reduced to Writing by the Author in A.H. 390-1, A.D. 1000,* translated and edited by C. Edward Sachau (London, William H. Allen and Co., 1879, pp. xvi, 464). J.-B. Chabot, *Synodicon Orientale ou Recueil de Synodes Nestoriens, Publié, Traduit et Annoté* (Paris, Imprimerie Nationale, 1902, pp. 695).

The Persian Empire. Many of the titles are in the preceding paragraph. William Ambrose Shedd, *Islam and the Oriental Churches: their Historical Relations* (Philadelphia, Presbyterian Board of Publication and Sabbath-School Work, 1904, pp. vii, 253); by a Presbyterian missionary to Persia.

Arabia. L. Duchesne, *Les Missions Chrétiennes au Sud de l'Empire Romain* (Ecole Française de Rome, Mélanges d'Archeologie et d'Histoire, 1896, pp. 79-122). Ign. Guidi, *L'Arabie Antéislamique* (Paris, Paul Geuthner, 1921, pp. 88); by an eminent scholar. Henry Yule, *Cathay and the Way Thither, being a Collection of Medieval Notices of China* (new edition, revised by Henri Cordier (London, The Hakluyt Society, 4 vols., 1925, 1926); standard. Henry Yule, *The Book of Ser Marco Polo,* third edition, revised by Henri Cordier (London, John Murray, 2 vols., 1921). Axel Moberg, *The Book of the Himyarites* (Lund, C. W. K. Gleerup, 1924, pp. clxxii, 61).

Central Asia. Several of the titles are in the first paragraph. Eduard Sachau, *Zur Ausbreitung des Christentums in Asien* (Abhandlungen der preuss. Ak. der Wissenschaften, phil. hist. Klasse, 1919, pp. 1-80); a scholarly summary. Alphonse Mingana, *The Early Spread of Christianity in Central Asia and the Far East: A New Document* (Manchester University Press, 1925, pp. 80). Paul Pelliot, *La Haute Asie* (neither date nor publisher, pp. 37). W. W. Rockhill, *The Journey of William of Rubruck to the Eastern Parts of the World, 1253-55* (London, The Hakluyt Society, 1900). E. Bretschneider, *Mediæval Researches from Eastern Asiatic Sources* (London, Kegan Paul, Trench, Trübner and Co., 2 vols., 1910).

China. A. C. Moule, *Christians in China before the Year 1550* (London, Society for Promoting Christian Knowledge, 1930, pp. xvi, 293); translations of all the pertinent documents with extensive footnotes; standard. K. S. Latourette, *A History of Christian Missions in China* (New York, The Macmillan Co., 1929, pp. xii, 930). E. Chavannes and P. Pelliot, *Un Traité Manichéen Retrouvé en Chine, Traduit et Annoté* (Paris, 1913, extract from *Journal Asiatique,* Nov.-Dec., 1911, and Jan.-Apr., 1913).

India. Walter F. Adeney, *The Greek and Eastern Churches* (New York, Charles Scribner's Sons, 1928 [preface 1908], pp. xiv, 634). Julius Richter, *Indische Missionsgeschichte* (Gütersloh, C. Bertelsmann, second edition, 1924, pp. vi, 570); the best comprehensive account of Protestant missions in India, with an important chapter on pre-Protestant missions. Rao Bahadur L. K. Anantakrishna Ayyar, *Anthropology of the Syrian Christians* (Ernakulam, Cochin Government Press, 1926, pp. xvii, 338); fairly good. A. Mingana, *The Early Spread of Christianity in India* (Manchester University Press, 1926, pp. 82). S. Gnana Prakasar, *A History of the Catholic Church in Ceylon* (Colombo, Literature Committee for the Catholic Union of Ceylon, 1924, pp. xiv, 283); by an Oblate father. Carl Clemen, *Der Einfluss des Christentums auf andere Religionen* (Leipzig, A. Deichertsche Verlagsbuchhandlung D. Werner Schall, 1933, pp. 122); well documented, brief, by a competent scholar.

CHAPTER VI

Christian Influences in the formation and development of Islam. P. L. Cheikho, *Le Christianisme et la Littérature Chrétienne en Arabie avant l'Islam* (Beirut, Imprimerie Catholique, 2 parts in 3 fascicules, 1912-1923); by a Jesuit, largely in Arabic, stressing Christian influence. J. Wellhausen, *Skizzen und Vorarbeiten* (third vol., Berlin, 1887). Charles Cutler Torrey, *The Jewish Foundation of Islam* (New York, Jewish Institute of Religion Press, 1933, pp. vii, 164); by an eminent

Protestant scholar, stressing Jewish and minimizing Christian influence. Richard Bell, *The Origin of Islam in Its Christian Environment* (London, Macmillan and Co., 1926, pp. vii, 224); by a Lecturer in Arabic in the University of Edinburgh. H. Lammens, *L'Arabie Occidentale avant l'Hégire* (Beirut, Imprimerie Catholique, 1928, pp. 343); by a scholarly Jesuit. Carl Clemens, *Der Einfluss Christentums auf andere Religionen* (Leipzig, 1933, pp. 122). Samuel M. Zwemer, *The Moslem Christ* (New York, American Tract Society, 1912, pp. 198). Margaret Smith, *Studies in Early Mysticism in the Near and Middle East* (London, The Shelton Press, 1931, pp. x, 276); scholarly, endeavouring to show a connexion between the rise and development of Sufism and Christian mysticism. Laurence E. Browne, *The Eclipse of Christianity in Asia* (Cambridge University Press, 1933, pp. 198); well done. Reynold A. Nicholson, *The Mystics of Islam* (London, G. Bell and Sons, 1914, pp. vii, 178); the fruit of twenty years of study.

The decline of Christianity in Moslem lands: generalizations. A. S. Tritton, *The Caliphs and Their Non-Muslim Subjects* (Oxford University Press, 1930, pp. 240); scholarly, unbiased. T. W. Arnold, *The Preaching of Islam: a History of the Propagation of the Muslim Faith* (New York, 1913, pp. xvi, 467); by an eminent scholar, sympathetic with Islam, and combating the popular impression that Islam was propagated almost entirely by force. Samuel M. Zwemer, *The Law of Apostasy from Islam* (London, Marshall Brothers, 1924, pp. 164).

Arabia. The Book of Governors. The Historica Monastica of Thomas Bishop of Marga, A.D. 840, edited and translated by E. A. W. Budge (London, Kegan Paul, Trench, Trübner and Co., 2 vols., 1893). *The Chronography of . . . Bar Hebræus . . .*, translated and edited by E. A. W. Budge (Oxford University Press, 2 vols., 1932).

Syria and Palestine. W. A. Shedd, *Islam and the Oriental Churches* (Philadelphia, Presbyterian Board of Publication and Sabbath-School Work, 1904, pp. vii, 253). H. Lammens, *Islām, Beliefs and Institutions,* translated from the French by E. Denison Ross (London, Methuen and Co., 1929, pp. ix, 256); by a Jesuit expert in Islam. F. W. Hasluck, edited by Margaret M. Hasluck, *Christianity and Islam under the Sultans* (Oxford, Clarendon Press, 2 vols., 1929); well documented. A. A. Vasiliev, *History of the Byzantine Empire* (Madison, University of Wisconsin Studies in the Social Sciences and History, 2 vols., 1928, 1929); a standard summary.

Georgia. Michel Tamarati, *L'Église Géorgienne des Origines jusqu'a nos Jours* (Rome, Imprimerie de la Société Typographico-Editrice Romaine, 1910, pp. xiv, 710); based on extensive research. S. C. Malan, *A Short History of the Georgian Church* (translated from the Russian by P. Ioselian, and edited with additional notes (London, Saunders, Otley and Co., 1866, pp. ix, 208); by a Georgian, uncritical.

East of the Euphrates. W. A. Wigram, *An Introduction to the History of the Assyrian Church and the Church of the Sassanid Persian Empire 100-640 A.D.* (London, Society for Promoting Christian Knowledge, 1910, pp. 318).

Egypt. Alfred S. Butler, *The Arab Conquest of Egypt and the Last Thirty Years of the Roman Dominion* (Oxford, The Clarendon Press, 1902, pp. xxxiv, 563); objective, scholarly, well documented. E. L. Butcher, *The Story of the Church of Egypt* (London, Smith, Elder and Co., 2 vols., 1897); uncritical, pro-Copt.

Nubia. E. A. W. Budge, *A History of Ethiopia, Nubia, and Abyssinia* (London, Methuen and Co., 2 vols., 1928). E. A. W. Budge, *The Egyptian Sûdân Its History and Monuments* (London, Kegan Paul, Trench, Trübner and Co., 2 vols., 1907). W. F. Adeney, *The Greek and Eastern Churches* (New York, Charles Scribner's Sons, preface, 1908, pp. xiv, 634). E. A. W. Budge, *Legends of Our Lady Mary the Perpetual Virgin and Her Mother Hannâ translated from the Ethiopic* (London, The Medici Society, 1932).

North Africa. E. L. Iselin, *Die Untergang der christlichen Kirche in Nordafrika* (Basel, Verlag der Baslermissionsbuchhandlung, 1918, pp. 69); not very important. H. Leclercq, *L'Afrique Chrétienne* (Paris, Librairie Victor Lecoffre, 2 vols., 1904); excellent. Marcellino da Civezza, *Storia Universale delle Missioni Francescane* (Rome, Prato, Florence, 11 vols., 1857-1895); a monumental work, emphasizing the romantic features of the story, not always critical. J. Mesnage, *Le Christianisme en Afrique* (Algiers, Adolphe Jourdan, 3 vols., 1914, 1915); important.

Spain. C. R. Haines, *Christianity and Islam in Spain, A.D. 756-1031* (London, Kegan Paul, Trench and Co., 1889, pp. viii, 182); scholarly, objective, based largely on original sources.

CHAPTER VII

The gains of Christianity against Islam. Byzantine Empire. The Chronography of Gregory Abu'l Faraj . . . Commonly Known as Bar Hebræus . . . translated from the Syriac by E. A. W. Budge (Oxford University Press, 2 vols., 1932). Alfred von Kremer, *Culturgeschichte des Orients unter den Chalifen* (Vienna, Wilhelm Braumüller, 2 vols., 1875, 1877).

Spain and Portugal. Ramón Menéndez Pidal, *The Cid and His Spain,* translated by Harold Sunderland (London, John Murray, 1934, pp. xiv, 474). Adelhelm Jann, *Die katholischen Missionen in Indien, China und Japan . . . vom 15 bis ins 18 Jahrhundert* (Paderborn, Ferdinand Schöningh, 1915, pp. xxviii, 540); excellent. Henry Charles Lea, *A History of the Inquisition in Spain* (New York, The Macmillan Co., 4 vols., 1906, 1907); standard, but biased against the Church. Henry Charles Lea, *The Moriscos in Spain: their Conversion and Expulsion* (Philadelphia, Lea Brothers and Co., 1901, pp. xii, 463); based on careful research, but also prejudiced against the Church. P. G. Bridge, *Ramon Lull, a Medieval Bakta* (Madras, Christian Literature Society for India, 1932, pp. 107); based largely on Peer's biography and translations of Lull's writings. J. Schmidlin, *Katholische Missionsgeschichte* (Steyl, Missionsdruckerei, 1924, pp. xi, 598); excellent, especially for its bibliographies. Leonhard Lemmens, *Die Heidenmissionen des Spätmittelalters* (Münster in Westf., Aschendorffsche Verlagsbuchhandlung, 1919, pp. x, 112); by a Franciscan, based upon careful use of the sources. Berthold Altaner, *Die Dominikanermissionen des 13 Jahrhunderts. Forschungen zur Geschichte der kirchlichen Unionen und der Mohammedaner und Heidenmission des Mittelalters* (Habelschwerdt, Shles., Frankes Buchhandlung, 1924, pp. xxiii, 248); based largely on original sources. C. R. Haines, *Christianity and Islam in Spain A.D. 756-1030* (London, Kegan Paul, Trench and Co., 1889, pp. viii, 182); scholarly, based largely upon original sources, and, in general, unbiased.

Sicily. Edmund Curtis, *Roger of Sicily and the Normans in Lower Italy, 1016-1154* (New York, G. P. Putnam's Sons, 1912, pp. xii, 483); semi-popular, scholarly. Ferdinand Chalandon, *Histoire de la Domination Normande en Italie et en Sicile* (Paris, Alphonse Picard et Fils, 2 vols., 1907); excellent.

The Crusades. Dana C. Munro, *The Kingdom of the Crusaders* (New York, D. Appleton-Century Co., 1935, pp. ix, 216); semi-popular lectures by a distinguished specialist. F. M. Powicke, *The Christian Life in the Middle Ages and Other Essays* (Oxford, The Clarendon Press, 1935, pp. vi, 176). W. F. Adeney, *The Greek and Eastern Churches* (New York, Charles Scribner's Sons, preface, 1908, pp. xiv, 634).

Persuasion, and the Missions of the Franciscans and Dominicans. L. E. Browne, *The Eclipse of Christianity in Asia from the Time of Muhammed till the Fourteenth Century* (Cambridge University Press, 1933, pp. 198); excellent. Luca Wadding, *Annales Minorum seu Trium Ordinum a S. Francesco Institutorum* (Rome, Typis Rochi Bernabo, 16 vols., 1731-1736); in addition, an index volume and a continuation volume have been published; a standard. Louis Bréhier, *L'Eglise et l'Orient au Moyen Age: les Croisades* (Paris, J. Gabalda et Fils, fifth edition, 1928, pp. xv, 399). Paul Sabatier, *Life of St. Francis of Assisi,* translated by Louise Seymour Houghton (New York, Charles Scribner's Sons, 1909, pp. xxxv, 498); a standard life, by a Protestant. Erhard Schlund, *St. Franziskus und sein Orden in den Heidenmission* (Düsseldorf, Missionsverwaltung der Franziskaner, pp. 63); a popular account by a Franciscan. Marcellino da Civezza, *Storia Universale delle Missioni Francescane* (Rome, Prato, Florence, 11 vols., 1857-1895). Leonhard Lemmens, *Geschichte der Franziskanermissionen* (Münster in Westf., Aschendorffsche Verlagsbuchhandlung, 1929, pp. xx, 376); carefully done by a Franciscan. Élie Marie, *Aux avantpostes de la Chrétienté. Histoire des Instituts Religieux et Missionnaires* (Paris, P. Lethielleux, 1930, pp. xii, 343); semi-popular, fairly comprehensive, with bibliographies. Michel Tamarati, *L'Église Géorgienne des Origines jusqu'a nos Jours* (Rome, Imprimerie de la Société Typographico-Editrice Romaine, 1910, pp. xv, 710); based on careful research. Henry Yule, *Cathay and the Way Thither: Being a Collection of Medieval Notices of China,* revised by Henri Cordier (London, The Hakluyt Society, 4 vols., 1925, 1926); long a standard. W. W. Rockhill, *The Journey of William of Rubruck to the Eastern Parts of the World, 1253-55, as Narrated by Himself* . . . (London, The Hakluyt Society, 1900). Henry H. Howorth, *History of the Mongols from the Ninth to the Nineteenth Century* (3 parts, London, 1876-1888). Henry Yule, *The Book of Ser Marco Polo the Venetian Concerning the Kingdoms and Marvels of the East,* third edition, revised by Henri Cordier (London, John Murray, 2 vols., 1921). A. C. Moule, *Christians in China before the Year 1550* (London, Society for Promoting Christian Knowledge, 1930, pp. xix, 293); translations, with notes, of the pertinent sources. Alphonse Mingana, *The Early Spread of Christianity in Central Asia and the Far East; a New Document* (Manchester University Press, 1925, pp. 80); excellent. E. A. Wallis Budge, *The Monks of Kûblâi Khân Emperor of China or the History of the Life and Travels of Rabban Swâmâ Envoy and Plenipotentiary of the Mongol Khâns to the Kings of Europe and Markôs who as Mâr Yahbhallâhâ III became Patriarch of the Nestorian Church in Asia,* translated from the Syriac (London, The Religious Tract Society, 1928, pp. xvi, 335); the best English translation of this important document.

The second retreat of Christianity before Islam. H. Yule, *Mirabilia Descripta. The Wonders of the East by Friar Jordanus of the Order of Preachers and Bishop of Columbum in India the Greater* (circa *1330*), translated (London, the Hakluyt Society, 1863, pp. xxvi, 68). W. Barthold, *Zur Geschichte des Christentums in Mittel-Asien bis zur mongolischen Eroberung,* enlarged and translated by R. Stübe (Tübingen, J. C. B. Mohr, 1901, pp. vii, 74). W. M. Ramsay, *The Cities and Bishoprics of Phrygia* (Oxford, the Clarendon Press, 2 vols., 1895, 1897); based upon archæological investigations by the author. T. W. Arnold, *The Preaching of Islam: a History of the Propagation of the Muslim Faith* (New York, 1913); scholarly, pro-Moslem.

CHAPTER VIII

Western Christendom in general. Samuel Dill, *Roman Society in Gaul in the Merovingian Age* (London, Macmillan and Co., 1926, pp. xiii, 566); delightfully written by an outstanding specialist. Bede Jarrett, *Social Theories of the Middle Ages 1200-1500* (Boston, Little, Brown and Co., 1926, pp. ix, 280); by a competent Roman Catholic scholar. Henry Osborn Taylor, *The Mediæval Mind. A History of the Development of Thought and Emotion in the Middle Ages* (London, Macmillan and Co., 1911, 2 vols.); a standard work. Ernst Troeltsch, *The Social Teachings of the Christian Churches,* translated by Olive Wyon (New York, The Macmillan Co., 1931, pp. 1019); also standard, first published (in German) in 1911. Charles Howard McIlwain, *The Growth of Political Thought in the West from the Greeks to the End of the Middle Ages* (New York, The Macmillan Co., 1932, pp. vii, 417); a well-documented, scholarly summary. Christopher Dawson, *Progress and Religion: An Historical Inquiry* (New York, Longmans, Green and Co., 1929, pp. xvii, 254); brilliant and suggestive, by a Roman Catholic layman. John Brown Paton, Percy William Bunting, and Alfred Ernest Garvie, editors, *Christ and Civilization: A Survey of the Influence of the Christian Religion upon the Course of Civilization* (London, National Council of Evangelical Free Churches, 1910, pp. xi, 546); semi-popular, by twelve scholars, warmly appreciative of the Christian faith. W. Cunningham, *Christianity and Economic Science* (New York, Longmans, Green and Co., 1914, pp. viii, 111); a careful and stimulating essay.

Western Europe: effect upon religion and morals. Theodore Jorgenson, *History of Norwegian Literature* (New York, The Macmillan Co., 1933, pp. xiii, 559); excellent. Albert Hauck, *Kirchengeschichte Deutschlands* (Leipzig, J. C. Hinrichs'sche Buchhandlung, 1922-1929, 5 vols.); standard, by a Protestant scholar. Edward Kylie, translator and editor, *The English Correspondence of Saint Boniface* (London, Chatto and Windus, 1911, pp. xiv, 212). J. P. Migne, *Patrologiæ . . . Ecclesiæ Latinæ . . .* (Paris, 1844-1864, 221 vols.); a standard collection of sources. George Ratzinger, *Geschichte der kirchlichen Armenpflege* (Freiburg im Breisgau, Herder, 2d ed., 1884, pp. xiv, 616); a pioneer standard work, concerned almost entirely with the activities of the Roman Catholic Church in Europe. F. M. Powicke, *The Christian Life in the Middle Ages and Other Essays* (Oxford, The Clarendon Press, 1935, pp. vi, 176). Francis Herbert Stead, *The Story of Social Christianity* (London, James Clarke and Co., no date, 2 vols.); laudatory of Christianity. Charles Henry Robinson, *The Conversion of Europe* (London, Longmans, Green and Co., 1917, pp. xxiii, 640); useful, but partly out of date. Edward L. Cutts, *Parish Priests and Their People in the Middle Ages in England* (London, Society for Promoting Christian Knowledge, 1898, pp. xvii, 579); objective, with extensive quotations and translations from the sources. G. G. Coulton, *Life in the Middle Ages* (Cambridge University Press, 2d ed., 1928-1930, 4 vols.); translations of original documents. J. Huizinga, *The Waning of the Middle Ages, a Study in the Forms of Life, Thought and Art in France and the Netherlands in the XIV and XV Centuries* (London, Edwin Arnold and Co., 1927, pp. vii, 328); based upon careful research, a translation and condensation of the second Dutch edition. J. A. MacCulloch, *Medieval Faith and Fable* (Boston, Marshall Jones and Co., 1933, pp. 345); a scholarly collection of incidents with references to the sources. Thomas Pollock Oakley, *English Penitential Discipline and Anglo-Saxon Law in Their Joint Influence* (New York, Columbia University Press, 1923, pp. 226); scholarly. Oscar D. Watkins, *A History of Penance* (London, Longmans, Green and Co., 2 vols., 1920); containing extensive excerpts from the sources. Henry Charles Lea, *A History of Auricular Confession and Indulgences in the Latin Church* (Philadelphia, Lea Brothers and Co., 1896, 3 vols.); based upon wide reading in the sources and slightly biased against the Church. G. R. Owst, *Preaching in Medieval England: An Introduction to Sermon Manuscripts of the Period c. 1350-1450* (Cambridge University Press, 1926, pp. xviii, 381); well written and based upon extensive research in original manuscripts. G. R. Owst, *Literature and Pulpit in Medieval England* (Cambridge University Press, 1933, pp. xvi, 616); scholarly and primarily from the approach of the historian of letters. Anscar Zawart, *The History of Franciscan Preaching and of Franciscan Preachers,* in *Franciscan Studies,* No. 7, Feb., 1928 (New York, Joseph F. Wagner, pp. 241-596). K. L. Wood-Legh, *Studies in Church Life in England under Edward III* (Cambridge University Press, 1934, pp. x, 181). Abbot Gasquet, *Parish Life in Mediaeval England* (London, Methuen and Co., 2d ed., 1907, pp. xxi, 279). A. S. Rappoport, *Mediæval Legends of Christ* (New York, Charles Scribner's Sons, 1935, pp. 312); scholarly.

Western Europe: effect upon social relations and customs. John Thomas McNeill, *The Celtic Penitentials and Their Influence on Continental Christianity* (Paris, Édouard Champion, 1923, pp. vi, 199); a doctoral dissertation of the University of Chicago. W. E. H. Lecky, *History of European Morals from Augustus to Charlemagne* (New York, D. Appleton and Co., 1884, 3d ed., 2 vols.); a standard work with a conviction against the utilitarian basis and supporting the intuitive theory of ethics. G. G. Coulton, *Five Centuries of Religion* (Cambridge University Press, Vols. 1-3, 1923-1936, to be in five volumes); based upon exhaustive research. H. F. Westlake, *The Parish Gilds of Mediæval England* (London, Society for Promoting Christian Knowledge, 1919, pp. vii, 242); scholarly. P. Boissonnade, *Life and Work in Medieval Europe,* translated by Eileen Power (New York, Alfred A. Knopf, 1927, pp. xix, 395); a semi-popular summary by an expert.

Western Europe: Christian charity. Bede Jarrett, *Mediæval Socialism* (London, T. C. and E. C. Jack, no date, pp. 94); a semi-popular summary by a competent Roman Catholic scholar. Léon Lallemand, *Histoire de la Charité* (Paris, Alphonse Picard et Fils, 1902-1912, 4 vols.); well documented, favourable to the Church, valuable for many citations of sources. Wilh. Liese, *Geschichte der Caritas* (Freiburg i. Br., Caritasverlag, 1922, 2 vols.); from a Roman Catholic viewpoint. G. Uhlhorn, *Die Christliche Liebesthätigkeit* (Stuttgart, D. Gundert, 1882-1890, 3 vols.); the period covered is from the beginning through the Reformation; an English translation of the first volume appeared in Edinburgh in 1883. W. Edward Chadwick, *The Church, the State and the Poor: A Series of Historical Sketches* (London, Robert Scott, 1914, pp. viii, 223); based only partly upon the sources; from a strongly Christian viewpoint. David Riesman, *The Story of Medicine in the Middle Ages* (New York, Paul B. Hoeber, 1935, pp. xii, 402); semi-popular. F. Meffert, *Caritas und Krankenwesen bis zum Ausgang des Mittelalters* (Freiburg i. Br., Caritasverlag, 1927, pp. xvii, 443); a good summary. Gustav Schnürer, *Kirche und Kultur im Mittelalter* (Paderborn, Ferdinand Schöningh, 2d ed., 1927-1929, 3 vols.). John Evans, *Life in Mediaeval France* (Oxford University Press, 1925, pp. 234); semi-popular, scholarly.

Western Europe: protests against social and economic injustice. Attitude toward slavery and serfdom. James Gairdner, *Lollardy and the Reformation in England: An Historical Survey* (London, Macmillan and Co., 1908-1911, 3 vols.); standard. Herbert Grundmann, *Religiöse Bewegungen im Mittelalter* (Berlin, Dr. Emil Ebering, 1935, pp. 510); one of *Historische Studien*. M. Beer, *Social Struggles in the Middle Ages,* trans. by H. J. Stenning (London, Leonard Parsons, no date, pp. 207); a scholarly summary. C. M. Kennedy, *The Influence of Christianity upon International Law* (Cambridge, Macmillan and Co., 1856, pp. xvi, 158); a Hulsean prize essay.

Western Europe: effect upon political theory. Otto Gierke, *Political Theories of the Middle Ages,* translated with an introduction by F. W. Maitland (Cambridge University Press, 1927, pp. lxxx, 197); a standard. R. W. and A. J. Carlyle, *A History of Mediæval Political Theory in the West* (Edinburgh, William Blackwood and Sons, 1928-1936, 6 vols.); based upon the sources. G. P. Gooch, *English Democratic Ideas in the Seventeenth Century* (Cambridge University Press, 1927, 2d ed., with supplementary notes and appendices by H. J. Laski, pp. x, 315). C. E. Osborne, *Christian Ideas in Political History* (London, John Murray, 1929, pp. xiv, 319). C. Loring Brace, *Gesta Christi, or a History of Humane Progress under Christianity* (London, Hodder and Stoughton, 1889, pp. xxiii, 520); very favourable to Christianity; using the sources but not always critical.

Western Europe: effect upon war. Edmund H. Oliver, *The Social Achievements of the Christian Church* (Toronto, Board of Evangelism and Social Service of the United Church of Canada, 1930, pp. 192); designed as a textbook and favourable to Christianity. Axel Olrik, *Viking Civilization* (New York, W. W. Norton and Co., 1930, pp. 246); popularly presented results of the researches of a distinguished specialist. Élie Marie, *Aux Avant-postes de la Chrétienté. Histoire des Instituts Religieux et Missionaires* (Paris, P. Lethielleux, 1930, pp. xii, 343); a competent popular account for youth. James Westfall Thompson, *Economic and Social History of the Middle Ages (300-1300)* (New York, The Century Co., 1928, pp. ix, 900); must be used with care. R. F. Wright, *Medieval Internationalism. The Contribution of the Medieval Church to International Law and Peace* (London, Williams and Norgate, 1930, pp. 240); strongly pro-Christian.

Western Europe: effect upon art. M. Didron, *Christian Iconography, or the His-*

tory of Christian Art in the Middle Ages, translated from the French by E. J. Millington (London, Henry G. Bohn, 1851, 2 vols.); old, but standard. Hans von Schubert, *Geschichte der christlichen Kirche im Frühmittelalter. Ein Handbuch* (Tübingen, J. C. B. Mohr, 1921, pp. xxiv, 808); excellent. Maud Joynt, *The Life of St. Gall* (London, Society for Promoting Christian Knowledge, 1927, pp. 168).

Western Europe: education and scholarship. Hastings Rashdall, *The Universities of Europe in the Middle Ages* (Oxford, The Clarendon Press, 1895, 2 vols.); standard. A revised edition of Rashdall, edited by F. M. Powicke and A. B. Emden, has appeared (Oxford, The Clarendon Press, 3 vols., 1936). A. C. McGiffert, *A History of Christian Thought* (New York, Charles Scribner's Sons, 1932, 1933, 2 vols.); by a distinguished liberal Protestant historian. Rose Graham, *English Ecclesiastical Studies* (London, Society for Promoting Christian Knowledge, 1929, pp. xiii, 463); scholarly. *Part of the Opus Tertium of Roger Bacon including a fragment now printed for the first time,* edited by A. G. Little (Aberdeen, The University Press, 1912, pp. xlviii, 92). Charles Homer Haskins, *The Renaissance of the Twelfth Century* (Harvard University Press, 1928, pp. x, 437); a semi-popular account by an expert. J. B. Bury, *The Idea of Progress. An Inquiry into Its Origin and Growth* (London, Macmillan and Co., 1920, pp. xv, 377).

Western Europe: literature. Gustav Schnürer, *Kirche und Kultur im Mittelalter* (Paderborn, Ferdinand Schöningh, 2d ed., 1927-1929, 3 vols.). Carl Clemen, *Der Einfluss des Christentums auf andere Religionen* (Leipzig, A. Deichertsche Verlagsbuchhandlung D. Werner Scholl, 1933, pp. 122); by an expert. Henry Dwight Sedgwick, *Italy in the Thirteenth Century* (Boston, Houghton Mifflin, 1912, 2 vols.); semi-popular and readable.

The Byzantine Empire. A. A. Vasiliev, *History of the Byzantine Empire* (University of Wisconsin, 1928, 1929, 2 vols.); by a Russian specialist. Steven Runciman, *Byzantine. Civilization* (New York, Longmans, Green and Co., 1933, pp. 320); an excellent summary. Walter F. Adeney, *The Greek and Eastern Churches* (New York, Charles Scribner's Sons, 1928, pp. xiv, 634). J. B. Bury, *A History of the Later Roman Empire from Arcadius to Irene (395 A.D. to 800 A.D.)* (London, Macmillan and Co., 1889, 2 vols.); by a distinguished specialist.

Greek Christianity in the Balkans and Russia. Matthew Spinka, *A History of Christianity in the Balkans* (Chicago, The American Society of Church History, 1933, pp. 202); excellent. Paul Milioukov, Ch. Seignobos and L. Eisenmann, *Histoire de Russie* (Paris, Ernest Leroux, 1932, 1933, 2 vols.). Paul Milukow, *Skizzen russischer Kulturgeschichte,* German ed. by E. Davidson (Leipzig, Otto Wigand, 1898, 1901, 2 vols.). David Roden Buxton, *Russian Mediæval Architecture* (Cambridge University Press, 1934, pp. xi, 112); carefully done, profusely illustrated. Alexandre Eck, *Le Moyen Age Russe* (Paris, Maison de Livre Étranger, 1933, pp. xiv, 570). George Vernadsky, *A History of Russia* (Yale University Press, pp. xix, 413); brief but authoritative.

Other Eastern Churches. A. Mingana, *The Early Spread of Christianity in India* (Manchester, The University Press, 1926, pp. 82); by an expert. Hilko Wiardo Schomerus, *Indien und das Christentum* (Halle-Saale, Buchhandlung des Waisenhauses, 1931-1933, 3 vols.); excellent summary of existing literature. Rao Bahadur

L. K. Anantakrishna Ayyar, *Anthropology of the Syrian Christians* (Ernakulam, Cochin Government Press, 1926, pp. xvii, 338); not always critical.

CHAPTER IX

Western Europe. J. A. MacCulloch, *Medieval Faith and Fable* (Boston, Marshall Jones and Co., 1933, pp. 345); a scholarly collection of incidents with references to the sources. Charles Henry Robinson, *The Conversion of Europe* (London, Longmans, Green and Co., 1917, pp. xxiii, 640); useful. Donald A. Mackenzie, *Scottish Folk-lore and Folk Life. Studies in Race-Culture and Tradition* (London, Blackie and Sons, 1935, pp. ix, 310); carefully done, with interesting hypotheses. Albert Hauck, *Kirchengeschichte Deutschlands* (Leipzig, J. C. Hinrichs'sche Buchhandlung, 5 vols., 1922-1929); standard, to the close of the Middle Ages, by a Protestant. Heinrich Timerding (editor), *Die christliche Frühzeit Deutschlands in die Berichten über die Bekehrer* (Jena, Eugen Diederichs, 1929, pp. 276, 226); a collection of lives of leading missionaries with preliminary notes and essay. Thomas B. Willson, *History of the Church and State in Norway from the Tenth to the Sixteenth Century* (Westminster, Archibald Constable and Co., 1903, pp. xii, 382); excellent, semi-popular. Carl Hallendorff and Adolf Schück, *History of Sweden* (London, Cassell and Co., 1929, pp. xxiv, 446); by two eminent Swedish historians; translated by Mrs. Lajla Yapp. A. S. Rappoport, *Mediaeval Legends of Christ* (New York, Charles Scribner's Sons, 1935, pp. 312); scholarly. Knut Gjerset, *History of the Norwegian People* (New York, The Macmillan Company, 2 vols., 1915); excellent. John Thomas McNeill, *The Celtic Penitentials and Their Influence on Continental Christianity* (Paris, Édouard Champion, 1923, pp. vi, 199); a doctoral dissertation. G. G. Coulton, *Life in the Middle Ages* (Cambridge University Press, vols. 1-3, 1923-1936, to be in five volumes); based upon careful research. M. Didron, *Christian Iconography, or a History of Christian Art in the Middle Ages,* translated from the French by E. J. Millington (London, Henry G. Bohn, 2 vols., 1851); an old standard work. *An Outline of Christianity. The Story of Our Civilization* (New York, Bethlehem Publishers, 5 vols., 1926); semi-popular, by various experts. Thomas Whittaker, *The Neo-Platonists. A Study in the History of Hellenism* (Cambridge University Press, 2d ed., 1918, pp. xv, 318); excellent. Arthur Cushman McGiffert, *A History of Christian Thought* (New York, Charles Scribner's Sons, 2 vols., 1932, 1933); a standard. Solomon Zeitlin, *Maimonides. A Biography* (New York, Bloch Publishing Co., 1935, pp. xi, 234); popular, sympathetic, fairly scholarly. Hans von Schubert, *Geschichte der christlichen Kirche im Frühmittelalter* (Tübingen, J. C. B. Mohr, 1921, pp. xxiv, 808); a standard handbook. R. W. and A. J. Carlyle, *A History of Mediæval Political Theory in the West* (Edinburgh, William Blackwood and Sons, 6 vols., 1928-1936); scholarly. Ernst Troeltsch, *The Social Teaching of the Christian Churches,* translated by Olive Wyon (New York, The Macmillan Company, 1931, pp. 1019). Edward L. Cutts, *Parish Priests and Their People in the Middle Ages in England* (London, Society for Promoting Christian Knowledge, 1898, pp. xvii, 579); objective. James Westfall Thompson, *Economic and Social History of the Middle Ages (300-1300)* (New York, The Century Co., 1928, pp. lx, 900). Henry Charles Lea, *History of Sacerdotal Celibacy in the Christian Church*

(New York, The Macmillan Company, 3d ed., 2 vols., 1907); largely based on the sources, with a bias against the Roman Catholic Church. Charles Howard McIlwain, *The Growth of Political Thought in the West from the Greeks to the End of the Middle Ages* (New York, The Macmillan Company, 1932, pp. vii, 417); well documented, scholarly. J. W. Willis Bund, *The Celtic Church of Wales* (London, D. Nutt, 1897, pp. vii, 530); based on the sources; taking positive views on some controversial issues. Henry Osborn Taylor, *The Mediæval Mind. A History of the Development of Thought and Emotion in the Middle Ages* (London, Macmillan and Co., 2 vols., 1911); standard. Axel Olrik, *Viking Civilization* (New York, W. W. Norton and Co., 1930, pp. 246); the popularly presented results of the researches of a distinguished specialist. Mary Wilhelmine Williams, *Social Scandinavia in the Viking Age* (New York, The Macmillan Company, 1920, pp. x, 451); excellent. Abbot Gasquet, *Parish Life in Medieval England* (London, Methuen and Co., 2d ed., 1907, pp. xxi, 279); excellent. John A. Duke, *The Columban Church* (Oxford University Press, 1932, pp. xii, 200). Alex. R. Macewen, *A History of the Church of Scotland* (London, Hodder and Stoughton, Vol. I, A.D. 397-1546, 1913, pp. xv, 487); a competent summary. Herbert B. Workman, *The Evolution of the Monastic Ideal from the Earliest Times down to the Coming of the Friars* (London, The Epworth Press, 2d ed., 1927, pp. xxi, 368); semi-popular, sympathetic with monasticism. Ernst Benz, *Ecclesia Spiritualis. Kirchenidee und Geschichtstheologie der franziskanischen Reformation* (Stuttgart, W. Kohlhammer, 1934, pp. xv, 481). Ellen Scott Davison, *Forerunners of Saint Francis and Other Studies,* edited by Gertrude R. B. Richards (Boston, Houghton Mifflin Co., 1927, pp. xvi, 425); well written, based upon careful research. G. Volpe, *Movimenti Religiosi e Sette Ereticali nella Società Medievale Italiana (Secoli* xi-xiv) (Florence, Vallecchi, 1926, pp. xii, 276). William Ralph Inge, *Christian Mysticism* (London, Methuen and Co., 6th ed., 1925, pp. xv, 379). J. Huizinga, *The Waning of the Middle Ages. A Study in the Forms of Life, Thought and Art in France and the Netherlands in the XIVth and XVth Centuries* (London, Edwin Arnold and Co., 1927, pp. xii, 328); a translation and condensation of the second Dutch edition.

The Eastern Churches. Steven Runciman, *Byzantine Civilization* (New York, Longmans, Green and Co., 1933, pp. 320); an excellent summary. A. A. Vasiliev, *History of the Byzantine Empire* (University of Wisconsin Studies in the Social Sciences and History, 2 vols., 1928, 1929); by an eminent authority. Walter F. Adeney, *The Greek and Eastern Churches* (New York, Charles Scribner's Sons, 1928, pp. xiv, 634); preface dated 1908; a standard summary. Matthew Spinka, *A History of Christianity in the Balkans* (Chicago, The American Society of Church History, 1933, pp. 202); thorough and competent. Paul Milukow, *Skizzen russischer Kulturgeschichte,* German edition by E. Davidson (Leipzig, Otto Wigand, 2 vols., 1898-1901). Victor N. Sharenkoff, *A Study of Manichæism in Bulgaria with Special Reference to the Bogomils* (New York, Carranza and Co., 1927, pp. xxv, 83); a doctoral dissertation, not always convincing. E. A. Wallis Budge, *A History of Ethiopia, Nubia and Abyssinia* (London, Methuen and Co., 2 vols., 1928). C. H. Walker, *The Abyssinian at Home* (London, The Sheldon Press, 1933, pp. xii, 220); by a British consular officer long resident in the country.

INDEX

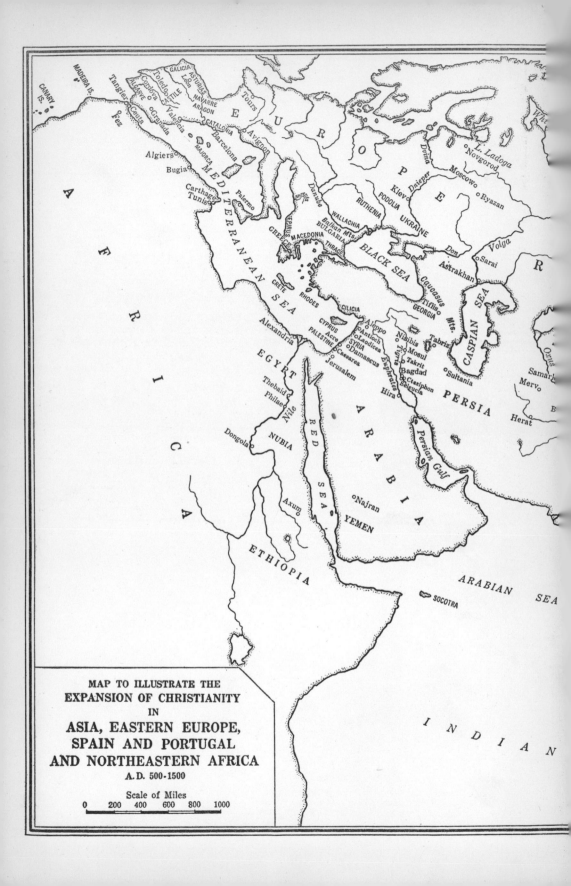

MAP TO ILLUSTRATE THE
EXPANSION OF CHRISTIANITY
IN
ASIA, EASTERN EUROPE,
SPAIN AND PORTUGAL
AND NORTHEASTERN AFRICA
A.D. 500-1500

Scale of Miles

0   200   400   600   800   1000